SHIVAJI
THE GREAT MARATHA

Ranjit Desai (1928–1992) was born in Kolhapur district of Maharashtra. He was considered a large-hearted littérateur whose writing engaged the readers at the highest level of emotional dialogue. He started writing when he settled in Kowad after his graduation. A writer of short stories, plays and novels, Ranjit Desai received an award for his very first short story, 'Bhairav', published in the magazine *Prasad* in 1946. He published his short story collection *Roop Mahal* in 1958 and stepped into the world of novels with *Bari* in the same year. He received many awards, including the Maharashtra Rajya Award (1963, for *Swami*), the Hari Narayan Apte Award (1963, for *Swami*), the Sahitya Akademi Award (1964, for *Swami*) and the Maharashtra Gaurav Puraskar (1990). The Government of India gave him the Padma Shri in 1973.

Vikrant Pande started translating from the Marathi with Ranjit Desai's classic novel *Raja Ravi Varma*, the story of India's most celebrated painter. He has since translated Milind Bokil's *Shala*, N.S. Inamdar's *Rau: The Great Love Story of Bajirao Mastani* and *Shahenshah: The Life of Aurangzeb*. A graduate of Indian Institute of Management–Bangalore, Vikrant worked in the corporate sector for twenty-five years before shifting to the field of education where he currently is a vice chancellor with TeamLease Skills University at Vadodara.

SHIVAJI
THE GREAT MARATHA

RANJIT DESAI

TRANSLATED FROM THE MARATHI BY
VIKRANT PANDE

HARPER PERENNIAL

NEW YORK • LONDON • TORONTO • SYDNEY • NEW DELHI

First published in India in 2017 by Harper Perennial
An imprint of HarperCollins *Publishers*
4th Floor, Tower A, Building No. 10, Phase II,
DLF Cyber City, Gurugram, Haryana -122002
www.harpercollins.co.in

In association with Mehta Publishing House

18

P-ISBN: 978-93-5277-439-5
E-ISBN: 978-93-5277-440-1

Typeset in 11.5/14 Linden Hill at
Manipal Digital Systems, Manipal

Printed and bound at
Replika Press Pvt. Ltd.

This book is printed on FSC® certified paper
which ensures responsible forest management.

Aai, tula samarpit

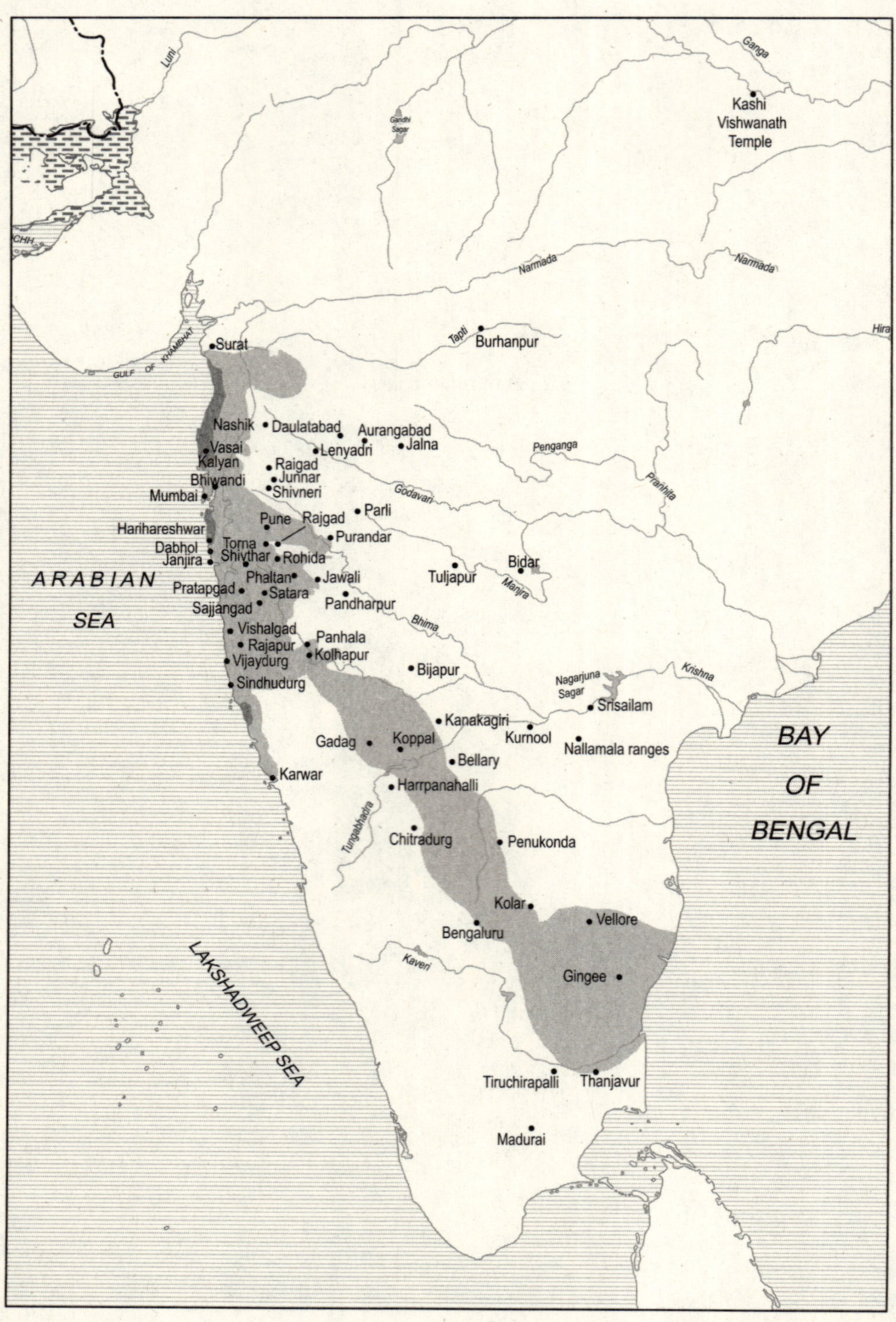
Luni
Ganga
Kashi
Vishwanath
Temple
Gandhi
Sagar
GULF OF KHAMBHAT
Narmada
Narmada
Tapti
Surat
Burhanpur
Hira
Nashik
Daulatabad
Aurangabad
Jalna
Lenyadri
Vasai
Kalyan
Raigad
Junnar
Shivneri
Bhiwandi
Mumbai
Penganga
Pranhita
Godavari
Pune
Rajgad
Parli
Harihareshwar
Purandar
Torna
Dabhol
Janjira
Shivthar
Rohida
Bidar
Tuljapur
Manjra
ARABIAN
SEA
Phaltan
Jawali
Pratapgad
Satara
Sajjangad
Pandharpur
Bhima
Vishalgad
Panhala
Rajapur
Kolhapur
Vijaydurg
Bijapur
Sindhudurg
Nagarjuna
Sagar
Krishna
Srisailam
Kanakagiri
Kurnool
Nallamala ranges
Gadag
Koppal
Bellary
Karwar
Harrpanahalli
BAY
OF
BENGAL
Tungabhadra
Chitradurg
Penukonda
Kolar
Bengaluru
Vellore
Kaveri
Gingee
LAKSHADWEEP SEA
Tiruchirapalli
Thanjavur
Madurai

Cast of Characters

Shahaji Bhosale	*Shivaji's father*
Jijabai	*Shivaji's mother*
Sambhaji	*Shivaji's elder brother*

Saibai (Nimbalkar):	Who gave birth to Sambhaji and Sakhubai	*Shivaji's wives*
Soyarabai (Mohite):	Who gave birth to Rajaram and one daughter	
Putlabai (Palkar)		
Gunwantabai (Ingle)		
Sagunabai (Shirke):	One daughter	
Sakwarbai (Gaikwad):	One daughter	
Lakshmibai (Vichare)		
Kashibai (Jadhav)		

Ekoji Raje	*Stepbrother of Shivaji*
Dadoji Konddev	*A trusted lieutenant of Shahaji, Shivaji's father, and advisor to Shivaji*
Vishwasrao	*Jijabai's elder relative, under whose care Shahaji left a pregnant Jijabai*
Lakhujirao Jadhav	*Jijabai's father and a Maratha general under Nizam Shah*
Achloji Raghoji Yeshwantrao	*Lakhuji's sons*
Nizam Shahi and Adil Shahi dynasty	*Earlier, Shahaji had served under the Nizam Shahi dynasty of Ahmadnagar but when Shah Jahan joined forces with Adil Shah of Bijapur, the Nizam Shahi rule almost came to an end. Shahaji later served under Mohammad Adil Shah of Bijapur, based in Bengaluru*
Ali Adil Shah	*Son of Mohammad Adil Shah*
Murar Jagdev	*Minister under Adil Shah*

Mahabat Khan	*General under Shah Jahan who routed the Nizam Shahi with the help of Adil Shah of Bijapur*
Khavas Khan	*One of the generals under Adil Shah*
Kheloji Bhosale	*Young relative of Shahaji. His wife was kidnapped by Mahabat Khan*
Gomaji Naik	*Advisor to Shivaji and deputed by Lakhujirao to teach Shivaji swordsmanship*
Dadaji Naras Prabhu	*Part of the initial group of men working with Shivaji*
Firangoji	*Close confidante and a sardar in Shivaji's army*
Yesaji Kank Baji Pasalkar Tanaji Malsure	*Early Mavals who joined Shivaji*
Shamrao Nilkant	*Peshwa (prime minister)*
Balkrishna Hanumante	*Mazumdar (treasurer)*
Sonopant Korde	*Dabir (secretary)*
Raghunath Ballal Korde	*Sabnis (the paymaster)*
Kanhoji Jedhe	*Shahaji's right-hand man sent to help Shivaji*
Moropant Pingle	*A Peshwa of Shivaji, who headed the ashta pradhans, council of eight ministers*
Siddi Hilal	*A brave Muslim chieftain in Shivaji's army. His son, Siddi Wahwah*
Bajaji Nimbalkar	*Shivaji's brother-in-law and Saibai's brother*
Mahadji	*Bajaji's son, married to Shivaji's daughter Sakhubai*
Netaji Palkar	*Second commander-in-chief, or Sarnobat, who later defected to Mughals and was rechristened Mohammad Quli Khan*
Prataprao Gujar	*Aka Kudtoji Gujar, one of Shivaji's commanders*
Afzal Khan	*Commander under Adil Shah of Bijapur*
Krishnaji Bhaskar	*Emissary of Afzal Khan*
Shaista Khan	*General in the Mughal army and maternal uncle of Aurangzeb*
Murarbaji Deshpande	*General with Shivaji and best known for his defence of Purandar Fort against Diler Khan of the Mughals*

Baji Prabhu Deshpande	*One of Shivaji's generals who helped him escape from Panhala Fort and later led the siege of Paavankhind to hold the enemy*
Shah Jahan	*Mughal emperor*
Shahzada Murad	*Aurangzeb's brother who commanded the Deccan for a while*
Aurangzeb	*Shah Jahan's son and later Mughal emperor*
Shahzada Muazzam	*Aurangzeb's son*
Mirza Raja Jai Singh	*Rajput general under Aurangzeb who forced the treaty of Purandar on Shivaji. Later he died mysteriously; some say he was poisoned by Aurangzeb. Aurangzeb had held him and his sons responsible for Shivaji's escape from Agra*
Kirat Singh Ram Singh	*Sons of Raja Jai Singh*
Samarth Ramdas Maharaj	*A saint whom Shivaji revered a lot and took advice from. He wrote the famous* Dasbodh. *Ramdas convinced Shivaji to get himself crowned as Chhatrapati*
Gyandev (Gyaneshwar) Sopandev Muktabai Namdev Eknath	*Poet saints of Maharashtra*

Some Places Mentioned in the Book

Junnar	*It is near Pune and was earlier the capital of the Nizam Shah where Shahaji, Shivaji's father, worked*
Shivneri	*A fort near Junnar, where Shivaji was born*
Torna	*A fort near Pune. The first fort captured by Shivaji*
Lenyadri	*It represents a series of about thirty rock-cut Buddhist caves, located near Junnar in Pune district*
Bijapur	*One of the Deccan sultanates, ruled by Adil Shah*
Phaltan	*A town in Satara district. It was ruled by the Nimbalkars. Saibai, Shivaji's first wife, was from the Nimbalkar family*
Daulatabad	*It is a fort town a little north-west of Aurangabad*
Burhanpur	*On the banks of River Tapi, in south-west Madhya Pradesh, it was an important Mughal post and an entry to the Deccan*
Satara	*Shivaji captured the forts of Parli and Satara. It is a town in Maharashtra on the confluence of River Krishna and its tributary Venna*
Rajapur	*A town in Ratnagiri district of Maharashtra*
Shikhar Shingnapur	*A shiva temple located at the top of Shingnapur hills near Satara*
Kanakagiri	*A temple town in Koppal district of Karnataka*
Rayari/Raigad	*Shivaji captured the fort of Rayari and renamed it Raigad. The village of Pachad is at the base of the fort. It was the capital of Shivaji's empire*
Tuljapur	*A town in Osmanabad district of Maharashtra is the home of the Tuljapur Bhawani temple*
Shivthar	*A cave near Mahad where Samarth Ramdas stayed for nearly twenty-two years. He dictated the Dasbodh to his disciple Kalyan Swami there*
Sajjangad	*A fort near Satara. It is the final resting place of Samarth Ramdas Swami*
Bidar	*A town in the north-eastern part of Karnataka*
Shringarpur	*A village in Ratnagiri district. During Shivaji's time it was held by the Surves*
Harihareshwar	*A town in Raigad district with a popular Shiva temple*

Chandan–Vandan	*Twin forts built to protect the route leading to Satara*
Godhkhind	*The narrow pass became famous when Baji Prabhu Deshpande defended it for many hours, allowing safe passage to Shivaji. It was later renamed Paavankhind*
Panhala	*The fort is near Kolhapur and Shivaji escaped from there when surrounded and reached Vishalgad. He was helped by Baji Prabhu Deshpande*
Rajgad	*A little south-west of Pune. The fort was earlier capital of Shivaji's empire*
Salher	*A fort in Nashik district*
Karwar	*A town on the west coast, in Uttara Kannada district of Karnataka*
Nallamala ranges	*The Nallamalas are a section of the Eastern Ghats which stretch primarily over Kurnool, Nellore, Guntur, Prakasam, Kadapa and Chittoor districts*
Srisailam	*The shrine of Mallikarjuna picturesquely sits on the flat top of Nallamala hills. It is near the River Krishna*
Bengaluru	*Then an important town in Karnataka. Shahaji ruled the jagir of Bengaluru under Adil Shah of Bijapur*
Goa	*The port of Goa ruled by the Portuguese*
Tiruchirapalli	*Important city in Tamil Nadu*
Thanjavur	*Temple town in Tamil Nadu ruled by Venkoji Raje, Shivaji's half-brother*

Important Dates and Years

19 February 1630	*Shivaji's birth at Shivneri Fort*
1630-31	*Famine in Maharashtra*
1637	*Shivaji arrives in Pune*
14 May 1640	*Marriage of Shivaji and Saibai*
15 April 1645	*Oath at Rohideshwar*
1646	*Shivaji captures Torna*
March 1647	*Death of Dadoji Konddev*
October 1648	*Shivaji defeats Fateh Khan*
1650	*Birth of Sakhubai*
1651-52	*Bajaji is taken back into Hindu fold*
1655	*Marriage of Sakhubai*
15 January 1656	*Capture of Jawali*
27 August 1656	*Sons of Chandrarao are killed*
14 May 1657	*Birth of Sambhaji*
5 September 1659	*Death of Saibai*
10 November 1659	*Shivaji kills Afzal Khan*
9 May 1660	*Shaista Khan comes to Pune*
13 July 1660	*Death of Baji Prabhu Deshpande*
1661-62	*Meeting of Shahaji and Shivaji*
2 February 1661	*Battle of Umbarkhindi*
5 April 1663	*Attack on Shaista Khan*
6 to 10 January 1664	*Looting of Surat*
October 1664	*Death of Baji Ghorpade*
15 November 1664	*Construction of Sindhudurg begins*
11 June 1665	*Treaty of Purandar*
30 September 1665	*Farman to Shivaji*
22 January 1665	*Death of Shah Jahan*
5 March 1666	*Shivaji leaves for Agra*
12 May 1666	*Durbar at Agra*
16 August 1666	*Escape from Agra*

September 1666	*Shivaji returns to Rajgad*
28 August 1667	*Mirza Raja Jai Singh dies*
27 March 1667	*Netaji Palkar converts to Islam*
August-September 1669	*Aurangzeb destroys Kashi Vishwanath Temple*
4 October 1670	*Second raid on Surat*
13 January 1672	*Diler Khan raids Pune*
August 1672	*Meeting with Samarth Ramdas*
24 February 1674	*Death of Prataprao Gujar*
19 March 1674	*Death of Kashibai*
6 June 1674	*Coronation of Shivaji*
17 June 1674	*Death of Jijabai*
21 May 1675	*Large part of Karwar annexed*
19 June 1676	*Netaji Palkar returns, and is reconverted to Hindu fold*
4 March 1677	*Meeting with Qutb Shah*
13 May 1677	*Capture of Jinji*
5 July 1677	*Sher Khan surrenders to Shivaji*
27 July 1677	*Ekoji Raje runs away*
August-September 1677	*Diler Khan replaces Bahadur Khan as chief of Mughals in the Deccan*
June 1678	*Shivaji captures Gadag*
13 December 1678	*Sambhaji joins Diler Khan*
25 February 1679	*Aurangzeb arrives in Aurangabad to wipe out the Marathas*
13 January 1680	*Meeting of Shivaji and Sambhaji*
3 April 1680	*Death of Shivaji*

BOOK
ONE

The village of Junnar, at the base of the Shivneri Fort, shone in the last rays of the setting sun. Shahaji and his younger son Sambhaji, along with a few horsemen, waited in a mango orchard a few kilometres away from Junnar. Not a single leaf stirred. As they stood observing the road, the coolness of the night had not enveloped the orchard yet. Not a soul was in sight, making Shahaji restless with every passing minute.

'Aba saheb, Maa saheb has arrived!' Sambhaji shouted, pointing across the road. They could see a few horsemen kicking up dust as they rode silhouetted against the slanting rays of the western sun. Soon, the horsemen stopped maintaining a respectable distance from Shahaji.

Jijabai, tired by the long ride, smiled weakly on seeing Sambhaji as she dismounted. A maid gave her a helping hand. Three months pregnant, Jijabai seemed visibly exhausted. Her face was flushed as she wiped the sweat off her forehead.

'If I keep moving like this from one place to another, halting at various places, it won't be long before your father traps us,' Shahaji snapped.

'I think you should carry on. I don't think I can bear the exertion of travel any further.'

'But leaving you in such a state and that too in a place like this ...'

'Your kinsman Vishwasrao lives close by. I can rest there—but you need to take care of yourself.'

Shahaji Raje erupted with anger. 'This is all your father's fault! What do you expect me to do? The enmity between the Jadhavs and the Bhosales have been going on for years; and you probably think I am only continuing the tradition.'

An unfortunate incident many years back, a skirmish in the court of the Nizam, had left family members dead on both sides but the Jadhavs held Shahaji responsible for the death of their son. The marriage of Jijabai with Shahaji had exacerbated the same and reached a point where they were ready to kill the other.

'What do you want me to say?' mumbled Jijabai.

'All right, I shall do as you wish. If your father cares about you, he will spare you. Else, he may take you away. It is your future and your luck. I am not going to interfere—are we agreed?'

Jijabai nodded while keeping her tears in check as she moved towards the waiting horsemen.

The news of Jijabai's arrival had reached Junnar. Vishwasrao personally came to receive Jijabai and Shahaji, who spoke as he stepped into the courtyard, 'Vishwasrao, pardon me for troubling you. I had no other choice.'

'Raje, it is my good fortune to serve you. I will take care of Rani saheb in the best possible manner I can.'

'If I were not sure of that, we would not be here!' Turning to Sambhaji, Shahaji said, 'Shall we? Or do you want to stay?'

Sambhaji Raje, avoiding his mother's gaze, meekly nodded his head.

'Good!' exclaimed a visibly relieved Shahaji.

'Would it be not advisable for the young one to stay back and join you after the danger abates a little?' Jijabai asked.

'Vishwasrao, did you hear that? It seems the young one is in danger and not me!'

'I did not mean that!' Jijabai retorted.

'I am going to take Shambhu with me. He has a lot to do. I am leaving behind Balakrishna Hanumante, Sankraji Nilkanth, Sonojipant Korde and a few others to look after you; and a few horsemen too. Once things are normal, we will bring you back. Until then, take care of your health.'

Jijabai hugged Shambhu when he tried to touch his mother's feet. He somehow managed to wriggle himself out of her embrace and moved away. Jijabai was unable to speak, trying to capture the sight of her son in her eyes but her tears blinded her. By the time she wiped them away, Sambhaji had left the haveli with Shahaji Raje. They did not turn back to look even once.

The clattering of the horse hooves reverberated in Jijabai's mind for a long time.

It was nightfall and oil lamps burned in a few households in Junnar. The mashaal near the temple flickered in the wind and a deep slumber seemed to envelop the village. Suddenly, the entire village woke to the clipping sound of horse hooves coming from all directions.

Vishwasrao had just finished eating and was relaxing on a swing in the courtyard. The weapons, hung on a wall, were shining in the golden light of the oil lamps. He stood up hearing the sounds of the hooves and turned to look at the open door when his guard came running in.

'We have been ambushed! Lakhujirao Jadhav has surrounded the village and is coming this way.'

'What a time for him to arrive!' remarked Vishwasrao as he unsheathed his sword and reached the door in four large steps to find Lakhujirao Jadhav standing there with a sword glistening in his right hand. Lakhujirao's face shone with anger.

'Where is that Bhosale?' Lakhujirao growled.

'First sheath your sword and come inside,' Vishwasrao replied calmly.

'Get out of my way!' Lakhujirao shouted again.

'Gentlemen do not enter others' homes with naked swords in their hands,' Vishwasrao said, maintaining his composure.

Lakhujirao stood his ground, his white sideburns glistening with sweat. He repeated, 'Where is that Bhosale?'

'He is not here.'

'Must be hiding here, I suppose.'

'The Bhosales have not produced any offspring who hide.'

'Then maybe they have produced those who run away,' Lakhujirao retorted scathingly.

'Enough of this, Jadhavrao! This is a Bhosale household and I will not tolerate such insults.'

'Huh! I am not requesting his whereabouts. I have my sword in my hands—move away!' he said, trying to move forward.

Vishwasrao raised his sword as a warning.

'What daring!' exclaimed Lakhujirao.

'Aba!'

Hearing a familiar voice, Lakhujirao lowered his sword to see Jijabai standing in the courtyard. Vishwasrao made way for him to enter but Lakhujirao was rooted on the spot as he stared at his daughter.

Jiu! How many memories were attached to that name! She was Lakhujirao's darling daughter, the Lakshmi of the Jadhav household. The day she married into the Bhosale family had been a dark and unfortunate one.

Lakhujirao's sword fell from his hand as he moved ahead in a trance, his lips muttering softly.

'Jiu ...'

'Aba!' Jijabai repeated, as she rushed to hug her father.

Vishwasrao, touching Lakhujirao's feet, said, 'Mamaji, please forgive me.'

'Vishwasrao, there is nothing to forgive. In fact, I was quite impressed to see your courage. That Bhosale may not be a courageous one, but one of his relatives does seem to be a tiger. I am happy to see that!'

He laughed loudly but realizing that he was the only one laughing, he stopped suddenly, embarrassed by his own joke. He hugged Jijabai again and asked, 'My dear, are you well?'

'What do you mean well, father?' Jijabai asked, her voice taking on an edge. Jijabai looked at her father with anguish in her eyes and sadness erupted in her as she continued, 'A daughter is like haldi. Anyone can take a pinch and smear it on another person's forehead. You sealed your daughter's fate on the day of Holi. The dust of that haldi is still floating in the air.'

'Why floating in the air? Since when did Lakhuji's daughter become so weak? If that Bhosale cannot manage his wife, I am capable of taking care of my daughter.'

'If you care for your daughter so much, then why are you raiding in the middle of the night? Had something happened and your daughter been widowed tonight, would you have been happy? Aba, you have Jiu's promise ...'

Covering her mouth with his hand, Lakhujirao stopped her mid-sentence and hugged her tightly .

'Don't trap me with your promises, Jiu. Your blood is mine but my allegiance is to the Jadhav family and vengeance is my destiny—I can only die for it! Daughter, you have my blessings. May you always remain happily married! Don't worry about your father. If I die, don't cry for me.'

Jijabai could not stop her tears as she listened to her father.

Lakhujirao said, 'Listen to me—just look around you. The whole province is suffering from famine. There is chaos everywhere and nobody cares about what happens to someone else. In such a situation, how can you stay alone? Come with me. Once things are stable, you may go wherever you wish.'

Jijabai shook her head in disagreement.

'No, Aba. I may be a Jadhav daughter but I am a Bhosale daughter-in-law now. I cannot stay in my father's house. If I come with you, I will insult the Bhosale household.'

Lakhujirao said exasperatedly, 'How can I leave my own daughter to her fate? Your husband has abandoned you and this father of yours should do nothing but watch silently?'

'Don't say that, Aba. There is much that you can do.'

'Tell me, my dear. What can I do?'

'Aba, take me to Shivneri. I will be fine there.'

'I agree. I will make arrangements for a carriage tomorrow. Instead of suffering this humid weather here, it is better that Jiu stays in the fort,' Lakhujirao said.

'I intended to do precisely that. I have but one request,' Vishwasrao said.

'I am yours to command. After all, my daughter is now part of your household.'

'This may sound impudent, and I know you probably hate your own destiny, but I believe that this Jadhav–Bhosale enmity is gift from God.'

'What do you mean?' asked Lakhujirao.

'If it were not for this enmity, you would not have stepped into our home!'

'Wah! Vishwasrao, you have a way with words!'

'I'd still like to make a request.'

'Yes?'

'We would be honoured if you and your soldiers dined here.'

'The soldiers have already eaten as we were not sure how long we would be riding. At my age, I eat only once a day. Well, you may take care of the horses ...'

'I have already taken care of them. But this is a rare occasion for us and a privilege. Rani saheb, please persuade your father.'

Jijabai hesitated. 'Aba ...'

'All right, Vishwasrao. It is quite late and I will not trouble you. Let us have a little bit of rice and milk.'

The kitchen burnt brightly with the light of silver lamps. A silver-carved wooden seat was set for Lakhujirao to sit on. As Lakhuji settled himself, Vishwasrao asked Jijabai to serve her father.

'Well played, Vishwasrao! You know I cannot refuse my dear Jiu anything.'

The pulao plates were bought forward as Jijabai lovingly served her father.

Lakhujirao could not hold his tears back and said, 'Serve me well, my dear. In this climate of hectic haste and the rush of politics, I am not sure when I will have the pleasure of a meal being served with such loving care again.'

The entire kitchen glowed with happiness while everyone enjoyed their meal.

In the morning, Jadhavrao's horsemen and Bhosale's men were ready and sardars like Balkrishna Hanumante, Nilkanth, Raghunath Ballal and Korde were waiting at the entrance. Vishwasrao's family presented Jiu with a piece of cloth for a blouse and a coconut as a parting gift. She got into the palanquin after touching both Vishwasrao's and Lakhujirao's feet and the group started ascending the slope, towards the fort, at a rapid pace.

Vishwasrao looked back after a while to see the village of Junnar spread in a wide arc. The climb ahead of Peer Darwaza was steep and Lakhujirao asked the bearers to be careful at each step as the palanquin creaked. They stopped at the door of the Shivai Devi temple and the curtains were moved.

Jijabai asked, 'Have we reached the fort?'

'Jiu,' Lakhujirao replied, 'First we will pay our respects to Shivai Devi and then move further up.'

Jijabai stepped out of the palanquin and began to walk ahead carefully. One of the maids was ready with the items for the ritual while Lakhuji and Vishwasrao walked a few steps behind.

Entering into the temple Vishwasrao said, 'Rani saheb, Shivai Devi is reputed to have many powers. Whatever you ask for will be granted.'

Jijabai prayed to the deity for a while and accepted the prasad in her cupped hands when Lakhujirao said, 'Dear, will you do something for me?' Then he paused for a moment, changing his mind, and said, 'I will tell you about it later.'

The sun was high up when they reached the fort and they could now see the palace ahead. As Jijabai stepped out of the palanquin, Lakhujirao said, pointing at the mountains in the direction of Pune, 'Jiu, you need not ever feel alone. You see Lenyadri there? It is our protector.'

Jijabai folded her hands in obeisance to the Lenyadri Ganesha, one of the Ashtavinayaks.

Jadhavrao left after seeing Jijabai off to the palace. Lakhuji could not hold back his tears when she touched his feet, and hugged her affectionately saying, 'Jiu, you are such a simple soul. Even if your husband does not invite me here, I shall come to see my grandchild. And here,' he said, as he took out a pouch hanging at his waist. 'Take this pouch of one hundred and one gold coins. I have made a promise to Shivai that if I am blessed with a grandson, I will donate these coins. My dear, this is my blessing for you—you shall have a child who will make you proud and who will never allow you to be sad. Take care now, and I shall return soon.'

A few of Vishwasrao's sardars were waiting. Lakhujirao said, 'With such dedicated men to look after Jiu, I am not worried. Take good care of her.'

Looking at Vishwasrao, Lakhujirao said, 'Vishwasrao, I can never repay my debt but ...'

'Please don't say anything. Leave everything to me and be assured.'

'I have full faith in you. Nevertheless, if you need anything, please call me. I will make myself available at the fort immediately. Ram, Ram.'

Vishwasrao bowed slightly and flapped his right arm in front of his chest three times in the traditional way of greeting. Lakhujirao accepted these mujras and Vishwasrao walked a few steps with him to say his goodbyes.

The sun was at its zenith when Lakhujirao stepped out of the fort.

The political situation was not very conducive. Lakhujirao worked under the Nizam Shah. Constant skirmishes were the order of the day, leading to a very turbulent and instable situation. A worried Jijabai could only pray for the well-being of her father and her husband.

It had been four months since Jijabai had arrived at the fort. Jijabai would get up in the morning, have a bath and complete her puja before sunrise. Then, she would help a little in the kitchen, read a few religious texts and have lunch, enjoy a siesta, and go for a little walk in the evening. Once every two days, she would walk all the way to the Shivai Devi Temple. Vishwasrao would plead, in vain, for her to take the palanquin.

One afternoon, while Jijabai rested in her room, her maid Lakshmibai sat on the carpet stitching a dress. Another maid sat on the floor massaging Jijabai's feet. Lakshmibai asked casually, 'Rani saheb ...'

'Lakshmibai, don't address me so formally. We are of the same age. Why don't you call me Jija?'

'I can't forget my position just because I love you.'

Jijabai sighed and said, 'Tell me.'

'Don't you feel like eating something special? I have not seen you ask for anything.'

She laughed. 'Frankly, I don't have any special taste buds. Instead, I feel like going for a horse ride, a sword dangling at my side, riding around the fort in the cool morning air. Look at the dense forest in the valley—how I wish I could go riding there!'

Lakhmibai laughed as she put her stitching down.

'Shall I tell you something?' Jijabai continued, 'I am unable to sleep in the afternoon.'

'Why?'

She blushed and, lovingly moving her hand over her stomach, she said, 'He keeps playing all the time.'

Lakshmibai got up immediately and made the traditional sign of breaking her knuckles over Jijabai's glowing face to ward off evil.

That evening, as Jijabai was strolling with Lakshmibai and other maids, the servant Vithu came running and announced Vishwasrao's arrival.

Vishwasrao came along with Hanumanta, an elderly gentleman. Jijabai said, as they bent in mujra, 'What's the matter, Vishwasrao? Is something wrong?'

'Rani saheb, it is not good news.'

Jijabai waited for him to continue.

'Shahaji Raje captured the territory of Bijapur; and hence, the Bijapurkars have sent Murar Jagdev to raid Pune. He has been traumatizing the city, burning palaces and torturing people. He has stabbed the heart and soul of Shahaji Raje's kingdom and run away.'

'What about Raje?' Jijabai asked, her throat dry.

'I am told he is safe and is somewhere near Phaltan.'

'Vishwasrao, it is our good fortune ...' Jijabai's voice trailed away.

After saluting her, Vishwasrao left and Jijabai allowed her tears to fall.

News never comes singly. Before Jijabai could get over the earlier news, she heard that Shahaji Raje's cousin Kheloji Bhosale's wife, on the way to Nashik for a dip in the Godavari River, had been kidnapped by Mahabat Khan. Jijabai was badly affected by the news and did not have the energy to climb up to the temple after that day.

Vishwasrao and the other sardars were constantly worried. Gomajipant was from her father's village and he could speak to her without any protocol or formality, but still his words did not comfort her. Lakshmibai was trying to find different ways to keep her mind free of such thoughts, but in vain.

She realized that since a few days, they all seemed unnaturally silent. Lakshmibai avoided her and the maids seemed to be carrying some burden with them in the way they walked. Vishwasrao, Gomaji and the others seemed to talk abruptly, almost stiltedly. Jijabai saw all of this but was unable to understand what was going on. The silence became unbearable after a couple of days and she confronted Vishwasrao.

'Vishwasrao, I have not come here just because I am related to you. You are like a brother to me—that is why I agreed to stay here.'

'I know that.'

'Then what are you hiding from me?'

'Why, did someone say something?'

'I don't need to be told. For the past two days, you seem to be avoiding me.'

'There seems to be some misunderstanding, Rani saheb.'

'Vishwasrao, I am not a child and have suffered many a blow. If you won't tell me the truth, I am leaving the fort right away.'

'Rani saheb ...'

'I am prepared to hear anything. I have the strength but I cannot bear to keep imagining things. Tell me what it is!'

'Maa saheb ...'

'Tell me ...'

Vishwasrao burst into tears.

'Vishwasrao, please control yourself,' Jijabai said, feeling desperate now and using the wall for support.

Vishwasrao wiped his tears and blurted out, 'Your Aba saheb ... Lakhujirao Jadhav ... has been murdered.'

'Murdered? Aba has been murdered? Who killed him?' Jijabai looked at Vishwasrao wide-eyed.

Vishwasrao had no words and tried to form a sentence as he licked his lips nervously. 'Lakhujirao had gone to Daulatabad with Achloji, Raghoji and Yeshwantrao—his three sons—to see the Sultan. He was not aware that a plot had been laid earlier. After accepting their salutes, the Sultan just got up and left the durbar without saying anything. Lakhujirao was unable to understand what had just occurred but before he could react ...'

'Continue, Vishwasrao, please continue. Don't stop for a second.'

'... at that moment, swords were drawn. They had no time to react and defend themselves. How can one protect oneself with just a small knife? Maa saheb, four Jadhavs have been murdered trying to serve the Sultan. Only Bahadurji, who was with his mother, is alive.'

Vishwasrao looked up to see Jijabai standing still as a statue, her back to the wall. She had a vacant look. A strange, hideous smile formed on her face. Vishwasrao could hear dry words ...

'Aba is dead. My home is no more. One enemy has raided our Pune. Another has taken away our daughter. And the Sultan, whom my father served loyally, has killed him in his own durbar.'

And then she screamed loudly. 'Vishwasrao, is there a god in this damned universe?'

He rushed to steady her as she slipped to the floor, unconscious. The entire palace erupted in turmoil. In the middle of the night, all one could hear from the palace were deep heart-rending sobs.

Jijabai was unable to recover from the news of her father's murder in cold blood. She would get up in the middle of the night, her whole body drenched with sweat and be startled even at the noise of a falling vessel. She would keep watching Lenyadri from her window and would start crying the moment someone tried talking to her.

Lakshmibai tried everything to take her mind off the matter but did not succeed. A few days later, Lakshmibai said exasperatedly, 'Rani saheb, are you the only one to feel this sorrow? Don't I feel sad for whatever has happened? I now am worried for your son. At the very least, take care of your son who is growing inside you. Don't you think your sadness will affect his health?'

Jijabai's body shook with fear. She had completely forgotten her child in the midst of her father's tragedy. She said, wiping her tears, 'Lakshmibai, I understand; thank you; but I will not allow my sorrow to affect anyone else.'

And from then onwards Jijabai started moving around as before, taking care of her unborn child. Soon, nine months drew to a close. Brahmins had been called for meals and special maids were now in charge of Jijabai. Experienced and carefully handpicked physicians were standing ready for any emergency. The nursery looked bright with freshly painted walls. The roof had a layer of pearls to reflect light from the oil lamps which burned day and night. A golden vessel with fresh water stood on a table nearby. As a sign of good omen, white mustard was strewn all over the floor. Everyone was waiting for the arrival of a new life.

The afternoon progressed towards the evening and a cool breeze had just begun. Vishwasrao, Gomaji Naik, the chief physician and some others sat making paan for themselves. Putting some lime on his betel leaf, Naik said, 'Sarkar, you seem quiet.'

'What can I say, Gomajipant? You remember when Maa saheb interceded to stop a fellow from being thrown over?'

'Yes, she can't tolerate such violent methods.'

'That is true, but crimes are on the rise each day. If there are no rains this year, the coming year is going to be very difficult for all us.'

'Shall I say something?' ventured Shastribua, the priest.

'Please.'

'I can clearly see famine in the future.'

'Why don't you say something about Rani saheb rather than making such predictions?' Vishwasrao commented sarcastically.

'Don't worry about Rani saheb's future. I am not worried on that count,' Shastribua said.

'I just checked her pulse today. The child is due any moment now ...' the physician muttered.

At that moment a maid came running to give news. 'Sarkar, Rani saheb is in the advanced stages of labour now. I have been asked to inform you.'

'I was sure of my diagnosis,' the physician mumbled in a low tone.

Everyone stood up in hurry but immediately realized that getting up was of no use, and they all sat down again. They could do precious little as nature took its course.

Time crawled. Hours went by and it was time to light the lamps but there was no news yet. The men grew more anxious with each passing moment, and all they could see was the maids and midwives rushing about.

It was approaching midnight. Vishwasrao was deep in thought as he paced up and down the corridor. The lamps were flickering in the wind and shadows played on the walls.

A maid came running, her face bright and smiling. 'Sarkar, it's a baby boy!'

Vishwasrao could not contain his happiness. He removed the pouch at his waist and poured the coins over the maid. Shastribua got busy calculating the exact time of the birth in his small diary. Vishwasrao reached Jijabai's room along with Shastribua. Vishwasrao showered the child with gold coins and said, 'Rani saheb, Shastribua is here.'

Jijabai managed a weak smile as she folded her palms to the priest. A carpet had been laid out for the shastri to sit on. He opened the almanac where the exact date and time had been marked and a low chant could be heard, 'Shri Ganeshaya namah ...'

Shastribua did some counting on his fingertips and after consulting the almanac, he started filling up the horoscope. The moment he completed the horoscope, he looked at Jijabai.

'Shastribua, tell me without any hesitation. Since the day I was pregnant, it has been chaos. Bloodshed, losing Pune, losing his grandfather ... all our relatives turned our enemies and we lost our jagir. His father is still running from enemies while his elder brother, still young, roams around with him. I have given birth to him in a place which is neither my husband's nor my parent's house. What more calamities can one think of? So tell me without hesitation.'

It was a sad outburst but Shastribua did not wince. He said with a relaxed smile, 'Rani saheb, please don't have such negative thoughts in your mind. The bad days are over. Your luck is smiling on you. You have delivered the sun god!'

Jijabai said, her voice tinged with sarcasm, 'All of you say the same thing while preparing the horoscope of a child.'

Stung by her reply, the shastri spoke in a voice loud and clear, 'Rani saheb, please believe me. Till now, this shastri has not been proved wrong. I predict not for the lure of gold but for the sake of my knowledge, my experience and my confidence. This horoscope too will not be proved wrong. This child will redeem the sins of the past. Rani saheb, don't forget Krishna was born to Devaki and Vasudev in Kamsa's prison when the weight of sin had reached its peak and the whole world was fed up.'

'May your words be true,' Jijabai said, sounding relieved. She looked at the child lying in her lap, happily sucking his wrist.

Fresh cool winds had started blowing since Jijabai had given birth. A few horsemen had been dispatched immediately to inform Shahaji Raje. New ornaments and clothes were being ordered to the fort. Lakshmibai opened a lovely silk sari with small violet embroidered dots and said, 'Rani saheb, isn't that gorgeous?'

'Yes, it is!'

'Then you will wear it at the naming ceremony.'

A royal palanquin came to the fort the next day and Vishwasrao rushed to receive the visitor. Shahaji Raje's mother and Jijabai's mother-in-law, Umabai saheb, had arrived.

Umabai's face showed the exhaustion of the long ride. Jijabai touched her feet the moment she entered the nursery. The child was fast asleep in the crib. She observed him with keen eyes and moving her hands in blessing over his head, said, 'He looks just like you. When is the naming ceremony?'

Lakshmibai replied, 'Tomorrow. Just yesterday Rani saheb was wishing that someone from the family would be in attendance.'

'I understand. Jiu, you have a handsome son. He will fulfil all your wishes.' She added, with a serious face, 'Have you informed his father?'

'Yes.'

'Do you think he is going to come? He has left the house to take care of his army. Damn the royal pursuit!'

Both Lakshmibai and Jijabai laughed out loud at Umabai's sudden outburst.

After a while, Umabai asked, 'And where is your elder one, my dear?'

'With his father.'

'What an idiot! And you are an idiot many times over to send such a young lad out. Is this the age for him to roam around in such danger? If I had been here, I would have told him ...' She let out a deep sigh and said, 'But who will listen to my advice?'

The next morning, the fort woke up to the sound of the shehnai. Decorative flags were fluttering at the entrance and the maids had beautified the grounds with rangoli patterns. The air was filled with the songs being sung by the ladies.

Jijabai asked Umabai shyly, 'What shall we name the baby?'

'What did you have in mind?'

'I had prayed to Shivai Devi. I wish to call him Shivaji.'

'And so it shall be!'

After the rituals, Jijabai bent down in the crib and whispered his name into the baby's ears, 'Shivaji!'

As per tradition, Jijabai's back was hammered with soft, friendly blows from all the ladies. The whole fort reverberated with the sounds of trumpets, horns and drums, and the baby's name was declared to every one present.

The palanquin was then readied outside the palace. Shivaji was now ready for devi darshan. Jijabai sat holding the baby in her lap inside the palanquin while Lakshmibai and the other maids walked alongside. Shivaji was placed in front of the devi. Sacred ash was smeared on his forehead and the priest blessed him.

Vishwasrao was becoming restless, wishing to return to the palace before nightfall. At that moment Jijabai handed over a velvet pouch to Vishwasrao. He asked, 'What is this?'

Jijabai, her eyes filled with tears, said, 'Aba had made a promise, while leaving, that if I had a boy, he would donate these hundred and one gold coins. He may have passed away but the promise should not be broken.' Jijabai could not speak any further, and she wiped her tears with the edge of her sari.

Vishwasrao opened the pouch with shivering hands and the coins flowed from his hand on to the floor. Gold coins were raining near the head and feet of the baby.

Shivaji was fast growing up in his grandmother's lap, in his mother's cosy arms and on the shoulders of the maids and other servants. If any passing vendor came to the fort with a new rattle or a toy, Vishwasrao would immediately buy it. The shastri, while returning from Junnar village, bought a metal chain much to the amusement of those present. He said, noticing their mocking smiles, 'Anklets of silver or gold do improve the baby's health. For good health, he needs this anklet made of pancharatna.'

And so, many days and nights passed devoted to the love and care of the baby. Soon it was time for the monsoon again and westerly winds started blowing. Clouds moved far above but were not in a mood to stop by, and the hot earth seemed to be sighing in the sun. Vishwasrao, fearing harder times ahead, moved the grain store in the fort to a safer, more fortified place.

One evening, Vishwasrao came to meet Jijabai in her private quarters. She was busy stitching something while Shivaji played with a toy.

'Rani saheb, we have good news! Raje saheb and his men are fast approaching the fort.'

'When are they likely to reach?' Jijabai asked excitedly.

'Any moment now!'

A fresh sitting arrangement was laid out in the inner courtyard with carpets, bolsters, pillows and dhurries. Jijabai changed her clothes hurriedly, putting on her jewellery. The sound of the trumpets announced the arrival of the visitors and Vishwasrao rushed to receive them as he adjusted his turban.

Everyone bent in an elaborate salute as Shahaji Raje entered the fort. He hugged Vishwasrao who said, 'We received the news very late. I apologize for not receiving you at the base of the fort.'

'I am not bothered about such formalities. Is everything all right?'

'Yes, Raje.'

Everyone entered the palace. There was frantic activity as the servants rushed around. Shahaji Raje washed his hands and feet and all the other men followed suit. They all went to the inner courtyard to sit down. Vishwasrao asked, 'I hope the journey was not difficult?'

'Vishwasrao, we have got so used to running and horse riding that we spend nights sleeping on horseback as well.'

Everyone burst out laughing and then stopped suddenly. Shivaji had come crawling out of the inner door. Everyone stared at the cute boy.

Raje said looking at him, 'Chotte Raje! I have come here just to see you.'

Shivaji looked at everyone once and he gave a sweet smile and ran towards Shahaji Raje.

Shastri said, 'Blood can always identify its own.'

Shahaji Raje picked up Shivaji affectionately, showering kisses on him and put him on his lap. Shivaji was now playing with his father's beard.

Vishwasrao smiled and said, 'He must be the first to dare touch your beard.'

'No, he's the second, I believe! But I understand that Chotte Raje has come here with a command.'

'Command?'

'I must visit the inner quarters.'

Shahaji Raje stood up and moved into the inner quarters with Shivaji. He was about to sit on the couch when Jijabai said smilingly, 'Sasubai is waiting for you.'

'Oh my god! I am so sorry. Please take me to her.'

Shahaji Raje took his mother's blessings. When finally Jijabai and Shahaji Raje got a chance to be alone, he asked, 'Jija, is everything all right?'

Jijabai's tears, held back for so long, now flowed freely and a deep sob escaped her.

'Rani saheb, I understand. Mama saheb being murdered in such a manner is a deep sorrow for me too. We may have had our enmity but I cannot tolerate such a dastardly act. I have left the Nizam Shahi court and have now taken a job under Mohammad Adil Shah now.'

'How long can this go on?'

'I don't know! Do you think I don't feel like staying with my family? But Rani saheb, I am sure with Shivba's good fortune, our bad days are numbered. I will settle down somewhere soon.'

Shahaji Raje stayed on for another week at the fort, until summons from the Mughal Badshah arrived. Shahaji Raje's eyes scanned the summons and let out a deep sigh, and said, 'Vishwasrao, our days of rest are over.'

'Why? What happened?'

'The Badshah is coming on a tour of the south. The troops are stationed in Burhanpur and I have been asked to report there. I will have to leave tomorrow itself.'

Raje took leave from Jijabai, kissed Shivaji and, leaving everything under Vishwasrao's supervision, left for Burhanpur to report to Emperor Shah Jahan.

Bal Shivaji was now a year old and the famine had become brutal. Villages were being orphaned and animals, left alone to graze, were seen roaming all over. Villagers had left their villages in search for better prospects. Gold had no value, being replaced by food grains as currency. Wherever one went, one could see groups of people waiting at the roadside to loot travellers. People, struggling for a handful of rice, did not hesitate to commit heinous crimes. Eagles and vultures were constantly circling in the sky and not a single healthy soul was visible—all one could see were dead animals and people. The surviving villages were being subjugated by the Mughal dynasty and soon, nearly the whole of the Deccan was under their control.

Vishwasrao maintained a strict vigil on the Shivneri Fort. The doors of the fort were always closed and nobody was allowed inside without proper enquiry. The water tanks were half-empty while the grain store was heavily guarded. Thus, one more year passed. The winter ended, giving way to the hot summer and everyone waited for the rains, praying fervently. One afternoon, a line of clouds was visible in the eastern sky as soft winds blew and clouds were rising. Bright lightning flashed across the sky and there was a low rumble in the distance. Shivaji stood with the others at the edge of the fort, watching the clouds. A mini tornado played with the dust and cold easterly winds started blowing.

Soon, lightning covered the sky accompanied by loud bursts of thunder. Shivaji clung to his mother in fear and Jijabai took him inside as a curtain of rain approached the fort. There was a hailstorm and everyone ran to protect themselves while Shivaji watched with wide-eyed curiosity. The hailstorm was followed by a torrential downpour and nullahs started filling to the brim. There was water everywhere but nobody complained. The sweet aroma of the wet soil permeated the air. There was an air of celebration as people welcomed the showers with relief.

Everyone came out the moment the rain stopped. A single shower had changed the landscape completely and a brilliant rainbow could be seen across the eastern sky. Shivaji pointed towards it and said, 'Aai, look!'

Jijabai remarked to Vishwasrao, who had just stepped into the courtyard, 'The danger seems over. I think the next year will bring good rains.'

'It seems so,' he said, sounding dejected.

Jijabai looked askance when Vishwasrao clarified, 'Rani saheb, we have rains but no people in the village to till the land.'

'Half the Junnar village is here in the fort itself.'

'I don't understand!'

'We have enough men here to give us a helping hand. Is it not our responsibility to ensure that the land is tilled and houses repaired before the villagers return? Let us all go down.'

The whole fort reverberated with enthusiasm. The dry grass growing on the village huts brought tears to Jijabai's eyes. The fort blacksmith, who till now had only forged weapons, was busy making agricultural implements. And one day after the bhoomi puja, the ceremonial prayers before tilling, the work began in earnest. The sowing was soon completed and within no time, the fields were green again. The forest on the hills looked dense and one could see the milky-white waterfalls on the Lenyadri and neighbouring mountain ranges. Soon, the villagers began to return and they could not contain their happiness seeing the green fields.

Whenever Vishwasrao stepped out, Shivaji would insist on accompanying him, come rain or shine. He loved the sight of green fields.

'It seems he is going to be a farmer,' Jijabai commented.

'And what is wrong with that? There are lords; then why not a farmer who is a lord?'

Jijabai laughed with deep satisfaction.

A year had passed since Shahaji Raje had left Adil Shah of Bijapur to join the Nizam. The Mughals had overrun Daulatabad but Shahaji Raje was not disappointed. He took the new Shah to Mauli. Adil Shah of Bijapur and the Mughals joined hands and it was not easy to fight them. The Nizam Shahi dynasty collapsed but Shahaji formed his own troops and attacked the Mughals. It was very rare for a Jagirdar to raise an army and face the might of the Mughals. Within two years, the stronger Mughal army had routed Shahaji's men, and Shahaji had to accept employment under the patronage of the Bijapurkars. Another six years would go by before he managed to move to a more prestigious position.

In the meanwhile, Shivaji was growing up at the Shivneri Fort. He had turned six now. He would watch the Lenyadri and surrounding provinces from the fort. Shastribua had started teaching him the script now. A year after Shahaji's new appointment, a messenger arrived from Bijapur. Soon, horsemen followed along with royal palanquins and a couple of bullock carts.

Jijabai read the message: Shahaji Raje had been awarded the jagir of Pune. He had sent his trustworthy and wise lieutenant Dadoji Konddev with the order to move to Pune. Dadoji was a fair-complexioned man, wearing a smart turban, long tunic and a crisp dhoti. His bearing was enhanced by a broad forehead and piercing eyes. He bent low on seeing Jijabai and she asked Shivaji, 'Raje, did you salute Dadoji?'

Shivaji Raje saluted as Dadoji replied, 'Rani saheb, it is we who are supposed to salute, not Raje.'

'There is a difference between you and the others. Don't you think I understand that? The person sent to take care of us must be someone who is extremely trustworthy.'

'Rani saheb, when shall we leave?'

'Whenever you say. Where is my lord these days?'

'Raje is busy on a campaign in Karnatak. Had he been free, he would have come himself.'

'He finally had to find employment under the same person who sacked his jagir.'

'Rani saheb, politics is not one-sided—it has many facets, and it changes with the times. The same Murar Jagdev, who burnt Pune, became a close friend of Shahaji Raje. Politics turned its tables again and Murar Jagdev was killed by Adil Shah ruthlessly.'

'And my lord?'

'Raje is treated with great honour in Adil Shah's durbar. He has a mansab of twelve thousand and has earned the title of Raja. He has the jagir of Pune and the neighbouring villages. He is enjoying his stay with honour and dignity in Bengaluru. Karnatak today is proud of him.'

Jijabai was ready to leave in the next two days. During the six years that she had stayed at the Shivneri Fort, every one there had become like family, and she was pained to leave close confidantes like Vishwasrao and Lakshmibai. With a heavy heart, Jijabai, along with Shivaji, had darshan of Shivai Devi before leaving.

By late afternoon, they had entered the devastated landscape of Pune. Shivaji felt as if he were entering some old, dilapidated town. The broken walls of ruined forts seemed to tell a story of a grandeur gone by. All one could see were collapsed structures everywhere with wild shrubs growing amok. The only sign of life was a few stray blossoms. People settled at the banks of the river looked with surprise, and a little trepidation, at the approaching caravan. Dadoji Konddev, alias Pant, raised his hand to signal the caravan to stop. The men unloaded the luggage from the bullock cart as Shivaji looked curiously at the ruins.

'Maa saheb, is this Pune?' he asked.

'Yes.'

'I can't see anyone here other than us.'

'They will come when you call them.'

'Where will we live? Where is the palace?'

'One doesn't always live in a readymade palace, Raje. Kings have palaces built for themselves!'

At a flat piece of ground near the banks, a shamiana was raised and small camps were set around it. The waters of the confluence of the Mula–Mutha Rivers shone in the light of the setting sun. The heir to the jagir had lit his first lamp in the ruins! In the days that followed, Shivaji would walk around with Dadoji observing the surroundings, and Dadoji Konddev could visualize the Pune of the future.

A few days later, Shivaji came in running shouting, 'Maa saheb, Pant has found an idol of a god.'

'Where?'

'Near the river.'

Pant seemed excited. They had cleared the rubble around to expose a hidden Ganesha idol. It was a beautiful, unbroken statue. Jijabai folded her hands in reverence when Pant said, 'Maa saheb, it is an auspicious beginning.'

'Yes, Pant. Let us build a beautiful temple here.'

Pant readily agreed and said, 'Maa saheb, we still haven't decided the location for the palace.'

'Let the palace be near the temple.'

The markings for the palace were made and after the bhoomi puja, Dadoji dug the ground first in a ceremonial gesture. Dadoji was not content that there was just one palace for the family. He decided to build another palace and the work began in earnest.

The palace construction was in full swing. Wells were being dug in search of water. Hundreds of people were involved in the work and hearing of the same, many craftsmen rushed to find employment there. The Pune palace had two large courtyards and a huge hall for audiences with the people of the city . There was a private hall and another set of private quarters for the queen, kitchen and a beautiful puja room, apart from stables and cowsheds. Dadoji named the palace Lal Mahal, adjacent to which was a ganapati temple.

Soon, the villagers started settling down. One day, Pant asked Jijabai, 'Maa saheb, may I take Raje to Shivapur?'

'Why?'

'I have decided to plant a mango orchard there. I want the first sapling to be planted by Raje.'

'It seems that you don't tell me everything these days!'

Dadoji was taken aback and said, 'What haven't I told you?'

Jijabai smiled and said, 'My lord has a younger wife now but I was not told of it; and that Tukabai Rani saheb has delivered a baby boy?'

'I must have forgotten in the rush of things here ...' muttered Dadoji, embarrassed.

Dadoji busied himself with the administration of the jagir and he extended monetary support to people to come and settle there. Villagers thronged the palace each day and Jijabai would listen to the sad tales of the women.

Shivaji absorbed everything as he grew up, watching the jagir take shape. Dadoji was teaching him archery, sword fighting and wrestling. Tough games were played out in the courtyard each evening and the peasant folk's children would participate along with Shivaji.

One day in the summers, Dadoji came in to announce the arrival of Mudhojirao Nimbalkar, an old confidante of Shahaji's. Jijabai had heard that

Mudhoji's jagir had been captured by Bijapurkars and that he had been kept under arrest in Satara. When Jijabai met him, she saw that he had come with his son Bajaji and daughter Saibai.

Bajaji bent low in mujra seeing Mudhoji salute Jijabai. Jijabai hugged Saibai as she touched her feet and asked, 'When did you all arrive?'

'We were released from jail thanks to Shahaji Raje. Now that we got our jagir at Phaltan back, we wanted to pay you a visit.'

'Having you around will be great help and support.'

'Maa saheb, you have brought Pune back to life—that is a great achievement.'

'I have done nothing! It is people like Dadoji who create the magic.'

'Doers will do but one needs the blessings of Devi to make things happen,' Mudhoji exclaimed, raising his hands upwards in prayer.

Pointing at Saibai, Maa saheb asked, 'What is her name?'

'Sai; and this is my son, Bajaji.'

The young Saibai, barely seven or eight years old, looked at Jijabai wide-eyed. She had a wheatish complexion and her sweet face was highlighted by a sharp nose, lovely lips, jet-black eyes and a slim neck.

Maa saheb requested the Nimbalkars to stay in Pune for a while and they agreed. Sai clung to Maa saheb like a shadow while Bajaji made friends with Shivaji. One evening, the courtyard was busy with the usual evening games when Shivaji and the instructor began their sword practice. Sai, watching from the balcony, came running in to Maa saheb's quarters where she sat chatting with Mudhoji.

'Maa saheb, there is a great fight going on outside!'

'Mudhoji, let us go and watch them practice. I haven't seen the games in quite a while now.'

Four pairs of men were practising sword fighting. Maa saheb asked the ustaad when he saluted, 'Nanu Ustaad, what is Raje learning these days?'

Nanu, despite his age, had the strong physique of an instructor. He said, 'Raje, pick up a lathi!'

Picking up a lathi, Shivaji started circling it around his head and showed his prowess with it. As it moved over his head, they could all hear the whirling sound.

Nanu Ustaad spat on his palms as he picked up his stick and took his position. Raje followed suit.

'Raje! Attack!'

Shivaji lifted the stick and started attacking vigorously. Nanu defended himself deftly taking a few steps back as he handled the hammering blows. Everyone looked at the fight wide-eyed and suddenly Nanu shouted, 'Raje ... careful now!'

Jijabai was worried seeing Raje defend himself, moving back with each attack. After a while, unable to defend a hard blow, Raje's stick fell out of his hands. Maa saheb said, sighing deeply, 'Nanu, be careful. You seem to forget he is just a child.'

'No, Maa saheb. There is no age barrier in this game. The one who attacks first wins. Raje's arms are not yet strong enough. But this is the only way to learn.'

A tall banana tree was placed on a hook in the middle of the courtyard. Raja was given a spear which was a few feet taller than him. A few silver rings shone where the metal joined the wood. Raje took a few steps back and waited for the instructions when Nanu shouted, 'Raje, move!'

Lunging forward in long leaps, Shivaji threw the spear deftly, piercing the tree right through the middle. Everyone cheered and Saibai sat there looking at Shivaji with great admiration.

A little further on the field, two banana trees were placed a few feet away from each other. Shivaji held two thin swords in his hand, waving them in the air with focused attention while a casual smile played on his lips. Then, in a flash, as he stood between the trees, he made his move. Nothing seemed to have happened. He saluted, looking at Maa saheb and Dadoji.

Both the trees stood in the same place. Saibai chuckled and looked askance at Maa saheb who said, 'Nanu Ustaad! Please explain what our Raje has done.'

Nanu Ustaad moved forward and pushed the trees. They both fell down, having been cut right through the middle. Unable to contain her surprise, Saibai, covering her face with her dupatta shyly, muttered, 'That was unbelievable!'

Jijabai hugged Saibai and, taking everyone around by surprise, asked, 'Sai, how would you like to have Raje as your husband?'

Saibai looked at Maa saheb once and then at Shivaji, who was busy sheathing his swords, and said loudly to no one in particular, 'Yes, he will do for a husband!'

Impressed by her innocent yet candid reply, Jijabai hugged her again and said in a gentle chiding tone, 'You silly girl! One never agrees so readily!'

Everyone laughed aloud. There was no formality in the air that evening.

Dadoji said, 'Maa saheb!'

'Yes, Dadoji?'

'Now that the matter is being discussed openly, I think we should formalize it. Raje is ten years old now. The pair of them would look beautiful together.'

'Nanu Ustaad, what do you say?' Jijabai asked.

Nanu nodded. 'I agree. A bride would add to the glory of this palace.'

Jijabai smiled in agreement. 'Should we not take the opinion of Nimbalkar mama? After all, she is his daughter,' she said, turning towards Mudhoji.

'Don't say that, Maa saheb. After all, she is yours. We owe our life to Maharaj—if you accept our daughter into your family, we would feel blessed to have returned a part of our debt.'

'If Jagdamba so wishes, then let it be so! It is our good fortune to continue with the old ties. Dadoji, send a message to Bengaluru at the earliest. Once we get Maharaj's formal approval, we shall start planning the wedding.'

Everyone saluted as Maa saheb stood up and left with Saibai holding her hand. Mudhoji sat there, watching them leave through tear-filled eyes.

The next day, two horsemen were dispatched at the crack of dawn towards Bengaluru, and Mudhoji returned to Phaltan with his son and daughter. In a week, the messenger returned, putting an end to an anxious wait. Dadoji reverently touched the bag containing the message to his forehead before opening it. He scanned the message quickly and his face lit up.

'Maharaj saheb has agreed to the alliance! Not only that, he has also given us permission to spend lavishly for the wedding. He has asked for the date so that he may be present for the festivities.'

'Pant, please inform Mudhojirao—we don't have much time now.'

Things began to move at a rapid pace. Shivaji's and Sai's horoscopes were well matched, clearing the niggling doubts Jijabai had in her mind! The priest chose an auspicious date. As the days went by, Pant had no time as each moment was earmarked for some task or the other. Seeing the activities around, Jijabai asked him, 'Pant! The scale of this wedding seems to be huge. Are we being extravagant?'

'Maa saheb, don't worry about the expenses. Helping a community financially alone does not make them feel like a part of the jagir. This is an opportunity to make the community into a family.'

Mudhoji was under a bit of stress. He had been recently made the Jagirdar of Phaltan. After making initial preparations, he returned to Pune to discuss the arrangements. He shuffled nervously as he stood near Jijabai and wondered how he should propose the topic of dowry. He said, clearing his throat once, 'Maa saheb, we have discussed the dates and other arrangements but we have not spoken about what we should be offering you.'

'Such discussions suit business dealings, Mudhoji, and this is a matter of blood relations. You are giving your daughter to us. What more can we ask for? However, you have to give just one more thing.'

'Ask, Maa saheb!' Mudhoji said happily.

'Give them your blessings and everything else will be fine.'

Mudhoji could not hold back his tears. 'Maa saheb, by accepting our daughter, you have redeemed our debt to you of the last seven generations. Allow us to do something so that we feel we too have contributed.'

'I only want you to ensure that all of Phaltan is here for the festivities.'

Jijabai had not exaggerated. The scale of activities was such that everyone could be accommodated. The kitchen had moved to the open courtyard, and a variety of items were being prepared. The palace was being decorated with new curtains and chandeliers and expert jewellers were working under Dadoji's supervision.

In the meantime, the news had arrived that Shahaji Raje would not be able to attend since he was busy with a military campaign. However, the wedding was to be carried out as per plan. Jijabai was depressed because Shahaji Raje's absence meant that Sambhaji too would not attend. It had been eleven years since she had seen her elder son. In anticipation, Jijabai had gotten clothes and jewellery made for him, but putting her sadness away with a sigh, she went back to the work at hand.

The marriage activities formally began with an invitation to the gods. Mudhojirao entered Pune with his people to the entire city reverberating with the sound of drums and trumpets. Everyday more than a thousand meals were being prepared for guests. The ceremony took place in the Lal Mahal which was filled with the auspicious chanting of the mangala ashtakas and at the right time, thousands of hands showered the couple with the auspicious blessings of raw rice.

Shivaji, wearing a lovely embroidered turban and a matching kurta, walked towards the palace. A large sandalwood tilak adorned his forehead and a sword hung from his waist. Saibai walked a step behind him. A shawl tied both of them together and the knot hung in middle swaying a little as they moved. As Raje touched Dadoji's feet, the old man could not hold back his tears. His whole body was shaking as he hugged Shivaji without a word.

The party moved ahead by the light of hundreds of maashals and lanterns. Dadoji, Mudhoji, Hanumante, Shastri, Korde and others walked in the front while different groups displaying their antics with swords and other weapons went ahead of them. The procession moved at a snail's pace and Sai dozed off, waking up intermittently to the sound of the crackers. Entering the Bhosale household in traditional fashion, she pushed a rice container placed at the threshold with her feet and crossed over as the rice spilled out.

The rains had now ended and Shahaji Raje sent a message to Dadoji Konddev to accompany Jijabai and Shivaji to Bengaluru. It was a long journey and Saibai was sent to her father's house in Phaltan. The horses and palanquins were made ready while an advance party ensured their comfort along the way. Shivaji was eagerly waiting to meet his father, while Jijabai could not contain her excitement at the prospect of seeing not just her husband but also Sambhaji.

On an auspicious day, the entourage left for Bengaluru with great fanfare. As they entered Karnatak, Shivaji was astonished by the change in topography, huge boulders on mountain tops. A cool breeze blew as they reached the outskirts of Bengaluru and messengers were dispatched to inform Shahaji Raje of their arrival.

The next day, Shivaji entered the city of Bengaluru. Adil Shah's flag fluttered on the huge and heavily guarded entrance. Sambhaji stood waiting to receive Dadoji, and when Dadoji signalled to Shivaji, they both got off their horses and walked a few steps. Shivaji saluted Sambhaji, bending low in mujra. Seeing his younger brother's formal approach, Sambhaji hugged him with great affection.

'Shivaji, we have all been eagerly waiting for you. Maharaj saheb has not been himself for the past two days because of his excitement.'

The palanquin arrived and Shambhu Raje stepped forward. The curtain was moved and Jijabai looked at Shambhu Raje with surprise and affection. He was wearing a churidar and carried a sword at his waist. He resembled his father and a faint moustache sprouted above his lips, his broad forehead smeared with white ash. He stepped forward and touched Maa saheb's feet. Jijabai could not hold herself back and hugged him, kissing him on his cheeks. Sambhaji extricated himself out of her embrace and said, 'Maharaj saheb is waiting for you.'

Sambhaji, Shivaji and Dadoji mounted their horses again and the procession moved into the city. There were huge palaces all around and Shivaji was struck by the beautiful architecture. Their way of dressing, their language—everything was different and impressive. The horses moved at a slow trot as they crossed a large ground in front of the palace. Servants, wearing bronze coloured clothing, stood at attention in the entrance. As Shivaji reached the steps, he looked up to see a tall, powerful personality standing there. His long hair reached his neck and his full beard gave him an aura of prestige. Sambhaji nudged his brother gently and performed an elaborate mujra to his father. But Shivaji was too busy staring at his father and did not bend in salute.

Shahaji Raje said, 'Welcome, Raje.'

Shivaji moved forward and sat on his knees. Touching the ground with both hands, he put his head on his father's feet.

Shahaji Raje lifted him and said, as he hugged him, 'Dadoji, perhaps the young Raje does not know how to perform a mujra?'

'I know, Aba saheb, but Maa saheb has taught me to touch the feet of my elders.'

'Oh, I see ... Raje, I see you ride without a saddle. It is difficult to ride bare back, isn't it?'

'It is not, Aba saheb. You just need strong thighs.'

'Wah, Raje! I am impressed!'

At that moment the palanquin carrying Jijabai arrived. She entered the palace escorted by the ladies and was surprised at its size, which was difficult to estimate from the outside. As she entered the second courtyard, Tukabai came forward to touch her feet.

'Younger Rani saheb, you need not do that.'

'You are elder to me. But how did you recognize me?'

'Who would not recognize the Lakshmi of the house? Where is Chotte Raje? I am keen to see him.'

At that moment, Ekoji Raje came in with his brothers and touched Jijabai's feet.

'It is so nice to have the entire family together after so many years!' Tukabai said.

'It was like the twelve-year-wait for Ram and Sita,' Jijabai said, smiling.

And so, time passed in Bengaluru. It had been a month since they had arrived in Bengaluru. One afternoon, Shahaji Raje summoned Shivaji. He went into the office to find two British traders there and weapons spread out on a table.

Shahaji Raje asked, pointing towards them, 'Raje, would you like a firangi gun?'

Shivaji's eyes were fixed on a gun with a long, narrow muzzle.

'Do you know how to fire one?' Shahaji asked.

'I don't, but I am sure I can learn.'

'Shabbash! Then we shall buy you one.'

The traders immediately held the firearm for Shivaji to hold and it was surprisingly light despite its long muzzle. They stepped out of the office into the courtyard where, at a distance, a coconut was kept on a wooden post. Shahaji Raje crouched on one knee, adjusting the gun in his hand and then, taking aim, fired. The coconut shattered into small pieces. He said, fondling the gun, 'This gun is very good, with hardly any recoil. It is yours now. Keep it as a memento from me. I will instruct the shikar havaldar to teach you how to fire it tomorrow.'

There was a deep bond between father and son and Shahaji Raje used to love Shivaji's company. He would introduce him to all the important sardars saying, 'You know, his birth heralded prosperity and ended our sorrows!'

Shivaji never tired of asking questions which Shahaji would try answering as best as possible.

One day, Shahaji Raje went into the inner quarters where Jijabai and Tukabai sat chatting. Joining the conversation, Shahaji said 'I was very keen to attend Shivaji's wedding but could not.'

'Then let us get him married again?' Tukabai suggested.

'What a good idea! After all, what's a marriage without my presence? But who do you have in mind for the bride?'

'I have already identified one. Have you seen Mohite's girl? What a beauty!' Tukabai said excitedly.

'I agree. Let us fix the marriage then!' said Shahaji Raje excitedly and left the room.

Jijabai was not happy with such quick decisions. 'It has only been a short while since we got him married ... '

'It suits a raja to have many wives.'

There is a saying that the king's wish is really a command. The arrangements were made within no time and the marriage took place with great fanfare. The bride and bridegroom were taken around in a golden palanquin and the entire city reverberated with gun and cannon fire. Shahaji Raje's wish had been fulfilled.

Shahaji Raje's life was one of richness and pomp. Days would pass by in elaborate morning rituals, baths, pujas, and discussions on poetry, dance and other arts. The palace would wake up to the chants of the priests and sleep to the sounds of dance. People would arrive on horseback and in palanquins.

For some, their arrival would be announced by a messenger and for others, the trumpets would be sounded.

Shivaji found all of this very new, and, one afternoon, he was sitting with Jijabai and Tukabai. Suddenly, he said, 'Aai, people used to visit us every day in Pune. But I don't see such people here. Why is that so?'

'Don't you see so many sardars and other visitors?'

'I am not talking about them. What about the Patils, farmers and other villagers?'

Tukabai laughed sarcastically. 'Shivaji Raje, this is the palace of a maharaj. How can such people visit him? It is appropriate that only a raja meet a raja.'

'If the common folk are scared of visiting and meeting him, what kind of raja is he? When Ram left for the forest, his entire city came to see him off. A fisherman hugged him. Isn't that king a real one, Aai?' asked Shivaji.

Tukabai's face turned grave and she did not reply.

Bengaluru was now becoming boring for Shivaji. The novelty had worn off, making him want to return to Pune and be with the peasant folk. A few days later, he went to meet his father to find him inspecting a couple of horses. The moment Shivaji arrived, Maharaj said to him, 'I am going to test you now. Tell me which one is the better horse.'

Both the horses were almost identical in height. Shivaji looked at them with an expert eye while his father looked at him with pride. He moved closer to one horse and touched its lips.

'Careful, Raje! He may bite.'

'He won't. He is a good horse.'

Mohammed, the syce, was surprised and exclaimed, 'Al-hum-dullilah! He may be young but he has a good eye.'

'How did the Raje identify the better horse?' The syce asked.

'He spends a lot of time in the stables and has great love for animals,' Dadoji explained.

'That is the true sign of a king in the making. Look at our Shambhu Raje! He knows Sanskrit very well, writes poetry in it, but he does not have these traits. He has become more of a Brahmin because of his involvement in the shastras,' Shahaji added.

Sambhaji blushed while Shahaji hugged his younger son and said, 'I am impressed. This horse is now yours.' And then looking at Pant he said, 'Have a ritual done to ward off evil eyes from him. I am afraid I myself may cast it upon him!'

That night, Ekoji made a fuss with his mother, demanding a horse for himself. She hugged him and, looking at Jijabai, said, 'How can you get one? Shivaji is dear to your father and you are the youngest and not that lucky.'

Tukabai's words pierced Jijabai's heart like an arrow but she did not utter a word.

After dinner, Tukabai and Jijabai came to their bedroom to find both Shivaji's and Sambhaji's beds empty. It was quite late in the night and she wondered where the boys could be at that hour. She sent the servants in search of them and when they were found, they came in looking guilty. Jijabai asked, 'Where were they?'

'They were in the dance mahal.'

'In the dance mahal?'

'Not inside. They were hiding behind a curtain, watching from the outside.'

'All right. You may go,' she said dismissing the servant.

Jijabai looked at both of them and asked in a harsh tone, 'Raje, is this true?'

Shivaji was quiet.

'Whose permission did you take before going there? Were you not told not to step out of the palace after dusk?'

Shivaji was now on the verge of tears and said, 'Dada Maharaj insisted. He wanted to have some fun.'

'Aren't you ashamed of yourself?'

Tukabai came in and saw Shivaji crying. She hugged him and said, 'Rani saheb, it is just a dance. What is wrong with that? If Raje's sons don't see the dance, who else will?'

'Bai, you may be younger than me but I am requesting you not to interfere.'

'Why make a fuss of such small things? These things happen.'

'It may be fine with you but I cannot tolerate such things. The children will be spoilt.'

Tukabai was furious and retorted, 'If you are so concerned about their behaviour, then instead of scolding them, you should be questioning him.' Jijabai knew she was referring to Shahaji.

'Yes, I will do that,' Jijabai said firmly. 'Elders need to set an example for the way they want their children to behave.'

Tukabai left the room fuming. Shivaji cried himself to sleep but Jijabai did not try to pacify him.

The next morning, Shahaji Raje came to the quarters where his entire family sat chatting. Sensing an opportunity, Tukabai said, 'Rani saheb does not like the lack of discipline in this household. She is afraid Shivaji will get spoilt here.' Waving a hand towards Jijabai, she continued, 'She says you need to change your habits if you want Shivaji to stay here.'

Shahaji Raje raised an eyebrow questioningly.

'It seems Shivaji Raje was watching the dances last night.'

'So?'

'Rani saheb insists they must be stopped immediately.'

'Is that so?' he asked, staring at Jijabai.

Jijabai chose to remain silent and Tukabai smiled victoriously. Shahaji Raje stood up suddenly and said, 'It is not possible for me to change my habits—I am too old now. If Rani saheb is afraid that my habits will spoil Shivaji Raje, then she is free to go whenever she wishes to.' He turned and left abruptly, leaving Jijabai in tears.

Jijabai could sense the bitterness in their relationship increase every day. She decided to move back to Pune rather than allow things to fester further. She steeled her heart and informed Shahaji Raje of her decision. The news of Shivaji going back to Pune spread like wildfire across the palace. In the period of a year and a half, father and son had grown close to each other and the separation would be hard. When Shivaji came to take Shahaji's blessings in the morning, he asked, 'I am told you are going back to Pune. Would you remember me?'

'Aba saheb!' Shivaji exclaimed and hugged him, tears in his eyes.

'No, Raje! Men don't cry,' Shahaji Raje said in voice choked with emotion. 'I will come to Pune soon.'

'Do you promise?' asked Shivaji, smiling.

'Absolutely! You are now the Jagirdar. Your wish is my command.'

'Where do I have a jagir?' asked Shivaji

Shahaji smiled. Looking at Dadoji, he said, 'Pant, why do we give our children horses to play with—guns, swords and other things? So that they may grow up and be men, isn't it? I have allocated thirty-six villages from my jagir in Shivaji's name. You may start the process and formalize it. Raje! Take care of your jagir now.'

Pant said, 'Raje! Touch your father's feet—you are very lucky to have such a father.'

Shivaji put his head on his father's feet. Shahaji Raje hugged him tightly and said, 'Pant, how will I manage when he goes away tomorrow? He is such a darling. You have taken very good care of him. I can now retire in peace.'

Pant could not hold back his tears of satisfaction and pride.

The next day, all documents regarding the jagir were readied. Shamrao Nilkanth was made Peshwa while Balkrishnapant, Naropant Dikshit's cousin, was made the deputy. Dadojipant was made the trustee of the jagir. The preparations for the return had begun in earnest.

Jijabai asked Shahaji Raje, hoping against hope, 'Shall I take Sambhaji with me for a few days?'

'No, Rani saheb. Sambhaji has grown up with me in a different world. Leave him here.'

'I hope you have forgiven me ...'

'I am not angry with you. That is why I am sending Shivaji Raje back with you. I shall take care of Shambhu Raje and you take care of Shivaji Raje.' He added with a smile, 'Let us see who does a better job!'

As Shivaji touched Shahaji's feet while leaving, Shahaji said, 'Pant! Take care of Raje. Make a man out of him. I am leaving my precious treasure in your hands—guard him with your life.'

Sambhaji Raje escorted them till the first stop on their journey. The next day, the caravan moved towards Pune and Sambhaji returned with his men to Bengaluru.

The news of Shivaji's arrival in Pune spread fast. Everyone rushed to meet Shivaji Raje, who seemed grown up now. The office of the Jagirdar had acquired a stature, since apart from the clerks, there were now the Peshwa and other officials. Dadoji took stock of everything that had occurred while they were in Bengaluru from Narhekar. He was helping Shivaji learn the ropes of the office including writing letters and documents.

A few days later, Mudhojirao Nimbalkar arrived.

'Welcome, Raje! How was your stay in Bengaluru?' asked Mudhojirao as he entered the private quarters.

Jijabai immediately asked, 'Where is our daughter-in-law?'

'There! We can see her palanquin arriving,' he said, pointing towards the courtyard. Dadoji got down the steps, adjusting his turban and tunic. Saibai entered the courtyard, after washing her feet. Her gait had changed as she now wore a sari. Despite her youth, she had acquired a grace in her gait. She looked at the maids and accepted their mujras as she walked.

Pulling her cheeks affectionately, Jijabai said, 'You have grown so much! Haven't you forgotten to touch the feet of your husband?'

Saibai lost all her controlled poise, chuckled and hugged Jijabai.

'Now you seem more yourself! But don't try to pretend to be someone else. Raje has acquired another wife in Bengaluru.'

'Let him!'

'She is better looking than you and much fairer.'

'Let her be! She will be my playmate.'

Mudhojirao said then, 'She knows how to behave like an elder queen.'

Navratri was approaching fast and these were days of celebration. All the swords, knives and other metal weapons were cleaned with salt and tamarind for the shastra puja. The lamps in the inner temple burned brightly, lighting up the statue of the goddess with eight hands. Each evening the courtyard would resound with chants of 'Jay Ambe! Jay Ambe!' and crowds would gather to see the festivities.

On Navami, the ceremonial horse arrived at the palace with much fanfare. The goat sacrifice was made, after which the horse crossed the thin stream of flowing blood and entered the courtyard. Shivaji took a sword, kept especially in the puja room for the past nine days, and touched it to his forehead reverently.

That evening as he paid his respects to Jijabai, who, putting a black mark on his cheeks to ward off evil, said, 'You are supposed to step out of the house on this day for victory. Destroy the enemy and come back with riches.'

A horse, decorated with finery, stood at the door. Shivaji saddled the horse and mounted, while his trusted soldiers followed. Shivaji reached the auspicious shami tree, the leaves of which had been traditionally worshipped since the Pandavas had hidden their weapons there during the Mahabharata war. It had a religious significance especially on Dussehra—the leaves were treated like gold on Dussehra and as per tradition, Raje was supposed to return home with these riches. As per ritual, Raje cut the leaves with his sword and he entered the palace rich with the booty.

Jijabai said, 'Raje, now without looking back, hit the threshold with your sword.'

Jijabai held a tray with a gold ring in it among rice grains. She picked up the ring and touched his forehead with it.

Raje asked, 'Maa saheb, what is this ring for?'

'This is not merely a ring, Raje. This is Lakshmi. You brought home riches and she came along with them. But you are not supposed to see her. After crossing the threshold, you are supposed to break her leg.'

'Break her leg?'

'Yes. Once you break her leg, she cannot leave the house!'

Raje smiled.

Jijabai said, 'Raje, you are an adult now. Remember—Lakshmi is never happy if you run after her. She follows people who do their duty. Always keep her behind you while you face calamities boldly. Never forget this. Dadoji must be waiting; go and pay your regards to him.'

Raje bowed to Jijabai and went in.

Shivaji donated a gold coin to each of the Brahmins as a token of charity. The office managers came next, followed by the stable managers, servants, household staff and others. Raje put his head on Dadoji's feet when Jijabai asked, 'Raje, did you not give a coin to Dadoji?'

Hugging Shivaji, Dadoji said, 'Maa saheb, this coin is my most precious one. What better gift can I ask for?'

Shivaji would usually accompany Dadoji as he went on inspection tours. He would also watch how Jijabai solved legal issues of people who approached her. The palace would be full of people singing bhajans and Raje would get engrossed listening to them. His body would tingle with pride and delight listening to the patriotic songs.

One morning Dadoji told him, 'Raje we need to go the Nane village.'

'When will you return?' Jijabai asked.

'We'll be away at least five or six days—there are a lot of accounts to be audited.'

Noticing Shivaji's long face, Dadoji said, 'Raje! This is your jagir. You took it from the elder Raje with lot of excitement. If you are bored of running it, let me know. I will inform Maharaj saheb accordingly.'

Such reprimands would always work on the young man and he would mount his horse quickly! While riding around the countryside, he would notice the tall forts which seemed to be kissing the skies. He would ask Pant, 'Whose forts are these?'

'Adil Shah's.'

'The jagir is ours. Then why are the forts his?'

'Raje, the jagir is not ours. We have been given the right to collect the taxes. But the ownership is Adil Shah's.'

Shivaji Raje was very popular in the jagir. Everyone would bow their heads on seeing Shahaji Raje's son arrive. The ryots would share their joys and sorrows with Dadoji, while Shivaji observed how Dadoji would use his discretion to solve their problems.

One evening, Raje sat alone in the courtyard, lost in his thoughts. He did not see Jijabai arrive.

She asked, 'Raje, what are you looking at with such intensity?'

'Maa saheb, I am watching an insect being taken away by the tiny ants.'

'What about it?'

'Look at the size of the insect! The insect is alive and struggling to get away but is unable to do anything with the ants that have surrounded it.'

Jijabai did not reply and when Raje turned back, he saw that she had left. He then turned to look at the door as he heard someone enter. It was a man with a fair and handsome face. He had a broad chest and was wearing a dhoti which covered his knees. He wore a coarse vest which was torn in many places. His shoulder seemed injured and the blood, which had oozed down to his palms, had dried. But there was no sign of any pain on his face. He walked swinging a heavy stick in his hand.

He looked around in the courtyard and seeing Shivaji, he bowed in mujra.

'Ram, Ram! Is this Shivaji's palace?'

'Yes, it is.'

'I would like to speak with him.'

'Sit down.'

'But ... '

'I said sit!' Seeing a servant nearby, Shivaji shouted, 'Go and fetch a doctor immediately.' Turning towards the man, he asked, 'What is your name?'

'Bhima. I am an ironsmith,' and then quickly added, 'Sarkar.'

Dadoji had arrived by then and Raje asked Bhima, 'What work did you have here?'

'I don't know how to put it. I am from Satara. There is a famine there and I had left my village to join the Mughals. As I was crossing a forest, they attacked me.'

'Who?'

'Those bloody wolves ... oh, sorry, Sarkar,' he said, realizing his use of profanity.

'Then ...?'

'There were three of them. I was alone with just a stick in that dense jungle. I swung my stick and hit hard. They backed a bit but one of them jumped and ripped my shoulder. I was furious and hit him so hard that he never got up.'

'And what about the others?'

'They ran away scared.'

Shivaji was amused by the story. 'What brings you here?'

'Oh, I forgot! I brought the tail of the wolf as proof of the battle. I was told I would get a reward if I showed up with one,' he said, smiling as he unhooked the tail tied to his belt.

Dadoji had started this practice to ward off the trouble created by the wolves. The physician arrived in the meantime and put a lotion on the wound. He was dressing the wound when Bhima asked, 'Are you Shivaji Raje?'

'Yes. Why do you ask?'

'I have heard a lot about you.'

Dadoji said, 'Kulkarni, take him to the office and give him his reward.'

'Wait,' said Raje and went inside. He came back carrying a sword and giving it to Bhima said, 'You were lucky to manage with just a lathi. Keep this sword with you.'

Bhima observed the sword carefully and moving his finger on the sharp edge, he said, 'This looks like a Rampuri.'

'You do know something about swords,' Raje remarked.

'Of course! This is what I do for a living—I make swords.'

'Will you work here?'

'Yes—just tell me what I need to do.'

'I will give you a blacksmith's workshop.'

Bhima touched Raje's feet and said, 'It would be my pleasure.'

'Sonopant,' Raje said, 'arrange a workshop for this person.'

Sonopant looked at Dadoji, who said, 'Sonopant, Raje has given a command. What are you waiting for?'

'As you wish,' said Sonopant reluctantly and took Bhima inside.

Everyone went back to their respective posts and Raje was alone with Dadoji.

'Raje, I understand Sonopant's hesitation. You should not appoint people in such a hurry. Bhima is an outsider—we don't know him at all!'

'Pant, he seems a fit, hardworking man. He has a broad, strong chest and is courageous. What else do you want? We have given him a chance and we shall know his calibre soon.'

That evening when Dadoji came to pay his regards to Jijabai he said, 'Maa saheb, I must say Raje is very perceptive. He was able to assess Bhima very well.'

Jijabai was happy to hear Dadoji praising Shivaji openly because he very rarely did so.

'I heard about that. He has an eye for spotting talented people.'

Dadoji said, 'Maa saheb, a famous poet has arrived from Kolhapur. If permission be granted, I shall ask him to come to the palace.'

'Please do! We shall all listen to a ballad this evening—Raje would love it!'

That evening, the courtyard was brightly lit with burning mashaals and lamps and a crowd eagerly waited for the singer, while the accompanying musicians tuned their respective instruments. Dadoji and other important members sat to the right of the baithak. On the left were Dadoji's family, Brahmin members of the court and behind them the other Maratha ladies.

The singer came into the courtyard and his troupe and he saluted before taking their seats. He gave a loud signal to the percussionist, the sitar player strummed his sitar, giving out a melodious sound, and the ambience was set for the evening. The mild whispers, which had prevailed till now subsided and the audience was eager for the performance to start. Bending in mujra once more, he began.

It was the story of Rani Padmini, the queen of Chittor. Allauddin Khilji, enamoured by what he had heard of Rani Padmini's beauty was desperate to see her and unable to control his lust, he invaded Chittor. Ratansen, the king, tried his best to save his kingdom but was captured by Allauddin. The invader agreed to spare Ratansen's life on the condition that Padmini would allow him to see her face once. When he entered her quarters, he saw Padmini sitting there, looking divine in her regal beauty. Unable to control his desire, he forgot the promise made to Ratansen and insisted on taking Padmini into his harem.

Obviously, Padmini refused to entertain Allauddin, and snubbed by such a rejection, he turned his rage on to Chittor. Rani Padmini had only one choice; she and the other ladies would perform johar, the Rajput women's ritual of entering the sacrificial fire and ensure that Khilji and his men would not be able to see even an inch of their bodies.

The singer was now singing with high emotions and the entire crowd sat mesmerized as the ballad progressed. Shivaji had a lump in his throat and was barely able to breathe. It was a tale of a victory for the righteous. The lust of the foreigners had made mothers and sisters surrender themselves to the sacrificial fire. But it seemed that God had turned a blind eye. The sacrifice of the women seemed in vain as the might of the Rajputs was laid to dust.

Unable to hear the story any further, Shivaji got up and left, tears flowing down his cheeks. He stood in his room with his back to the door. Jijabai asked, as she entered, 'Raje, what happened?'

He turned to face her. His face was swollen as his eyes welled up with tears again. 'Maa saheb, even a person with a heart of stone cannot listen to such poignant stories. I cannot bear it anymore!'

'Padmini herself had to bear this burden. There is no species more shameless than us human beings. When the daughters of Dahir were put under arrest by the Khalifa, nobody objected. Padmini was lucky to perform Johar and escape. But there are thousands of such Padminis who are silently tolerating such barbaric acts, praying to their gods. My own sister-in-law had gone for a bath in the Godavari when she was kidnapped in broad daylight by Mahabat Khan. What did we do then?'

Shivaji asked, 'Then why do our men go around proudly twirling their moustaches?'

'It is easy to talk of these things, Raje. There is no value for false pride.'

'When will all this stop?'

'When there is someone to stop it. Those who can are enjoying royal patronage while the poor ryot, the tenant farmer, has gotten used to being a slave.'

'Maa saheb, I will stop these atrocities.'

'Raje, if only we could see our dreams being fulfilled, such things would not occur. Now wipe your tears and go back to the courtyard. It does not suit you to walk away in the middle of a performance. The singer will feel insulted. You must stay till the end.'

For many days after, Shivaji continued to be haunted by thoughts of Padmini. The words of his mother rang in his ears—he knew he had to do something. He had always had the knack of gathering the right kind of people around him. The circle of his friends and relatives was broadening and one of these was Yesaji Kank. Others around him included Baji Pasalkar and others; a mix of both young and mature men. Baji Pasalkar was nearly sixty years of age but was a close friend of Shivaji's, who had not even fifteen then.

With such men for company, Raje would go around his jagir, meeting the common folk. Earlier, the villagers would run into the forest hearing hoof beats, fearing the Mughals, but now they would shout 'Raje has arrived' and would bow before him. They would look at their young Raje with pride and affection.

One such winter evening, Raje trotted along with his men. The hoof beats could be heard echoing in the valley. He heard a faint voice, 'Raje ...'

He looked all around when Yesaji pointed in the distance, 'Look!'

A man was running across the field towards them. He stumbled once and got up again. He was a balding man with grey hair on the sides, his face wrinkled with age and he fell at Shivaji's feet as soon as he reached him. His body shuddered with exhaustion and deep sobs. Yesaji tried to lift him but he would not leave Raje's feet.

'Get up, please. Tell me what happened.'

'Raje, ask me what has not happened.' He was in tears again and wiped them before continuing. 'I am shattered. My daughter had gone to the river to fetch water when she was kidnapped and raped. She has now committed suicide. I am orphaned without my child.'

'Who has dared to commit this act? Do you know his name?' Raje asked, shocked.

'Yes. The entire community saw but nobody wants to open their mouths. The protector has become the destroyer—it was the village Patil, the headman, himself.'

'Yesaji, go to village and fetch the Patil.'

Yesaji galloped away at full speed towards the village. Raje consoled the man and got all information from him. After a long time, Yesaji returned alone, his face flushed.

'What happened? Did you not find the Patil?'

'I did.'

'Then why did he not come along?' Raje asked in a firm voice.

Yesaji licked his lips trying to form the right reply. 'This Patil is an arrogant fellow and doesn't care two hoots. When I told him that you had commanded his presence, he said, 'Tell Shivaji that he may be a raja in name but I am a real Patil. Tell him the village is mine and I shall do what I feel like.'

'Oh, is that so?' Raje said, smiling.

Baji said, anger rising in his voice, 'Yesaji, did you come back to give such a message? Is your sword a decoration?'

'Baji, what Yesaji did was right. There would be no difference between the Mughals and us otherwise.'

'Raje!' the man said, now despondent.

'Don't worry. Yesaji, ask one of the soldiers to take this man on horseback.'

They all returned to Pune. The poor fellow had introduced himself as Ramji Khade. Raje said as they reached Pune, 'Yesaji, take fifty horsemen and go to the village. Arrest the Patil and present him to me tomorrow morning.'

Yesaji was all smiles. The next morning Raje dressed up after his bath. He was wearing a churidar with an embroidered shirt. A small knife was put into his cummerbund and a sword hung on one hip. He looked in the mirror as he adjusted his cap and smiled at seeing Jijabai standing behind him.

Jijabai asked, 'What is the commotion outside? I asked Dadoji but he does not know. The whole courtyard is full of people and why are you dressed up so?'

Shivaji smiled and said, 'It suits a raja.'

All the office staff had assembled in the courtyard. Shivaji took his seat and said, 'Yesaji, please produce the Patil.'

The Patil was pushed forward, his arms tied behind him.

'Ramji, is this the same Patil?'

'Yes, Maharaj.'

'Raje ...' said the Patil in a trembling voice. He was clearly petrified.

Raje smiled. 'Patil, you may be a real Patil and I may be a raja in name only but I am a son of the soil. I respect another woman like my mother or sister. I don't consider the kingdom my property.'

He looked at Yesaji and asked, 'Has his crime been investigated?'

'Yes, Maharaj.'

'Patil, the village people are like your children. And you were made Patil to take care of them but you go about raping them! You seem to be carrying on the traditions of the Mughals.'

The Patil rushed forward and fell at Pant's feet.

'Pant, help me. I need justice.'

'Raje,' Pant began.

'Pant, I suggest you don't interfere ... Patil, we will give you a hearing by jury on one condition.'

'What condition?' asked Patil, seeing a small ray of hope.

'The condition is that you need to get the girl to speak in court. I am sure she too has something to say in her defence.'

'That is unfair!' Patil shouted. 'Since when can a dead person appear in court?'

'Enough!' Raje said, staring at him intently. 'The jury is for ordinary crimes; not for criminals like you.'

The Patil said beseechingly, 'Pant, I made a mistake. Please pardon me.'

'Silence!' Raje shouted, his face red with anger. 'Were you deaf when the poor girl screamed for mercy? Yesaji! Break this criminal's legs and arms and take him around the town on a donkey. He is, after all, the village Patil! He should be sent home with due respect. Take him now, and inform me after the punishment has been meted out.'

Raje walked into the inner quarters, followed by Jijabai and Dadoji.

'Raje, isn't his punishment too severe?' Dadoji asked.

Shivaji turned suddenly and said, 'Pant, please pardon me for interrupting you then, but I believe that this person deserves it.'

'But Shivaji!'

'Maa saheb! Do you remember Padmini? Or your sister-in-law? This needs to stop. If I cannot implement these things then I don't need this jagir and I don't need to be a raja.'

An angry Shivaji walked out of the room and a stunned Jijabai exclaimed, 'Look at his temper!'

Dadoji wiped his moist eyes and said, 'Maa saheb! I am finally content today. How I wish the elder Maharaj was here to see this! Today, Shivaji behaved like a true king. I shall now go and pay my respects to the Almighty.'

The news that the Patil's arms and legs had been broken spread like wildfire. Everyone had a word of praise for Raje while the Patils and Deshmukhs were a scared lot now. No one dared to dismiss Shivaji as a young lad. He had grown in authority now.

'Maa saheb!' Shivaji Raje said, entering his mother's quarters, 'I am leaving for Rohideshwar for darshan.'

'Is Dadoji going along?'

'No.'

'Then who else is?'

'Baji, Yesaji, Chimnaji and Balaji are all coming.'

'Has Pant been informed?'

'Yes, and he has given his consent.'

'All right. When will you return?'

'The day after tomorrow.'

'And where will you stay?'

'We will be staying in the village itself. Baji has a house there.'

'Are you going to stay in his house?'

'Why, what is wrong with that?'

'Raje, do you realize it is a poor man's house? And if a raja stays there, the whole household wealth will be spent in a single evening. And what about your horsemen?'

'They will stay in the village too.'

'Then you are going to punish the whole village!'

'What do you suggest I do?'

'Raje, you may stay in Baji's house but send an advance party with all the necessary items for your stay. That way, they will not be constrained and yet can treat you like a royal guest!'

Shivaji left beaming with joy.

Raje enjoyed visiting places like Alandi, Jejuri and other such temple towns. Rohideshwar was one such place. There was a Shankar temple in the middle of a dense village on the top of a mountain. Shivaji would get enraptured by the beauty of nature and he had become friends with people like Dadaji Naras Prabhu in his many visits to Rohideshwar.

It was afternoon and the temple looked serene. The cool breeze blowing around soothed the visitors.

'Raje, you seem to be silent,' Chimnaji observed.

'What can I say, Chimnaji? A person who is a raja in name only does not have the right to say something or do something.'

'Who is the raja in name?'

'Me! Who else? See how the countryside seems listless. Earlier it was the Nizam Shahi rulers and now it is Adil Shah's reign. But there has been no change in the country. The royal troops come and loot the place, filling their coffers. The common man swallows his pride while the royals loot the villages, and take away the women and young girls.'

'Raje, nobody likes this, but these are poor peasants.'

'Yesaji, I don't know how strong the ordinary peasant is, but if a peasant can kill a wolf with a mere stick and such peasants join forces then ...'

'Then what, Raje ...?'

'Then ... what can I say?' Raje said, puffing his chest with pride. 'Then by God's blessing, our people do not have to hide in these mountains. They can roam around without fear.'

'But how will this happen?'

'All these Jagirdars, Patils, Deshmukhs, Kulkarnis; if they all join together imagine the strength!'

'So you think we can defeat the Bijapurkars?' Balaji asked.

'What army did Lord Ram have? Ravan was a great yogi but he was defeated with the help of monkeys. Balaji, what we lack is faith.'

'Keep talking, Raja,' Subhana said. 'It is music to my ears.'

'Huh!' Raje smiled. 'Subhana, all singers speak of God and tell people where he resides. But that does not make people meet God.'

'But I have found my god ...' Subhana said.

'Where?'

'In you!'

'You are naïve, Subhana. Just saying so does not make one a god.'

'Then tell us what needs to be done. One command and the whole village will be with you. They worship you. The Deshmukhs, Desais, Deshpandes and the others are with you. If they had not been, they would not have kept quiet when you dealt with that Patil. They are all waiting for directions from you ...'

Raje got up and said, 'Subhana, my head is reeling with all these thoughts. Let's go talk to Yesaji.'

The small village where Yesaji stayed had a population of a mere hundred- or hundred-and-fifty-odd people. They were all waiting for Raje.

'Raje, you have blessed the village, thanks to the goodness of Yesaji. Let us go to my mansion,' the village Patil requested when they reached the village.

'Why? Is Yesaji driving us away from his humble home?'

'It is not befitting that you stay with Yesaji.'

'Patil, I am Yesaji's guest. I will stay with you the next time.'

They entered Yesaji's cottage. The courtyard was decorated with simple rugs. Raje washed his feet and sat down on a parapet. He stood up and folded his hands on seeing Yesaji's mother and wife. Yesaji's mother bent down to touch his feet, but, holding her hands, Shivaji said, 'Mother, to you, I am like Yesaji. I need your blessings.'

The whole village had assembled that evening. They were discussing their crops and the other problems they faced. Everyone was happy to see Raje share a close bond with Yesaji and wanted to share their thoughts. The village Patil remembered something and said, 'Call that girl Manu.'

A young twelve- or thirteen-year-old beautiful Konkani girl came forward and fell at Raje's feet.

'Who is she?' he asked.

'Maharaj, her name is Manohari.'

'Manohari? It sounds unfamiliar.'

'She is from the Manohar Fort and has been named after it. She came here yesterday.'

'Why?'

'The kiledar is a Muslim. He had his eye on her, poor orphan that she is, and ordered her to be sent to his harem. The villagers conspired to help her and sent her here in the night. I am sure that you will find a way to take care of her.'

Raje smiled. He said, 'Send her to Maa saheb. She deals with all these issues. I cannot tolerate the fact that an orphaned Hindu girl is being exploited in such a manner.'

After dinner, Shivaji relaxed on a cot in the courtyard. The cool night breeze was soothing but sleep eluded him for a long time. In the wee hours of the morning, Shivaji took his leave from Yesaji and the horses galloped in the direction of Pune. A flock of birds seemed to be following them. Once in a while, a sambar would rush across the path to the other side. The sun rose and the mountains were lit with the rays of the dawn. Shivaji enjoyed the sights as he rode and he noticed a village nestled in the valley. A lot of men seemed to have assembled near the village. Raje raised his hand for the troops to halt.

'Baji, please check why these people have assembled at dawn.'

The villagers were scared when they heard the approaching horses. Raje dismounted and the men touched his feet. There was a cow lying down on the ground.

'What happened?'

An old man, who sat caressing his dead cow, said wiping his tears, 'Raja, a tiger killed my cow.'

'And the tiger?'

'He is somewhere in the jungle. But who can find him? Our whole life is wasted. The Badshah's men come and take away our crops. Now, the tiger comes and takes away our cow. How do we live? This is the third animal we lost this month.'

'Baji! Yesaji! Let us drive the tiger out by creating noise. I have my rifle.'

'A tiger who kills a cow cannot be spared,' remarked Balaji Narhekar.

The news of Shivaji Raje's plan to shoot the tiger spread quickly in the small village. Shivaji's men assessed the terrain and got some people together who had good knowledge of the jungle. The area where the tiger was expected to be hiding was marked.

'When you hear the gunshot, do not move forward but hide in the bushes. Move forward only when you hear the trumpets,' Shivaji warned.

The men designated to create the noise moved into the jungle. Raje checked his sword, spear and his knife. He moved forward to take his position followed by Baji, Yesaji, Balaji, Chimnaji and others. He selected a big bush to hide behind and waited after readying his rifle. Everyone waited for the people to begin their shouting to push the tiger out of hiding.

The jungle was bathed in pin-drop silence. As the sun rose higher in the sky, the shouting began all of a sudden. The noise of the shouts and the utensils being banged could be heard as they descended the mountain. Flocks of birds flew up and circled around. Herds of sheep ran down the slopes.

Baji pointed towards a bush hearing a shuffling sound. Raje looked in that direction to see a few wild boars emerge out of the bush, their hair straight, baring their teeth. They rushed unaware of the men hiding behind the bush.

The tiger, having enjoyed his kill, was now enjoying a siesta when he was disturbed by the noise of the utensils banging. There were stones falling all around and the noise was increasing in intensity. The tiger angrily moved out of his cave and growled, his tail raised high as he climbed down the slopes. He turned back every now and then towards the noise which seemed to be nearing closer.

The noise suddenly stopped and then again it increased with more intensity. A few monkeys screeched in warning as they flitted from one tree top to another. Pointing at them, Raje said, 'Baji, I think the tiger is coming our way.'

Shivaji sat in position without moving an inch. The noise was closer, and suddenly, out of the blue, the tiger emerged into the clearing. The huge animal was nervous and flicked his tail angrily. His stripes shone in the sunlight and the muscles rippled with each step. He was now right in front of the bush where Raje and his men were hiding.

Raje balanced the rifle with one hand on his thigh and shoved the barrel through the bushes. A shot rang out the moment the tiger came within shooting distance. The loud roar of the tiger followed the shot and the jungle reverberated with the sounds. The bush was filled with the smoke emanating from the rifle barrel. The men chasing the tiger, hid in the bushes, waiting for the signal. Raje saw the tiger groaning as he rolled on the ground. The beast was trying to get up but fell back each time. His backbone was hit and it was impossible for him to get up. The jungle shook with the painful roar of the tiger.

'He has been hit,' shouted Baji loudly.

'Shhhh ...' Raje scolded him.

The tiger's growling subsided slowly and his stomach heaved slowly with his laborious breathing. Raje came out of the hiding in careful steps. 'My spear ...'

'But Raje ...' Yesaji mumbled.

'Hit him only if I miss. Come.'

The tiger opened his eyes and saw his enemy walking towards him. He growled loudly and, at that moment, Shivaji's spear pierced his heart and his neck slumped back instantly. Baji picked up his spear but Raje indicated to him to stop. The tiger was dead.

Yesaji said, 'It is a tigress.' The next moment he blew the trumpet to announce the death of the beast. The villagers ran down the slopes shouting with happiness and assembled around Shivaji Raje. Forgetting protocol, many hugged Shivaji in appreciation of his valour. One of them had picked up two cubs and put them in front of Raje. He stretched his hand to pick up one of the cubs but the tiny cub hissed and bared his teeth. He managed to catch the cub and cuddled it forcibly and said, 'The tigress was stuck in this place because of her cubs. Havaldar, take these cubs with us. They will be a good addition to our zoo.'

One of the old men plucked away the whiskers from the tigress and burnt them. There was a belief that the whiskers were very poisonous. He spat on the animal saying, 'A tiger has finally met his match today.'

The tigress was tied to two poles and it took ten men to lift the huge beast. Everyone shouted with joy, 'Shivaji Maharaj ki jai!'

Everyone lifted Raje high up in the air and he was carried around with every one vying to hold him high on their shoulders. Shivaji was embarrassed while Yesaji, Chimnaji and Baji laughed on seeing the funny procession. While departing from the village, Raje asked what the name of the village was.

The old man said, 'What name? It has not even been a year since we settled here.'

'Then let us name it Waghmar.'

All of Pune gathered to see the dead tigress. The animal lay in the open courtyard of the Lal Mahal palace, and Shivaji was resting in his room in the evening when Dadojipant arrived in the main hall.

'What a huge animal!' Jijabai said. 'I am told that Shivaji killed it all alone.'

'Yes.'

'What a daring boy!'

'That is precisely what I wanted to say—this bravado needs to be contained in time,' Dadoji said.

'I thought you were praising him!'

'I too feel proud of him, Maa saheb, but that does not mean I forget my responsibility. I am responsible for this episode. He said he was going to Rohideshwar for darshan which is why I agreed to let him go. I had not anticipated a shikar in between.'

'I think you are mistaken, Pant. I enquired and found that a cow killed by the tiger was the reason. Raje could not bear to see the troubled villagers and volunteered. I thought you would be proud of his actions.'

'I am ashamed to say this, Maa saheb. My whole body was numb the moment I heard of the shikar. I could not move a step. Maa saheb, one can tolerate many personal tragedies, and you too have done that. But you know thousands of people are dependent on Raje. We cannot put these people's futures at risk with such bravado.' He wiped his tears before continuing, 'Maa saheb! Only you can convince Raje. If this habit is not nipped in the bud, it will become difficult later.'

Pant left the room with tired footsteps. He had never been so outspoken before but he had not exaggerated the situation. Maa saheb was now furious. She entered Raje's room fuming and asked, 'Raje, whose permission did you take before going for shikar?'

'Maa saheb, I was gifted the rifle by Aba saheb as he had confidence in me. And you know I never miss my aim. But I knew Pant would complain and that you would ...'

'Shivaji!' Maa saheb said, her voice taking on an edge. 'Do you know what you are saying? Apologize!'

Raje gulped once and said, 'But ...'

'Don't utter another word till you ask for pardon.'

Raje eyes were filled with tears and he somehow managed to mutter, 'I am sorry. Please pardon me.'

'You need to ask for Dadoji's pardon. Go and ask his forgiveness and promise that you will not do this again.'

'As you wish.'

Seeing his angry and hurt face, red with tears and insult, Maa saheb's heart melted and she hugged Raje, but he wriggled out of her embrace.

'Where are you going?'

Without turning back he said, 'To meet Pant.'

Pant was sitting in his room and the moment he saw Raje, he stood up.

Shivaji could not say anything and he touched Pant's feet and said, 'I shall never do this again. Please pardon me.'

'I have already pardoned you, Raje. Who does not make mistakes? If you remember the mistake, you will not repeat it.'

The moment Pant finished speaking, Raje returned to his quarters. He could not hold back his tears now. The lamps had been lit for the evening but he continued to stay in his quarters and refused dinner when Saibai enquired if he were hungry. The next morning he woke up and finished his morning chores. Saibai and he were playing with the tiger cubs when Jijabai entered.

He tried to turn the other way in order the hide the cubs when she said, 'Raje, since when have you started turning your back to your mother? If you are so troubled by seeing my face, I shall go away. If you are not hungry, let me know. I shall also not eat today. I had come here only to enquire about you.'

Shivaji realized that Maa saheb had not eaten since last night either. His eyes brimmed with tears as he embraced her.

'Raje, wipe your tears. Rajas do not cry. And surely not in front of their wives! You told me about the shikar last evening but did not say anything regarding the cubs. I have come to see them. Where are they?'

Raje looked towards the cot. Maa saheb stepped forward and saw the two cubs sleeping peacefully curled up on the bed.

'They are so sweet! I am putting them in my daughter-in-law's custody,' she said, looking at Saibai.

Saibai beamed with pride and walked out of the room with a swagger.

Shivaji was relieved that his mother was not angry anymore.

In a few months, the summers arrived. During this time, the family usually moved from the Lal Mahal Palace to the palace at Khedbare. Dadoji had planted mango trees in the orchards at Shivapur and Shivaji would often accompany him while he visited them. The family moved back from Khedbare to Pune after the summer. That summer, Shivaji seemed to be in a hurry to get back to Pune and Jijabai was unable to understand his behaviour. Ever since the Patil episode, he would often sit alone, lost in thought, or he would be out on tours. He made a visit to Rohideshwar within a few days of reaching Pune, while Pant had gone to Junnar at that time.

'There is nothing wrong in his visits, but something's not quite right,' Pant said while talking to Jijabai.

'What makes you say that?' she asked.

'Have you noticed the men surrounding Raje these days? Netaji, Yesaji, Tanaji, Baji, Balaji, Chimnaji—how many shall I count? On each trip I see a new face added to his group. Dadaji Naras Prabhu too sticks to him like a shadow.'

'What are you alluding to?'

'I am not able to understand it, Maa saheb! I would understand if these men were of Raje's age. But I see men of all ages. And not only that but also Brahmins, Marathas, Mahars, Prabhus—all types of castes and sub-castes. There are also the Deshmukhs, Deshpandes, farmers and others. I am unable to understand it ...'

'I think you are worrying yourself unnecessarily, Dadoji. I think it just means that Raje attracts people of all kind and nothing else. And there is nothing wrong with that.'

Dadoji was silent but not convinced. And Dadoji's doubts were not without reason. The Shivapur Palace was always overflowing with farmers early in the morning. Raje came out followed by Naras Prabhu, Gupte, Yesaji, Tanaji, Balaji, Chimnaji and others. Bhima the blacksmith stood there, bowing down in mujra.

'Bhima, how is the work progressing?'

'Fifty swords and a hundred spears are ready.'

'Shabbash! What about the other blacksmiths?

'They too will have made similar numbers.'

'Come on, let's go.'

They all left for Rohideshwar and reached by late afternoon. Shivaji's face beamed with a different kind of radiance. They entered the temple after washing their hands and feet at the stream. Dadaji Naras Prabhu and the priest performed the puja and Shivaji prostrated in front of the idol. He said, 'Dadaji, think once again.'

'I have decided long ago,' Dadaji said. 'If I have to live, I will live like a lion. I don't want to lead the life of a lamb.'

'Step forward.'

Raje placed Dadaji's palm in his own and putting it on the lingam said, 'Har Har Mahadev! With your blessing, we take the oath for a Hindavi Swaraj. With your blessing, we take the oath for a Hindavi Swaraj and will proceed with your guidance. We shall not leave each other's friendship till the task is done. We shall not forget our oath.'

He then removed the leaves from the lingam and touched them to his forehead. Dadaji followed suit. A coconut was broken and the priest came out carrying prasad. A hundred-odd followers waited outside the temple expectantly. Raje sat on the footsteps of the temple while prasad was distributed. Yesaji, Baji, Tanaji and others were also waiting expectantly.

Shivaji said, 'Yesaji, I have taken an oath today. This idol is a swayambhu and our desire is for a Hindavi Swaraj. We shall be granted that wish but we have a great responsibility towards it.'

Netaji was a close confidante of Raje and much older than him. He said, 'What are we afraid of?'

'There is no fear. I am wondering what our first step should be, and when and where.'

'What is there to think? We have taken an oath in front of the Lord. Let this be the first place.'

'What do you mean?'

'We shall first capture the Rohideshwar Fort and free the Lord.'

'I like the idea. But how feasible is it?'

'I have done a reconnaissance. There are not more than two hundred soldiers there—we would not face much resistance.'

'What do you say, Dadaji?'

Dadaji nodded in agreement.

'Rohideshwar will be our first goal. Our flag shall fly high on Rohideshwar tomorrow.'

Shouts of 'Har Har Mahadev!' reverberated in the air and Shivaji, addressing Yesaji and Tanaji, said, 'Assemble your men at the base of the fort tonight. I shall arrive before dawn and we will need to act in total silence.'

Though it was past midnight, Shivaji was wide awake inspecting the swords and spears made by the blacksmiths. Four blacksmiths had worked day and night to ready the weapons within a fortnight.

'Raje, if you had given us some extra time, we would have created wonders,' Bhima said.

'Bhima, what you have done is no less.' He removed the gold bangle he was wearing and handed it to Bhima and said, 'Share this among the four of you.'

'Raje, you think we will break this up? We will use it for puja! I have one request though,' Bhima said, touching Shivaji's feet.

'What is it, Bhima?'

'Take me along with you tomorrow. Raje, I know how to use a sword and my spear is not for killing wolves!'

Shivaji was overwhelmed. He asked Bhima to get up and patted his back saying, 'Bhima, I am looking for men like you. We shall leave together in the morning.'

Shivaji was ready in the wee hours of the morning. Before leaving, he closed his eyes in prayer for a moment. The eastern sky was still dark and there was no sign of dawn yet. They reached the foothills of Rohideshwar as the dawn broke on the eastern horizon. Everyone was waiting for his arrival.

Shivaji asked, as he dismounted, 'Tanaji, how many men do we have here?'

'Approximately twelve hundred.'

The arms were distributed among the men. It was slowly becoming bright now and the jungle was filled with the twittering of birds.

Shivaji asked Yesaji, 'How many porters do we have?'

'Fifty.'

'Are they enough?'

'More than enough. I have asked them to surround the fort. The moment they get the signal they will climb the fort.'

'And you?'

'Tanaji and I will be with you. Once we get the signal, we shall go up the jungle route. My men are already there.'

'And the fort?'

'Is sleeping peacefully! Subhana has reached the fort last evening—his aunt lives there.'

Everyone present smiled. The blowing of the trumpets announced the opening of the fort doors in the morning. One of the porters, carrying a load on his head moved forward, followed by another.

A few more people proceeded and Bhima lifted his load. Shivaji asked, 'Have you taken your sword?'

Bhima smiled and pointed to his head.

By the time the sun had risen, the only people left in the jungle were Shivaji, Dadaji, Yesaji and fifty farmer-soldiers. The forest was now drenched in light and the fresh, young leaf buds glistened in the morning sun. Yesaji looked at Raje as he unsheathed his sword and touched it to his forehead reverently. He started walking towards the fort, each step taken carefully.

The guards at the gate sat on the steps, smoking a chillum. The porters were moving in slowly. The monsoon was around the corner and there was a lot of masonry work going on at the fort. One of the guards, seeing a larger than normal crowd, commented, 'Looks like these idiots were sleeping till now. Look how many of them are getting into the fort!'

A porter entered, followed by three men wearing ceremonial clothes with swords hanging at their side and spears in their hands. They did not bother to look at the guards, but a guard shouted and stopped them. 'Hey you!'

'Yes, sir?' one of the men asked.

'How can you enter without permission? Where are you from and what are you doing here?'

'We are here to make arrangements for the marriage.'

The guard asked, 'Aren't we invited?'

'How can we have the marriage without you?' And thus, the men entered the fort.

One of the guards didn't quite trust the men and was restless. He was suspicious of the armed men claiming to attend a marriage. At that moment, one more porter arrived at the gate and he shouted, 'Stop!'

The man stopped.

'Where are you carrying the load to?'

'Inside the fort, sir.'

'That I can see. Whose house are you going to?'

'The fort-keeper's house, sir.'

'Is this what the fort-keeper ordered yesterday?'

The guard shouted, 'Open the bags!'

The other guards laughed and one of them said, 'Ramji, why are you troubling this poor soul? Let him go.'

Ramji ignored them and repeated, 'Open the bags!'

The porter realized that his game was up and he bent down and suddenly let out a loud whistle. Before the guard could react, the porter had taken a sword out of the bags. The guard could not believe his eyes and ran towards his companions. He had barely taken two steps when he fell down screaming.

The guards smoking the chillum were stunned for a moment and then recovered enough to run and pick up their arms. Bhima was ready with his sword as he ran towards them. A mild scuffle ensued and soon the whole fort reverberated with the sound of trumpets. Shouts of 'Har Har Mahadev!' boomed from all over the fort. Within a few minutes, all the posts inside the fort were captured.

The fort-keeper was still half asleep as he stumbled out of his room. There were shouts of 'Shivaji aalaa! Shivaji is here!' and before he could pick his sword, he was surrounded and taken into custody. Shivaji Raje entered the fort and there was complete silence as the men from the fort were too stunned to react. They had never expected an attack of this kind.

The fort-keeper was presented to Shivaji and as he stood there shivering; he tried to vent his anger and shouted, 'Let me warn you—this will not last long!'

'Yesaji, is there a cannon in the fort?'

'Yes, there is.'

'Put his head in the cannon,' Shivaji ordered coolly.

The fort-keeper fell at Shivaji's feet, pleading, 'Raje, please pardon me! This is your fort now. If you command, I will serve you hereafter.'

Raje laughed and turned to Dadaji saying, 'Did you see that? These are the men who pledge their allegiance to Adil Shah! Keep this fellow in custody and stay here till other things are arranged. Balaji, Chimnaji, take account of the things like food stock and grains. I will go to Pune tomorrow and return soon.'

The women in the fort came and fell at Shivaji's feet, worried about their future, and he comforted each one of them and asked them not to worry. He instructed his men to take the wounded to the palace at Shivapur and nurse them. At the main door, he noticed the green Adil Shahi flag fluttering in the wing. He said, 'Dadaji, are we carrying our flag?'

'Here it is,' said Dadaji, giving him the saffron flag.

'Dadaji, with the Lord's blessing, we have taken our first steps. We shall thus use the Lord's flag as ours. We will establish his kingdom!'

He walked up the steps to the flagpole and removed the Adil Shahi flag and hoisted his own. A saffron flag now fluttered in the wind, the clear blue sky adding to its beauty.

Dadoji was late to his duties and the moment he entered the room, Shamrao Nilkanth, Sonopant Dabir and Ballal Sabnis got to their feet. 'I was delayed for the puja today. Where is our physician? I did not get my medicine last evening,' he said.

Shamrao Nilkanth said, 'He has been in Shivapur for the past four days.'

'Why?'

At that moment, the guards sitting outside and enjoying the warm sun, heard hoof beats clattering outside. They got up hurriedly, holding their spears aloft as they saw a rider approach at full speed. He dismounted at the gates and handed the reins over to a guard nearby. Without even waiting to dust off his tunic, he entered the office. He performed his mujra to Dadoji who asked, 'What is the matter?'

The rider looked around, hesitated and said, 'Pant, would you please come outside for a moment?'

Pant asked irritably, 'You may speak freely. There are no outsiders here.'

The rider came forward and whispered in his ear. Pant shrieked, 'What are you blabbering? Are you drunk?'

'No, Pant. In the palace, the wounded ...' He trailed off, unable to complete his sentence as Dadojipant had walked out in a trance without even wearing his sandals.

Jijabai was busy in the kitchen instructing the cooks. She came into the inner quarters the moment she got the message from Pant.

'What is it, Pant?'

'I warned you, Maa saheb! Raje had indeed been acting strange for the past few days. No doubt he wanted to stay in Shivapur and get the palace cleared of people.'

'Pant, do not speak in riddles. I do not understand!'

'I wish I could tell you properly had the events occurred so,' Pant said. 'Maa saheb, have you heard about the exploits of Raje? He has captured Rohideshwar!'

'Rohideshwar? Are you sure?'

'Maa saheb, I am not sure if I will remain sane now. Raje's frequent trips to Rohideshwar, his mingling with people like Dadaji Naras Prabhu and the way he had gathered the farmers— I can now fathom the meaning of it all. The Shivapur Palace is full of wounded men.'

'And Raje?'

'Thank goodness he is unharmed.'

Jijabai heaved a sigh of relief and asked with a smile on her face, 'How did all this happen?'

'Maa saheb, they attacked Rohideshwar with twelve hundred men, captured the fort-keeper and there is now no sign of Adil Shah's rule at the fort.'

'We shall hear the details once Shivaji arrives.'

Dadoji came out of the room. Jijabai was proud of Shivaji's daring but she felt a certain disquiet. She went into the kitchen and found Saibai and Manohari there. 'Your husband is returning home after a daredevil exploit and you must welcome him—he has captured Rohideshwar!'

Shivaji's exploits at Rohideshwar had spread to everyone's lips. Horse hooves were heard from a distance and everyone waited with anticipation. Raje dismounted and his feet were washed by women and he was served a spoon of curd rice to welcome him. He was about to step in when he saw Saibai walking towards him wearing a traditional yellow sari. Saibai reached him and lifted her hand to apply the traditional tilak on his forehead. As Shivaji bent his head, Saibai looked at his forehead wet with sweat, his long sharp nose and earrings dangling in his ears—he was a beautiful sight. She blushed and realized that Raje was staring at her. She hurriedly gave him the traditional betel leaf and performed the aarti. Raje was smiling as he put the betel leaf back in the tray. He stepped into the courtyard and prostrated before Maa saheb.

Blessing him she said, 'May you ever be victorious!'

Raje noticed Manohari standing next to Maa saheb and asked, 'Haven't I seen her before?'

Jijabai smiled and said, 'Raje, don't you remember? She was the girl whom the kiledar wanted to ...'

'Oh, I remember now! Manohari, isn't it?'

'That is right. You changed her fate, you know!'

Shivaji came into the inner courtyard where Tanaji and Dadaji Naras Prabhu were waiting. He asked, 'Where is Dadoji?'

'In his office.'

Dadoji stood up the moment they reached the office. He was alone and, ignoring Shivaji's salute, he continued to stare at him for a while and said, 'Raje, should you not inform us before committing such deeds?'

Raje was silent.

'Did you not consider me trustworthy enough to be taken into confidence?'

'Dadoji, you are mistaken!'

'I have seen enough to know that you acted from the heart. Do you realize the reaction your actions will have?'

'We shall bear them happily!' Raje said casually.

'Huh! It is easier said than done. You have captured Rohideshwar and taken up cudgels against the Badshah himself!'

'What Badshah are you talking about?' Shivaji asked, erupting in anger. 'Where neither job, nor religion nor god is safe ...'

'What job?'

'I am told that you and the elder Maharaj were questioned in his durbar?'

'That was a misunderstanding.'

'Misunderstanding? Huh, I understand the meaning of royal misunderstanding! Murar Jagdev was tortured before he died. Similarly, my grandfather, Lakhujirao Jadhavrao, was hacked to pieces in the presence of a full durbar. It is time we stopped tolerating these insults.'

'You believe the ways and means you follow will put an end to such things?'

'If the Lord wishes, they will.'

Dadoji looked angrily at Dadaji and shouted, 'And you? At least you should have had some sense. You are a paid employee of Adil Shah, a Deshpande at Rohideshwar. Why did you participate in this childish act?'

Shivaji said, his voice firm, 'Pant, this was not a childish act.'

'Raje, you are young and I have seen many seasons go by. Don't try to teach me politics now. The elder Maharaj had once revolted in a similar manner and he also had the support of his men. But do you know what happened in the end? Those dreams were shattered. If the elder Maharaj suffered so then ...'

'One misfortune may lead to the beginning of prosperity.'

'Raje, that is rhetorical! You will remember later ... the step you are taking may ...'

Shivaji pleaded, 'Pant, stop! Misfortune can befall anyone. I have started something with the Lord's blessings. If you cannot support me, I beg you not to curse me.' Turning, he left before Dadoji could react.

It was evening now and Shivaji sat alone in Jijabai's quarters.

She said, 'Dadoji has taken your words to heart. Please show some forbearance for the next few days.'

'Maa saheb, I don't think I can do that now.'

'Why?'

'I have deliberately stepped on a snake. I have to consolidate my power before the news reaches the other forts and they fortify them.'

'And what if the Bijapurkars attack our jagir?'

'I have thought about that. Speed is not one of their virtues and we will keep them engaged in correspondence.'

Jijabai sighed. 'You know best. But remember that I don't have anyone but you. Don't do anything hastily.'

Raje got up and said, 'Maa saheb. I shall take your leave. I need to get back to the fort early in the morning and ensure that all arrangements are in place.'

'Wait!' Jijabai said as she took out a small pouch from a trunk. 'These are two thousand hons; my own. I have no use for them but you may need them.'

Shivaji could not suppress his tears. 'Maa saheb, these are not just two thousand hons. They are priceless and can take care of any calamity which befalls the Swaraj.' Shivaji touched Maa saheb's feet and she caressed his back with affection.

The next morning, Shivaji met Pant in his office. He was welcomed with a smile, much to Shivaji's relief. He said, 'Pant, I shall go to Rohideshwar and return soon. I wish to take some of the senior officials with me.'

'You may take them. After all, these people have been sent to you by the elder Maharaj to manage your jagir.'

As he was about to step out, Pant said, 'Raje, you are new to the fort and there is the possibility of sabotage. Be careful!'

The next day, seeing a couple of riders being dispatched early in the morning, Jijabai asked, 'Where are these riders going?'

'To Bengaluru.'

'What for?'

'Maa saheb, it is my duty to inform the elder Maharaj about what has happened here. Things may have been beyond my control but he should know.'

Shivaji started work at Rohideshwar in earnest. The ramparts were repaired and made stronger; a new account was opened in the office at Pune maintaining the affairs of the Swaraj. The Mavals, people residing in the Maval region east of the Sahyadris, now freely called upon their prince to pledge their loyalty and, soon, a list of three thousand men was ready. Pant observed all this stoically, neither encouraging nor discouraging the work. He kept himself busy managing the affairs of the jagir.

A few months had elapsed when Pant asked Shivaji, 'Raje, on what basis are these Mavals fighting on your behalf?'

'It is their integrity and determination. They have lots of it.'

'That won't suffice. An army marches on its stomach, Raje.'

'Pant, I get your point but don't worry; I shall not bother you for money.'

'Don't be upset, Raje! How are you going to manage the repairs and the salaries of the Mavals from the revenue you get from these thirty-six villages in the sub-jagir?'

'Tukaram said the Lord has the ability to make a lame person walk.'

Shivaji knew that his confident posture was not enough. After all, without money it was not possible to manage an uprising. He was troubled as he knew he did not have all the answers.

Jijabai noticed his discomfort and asked, 'Raje, Rohideshwar is being renovated, and yet you look despondent. Is anything bothering you?'

'Nothing, Maa saheb! I might only have seemed preoccupied.'

'Shivaji! You cannot hide anything from a mother and a guru; and you should not try either!'

Raje let out a deep sigh and recounted the meeting he had with Pant.

Jijabai said, 'Don't bother yourself with imagining things in the future. There are two types of people. One type thinks of cause and effect and are cautious in their approach, always afraid of failure. They lead a steady life but don't achieve much. The other kind are the ones who act on instinct and do not care much for results. Look at your father! He likes to plunge into things without a care. You have inherited the same kind of personality.'

'But what if this bravery turns out to be mere bravado?'

'Who can say if it will? Your father led a revolt and faced the Mughals and Adil Shah's troops alone. The revolt was crushed but that does not make him a failure. Gyaneshwar brought the Gita to the masses in Marathi but he was shunned by the same people. Does that make him a failure? The temple at Alandi is proof of his greatness. Nothing is achieved by a person who is always scared of the results—keep this in mind.'

'Maa saheb!'

'Raje, you have started your work with great devotion to the Lord. He will give you the strength to see your work completed. Have no doubt about that. Raje, you can create what you dream of. This is your destiny. As the sacred sanctum is graced by the Lord, so is the mind by one's loyalty, bravery and faith. Don't allow fear to enter your vision.'

Jijabai's words were a balm to Shivaji's tired soul and he got up with renewed confidence. He had his sights on Torna now; the fort was at a height and difficult to climb but it had been neglected for a long time. He marched straight to the fort and caught the fort-keeper unawares. Soon after, he was able to capture the Durga Devi Fort too, which was a little south-east of the Torna Fort. Shivaji ordered the re-fortification of both the forts immediately.

They say it does not take long for household affairs to become public and so the proclamation of Swaraj too reverberated in the Sahyadris. Traitors like the Bandal Deshmukhs managed to send their reports to the Amin at the Subhanmangal Fort. The Amin could not believe his ears and sent a report to Bijapur against Shivaji. He also complained about one babaji Naras Prabhu Gupte having defected to the Shivaji camp.

The repair work was progressing but it was impossible to manage with the meagre wealth in the fort's treasury. Shivaji was seized with anxiety about the way forward and he sat in Pune, wondering about his course of action. He said, while he conferred with Jijabai, 'Maa saheb, we may have to stop the repair work at Torna.'

Jijabai could not bear to see the work stopped midway. She asked in desperation, 'Raje, can we raise some money selling some of our jewellery and utensils?'

'I would have done it already had that been a solution. A fort like Torna needs a lot of money for its upkeep and I may have to stop the work for the time being.'

Shivaji left for his quarters with a heavy heart. Troubled by his thoughts, he could not sleep all night. In the morning, he was surprised to find Tanaji waiting for him outside his quarters. Tanaji looked fresh and cheerful despite an all-night journey. Shivaji asked him anxiously, 'Tanaji, whats's the matter?'

Tanaji whispered something in Shivaji's ears, making him smile brightly. 'These are indeed the Lord's blessings. Wait! I need to tell Maa saheb—she too has been worried.'

Jijabai was awake and reading Eknath's Ramayana. Raje stopped at the doorstep watching the scene inside. A lamp burned to her right while Saibai was removing the soot from the wick lamp. Jijabai sat there, reading the lines from the book in front of her. She finished the chapter and touched the book to her forehead reverentially. She looked at Saibai and asked her, 'Why do you get up so early in the morning?'

At that moment, Shivaji called out, 'Maa saheb!'

Getting up, she said, 'Shivaji! I have not been able to sleep the whole night.' She was surprised to see Raje's smiling face and asked, 'You are smiling! What is it?'

'Maa saheb, I have good news. Tanaji came in just now. They have found a huge stock of jewels hidden in the fort, including huge containers full of gold coins.'

'The Lord has saved us!'

Shivaji asked Tanaji to bring the treasure to Pune when Tanaji said, 'Raje, I would rather that you came along.'

'Tanaji, I have no doubts about your capabilities. Take some soldiers and get the treasure here. I am not required to come along.'

The treasure arrived at Lal Mahal and the jewels and other valuables were duly counted and noted. When Dadoji came to know about this, he said, 'It seems Lakshmi has showered her blessings in our time of need. Use this money but ensure that all estimates are in place before you begin to spend.'

Delighted with Dadoji's approval, Shivaji began work on the three forts with renewed vigour. He bought weapons and rifles and he would go to all the three forts every now and then and rarely be seen in Pune. One day, when Shivaji was in Shivapur Palace, he received an urgent message to reach Pune. He found Dadoji and others waiting for him eagerly, their faces looking grim.

'What happened?' Shivaji asked.

Dadoji produced a letter from Bijapurkar saying, 'Raje, we cannot take everything lightly. Read this and you would understand why we are all worried. Read it aloud so that Maa saheb can also hear it.'

The letter was addressed to Dadaji Naras Prabhu's father, Babaji.

'We have been informed that you had helped your honourable Shivaji Raje, son of Shahaji Raje, and that he has been disloyal, using a band of Maval men to capture the Rohideshwar Fort. If you do not accept the transgression, you will be taken to Bijapur and beheaded, and your jagir repossessed. Please note the same and present yourself at the durbar forthwith ...'

Looking at Babaji, Shivaji said, 'Babaji, it looks like you are going to be beheaded!'

'Raje, this is a royal farman and not a joke.'

'We have nothing to worry when we have blessings of elders like you. We have taken an oath to create a Hindavi Swaraj and I have trust in my Lord.'

'Raje, your trust in the Lord may not be of much use. Do you think fighting against Adil Shah is a joke? You have just sprouted a moustache, but my hair is grey with experience ...'

'Oh, my age! I have heard this comment far too many times! Babaji, when Krishna came to Mathura from Gokul, how old was he? What was Ram's age when he decided to go for a yagna? How old was Gyaneshwar when he wrote the Gyaneshwari?'

'Raje, you are talking about gods. But for ordinary people ...'

'Who is ordinary? It is our own fallacy to think that we are ordinary. We are here to create a kingdom of the Lord. So we need to follow His example. If we think of ourselves as old or incapable, we can never fulfil our dreams.'

Babaji said, 'Raje, tell me what I should do.'

Shivaji said, 'I am nobody to advise you. You may ask for pardon and be relieved of the punishment.'

Babaji asked in a quivering voice, 'Ask for pardon? Should I also beg for my life to be spared? Raje, this too is an old Maval heart. Whatever has to happen, let it happen!'

Dadaji was looking at his father with renewed pride. Dadoji let out a deep sigh of exasperation.

'Dadoji, please don't be worried. I will send my Peshwa to Bijapur with a message.'

'And what would the message be if I may ask?'

'Dadoji, I have learnt a lot from you. The message will say, "The forts here are unprotected. The territory too is under threat. Hence, I have taken control of the forts to ensure that the jagir is well protected. I will not be disloyal to my position under the Shah." Such a message will satisfy the Badshah.'

'For how long?' Dadoji asked.

'As long as possible,' Raje said.

'What if Maharaj saheb finds out?'

'I ensured that he has already been informed. He has not replied yet and I believe he would have, had he been worried. The fact that he has not means he is fine. And incidentally, he is not in Bijapur but in Bengaluru.'

Dadoji asked, 'Raje, where will Babaji stay?'

'Why?'

'The Amin may not remain a silent spectator now. There could be a chance of him being arrested.'

'If Babaji feels comfortable staying here, he is welcome. It would be my pleasure, and I will have one more elder to bless me.'

Jijabai was surprised to find Shivaji back from Shivapur. Since Rohideshwar had been captured, he would spend most of his time at Shivapur. He would come back once a while, meet her and then go back again. When they were alone in her chamber, he said, 'Maa saheb, it seems we will have to first fight our own people before we fight outsiders.'

'Whom are you referring to?'

'My own Mama saheb.'

'Mudhojirao?' Jijabai asked.

'Yes. He was not able to tolerate the proclamation of Swaraj at the Rohideshwar Fort. After all, he is a loyal servant of Adil Shah! He has started going around the Maval region and is usurping people against me.'

'What are you planning then?'

'What else can I do? I have sent some soldiers to Phaltan. I too will be going there. Let him taste the might of the Bhosales.'

Jijabai got up and said, her voice quivering, 'Shivaji! I beg of you, hold on to your temper and don't get carried away. The Bhosale–Jadhav families fought with and destroyed each other. Blood relations are meant for mutual support and not for fighting.'

'I am not making enemies. He is the one who is taking the lead.'

'That does not mean we cannot make amends. It is easy to start and aggravate hostility but difficult to face it. That needs tremendous strength.'

'Do you suggest I just sit and watch?' Shivaji asked.

'No. Go to meet him with the intention of destroying the enmity and come back victorious. Remember also that Mudhojirao is Sai's father.'

'I will do as you say, Maa saheb. Wish me luck!'

Raje reached the outskirts of Phaltan where a few of his men were waiting for him. The entire village was silent and Raje's cavalry was nowhere to be seen. He asked, 'Where is Nimbalkar?'

'He ran away the moment he got a whiff of the impending danger. We have sent a few horsemen after him.'

'I will wait here till they find him,' Shivaji said, pointing in the direction of a few trees which provided shade in the hot sun. He did not have to wait very long. The rising dust in the distance indicated that a group of horsemen was arriving. There were two horses leading the group—Mudhojirao sat on one of them and on the other Yesaji. As they came nearer, Shivaji bent in mujra. Mudhojirao seemed in a bad temper. Shivaji asked Yesaji, 'Where did you find Mama saheb?'

'Around thirty miles from here.'

'Was there any resistance?'

'No. We surrounded them from all sides. They surrendered without any trouble.'

'Mama saheb, where were you rushing to in such a hurry?'

'Bijapur. Where else do you think?'

'You could have complained to Pune against me. It is much closer than Bijapur.'

'It might be closer but we need men who are close to us.'

'Mama saheb! You believe that Bijapur is closer to you than us? You seem to have forgotten that they are the same people who put you behind bars for ten years. It was due to Maharaj saheb's efforts that you were again a free man and you got your jagir back.'

'Raje, I am going to suffer due to your revolt and I am tired of all this.'

'And so you decided to take this route? When are the Marathas going to wash away their sins? The Jadhavs fought against the Bhosales. If only they had worked together! We are working hard to ensure that no innocent person is thrown into jail for ten years again. We are against the torture and barbaric attitude of the Mughals.'

'Raje, you talk about wanting our blessings, but you never asked for them when you captured Rohideshwar. You never even asked us what we thought.'

'This is the usual Maratha habit! You don't hesitate to lick the feet of the man who put handcuffs on you but are willing to take up cudgels against some imagined insult. Mama saheb, not only you, but even Maa saheb and Dadoji were unaware of my plans for Rohideshwar.'

Mudhojirao now looked down with embarrassment. Shivaji spoke, his voice filled with emotions, 'Mama saheb, I have not captured you. If you fear the might of the Mughals, you are free not to join us. But don't stop our campaign—this is my humble request.'

Mudhojirao said, 'Raje, don't embarrass me further. You have shown maturity far beyond your years and I feel ashamed. I promise you ... I shall never come in your way again.'

Shivaji smiled and said, 'I consider this your blessing. It is getting dark now and I will take your leave.'

'No, you should not travel in the night. Go in the morning, or I will assume that you are still angry with us.'

'Mama saheb, Maa saheb is waiting for me and will not eat a morsel till I return. If you would consider coming back with me, she will be really pleased.'

'You are right! Let's go,' Mudhojirao said.

It was past midnight when they entered Pune. Dadoji was in the office and Jijabai came out and smiled the moment she saw Mudhojirao with Shivaji.

Mudhojirao was silent. He bent to touch Maa saheb's feet but she stepped back hurriedly and exclaimed, 'What are you doing? You are elder to me!'

'I am too small a person, Rani saheb. I have realized this too late. Raje is much younger, and hence I did not touch his feet. My timid heart has been defeated today.'

Saibai came running and hugged her father tightly.

Maa saheb said, 'She cried and created such a fuss! She was not willing to believe that all would be well. Raje, it was good that you brought Mama saheb along. Else, she would have believed the worst. Come on in now.'

As he stepped out of the office, Dadoji said, 'Raje, you have performed an act braver than the capture of Rohideshwar. I am proud of you!'

But this satisfaction did not last long. Upon Mudhojirao's return to Phaltan, a royal farman from Bijapur, expressing the Shah's displeasure, reached him. Under the charge of abetting criminals, Ambar Khan, one of Adil Shah's sardars, came marching into Phaltan without warning. Mudhojirao fell as he tried to resist and Bajaji was captured. It was a few days after this episode when disastrous news reached Pune; Bajaji, Sai's brother, had been forced to convert to Islam. Adil Shah laughed with scorn knowing that the person whose sister was married to Shahaji Raje's son was now a convert. Adil Shah had his daughter married to Bajaji out of sheer happiness. Sai was inconsolable.

'Sai, don't take it to heart. Bajaji may have been made a Muslim but he is still ours. We don't consider him an outsider.'

'How can that be?' Saibai asked.

Shivaji let out a sigh and said, 'There is no reason why we can't take him back into our religion. Thousands have suffered because our religious leaders do not allow that. I realize this tragedy today and I promise you—I shall not rest in peace till Bajaji is one of us again.'

Sai's body trembled with gratitude. She remained silent as she put her palm in Shivaji's. No words were exchanged but a lot was said in that gesture.

Babaji Naras Prabhu had now shifted residence to Pune's Lal Mahal Palace to avoid being arrested. Dadoji was worried for him as he was for Shivaji, knowing he may have to face Adil Shah's wrath sooner or later. The repairs to the forts were almost complete and they were now being strengthened with cannons. They had fortified all the easy routes to the forts as well. The initial population of a thousand-odd people at Rohideshwar had now increased to nearly six thousand, which increased worries for Shivaji too, knowing that he had to take care of them.

The biggest worry for Shivaji was that Dadoji was getting old. He had aged considerably, especially in the light of recent events, but Shivaji was unable to find a solution to mitigate his fears. He would try and spend as much time with Dadoji whenever he visited Pune. Dadoji busied himself in the affairs of the jagir and spent the rest of his time in prayers.

One day, Shivaji returned from Torna carrying a walking stick. Giving it to Dadoji, he said, 'Pant, this is a special cane. Very rarely do you get them so straight and I got this one especially for you.'

Pant examined the cane and said, 'Raje, it is nice but ... one needs the support of a son and not a cane in their old age.'

'Pant, why don't you take the medicine prescribed by the vaidyaraj?'

'Don't worry. Nothing is wrong with me. Now all I look forward to is ...' he said, pointing heavenwards.

Such talk from Pant would worry Shivaji but his preoccupation with Swaraj prevented him from dwelling on matters at home for long. Soon, he managed to capture the Rohida Fort and one more saffron flag fluttered in the wind now.

Rohideshwar, Torna and now Rohida—Shivaji was now moving forward rapidly. He had the backing of Jijabai but there had been no communication from Shahaji Raje except for a brief note saying, 'Take care of Shivaji Raje; keep that in mind.'

Dadoji would hardly get any sleep, staying awake at night. He remembered the days he had spent in Adil Shah's court and how he had earned his standing there. He had gained the confidence of Shahaji and was asked to accompany a pregnant Jijabai to Pune. He smiled, thinking of the trust reposed in him by Shahaji Raje. Dadoji sighed with relief in the knowledge that he had executed his responsibility with diligence and integrity.

It had been an eventful start at Pune, right from finding the right men to managing the few years of famine. He was worried that the jagir he had so lovingly built should not get destroyed in Shivaji Raje's attempt to create a Swaraj. Dadoji tossed and turned as the thoughts kept turning in his mind ... Raje ... he had been merely six when they had entered Pune. He was a rare, talented and precocious child. If only Raje had not started this dangerous game of capturing forts, he would have easily won the title of Jagirdar! He learnt to fight with every weapon but did not go hunting in the forest. What he dreamt was of Swaraj and he dreamt with eyes wide open. And what would the result be?

The fate of Shahaji Raje's revolt was no different from the one in Hampi, Devagiri or anywhere else. They were crushed by the mighty Mughals. Would Shivaji's dream be fulfilled? And what if the dream were shattered? Dadoji could not imagine facing the elder Maharaj who had explicitly asked him to take care of Shivaji.

'Not my fault!' shrieked Dadoji loudly as he woke up from his dream. Gangabai, who was sleeping next to him, saw him drenched with sweat and asked, 'What happened?'

'Nothing,' Dadoji replied and turned the other way. He wiped his brow and drank a little water. He looked at the small temple inside the room where a lamp flickered. Folding his hands, he prayed for a while and felt better. After a while he dozed off.

Shivaji returned in the late afternoon along with other riders. As he stepped into the courtyard, Balkrishna said, 'Raje, Pant has asked to see you.'

Shivaji walked towards the office wondering why Pant wanted him urgently. Dadoji was in his chair, busy writing. He said, without looking up, 'Come in, Raje. I was waiting for you. I believe you were in Shivapur. Did you see the forest that has been cleared?'

'Which forest?'

'Raje, you are not young now. Earlier, during the famine, you had urged a few hundred men to settle there. It looks like your memory is failing you!'

'I don't understand ...'

Pant smiled. 'Nowadays you are not bothered about your work and it is likely that you forgot. Raje, I am told by Shamrao Nilkant that the land near Shivapur has been reserved for rehabilitation of people.'

Shivaji said, looking at the floor, 'I am sorry. I had forgotten ...'

Pant said, 'Raje, you cannot build a Swaraj on the base of a weak foundation. Before you find people who are willing to lay down their lives for you, you need to make their homes safe and strong. Once you do that, people will automatically be drawn to you. I believe you had gone to Rohideshwar.'

Raje had gone to Rohideshwar when stationed at Shivapur but wondered who told Dadoji about it. Raje had gathered his Maval troops there. Was Dadoji aware of that too?

Dadoji gave a wry smile and asked, 'Raje, how many Mavals did you gather at Rohideshwar?'

Raje let out a sigh and said, 'Seven thousand.'

'How many of them are going to stick with you?'

Raje raised his head up suddenly and anger flickered past his eyes for a moment. He said, 'Pant, I am trying my best. I can do without your mocking remarks.'

'I am not taunting you,' Dadoji said, his voice rising. 'Do you think you were able to gather so many men on your own?'

'Who else do you think helped?'

'Elder Maharaj saheb.'

'Pant!'

'Listen, Raje. The region is not yet stable. You do not have the wherewithal to take up cudgels against the Shah and you cannot create a kingdom without wealth. The people you have gathered have come to help the Maharaj saheb's son—not Shivaji. You need to build your credibility before you can attract men.'

'I don't mind waiting.'

'Do you think Adil Shah will wait? Raje, what is your plan? What are your next steps? Let me hear what you have planned.'

Shivaji took a deep breath and said, 'Kondana.'

'Kondana? That is like slapping Adil Shah on the face. And you think capturing Kondana is child's play?'

'I cannot capture it by might alone but with some strategy and negotiations.'

'If it is possible, do so,' Pant said.

Shivaji could not believe what he was hearing. He knew he had Dadoji's implicit support.

'Raje, I am confident that whatever you do, you will think through it fully. I called you to have a look at this,' he said, giving Shivaji a piece of paper.

Raje took the paper in his hand and asked, 'What is it?'

'A full report of the revenues from your twelve Mavals.'

'Why should I see this? You are taking care of it, isn't it?'

'Raje, please don't mistake me. Money is an important part of the Swaraj-building exercise. You need to understand where money comes from.'

'Dadoji!'

Pant's voice was choked with emotions as he said, after taking a deep breath, 'Raje, I am like a ripe old leaf. I don't know how long I will last and I am tired and old. Investigate out these men before you take them. Listen to everyone but do what you heart tells you. When I arrived in Pune with you, you were a young lad. The entire region was undisciplined and chaotic. We brought it under control using all the means at our disposal. I used to take you along everywhere and we roamed the villages and all the twelve Mavals. I made you familiar with the trees and bushes in the region. My work is showing results now and I am pleased. I wish Jagdamba blesses you with immense luck. There is no other desire in this frail body ... you must be tired now. Go and meet Maa saheb. She must be waiting for you.'

That evening, after his meal, Shivaji sat in his room when he heard a shout, 'Shivaji!'

Soon, Jijabai came in looking tense and said, 'Dadoji is shivering. Hurry!'

They rushed to Dadoji's room and Manohari and the others had gathered outside his quarters.

Dadoji was lying on his bed. Shivaji rushed to the bed and asked, 'Pant, what happened?' He shouted at the crowd, 'Someone get a physician fast.'

Pant raised a weak hand and said, 'No. There is no need now.'

Maa saheb put her hand to her mouth and said, 'I hope he has not consumed something.'

Shivaji looked at Maa saheb with surprise and a cold shiver ran through his body. He looked at Pant and asked, 'Pant, is that true?'

Dadoji was silent for a moment and then said, 'Yes, it is. There is no use in getting the physician now.'

'Dadoji, why did you do this? Why are you punishing us like this? What crime have we committed?' He looked into Dadoji's eyes and said, 'Pant, if you are so tired of our fight for Swaraj, you should have told me so. I would have personally destroyed the Swaraj I built with my own hands ...'

He put his head on Dadoji's chest as tears flowed down his cheeks. Pant patted his head with shivering hands. He said, 'Raje, don't utter such words. I don't have much time and have a lot to tell you, so listen.'

Shivaji lifted his head. Dadoji continued, 'I am not angry at you and I am not going away disgusted. But I am an old man now and don't have the bravery of youth. A mountain stream rushes through the valley, making friends with rocks and boulders on its way and becomes a river before it meets the ocean. The stream is not worried of the tumbles and falls it encounters on its way. But I am an old man—like a placid pond. Ponds shrink under the hot rays of the sun. I don't have the energy you have, Raje ...'

'Pant!'

'Listen to me, Raje! In the game you are playing, if you win, you will be remembered across the ages. But if you lose ... Raje, everyone praises the victor but very few are willing to stand behind the defeated. A freedom fighter may soon be labelled a looter or a criminal. I worked all my life with dedication and integrity for the elder Maharaj. I am afraid of defeat in the evening of my life. Raje, a coloured cloth can afford to hide many stains but a white cloth cannot afford even a small smear. It can be seen by anyone.'

Shivaji could not stop his tears. He said, 'Pant, you were the one who taught me to welcome defeat with the same stoicism as victory.'

Pant shook his left hand and said, 'No, Raje. I am not afraid of such a defeat. When Maharaj saheb sent me from Bengaluru to take care of you and Maa saheb, he said, "Dadoji, my treasure is in your hands now. Take care of it as you would your own life. I am entrusting this task to you with full confidence." I was mindful of just one thing—that I should not let him down ... Raje! Water!'

Raje gave him a sip of water and wiped his brow.

Dadoji said, 'Maa saheb, there is some gangajal and tulsi in the temple. Raje, put my head in your lap.'

Raje wiped his tears and gently placed Dadoji's head in his lap. Looking at Jijabai, Dadoji said, 'Maa saheb! I am lucky to see the tears in Raje's eyes at the end of my life. Even gods will be jealous of this!'

Pant took the gangajal and put a tulsi leaf on his tongue. The sobs from the women in the room were getting louder. Shivaji sat silently, holding Dadoji's head in his lap. Dadoji said, each word now taking a lot of effort, 'Maa saheb, take care of Raje. He is grown up now ... you will see his valour and his good fortune ... don't be timid like me ... Raje ... !'

Shivaji's tears fell on Dadoji's forehead. His lips quivered and he heard the words, 'Don't cry. I take your leave now ...'

Pant raised his hand to wipe Shivaji's tears as he spoke his final words, 'Raje!' The hand raised to wipe the tears fell down limply.

BOOK
TWO

Shivaji could not bear the loss of Dadoji. He remembered his teachings, his voice, his remonstrations, his praise and everything else besides. Dadoji's presence had never allowed him to miss his own father and now he had left a void that was impossible to fill. He would never see Dadoji walking around in Lal Mahal again. He would not see the old, frail Dadoji sitting in one of the rooms reciting Sanskrit shlokas again. Dadoji's place in his office, where he sat terrifying every one with his meticulous and demanding work, would be empty forever. The very utterance of Dadoji's name was enough to send tears rolling down Shivaji's and Maa saheb's cheeks and Shivaji did not feel like staying in Lal Mahal Palace.

But he did not have much time to think of his own sadness. It was important that he stabilized his Swaraj before Bijapurkars took notice. The treasury had twenty-five thousand hons and Raje sent a message to Shahaji, along with the news of Dadoji's demise, requesting permission to use the money. Shahaji Raje sent his approval immediately. Shivaji's plan was to negotiate for the fort of Kondana. Bapuji Narhekar of Khedbare, who was also Shivaji's havaldar in Pune, was a good friend of the Kondana fort-keeper, Siddi Ambar. He used this friendship to turn Siddi Ambar into an ally and on an auspicious day, Kondana became a part of the Swaraj. Siddi Ambar continued to manage Kondana as a fort-keeper for Shivaji.

With the growing Swaraj, Shivaji moved to Khedbare from Pune. His next target was the fort at Purandar. The provinces of Baramati, Supe and Indapur were already under his control and, in order to take care of them, he needed Purandar. The fort was managed by Nilkantrao, a favourite of

Shahaji Raje and Dadoji and Shivaji thus hesitated to attack Purandar. Soon after, Nilkantrao passed away and left behind three sons—Niloji, Sankraji and Pilaji. After his father's death, Niloji became the fort-keeper but was unwilling to give his brothers their share of the wealth. Pilaji and Sankraji started visiting Shivaji, hoping to use his influence to get what was theirs.

Reassuring both brothers Shivaji said, 'Pilaji, I would love to help you but I am helpless. If you invite me to the fort, I can put in a word to Nilojirao then.'

'Raje, Diwali is just a few days away. We can invite you on that pretext,' Pilaji said.

'That is fine. I will be camping at the foothills for darshan at the temple there. I can spend the five days of Diwali at the fort.'

The plan was thus finalized. As planned, Shivaji reached a day before Diwali. The three brothers waited to receive him at the temple. Yesaji, Tanaji, Jiva Mahala, Sambhaji and Kavji had accompanied Shivaji and were also present. Raje had darshan and sat down on the bench in the temple premises.

Niloji said, 'I found out that you are here at the base of the fort, and I have come to invite you to the fort for Diwali. I request that you bless us with your presence at the fort.'

'Why not? But I cannot come alone during these festival days. I have these men with me.'

'Your men are my guests too. Please do not hesitate to invite them,' Niloji said.

Shivaji accepted the invitation. He had a hundred and fifty soldiers along with him, all dependable and strong. Shivaji observed the terrain carefully as they climbed up the hill. The fort was strong and sturdy and the walls were thick and formidable. As they entered the gate, a magnificent palace came into view. The inner fort was surrounded by mountains on three sides and was an impressive structure. Shivaji noticed cannons placed at each gate but he also saw that the number of soldiers were proportionately lesser than expected.

During the feast in the night, Niloji asked Raje hesitatingly, 'Raje, would you like a little wine? It is a festival day after all ...'

'Niloji, I don't mean to insult you by refusing but I don't have such habits. I am fine with a little sherbet.'

Niloji was enjoying his wine and Pilaji and Sankraji sat looking expectantly at Shivaji. A little drunk by then, Niloji said, 'Raje, you have captured many forts but have you seen one like Purandar?'

'I haven't seen one so formidable and strong. But I can help you if you need me.'

'No, Raje. Let us keep politics and friendship apart. I am a loyal servant of Adil Shah. I don't want to spoil that relationship.'

Shivaji laughed. 'I won't insist but won't you at least allow shelter to your own family members?'

'Raje, there is no question of distribution of wealth. I am the eldest; and hence, I am the owner. My brothers can stay here if they want. Else, they can go to hell.'

'Wait a moment!' Shivaji intervened. 'It is a festival day. Let us not get bitter today.'

The argument ended for the time being. Shivaji stayed back at the fort that night and met Pilaji as he was inspecting the fort the next day. Pilaji seemed disappointed and asked, 'Raje, what next?'

'You heard him. I don't think Nilojirao will do anything for you.'

'Raje, if you too believe ...'

'Pilaji, there is only one way out. If you are ready, then capture Niloji tonight. My men are there to support you. Think about it and then let me know.'

Pilaji agreed instantly.

That night, Nilojirao was totally drunk as he went to his quarters, his steps unsteady. Shivaji retired to his room while Pilaji and Sankraji, with Shivaji's men in tow, captured the drunk and sleepy Niloji without any resistance. Shivaji woke up in the morning to find Niloji tied to a pole. He was fuming and shouted, 'Raje, this is treachery. You have taken advantage of our friendship!'

'You are mistaken, Niloji. I have not been disloyal. Had you been fair, your brothers would not have arrested you. Pilaji, please ensure that Niloji is kept under guard. We shall decide the next steps later.'

Pilaji and Sankraji were ecstatic. The next day, Shivaji called for Pilaji and Sankraji. 'I would like you both to come to my palace for the auspicious day of Gudi Padwa, the New Year. We shall return tomorrow morning.'

'As you wish.'

That evening, Shivaji returned to the Shivapur Palace with Pilaji and Sankraji. The advance party had already reached and Jijabai was waiting for Raje. They had a relaxed meal chatting away. Pilaji and Sankraji slept soundly and Raje returned to his quarters.

The next day Shivaji moved towards Purandar along with Pilaji and Sankraji. There was a nip in the air and the path shone with the morning dew on the grass reflecting the sun. Purandar could be seen through the fine mist which hung in the air, and a light fog covered parts of the mountains. Shivaji dismounted at the first post and walked along with Pilaji and Sankraji, chatting merrily. The main door came into view and Pilaji and Sankraji were astonished to find the Adil Shahi flag missing. Instead of the moon and stars flag, a huge saffron flag fluttered in the air. The brothers were dumbfounded. As Murarji saluted, Shivaji asked, 'Is everything under control?'

'Yes,' said Murarji.

'Shabbash! And where is Yesaji?'

'He is guarding the explosives store.'

'Let us go.'

'Raje, what is happening?' shouted Sankraji.

'Why? Are you surprised? The main gate has my flag, the guards are mine. Hence, the fort too must be mine!'

'This is treachery!' screamed Pilaji.

'No, Pilaji. The treachery was committed by you two towards Niloji. I am just playing politics. You are getting confused between friendship and politics.'

He clapped once and a few guards came running. Raje shouted, pointing at Pilaji and Sankraji, 'Arrest them!'

Shivaji looked at them with pity as they were led away. He inspected the fort thoroughly and ensured that it was well protected. The explosive store was full and there were a lot of cannons, rifles and weapons. It had been a great gift on Gudi Padwa!

In the afternoon, Shivaji met the three brothers together. He told Niloji, 'I hope you three will now live together in peace.'

'That is not possible now,' shouted Niloji.

Raje looked at Yesaji and said, 'Throw them in a room together. If they don't come to an agreement by evening, then the fort has already been lost and they will lose their incomes too.'

Balaji arrived within an hour and said, 'They will agree to whatever you say.'

The three brothers were assembled again in front of Shivaji.

'Niloji, don't be afraid. I'm sure you have now realized the dangers of a family fight. Had it been a Muslim in place of me, he would already have beheaded all of you. We will ensure that you don't lose your income and revenue shares—be happy with that. I shall keep the fort and you will manage your respective territories at the base of the fort. If you work with integrity, I shall ensure that you are protected.'

The three brothers took their oaths to Raje and he ensured that their revenue share was agreed upon and he departed to meet Maa saheb who had come to the fort with Saibai. Shivaji took Maa saheb on a tour of the fort. Saibai had not seen such a fort before and was impressed. Maa saheb walked around accompanied by Netaji and Tanaji. Saibai went a little closer to the edge and Shivaji came forward to warn her, 'Don't go so close to the edge.'

The wind blew hard, ruffling Sai's hair. 'I am so happy. I feel like ...'

'What?'

'I feel like riding a horse and inspecting the fort. Riding with you ...'

'What would people say?'

'What will they say? After all, you held my hand in front of everyone when you took your marriage vows. If we ride a horse together, is it that scandalous?'

'That was a different matter.'

'Why?'

'I was young then.'

Saibai was silent and grumpy. Shivaji smiled and at that moment Maa saheb arrived. It was yet time for the sun to set. Maa saheb sat on the parapet and said, 'Raje, my legs are feeling tired.'

'Then shall I order a palanquin?'

'No need for a palanquin ... Yesaji, why don't you get a horse? I too feel like riding a horse today.'

Shivaji's face flushed with embarrassment and Saibai blushed. He realized that the wind had carried their conversation to Maa saheb. The horses arrived and the group went around the fort followed by Tanaji, Yesaji, Netaji and the others.

As they toured, Saibai said, 'May I ask something? Why can't we stay here at the fort instead of staying at Pune or Shivapur?'

'Are you sure you would like it here? It is not easy in the rainy season.'

'I am quite sure.'

'Sai, our thoughts match so much. I too was thinking of the same thing when I came here,' Jijabai said.

Everyone returned to the palace in the evening and Shivaji sat near Maa saheb and asked, 'Maa saheb, did you like the fort?'

'It is very beautiful! Raje, likewise you should be taking some interest in your familial life too.'

'Why, have I neglected something?' Shivaji asked, a little surprised.

Jijabai glanced towards Saibai and smiled. 'She is pregnant. Should you not enquire about her needs?'

Shivaji looked at Saibai in surprise and she blushed and ran from the room. Shivaji came to his senses hearing Jijabai laugh and his face was flushed. He changed the topic saying, 'Will you step outside for a moment?'

Jijabai got up and stepped into the courtyard. Shivaji indicated to Yesaji, who brought a tray to Maa saheb. It had a shawl and a sword. Maa saheb looked questioningly when Shivaji said, 'Maa saheb, I have captured Purandar, and with Chakan I will get the twelve Mavals under my control. If I did not have the support of men like Netaji, Yesaji, Tanaji and the others, I would never have been able to fulfil this dream. Netaji ...'

Netaji came forward and bent in mujra.

'Maa saheb, I would like to honour Netaji as the fort-keeper of this fort and I want you to bestow the honour on Netaji. I value his dedication and sincerity greatly.'

Maa saheb presented the traditional shawl and sword to Netaji, who was overwhelmed with emotions.

Maa saheb said, 'Netaji, it is very difficult to win Raje's trust, and I hope you safeguard it with your life.'

Shivaji said, 'Netaji, make the fort strong. I feel we should all live in Purandar, so have a mini-palace built on the other side.'

'Raje!' Maa saheb exclaimed.

'Maa saheb, we are everywhere—we now have Rohideshwar, Torna, Kondana and Purandar. Staying in the plains is not safe. I am not sure when Adil Shah may march on us. It is better and safer to stay at a place like this.'

Everyone agreed with Raje's view and they all left the next day and moved towards Pune.

Now the only thing he had in mind was Chakan!

Shivaji sat in the royal hall at Purandar while Tanaji and his other sardars waited for instructions. He asked, 'Tanaji, we have three thousand cavalry and five thousand foot soldiers. But to take care of the entire region and the forts, this is not sufficient. We need more cavalry.'

'We are increasing the numbers slowly,' Tanaji said.

'Slowly is not good enough. The leader who does not have enough horsemen cannot defend his land.' Changing the topic suddenly, he said, 'Tanaji we shall depart tomorrow. Yesaji, Baji, Chimnaji, Balaji and the others will also accompany us.'

'How many soldiers will you need with you?' Yesaji asked.

'Two or three hundred.'

'Are we going to Rohideshwar?' asked Chimnaji.

'We shall go wherever Jagdamba asks us to go,' Shivaji replied. The sardars knew by now that Raje would not share all the information till they reached the destination.

Shivaji took the road leading to Chakan the next morning. Yesaji and Tanaji were surprised and were unable to understand his mind but they dared not ask till they reached Chakan, galloping all the way. Nobody expected Shivaji to reach the fort with such a small number of men. The fort havaldar could not believe his eyes and was in a dilemma whether he should allow Shivaji to enter or not. The door was open but Shivaji did not enter. He dismounted at the gate and as the havaldar came running out, he said, 'Send a message to Firangoji that I am here'.

'Yes, sir,' the havaldar said and returned with the message that Raje was invited inside.

Firangoji Narsala was confused on hearing that Shivaji had come to see him. Why has he come here? What if Adil Shah finds out about this meeting?

He heard the hood beats and looked out of the window to see Shivaji arriving on a beautiful white horse. The saddle, adorned with a red silk cloth, looked brilliant against the white horse. Shivaji was wearing an embroidered turban and a pearl necklace swayed gently on his chest. The soft beard added to his majesty. Firangoji adjusted his turban and went hurriedly down the steps.

Firangoji folded his hands in namaskar and Shivaij returned his greetings. Firangoji led them into the inner courtyard. He looked back to see the courtyard filling with Shivaji's horsemen. He was restless and not sure what he should say. Shivaji said, 'Balaji, it looks like Firangoji does not like our arrival here.'

Firangoji said, 'No, it is just that ...'

'What?'

'I wonder what made you grace our household today.' He swallowed nervously and continued, 'Raje, what is on your mind?'

Firangoji was middle-aged and powerfully built. The edges of his bushy moustaches were sharp and pointed and his face had a glow. He did not seem scared. Shivaji answered in a casual tone, 'I came to meet you.'

'That is not true. What is your real purpose, Raje? I may live in Chakan but I have my eyes and ears on the Maval and know that you have already taken charge of Torna and Purandar, and I also know how you managed to get them. Raje, let me make it clear—I will not tolerate any such things here.'

Shivaji whispered something to Tanaji and Yesaji and they left the room and Balaji and Chimnaji continued to sit. Firangoji looked outside and saw the horsemen moving out. He was surprised and looked at Raje askance. Shivaji smiled, stretching himself to relax.

Firangoji asked, 'Where have your men gone?'

'Outside. They had come in without your permission. I asked them to leave.'

There was a thud and Firangoji rushed to the window to see the door to the fort being closed. Firangoji asked, 'Who ordered the door to be shut?'

'I did. Now there are just three of us inside the fort. We cannot leave the fort without your permission, Firangoji.'

Firangoji was now completely at a loss. He knew he was safe; and yet, he was uncertain of Shivaji's real motive. He asked, 'Raje, tell me the truth. Tell me what you want.'

'I want to create a Swaraj.'

'What purpose will creating the Swaraj serve?'

'To establish my kingdom here. It is the Lord's wish as well.'

'Is it true that you found a lot of treasure at the Purandar Fort?'

'Yes. Firangoji, what is your religion?'

He was a little taken aback and said, 'I am a Hindu!'

'Are your temples safe? Is your god safe?'

'Raje!' Firangoji exclaimed, a little irritated now.

'Why don't you convert and become a Muslim instead? If you send one of your daughters to the royal palace, you may even be made a Subedar.'

'Raje, be careful of what you speak. Did Shahaji Raje become Muslim?'

'No,' said Raje, unperturbed. 'And that is why he had to suffer so much. He had no choice but to be arrested. Murar Jagdev's legs and hands were broken, but not of the Mughal sardars. Do you know why Amin complains against you in the Mughal court? Do you want to know what your fault is? I will tell you—there is only one fault—that you are a Hindu but the emperor is a Muslim.'

'Do you understand their strength, their might?'

'Huh!' exclaimed Shivaji, 'Firangoji, where did these Mughals come from? Babar, thrown out of his own country, made himself an emperor here. On whose support did he become one? Was it not people like you and me? If foreigners can do this here, can we not do it for ourselves?'

'Yes, but don't you think elder Maharaj saheb would be punished in this process?'

'He is aware of the consequences or he would not have asked me to go ahead.'

Firangoji was silent.

'Firangoji, I can be quite content managing my jagir here. But I am not here to sit quiet. I want a kingdom where each religion can be happy; where women and children can roam freely without any fear; where the poor do not feel orphaned. I want to create one such kingdom or there is no point in living—I would rather be dead. Anyone who wishes to join me should be prepared to sacrifice his family for the sake of building the nation.'

'Enough of this! Let us go.'

'Where to?'

'No point in breaking our heads over this. Let us go to Pune. If your mother gives her consent, I shall do whatever you say.'

Shivaji Raje could not contain his happiness. He got up and hugged Firangoji without saying a word. They prepared to return to Pune. The fort gate was opened and while leaving, Firangoji indicated to the guards by pointing at the havaldar, 'Arrest him. I shall deal with him when I return.'

The order was executed immediately. Shivaji asked, 'Why are you taking out your anger on that poor soul?'

'Raje, this fort is under my command. How can I tolerate a fellow who falls prey to guile and allows people to come in?'

Raje smiled and kept quiet.

On reaching Pune, Firangoji met Jijabai. She said, 'We have been waiting a long time for you to come. Without you, this kingdom is incomplete.'

Firangoji was taken aback at her direct speech and asked, 'Rani saheb, does that mean you are in agreement with Raje?'

'Do you think a child can go ahead without his mother's permission?'

'My doubts are cleared. Raje, Chakan is yours. You may hand it over to whomever you think fit. I have no objection.'

'Firangoji, we didn't want the fort. We wanted you. It is only a man like you who can manage a fort like Chakan. Take our royal insignia and a few soldiers when you return. You are now the fort-keeper entitled to the pride of Swaraj. The fort shall remain under your command as before.'

Firangoji returned to Chakan after taking Jijabai's blessings. Soon, the saffron flag fluttered over Chakan as well.

A few days later, as Shivaji was busy looking at a report on the status of the repairs at the Purandar Fort, Shamrao Nilkanth came to say, 'Baji Pasalkar has come.'

'Baji?' Raje got up wondering why Baji had come in suddenly. He came at the door to see Baji standing there. 'Baji, please sit,' Raje said.

Baji kept standing, his face creased with anxiety and he did not wear his usual smile. He said, 'I wanted to pay my regards to Maa saheb.'

As soon they entered her chamber, Jijabai asked, 'Baji, what is the matter?'

'I beg your pardon to come in unannounced,' Baji said, 'It is urgent news I bring. The moment Raje captured Chakan, the Amin of Shirval sent a complaint to the Badshah. He has deputed Fateh Khan to take care of the situation and I am told that he has left Bijapur.'

Shivaji let out a deep sigh and said, smiling, 'Baji, you know, I got scared when I saw you come in like this. I wondered what the bad news could be but this news is not surprising at all. In fact, it is later than expected. I am ready to face that Khan.'

'Raje, it is fine at your age to show such courage, but this old man with grey hair needs to think twice before taking any steps.'

'Baji, I don't want to put you in any trouble. Maa saheb, all I need are your blessings. I will take care of the rest,' said Shivaji, a mischievous look in his eyes as he bent to touch Maa saheb's feet.

Baji, rubbing his moustache with the back of his fist, said, 'Raje, my wrists still command the same power as before. I am not used to being a mere bystander, observing from afar!'

'Then get up, Baji! Let us gather everyone. It is your responsibility to ensure that we win our first battle at Purandar.'

Baji bowed in mujra and moved to make arrangements at Purandar.

Shivaji did not have a single moment's rest now. He dispatched Tanaji and others to Purandar and the royal treasury was moved from Pune to Torna for safekeeping.

Maa saheb said, 'Raje, I too shall come to Purandar.'

'No, Maa saheb. I shall ask Firangoji to stay back here with you. I am quite sure that Khan would not cross Katraj; and in case he does, I shall warn you in advance. I have no doubt I will be victorious. In fact, I am quite eager to see the outcome of this first clash.'

'Raje, I am sure you will emerge victorious but be careful!'

'Rest assured that I will be careful. My dreams are far too big now and I cannot get emotional and put my life in danger.'

Raje chose an auspicious date, within a few weeks of receiving the news, and reached Purandar with Baji Pasalkar, and the excitement was palpable. There was adequate ammunition for the cannons positioned at strategic places. Piles of stones of various sizes were stacked along the walls for the catapults and hundreds of soldiers walked along the ramparts keeping guard. Within a day of reaching the fort, they began to receive news of Khan's movements.

Khan camped at Khalat–Belsar and sent one of his sardars, Balaji Haibatrao, with troops to Shirval, which was under the command of the Amin. Balaji reached Shirval along with his men and camped in the small Subhanmangal Fort.

'Raje, we are ready to face Balaji Haibatrao,' one of the sardars said.

'I don't want to wait for him—we must move ahead and intercept him.'

Kavji Malhar stepped forward and said, 'Raje, you are absolutely right. I am familiar with the fort at Shirval. Give me the chance to lead!'

'Shabbash, Kavji! You are the first volunteer; and hence, this right is yours. Capture Balaji before he settles there. Move tonight.'

Baji Pasalkar was the eldest there and he said, 'Raje, it is amavasya tonight. Would it not be advisable to move tomorrow?'

'It may be amavasya tonight but tomorrow is pratipada, the first day of the lunar month, and a victory on pratipada would be even more auspicious. To achieve that, we need to move tonight.'

The men got ready while the fort was illuminated by the light of the mashaals. The stars lit up the moonless sky as Kavji and his men got down the fort. Shivaji came to see them off and said, 'Kavji, this is our first foray. I need a victory but I want all of you back for us to celebrate together. Take care!'

The men moved towards the Subhanmangal Fort at the crack of dawn. Seeing the Maratha troops, the Adil Shahi troops ran to take refuge inside the fort. Kavji was emboldened seeing Shirval being abandoned by the Adil Shahi troops and he attacked Subhanmangal mercilessly.

The Adil Shahi troops peering from the ramparts were targeted by arrows shot expertly from below while the others continued battering the walls with iron rods and ploughs. Kavji was busy hammering away at the iron gates. The men inside the fort first threw boulders and then, in panic, they started throwing whatever they could lay their hands on including kitchen utensils. The sardars inside the fort crowded into the inner rooms fearing imminent death.

Soon, the door of the fort was broken open and shouts of 'Har Har Mahadev!' rent the air. Combat ensued everywhere and the houses inside were torched. Huge clouds of smoke rose from Subhanmangal and there was chaos all over. Suddenly, Kavji spotted Balaji Haibatrao who had started running the moment he realized that he had been overpowered. Kavji balanced his spear in his right hand and ran behind him. Balaji was about to take cover in a room when the spear hurled by Kavji found its mark and he fell. The news of his death spread like wildfire and there was further chaos. Within the next hour, the fort was captured. By evening, the Maratha flag fluttered at Subhanmangal Fort and Shivaji got the news soon after.

They had captured a lot of horses, elephants, jewellery, palanquins and weapons. The men stood in front of Raje as the loot was arranged for display. Shivaji said, 'Shabbash, Kavji! You have won the first battle for our Swaraj. Fateh Khan will soon be forced to come out of Khalat–Belsar as a snake is out of its hole. He will surely challenge us here, and we will await his arrival.'

Shivaji's estimate turned out right. Fateh Khan, hearing the massacre at Shirval, marched towards Purandar and started climbing the steep slopes. Shivaji stood at the ramparts, observing the approaching enemy, while Baji Pasalkar walked back and forth at the edge, contemplating the next action. The moment the enemy was within striking distance, the cannons roared and Maratha soldiers streamed out of the fort with shouts of 'Har Har Mahadev!' The enemy was bombarded with cannon balls and huge boulders from catapults.

There was chaos within Fateh Khan's troops. Those who had managed to reach the doors of the fort were massacred while the rest ran for their lives. Shivaji saw Baji Pasalkar jumping on a horse when he asked, 'Baji, where are you going?'

'Raje, I have spent my lifetime waiting for victory. How can I just sit and watch? I shall return only when we are victorious.'

He spurred his horse forward before Shivaji could say anything. Fateh Khan was desperately trying to assemble his troops back to fight. Baji charged right into the Muslim troops, attacking Muser Khan, Fateh Khan's right-hand man. Godaji Jagtap came to his aid and flung his spear at Muser Khan, at his thigh. Khan, wild with anger and pain, pulled the spear out and broke it into two pieces. He charged at Godaji with his sword while Godaji waited for the opportune moment to strike back. His sword pierced his shoulders and Muser Khan fell down. Seeing him critically wounded, Fateh Khan lost his nerve and began to retreat.

Baji Pasalkar shouted at his men, seeing him running away, 'Don't leave a single enemy alive. Let them know that if you dare enter Maval, you cannot escape alive.'

The Maratha soldiers, already heady with the victory at hand, ran after Khan. They chased the Muslims right up to Belsar and there was massacre at the cantonment. The Maratha troops chasing Khan could be seen from the fort and Shivaji waited to welcome the victorious warriors.

The Maratha soldiers returned to the base of the fort the next evening, having defeated the Mughals at Belsar. Shivaji stepped forward to receive Godaji Jagtap. 'Godaji, we won!'

'Yes,' Godaji said, nodding but there was no happiness in his voice.

'What happened?'

'Baji is wounded.'

Shivaji noticed a palanquin being placed carefully on the ground and rushed toward it.

Baji lay inside with his eyes closed and his clothes were soaked with blood. His white hair was ruffled and there were streaks of blood all over his face and forehead. His whiskers shivered as he tried to speak.

Shivaji exclaimed, 'Baji!'

Baji opened his eyes and smiled when he saw Shivaji looking at him. He squeezed Raje's hand and said, 'Raje, we have won!'

'Baji, what have you done to yourself? We were sure of the victory. Where could that Fateh Khan have hidden? Why did you put yourself into this situation?'

Baji said, 'Raje, we have won. What is there to feel sad about? I am an old man. I could not have asked for a better way to die. Smile, Raje. I have been holding myself to see that smile of victory on your face. Fulfil this last wish of mine.'

Shivaji forced a smile and the next moment he felt Baji's hand go limp. Shivaji covered his face with the shawl and got up, wiping his tears. He said, 'Godaji, we have managed to get victory on the pratipada. But we shall never get back this crescent moon. Even the full moon at poornima shall miss this lovely crescent.'

Shivaji honoured all those who had fought in the war at Purandar. The entire Maval region was drenched in happiness after the victory at Khalat–Belsar. But their happiness was not to last for long. There was an urgent message from Bengaluru and Shivaji was disturbed on reading the message. He told Jijabai, 'Maa saheb, I have received a message from Dada Maharaj in Bengaluru.'

'What is Sambhaji saying?'

'It seems the entire Bhosale family is a pet enemy of Adil Shah's. We had Fateh Khan and Balaji attacking us; and likewise, Farhad Khan and Tanaji Durre were sent by Adil Shah to attack Bengaluru. But Dada Maharaj repulsed their attack and Farhad Khan had to return empty-handed.'

'By God's grace, this is good news then!'

Shivaji let out a deep sigh and said, 'No, Maa saheb! This is going to cost us heavily. While we were busy defeating Fateh Khan, Maharaj saheb in the south was getting caught in Adil Shah's trap. Mustafa Khan has betrayed and arrested Maharaj saheb.'

'Shivaji, what are you saying? Is that true?' exclaimed Jijabai.

'Maa saheb, listen to the tale of our misfortune. Baji Ghorpade of Mudhol entered the palace in the middle of the night when Aba saheb slept. There was a fight between Ghorpade and Aba saheb, and Shahaji Raje, who would enter the court atop an elephant and whose prestige was known far and wide, was chained by his ankles and marched like a common criminal into Bijapur. He was presented in Adil Shah's durbar by Afzal Khan on the day of Nawroz.'

Tears welled up in Maa saheb's eyes. Her voice was shaking when she asked, 'What happened then?'

'What more was to happen? Maharaj saheb is a prisoner of Adil Shah. Maa saheb! Afzal Khan and Ghorpade will have to suffer. It is not a joke to put Shivaji's father in chains. Anyone who dares to do such a thing will have to pay for it.'

'Whatever has to happen will happen, Shivaji. What are you planning now?'

'I am not sure, Maa saheb. I have instigated the enemy, and they are baying for my blood. I don't think they would release Maharaj saheb unless we surrender.'

Shivaji clenched his fist in anger and said, 'Adil Shah has played a dirty trick. I feel I should send a message to Dada Maharaj and attack Bijapur right away.'

'Do you think Adil Shah would attack us?' asked Jijabai.

'Adil Shah would not act in haste either. He is aware that any harm done to Maharaj saheb will not be tolerated by other Hindu sardars including us—he knows that very well,' Shivaji said.

Raje managed to console Jijabai but he was unable to quieten his own mind. Each day brought more worries. He did not dare to see Jijabai's face, creased with worries of an unknown fear. Shivaji remembered Murar Jagdev. He too had been a maharaj like Shahaji Raje but Adil Shah had not spared him. Capturing Purandar had meant thumbing a nose at Adil Shah.

Lying on his bed, Shivaji was lost in these thoughts when Saibai entered the room.

She asked, 'Why aren't you sleeping yet?'

Shivaji paced the room. 'I am not able to sleep. I keep worrying about Maharaj saheb. I cannot imagine what Maa saheb must be going through. Each day while combing her hair and putting the sindoor, she must shudder while thinking of any mishap.'

'For his safey, Maa saheb has called a few Brahmins for lunch, and there is a puja at the Ganesh temple. I too am fasting.'

'God helps those who help themselves, Sai. Merely feeding Brahmins will not help. There needs to be some action.'

'What are you planning?'

'There is no point in just sitting here idly. Rather than surrender, I am tempted to march on Bijapur.'

'Are you sure of a victory?'

'I doubt it. But isn't it better than leading a life of cowardice? What do you say?'

Saibai thought for a moment and said, 'What can a woman like me say about politics but I feel ...'

'Tell me!'

'No, leave it. You will laugh at me.'

'No, tell me. I won't laugh.'

'I don't understand politics but I can follow a game of chess. If you are not confident of winning, you should not make that move in chess. You need not defeat a rook with a queen. You can send a knight or a bishop instead.'

Shivaji was surprised at the analogy and stopped pacing. 'You can defeat a rook with a knight or a bishop ...' he mumbled.

He rushed to put on his sandals and said, 'Sai, wake up Maa saheb and I will assemble others. We have found a solution!'

The palace was lit with oil lamps and the key officials waited in the office.

Maa saheb asked, 'Raje, what is this urgent meeting all about?'

Shivaji looked at everyone assembled in the room and said, 'How would you react if I told you that I have decided to attack Bijapur?'

'I would say it is suicidal.'

Raje looked at Nilojipant and asked, 'Where is Shahzada Murad these days?'

'He is camping at Ahmedabad.'

'Nilojipant, send word to Shahzada. Say that I would consider it my privilege to work under him. I would have come to pay my regards personally but for the fact that Adil Shah has arrested my father. I shall make myself available the moment I hear from him.'

'Wah, Raje! It is a superb diplomatic move,' the finance minister commented.

A rider with the message was dispatched that very night to Ahmedabad.

A few days later, Jijabai was surprised to see Shivaji in her quarters early in the morning.

'Raje, why are you up so early? You look like you haven't slept well.'

'Maa saheb, I have been worried the whole night. It has been many days since we sent the message to Ahmedabad and we have not received a reply yet. I am not sure what that Afzal Khan and Baji Ghorpade are up to. But I am sure Maharaj saheb will be released safely.'

'I hope your words come true. I have been on tenterhooks ever since we got the news. If I see a rider coming into the fort, I wonder if there is bad news. If someone shouts loudly, I get startled. I have been praying to the Lord non-stop and I hope He showers his blessings.'

'I have been wanting to visit Alandi for a few days, and I woke up this morning with that thought.'

'Please do go. After all, the Lord is our saviour in such hard times.'

It was a pleasant summer morning. Shivaji and his men crossed many streams and rivulets on their way and reached the banks of Indrayani by noon. Shivaji folded his hands in salutation on seeing the temple of Gyaneshwar. A hundred-odd horsemen stood outside at the temple while Shivaji entered the temple with a few select men. He touched the steps of the temple reverently and went in.

The temple priest came forward with his tray with flowers in it.

Shivaji placed a bag of coins and precious stones in the priest's tray. As soon as Shivaji turned to leave the temple, he found a huge crowd waiting for him outside. Yesaji came forward and after saluting said, 'Tukobarai is coming here.'

'This is really a lucky day for us,' Shivaji said, coming out of the sanctum sanctorum. He scanned the temple courtyard with hungry eyes searching for Tukaram Maharaj.

A crowd danced and swayed as trees move in the wind. The wave was led by Tukaram, his frame drum providing the beats. His eyes were closed and he sported a big tilak on his forehead. He was barefoot and wore a short dhoti covering his knees. He wore a short half-sleeved shirt while his head was covered with a small flat turban. The crowd came to the temple steps and broke up into two sections. In the middle stood Tukaram, singing and dancing to the beats of his kanjira, unaware of anything around him. The dance stopped momentarily while Tukaram looked at the idol lovingly. The beats were now softer and the mridangam had stopped playing.

Tukaram prostrated himself in front of the idol and when he got up, the crowd surged forward to touch his feet. The moment they saw Shivaji, they gave way. Raje put his head reverently at Tukaram's feet.

Pulling him up, Tukaram said, 'Raje! How many times have I told you not to do this? Why would a raja like you touch the feet of a poor man like me?'

'Maharaj!'

'I am not a Maharaj,' he said. Pointing to Gyaneshwar's idol he said, 'He is.'

Raje felt awkward and was silent for a while. Tukaram looked at Shivaji's face lovingly and exclaimed, 'Aha! What lovely face you have. I am reminded of Gyandev when I see you. He opened up the doors of knowledge—you will fulfil his mission.'

Tukaram made his way through the crowd holding Shivaji's hand. Shivaji was overwhelmed by the love and affection being showered on him. They came into a wide courtyard and someone spread a coarse blanket on the ground.

Shivaji said, 'Maharaj, I have a request. I wish you would bless our house by visiting us once. Let me know and I shall send for a palanquin and other help.'

Tukaram Maharaj laughed loudly and, wiping a tear from his eye, said, 'Why are you taking all these troubles?'

'We would like to have darshan of your good self. We would love to have you in our palace.'

'Raje, what darshan are you talking about? What is the pleasure in seeing this man in this dirty old attire?'

Shivaji was a bit despondent hearing Tukaram. However, Maharaj realized Shivaji's feelings and said, 'Raje, don't get upset. What can I ask for? If I ask for food, then the alms I get are more than sufficient. Even the weight of these tattered clothes is but a burden for my body. I have the earth as my bed and the sky as my blanket. People go to kings for recognition, but I feel suffocated. What will a common man like me do there?'

Shivaji looked up, his face confused.

Tukaram patted his shoulders with his trembling hands and said, 'Raje, you are a shrimant. You are a shriman yogi, a born gyani. Your face is like Gyandev. Why would an ordinary man come to your place? Only the blessed have a place there. This was the behind.'

Raje then touched Tukaram's feet and said, 'Maharaj, I need your grace.'

'Don't worry about grace. Your mission is pure. You will receive the grace you need at the right time from the right person. The mridangam cannot produce music when you simply beat it. Similarly, a cymbal needs another cymbal to get the melodious music out of it. You will find your guru—don't be impatient.'

Raje was overwhelmed on hearing the saint. It was late afternoon when Shivaji took leave from Tukaram Maharaj, who hugged him affectionately and said, 'Don't worry, Raje. Everything will be taken care of. Gyandev will ensure that you are well.'

It was late evening when Shivaji returned to Pune. He was about to enter his quarters when he saw Jijabai in the front courtyard.

She said, 'The message from Ahmedabad arrived while you were in Alandi.'

'That is good news!' Shivaji exclaimed. 'After all, his blessings couldn't have been in vain! Maa saheb, you should have come along. We had the good fortune of meeting Tukaram Maharaj.'

'Really?' Jijabai said, folding her hands in namaskar at the thought of the great saint.

'What a meeting! In those few moments, I learnt a lot. He assured me all our troubles will vanish.' Shivaji eagerly read the message the moment he reached the office. Murad had replied and said, 'We are in receipt of your request to join our forces. In case you decide to go ahead, please send your lawyer first so that we may get the necessary papers in place before you visit us. We shall then proceed further.'

Shivaji started the correspondence with Murad and word reached Adil Shah. He was already bedridden then and the news of Shivaji's forces joining hands with the mighty Mughal army was not helping. He had no intentions of taking on the Mughal might. At the same time, a letter from Murad reached Shahaji. It was not possible for the Bijapur Badshah to hide the letter. It was, after all, a letter from the Mughal emperor himself. It said, 'We are writing to you further to our partnership with Shivaji. We are thus sending you a royal farman and some clothes as a token of our appreciation and to welcome you to the Mughal durbar. Please acknowledge the same.'

It was clearly an invitation from the Mughal emperor and an indication that Shahaji was now officially a Mughal representative. It indirectly meant that taking care of him was now Adil Shah's responsibility. Adil Shah had no choice but to invite Shahaji to his court. He had to release him, no doubt, but he put a few conditions as a face-saving measure; Shivaji would have to return the Kondana Fort and Sambhaji would have to give back Bengaluru and the fort at Kandarpi. Shahaji sent dispatches to both Sambhaji and Shivaji agreeing to the terms.

It had been ten months since his arrest. To soften the affront of the long imprisonment, Adil Shah offered Shahaji elephants and horses and bestowed on him the honorific of 'Farzand'. Shahaji, in the meanwhile, having suffered so much, was getting increasingly disenchanted working under Adil Shah's regime.

Shivaji received Shahaji's letter and there were celebrations everywhere. Shivaji was unhappy at having to return Kondana but it was a compromise he was making for his father. He went for darshan to the Ganesha temple with Jijabai, Saibai and some others. He said, touching his head reverently on the floor, 'The Lord has taken care of us.'

Sonopant observed, 'I wonder when we will find happiness with no strings attached.'

'This is pure happiness, Sonopant. There is no loss if we give up Kondana now. We have two hundred more forts to capture and we shall reclaim Kondana later. I don't care if I have to give up a hundred such Kondanas for Maharaj's sake.'

While returning from the temple Jijabai told Sonopant, 'Let there be a deepotsav, a celebration of lights, at the temple today. Light a thousand lamps!'

The temple was brightly lit with oil lamps spreading their light and happiness all over the courtyard.

Jijabai returned from darshan late in the evening and said, 'Raje, it has been a hectic day. I suggest you rest now. Your wise thinking has saved us from calamity.'

'The credit does not belong to me,' Shivaji said, looking at Saibai. 'Your daughter-in-law deserves the credit. She was the one who suggested the plan.'

'She is really smart, isn't she?' Jijabai said, adoring Saibai a little more.

Having returned the Kondana Fort to Adil Shah, Shivaji was quite certain that Adil Shah would not act aggressively for a while, and Shivaji could afford to breathe easy for a while. He had never felt so relaxed during the last few years. He had been busy guarding various forts and training his troops. Dadoji Konddev had set up a revenue-sharing system years ago which Shivaji ensured was properly implemented. Work began on building a dam at the Kondhve village to prevent water shortages in Pune. Raje also supervised building of another dam at Shivapur. Jijabai would take care of the problems at the palace and would make decisions if there were any arguments or disputes.

Shivaji would spend his spare time supervising the work at Purandar. The region of Khalat–Belsar flourished and the people were happy and could take loans to develop land. The common man had access to Raje and he could come and complain if there was any misuse of power by officials.

Shivaji had rules for both his troops and the common public. There would be regular inspections for the troops. No one was allowed to own horses as they were considered the property of the king. The soldiers were not allowed to marry or keep a harem. The death sentence was the punishment for disobeying these rules.

Shivaji returned one day from Purandar to find everyone in a great state of excitement. He called Manohari when he saw her hurrying inside, 'Manohari, what is all the commotion?'

Manohari smiled, adjusting the water pitcher in her hand, and rushed inside without answering. Shivaji was unable to understand her strange behaviour. He reached Maa saheb's quarters but there was no one there. Just then, Jijabai entered.

'Maa saheb, what is all this excitement?' he asked.

'Raje,' Jijabai said, smiling, 'We have been busy since last night. I have been telling you not to go out for these few days.'

'What happened?'

'You are now Aba saheb! Raje, you have been blessed with a daughter. You have come back at the right time. I just got prasad from the temple and you can now distribute it.'

Raje could not contain his happiness and went to meet Saibai. The child was sleeping in the cot; he looked at her beautiful face and then, turning towards Saibai, asked, 'Who does she resemble?'

Saibai, weak from the delivery, managed a smile and said, 'She looks just like you.'

She continued, 'May I ask you something? Are you a little disappointed that it is a girl and not a boy?'

'Oh, not at all. I hope she follows your example.'

'Meaning?'

Shivaji pondered for a moment and, looking at her said, 'I hope she is someone who is able to forget her sorrows for the sake of someone else's happiness.'

He left the room and Saibai had a faint smile playing on her lips. There were celebrations everywhere in the Lal Mahal Palace and the naming ceremony was conducted with great fanfare. She was named Sakhubai. Her birth had been at an auspicious time. Shahaji had been released from captivity; Shivaji was busy managing the affairs of the kingdom; and there was a general feeling of well-being and happiness among the people. Sakhu grew quickly, laughing and playing, and being pampered by one and all.

Six months after Sakhu's birth, the news of Kanhoji Jedhe's impending arrival reached the palace. He was Shahaji Raje's right-hand man and when Shahaji had been arrested, he too had been put under captivity and was released along with Shahaji. The elder Maharaj had felt guilty that Kanhoji had to suffer imprisonment because of him and wanted Kanhoji to move away from Adil Shah's court. He had, thus, sent Kanhoji to Pune. While departing Shahaji had said, 'Kanhoji, my son Shivaji is in Pune. I want you to serve under him and protect him. Don't hesitate to repel any attack including any from Adil Shah's troops. May God be with you!'

Kanhoji took an oath to protect Shivaji till death and then proceeded to Pune. Shivaji looked forward to meeting Kanhoji. When Kanhoji arrived in Pune, a special palanquin accompanied him—Shahaji had sent Soyarabai, the girl Shivaji had married in Bengaluru, along with Kanhoji to Pune. The younger queen of Shivaji was welcomed into the palace with great fanfare. Kanhoji performed an elaborate mujra seeing Jijabai.

Shivaji welcomed him saying, 'Kanhoji, I am glad to see you!'

'Raje, Maharaj is proud of your actions and has sent me to help you in your mission.'

'I am aware of your loyalty,' and pointing towards Baji, he said, 'Baji fought Fateh Khan and defeated him. We call him Sawai Baji now.'

'One needs the right leader to show one's bravery. Raje, I brought a few brave soldiers along with me. They are the chosen few and are well-versed in the techniques of war. They will sacrifice their lives for their leader and their loyalty is beyond doubt.'

Yesaji came in at that moment and seeing him in tears, Shivaji asked, 'Yesaji, what happened?'

'It is bad news, Maharaj.'

'What happened?'

'Tukaram Maharaj has left for his heavenly abode.'

Shivaji's memories of his visit to Alandi came flooding back. The news was a shock to him. He said, his voice choked with emotions, as tears flowed down his cheeks, 'We have lost a great soul. That simple yet realized soul! The body had worn itself out and yet his compassion was unparalleled. I will never forget that radiant face. We rule forts and regions with our might, but these saints—they rule the whole world. Gyandev, Sopandev, Muktabai, Namdev, Eknath—how many shall I name? They have kept the flame of goodness burning despite all odds. They have managed to take the purity of religion to the poorest of the poor. Kanhoji, we must ensure that such saints are treated with the utmost respect. Without them, our mission and the pursuit of this kingdom are of no use.'

Shivaji did not try to check the tears flowing down his cheeks as he spoke, reminiscing about Tukaram Maharaj.

Within a few days, Kanhoji left for Rohideshwar.

Shivaji had some time to devote for other matters as things had stabilized a bit. His strength was increasing by the day. A few weeks after Kanhoji's departure, Maa saheb said, 'Raje, I have an unfulfilled desire.'

'Tell me what it is, Maa saheb!'

'When your father was arrested in Bijapur, I had promised the Lord that when he is released, I will pay my respects at Mahabaleshwar, but I have yet not been able to go.'

'I shall be happy to come with you.'

They made plans to leave for Mahabaleshwar. They met the saint Gopal Bhatt there and took his blessings. They prayed at the temple and donated jewels and clothes. While at Mahabaleshwar, Shivaji observed the dense jungles and valleys in Jawali and Koyna. He was impressed by the lovely valleys surrounded and protected by forts like Mahabaleshwar, Makrandgad and Mangalgad. Even Adil Shah would not venture into these forests so easily.

The person who controlled Jawali could keep his kingdom safe because it was almost impossible to capture the dense gorges. Jawali was under the rule of the Mores, who carried the title of 'Chandrarao.' The current ruler Chandrarao Yeshwant More was ruling thanks to Shivaji's beneficence. However, Shivaji was not too sure of his loyalties. Shivaji returned from Mahabaleshwar but the jungles of Jawali lingered in his thoughts for a long time.

Shivaji stood alone on the terrace at Lal Mahal. He wondered where everyone was and there was no one to be seen outside in the courtyard too. He saw someone lighting the thousand-wick lamp and asked, 'Who is there?'

'It is me, Manohari, sir.'

She bent in namaskar and Shivaji asked, 'Where is everybody today? I am not able to see my dear Sakhubai either.'

'Yesajirao has taken her for a marriage ceremony.'

'And what about Maa saheb?'

'She is here. Shall I call for her?'

'No, leave it.'

Shivaji turned at the sound of trumpets. There was a procession entering the courtyard.

'It looks like the marriage party has arrived.'

'Go and inform Maa saheb. I will wait for her downstairs.'

The procession reached the middle of the courtyard and Shivaji saw Jiva Mahala dancing to the beats of the drums while swinging his two swords. He was displaying his acrobatics by slicing up coconuts in the air. He would jump and in one sweep break open the coconuts while the crowd encouraged him. The bride and bridegroom arrived. Raje watched them for a while and then went inside to wear his turban.

Sakhubai sat in Yesaji's lap. He said, indicating to the newly-weds who were touching his feet, 'Maharaj, this is Ramu Kaka's son Bhima and she is Ganga, the daughter of Sarjewar.'

'Oh, it seems to be a case of a wedding within the family itself!' Turning towards Sarjewar, Raje said, 'I am angry at you.'

Sarjewar stepped forward adjusting his turban worriedly.

'Please pardon me, Maharaj. But what crime did I commit?'

'You did not invite me to your daughter's wedding.'

'Maharaj, this is a poor man's wedding. How could I dare to call you?'

Shivaji pointed at Sakhubai, perched on Yesaji's shoulders, and said, 'So you decided to invite the small rat instead?'

Everyone laughed at the joke and Raje, turning to Jiva Mahala, said, 'Jiva, I did not know you could do these acrobatics so well.'

Yesaji answered, 'Maharaj, he is well-known for this. He is invited to each marriage to display his skills.'

Jiva was a little nervous and said in a meek voice, 'Maharaj, this is all I know.'

Shivaji said, 'It does not matter what you know. What matters is you know it better than anyone else.'

He turned to the newly wed groom and said, 'So Bhimarao, you are lucky to get such a lovely girl as your wife. Will you be joining our new campaign?'

'Of course, Maharaj,' Bhima said confidently.

Shivaji asked, 'You may be ready but have you taken permission from your new wife?'

Sarjerao replied, brushing his thick moustache with his fist, 'Maharaj, she will not say a word. She is a daughter of Sarjerao. She has not married a man but a sword. She knows that if some calamity ...'

'Shut up, Sarjerao! Hold your tongue,' Shivaji shouted. 'Today is an auspicious day and not one for talk of calamities. I hope the dear girl has a long married life.'

The newly-weds stepped forward and bent low in namaskar. The wedding party then left the courtyard to the sound of trumpets and other musical instruments.

A few days later, Raje told Maa saheb, 'I feel like making a visit to Shikhar Shingnapur. Would you like to come along?'

'All right, let us leave in a few days.'

Shikhar Shingnapur was a Shiva temple on a hilltop a few miles from Phaltan and it was the seat of the family deity of the Bhosale family. A few horsemen had gone ahead as an advance party and the palanquins were ready to leave when Saibai asked, 'May I come along?'

'Sakhu is too small for the journey. It is better you stay back.'

'Can you not go later? I too would love to come.'

'That is not possible. I may not take you along this time but when I come back, I will bring back a lovely gift for you.'

'What would that be?' she asked, filled with curiosity.

'Let that be the Lord's wish. You will know when you see it.'

The camp near the base of the hills looked like a mini cantonment. There were soldiers posted at all strategic points on patrol duty.

Jijabai asked, 'Raje, does such a huge number of troops need to accompany us?'

'They all wanted to take the opportunity to have darshan and it is a good change for them too.'

They performed the abhishek at the temple the next day. While taking prasad, Shivaji said, 'Maa saheb, Bajaji Nimbalkar has come to meet you.'

'Is that so? Where is he?'

'He is waiting for us at the camp in the foothills.'

Bajaji Nimbalkar, Saibai's brother, had been forced to become a Muslim and had been in the employment of Adil Shah. After the death of his Muslim wife, he lost Adil Shah's patronage and had returned to Phaltan a disillusioned man. His first wife had died of shock when she had found out that he had been forced to convert. He was now waiting with his son Mahadji to meet Raje.

Bajaji's horsemen stood at the edge of the camp. Bajaji himself stood with his hands folded, waiting for Jijabai to step out of her palanquin. He wore a Muslim-style turban, a little scrubby beard at his chin and a loose garment with a flowing pyjama.

Jijabai's heart hurt to see him in Muslim garb. She said, 'Bajaji, you remembered us now? After so many years?'

Bajaji flung himself at her feet. She could feel his tears flowing down.

'Get up, Bajaji. Let bygones be bygones. I am happy that you have come back.'

Bajaji pleaded, 'Maa saheb, pardon me and only then will I get up.'

'Don't be so obstinate and demean yourself. Get up now!'

Bajaji got up and wiped his tears. He said, 'Maa saheb, I am not ashamed of falling at your feet in front of a million people. I do not have any self-esteem left in any case. Maa saheb, I may have become a Muslim but I am still a Hindu at heart. I am Sai's brother.' Pulling the five-year-old Mahadji towards him, he continued, 'I am willing to do anything for this poor lad. Who will otherwise take care of him?'

He sobbed relentlessly. Jijabai, Shivaji and others watching him were overwhelmed and in tears themselves. Jijabai hugged him affectionately and said, 'Don't lose heart. After all, you are one of us and will always remain so. You were made a Muslim but that was not your fault. Maybe it is a test for Raje. Come, I am sure he will find a way out.'

As Shivaji and Maa saheb walked towards the camp, Jijabai said, 'I understand now—this trip was all about meeting Bajaji, wasn't it?'

Raje merely smiled in response.

That evening, a meeting was held in Shivaji's tent. Those assembled were the key sardars and some important Brahmins. Shivaji said, 'My brother-in-law Bajaji Nimbalkar has been forcibly converted to Islam. I want us to take him back into the Hindu fold. Please suggest how we can do that and we shall meet tomorrow morning to decide the next steps.'

The Brahmins murmured among themselves while the sardars were dumbstruck. They did not know of a single case where a convert had been reconverted back to Hinduism.

The next morning, Shivaji finished his morning rituals and puja and took his seat on a high platform in his tent. The whole assembly had gathered and the Brahmins stood on the right and the sardars on the left. He saw Maa saheb entering the tent and got up. Everyone followed suit and bent in mujra. The assembly was silent as they waited for Raje to speak.

'I am eager to hear the recourse the learned men have thought of based on our discussion last evening.'

The main pandit stepped forward. He said, 'While it is not impossible to take him back into the Hindu fold, to do so would be against tradition. We are not in favour of doing things against tradition and this is our unanimous opinion.'

Everyone was visibly disturbed with the clear opinion placed forth by the Brahmins. Jijabai's face fell but Shivaji seemed unperturbed. He continued to wear his usual smile and said, 'I expected this answer from you.'

The pandits were happy because they felt that Raje had accepted their decision. But to their surprise, Shivaji said, realizing that they had not got his sarcasm, 'I am not against religious decisions but the time has come to give up your unreligious thoughts—this is my request.'

A senior pandit asked, 'Unreligious thoughts? Ours? What are you hinting at, Maharaj?'

'I am not saying you are not religious but your thoughts are. I do not like to meddle in religious matters but I understand that with changing times, religion needs to adapt. Today, thousands are being converted to the Muslim religion by force. All the Muslims have to do is throw a piece of meat in a village well for the entire village to be polluted, forcing them to turn Muslims. Our country is slowly being swallowed by these Muslims while the Hindu religion has a one-way policy. One can leave easily but can never come back. I don't understand the logic. If we continue this way, soon there will only be a few Hindus left.'

A senior pandit got up and said, 'Maharaj, this is not politics that you can change sides at whim.'

'Then you better learn to change sides,' Shivaji's voice, tinged with anger, cut across the crowd. 'Religion has been made rigid by people like you. Even Gyaneshwar said, "Let the ignorant lose their ignorance and become learned. Let one take whatever path he or she chooses as long as it leads to the Lord." But Gyaneshwar was a sanyasi and did not have a place among religious leaders. When Eknath spoke of universal brotherhood, he was shunned by all and tortured all his life. But when he died, people built temples in his name. If a religion creates discord and takes people away from it, what kind of religion is it?'

'Raje, we have given you our unanimous opinion. Please remember that the king is not above religion and we believe that you are insulting the religion here.'

Shivaji said, 'Shastribua, I am forced to speak up. Knowledge is not wisdom and our religion is like a blind elephant. Rather than allowing people to flourish, it is crushing people under foot. I want you to consider this carefully. When our Hindu religion was being challenged and temples were being broken down, why didn't any one of you come forward to protect the temples? Where were you then?'

'It is not wise to fight against the might of the enemy,' one of the pandits replied.

'Isn't it shameful for you to admit this so candidly? When pandits from Kashi sat down with Emperor Akbar and created the Din-i Ilahi, was there any uproar? You can happily take a coin from a Muslim, wash it and use it. But you cannot take a person back? Isn't it ironical that the Ganga, which is supposed to wash away sins of your past, cannot wash away the crime of a convert? What kind of religion are we talking about? Shastribua, are we not going wrong somewhere?'

'What if we are not in agreement with you?'

'Then I would have recourse to humanity. If religion fails, the king has to look to humanity to take care of his people.'

'Are you suggesting that you would force this matter?'

'Yes, if need be. I believe that a religion which has forgotten basic humanity is not worth being considered a religion at all. I am bound by my dharma, which is far bigger than religious dharma. I cannot desert my subjects.'

The pandits looked at each other in astonishment.

Jijabai was wondering how to intervene when one of the pandits stepped forward and said, 'Raje, if Bajaji is willing to perform prayaschitta, an atonement for his sins, he can be taken back into the Hindu fold.'

'I am sure he will be willing to atone for his sins. He has never denied that,' Shivaji said with a deep sigh. 'You are all learned pandits and it is your right to suggest the appropriate way forward. Religion should be like a flowing stream. It should be capable of washing away the sins of society. It does not take time for people to forget religion. Our flag was apparently created by Lord Indra himself and the same saffron flag was carried forward by Gyandev and Eknath. It represents humanity and we need to ensure that we live up to its meaning. You need to confront this dilemma!'

Shivaji had won the argument. The pandits were busy discussing among themselves. The sardars were clearly happy while Jijabai could not hold back her tears. The main pandit stepped forward and said, 'Maharaj, we are ready to convert Bajaji back to Hinduism.'

Everyone sighed with relief. Shivaji said, 'Shastribua, I will always be grateful to you for your support in this endeavour. There will be many unfortunate souls like Bajaji who may come to you for your help. Please show them the right path. There is no religion without compassion. In fact, without compassion there is no humanity.'

The process of purifying Bajaji started in earnest. Pandits and religious scholars from nearby villages were invited and Bajaji completed his prayaschitta. He was finally relieved of his sins. After the traditional yagna, havan and other rituals, Bajaji was welcomed back into the fold.

Jijabai returned to Pune with eager steps. Shivaji entered Pune along with Bajaji Nimbalkar. The royal palanquin followed them.

As he entered his quarters, Shivaji, on seeing Saibai, said, 'Did I not tell you that I would bring you a precious gift? Come and see!' Looking towards the door, he shouted, 'Bajaji, come inside.'

Bajaji stepped into the room. Saibai could not believe her eyes and rushed to hug her brother. Both of them had tears of joy in their eyes.

Shivaji said, 'Bajaji, now don't go about wandering in the forest, forgetting your own people. And Sai, this Bajaji is not going to be satisfied with just love. He has been tortured for the past four days with all kinds of penance. Now go and feed him properly.'

The feast that evening had a different flavour altogether. The seating arrangement was as per protocol and Raje, Bajaji, Mahadji and Netaji sat in one line while on the other side sat the Brahmins including Balaji, Chimnaji and others. The food served was similar yet different to suit particular Brahminical customs. Jijabai supervised the entire proceedings and ensured that everyone was well fed.

Raje returned late in the night to his quarters to find Saibai sitting on the carpet, waiting for him.

'Why haven't you slept yet?' he asked.

She did not say a word but came and sat next to him. She suddenly bent down and put her head at his feet. Raje moved back and asked, confused, 'What is this, Saibai?'

She looked at him with tear-filled eyes and said, 'No one has ever given me such a precious gift. I am truly blessed.'

Raje could not reply but just hugged her affectionately while Saibai continued to cry unabashedly. He patted her back gently and then pushing her away to look at her face said, 'I cannot understand you women at all. You cry when you are sad and also when you are happy. It is beyond my understanding!'

Saibai could not hide her smile despite her tears. Raje looked at her while a contented smile played on his lips.

It was one winter morning when Shivaji, having just returned from Purandar, was informed about the arrival of Kanhoji and Dadaji Naras Prabhu.

As soon as he met Shivaji, Kanhoji said, 'Raje, we have received orders from Afzal Khan to ask the chief of the Jawali region to surrender or else I have been ordered to capture it.'

'Why this sudden rush?'

'Raje, you nominated the young Yeshwantrao More to manage the region. Quite obviously, Adil Ahah does not like that because it undermines his role in what is principally his territory.'

'So what are you supposed to do?'

'Afzal Khan was given the job by Adil Shah and that Afzal Khan is a clever fox! He is scared of entering the dense jungles. I am, after all, in his employment and an easy target for this responsibility.'

'So you have been asked to march over and capture the region?'

'Those are the orders, and one cannot take chances with Khan.'

'Yes, I am aware. I have not forgotten his audacity at putting Maharaj behind bars.'

'Raje, I will buy time with Khan. But you need to find a way to take charge before Chandrarao takes Khan's side.'

'Jawali is not an easy target. It is situated in labyrinthine wilderness and Adil Shah's army has suffered badly there at our hands.'

'My troops know the region very well. Raje, you nominated that Yeshwant More as Chandrarao but now he has become too big for his shoes.'

'Let us first try to use reconciliatory means. If that does not work, we will march on him.'

After Kanhoji left, Shivaji sent his spies to Jawali and they sent back news of the atrocities being committed by More's sardars. Shivaji, in the meanwhile, focused on the work at Purandar.

Six months had passed since Bajaji had been taken back into the Hindu fold, when he came visiting Shivaji. He had been, in the meanwhile, busy arranging a suitable match for his son Mahadji. Bajaji had been to Junnar to meet a prospective bride and had decided to pay a visit to Raje on his return.

'Come in, Bajaji,' Shivaji said. 'I believe you went to meet a prospective bride?'

'Yes.'

'So have you fixed the marriage?

'No.'

'Why, did you not like the girl?'

'We did, but the girl's family has refused.'

Shivaji turned serious. 'And what is the reason for their refusal?'

Bajaji kept looking at the floor and tears flowed down his cheeks. Shivaji got up and placing his hand on Bajaji's shoulders said, 'Bajaji, are you upset over someone refusing his daughter for your son? Wipe your tears now. I am sure we will find better brides for your Mahadji.'

Bajaji said, wiping his tears, 'Raje, it is not as easy as you think. You may have taken me back into the Hindu fold but no one else is willing to take the risk.'

Shivaji was quiet, not knowing how to react. At that moment, Sakhubai came running in shouting 'Aba saheb!' She was wearing a green skirt and a matching green blouse. She stopped abruptly on seeing Bajaji inside. Shivaji smiled and said, 'Oh, is our Sakhu feeling shy? Come and touch Nimbalkar mama's feet.'

Sakhu came in and touched his feet. She hugged Raje and said, 'Aba saheb! I want a doll.'

'You are not going to get a doll now.'

Sakhu hid her face in her palms. Looking into her eyes, Raje lifted her chin and said, 'You now need a partner and not a doll. Bajaji, would you take her as your daughter-in-law?'

Bajaji was astonished at the sudden proposal and exclaimed, wide-eyed, 'Maharaj!'

'I am asking you in all seriousness. Would she suit you as your daughter-in-law?'

Bajaji trembled and could not hold back his tears. He rushed forward and fell at Shivaji's feet.

Shivaji hugged him saying, 'Bajaji, you are my daughter's father-in-law. You cannot touch my feet!'

Sakhubai ran away, her face flushed with embarrassment.

Bajaji said, wiping his tears, 'Raje, you are truly large-hearted.'

'Bajaji, while going down, ask your sister to come up here.'

Saibai came in a little later and asked, 'You called for me?'

'I needed your opinion on something important.'

'Which campaign are you planning to go on now?'

'What more important work can be there for a father of a daughter than her marriage?'

'Whose marriage?'

'Our Sakhu's. I have found a suitable match; very rarely does one get such.'

'Oh, is that so? Then let us go ahead and fix up the marriage.'

'Are you sure? I don't want you complaining later.'

'I won't. Who is the groom, by the way?'

'The groom is Bajaji's son, Mahadji.'

Saibai kept staring at Raje. She did not utter a word. Raje asked, 'Why? Do you not like the match?'

'May I ask you something?'

'Please.'

'Are you doing this for my sake?'

'I am not doing this for your sake, but I have the strength to do so because of you. Shall I go ahead?'

'If you have decided to go ahead, I am more than happy. I am sure Sakhu will be happy there.'

'Sai, I am quite sure of this.'

Sai saw Shivaji coming near her. She said, 'I will leave now. Maa saheb has given me some important work in the kitchen and the younger queen is all alone there.'

Raje smiled in response.

Bajaji's joy knew no bounds. He shared the news with whomever he met, and within a few hours the entire palace was abuzz with the news of Sakhu's marriage.

Jijabai was sleeping in her quarters in the afternoon as the younger Soyarabai sat near her bedside. When she woke, Soyarabai gave the news to Jijabai and she could not believe her ears. She asked, 'Who told you this?'

'The news is all over the palace!'

Jijabai got up and sent a message of her arrival to Shivaji's quarters. Shivaji waited for her while Saibai stood in one corner. The moment Jijabai came in Shivaji said, 'Maa saheb, had you called for me, I would have come to meet you.'

Jijabai looked at him and said, 'Raje, I was under the impression that my opinion is considered before deciding anything in this household?'

'That is true.'

'Then how is it that you have gone ahead and finalized Sakhu's marriage?'

'Maa saheb, it is with your wish and blessing that we were able to get Bajaji back into our family. I assumed that you would not object to this proposal and rather, you would appreciate it.'

Jijabai did not know how to respond and said, 'Mahadji's marriage could have got fixed anywhere. There are enough good families around.'

'Then why not with Sakhu, Maa saheb?' Shivaji asked.

She turned to Saibai and asked, 'Are you in favour of this proposal?'

Saibai looked down at her feet and did not answer and Jijabai understood that she was in agreement. She looked at Shivaji. He would normally not dare return her gaze but he stood there, looking at her with a new confidence in his eyes. He said, 'Maa saheb, don't tell me that you don't like the idea because Bajaji has been reconverted to the Hindu fold and that it is below our dignity to give our daughter's hand to his son?'

'And so you went ahead and finalized the marriage? You know that no one would object to your decision!'

'This isn't because no one will object but because Sakhu is my favourite. I have chosen a house where she will be loved and treated with respect. I am not sure if we would have found such a household elsewhere.'

'Shivaji!'

Shivaji continued, his voice getting emotional, 'Maa saheb, people do not become truly ours just because we take them back into our religion. We need to welcome them into the house as well. We need to win their confidence. Bajaji is one of us, he was made a Muslim by force. You felt hurt and got him back, but that alone did not help. He was unable to find a proper bride for his son, and I wanted to show what I meant by the true spirit of humanity.'

Jijabai let out a deep sigh and said, smiling, 'Raje, I must admit that I got carried away for a moment. You are, of course, right.'

'Maa saheb, I knew you would agree,' Shivaji said, beaming happily. 'A narrow mud path walked on by kings becomes a regular road within no time. There will be a little bit of gossip and debate but, eventually, people will accept the path we have chosen—I am quite sure of it!'

'Shivaji, may the evil eye never touch you. You have cleared away all the doubts I had in my mind.'

'Then let there be no delay, Maa saheb. Let us begin the preparations at once.'

The preparations started the next day itself. The guest list was prepared and Sakhubai's marriage in Pune was conducted with great fanfare.

Bajaji Nimbalkar took Raje's leave and went back to Phaltan. Since Sakhu had not yet come of age, she stayed back in Pune.

Shivaji was inspecting the branding of the newly bought horses when Tanaji came in and saluted saying, 'Maharaj, Kanhoji Jedhe has come along with other sardars.'

Shivaji knew it had to be something important. He mounted his horse and rode towards the palace.

Those assembled included Kanhoji Jedhe, Yesaji Kank, Baji Jedhe, Dadaji Naras Prabhu, Bajaji, Chimnaji and others. Shivaji commented, 'Well, this seems like a special meeting indeed!'

They all bent in mujra and waited for Jijabai to arrive. After Jijabai took her seat, Kanhoji said, 'Raje, Chandrarao is becoming intolerable now.'

'What happened?'

'Earlier, he captured Shirmalkar Deshmukh's territory. He has now encroached into our territory and is becoming more unmanageable with each passing day. To make matters worse, one of his sardars has unsavoury designs on innocent and helpless widows with his implicit support!'

'I wonder, Kanhoji, why you don't go ahead and attack him. I would not take offence.'

Kanhoji replied, licking his lips, 'Raje, we may be your men in our hearts, but officially, we still serve Adil Shah.'

Shivaji smiled, 'I am waiting for the right time. Kanhoji, keep me informed about Afzal Khan's movements.'

'Raje, rest assured, I don't think Afzal Khan is planning to march on you in the near future.'

'He is not doing us any favour,' Shivaji said. 'He is aware of the status Maharaj saheb has received as Farzand in the Bijapur durbar. He would not attack Maharaj saheb's son so casually. He is too cunning for that, the sly fox. I have not been going to Purandar for the past two years for nothing. I have been watching Afzal Khan working on the Wai region after being appointed the Subedar. He has been trying to win the Marathas by being nice to them and More is a mere puppet in his hands. If I attack Jawali, Khan would not hesitate to come from Wai and repulse the attack. I will have to wait and watch.'

'But how long will this go on?' Jijabai asked.

'Not for long. I am told that the Badshah is ill, and that Khan has been posted to Kanakagiri and may move away. The moment he leaves, I will plan my attack.'

Shivaji then decided to move base to Purandar on an auspicious day. The family was housed in a safe place. Within a few days of moving, he received a message saying that Afzal Khan had been called back to Bijapur and posted to Kanakagiri. Thus, Shivaji got the opportunity he had been waiting for. He immediately drafted a letter to More:

' ... you call yourself king but I am the only raja by the grace of Lord Shambhu. You are thus asked to not call yourself raja and work for my kingdom. You are also hereby asked to move out of Jawali and surrender to us. We assure you that there will be no bloodshed but we warn you that in case you try to capture our messenger, we shall not hesitate to kill you ...'

More replied saying, 'My name is Chandrarao and we have been kings for generations now. You have become a king only yesterday and we do not believe you deserve any title. If you wish, you may try your luck and come here.'

Tanaji and Yesaji were fuming and brushed their moustaches with their wrists, waiting for Shivaji's response. Shivaji continued reading ...

'... if you attack us, we will not spare anyone. We have adequate ammunition to destroy your forces. You are most welcome here at your own risk.'

Everyone was fuming at the arrogance and audacity of More. Shivaji smiled, 'More has cordially invited us to Jawali. How can we refuse his invitation?'

Their own smiles spreading, the sardars waited eagerly for the orders to start marching.

After finishing darshan at Mahabaleshwar, Shivaji sat with his sardars discussing the strategy. The forest in Jawali was a treacherous one. The gorge was full of thick, thorny bushes and it was so dense that an ordinary man would hesitate to enter it even during the day. It was in the same forest that the Ranes had vanquished the Khilji, Bahamni and Adil Shahi forces. The narrow paths were such that a single man in the gorge could hold a hundred men at bay.

Shivaji called Raghunath Ballal and said, 'Chandrarao More will have to be killed. The one who controls Jawali will also control the Wai province. I want you to lead our men.'

Raghunath Ballal gladly accepted the challenge and entered the valley under the pretext of a meeting with Chandrarao More. Raghunath was accompanied by a select few horsemen and a hundred foot soldiers. He asked his men to wait at strategic points before entering the dense gorge.

Yeshwantrao More was happy to hear that Shivaji had sent a messenger—the same Shivaji who had earlier ordered him to surrender! He decided to meet Shivaji's men the next evening.

The inner courtyard in Chandrarao's mansion as brightly lit with oil lamps. A tall soldier stood on the right of Chandrarao sporting a tilak on his forehead. He looked at Raghunath as he entered the courtyard, along with Hanumantrao, Yeshwantrao's manager, and a daredevil like Sambhaji Kavji.

Yeshwantrao asked, 'Who is it?'

'It is Shivaji's messenger, sir.'

They entered the courtyard and saluted.

Sipping from his wine glass, Yeshwantrao rudely asked , 'Who the hell are you?'

Hanumantrao began, 'Maharaj, he is ...'

'Shut up. Let him speak.'

Raghunath cleared his throat and said, 'I am Raghunath Ballal Korde and I am Shivaji Raje's secretary, lawyer and messenger. Raje said ...'

'Who are you calling Raje here?' Yeshwantrao interrupted. 'There is only one Raje here and that is me!'

'That is your opinion but I don't agree, sir. It is due to Shivaji Maharaj's grace that you had the chance to sit on this throne and received the title of Chandrarao. I request you not to forget that.'

Yeshwantrao's laughter echoed in the courtyard. 'Oh, it seems I must thank Shivaji profusely. If he had such powers then why did he not choose to sit on the throne himself?'

Everyone joined in the laughter. Sambhaji Kavji's hand gripped his sword hilt while Raghunathpant looked at him sharply. He did not want Sambhaji to react.

'Let bygones be bygones. Shivaji Raje wishes that you mend fences with him.'

'That might suit him but not me. Give him my message—if he dares step into the Jawali gorge, he will not return.'

Yeshwantrao got up to leave and to signal the end of the interview.

Raghunath was a little restless and said, 'What about a marriage proposal?'

Laughing, Yeshwantrao sat down and said, 'You want to propose an alliance with that Bhosale family?' His voice took on an edge and he added, 'Go and tell this to your Shivaji—the More family traces its lineage from the Chandragupta family and we have been kings for generations now.' He laughed scornfully before continuing, 'But we can find a way. I have a daughter whom we can consider for an alliance that may suit us.'

The assembly was silent and the screech of an owl was heard nearby. Yeshwantaro said, 'Think about it. The owl too seems to be in agreement!'

Raghunath retorted, without losing his temper, 'We consider the sound a bad omen, a harbinger of death in fact.'

'It may be true. Who knows, it may have been predicting your death? Hanumantrao, capture him and chop off his head!' he screamed.

'Now, wait a moment!' Raghunath shouted. Everyone was stunned.

He continued, 'I have been tolerating your nonsense for a long time, Chandrarao. Listen to me carefully. You have just lost a golden opportunity. At this moment, as we speak, Raje and his troops have surrounded the Jawali jungle and the owl you heard was heralding your imminent death.'

Hanumant More unsheathed his sword and attacked Raghunath. Sambhaji Kavji was ready and repulsed his attack, felling him in one blow. Sambhaji and Raghunath rushed out of the palace at once. A blast was heard deep in the jungle as shouts of 'Har Har Mahadev!' rent the air. The battle had begun. The troops were able to take charge of the Jawali area but in the midst of all the commotion, Yeshwantrao managed to escape to Rayari along with his wife and son.

Shivaji soon took charge of the stables, jewellery and other precious royal items. A brave More soldier Murarbaji Deshpande had been captured and was presented to Raje tied up in ropes. Seeing the brave soldier defiantly fighting the ropes, Shivaji asked the soldiers to release the bonds. He said, 'Murarbaji, I have seen the bravery with which you defended your king. We admire such brave men and would like you to join my army.'

Murarbaji was convinced that Shivaji meant what he had said and agreed and it was an important victory in the Jawali fight. It took almost a fortnight for Shivaji bring the Jawali gorge under his control. He ensured that all of More's men were taken care of and given the right responsibilities. Krishnaji Babaji was an experienced and senior leader and was made a Subedar. Viro Ram was made Mazumdar, or the treasurer. Shivaji also began allocating land to people it rightfully belonged to.

A long-cherished dream had now been realized for Shivaji—he had finally got hold of the valley. Various forts like Chambhargad, Songad, Chandragad and Makrandgad guarded the valley. The gorge was further surrounded by dense jungles making it inaccessible to enemy attack. Mahabaleshwar also stood like a huge rock protecting it.

Shivaji summoned Moropant Pingle and pointing at the mountain on one side said, 'Moropant, I am told that you are an expert at building forts. I would like to assign you the task of building a fort on this mountain that we all will be proud of. Will you take on the job?'

Moropant accepted the responsibility readily and said, 'Without a doubt, Maharaj. I shall build this fort. But I must praise your foresight.'

'Really? Why do you say that?'

'Maharaj, no one else would have thought of building a fort there when there are already strong ones like Chambhargad and Songad nearby. Why would one think of another fort?'

'Why, tell me?' Shivaji asked, wanting to hear his reply.

'You have realized the inherent strength of this place and have thought of building a fort right in the middle while there are others surrounding it. It would be difficult to find another place as safe and secure as this.'

'Well done! You were right in assessing my view. I find it inconvenient to make a visit to Tuljapur every time I wish to pray to Bhawani Mata. I would like us to build her temple here so that we can pray daily.'

Having set things in order, Shivaji started preparations to chastise More who was holed up in Rayari. Shivaji left Jawali and reached Rayari. During that fortnight, while Shivaji was taking formal possession of Jawali, Yeshwantrao had managed to escape to Rayari, along with the members of his family.

Rayari was a fort which seemed to kiss the skies. More had reached the fort without any prior intimation and the fort was not stocked well for food grains and other necessities. Shivaji's soldiers surrounded the fort as soon as they reached. Yeshwantrao More tried to attack from the fort but it was evident that he was on a fool's errand. The fort was strong and difficult to capture but the troops were inherently ill-trained and undisciplined. It had been three months since Shivaji's soldiers had surrounded the fort and by the time the monsoon arrived, it had become impossible to stay inside the fort. Shivaji sent Yeshwantrao a message through More's confidante.

More had been waiting for a signal and the moment he received the message, he came down with his wife and son. Shivaji welcomed Yeshwantrao and treated him with due respect. More, however, did not appreciate the value of Raje's treatment and, in fact, thought that Shivaji was merely trying to pacify him. After seeing More's reaction, Shivaji decided to take charge of the fort himself.

The Rayari Fort was a strategic location; it was on the main route from Ratnagiri to the Deccan and was also close to the sea. Control of Rayari meant that one would control the traffic through the many valleys and landscape around. The fort and its height ensured that it was near impossible to capture—it was many times taller than the fort at Daulatabad and Shivaji decided to rename it Raigad.

One day Kanhoji presented himself and said, 'Maharaj, you had pardoned Yeshwantrao and his brother, Prataprao. They tried to escape today. We were able to catch Yeshwantrao but Prataprao got away.'

'Bring Yeshwantrao here.'

Yeshwantrao was paraded, chained and handcuffed. Shivaji looked at him in contempt and asked, 'Yeshwantrao, where were you planning to run away to?'

He smiled and said, deliberately forgetting protocol and using derogatory language, 'I planned to go to a place where you are not present.'

'Yeshwantrao, don't forget that you are my prisoner.'

'Huh! A lion does not eat grass just because he is defeated. I may have lost to you in battle but I will not beg for my life. Chandrarao is a title which generations before me have worn with pride. I am not here to beg for mercy.'

Shivaji's face was hard. He said, 'One does not become great just because one has great ancestors. You were drunk and hopeless on most days. You enjoyed the sadistic pleasures of killing innocent people and throwing them to the wolves. You have no right to call yourself a Chandrarao. I gave you a chance but you do not want to change your ways.'

Raje turned to Jedhe and said, 'I don't think he has the inclination to change himself. Take him away and behead him.'

The next day, Yeshwantrao was beheaded and his wife and children were sent to Pune.

Pune's Lal Mahal Palace was bereft of royal presences ever since Shivaji had shifted base to the Purandar Fort. More's captive children, Krishnaji and Baji, were now growing up with Chandrarao's wife in Lal Mahal.

Shivaji reached Pune after getting an urgent message. 'What happened,' he asked Chitnis, the office manager, after reaching Pune.

'Raje, I beg your pardon. Baji More has run away.'

Shivaji erupted with anger and asked, 'How did this happen?'

Chitnis did not know how to respond. He replied in a tremulous voice, 'Raje, we had taken the utmost precautions and as per your instructions, we were taking good care of these children. They left the palace under the pretext of a Ganapati darshan but they managed to bribe some of our soldiers and escaped. We did not realize that Baji was working on his plan with Mudholkar Ghorpade.'

'And then? Tell me what happened!' Raje's anger was now evident.

'The day before yesterday when they went for their usual darshan, the children vanished. We managed to catch Krishnaji but Baji managed to escape. We have not been able to find him.'

Krishnaji More was produced before Shivaji. He was a young boy, sixteen or seventeen years old. He looked at Raje with pride and arrogance and was not scared of him. In fact, he had a slight smile on his lips. Shivaji asked, 'Where is Baji?'

Krishnaji laughed and said, 'He has escaped. He is not going to be found now.'

'Wah! What allegiance and loyalty you have displayed for the courtesies extended to you.'

'You too have benefited from our courtesies, don't forget that. Don't you know that the benefits you enjoy at Jawali are because of us?'

'Silence! I was treating you like a child thus far but you seem to be showing your true colours. You seem to have forgotten your father's fate.'

'Of course I remember! I am not scared of treading the same path—I will not forgive our enemies.'

'Take this arrogant brat away and behead him. After all, even if you feed him milk, a snake can only beget a snake.'

'Raje!' Chitnis exclaimed, hearing the harsh punishment.

Raje turned in anger and said, 'These are my orders and I expect you to obey them. The people who helped them should also be arrested and put behind bars.'

Krishnaji was taken away and beheaded as per Shivaji's orders and in the afternoon, Shivaji woke up to wailing sounds coming from one part of the palace.

Shivaji felt uneasy once the beheading had taken place and everyone was scared of meeting him because he would get angry at the slightest of reasons.

Two days later, a messenger came in with the news of Jijabai's arrival.

'Maa saheb?' He asked surprised, 'Where is she?'

'She will arrive at the gates any moment.'

Shivaji got up hurriedly. Jijabai stepped out of the palanquin but when Shivaji bent to touch her feet, she did not smile. She entered her quarters silently and Shivaji followed her.

Jijabai took some time to wash her hands and feet. Shivaji sat there, wondering why she had returned in such hurry. He was eager to know and asked her the moment she stepped into the room, 'I am dying of curiosity—why have you come without letting me know? Is everything all right?'

'Raje, I have been worried for the past two days—after hearing about More's son.'

'Maa saheb, you heard about the beheading but do you not want to know why?'

'That is the reason I have come here—tell me.'

'Maa saheb, I had the boys settled here and treated them with love and care. And yet, they were plotting to escape and even managed to get Ghorpade to help them. In fact, Baji escaped as well!'

'Is that all?'

'No! Krishnaji was not at all ashamed of his actions. On the contrary, he was arrogant and answered back when I questioned him. Anyone in that position would have begged forgiveness at my feet.'

Maa saheb laughed sarcastically and said, 'Raje, I would not have done what you did. I would have let the lad go.'

'Maa saheb!' exclaimed Raje.

'Raje, you were consumed with anger. You wanted him to fall at your feet and beg for forgiveness. Why? Just because you captured Jawali? Raje, it is easy to accept defeat but much more difficult to live with victory. I am disappointed that you were prey to the arrogance which follows success.'

Maa saheb's words carried a deep sense of regret and discomposure and she seemed deeply affected by the incident. Shivaji's throat went dry and he was unable to say anything—he did not have the courage to meet her gaze.

Sighing deeply, Jijabai said, 'Raje, I know that More was not willing to come to you despite your request for a friendly alliance. It was imperative for you to capture Jawali before More turned to Khan for help. I know why you beheaded him—he had acted in a manner which deserved such a punishment. But his children? What had they done to deserve such a punishment? You could have turned them into allies.'

'Maa saheb, that was impossible. They would have grown up to become poisonous snakes. They would have bitten us one day.'

'You can call a defeated man by any name, a snake or a dog. But if you call him a tiger's cub, then the same emotions would be termed as pride or bravery. Raje, do you remember? When you went hunting, you brought back two tiger cubs? You knew that they would become ferocious tigers one day, and yet you gave them milk and treated them with love and care. If you can treat an animal with such respect, why can't you treat humans the same way? If power is going to corrupt your wisdom, then such power is useless. You are then just like the sultans. Raje, I did not expect such behaviour from you.'

Each one of Jijabai's words pierced Shivaji's heart. He felt suffocated and was teary-eyed.

Jijabai continued, 'Raje, how will I go and face that poor lady? What will I say when she asks me why you killed her son? Raje, it will be a great kindness if you killed her too. At least she will not have to bear the daily anguish of her son's death.'

Shivaji could hear no more. He exclaimed, 'Enough, Maa saheb! No more! I am already dying of shame.'

He fell down and hugged her legs saying, 'Maa saheb, I made a terrible mistake. Please pardon me. I forgot myself and was swayed by my power. I have committed a crime—I promise you, I will never behave like this in the future.'

Jijabai hugged him affectionately and both of them wept together.

Six months had now passed since the capture of Jawali and Shivaji and Jijabai had shifted to Purandar. Ever since Shivaji had merged Jawali into his expanding kingdom, its boundaries stretched to the Arabian Sea and it was important that the region was protected both from internal and external threats. He was busy appointing new officials and increasing the cavalry. He minted a few coins and appointed important officials including the Peshwa, Mazumdar, Dabir, Sabnis, Surnis among others. The construction work at Raigad was in full swing and the office was shifted to Rajgad while Shivaji camped at Purandar.

A week later, when he had gone for darshan at the centuries-old Narayan temple at the base of Purandar Fort, he was informed that Timaji Kulkarni from Supe had come to meet him. Timaji was a revenue official and a landlord but his privileges had been taken away by Sambhaji Mohite, Shahaji's brother-in-law and Shivaji's foster uncle. Sambhaji had been bribed a horse and a hundred and fifty rupees by Timaji's enemies. Timaji appealed to Shahaji who had directed him to Shivaji. The Supe pargana was under Shahaji and he had handed it over to his younger queen, Tukabai's brother Sambhaji. He was, however, corrupt and misusing his powers. Shivaji had kept quiet knowing that Sambhaji was his father's brother-in-law. He assured Kulkarni that he would look into the matter.

The next day Shivaji was in his office when he heard a melodious voice singing bhajans. He looked out of the window to see a saffron-clad young fakir singing in a clear voice.

'Wah!' Shivaji exclaimed, listening to the lovely voice. 'Who is that sanyasi?'

One of the office clerks answered, 'He is a Ramdasi. Many such beggars and bhikshus come to our doorstep each day.'

'No, there is a difference between a Ramdasi and a beggar or even a sanyasi. A Ramdasi is a follower and disciple of our great Ramdas Maharaj. They go about spreading Ramdas Maharaj's message in society. They try to influence society towards the greater good and do great social work.'

'These Ramdasis are spread all over our kingdom.'

'I am aware of that. A lot of people have joined our cause after hearing the great man. I would like to meet him.'

'I will order him to come over right away,' Sonopant said, getting up.

'No, no. I will go and meet him. A Ramdasi is, after all, a representative of the Maharaj himself. I have no right to summon him.'

The Ramdasi was a little surprised to see Raje come out to meet him. Shivaji folded his hands and asked, 'Swami, do I know you?'

'I am a Ramdasi and people call me Kalyan. I came here for some alms.'

'Which abhang were you singing?'

'Raje, it was not an abhang. These are Gurudev's shlokas. He is at Shivthar–Khalit and is writing a book. He has decided not to move from there till he finishes the task.'

'I would love to hear some more of his shlokas if you would oblige me by singing,' Shivaji requested.

The Ramdasi sang a few more shlokas in his clear, mellifluous voice.

Shivaji was in tears listening to him and said, 'See, Sonopant! Look at the beauty and clarity of Ramdas Samarth Maharaj's thoughts.'

'I feel like running to him and falling at his feet. Kalyan, how is Samarth?'

'He is well, thanks to the Lord's blessings. He says often times ...'

'What does he say?' Shivaji asked eagerly, interrupting him.

Ramdasi Kalyan smiled and said, 'Samarth says that your worries are over now. The Mughal kingdom is about to end and the Swaraj will begin soon. Peace and justice will reign supreme in Shivba's kingdom.'

Shivaji was thrilled to bits. He said, 'Pant! Samarth has put such huge responsibility on my shoulders. Kalyan, please give my regards to him. Tell him that the dream of our Swaraj is yet to be fulfilled and we need his blessings. I am eager to see him and when I visit Raigad, I shall meet him. If you need anything, please do not hesitate to ask. I shall ensure that we fulfil your wishes.'

Shivaji came into the palace to find Vichare and Gaikwad there. Saibai was in the royal quarters and she said, 'I was looking for you.'

'Why?'

'Maa saheb wants to talk to you.'

'Is it urgent?'

Hiding a smile, Saibai said, 'I am not sure.'

Shivaji followed Saibai into Jijabai's palace and asked, 'Maa saheb, you called for me?'

'I will tell you if you promise not to get angry.'

'I never get angry by your command, Maa saheb. Please tell me.'

'Vichare and Gaikwad have come with proposals for you to marry their daughters.'

'Maa saheb, I have married thrice, isn't that enough?' A few months after Sakhu's birth, Shivaji had married Putlabai in a political alliance.

'Raje, this is a part of politics and running a kingdom. A marriage is an alliance with a family and not a person. Royals never marry one person. It is custom to have many wives.'

Shivaji smiled sarcastically and said, 'I don't believe in royal customs. I would rather follow the footsteps of Lord Ram. Maa saheb, it is a Mughal tradition to have many wives.'

'Raje, I have given my word to them.'

'What can I say then? Better go ahead,' Shivaji said, with a deep sigh.

Within a span of three to four months, Raje had alliances with Gaikwad, Jadhav and Ingle. Thus, Sakwarbai, Kashibai and Gunwantabai joined the rest of Shivaji's retinue of Saibai, Soyarabai and Putlabai.

A fortnight before Diwali, Shivaji left Purandar with a select team of horsemen. His destination was the Karhe plateau. He reached the Supe pargana and climbed up to the fort. Seeing Shivaji Raje, the guards saluted him and allowed him to enter. After all, the area was Shahaji's jagir and the Jagirdar's son had come on a personal visit to the fort. There was no one to stop him and his troops. Shivaji instructed his men to surround the fort and then entered with a few guards.

Assuming his role of a foster uncle, Sambhaji Mohite came to meet Shivaji. Raje bent in mujra as Sambhaji asked, 'Raje, what brings you here without any prior intimation?'

'Mama saheb, Diwali is fast approaching. I came to take the blessings of my elders.'

'Better late than never! At least you have remembered some of your elders now,' Sambhaji said, laughing sarcastically. 'It seems like someone from Bengaluru has pulled your ears.'

Sambhaji Mohite was being his usual arrogant self. Raje stifled a smile and said, 'You are right about that but it is your ears which are being pulled.'

'Raje, don't forget protocol! What kind of language is this?'

'Timaji Kulkarni has complained to Maharaj saheb and he came to meet me too. I have come to request that you return his privileges—which you took away forcibly.'

'You have come here on his request? I have been nominated here by Maharaj saheb. Who are you to question me? The Supe pargana is under Maharaj's jagir.'

'I agree, but you are forgetting that I am Maharaj's younger son. It is my responsibility to ensure that his jagir is well-maintained and that there are no complaints. I would prefer to solve this issue amicably.'

'Who are you and why should I heed your wish? You have come here to take my blessings. Take them and get going.'

'Then I have a right to ask for my reward.'

'Ask!'

'I want you to hand over the Supe and Thane parganas and join me.'

Sambhaji Mohite laughed out loud and said, his voice taking on a hard note, 'Raje, you are younger than me and also my nephew, which is why I am pardoning you. Someone else in your place would have lost his life for showing such temerity.'

Shivaji said, trying to control his rising anger, 'Mama saheb, it is not possible for you to do that. But I can do that to you easily.'

'What do you mean?'

'Mama saheb, at this moment, your fort has been surrounded by my men. You are under arrest.'

'Raje!' Mohite exclaimed, his eyes wide with anger and surprise. He rushed to pull out a sword hanging on the wall. Shivaji's men, quick to react, arrested him. Sambhaji shouted, 'Raje, you will not be pardoned so easily. I will tell Maharaj saheb.'

'You may try telling him. I know him well enough and your atrocities are known to him. You still have a chance to mend your ways and join me.'

'Huh! You expect me to serve under my nephew?'

'Then you are free to go to Bengaluru.'

'What about my things here?'

'They are in my custody now. Be happy that I have spared your life. You may leave now.'

Shivaji returned victoriously, having taken control of Supe Fort, to celebrate Diwali.

The Purandar Fort was enveloped in deep sorrow by the news from Bengaluru that Sambhaji, Shivaji's elder brother, had died in battle. He was seven years elder to Shivaji; thirty-five years of age. Sambhaji and Afzal Khan were attacking Kanakagiri when Afzal Khan asked Sambhaji to lead the charge. Assuming that he had the support of Afzal Khan, Sambhaji went ahead and

Afzal Khan finally had his chance to take his revenge on the Bhosale family. He did not extend any support to Sambhaji and he died when he was hit by a cannon ball.

Shivaji rushed to Jijabai's quarters. He could not hold back his tears and mother and son did not know whom to console and both wept, sobbing bitterly at the loss. Jijabai could not forget the image of Sambhaji seeing them off when they had left Bengaluru. Maharaj saheb had challenged her then saying, 'You take care of Shivaji and I will bring up Sambhaji. Let us see who wins!'

Dear Sambhaji! She had been able to enjoy his company only for a brief while. He was a lad of six or seven years when she had left for Pune. She remembered his blurred face as he followed his father when they had taken leave from Junnar. She could not forget her darling Shambhu bal as he waited for them when they reached Bengaluru. Or Sambhaji Raje who had seen them off a little distance from Bengaluru with tears in his eyes! That was her last memory of him.

Two years ago, they had received news of Sambhaji having been blessed with a son. Had she insisted on going to Bengaluru to see her grandchild, she would have been able to meet Sambhaji. But that was not to be! Sambhaji was a dream which was near yet untouchable. He grew up in her dreams and before she could touch him, he vanished in the early morning mist!

Shivaji Raje was aware that his mother's health was delicate following Sambhaji's death. He kept an eye on her as he continued focusing on the administration from the fort. Time would heal them, albeit superficially. The anguish of her loss was something Jijabai would always have to live with. Jijabai displayed the courage to take charge of her life, giving Shivaji the confidence to get back to his work wholeheartedly.

Shivaji was inspecting the construction work at the highest point of Purandar when Netaji Palkar came in and said, 'Maharaj, we have completed the work for housing the cannons.'

'Come, let us have a look.'

Yesaji, Tanaji, Shiva and Jiva Mahala were also present. The room housing the artillery was in one corner of the fort. Shivaji had employed three cannon experts, Ambaji More and two brothers. He had given them a mansab amounting to three thousand rupees in return for their work.

Shivaji said, 'Ambajirao, the real test is when the cannon balls destroy the enemy to pieces. Yesaji, provide all the support Ambaji needs. I am eager to see the cannons when they are ready.'

At that moment, Firangoji came and saluted.

'Firangoji, when did you arrive? I was missing you. Come, we have a lot to discuss.'

Firangoji moved ahead to assemble the men. He knew Shivaji had something important to discuss.

The men assembled in the main office as per Shivaji's instructions and included Tanaji, Yesaji, Firangoji, Raghunath Ballal, Atre, Dadaji Ranjekar and some others. Sonopant Dabir and Shamrao Nilkanth too were present. However, no one was aware about the reason for the meeting.

Shivaji said, 'I called you all here with a purpose. Ever since we captured the Karhe plateau, we have managed to secure a significant part of our kingdom. The capture of Jawali has allowed us to reach the ocean shores. Bijapur is in a shambles now that Adil Shah is dead and Shahzada Aurangzeb is stuck up in the Deccan due to his father's illness. This is a rare opportunity for us—we should take advantage of the situation when both our prime enemies are weak and occupied elsewhere.'

At that moment, an attendant entered the room and said, 'Maharaj, a sanyasi has come asking for you.'

'What is his name?'

'He calls himself Niranjan.'

Raje got up and went out hurriedly to escort the sanyasi inside. The other sardars were a little surprised when Tanaji said, 'Raje has great regard for sadhus and saints. If someone like that comes to his door, he will leave everything else and attend to him.'

Raje did not return for a long time. A little while later, he called Sonopant Dabir his side. When Sonopant went in to meet Raje, he was asked to provide five hundred coins to the sanyasi.

Sonopant was taken aback at the amount and exclaimed, 'Five hundred, Maharaj?'

'Yes. He is going on a yatra. He may return anytime. Please ensure that, whenever he does, I have his darshan, even if it means disturbing my sleep.'

The sanyasi left along with Sonopant.

Shivaji returned to the assembly and continued as if there had been no break, 'And so we need to take advantage of the situation when our enemy is weak. We need to move fast.'

Atre said, 'Raje, your wish is our command. Tell us and it shall be done.'

'Atre, do you remember you had gone to the Dabhol province?'

'Yes, Maharaj.'

'I suggest that you take charge of capturing the Mustafabad Port and the area around it.'

Atre got up excitedly and the others looked at Shivaji Raje expectantly. He told Firangoji, 'Stand ready at Chakan because I might come that side. Yesaji, Tanaji, keep your horsemen ready and be prepared to march whenever you get the message.'

Everyone now knew that a big move was being planned and was ready to swing into action.

Firangoji said, 'Raje, I would like permission to leave right away.'

'Firangoji, you are a part of the family. Why don't you stay for a few more days?'

'No, Raje. It is not good to stay away from the fort for long.'

'I too cannot move from here. But now that you are going, I am giving you the responsibility of Sakhubai's safety. She will accompany you.'

'As you command.'

Sakhubai and Mahadji were ready to leave after the meal. Sakhubai touched Raje's feet and he hugged her affectionately and blessed her. He was unable to say anything as he was overwhelmed by seeing her leave. He came down to see them off. He kept looking for a long time after they had left. The dust of the horsemen blurred the path they had taken.

As per Shivaji's orders, Atre marched to Dabhol and captured the port of Mustafabad and the saffron flags fluttered on the forts nearby. Shivaji dispatched Sonopant towards Aurangabad, aware that Shahzada Aurangzeb was in Bidar. Raje's plan was to take back the Junnar–Ahmadnagar area which he had had to return when Shahaji Raje was captured. But while Aurangzeb agreed to acknowledge the capture of Dabhol, he did not mention Junnar–Ahmadnagar. Shivaji was upset and decided to carry out the bold step of teaching the Mughal emperor a lesson.

The messages from his spies had been coming in regularly and Shivaji was getting news from Kalyan–Bhiwandi area as they roamed around in disguise. The sanyasis and fakirs were Shivaji's men too and they roamed freely in the

Junnar–Ahmadnagar area. It was Shivaji's brilliant idea to take the help of sanyasis and other fakirs, whom no one would suspect, to get information from across the regions.

It was a summer morning when Shivaji left Purandar with Maa saheb's blessings. He rode to Chakan and the troops assembled there under Firangoji's command. Their target was the marketplace of Junnar, which was now under the control of the Mughals. It was protected by strong walls and no one ever dreamt that Shivaji would besiege it one day. It was Shivaji's birthplace and dear to him! The fort of Junnar, as informed by the spies, was unguarded for such an attack and, within no time at all, they had captured the fort. The loot included three lakh coins, expensive jewellery, clothes and other valuables including a stable of famously well-bred horses. Within no time, the troops had looted the fort and Shivaji marched back to Chakan. The Bijapur sultanate had never dared to look at Junnar but Shivaji had dared to challenge the Mughal emperor.

Shivaji marched to Ahmadnagar within a few days of his attack on Junnar. Ahmadnagar was a key post for the Mughals, but it was not as ill-defended as Junnar. The moment they heard of Shivaji's troops marching towards the fort, the commander Nasir Khan decided to counter the offensive but the Maratha troops defeated him. The loot in Ahmadnagar was much lower in comparison to Junnar but the fact that they had defeated a key post of the Mughal empire was a lesson in itself for the Mughals.

The news reached Bidar where Aurangzeb was camped and he was wild with anger. It was a challenge to Mughal supremacy and he sent instructions to Multaf Khan, Nasir Khan and Mir Jumla to take care of the Maratha rat. The message was clear: Destroy Shivaji's province and kill whoever opposed the Mughal rule. By the time Aurangzeb's message had been sent out, Shivaji was back in Pune.

Shivaji was aware of Aurangzeb's might and his anger—he knew that Aurangzeb had capable generals like Kartalab Khan, Hoshdar Khan, Raikiran Singh, Shaista Khan, among others. However, Shivaji had another plan in place. He sent his messenger to meet Aurangzeb at Burhanpur. The diplomat conveyed the message that Raje was deeply regretful of his capture of Junnar–Ahmadnagar but did not say a word about returning either. Aurangzeb pretended that he too would forget the episode as his energies were focused on Agra where his father, Emperor Shah Jahan, was ill. After all, Allah had given him a rare opportunity to fulfil his desire to grab the throne and he had no option but to act as if he had forgiven Shivaji.

There was much to celebrate when Shivaji reached Purandar. The sound of cannons announced that Saibai had delivered a baby boy. Shivaji Raje had been blessed with his first son, the heir to the throne!

The invitations for the naming ceremony were sent out. They asked Jijabai to suggest a suitable name and after hesitating a moment, her eyes filled with tears and she said, 'Shivaji, let us name him after your Dada Maharaj.'

And so, the boy was named Sambhaji. Jijabai picked up the young Sambhaji and hugged him affectionately. She felt that her lost Sambhaji had been returned to her. Sambhaji's birth heralded good fortune and by the time the rains had ended, Shivaji was able to recapture Kondana. He had surrendered Kondana to secure the release of Shahaji and was relieved to have it back into the Swaraj fold.

Sambhaji was growing fast and Shivaji was busy expanding the Swaraj. Atre had captured Danda–Rajpuri and was on the way to Janjira. The expansion, however, came at a heavy cost to the exchequer. Raigad and Pratapgad were being fortified and that took huge amounts of cash. Moropant Pingle came to meet Shivaji at Purandar.

Shivaji said, with a deep sigh, 'Moropant, it looks like we may have to stop work for some time. We bring in a lot of treasure but I don't know how it gets over so fast.'

'Maharaj, our ambition is not small. We are, after all, building such huge forts.'

'I understand, Moropant. Anyway, I will ensure that the work is done under your supervision even though you may have to go slow for some time.'

Shivaji was not happy giving such instructions and he stepped out of the palace to find a sanyasi waiting for him in the courtyard. He asked, 'Is that Ram Sharan?'

'Yes, Maharaj.'

Shivaji indicated to him to follow and they walked along the courtyard for a while. When Shivaji came back, he was smiling. He told Moropant, 'I told you to go slow with the work, but you need not worry. I will take care of the finances.'

Moropant went back happily.

The next day Shivaji went to meet Jijabai and said, 'Maa saheb, I have received news that the royal treasury from Kalyan will be moved to another place soon. It is a golden opportunity for us to attack and take the treasure.'

He left the next day.

The sardar of Kalyan, Subedar Ahmad, was unaware of the impending attack. He was relaxing after having dispatched the royal treasure belonging to the Adil Shahi durbar. It was being escorted by soldiers all the way to Bijapur. His son Mullah Yayha along with his wife had also accompanied the caravan.

The caravan moved slowly through the dense jungle and the rumbling of the wheels pierced the silence of the forest. Mullah led the caravan on a horse and he would turn back once a while to see the caravan following him. His young bride would peep through the curtains of her palanquin to enjoy the beauty of the forest. They had no idea that they were being watched by hundreds of eyes from both sides of the forest.

The road was uphill and the caravan struggled with the heavy load, moving slowly. The bullocks were being pushed hard by the drivers and the noise of the whips echoed in the silence. The slopes were steep and the horsemen dismounted and walked slowly along the path. The soldiers had to give a helping hand to push the carts, and they were sweating even though the weather was cold. They were eager to cross the ghat as soon as possible. Suddenly, shouts of 'Har Har Mahadev!' rang across from all sides as the Maratha soldiers attacked. The fight which ensued was brief and within no time, the Kalyan treasure was captured.

The town of Kalyan was silent in the afternoon. The bazaars were empty and at that moment, a few Maratha horsemen landed at the gates taking the guards by surprise. Within minutes, the town was surrounded and Subedar Mullah Ahmad arrested. Shortly, a saffron flag fluttered from the top of the town hall. Bhiwandi was being captured at the same time the soldiers had captured Kalyan. Shivaji got the news of both the captures while he was en route to Kalyan.

In Kalyan, a lovely shamiana had been set up for Shivaji Raje. He looked at the saffron flag fluttering in Kalyan and smiled. Everyone bent low in mujra and Abaji, the sardar who had led the attack, ran to hold the reins for

Shivaji's horse. Shivaji dismounted and said, patting Abaji's back, 'Abaji, it isn't appropriate that you hold the reins!'

'Why, Maharaj?'

'The Subedar of Kalyan does not perform such tasks!'

'I am honoured, Maharaj. But even if you grant me ten such subas, I would still consider it my privilege to help you dismount.'

'Abaji! You and your men have done a commendable job. I am pleased. Did we lose any of our men?'

'Only fifteen, Maharaj.'

Shivaji smiled dejectedly and said, 'Abaji, even the loss of one person is a lot for me. Can we not win any battle without losing a single drop of blood? Anyway, let us not go against what Jagdamba may have decreed.'

Shivaji took a tour of Kalyan after a brief rest. The town looked pleasant against the backdrop of the ocean nearby. He came back to the shamiana which was decorated as a temporary durbar and the floor was covered with a soft carpet. Incense sticks burning in one corner spread a lovely fragrance all around. Shivaji said, 'Abaji, you have given me a royal welcome! If I stay in such a shamiana for a long time, I too will develop royal tastes!'

He sat on the high platform while the royal treasure was displayed and the inventory was carefully noted. Shivaji ordered compensation for families of all those who had suffered in the clash. Those who had shown valour were felicitated. Abaji Mahadev was officially made the Subedar of Kalyan. Dadaji Krishna and Sakho Krishna, the two other sardars who had done a commendable job, were given the task of managing Bhiwandi and Kalyan. The Muslim Subedar and his son were asked to march forward. Shivaji was impressed seeing the father and son. They were of Arab descent and were fair-complexioned, tall and handsome men. They looked at Shivaji with a mixture of pride and anger in their eyes. Shivaji ordered them to be released and asked them to leave for Bijapur. The duo was astonished as they had not expected anything other than a death sentence.

Abaji Mahadev stepped forward and bent down in mujra and Shivaji asked, 'What is it, Abaji?'

'I have one more prisoner to be presented.'

'Who is it?'

'The daughter-in-law of the Subedar.'

'Abaji!' Raje exclaimed in anger.

Abaji hesitated for a moment and said, 'Maharaj, please don't misunderstand me. She was travelling with her husband when we looted the caravan and was arrested along with the others. How could we decide her fate without informing you?'

Shivaji said, 'Abaji, you could have taken the decision yourself. I would not have blamed you. But it seems this daughter-in-law is someone special.'

'Yes, Maharaj. You would not find such a beauty easily—she is lovelier than the flowers you see. Her radiance spreads a divine fragrance everywhere.'

'Wah, Abaji! You have become a poet now. Please present her before me—I am curious to see such a beauty.'

The durbar was rapt with attention. Abaji clapped twice and the curtain of the palanquin was moved. The Subedar's daughter-in-law stepped out along with two maids. She wore a thin veil and her hands, with lovely mehendi on them, shivered in fear. The toes of her lovely fair feet dug deep into the soft carpet.

Shivaji let out a deep sigh and closed his eyes for a moment. He came close to her, walking slowly. She could see his feet as she kept looking down. Shivaji glanced at the crowd to see the father and son glaring at him, their eyes burning with anger. Shivaji lifted her veil and placed it on her head. Everyone present in the durbar gasped at seeing her radiant beauty. Shivaji looked at her face while she continued looking at the floor, tears flowing down her cheeks. Shivaji was disturbed seeing her tears and went back to sit on his chair.

The Subedar's daughter-in-law was surprised to see Shivaji turn back. She looked up to meet his gaze. He was wearing a saffron cap while his forehead had the traditional tilak. Most people were unable to look into his eyes but she continued to return his stare. Shivaji turned his eyes to Abaji and said, 'Abaji, this girl is really beautiful. I do not know what to do with her. What do you suggest?'

'Maharaj ...' Abaji hesitated.

'Please speak your mind without hesitation.'

'Maharaj, as per tradition, she can join the dancing girls troupe. That itself would be a reward for her. This is the way the enemy treats our women. No one showed Rani Padmini any mercy. In fact, such ladies fill up the harem of the Badshah. She is the daughter of an enemy—even if you make her the mistress of an ordinary soldier, you cannot be blamed. It will not be against protocol.'

'Enough, Abaji! One sin cannot be eliminated by another. I believe in recognizing the law of humanity rather than what society and protocols say. Our flag carries the saffron colour of the Lord. It is representative of the Lord

Himself. I was stunned seeing the beauty of this girl. I had never seen such pristine beauty.' Pointing a finger at her, he said, 'Seeing her, I wondered ...' Shivaji could not continue as his voice was choked with emotions.

'What is it, Maharaj?' Abaji asked.

'How do I put it? I wondered had Maa saheb been so beautiful, I too would have had the fortune of being handsome. Abaji, she reminds me of my Maa saheb. Please treat her with the utmost respect and dignity—treat her the same way as you would treat Maa saheb. Please send her back with that respect and care.'

The Subedar and his son looked at each other, astonished at Shivaji's compassion while the daughter-in-law had tears of joy in her eyes. She bent in an elaborate, respectful salaam and Raje folded his hands in response. He got up and the entire durbar saluted, and the Subedar and his son followed suit.

Shivaji returned to Purandar after finishing his tasks at Kalyan and was surprised to be received by Jijabai at the main door. She waited with a traditional thali in her hands to welcome him. He touched her feet and said, 'Maa saheb, I did not know that you would be waiting for me here. I wondered ...'

'I know you are surprised. Raje, without caring for social protocols, you have conducted yourself in a praiseworthy manner. I heard of your conduct at Kalyan and you are a real raja now. I had to come here to welcome such a raja.'

She could not speak further, engulfed by emotions, and hugged Shivaji. It was an emotional moment for everyone present. By the time Shivaji came to his quarters, it was late. Shambhu had slept while Saibai seemed tired. Shivaji said, 'Sai, you don't seem well. Please go to sleep.'

'How could I sleep? I have heard of the way you treated the daughter-in-law of the Kalyan Subedar. I am curious—is she really that beautiful?'

'Yes, truly beautiful.'

'Then?'

'She may be incredibly lovely but not as beautiful as you are,' said Shivaji.

'You are just trying to humour me.'

Shivaji turned her face towards him and said, 'I am not joking. Beauty lies in the eye of the beholder but true beauty is the one where the hearts meet.

She may have been beautiful but she cannot capture my heart. Without love, beauty is not complete.'

Sai could not hold his gaze, full of emotions. She put her head on his shoulders and before she could realize what was happening, she dissolved in his embrace.

Shivaji returned to Purandar after ensuring that the capture of Kalyan–Bhiwandi was complete. A few days later Abaji Mahadev came to report.

'Raje, you had asked me to find you experts who could build ships.'

'Why, have you found them?'

'Yes, they are waiting downstairs—four hundred of them!'

'Make arrangements for their stay. I shall see them tomorrow.'

The arrival of the shipbuilders was a topic of discussion for everyone. They had not seen so many Europeans in one place.

Jijabai asked, 'Why have you gathered so many firangis?'

'Maa saheb, our borders have reached the ocean now. We need to build strong ships and these men are experts at building ships.'

The next day, the Europeans were brought into the court. They removed their huge hats and bent low to salute. Abaji introduced the leader saying, 'Raje, this is Louis Vartav. He is an expert ship builder.'

Shivaji asked him a few questions through an interpreter and he appointed them to the task promptly. It was decided they would be based in Kalyan, and as they were leaving, Shivaji said, 'Take good care of them. And ensure that you get your best men to work under their guidance.'

The firangis had hardly begun their work when Shivaji received an urgent message to come to Kalyan.

Abaji said, once Shivaji arrived, 'Maharaj, we treated as best as possible but one day, as misfortune would have it, one of their friends came from Goa to meet them. God knows what happened but they all vanished overnight. I am told that they have all gone to Mumbai.'

Shivaji asked, unperturbed, 'What about the work?'

'It is halted completely. That is why I called you so urgently.'

'Will you be able to complete the task? You will be rewarded well if you do,' Shivaji asked the supervisor.

'Don't worry, Maharaj. We can do this better than the firangis. I will not let you down,' the supervisor replied.

'Abaji, I had a premonition that this may happen, and that's why I asked you to put your best men under them. These firangis are loyal to their king alone. They don't care whether they are paid well or not by someone else. When the call comes, they are willing to stake everything for the sake of their king—unlike our own men who are happy to serve under the Mughals. They must have realized that we are their enemy and that they may have to fight us one day. They are not foolish enough to help the enemy to build ships. But let us get on with our job.'

Shivaji returned to Purandar and within a few weeks captured Mahuli, one of the last forts that Shahaji had captured from the Nizam. The boundaries of the Maratha empire were spreading now and it was necessary to ensure that the Swaraj was well protected. Shivaji made a few changes in key posts; he appointed Moropant Pingle as the Peshwa in place of Shamrao Nilkanth. Nilo Sondev was made Mazumdar; Netaji Palkar was appointed as the Sarnobat, or the chief of artillery, while Abaji Mahadev was named Surnis, or the general record-keeper and superintendent of correspondence. Law and order and other general affairs were managed by Jijabai. The main office was shifted to Rajgad and Jijabai managed her duties from there.

Shivaji's cavalry had increased to ten thousand and his foot soldiers to a similar number. Yesaji Kank was made the commander of the troops. He controlled forty forts now and was constantly busy with some campaign or the other. When Shivaji returned from a campaign in Karnatak he received the news that the Bijapur and Mughal durbars had been getting increasingly restless about his progress.

Aurangzeb was eager to go back north and was camped at Burhanpur. He had not forgotten the looting of Junnar by the Maratha forces. Bijapur had changed a lot since the death of Mohammad Adil Shah. His eldest queen Badi Saheba now managed the state. In a reckless attempt to victimize her counsellors and ministers, she had had all the key aides murdered and even managed a plot to kill. Khan Muhammad and Bahlol Khan. Fateh Khan, who had attacked Purandar, was poisoned to death. Bijapur had thus lost one of its main commanders and was now weak. Shivaji was keen to take advantage of this and planned an attack. The Bijapur durbar had warned Shahaji Raje to check Shivaji but Shahaji Raje feigned an inability to have any influence on the behaviour of his wife and his wayward son. In fact, he went to the extent of suggesting that they nominate an able commander to counter Shivaji's advances. Badi Saheba named Khan Afzal Subedar and nominated Rustam Zaman, son of Ranadullah Khan, to annihilate the powerful Sawant Kudal.

Kudalkar Lakham Sawant was a Desai in the Adil Shah regime but had a mind of his own. The others like the Surves of Shringarpur, Gowalekars and the Sawants of the Kudal pargana were also independent and managed their own affairs. When Kudalkar Lakham Sawant learnt of Rustam Zaman marching on him, he decided to counter his attack. At the same time, they sent a messenger to Shivaji Raje for help. Shivaji answered the call and his troops repelled Rustam Zaman's attack. The Sawants decided to join forces with the Swaraj and gave the fort of Phonda to Raje. The province of Kudal, as dear to the Bijapurkars as Jawali, came under Shivaji and this was a strategically important acquisition.

Shivaji then captured Tale Ghosale and found Gowalekars waiting to join the Swaraj. Gowalekar presented to Shivaji a long, broad-bladed sword made by the Europeans. Shivaji was impressed seeing the lovely weapon and said, 'Sawant, I am happy that you are presenting me this sword but I believe that one should earn and not take these as gifts. How do I redeem this gift?'

In return, Shivaji presented Gowalekar with three hundred coins and some royal gifts. The sword was then named Bhawani.

One relentless campaign after another had taken a toll on Shivaji's health and the royal physician insisted he slow down a little. He decided to rest at Harihareshwar, a beautiful place by the seaside. He recovered from his fever but the weakness remained. After a few weeks, he returned to Rajgad. The queens too rushed from Pune to Rajgad. One day, Aurangzeb's messenger arrived. Aurgangzeb had decided to move to Delhi and written, 'You are hereby requested to meet me as soon as possible. If you are unable to present yourself, you may send your Diwan Shamrao Nilkanth along with your troops. I will capture Delhi and in return make you wealthier than you would have ever imagined.'

Shivaji's advisors thought that it was a golden opportunity. After all, the mighty Aurangzeb had personally asked for help.

Shivaji only smiled and said, 'I don't think that we should support the Mughals in their fights. I am not in favour of extending any help to Aurangzeb.'

Shivaji's inability to help was conveyed to Aurangzeb and he was quite expectedly annoyed. But he did not have the time to exact revenge—it would have to wait for some other day. He had a task at hand—dislodging his father and taking charge of Delhi.

Aurangzeb reached Agra and within three months, he had put his father in jail. He managed to kill his brothers and occupy the Delhi throne, being crowned the Mughal emperor. Shivaji did not want him to continue his enmity and sent his messenger Sonopant to Delhi to welcome the new emperor.

Jijabai said, 'I think you have managed to stall the enemy.'

'I don't think so, Maa saheb. He is not going to forget the insult so easily. He is a cunning politician. He would act as if he had forgiven the past and I am fine with it for the moment. I am not worried of him right now but ...'

'What are you worried about?'

'There are ominous murmurs of revenge in the Bijapur court. I don't know when they will show their true colours. Their commander-in-chief, the erstwhile Subedar of Wai, is itching to find a reason to attack us.'

However, at that point, Shivaji could not afford to think of Afzal Khan as his mind was preoccupied with Sai's health, which had been steadily deteriorating ever since the birth of Sambhaji. Shivaji decided to move her to Pratapgad for recuperation.

Badi Saheba sat in her durbar, fuming with anger. She wanted the Maratha menace to end. Shivaji had managed to capture their forts, taken charge of the harbour, attacked many provinces, looted the Kalyan treasury while Bijapur had sat and merely watched—she could tolerate no more. A tray with the traditional paan kept in the hall was ready for a brave commander, who would dare to take the challenge. Anyone who picked up the paan, and hence taken up the challenge, would lead the campaign against Shivaji.

The Bijapur court had able commanders like Ankush Khan, Rustam Zaman, Yakut Khan, Siddi Hilal and other loyal ones like Baji Ghorpade, Mambaji Bhosale and others. They were all silent and looked down on the floor at the carpet. They did not dare to meet Badi Begum's angry glare.

She thundered, 'Usne azmat-e-shahi ko lalkara hai. He has challenged the might of Bijapur. We need to defeat him for the sake of our religion and our kingdom. The royal durbar is looking for a brave volunteer to step forward.'

She scanned those present in the durbar and her voice boomed again, 'Is there a man among you who is ready to stake his life for the protection of our kingdom?'

Everyone was silent. They continued to look down when suddenly Afzal Khan walked confidently towards the throne. He was a hugely built man. There was a sort of brutish arrogance as he walked, his eyes confident as he came and stood in front of the throne. His left hand held the sword's handle. He bent low in salute and then looked at those assembled in the court with contempt and said, 'Jille Subhani, I am at your service. I am itching to kill enemies of the state, so please tell me who I should destroy.'

'Shivaji ... the rebel of the Deccan!'

Khan smiled and said, 'Is that all? I am surprised that there is no one here who can fight against him. Begum Huzoor, I will take care of that scoundrel Shivaji. Who is this Maratha rat anyway? I will drag him to this court soon!' and he picked up the paan from the royal tray.

The crowd erupted with cries of 'Subhanallah, Subhanallah!' Badi Begum then gave her jewel-encrusted sword to Afzal Khan as a token of appreciation.

Khan had the support of many sardars and his son Fazal Khan. His two younger sons were also part of the force. Soon, a huge army was being readied and it lumbered its way towards the Maratha Swaraj. The zenana khana consisted of many palanquins and elephants pulled heavy cannons while the green Adil Shahi flag fluttered from the howdah on the lead elephant. The entire contingent marched in the hot, dusty summer and they had only one objective: Shivaji.

They had moved barely a few miles from Bijapur when Khan indicated that they should camp. He assembled all the sardars in his tent that night. His mediator, Krishnaji Bhaskar, stood near him. Khan looked at the assembly and said, 'I don't want to reach Shivaji by the shortest way possible. We will go via Tuljapur, Pandharpur and then reach Wai.'

'Please pardon my interruption but why choose a long route to a short one?' Krishnaji Bhaskar asked, wondering why Khan would choose such a circuitous route.

Afzal Khan smiled and moving his hand over his beard, he looked at Krishnaji Bhaskar. He said, 'I am not sure when the rains will start. This contingent is huge. We don't want to get stuck in rains. The route via Pandharpur is dry.'

Everyone nodded in agreement while Khan avoided revealing his actual plan. The next day they marched towards Tuljapur, which was nestled amidst the hills, and one could see the golden spire of the Bhawani temple from a distance. The people of Tuljapur got the news of Khan's imminent arrival and ran helter-skelter. The contingent reached the town and Khan got down from his elephant, surfing the area. He asked, 'The Hindus consider this a sacred place, don't they?'

Krishnaji Bhaskar read his mind and said, his hands folded, 'Khan saheb, we Hindus consider this sacred. It is akin to Mecca.'

'Silence! How dare you compare Mecca with the Tulja of these Kaffirs, these non-believers? Isn't this the favourite deity of that rat Shivaji?'

'Yes, sir. I am afraid that our Hindu sardars would be quite upset if you destroy their sacred place.' Krishnaji tried another tactic.

Khan roared back, 'Does anyone have the strength to oppose me? I shall behead anyone who does. Krishnaji, I am the Subedar of Wai. I did not touch a single temple there and that was my mistake. This Shivaji has become too big for his boots and all the Kaffirs have joined him. Let them know that Khan is an annihilator of the ungrateful and the treacherous. He is an idol breaker by breed and a killer of killers!'

Afzal Khan had shown his true colours. He was, after all, a follower of Islam, a destroyer of Kaffirs. He pointed towards the temple and shouted, 'Destroy! Loot the town!'

The troops attacked the town with the shouts of 'Deen! Deen!' Within a few hours, the town had been razed to the ground. Khan reached the temple and walked in with slow, deliberate steps. The priests fell at his feet, begging for mercy, but he brushed them off. He was looking at the deity. There were a few statues in the way and he broke them with his sword. He reached the sanctum sanctorum and stared at the Goddess. The Tuljapur Bhawani stood in Her pristine glory with Her eight hands. The Mahishasur lay at feet pierced by a spear from one of Her hands. Khan laughed out loud and his booming voice rang across the silent temple. He shouted, 'Ei But-e-Kafran! Batao teri karamaat! Batao teri azmaat! Show me your prowess, you Goddess of the natives. Let me see your prowess.'

He raised his hands and in one fell swoop, his sword fell on the deity. The idol broke into pieces and Khan's laughter could be heard with each blow. The temple was looted and Khan slaughtered a cow in front of the temple. His anger had subsided for the time being. He had managed to destroy Shivaji's favourite deity. He had but one objective in mind now: Pandharpur!

Shivaji was camped at the base of Rajgad in a village called Shivapattan that he had created himself. He had sent Saibai, along with Jijabai, to Pratapgad for a change of weather with the hope that it would improve her health. Since there was no change in her health, Shivaji moved her to the haveli in Shivapattan. Sambhaji was growing up fast and constantly ran around the haveli. Saibai was unable to move from her bed due to acute weakness, ever since her illness after the delivery.

Shivaji sat near Sai's bed. He stood up as Jijabai entered the room followed by two maids. They performed the traditional sign to ward off the evil eye and put a tilak on Sai's forehead.

Jijabai said, 'I have got some prasad from Shingnapur. Let us hope that the Lord's blessings bring back her health.'

Shivaji was silent. Jijabai asked, 'Any news about Khan?'

'He has left Bijapur,' he said.

'I believe you called for Firangoji?'

'Has he arrived?'

'He came in a while ago. You were here in Sai's room, so I did not send for you.'

Shivaji stepped out to see Firangoji playing with the young Shambhu. Tanaji, Raghunathpant and some others had also come with Firangoji.

Shivaji sat on a chair when Firangoji asked, 'Raje, you have called us for a special meeting?'

'It is only during emergencies and crises that we remember our dearest ones, don't we?'

'So what is the crisis, Raje?'

'Afzal Khan has left Bijapur. He is marching here,' growled Mankoji.

'What for?' Firangoji asked.

'For the wedding invitation you sent!' taunted Mankoji.

Shivaji smiled and said, 'Mankoji, Firangoji is a simple man. He does not like such taunts. Firangoji, Afzal Khan is marching to attack us. He has a cavalry of ten thousand and an equal number of foot soldiers.'

Firangoji brushed his bushy moustache with his left wrist and said, 'Let him know we are waiting. He can do us no harm.'

'We need to have a plan in place. Let us not get carried away.'

At that moment, a servant announced the arrival of Vishwasrao, the head of intelligence.

Jijabai entered the room with Vishwasrao. She asked, 'Vishwasrao, do you have any good news?'

He did not reply and kept looking at the floor.

Shivaji asked, 'What happened?'

'Maharaj, Khan took a circuitous route and reached Tuljapur.'

'Tuljapur?' exclaimed Maa saheb.

'Yes. He looted the town and destroyed the Bhawani temple.'

Jijabai had tears in her eyes. A shiver went through Shivaji's body. His eyes were red with anger and he said, 'Vishwasrao, Khan has destroyed our family deity. We shall not spare him.'

Vishwasrao said, 'Maharaj, he has turned towards Pandharpur now.'

Jijabai muttered, 'He doesn't seem to have completed his quota of sins yet.'

'We cannot have any dialogue with a person who destroyed our family deity,' Firangoji said.

'Well said, Firangoji. We shall find a way to tackle this Khan.' Turning towards Vishwasrao he said, 'Keep us posted about his movements. I am sure he will camp at Wai—he is the Subedar of Wai. Place your sanyasis, fakirs, beggars and other spies all along the route. If he is on a recruitment drive, then put your men in his ranks. I want to know of each and every step he takes.'

Vishwasrao saluted and left. Jijabai had a worried look on her face.

Shivaji said, 'It is our good fortune that he is coming at a wrong time for us.'

Everyone looked askance at Shivaji's comment.

He clarified, 'Nature will help us this time. He will camp at Wai just as it starts raining. It will give us enough time to prepare and by the time the monsoon ends, we shall be ready. Firangoji, I want you to ensure that the Chakan Fort is well prepared. I want to ensure that all our forts are ready for attack.'

The next day, Shivaji moved from Shivapattan to Rajgad. He was receiving regular news about Khan's movements and soon, within a month, he got the news he feared the most—Khan had destroyed the temple at Pandharpur.

There was a general sense of disquiet everywhere and Shivaji's sardars were busy gathering their troops at their forts and the forts themselves were being fortified.

One afternoon, Kanhoji Jedhe reached the fort with his five sons. Shivaji wondered why he had arrived with all his sons. Shivaji asked, 'You must be drenched and uncomfortable in the rains.'

'When the mind is uncomfortable, who cares for clothes, Raje?'

'Why, what happened?'

Jedhe stretched his hand holding a royal farman. He said, 'I have received the Shahi farman. That is why I had to come here.'

Raje said, looking at the farman, 'Read it out aloud.'

The farman read, 'After the death of Sultan Muhammad Badshah, Ali Adil Shah is now the Badshah of Bijapur. This farman has been written for Kanhoji Jedhe and his family.

'Shivaji has captured many forts and tortured the Muslim citizens under the patronage of Bijapur. We have thus commanded the Subedar of Wai, Afzal Khan, to teach him a lesson. You are ordered to join forces with Afzal Khan. You are hereby asked not to extend any support or patronage to Shivaji's forces. You are asked to destroy Shivaji. You will be rewarded well for your efforts and will be suitably honoured. Please treat this as an order and implement it with immediate effect.'

The silence in the courtyard was complete. No one said anything.

Shivaji said, 'Kanhoji, it is a nicely worded order. One does not hear such eloquent farmans these days.'

'Raje, I am worried sick and you are praising the wording of the farman?' Kanhoji said.

Shivaji said, looking at Jijabai, 'Isn't it clear from the farman that I have no future? One cannot be expected to jump on to a leaking boat, no?'

'Raje,' Firangoji appealed. 'Does that mean we should join Khan's forces?'

'I cannot ask you to jump into the valley of death with me. Saving one's life is not a crime.'

'Raje, what are you saying?'

'I am not saying anything new. Your neighbours Khandoji Khopade, Deshmukhs like Jadgale Deshmukh, as well as Utravalikar have done the same.'

Shivaji clarified, 'You may not know but let me tell you; they too received such Shahi farmans and they have joined forces with Khan.'

'Raje, just because they are disloyal does not mean I will follow suit. There is a God up there, watching us.'

'Who is afraid of the Lord?' Raje said in an anguished tone, 'Our deity Bhawani at Tuljapur has been destroyed and now Khan has despoiled

Vithoba at Pandharpur. But has that stopped anyone from joining him? Look at Baji Ghorpade, Pandhare Naik, Kalyanji Yadav, Zunzarrao Ghatge, Prataprao More and my own step-uncle, Mambajirao Bhosale! Aren't they our own family? But they have not bothered to support our religion. I suggest you save your life. You can save your province too.'

Shivaji's words pierced Jedhe's heart. He said, 'Raje, I have served under the elder Maharaj. I can never be disloyal to him.'

'Jedhe, I am young and many call my dream childish. I do not wish that you join this game.'

'Raje, this Maratha cares nothing for his life. When I received the farman, I told my sons that we need to go and meet you. I have not bothered about my province or any other thing—I don't care if I don't have it anymore.'

He bent down to touch Shivaji's feet. Shivaji hugged him tightly and said, 'Jedhe, I am blessed to have a friend like you. I was hoping that you would come to my aid but did not want to put you in an awkward position.'

'Raje, what is your command?'

'I am going to give you a big task. I want you to gather all the Deshmukhs together. But ensure that they understand the real situation.'

'Consider it done. I will leave right away.'

Maa saheb said, 'Wait! You have come with your sons. Why don't you stay back for a night?'

'Maa saheb, I consider this my own house, but right now I have a job to do. Please allow me to start right away.'

He saluted and took his leave from Shivaji and Jijabai.

Soon, the spies brought the news that Bajaji Nimbalkar had been captured by Afzal Khan. Bajaji had not done any wrong except that he had reconverted to the Hindu religion. Khan had threatened to crush Bajaji under an elephant's feet. Shivaji's daughter Sakhubai was married to Bajaji's son.

Saibai was worried sick hearing the news and her health deteriorated again. She said, 'I cannot ask you to do anything more for my brother. You have already done so much.'

'Sai, you don't have to say this. Bajaji is your brother and our Sakhu is now a part of their family. I promise you, I will take care of him.'

'Will you really?' Sai asked.

'Yes, but on one condition—you have to stop crying.'

She immediately wiped her tears and Shivaji paced the room, wondering how he would fulfil his promise.

Soon, he sent a message to Pandhare Naik, a loyal sardar of Shahaji, who managed to convince Khan to release Bajaji in exchange for sixty thousand coins. Bajaji narrowly escaped a horrible death and Shivaji was relieved that he had managed to keep his promise to Saibai.

Rajgad was filling with different sardars who arrived every day. The work progressed in earnest, the pouring rains notwithstanding. Baji Prabhu Deshpande presented himself to Shivaji who asked him, 'Baji, is Mohangad ready?'

When the news of Khan leaving Bijapur had reached Shivaji, he had given orders to fortify Mohangad and the task was being handled under the supervision of Baji.

Baji Prabhu said, 'It is ready, Raje. You need not worry.'

The rains stopped for a while and Shivaji took the opportunity to place a cannon at Sanjivini Point at Rajgad. It was a strategic point and a cannon there would ensure that the enemy would be truly repulsed. Shivaji was personally supervising the work when one of the wheels of the cart carrying the cannon got stuck in the mud. The cart did not move an inch despite much pushing and pulling. Baji Prabhu, Tanaji, Sambhaji Kavji and some others were watching from a distance. Sambhaji, rolling up his sleeves, advanced towards the cart when Yesaji said, 'What are you up to, Sambhaji?'

'Let me try.'

Sambhaji Kavji asked the men to move away and said, 'When I lift the wheels, push the cart forward.'

Sambhaji took a deep breath, spat on his palms and got down to work. His chest was swollen and the muscles in his arms were bulging with the effort, the veins standing out, threatening to burst. The wheels creaked and before the others realized what was happening, the wheels had been taken out of the mud. The men pulled the cart forward to the shouts of 'Har Har Mahadev!'

Raje looked at Sambhaji and said, his voice full of approval, 'Sambhaji, I have seen your strong body before but today I've had the chance to see the strength within it.'

'Maharaj, this fellow is really strong. He can eat half a goat for one meal. He is able to pull a horse on his own!' said Tanaji.

'Tanaji, be careful. I don't want the evil eye to fall upon him—let us not praise him too openly!'

'But how can the evil eye fall on him? His huge frame won't fit into one eye!'

Everyone laughed heartily at Tanaji's joke.

After ensuring that Shivapattan and Rajgad were ready, Shivaji decided to visit Jawali to see the preparations there.

Jijabai said, 'Raje, must you go in such weather?'

'Maa saheb, Khan has not reached Wai yet and this is a good chance for me to see how things are in Jawali. Please stay here as this place is safe.'

'How can we feel safe when you are out of the fort?'

'Maa saheb, your duty is as important as mine. You need to take care of Shambhu Raje, the heir to the throne. I am, in any case, available at your call.'

It was easy to say goodbye to Jijabai but not to Saibai. She had been bedridden and received Shivaji with a weak smile. She said, 'Don't worry about me. Go without hesitation and defeat that Khan.'

'You think defeating him is so easy?'

'I don't know, but I do know that since the day he desecrated the Tulja Bhawani and Vithoba, his days have been numbered.'

Shivaji touched Maa saheb's feet before departing in the torrential rains. At the same time, Khan and his cantonment were slowly moving towards Wai. Jawali had taken on a look of a cantonment. Shivaji personally visited each village despite the relentless rain and the long barrelled cannons from Kalyan were placed in position at Pratapgad.

The monsoon soon ended and the valley looked green and captivating. At night, the sight of the burning maashals everywhere was captivating. Shivaji camped at Pratapgad and had decided that he would not leave Jawali, irrespective of Khan's movements. He was sure that Khan would camp at Wai and the town was a stone's throw from Pratapgad. And yet, the dense gorge and jungles made getting to Pratapgad almost impossible. It was an appropriate place to confront an enemy like Khan and Shivaji settled down to wait for Khan to make the first move.

At this time, Shivaji also received an invitation from Aurangzeb, asking him to come to Delhi for his coronation. This was an expected move since Aurangzeb knew how to play the role of a good host and would not show his true colours on such an occasion.

Soon thereafter, Shivaji received a summons from Rajgad that Saibai's health had deteriorated greatly, and with a heavy heart, he left Pratapgad.

On seeing Firangoji's worried face, as he dismounted, Shivaji asked, 'Firangoji, how is Rani saheb?'

'Not good ...'

It was evening and the mashaals burnt brightly. Normally, Shivaji's arrival would herald an atmosphere of happiness. There would be men scurrying around everywhere. But this evening was silent. There was not a smile on a single face. As he stepped into the palace, Shivaji noticed that the sardars, Peshwa and Amatya were standing with their heads down, their hands clasped behind their backs.

The moment Shivaji touched Jijabai's feet, she burst into tears.

'Maa saheb, have faith in the Lord.'

'Raje, we have tried everything possible from medicines to pujas. I have prayed to the Lord, promised him different rituals and penances and held kirtans. I am willing to give my life for her—if only she would get better!'

'Maa saheb, control yourself. If such wishes could be granted, then I too would give up my life for Sai. But the Lord moves in mysterious ways.'

He then entered Saibai's quarters. Saibai managed a weak smile and said, 'You came all the way to see me, did you? There is nothing to worry about really.'

Shivaji touched her forehead—her fever was raging. He said, 'I did not come because I received an urgent message, Sai. I was feeling restless and wanted to see you.'

'I am so happy to see you,' she said. Tears fell down her cheeks onto her pillow. Shivaji could not bear the sight of her tears and said, 'What is this, Sai? Why are you crying?'

Sai pulled herself up, trying to sit and said, 'I am happy to see you. Let my tears flow. I had never imagined that I would have the fortune of seeing your feet again.'

'Don't worry, I am not going anywhere till you get better. You just rest now.'

Shivaji went to his room. The curtains blew in the soft breeze and the chief physician gave him an update on Saibai's health. The situation did not look encouraging and Manohari came in when the physician said, 'We have tried everything possible, Maharaj. But the weakness does not seem to get better. In fact, she is becoming weaker day by day.'

Shivaji stood at the window, looking outside, and did not respond. Unable to be alone, he went to Jijabai's quarters.

Jijabai sat on her bed with a pandit, looking at an astrological almanac.

Shivaji asked, 'What are you studying, Maa saheb?'

'I am looking at Sai's horoscope.'

The priest said, 'There is nothing to worry about, Raje. She should recover from here. The next few days are risky but then it should all be well.'

That night, Shivaji was relieved to see Saibai sleep soundly. He woke up to the sound of the morning bugles and the sunlight was streaming in from the eastern window.

He met Jijabai after his bath and she too seemed relieved.

As he returned from the temple, a servant came in running and said, 'Hurry! Rani saheb is feeling restless.'

Shivaji ran towards Saibai's quarters. Seeing the physician there, he asked, 'Vaidyaraj?'

The physician could not utter a word. Instead, tears were flowing down his cheeks. Shivaji said, his voice choked with emotions, 'Don't cry. Just tell me the truth!'

'I feel helpless; there is nothing I am able to do to help.'

Shivaji touched Saibai's forehead, and it was burning hot. She opened her eyes and he held her hand—her palms felt cold.

Saibai asked, 'What did the physician say?'

'He said there is nothing to worry.'

Saibai gave a weak smile and said, 'He is right. Now there is nothing more to worry about!'

Shivaji could not hold back his tears now and exclaimed, 'Sai!'

'I know everything—we would not have been left alone otherwise. I don't want to say goodbye with tears in our eyes. I want to see you smile.'

'Sai, we have just begun the consolidation of our Swaraj. Do you not want to see my dreams being fulfilled? There is lot of work to do and I need you here.'

'I never wait to see the end, do I? Even when we played chess, you always complained that I would get up halfway through. I am leaving this world similarly. I could not feed my child my milk, I could not give him my love. I feel that I have not been able to do anything properly.'

'Sai ...' Shivaji's voice choked.

'I am worried Shambhu will be orphaned. Take care of him because he now has no one but you. You are both his mother and his father.'

Shivaji's tears continued unabashed. He said, 'Sai, I promise you, I will love him with all my life.' Raje covered his face with his hands and was unable to breathe. He heard Sai's soft voice ask, 'Won't you look at me once?'

Sai's voice sounded strange and Shivaji removed his hands to look at her. A smile played on her lips and the next moment, her neck went limp. The light had gone out of her eyes. He gently closed her eyes. She was in her eternal sleep now.

As he walked out of the room, as if in a trance, he mumbled, 'Maa saheb! Rani saheb has left us and gone on her solitary journey.'

Cries of despair rent the palace as the tragic news spread.

It was well past midnight. The thousand-wick lamp burnt brightly. Shivaji was restless, and sleep eluded him as he stood at the window, soothed by the cool breeze. Looking at the brightly lit sky he muttered, 'There may be a million stars in the sky, and yet the moon has its own place!'

The wicks fluttered in a sudden burst of cool breeze and Shivaiji felt a presence in the room. He could hear the soft tinkling of anklets and heard gentle footsteps on the carpet. A shiver went through his body as he turned around. There was no one in the room. The curtains swayed in the soft breeze. The wicks continued to flutter and dance in the breeze. There was no sound. It must have been his imagination.

He let out a deep sigh and continued to look at the stars in the sky. His right hand rested on the pillar and he brushed his hair with his left hand. He heard the same sound again—the unmistakable sound of anklets. The curtains shook once again and he heard footsteps on the carpet. It was undoubtedly Saibai's presence in the room. He did not turn back but said, his voice choking, 'Sai! Don't you believe me? I know you are worried for Shambhu and I know I could not make you a part of my life for very long. But I assure you that my promise will never be broken. Please believe me.'

The breeze stopped and the tinkling of the anklets faded away. There was pin-drop silence in the room and the curtains did not move anymore. Raje rested his forehead on the pillar and said, 'Sai, it is not Shambhu who is orphaned—it is I!'

BOOK
THREE

Dussehra went by quietly as everyone was still mourning Saibai. In the meanwhile, Afzal Khan had reached Wai and had camped on the banks of the Krishna River. Shivaji had to bury his personal sorrow and focus on the impending threat posed by Khan. All the forts had been instructed that if Khan reached their foothills, they should not resist and, instead, should join forces with Khan.

Sonopant Dabir asked, 'Raje, isn't such an instruction telling the people to surrender before they fight?'

'Yes, it is! I don't want our people to be killed by Khan's men. I don't want the common man to suffer. If they resist, Khan won't hesitate to kill them.'

Within a few weeks, Khan managed to take charge of a large part of the province, capturing the Supe region, Shirval and Sawad. The dangerous Saif Khan took over Tal Konkan but there was no resistance whatsoever anywhere. Afzal Khan had been quite sure that Shivaji would come out and fight. He had, after all, captured a large part of Shivaji's territory. But Shivaji was nowhere to be seen. This strange behaviour worried Khan.

Shivaji was aware of the atrocities being committed by Khan's troops despite the fact that there had been no resistance—it was a painful fact he had to live with. Mankoji Dahatonde was a loyal soldier who had come with Dadoji Konddev from Bengaluru, and was the first to take charge of the cavalry. Since Mankoji was becoming old, Shivaji had designated Netaji Palkar as the cavalry in-charge and Mankoji had taken on the role of an advisor.

Mankoji commented, 'Raje, I want us to teach this Khan a lesson. That's the only way he's going to come to his senses.'

Everyone was itching for some action and Mankoji's comments were echoed by many others. Shivaji listened patiently before saying, 'Mankoji, don't you think I want to trample Khan? But I would be foolish to meet him in the plains—we would certainly get routed. He is enticing me to come out and fight.'

'What do we do now?' Yesaji asked.

'Wait for him to enter Jawali.'

The evening assembly was in progress. Netaji Palkar, Atre, Mankoji, Moropant Pingle and other such capable men waited in attendance. Shivaji laid out his plan to confront Khan.

One of the sardars asked, 'What if we try for a compromise?'

'Compromise?' Shivaji smiled. 'Have you forgotten he has taken an oath to bring me to Bijapur, alive, dragging behind his horse? I would meet the same fate as Dada Maharaj. There is no question of any treaty now. We will either kill him or die ourselves!'

He continued, seeing Jijabai's concerned look, 'Maa saheb, I remember an episode from the Mahabharata when Krishna tells Arjun, "If you win, you will enjoy heaven here. If you lose, you will go to heaven." If I compromise, he will still destroy our land. It is better to fight now and if nothing else, we will die as warriors who fought for their motherland.'

They all agreed that the best course was to confront Khan in the dense jungles of Jawali.

Jijabai could not sleep that night. And as he took her blessings the next morning, Shivaji said, 'I had a dream just before dawn ... I had a vision of Bhawani appearing before me and saying, "May you be victorious! You are destined to kill Afzal Khan. My blessings are with you—go do your duty." When I woke up, the sun was rising on the eastern horizon.'

'That is good to hear! I am sure Bhawani will take care of you, Shivba. But I have decided that I too will accompany you.'

'Maa saheb!'

'Raje, I don't care about what happens henceforth. I don't want to lose sight of you now.'

'Maa saheb, you may not lose me but you may lose our Swaraj. I can take this risk because I have full faith in you.'

'Faith in me for what?' Jijabai asked, knowing exactly what he meant.

'After all, this is a battle. I am sure I will kill Khan, but in case I ...'

'Shivaji!' Jijabai screamed.

Shivaji continued, 'Maa saheb, this is no time to cry. I want you to listen carefully. In case I do not come back alive, I entrust the responsibility for Shambhu to you. I cannot be his mother and that's why I am asking you to stay back and take care of him.'

Maa saheb hugged Shivaji, who tried to force a smile through his tear-filled eyes.

She said, 'Shivba, remember he betrayed your Dada Maharaj! Come home victorious!'

'I will return soon, Maa saheb. I shall kill Afzal Khan and return for your blessings.'

The assembly of Firangoji, Sonopant and others were waiting. Shivaji looked at Firangoji and said, 'Sambhaji Raje and Maa saheb are now in your care. If I come back after killing Afzal Khan, then we continue as before. If I don't, I am asking you to serve under Sambhaji Raje and take care of him. I want you to carry forward the Maharashtra Rajya we have created. Take care—I will return soon!'

It was sundown by the time Shivaji reached Pratapgad. He looked around as he climbed up the steps. The fort was completely protected with cannons at strategic points. The Koyna gorge shone in the dying rays of the evening sun. Mahabaleshwar could be clearly seen on the other side.

Shivaji's quarters were at the highest point in the fort. The rooms were simple yet elegantly done. He was surprised at seeing Manohari in the room.

'Manohari, what are you doing here?'

'Maa saheb asked me to come. She said there won't be anyone to take care of your clothes otherwise.'

Shivaji smiled. 'Well, if it is Maa saheb's will, I am no one to object. Go ahead and get things arranged. I will return later.'

Shivaji was about to leave when Manohari stepped forward and opened her fist to show him a ring.

'Isn't that Sai's? What are you doing with it?'

'Rani saheb had asked me to give it to you. I did not find time and hence carried it here for you.'

Shivaji said, letting out a deep sigh, 'I had given this to Rani saheb as a token of my love. Wear it in her memory.'

He turned and left abruptly and Manohari kept staring at his back.

The fort bubbled with fresh energy and enthusiasm. Shivaji received a message saying that Kanhoji Jedhe was on his way. Kanhoji had kept his word and had brought along people like Shitole, Gaekwad, Dohar, Marne, Maral, Shirmalkar and other Deshmukhs. Kanhoji had also brought the love, affection and enthusiasm of the population with him. Shivaji's confidence improved dramatically seeing the support of these people. Shivaji's cavalry had increased to seven thousand and the foot soldiers to more than three thousand in number.

Kanhoji said, 'Raje, you seem prepared for a big fight. Khan, no doubt, will have a huge army.'

'Kanhoji, the Jawali region has an advantage in our favour. Here, one of our soldiers is equal to a hundred of the enemy's. We have the blessings of Mahabaleshwar too. This fight is going to decide whether we serve under our oppressors forever or we declare Swaraj once and for all!'

'But do you expect Khan to come here?'

'He will be forced to. His army includes people like Prataprao More, who is itching to reclaim Jawali. Khan has a lot of people who know this region well. Accounting for their knowledge and his arrogance, I know he will attack us. If he does not, we will find ways to make him come here.'

While Shivaji sat in Pratapgad deciding the next course of action, Khan too was frustrated, hungering for battle. He had captured most of Shivaji's territory but the Maratha rat had stayed put in Jawali. He received daily updates from his spies in Jawali and knew that the longer he waited, the stronger Shivaji would become. He decided to test Shivaji and sent his lawyer and messenger Krishnaji Bhaskar to meet Shivaji at Pratapgad.

The messenger of the mighty Afzal Khan was coming to Pratapgad on his own—without an invitation from Shivaji! It was indeed a test of nerves!

No one could believe that Khan had sent a messenger on his own. Krishnaji Bhaskar was a tall, slim and handsome man with penetrating grey eyes.

He wore a turban and a yellow, silk robe with a dhoti to match. Krishnaji observed the surroundings as he walked up to the fort. He could see that the security was tight. The cannons were placed strategically and the heaps of boulders and cannon balls arranged at select locations spoke of the Maratha preparedness for an attack. He could not hide his smile and commented, 'You seem ready for a major confrontation.'

'No, this is merely Raje's way of protecting every fort.'

Krishnaji Bhaskar had darshan at Kedareshwar and then entered the courtyard where arrangements for seating had been made. Accepting Krishnaji's salute, Shivaji said, 'It is my good fortune that Afzal Khan has remembered us.'

Krishnaji said, 'Raje, Khan has a lot of respect for you. Else, he would not have sent me.'

'Please convey our regards to Khan saheb. He is, after all, a father figure to me, just like my Maharaj saheb. I would consider it my privilege if I had the chance to meet him.'

Krishnaji Bhaskar produced a letter by Khan. The letter read, 'Adil Shah is disturbed by your impertinence. After the downfall of Adil Shah, he has given, in a treaty to the Mughals, the territory conquered by him. You have captured a lot of that mountainous terrain, much against our wishes, and taken control of the territory given to Chandrarao. You have also destroyed mosques while capturing Kalyan–Bhiwandi and taken the liberty of arresting the kaji and the mullah there. It is, thus, our command that you give back all the forts and territory you have captured with immediate effect. This includes Sinhagad, Lohgad, Purandar, Chakan, Neera and Bhima.'

'It appears that I have no other option now but to comply,' Shivaji commented.

'Raje, if you ask me, I would suggest that you make peace with Khan,' Krishnaji Bhaskar said.

'And if I decide not to?'

'Then his forces will descend upon you. You are aware of his might—he will ruin you.'

'I am aware. But he seems to be forgetting that I am Shahaji Raje's son. My brother has already been killed and I am sure Bijapur's Farzand would not tolerate the loss of another son.'

Krishnaji Bhaskar was taken aback. This was a new ploy and, changing tactics, he said, 'There is no need to take your problems to Bijapur. You may come to Wai and sort out your differences with Khan.'

'Khan looks at things only from his own perspective. It would not be difficult to find out whether we really destroyed the masjid at Kalyan or anywhere else. But he chooses to see things only the way he wants to.'

'I would suggest that you do not go into minute details but look at the larger picture.'

'I do not have anything against anyone, Krishnaji. I request you to stay here a few days while we think of a rational solution.'

'As you command,' Krishnaji Bhaskar said, bending low.

Krishnaji Bhaskar was soon accommodated in an independent haveli and Shivaji returned to his quarters. Everyone was curious to know what was on Raje's mind. The next day, he called his loyal team to a private conference. They discussed Khan's letter and most were of the opinion that Raje should meet Khan at Wai and negotiate a peaceful retreat.

Shivaji retorted, 'Do you think Khan is a simpleton? That he will merely accept my proposal? He has taken a public oath in the Bijapur durbar to kill me. Remember, it was he who killed Kasturi Ranga of Shira after inviting him to a friendly meeting. The same Khan murdered Khan Muhammad and also betrayed Dada Maharaj. If we have to meet him, we have to find a way to bring him here.'

'But do you think he will come?'

'If Jagdamba so decrees, he will.'

Shivaji went to meet Pantaji Gopinath in his room. Pantaji was a shrewd strategist and a close family member. He was fondly called as Pantaji Kaka. Shivaji said, 'Pantaji, Khan's messenger Krishnaji Bhaskar has now visited us. As per protocol, we too should send our emissary to Khan's camp. I have nominated you. Go with Krishnaji and meet Afzal in his camp. Your job is to convince Khan to meet us here in Jawali.'

Raje then called Krishnaji Bhaskar and told him, 'Krishnaji, I have prepared a reply to Khan's letter, but it would not be appropriate to send the letter with you. As per protocol, I am sending my emissary, Pantaji Gopinath, with the letter.'

'As you wish, Raje,' Krishnaji Bhaskar said, saluting.

Before he left, Shivaji met Pantaji and said, 'I am sure you will have a dialogue with Khan. Listen to him carefully and try to understand how his mind works. Don't argue and if possible, agree with whatever he says. I am sending a few men with you who can keep their eyes and ears open—find out Khan's motive and then come back. I am sure Bhawani Mata will protect you.'

The moment Khan got the news of Krishnaji Bhaskar's return, he called for him.

'Kaho Krishnaji! How was your meeting with Shivaji?'

'I handed your letter over to Shivaji and he seemed quite disturbed by it.'

Khan was happy as he had expected Shivaji to get nervous. 'So has he agreed to come here?'

'No, he is scared, I think. I told him that he should fear your wrath and that he would not be spared if you attack him.'

'How did he respond?'

'Shivaji said, "Tell Khan that Farzand Shahaji will not be happy to lose his second son."'

Khan's hookah slipped on hearing the response but he recovered immediately and said, laughing loudly, 'Our enemy seems to be a very smart and talented one!'

Krishnaji Bhaskar also told Khan that Shivaji's messenger had come back with him, leaving Khan unable to put his finger on Shivaji's plan of action.

The next day, Pantaji Gopinath presented himself to Khan. Pantaji requested for a private audience and as soon as they were alone, he said, 'Your letter was received by Raje and he has sent a reply.'

'Please read it out to me.'

Pantaji read, 'Your wish is my command. Only you can be as large-hearted and magnanimous enough as to pardon my transgressions and I am willing to return all the forts including Jawali. You have such a dominating personality that it makes it impossible for me to even look in your eyes. I am willing to meet you whenever you command me to and lay down my arms.'

Khan's happiness knew no bounds. He tried masking his satisfaction and said, 'When is Raje coming to meet me?'

'I beg your pardon, sir, but Raje is mortally scared to come and meet you here. As a token of his love and respect, he has sent you a few gifts. If you so command, may I ...'

'Please go ahead.'

Pantaji Gopinath clapped once and two men entered the room, carrying a tray. Pantaji uncovered the tray. A dagger lay on it, its handle studded with lovely gems and precious stones. Apart from the dagger, Khan also noticed a lovely pearl necklace.

Pantaji said, as he noticed Khan admiring the necklace, 'Forgive my impertinence, sir, but I know you employ many jewellers who can estimate the price of the dagger. The pearl necklace, however, is beyond compare.'

Khan touched the necklace. Each pearl was huge, the size of a large marble. He murmured, 'How did Shivaji manage to amass such wealth?'

'Huzoor, this is all because of your blessings—these items are just a drop in the ocean.'

'But why is he giving me such expensive gifts?'

'You are, after all, a friend of Farzand Shahaji Raje. You are a father figure to Raje and he would do anything for your blessings.'

Khan fondled his beard as he continued to look at the necklace.

Pantaji Gopinath continued, 'Raje is afraid to meet you here in Wai. If you only say the word, he will come running to see you in Jawali.'

Khan looked at Pantaji Gopinath and then looked at the pearl necklace. He said, 'Shivaji Raje is a haramzada. A Kaffir! Jawali is a dangerous place and I think he will betray us there.'

Pantaji Gopinath laughed which irked Khan.

'Why do you laugh?'

'I heard that you are fearless, sir. Come to Jawali with all your men and it will be Raje's pleasure to welcome them all. He doesn't stand a chance against your might. After all, an ant cannot fight an elephant. Raje would be honoured if you were willing to pardon him and employ him. He is willing to pay one crore hons for the appointment.'

'One crore hons!' Khan exclaimed.

'Raje dare not fight, but he can arrange for the sum you ask for.'

Khan had let Bajaji go for a mere sixty thousand. The sum of a crore hons was beyond his imagination. He drooled with greed and said, 'As a Brahmin, can you give me an assurance on Shivaji's behalf? I will certainly meet him then.'

Pantaji Gopinath swore an oath to assure Khan of Raje's good intentions. Khan was enchanted by the prospect of receiving such a huge sum and he requested Pantaji Gopinath to stay for a few days while he went over the proposal.

Pantaji Gopinath was given accommodation in the cantonment and was enjoying Khan's hospitality. Krishnaji Bhaskar introduced him to many sardars while Raje's men walked freely around the cantonment, absorbing each and every detail.

Khan called for a special meeting and discussed the issue of Shivaji's invitation to meet in Jawali. The unanimous opinion from the sardars was that it was dangerous to enter Jawali and that Shivaji was very likely to betray them. Khan asked Krishnaji Bhaskar for his opinion. 'Do you think Shivaji will leave Jawali to meet me?'

'Huzoor, my instinct is that whatever happens, he will not leave Jawali. He feels safe at Pratapgad.'

Khan touched his beard, thinking aloud, 'Shivaji is a haramzada. He would never agree to a direct confrontation. We shall go to Jawali. He cannot escape in any case.'

Once the others were dismissed, Khan asked Krishnaji Bhaskar, 'Krishnaji, do you really think Shivaji has so much wealth?'

'Huzoor, Shivaji is a born thief. He looted Jawali, and managed to rob the Kalyan treasury when he captured Kalyan–Bhiwandi. He appropriated the Mughal treasury when he took over Junnar. I had gone merely as your emissary but when I was leaving, he gifted me precious clothes, a pearl necklace, a gold bangle, a medal, an Arabian horse and five thousand coins.'

Khan was wide-eyed at the description.

'I am not exaggerating, Huzoor,' Krishnaji reiterated.

'Krishnaji, we will first capture his wealth and then Shivaji. Where can this fellow hide anyway?'

Khan laughed loudly and Krishnaji reluctantly joined in. The next day, Pantaji Gopinath was sent back to Pratapgad, as per protocol, with due respect.

Everyone was eagerly waiting for Pantaji to return. Shivaji asked, once he reached Pratapgad, 'Pant, what did Khan say?'

'Raje, Khan was mighty pleased with your gifts. He is willing to meet you in Jawali but he will not come alone. He will bring his entire army along.'

'We will be happy to welcome them. Pant, you must be tired. Go get some rest now.'

Pant bent low in mujra and left.

Shivaji stood at the ramparts of the fort, looking down at the Jawali gorge. Winter was setting in and the cool breeze ruffled his hair. He was entranced by the beauty of the valley and the dense forests and by the time he realized the time, it was dark. The guards had lit the mashaals and were at their positions guarding the fort. After dinner, he summoned Tanaji and Pantaji.

He said, as Pantaji entered, 'Pant, please sit down. I need to talk you at length.'

Pant did not sit and continued to stand after seeing Raje pacing the room. Shivaji suddenly stopped and turning towards Pantaji said, 'I wanted to speak to you privately about your experience with Khan. Tell me, what is your opinion?'

Pantaji described his entire journey from the start. He said, 'Raje, this Khan is a shrewd fellow. He is intelligent and has a sharp mind in his strong body. But ...'

'What?' Raje asked.

'You were right—the moment I showed him your gifts, I could see his greed.'

'Is Khan really interested in an alliance or ...'

'Raje, Khan is a treacherous man. He is only waiting for an opportunity to betray your trust. He wants to pose as a friend but his plan is to capture you and take you to Bijapur.'

'What do you think we should do?'

'Khan is greedy. We must take advantage of his greed and invite him to Jawali. We need to arrange a private meeting between the two of you. That will be your chance to kill him, destroy his camp and take back your Swaraj.'

Shivaji agreed with this and gifted Pantaji five thousand coins. He said, getting up, 'Pant, go back to Khan and tell him that Shivaji is scared and wants to meet him in Jawali. Tell him I would be most happy to receive his patronage and am ready to work under the Badshah as a mere employee if Khan promises to take care of me.'

Pantaji Gopinath left for Khan's camp the very next day. Shivaji had no doubt that Khan would come to Jawali. Each sardar was given charge of a designated area in the Jawali gorge and a map of Jawali was spread out in the fort. Raje pointed out the strategic places for each sardar and they prepared themselves for the impending attack. Shivaji also took a tour of the Koyna valley and the village of Par, a few miles south of Pratapgad, was chosen as the location for the cantonment. The entire area was cleaned and made ready.

In the meanwhile, Pantaji Gopinath engaged Khan. Pantaji said, 'Raje is requesting you to come to Jawali. He is willing to leave with you after the meeting.'

Khan agreed and while departing, Gopinath made another request, 'I am sure that Raje will not leave anything wanting but he desires to gift you something very precious. If you bring your jewellers and traders with you, it would be most convenient for Raje to buy something valuable and honour you and your sardars there.'

'Beshak! Beshak! The jewellers shall surely accompany me.'

Khan sent one of his close aides along with Pantaji to oversee the preparations for the meeting. In order to impress and convince Khan of his intentions, Shivaji had not spared any effort. The grounds near Par were prepared for the cantonment to be set up as it was the only flat and clear space in the entire Koyna jungle. Shivaji's spies were positioned at strategic places, their duties assigned to them.

Shivaji selected a place at the base of the fort for the meeting. It was a place which could be monitored and seen clearly from the fort.

Khan's men accompanying Pantaji Gopinath surveyed the village of Par and were convinced that they would be able to capture the fort easily. Shivaji ensured that the men were compensated well and they all went back satisfied. Khan asked his army to prepare for the move. He had a cavalry of ten thousand men and formidable artillery. It was a difficult task for such an army to negotiate the narrow and steep slopes leading to Jawali.

The caravan finally entered the Koyna valley and Khan was quite pleased seeing the place made ready for their camp. The soldiers got busy setting up the cantonment. The traders accompanying Khan set up their shops near the cantonment as they waited to strike a good deal. Everyone was convinced that Shivaji would buy precious goods in huge quantities to please Khan and his sardars.

Khan's camp could be clearly seen from the fort. The moment Khan settled into the camp, Shivaji sent word to his troops to move closer. Some were stationed at Dhawleghat and some others near Chandragad, while Netaji Palkar guarded the route to Mahabaleshwar. There were Bandals on patrol in Jawali and the Bachigholighat was being guarded by Silamkar.

Afzal Khan was completely unaware that he had been surrounded. He dreamt of capturing Shivaji under the pretext of a friendly meeting. And even if Shivaji managed to escape, Khan was confident that his men would capture the fort. He had faith in his huge artillery. A smile spread across his face at the thought that Shivaji had no place to hide now!

Messengers from both camps finalized the details and conditions for the meeting. Both parties would be allowed to carry arms. They would be allowed two bodyguards each into the camp. Khan would arrive first and wait for Shivaji. They were allowed to bring ten soldiers with them who would be stationed at a distance of a hundred yards, the distance of an arrow's flight. They both would meet alone inside the tent. Both the parties agreed to the conditions and the meeting was fixed for two days after Khan's arrival.

Shivaji inspected the tent a day before the meeting. It was a crucial meeting because it would decide whether he would emerge victorious or dead. He looked at everything carefully and returned to the fort. He sent a word to Jijabai with a trusted soldier as he was aware everyone was anxious and nervously waiting for the next day.

Soon, it was nightfall. The crescent moon on its sixth day shone brightly in the sky. Hundreds of lamps burnt in Khan's camp. One of Raje's spies reached the fort in a hurry and waited for an audience with Shivaji.

Bahirji, the spy, recounted, 'Khan is a huge fellow. He is more than six feet tall and likely as wide. He bends an iron rod with complete ease and then straightens it out as well—that is the measure of his strength. I have seen him lifting a cannon with his own hands! He may not have much intelligence but plenty of brawn.'

'Who has been nominated as his personal bodyguard?'

'He does not trust anyone other than Syed Banda. We are told that he will accompany Khan.'

'Who is this Syed Banda?'

'He is tall or big as Khan and is extremely strong. He is known to use the sword skilfully.'

'Who is the other bodyguard?'

'Khan feels he does not need anyone else—he is sure of his victory.'

'Your information has been immensely valuable. If you find out anything else, let me know immediately.'

Bahirji bowed and left.

Shivaji was lost in thought for a moment and then he smiled and went into the courtyard. Mankoji Dahatonde, Ranjekar, Subhanji Ingle, Yesaji Kank, Tanaji Malsure and Sambhaji Kavji were all waiting.

'Mankoji, what news do you have?'

Tanaji said, 'We are tired of waiting. Please command us.'

'I deliberately asked you to stay back. You and your people have to take your positions before sunrise without being seen. Hiroji, Tanaji, Yesaji—I want your men to be in the bushes next to the shamiana. My attention is not on Khan alone because we cannot meet our goal merely by killing Khan. We need to capture his huge wealth, his tents, the hundred-odd cannons, horses, elephants, camels—the entire lot. We need all those things to make our dream come true. Don't leave anything behind.'

All the sardars were completely focused on what Shivaji was saying.

Shivaji asked, 'I am allowed to take two bodyguards with me. Whom shall I take?'

Everyone looked at Raje with expectant eyes.

'I understand that each one of you is eager to accompany me, but I have selected my team.'

'Who are they?' Mankoji asked eagerly.

'Sambhaji Kavji—he is the only one who can match Khan's strength.'

Sambhaji's chest swelled with pride and Raje looked at him and said, 'Sambhaji, please don't get carried away. We need both intelligence and strength—they are equally important.'

Raje's eyes scanned the group and he asked, 'I don't see Jiva here?'

Jiva Mahala was immediately summoned and Shivaji asked, 'Jiva, will you come with me tomorrow?'

Jiva was as surprised as the rest of the group and he said happily, 'I would consider it my good fortune, Raje!'

'Good! Jiva, I shall brief you in the morning.'

The men left soon after and by the time Manohari had come to put out the lamps, Shivaji was fast asleep.

Shivaji woke up to find the room bathed in a mild glow. Two lamps flickered in one corner of the room and the cool breeze of the morning wafted across the room. He stepped out of his room after his morning prayers. The fort was still in darkness and the eastern sky had not yet lit up. He summoned ten specific men and gave them detailed instructions. They all looked at Raje with respect, knowing full well the kind of risk he was going to undertake. They saluted and disappeared in the darkness.

The Jawali gorge woke up to the morning slowly. The chirping of the birds filled the valley and the eastern sky turned light. At the break of dawn, Shivaji, along with his men, went for darshan at Kedareshwar. He came back after the puja with a bright tilak on his forehead. His long hair covered his neck and earrings shone in his ears. The sound of trumpeting elephants could be heard in the distance. The meandering Koyna River was still covered in a faint mist and wisps of clouds covered the peaks, enhancing their beauty. Mahabaleshwar shone in the rays of the morning sun and Raje bent low in namaskar to the Lord at Mahabaleshwar and then turned back to his palace.

Raje inspected the arrangements at the fort personally. As instructed, each cannon was supplied with adequate ammunition. The men were waiting to make their move, their faces glowing with excitement. They knew the risk they all were taking.

Shivaji said, 'I have no doubt that I shall return victorious. But in case I don't return, I don't want you to lose hope. I am telling you what I have told the others—our army is spread across the entire jungle right from the base of Pratapgad to Supe. I want you to wipe out Khan and his entire army and capture Rajgad after defeating him. Mankoji, I need you to take charge if I do not return. Ensure Sambhaji Raje is on the throne and continue to work towards my dream.'

All the soldiers and the sardars became emotional after hearing this and Yesaji said, wiping his eyes, 'Raje, we derive all our strength from you.'

'Yesaji, you have to stop thinking like this. You must be loyal to the kingdom. The question is not whether Shivaji survives or not. If the kingdom survives, then ten such Shivajis can be created.'

It was nearly noon when Shivaji dispatched Pantaji Gopinath to escort Khan to the meeting. He said, 'Pantaji, ensure that Khan follows all the rules that have been agreed to for the meeting. And don't leave him out of your sight till I meet him.'

'Raje, don't worry. I will ensure that he is alone. He is a cunning rascal and will not hesitate to betray his promises. This meeting is the only chance you will have and so do what you can, that is my only advice. I will take your leave now and see you when I return with Khan. Take care.'

Shivaji hugged Pantaji tightly before he left.

Shivaji left for his quarters along with Jiva Mahala and Sambhaji Kavji.

'Jiva, I have a small job for you. Do you have your scissors with you?'

'Yes.'

'Bring them.'

Jiva got the scissors and Raje sat on a stool. He casually said, 'Jiva, trim my beard. Make it so small that it cannot be pulled by hand.'

Jiva trimmed Raje's beard and Raje said, caressing his beard, 'Now listen to me carefully. Sambhaji, Jiva—both of you will be standing at the entrance of the shamiana. Keep an eye on Syed Banda. Don't bother about me. Is that understood?'

'Yes.'

'And Sambhaji, you keep an eye on Khan. Follow me like a shadow and never allow me out of your sight.'

'Yes.'

After a light meal, Shivaji went into his room to get dressed and his clothes were laid out for him on the bed. He first put on a brocaded armour on top of which he put on his shirt. He wore his head gear which he covered with his turban. He wrapped a shawl around him and tucked a scorpion-shaped dagger into his right palm. He removed his earrings and, handing over the Bhawani sword to Jiva, said, 'If there is need, don't hesitate to use it.'

He then picked up the weapon specifically made for the meeting; it was a tight-fitting glove with four sharp and pointed nails. It was called 'wagh nakh' or the tiger claws and was capable of inflicting as much damage on the human body as a tiger could. The glove had a golden border with diamonds shining on it. On curling the fist, all one could see were the lovely rings on the fingers. The sharp claws would snugly fit into the palm.

The trumpets were sounded. Khan began to move towards the rendezvous.

Shivaji was about to step out of the room when Manohari came in and, without saying a word, put her head at his feet. Shivaji said, patting her head gently, 'Silly girl! I will return. I promise.'

Shivaji left the palace acknowledging the mujras he encountered at each step. He reached Kedareshwar as the sun rose high in the sky. He prayed to the Lord and then stepped out to have a look at the cantonment below. Khan had left the cantonment and was on his way to the meeting.

Khan was in a happy mood and the cantonment was rejoicing his victory in advance. They were enjoying a feast. Khan stepped into a royal palanquin, while a contingent of fifteen hundred soldiers waiting in attendance moved ahead. Seeing the horsemen move, Pantaji ran forward to make a request of Khan.

'Sir, we need to abide by the terms of the meeting. The moment Raje sees your fifteen hundred cavalry, he may run back into the fort. It would then be impossible for the meeting to take place.'

Khan laughed. He knew he was taking a risk but responded immediately by saying, 'You are absolutely right.'

He ordered Krishnaji Bhaskar to ask the soldiers to stop and his palanquin moved forward alone towards the meeting place. Khan reached the meeting point and stepped out of the palanquin as it was lowered in front of the shamiana.

Khan observed the shamiana as he stood outside with his hands on his hips. The golden crescent-shaped dome shone brightly in the hot sun, and slender, elaborately decorated pillars supported the shamiana. The ropes were of fine but strong silk while rich and heavy curtains swayed in the wind. Khan looked at the beautiful shamiana in wonder. His feet sunk into the soft and thick carpet on the ground. The curtains had pearls dangling on the border and was embroidered all over. The seats were decorated with dark green silk and the chandeliers reflected the light inside the tent. A faint smell of camphor wafted inside as it burned in a brass container. A Muradabadi spittoon and a Burhanpuri hookah complemented the decor.

Pantaji Gopinath requested Khan to take his seat. Khan came to his senses on hearing his words and said, 'What does Shivaji think of himself? Is he trying to outdo the Badshah? Look at the pearls and the decor!'

Pantaji replied, 'I had told Shivaji Raje that it is not his property. It belongs to the Badshah and shall be returned.'

Khan laughed out loud and said, taking his seat, 'Bring your Raje here as soon as possible.'

Pantaji sent an urgent message to the fort. Shivaji looked at Mankoji for a brief moment. Now old and weak with age, Mankoji had taken care of Shivaji since he was six years old and had loved him as a father would. His body shivered at the sight of Raje and tears welled up in his eyes.

Shivaji touched his feet and said, 'Mankoji, you are like my Maharaj saheb. Please give me your blessings.'

'Shivba!' Mankoji exclaimed, hugging him. 'Raje, may you be victorious today!'

'Don't worry; Bhawani will take care of me. If something happens today, take care of the kingdom.'

Shivaji glanced at the cannon which would signal the attack. He took the tiger claws from Jiva and touched the glove to his forehead before slipping it on to his left hand. He curled his fist tightly and walked down to the horse waiting at the door. He asked Jiva and Sambhaji to get their horses to the shamiana and decided to walk down the steps with his bodyguards and ten chosen men.

The shamiana was visible now and Khan's ten men stood in one corner as per the rules— an arrow's flight away. Shivaji's ten men stood at the appropriate distance and took their positions. Shivaji then moved towards the shamiana with Jiva and Sambhaji. Krishnaji Bhaskar stepped forward and saluted Raje. Shivaji reached the door and peeped through the curtains and stepped back immediately.

Pantaji Gopinath quickly came to him when Shivaji asked, 'Pant, who is inside with Khan?'

'Banda Syed.'

'Ask him to step outside and take his place as per the rules.'

Khan was both eager and impatient by then. He had a twisted smile on his face when he heard Gopinath's request and ordered Banda Syed to stand outside. Shivaji asked Jiva and Sambhaji to wait at the door and stepped inside with Krishnaji.

Shivaji observed Khan minutely the moment he stepped in. Khan wore a lovely turban with diamonds encrusted in it. He had a faint smile on his lips as he stared at Shivaji. He stood up to his full height, accentuating the difference between the two men. Shivaji looked puny in front of the giant.

Pantaji Gopinath made the introductions. 'Vizarmatab Huzoor Afzal Khan Madamshahi!'

Krishnaji Bhaskar said, 'Maharaj Shivaji Raje Bhosale.'

Khan smiled and said, pointing a finger, 'Is this who everyone calls Shivaji?'

Both the messengers nodded, not knowing how to react.

Shivaji looked at Khan without a hint of fear in his eyes and retorted, 'Is this the person whom everyone calls Khan?'

The messengers nodded involuntarily and without further ado, they stepped out of the shamiana.

There were just two of them in the shamiana now. Khan spread out his huge arms and welcoming him said, 'Aao, Raje.'

Raje walked towards Khan with slow and deliberate steps. He remembered Jagdamba once as Afzal Khan embraced him. Shivaji placed his head on the right side of Khan's chest as Khan continued to hug him. Khan, quickly mustering all his strength and laughing rudely, pressed Shivaji's head to the left of his chest while he tried to crush it into his armpit. He had a victorious smile on his lips. At that moment the smile vanished and his face turned harsh with anger, as he pulled out his dagger to stab Raje in the back.

The armour below Shivaji's kurta prevented the dagger from piercing him and it slipped down. At the same time, Shivaji opened his 'tiger claws' and plunged it deep into Khan's right side and pulled it sideways with all his strength. Khan stepped back in pain, allowing Shivaji to slip out of his embrace. He jumped to one side but Khan managed to hit him on the side of his head. The blow was so strong that it broke open the head gear armour Shivaji was wearing and left a wound on Shivaji's head.

Startled by the narrow escape, Shivaji took a moment to recover when Khan shouted, 'Treachery ... treachery!'

Sambhaji Kavji and Jiva, standing at attention at the door, leapt into the tent immediately to find Raje standing on one side, stunned by the attack. Banda Syed entered at the same time from the other door, adjusting his sword. Jiva did not waste a moment and took his position crouching near Shivaji's legs. Banda Syed was distracted by Jiva's movements and Jiva took this opportunity to severe Syed's hand with one stroke of his sword. His scream echoed in the tent and before Syed realized what was happening, the next blow from Jiva was fatal.

Sambhaji was watching Khan closely as he stumbled out of the tent, bleeding from the stomach. He stumbled and managed to reach his palanquin but, before the bearers could lift the palanquin, Sambhaji's sword had pierced Khan's chest.

The soldiers hiding in the bushes came out instantly and a fierce battle ensued. Shivaji, in the meanwhile, stepped out of the tent. Jiva handed over the Bhawani sword to Shivaji and the other horsemen were ready and mounted.

Krishnaji Bhaskar ran towards Shivaji shouting, 'Raje, you have betrayed us!'

Shivaji, thwarting Krishnaji's attack, shouted, 'Pantaji, please go away.'

Krishnaji Bhaskar could not control his anger and attacked again. Shivaji had no choice—his blow was fatal as Krishnaji fell to the ground.

Shivaji saw that Jiva had mounted his horse but Sambhaji Kavji was nowhere to be seen. At that moment, Sambhaji Kavji emerged, holding Khan's severed head in his hand. The moment Sambhaji had mounted, Shivaji spurred his horse and the three horses galloped towards the fort.

Everyone in the fort was watching the action below with bated breath. Shivaji dismounted at the first gate and ran up the steps. The cannons were waiting for his signal and everyone was watching him wide-eyed. His white kurta was torn at the back and was blowing in the wind. The front was drenched in blood and his hair was dishevelled.

He shouted, 'What are you staring at? Fire the cannons!'

The door of the fort closed in an instant as the cannons were fired. Shivaji could hear the cries of 'Har Har Mahadev!' echo in the gorge below. Mankoji stood in the courtyard shivering like a dry leaf in the wind. He had been tormented with wild and ill omens and he had seen Shivaji climb the stairs, his chest drenched with blood.

Shivaji said, allaying his fears, 'Mankoji, nothing has happened to me. We have won. Khan has been killed.'

Manohari rushed out hearing the cannons and then glancing at Raje's head, covered her mouth and turned away.

As a sob escaped Manohari's mouth, Shivaji said, 'Manu, this is not my blood. It is the blood of the enemy—I am absolutely fine.'

Manohari turned around hearing these words, joy filling her heart and her eyes filling with tears.

Shivaji returned to the fort after darshan at Kedareshwar. The cannons at the other forts were active and one could hear their fire. The news of Khan's death had spread all over Jawali.

Mankoji observed the chaos which had erupted in the cantonment below. Khan's men had not yet eaten and the sardars were contemplating a little siesta in the afternoon when they heard the loud noise of the cannons. They assumed it to be a welcome signal for the meeting. They were relaxing, going about their chores when shouts of 'Har Har Mahadev!' filled the air in the jungles around.

Only a few moments ago, the jungles were quiet and serene with the occasional chirping of the birds. Now they were buzzing with the brave Maratha soldiers pouring out of every corner. It was chaos everywhere. Bajirao and Sarjerao had taken charge of the attack, eliminating nearly fifteen hundred soldiers stationed near the meeting camp. Jedhe and Bandal took care of the army near the Parghat with Moropant's support.

The Bijapur cantonment was being systematically massacred and Afzal Khan's son Fazal Khan managed to escape but his two other sons were captured. The cantonment, which was enjoying the luxuries of life only a few hours ago, was now littered with dead bodies and shouts of agony and despair. By late afternoon, the rampage was over. A Maratha horseman galloped towards the fort to reach the news as soon as possible.

Having changed his clothes, Shivaji was at the ramparts observing the massacre below when he saw a horseman gallop towards him. He asked, before the man dismounted, 'What news do you bring?'

The messenger bent in mujra, his face beaming with joy, and said, 'The enemy has been routed, Maharaj. You have won!'

Filled with joy, Shivaji turned. The fort was overflowing with revelry. On the other side, the Maratha soldiers were busy attacking and taking charge of Wai, Supe, Shirval and Saswad.

That evening Khan's decapitated head lay in the courtyard. Everyone had assembled around. Shivaji instructed Sambhaji Kavji, 'Sambhaji, I asked you to use your brains more than your brawn. Look at Jiva! He did what I told him. I was a little shaken with Khan's blow but Jiva did not bother to look at me. He kept his eyes on Syed Banda. Had Jiva gotten distracted even for a moment, you would not have found me alive despite our victory. But you ran after Khan, leaving me alone. You beheaded him despite no such orders from me. Sambhaji, in such times, each moment is important. Khan wasn't going to run away anywhere, was he?'

Pantaji Gopinath came in and said, 'Raje, we have captured a few of their men. Would you like to meet them?'

Afzal Khan's two sons were scared for their lives, and the captured sardars were also sure that their fate was death.

Shivaji patted Yesaji's back and said, 'Yesaji, the battle is over and so is our enmity. Release all the prisoners and send them off with the respect that is due to them.'

The mashaals were burning brightly when Raje reached the base of the fort. He inspected the injured troops and the dead were cremated with honours. Shivaji let out a deep sigh at the loss of his men and then returned to the fort.

Khan's dead body was kept for inspection. Shivaji said, 'This mlechcha, this barbarian, despoiled our family deity. Send his head to Maa saheb and then bury his head there in the royal courtyard. In the place where he fell, give him a burial fit for a commander of the Bijapur kingdom.'

There was no time to rest now. The Mavals in the region would stream in to offer their congratulations. The gates, normally closed after sunset, were thrown open in welcome and the fort was filled with visitors and devotees. The sky was lit with the seventh day of the moon while rows of mashaals could be seen right from the village at Par to the base of the fort. It was as if the Jawali gorge were celebrating a festival of lights, and soon, news of the capture of Wai reached the fort.

Jiva Mahala was, in the meanwhile, on his way to show Jijabai Khan's head.

At Rajgad, time seemed to crawl and the hours seemed interminably long. Despite the usual hustle and bustle, there was a strange silence everywhere. A puja was taking place at each temple in the fort, and Firangoji sat on the ramparts, his eyes scanning the eastern horizon. Everyone waited for news from Pratapgad.

The silence outside permeated into the palace. Jijabai was in the temple, not having touched a drop of water since early that morning. She sat there, looking at the idol of Bhawani Mata, while tall lamps burned on both sides. There was a pearl necklace on the right side of the idol and on the left side lay a tray on which a beautiful dagger shone in its emerald-encrusted beauty.

Jijabai's attention was focused on the Goddess. Her lips quivered and tears fell down her cheeks like the prajakta flowers in bloom. She recalled each moment of the thirty years of Shivaji's life. How many dreams she had dreamt with the young lad; how many plans she had made with him! News from Pratapgad could arrive any moment and she had no way of knowing what it would be. Jijabai continued her puja, asking, pleading and cajoling Bhawani Mata but the Goddess was silent. She continued to smile benevolently at Jijabai.

It was past noon, the sun was inching towards the western horizon but there was no news yet. What was taking so long? What was happening?

A maid came running in. 'Maa saheb, Maa saheb!'

A shiver ran through Jijabai's body and her heart skipped a beat but all she could do was continue staring at the idol.

'Maa saheb! It is good news! Raje has reached the fort. The cannons have been sounded!'

A huge shout of joy went up outside and Jijabai bent to touch her forehead on the temple floor. She got up and said, 'Come here.'

The maid stepped forward and Jijabai said, 'Spread your sari.'

The maid spread her pallu in the traditional way of receiving gifts and Jijabai lifted the tray filled with gold coins and poured them into the woman's pallu. She picked up the dagger and touching it to her forehead once, she put it at the goddess' feet. The joy at Rajgad knew no bounds. Everyone hugged baby Sambhaji and he was smothered with kisses.

It was dawn at Rajgad when Firangoji announced the arrival of Jiva Mahala.

Saluting, Jiva said, 'Maa saheb, Raje is fine and will be coming here shortly. We utterly routed Khan. He has sent you this and requested that it may find its place in a corner of the garden in the fort.'

And so saying, he uncovered the tray. Everyone gasped and Jijabai continued to look on, without blinking, at the decapitated head of Afzal Khan.

It was this Khan who'd had the temerity to handcuff the elder Maharaj. It was this Khan who'd killed her beloved Sambhaji. It was this Khan who had marched here to capture Shivaji. It was he who was responsible for her worries for the past few months. It was he who had despoiled the Bhawani temple at Tuljapur.

However, Jijabai swallowed her anger and said, 'Firangoji, let bygones be bygones. As per Raje's command, please ensure that we give him a burial befitting a commander of Afzal Khan's stature. He may have been our enemy but he was a bold enemy. He had gotten carried away by the arrogance of his power and blindness of his faith. Now that he is dead, our enmity is over.'

Khan's head was buried with due respect and everyone waited for Raje's arrival. The first gate of the fort was decorated with a traditional garland of mango leaves. Each door, thereafter, wore a similar garland. The traditional gudi, usually used to celebrate the New Year, was put up to welcome Raje.

It was mid-afternoon when the news of Raje's arrival reached the fort. He dismounted at the first gate where he was welcomed with an affectionate hug by Firangoji. Shivaji washed his feet and began climbing the steps with his fifteen-hundred-odd soldiers. Stopping briefly for darshan at the temple, he entered the palace. The ladies of the royal household stood waiting with lamps in traditional trays to welcome him, but Shivaji wanted to meet Jijabai first.

Tears welled up in her eyes while her face shone with pride. She hugged him and the tears would not stop.

Shivaji said, 'Maa saheb, I am here now. Thanks to your blessings and Bhawani's protection, I have come back unscathed. This is not the time to shed tears!'

Jijabai wiped her tears and said, 'One doesn't cry only when they are unhappy, Raje. These are tears of joy!'

'I am blessed to see them then!'

Shivaji held a special durbar the next day. The wounded were given special allowances and the victorious were duly honoured. Some were given special tasks and positions in Shivaji's government. The campaign against Khan had yielded rich dividends. Shivaji had captured seventy-five elephants, four thousand horses, twelve hundred camels, a few hundred cannons, expensive clothes, jewellery and gems. Khan had lost three thousand men while only a few hundred of Raje's troops had died in the battle. The entire province had been freed from Khan's clutches in a single day.

Later, Jijabai said, 'Raje, I don't remember the number of promises I must have made to the Lord for your safety. I shall try and fulfil them to whatever extent I can remember!'

Shivaji smiled. 'Maa saheb, it would be my pleasure to help you fulfil all of them. However, this is an opportune moment for me while the Bijapur durbar is reeling from the news of Afzal's death. I want to take advantage of the situation—I will leave on a campaign tomorrow to capture the other forts controlled by Bijapur. This is the only chance I have.'

He paused for a moment as a bold thought crossed his mind. 'Maa saheb, this victory is not our greatest yet. It is but a step towards our ultimate goal. The real battle has not yet begun—that would be when we defeat Aurangzeb.'

The next morning, Raje left for his campaign. His target: the majestic Panhala Fort!

After leaving Raigad, Shivaji reached Wai. The forces that had fought Khan's troops had been asked to assemble at Wai. The victorious commander, Netaji Palkar, presented himself. Shivaji honoured him and said, 'Kaka, your valour has been a matter of great pride for me. I don't mind that Fazal Khan ran away but I was disappointed that the treacherous Khandoji managed to escape.'

'Where will he hide, Raje? He must come back one day. However, I need to speak to you about another matter.'

'What is it?'

'The captured sardars—Jadhavrao, Pandhare, Khagte and Siddi Hilal—have all surrendered and they would like to meet you.'

When the sardars were brought in, Shivaji said, 'I have pardoned all of you even though you were enamoured by using the enemy's strength against your own people. But my enmity was with Khan—I have nothing against you. You are free to go wherever you wish to.'

The sardars could not believe their ears. Jadhav stepped forward, 'Raje, we had no choice but to work under the Badshah. But we are keen to be a part of the Swaraj now. We would feel obliged if we get a chance to work under you ...'

'The Swaraj needs all the help it can get. I am pleased that you are offering me your services.'

Jadhav, Pandhare and Khagte stepped forward at once but Siddi Hilal hesitated and stood in a corner, unsure.

Shivaji went to him and said, 'Hilal, I am aware of your strength and capabilities. I have nothing against any religion and I treat Hindus and Muslims without any discrimination. I would be pleased if you would join us.'

Hilal was overwhelmed with emotion and laid his sword at Raje's feet. Raje picked it up and sheathed it at Hilal's waist.

He addressed the group and said, 'I am going ahead with my campaign. Continue to hold your positions and when I return, I shall allocate appropriate responsibilities to each one of you.'

He said, addressing Moropant, 'Pant, ensure that the privileges given to people in Pune, Indapur, Chakan, Supe and Baramati during Afzal Khan's time continue as before. Once I return from inspecting the territory, I will give you new orders.'

Turning towards Netaji, he said, 'Kaka, whatever damage Khan has done to our land must be compensated by conquering Adil Shah's territory. We shall start at Chandan–Vandan and stop when we reach Panhala.'

Netaji was overjoyed at hearing the plan and gave orders for the army to march. The town of Wai reverberated with the sound of the trumpets as the huge army marched out.

After taking charge of the Chandan–Vandan forts, Shivaji's forces occupied the Wai region. The ryots had not yet recovered from the news of Afzal Khan's defeat. The words 'Shivaji is coming!' were enough to terrorize people in Adil Shah's territories and would bend their knees before him.

The fort at Panhala was nearly six kilometres from Kolhapur. Shivaji's dream was now within his grasp. His troops marched towards Panhala and surrounded the fort. The kiledar, with just a small platoon to guard his fort, sealed the doors and started attacking the Maratha troops. Shivaji's army returned the attack with vigour and started picking off soldiers guarding the ramparts with their rifles. Within two days, the Marathas had taken over the fort.

It was nearly dawn when a rider approached the camp to inform Shivaji, who had been pacing his tent waiting for the news, about the victory.

Yesaji said, 'Raje, please rest a while, I will go and inspect the fort. You have not slept the whole night.'

'Yesaji, this news is balm to my tired soul and I am eager to see the fort. Come, let us go.'

Shivaji mounted his horse and the cool morning breeze soothed his skin. The morning mist was everywhere and the mashaals flickered in the cold wind. After an inspection of the fort, Raje stood at the eastern ramparts, looking at the landscape below. It had been his dream to look at the Malvan valley standing atop the fort, while the saffron Maratha flags fluttered in the wind. At that moment, the sun broke through the veil of the mist, lighting up the valley below. Raje put his palms together to pray to the sun god.

The fort was huge and well maintained with four large gates. The store was adequate enough to contain six thousand tons of grain. A fresh water spring gurgled nearby, providing a perennial water supply. The buildings inside the fort were both aesthetic and architecturally sound. Bijapur's most prized fort had been added to the list of growing acquisitions of the Swaraj!

The entire durbar at Bijapur was waiting for Afzal Khan to make good on his claim of 'capturing that Maratha rat' and bringing him back to Bijapur when they received the news of Afzal's defeat and death. The durbar woke up from its dreams of victory and the Badshah left the court hurriedly and Badi Begum was taken ill. To add to their anxieties, news reached them that Shivaji's men were collecting revenue from their territories. The final blow was the news of Panhala Fort being captured.

Shivaji had acted swiftly, capturing Panhala within eighteen days of defeating Afzal Khan. The Adil Shahi court was clearly worried and tried to figure out how to protect themselves from the increasing Maratha ambition.

After sending a dispatch of horsemen to Aurangzeb the Mughal Emperor in Delhi, appealing to his succour, Adil Shah decided to attack Shivaji. Afzal Khan's son Fazal Khan was waiting for an opportunity to take revenge, and the second attack was planned under the leadership of Fazal Khan and Rustam Zaman. Adil Shah's sardars—Sadat Khan, Fateh Khan, Santaji Ghorpade and Sarjerao Ghatje—also joined the campaign.

The moment Raje heard of the impending attack, he moved his troops from the Pune region. The sardars, along with new ones like Siddi Hilal, waited patiently. When Fazal's troops reached Kolhapur, the Maratha troops attacked first. Fazal lost his nerve seeing the huge Maratha force approaching them in swirling clouds of dust and before the Bijapur army realized what was happening, the Maratha forces descended on the Muslim troops, and the shouts of 'Har Har Mahadev!' drowned the meek 'Deen Deen!' of the Muslim soldiers. Fazal's troops ran for their lives and the Maratha troops returned to Kolhapur after chasing them a short distance. Shivaji managed to capture twelve elephants and two thousand horses.

Shivaji was sure that Adil Shah would not have the courage to attack again and began to take the Konkan, and the troops marched towards the

Rajapur Port under the leadership of Daroji. Rajapur was controlled by Rustam Zaman, and Shivaji's objective was to capture the three ships that belonged to Afzal and not touch the fort town itself. However, British soldiers tried to retain possession of one of the ships. Daroji was enraged on hearing this and ordered the capture of the British official Gifford and his agent.

Shivaji was camping at Miraj when British representatives came to negotiate for the captured British soldiers, and Gangadharpant brought the representative to Raje. Shivaji had recognized that the British were cunning but he was also aware that they were friends with Rustam Zaman. Shivaji released Gifford and the middlemen for the written agreement that they would not support the Siddi Nawab of Janjira or anyone who was against Shivaji's expansion and rule.

Adil Shah, in the meanwhile, was growing more despondent with each passing day. He had seen Shivaji loot many towns, capture multiple forts, defeat Fazal and continue to grow more powerful. The news that Shivaji was planning to attack Bijapur itself, dethrone Adil Shah and nominate someone else was the proverbial last straw. Ali Adil Shah ran to Siddi Johar, the valiant sardar of Kurnool, for help.

Siddi Johar was an expert at politics and decisive in nature. Adil Shah honoured him with the title of Salabat Khan, and asked him to attack Shivaji with an army of twenty thousand cavalry and forty thousand foot soldiers. Fazal Khan and Rustam Zaman also joined Siddi Johar's campaign to avenge their defeat.

Raje was in Miraj when Siddi Johar marched from Bijapur. Netaji was stationed in the Bijapur sector. Daroji had left Rajapur and had moved towards the Achare, Vergule and Kudal provinces. Two of Shivaji's units were busy in the interiors when Shivaji received the news of Siddi Johar's campaign.

It was an unexpected move and left Shivaji a little perturbed. He moved out of Miraj and asked Daroji and Netaji to meet him as soon as possible. After darshan at the Kolhapur Mahalakshmi Temple, he reached Panhalgad the day after Gudi Padwa. The fort was decorated with the traditional gudis strung across the arches welcoming the New Year. Adil Shah's troops seemed bent on ensuring that the Swaraj's victory did not last long. The news of the Mughal sardar Shaista Khan marching towards Panhala with seventy-five thousand soldiers was another damaging blow.

The Adil Shahi and Mughal forces had planned their attack in order to rout the Marathas. Shaista Khan had reached Ahmadnagar while Siddi was closing in fast. There was no news of Daroji's and Netaji's whereabouts.

Shivaji spared no effort to fortify Panhalgad. A week later Trayambakrao's accountant came running in and said, 'Raje, we have news—the Muslims will be here soon.'

'What are you afraid of? We have faced the enemy before and the Goddess has protected us.'

As he stood on the southern ramparts, looking towards Kolhapur, Shivaji could see a cloud of dust on the horizon. The enemy was approaching fast.

Siddi's forty-thousand-strong army reached Panhala and laid siege to the fort. The eastern flank was managed by Siddi Johar, Fazal Khan and Rustam Zaman while the western side was held by Sadat Khan, Masood and Baji Ghorpade.

Shivaji's men took their positions. The cannons were ready to fire the first salvo. When the enemy was within hitting range, Shivaji raised his hand to signal the attack.

Johar had to retreat. There was chaos in the Muslim flanks as the cannon fire routed them. The reach of the cannons sort of determined the distance to which Johar's troops could advance. Siddi Johar was enraged and concentrated on tightening the siege.

The lion of the Sahyadris was now being trapped in his own fort.

At Raigad, Jijabai was anxious on hearing of the siege. Netaji Palkar, who was busy wreaking havoc in the Bijapur region, heard of Siddi Johar's attack at Panhalgad and decided to turn the tables by attacking and looting Shahapur near Bijapur and looted it at his will.

Netaji had assumed that, seeing his town near the capital attacked, Ali Adil Shah would ask Siddi Johar to return. Ali Adil Shah was about to decide likewise when he got the news from his spies that Netaji had but a small platoon of soldiers. He sent Khavas Khan with an army of five thousand soldiers to subdue Netaji. Realizing that he had no chance of a victory, Netaji retreated hastily. With Shivaji trapped in the fort at Panhala, this was yet another blow to the Maratha morale.

Jijabai was receiving depressing news from all over. Shaista Khan had reached Shirval, the heart of the Maratha kingdom, with his huge army. There was a lady, the bold and daring widow of Udaram Deshmukh of Mahur, who was fighting with Shaista Khan. Aurangzeb had given her the title of Raibaghan, the royal tigress. To make matters much worse, Trayambakrao Bhosale, Babaji Bhosale, Dattajirao Jadhav and Shivaji Raje's maternal uncle, Rustamrao Jadhav were also fighting against Raje. Even family had turned against them now and Jijabai's heart broke hearing about developments like this.

Even though Panhala had been under siege for more than a month now, Jijabai's spies were unable to penetrate the barricade and reach the fort. But Jijabai did not lose hope and ordered her troops to use guerrilla tactics to harass the enemy. Shaista Khan left Shivapur and reached Pune. He camped in Shivaji's Lal Mahal Palace while his cantonment was spread far and wide on the banks of the Mula and Mutha Rivers.

More than three months slipped by while Shivaji continued to be trapped in Panhala. Jijabai made up her mind: She decided to gather whatever forces she could and lead the forces herself. The council of ministers were in a dilemma.

Moropant tried to reason with her when Jijabai asked, 'Pant, do you think I want to do this? Raje is stuck with a small band of troops in Panhala Fort. Khan grows stronger by the day. Should we merely sit and watch Khan capture Panhala?'

'Maa saheb, I beg your pardon, but it is not wise to attack the enemy with such a small force.'

'What is the risk? If we win, Raje will be safe and if not, I would die. That is all! The Swaraj needs Raje and not Maa saheb.'

Moropant had tears in his eyes. 'Maa saheb, this is something that only Raje can answer—not us.'

The news of Netaji Palkar's arrival at the fort brought Jijabai some comfort. Netaji Palkar and Siddi Hilal came to pay their respects to Jijabai. She accepted their mujra and asked, 'Any news of Raje?'

Netaji looked at the floor and said, avoiding her gaze, 'Siddi Johar has tightened the noose around Panhala. We don't know what to do.'

'Oh, that is easy,' Jijabai said, with a wry smile. 'Surve, Sawant and others have joined the enemy. You too can do that. I am aware this is a possibility and that's why I have decided to personally attack Siddi Johar.'

'Maa saheb!'

'Netaji, you are family. Raje trusts you and has made you Senapati. I do not understand why you are praising Johar's strategy!'

No one had ever seen Jijabai in such an explosive mood. 'Netaji, the responsibility of Swaraj does not rest with Raje alone. I am deeply disappointed to see two of his most trusted sardars standing in front of me, wringing their hands helplessly. Netaji, have some respect for the sword hanging at your waist and the bond you have with your family!'

Each word penetrated Siddi Hilal's and Netaji's hearts. Netaji unsheathed his sword and said, 'Maa saheb, in the name of this sword, I swear that I shall only show you my face when I come back with Raje. This is our duty and Maa saheb need not carry out the task.'

Netaji Palkar and Siddi Hilal stayed at the fort for two days, allowing their troops to rest before leaving for Panhala.

It was sunrise when Raje returned from darshan at Someshwar at the Panhalgad Fort. No one spoke a word. Raje dismounted and went to the ramparts. The view was as before—dense jungles were spread across and Siddi Johar's cantonment could be seen in a little clearing on one side. Raje let out a deep sigh and said, 'Trayambakrao, it looks like Siddi won't give up easily.'

'We have been besieged for months but there is no respite. In fact, he seems to be gaining strength every passing day.'

'We have a thousand-odd men at the fort. Do we have enough rations?'

'We have enough wheat, rice and other items. We can stay here as long as we want.'

'But Raje, we have no news of Netaji,' Baji Prabhu said, expressing his fears.

'Baji, Netaji is our Senapati. He knows we have been surrounded and we don't know what Netaji is going through. Now there are only two avenues of hope for us.'

'Two?'

'Yes. Netaji and the mighty Sahyadris!'

'Sahyadris?' Gangadharpant asked.

'Yes. The rains will begin any day now, and Siddi Johar's huge army will not be able to tolerate the incessant downpour.' Suddenly changing the topic, Raje asked, 'Trayambakrao, I hope we have enough ammunition.'

'Yes, we have enough.'

'Then we don't need to worry. As long as our cannons are booming, Siddi Johar will have to mark his time. He cannot come any closer.'

But Raje's estimation of Siddi Johar was off the mark. After surrounding Panhala, he had sent a small band of troops to the Rajapur Port to meet the British. He had requested help with trained manpower to work cannons and, also, to be given long-range cannons, which could be fired from a greater distance.

The British welcomed Siddi's messenger. They saw a new opportunity for trade and grabbed the opportunity. They agreed to help Siddi Johar, conveniently ignoring their pact with Shivaji. Gifford, who had been pardoned by Shivaji, was now, along with Migham and other ammunition experts, sent to Panhala with two long-range cannons in tow. Shivaji was unaware of these developments.

One morning, Trayambakrao came in and announced, 'Raje, the British have betrayed us and have joined Siddi Johar.'

'That is impossible!' exclaimed Shivaji.

'Maharaj, it is a fact. Their long-range cannons are targeting our fort right now.'

As they walked to the ramparts, Trayambakrao pointed in the direction of the cannons. Shivaji curled his fists in anger and said, 'These Britishers are the scum of the earth! It has not even been three months since we pardoned these men. We released their people and their loot, and they now have the temerity to disregard the agreement and attack us!'

However, Raje's anger vanished as fast as it came. The change was so sudden that the people around him were taken aback. He smiled and said, 'Baji, they are, after all, merchants. They have found an opportune moment for a deal. If fate is on our side, they will soon recognize that the deal is going to be too expensive for them. Trayambakrao, keep the cannons in top condition and ensure that each soldier is ready to fight. If the Lord wishes, we shall emerge victorious from this situation too.'

At that moment, the British fired their salvo and a cannonball landed close to the fort walls. Shivaji commanded, pointing to a foreign-made cannon christened Kali, 'Trayambakrao, let me see what Kali is capable of. Light her fuse.'

Kali roared into action and the British were given a suitable reply. The cannons from the fort continued their shelling and they had the advantage of height. The enemy cannons were unable to reach them and were falling short.

Shivaji looked heavenwards for the rain gods to protect them. Within a week, cool winds blowing in from the east heralded the monsoon, bringing a smile to Shivaji's face. But Siddi Johar was an experienced hand and not one to give up because of rain. He had, in anticipation, already started constructing rain shelters.

Within a week, Johar's spies brought the news of Netaji's troops marching towards them. Shivaji's Senapati was attacking them and Siddi Johar understood Netaji's ploy. Netaji would try and breach their security and enable Shivaji's escape. In order to prevent this, Siddi Johar sent a platoon to intercept Netaji's progress before they reached Panhala. He also tightened the security around the siege to ensure there was no breach.

Shivaji stood at the fort, watching the scene unfold as Netaji arrived. Netaji had Siddi Hilal and his son Wahwah with him. Netaji and Siddi Johar's troops clashed but Netaji was unable to make a breach. Wahwah was wounded and fell down and while trying to save his son, Siddi Hilal was captured. Netaji had to retreat to contain further losses and with that, Shivaji's last hope was gone.

The sun was setting in the western sky. Raje stood at the ramparts with a heavy heart. He prayed to the sun god as the western sky was lit with a golden-orange hue. A solitary cloud, golden with the dying rays of the sun, was slowly vanishing in the darkness. In a few moments, it was dark. Shivaji turned back with a deep sigh of dejection.

The monsoon was in full swing but there had been no change in Siddi Johar's resolve. The rains continued to pour and drench the cantonment. Strong winds blew everywhere but Siddi Johar stood his ground. The hope of escape was diminishing every day.

Shivaji grudgingly admired Siddi's perseverance and pitied his own fate. He sent out feelers to the enemy but Siddi Johar was adamant. He would agree to only one condition—the surrender of Shivaji and nothing else.

It was a dark night and the guards at Panhala were alert. They could not see anything in the inky darkness. Sidu Havaldar was guarding the northern side of the fort when he heard something sliding down. He had two soldiers with him and they all stopped to hear the noise. They could not see a thing in the darkness. All they could hear was the sound of the wind blowing and the pouring rain.

'Careful!'

The sound had not come from the fort. It was from somewhere down the hill. He unsheathed his sword and strained his ears. He could hear a faint sound again.

He shouted, 'Who is it?'

There was no response. He shouted loudly again, against the noise of the rain, 'Who is it?'

'Send a rope down!' he heard in response.

In the pouring rain, a shiver ran down his spine. He asked one of the guards to gather other soldiers and within moments, fifty-odd men had appeared.

A rope was sent down and Sidu shouted, 'Rope coming your way!'

Two guards stepped forward. They held the rope and pushed their legs against the wall to steady themselves as they hauled the person up. A few minutes later, a hand appeared at the edge and the soldiers pulled it and a man emerged from the darkness.

Trayambakrao, the fort-keeper, asked, 'Anyone else with you?'

The man was panting with the effort of climbing up. He said, pausing for a breath, 'No one.'

They came into the courtyard and a few mashaals were lit. It was a sanyasi!

Trayambakrao asked, 'Who are you?'

'A sanyasi, Maharaj. I come with Samarth Maharaj's blessings,' the sanyasi replied. Seeing no reaction, he said, 'Raje might get angry if you don't take me to him right now.'

Trayambakrao was taken aback at the confidence with which the sanyasi spoke. He reluctantly sent a message to Shivaji and as soon as Shivaji came in, the sanyasi stepped forward.

Shivaji's face lit up. He said, 'Trayambakrao, you may go and rest now. I will look into this matter.'

Trayambakrao saluted and left. Raje hugged the wet and dripping sanyasi affectionately and said, 'Mahadev! You have arrived out of nowhere! Wait a minute.'

He went inside and opened a trunk. Taking out some dry clothes, he said, 'Wear these. You are shivering. I will ask for a fire to be lit. Make yourself comfortable before we speak!'

A small fire was lit in a small room. Shivaji sat on a blanket and pulled Mahadev down beside him. The rains were incessantly pelting the roof above.

'Tell me, Mahadev. What news do you bring?' Shivaji asked.

'Maharaj, Maa saheb is worried sick. Shaista Khan is enjoying his stay at the Lal Mahal Palace in Pune and has been looting the territory there.'

'And what about the forts?'

'The forts are strong and well-protected. They have surrounded Chakan but Firangoji is fighting back. Maa saheb is worried that you have been surrounded and was planning to come herself to rescue you.'

The flames from the fire were dancing around. Raje said, warming his hands on the fire, 'The eagle may fly high up in the sky but she has her eyes on her chicks. It is just the opposite here. Here, I am flying around and Maa saheb is stuck in the fort, watching all this helplessly. I can't imagine what she must be going through. But you tell me more.'

'Netaji was forced to go back.'

'Yes, I saw that. He had no choice. But how did you manage to get in?'

'Maa saheb had sent many spies but they were unable to get through. Siddi Johar does not care if you are a sanyasi, beggar or whatever else. The security is very strong and they ensure that the change of guard takes place even if it is pouring cats and dogs.'

'Then how did you sneak in?'

'When I reached the area, they were busy incorporating a platoon from Surve's troops. I paid a bribe of fifty coins to join the platoon and then managed to come here.'

'Well done!'

'I was with them for a month. But I did not have a chance to break the security ring. Finally, I found one place. There is news all over the camp that Shivaji Raje is going to surrender and I was eager to reach here at the earliest. While it was raining heavily, I snuck out.'

'Then how did you change into these sanyasi's clothes?'

'I had carried them with me.'

'God bless you! Tell me, how is the path you took?'

'At one place the security can be breached. The soldiers are a few hundred feet away.'

'You call that wide enough?'

'At other places, they are literally touching each other.'

'Let us discuss this in the morning. You must be tired now. Get some rest.'

The news that someone had come up the fort using a rope was all over the fort but no one knew any other details. Mahadev entered Shivaji's chamber and saluted. Shivaji smiled looking at him. He was tall and lanky and Shivaji's clothes didn't fit Mahadev at all. The trouser bottoms were at his knees and the robe was at his waist. Shiva, the barber came in at that moment.

Shiva looked at Mahadev and tried to suppress a smile. He said, caressing his beard, 'After all, they are royal clothes. How can they fit anyone else?'

'Why, if you were to wear them, no one will be able to make out whether it is you or me. Mahadev and I are built differently and that's why you're able to discern the difference.'

Baji Prabhu, Trayambakrao, Gangadharpant and the others arrived at that moment.

Shivaji said, 'Tell me, Trayambakrao. How does one find a way out of this security ring?'

'Raje, I am not able to think of a solution. Siddi Johar will not agree to anything less than your surrender.'

'Then we have no other choice,' Raje said, letting out a deep sigh.

'Raje!' Baji Prabhu did not know what to say and tears rolled down his face.

'What is it, Baji?'

'Raje, we have failed you.'

Shivaji's heart ached at seeing a huge, strong man like Baji Prabhu shedding tears. He said, 'Baji, our luck may not be on our side, but we have to find a way.'

He continued, 'Mahadev mentioned a gap in the security towards the north. We can take advantage of the same during the night and escape.'

Trayambakrao said, 'Then don't wait. We can take care of the fort—your survival is of the utmost importance.'

'I know. But we need to be careful. We cannot allow the enemy be alerted of our movements.'

'We will kill anyone who comes in our way,' Baji erupted.

'That is fine but we cannot stop till we reach Vishalgad, a distance of approximately twenty-five kilometres. Will we be able to reach without being spotted?'

'Raje,' Baji said, 'once you are out of the security ring, it is our job to ensure you reach Vishalgad.'

'All right then. Let the Lord decide what he has in store for us.'

That night, one person left with Mahadev. They returned early the next morning, drenched to the bone. They had surveyed the area and ensured that the way out was safe. The day after, Gangadharpant went to meet Siddi Johar with a proposal for a ceasefire.

Shivaji slept soundly that night. The next morning, he explained his plans to everyone gathered. 'Trayambakrao, ready two palanquins. Baji, you need to get your men organized—select your best. Gangadharpant, is the letter ready?'

Gangadharpant had drafted a letter saying, 'I request that Salabat Khan pleads on our behalf with Ali Adil Shah for a pardon. I will then surrender myself to you.'

Gangadharpant and four other men reached the Char Darwaza gate of the Panhala Fort, and Trayambakrao gave the orders for the door to be opened for the first time in one hundred and twenty-five days. Gangadharpant descended the hill with a white flag signifying peace. The enemy troops saw the flag and sent a message to Siddi Johar. Fazal Khan came out of his tent feeling proud that the enemy had been made to surrender.

Gangadharpant handed over the letter with exaggerated courtesy and humility. Siddi read the letter and was happy to know that Shivaji had finally agreed to surrender and that he had brought the enemy to his knees. Siddi asked, 'Will Raja saheb present himself?'

'If you assure his safety, he will make himself available tomorrow.'

'I smell a rat,' Fazal commented. 'He started similar discussions during Abbajaan's time as well.'

Siddi Johar laughed and said, 'Fazal, the discussions during Afzal Khan's time may have been similar but he was not surrounded in this fashion. It was your Abbajaan who had gone to meet Shivaji. This time, Shivaji is coming here—we have left him no choice.'

While leaving Gangadhar said, 'Raje will present himself tomorrow.'

The news spread across the cantonment, and it was a relief to the soldiers suffering in the heavy rains. There was a significant lax in security once the soldiers knew that Shivaji was to surrender the next day. Fazal Khan was busy dreaming of the next day and Siddi Johar was busy imagining the huge reception he would get when he returned to Bijapur. Through it, the rains continued to lash incessantly.

Gangadharpant returned from Siddi Johar's camp and told Shivaji what had happened.

Shivaji smiled. 'Pant, things have gone according to plan. Now, let the news of the surrender tomorrow spread here at Panhala. If our plan works, all will be well. Else, I may actually have to surrender tomorrow!'

Next day, by late afternoon, Baji had his men ready and Shivaji was pacing in his room. Gangadharpant and Trayambakrao were busy readying everything to accompany Raje. The rain continued to pour as before. Shivaji summoned Shiva the barber.

'Shiva, when we leave the fort, one more palanquin must leave carrying another Shivaji.'

'Maharaj, I do not understand,' Shiva said.

Raje hesitated for a moment. 'Shiva, after I leave, another palanquin will leave the fort. It will follow the royal path and will be received by Johar's men. They will assume that they have caught Shivaji.'

'What exactly is the problem?' Shiva asked.

'We need one more Shivaji—someone who resembles me.'

Shiva beamed with joy and said, 'I would be a fool to refuse such an offer!'

Shiva the barber had the same height and physique as Shivaji and Raje had often spoken of the similarity between the two. Shiva too had grown a beard like Raje's, and his friends teased him saying 'Welcome, Raje!'

Shivaji said, seeing Shiva's eagerness, 'Shiva, it is not easy to be Shivaji. I will escape, but what about you? That thought disturbs me.'

Shiva touched Shivaji's feet and said, 'Maharaj, I swear in Bhawani Mata's name, please don't have an iota of doubt. For only if you are alive can a million Shivas be born. My life would be blessed if I am able to carry out this assignment.'

'Come, let us then see what this Shivaji looks like!'

Shivaji gave Shiva his own clothes to wear. The barber touched the clothes to his forehead before putting on an embroidered coat. Shivaji adjusted a rich turban on Shiva's head and tied a stone-studded sword to his waist with a dagger on the other side of the waist. Shiva was becoming increasingly restless as he wore each garment and his heart was beating rapidly.

Raje took a piece of pearl jewellery and stuck it on to the turban. Taking off his jewel studded shoes he said, 'Shiva, put these on.'

Shiva took a step back and holding the shoes close to his chest, he said, 'Maharaj, I don't deserve to even stand near them. How can I wear them?'

Shivaji said, his voice stern, 'Shiva! Wear them. I can't bear to see a crying Shivaji. If you cry, my reputation will be ruined!'

Shiva's chest swelled. He had a smile in his eyes as he put Shivaji's shoes on. He rested his hand on the sword's hilt and said, 'Who says I am crying?'

Shivaji laughed and he took off his pearl necklace and put it on Shiva. Bringing out a rudraksh necklace, he touched it to his forehead reverently before handing it over to Shiva saying, 'Shiva, this is Bhawani's prasad—our true wealth. It is a sign of the Devi's kripa. Don't think it is worthless. If nothing else works, this will help you to outwit Siddi.'

Shivaji stepped back to admire his new avatar. The guard came in to announce the arrival of Gangadharpant .

Shivaji quietly stepped into the other room as Gangadharpant and Baji Prabhu entered. Pant said, 'Raje, everything is ready.'

Shiva turned around and said, 'I am ready too.'

Baji Prabhu said, 'Maharaj!' and then, realizing his mistake, he exclaimed, 'Oh, it's you, Shiva!'

Shiva smiled. Raje stepped in from the other room and asked, 'Baji, what do you think of this copy?'

'Maharaj, anyone who has not seen you at close quarters would easily be fooled. But Shiva, Raje does not stand with such drooping shoulders.'

Shiva stood ramrod straight and everyone burst out laughing.

Shivaji said, 'Shiva, I forgot one thing.'

He removed his earrings and put one of them on to Shiva's ear. As he turned to put the other ring, he could not hold his emotions back and tears flowed down his cheeks. A sob escaped his lips as he handed the earring to Shiva.

Shiva exclaimed, 'Maharaj!'

Raje hugged Shiva tightly and did not say a word. His tears drenched Shiva's shoulders. Raje said, 'Shiva, I hate what I must do. I have to sacrifice people like you at each step. You are willing to embrace death for me, and here I am, putting earrings on you! What will I get finally? What an irony!'

Shiva struggled out of Raje's embrace and said, 'Raje, there are many people who cry when someone dies. But very few who are willing to cry for a living person. Maharaj, you are shedding tears for someone like me. What more can I ask for? I am willing to give my life for each one of your tears. Don't weep for me.'

Raje gathered his emotions and wiped his eyes. He asked, 'Gangadharpant, have you sent the spies ahead?'

'Yes, they left the moment it was dark. But Raje, there is a storm brewing outside.'

'Mother Nature is here to protect me. It is a full moon tonight but she has ensured that the moon does not expose me.'

Everyone ate their meal and was ready to move. It was late that night when Shivaji came out of his quarters. The rains continued to lash, the wind blew hard and the palanquin was ready and waiting. Raje hugged Shiva and addressing Trayambakrao he said, 'Close the doors the moment I leave. Send Shiva off on the other route. Keep fighting and protect the fort for as many days as you can.'

Pant replied, 'Raje, don't worry. Just take care of yourself.'

Raje said, 'Baji is with me. I am not worried. I shall take your leave now.'

Siva sat in the palanquin and the group moved out towards the exit. He was followed by six hundred foot soldiers and fifteen cavalry troops. The door closed the moment they left.

Shivaji and his palanquin began their descent from the other route.

Raje's palanquin moved forward in the torrential rain. Baji and other soldiers ran alongside. In order to avoid noise, none of the bearers were wearing shoes. In any case, the shoes would not have lasted in the muddy, rocky and rough terrain. Each moment was critical and they made as much speed as possible.

The enemy's security ring could be seen now. Spies would go ahead and keep Raje informed every fifty steps. They slowed down a little seeing a post ahead. Swords were silently unsheathed as everyone waited with bated breath. They proceeded with utmost care not to make any noise. Their footsteps in the puddles sounded louder than the falling rain. They had crossed the post when they heard a loud voice asking, 'Who's there?'

Baji hissed, 'Keep moving.'

The speed, which had slacked for a while, picked up again. The voice was heard again, 'Who's there?'

Raje's palanquin had crossed the security ring by then. The palanquin bearers were running now. They heard voices, 'Stop!'

Baji's order to keep moving was louder than the order to stop. The enemy was now convinced, and Shivaji's men heard one of the soldiers shouting, 'The enemy has run away!'

'How did he escape?'

Siddi Johar had been sitting on a royal seat, drunk and about to go to sleep, when the news of Shivaji's escape reached him. Like a cobra enjoying the warm sun in a jungle, but which stands up, hissing, when a stone is thrown at it, Siddi Johar sat upright in a flash, his eyes red with anger. He pounded the messenger with blows and slaps. Fazal and Masood Khan came running in.

Fazal said, 'I knew it! I warned you!'

'Khamosh!' Siddi Johar shouted angrily.

Fazal was about to say something but seeing Siddi Johar's face, he swallowed his words.

Siddi Johar looked at Masood and said, 'Masood, Shivaji ka peecha karo! Go! Don't come back till you find him.'

Masood did not delay a single moment and gathered a thousand horsemen and foot soldiers. They covered a large distance but were not able to see Shivaji and his men anywhere. Suddenly they heard a scream, 'Enemy!'

Masood's hopes rose, and he spurred his horse on. A palanquin had been surrounded by his horsemen. He saw Raje sitting in the palanquin and Masood was overjoyed. He had trapped the Maratha king Shivaji without much effort!

The palanquin reached the cantonment among tight security. Everyone was thrilled on hearing the news and a guard ran to inform Siddi of the capture.

'Shivaji has been caught, Huzoor! Masood is coming back with him.'

Siddi stared at the messenger and a smile played on his lips, his white teeth shining in the darkness. He took a gold leaf from his turban and threw it at the messenger. Fazal Khan was watching the scene unfold when Siddi said, 'Fazal, no one has escaped from the clutches of the Kurnool lion. And this Shivaji thought he can ... ha!'

They heard the soldiers at the door of the tent. Siddi and Fazal turned to look when Masood walked in. He was followed by Shivaji Raje who walked in as if nothing had happened. Raje looked at everyone and stared at Siddi Johar, who was surprised at his temerity.

Siddi smiled and said, 'Raje, it looks like you were trying to escape.'

'Yes, that was the plan.'

'What happened then?'

'Well, I got caught!'

Siddi laughed. 'Raje, you are a daredevil. Come, take a seat.'

Fazal was seething with anger on seeing Shivaji. This was the same Shivaji who had murdered his Abbajaan. And Siddi was treating him with such courtesies!

'Johar,' Fazal shouted, 'why are you praising this enemy of the sultanate? Take your sword and ...'

'Fazal, hold your tongue! Shivaji is not an ordinary sardar like you or me. He is a king. His fate will be decided by the Badshah. Raje is my guest. Raje, take a seat please.'

'Thank you!'

'Rajasaab sharaab piyoge?' Siddi asked, looking at his wet clothes.

Siddi handed over a tumbler to him and poured some amber liquid into it. Raje did not touch the tumbler but looked at Siddi and asked, 'Aap nahin piyoge?'

Siddi smiled. Wanting to reassure Shivaji, he picked the same jar and poured himself a drink and sipped a little. Raje too followed suit, smiling as he did.

Siddi Johar was staring at Raje. He was amused and admired Raje's courage. He asked, 'Rajasaab, agar aap bhag jaate, toh kahan jaate?'

'Vishalgad. Had I reached there, you would not have been able to do anything.'

'Bilkul sach, Rajasaab. I am sorry your kismet is not supporting you.'

Raje smiled and said, 'But my Lord is with me.'

Siddi asked, 'What if you had been killed in the battle?'

At that moment, a messenger entered the tent and whispered something in Siddi's ear. Anger boiled over Siddi's face and he asked, as he unsheathed his sword, 'Who are you?'

'Shivaji.'

'Liar! The real Shivaji has escaped!'

'Shivaji Raje is not so naïve that he would be caught by you. By now, Raje has gone far away.'

'Who are you then? Speak up!'

Shiva looked at Siddi and said, 'I am called Shiva the barber.'

'Treachery!' screamed Fazal.

Siddi stood there, shivering with anger. He touched his sword to Shiva's chest and said, 'Do you know the consequences of this?'

Shiva pushed the sword away without flinching and said, 'Had I not known, I would not have undertaken this enterprise. If I were worried for my life, I had this dagger to help me in the palanquin.'

'Haramkhor!' shouted Fazal.

Shiva laughed and said, 'Fazal, there is no point in getting angry now. Raje has escaped long ago and I am fortunate to have worn Raje's clothes for a brief while. Even to pretend to be Shivaji is a reward for me—this Shiva is blessed.'

'Khamosh, kambhakt!' Siddi screamed. He plunged his sword deep into Shiva's chest and Shiva's face contorted with pain.

He stumbled but managed to support himself on a pillar to steady himself. He said, 'I may only be pretending to be Shivaji but I am not going to show my back to the enemy either. Raje, this is my final salute to you!' And so saying, he collapsed on to the floor.

The news of Raje's escape created turmoil in Khan's camp. Masood rued his luck for having captured a fake Shivaji, and gathered his forces again and marched towards Vishalgad. Siddi Johar did not know what to do next. He wondered if the real Shivaji was still at the Panhala Fort and ordered the security ring to tighten further.

Dawn broke on the eastern horizon as Raje's palanquin moved towards Vishalgad. The storm had lessened but the rains continued unabated. Raje had tears in his eyes seeing the risk his men were willing to take for him. Vishalgad was still hours away.

It was morning when they got the news of Masood and his men pursuing them. The men, tired to the bone after running the whole night, were determined to reach Vishalgad at the earliest. They reached Godhkhind, a narrow pass near Gajapur, and it was nearly ten kilometres to Vishalgad. The enemy could be sighted now. At this moment, they got the news that Surve and Jaswant Singh had surrounded Vishalgad, and in order to reach the fort, they would have to break through their ranks. Raje had barely six hundred foot soldiers with him and they were exhausted after running more than forty-eight kilometres through the night. How would they break through Surve's siege? And Masood was following them!

Raje had never faced such a situation earlier. Baji Prabhu ordered the palanquin to be lowered and Raje stepped out.

Baji said, 'Maharaj, there is no time to spare. I suggest that you move ahead with a few soldiers. Break through Surve's flank and reach the fort.'

'And what about you, Baji?'

'Me? I will be waiting here. We will not allow the enemy to cross this place.'

'No, Baji. You have played with fire to get me here. Whatever happens, let us face it together.'

'Raje,' Baji said, 'each moment is crucial. I request you to move ahead. You need to fulfil our mission. If the enemy reaches you, all our efforts will be wasted.'

Raje hugged Baji who then saluted and said, 'Raje, hurry! We will take care of the enemy. I will die knowing that our families will be taken care of by you. I have no worries. But Raje ...'

'What is it, Baji?' Raje asked, holding back his tears.

'Raje, fire a cannon the moment you reach the fort. Take care, Raje!'

Raje hugged Baji again. Baji extricated himself and stood at attention as Raje moved ahead with a few soldiers towards Vishalgad. Baji kept looking at them till they disappeared from his sight and then turned to his men. The soldiers were waiting for instructions.

'What are you staring at me for? Till Raje reaches the fort, not a single enemy must cross this place. Now say with me—Har Har Mahadev!'

The cries of 'Har Har Mahadev!' rent the air and a surge of energy flowed through everyone. Their swords were drawn and Baji Prabhu waited for the enemy to reach them.

Masood and his troops were advancing to the shouts of 'Deen! Deen!'

The gorge at Gajapur was true to its name. It was called Godhkhind and there were high mountain walls on both sides with a narrow path in between. The gorge was almost a hundred and fifty yards long. As Masood's men reached the gorge, Baji Prabhu's soldiers pounced on them—the massacre had begun. The soldiers moved back and forth, fighting each other. Masood's men were trying their best to move forward and were effectively resisted by Baji's men.

An hour passed and Suryarao came forward to lead the attack. Raje's men had taken an oath of valour. They knew that their job was to get Raje to the fort safely. Surve's men were not able to repulse the determined attack and soon they were fighting a losing battle. The shouts of 'Har Har Mahadev!' reached the fort and Raje with his wounded soldiers ran towards Vishalgad.

The saffron flag at the fort fluttered in the rain and the fort was within grasp now. While Raje had managed to escape, Baji and his men were fighting a losing battle in the gorge. Only a handful of the three hundred were alive. There was no one who was not wounded and the blood staining the gorge would have put a Holi celebration to shame.

Baji was wounded all over but he continued to swirl his sword at the enemy. The knot of hair tied at the back of his head was swinging as he moved from one place to another. They had managed to frustrate Masood and his men for more than three hours but Masood was not one to give up easily. He ordered for a gun to be brought. The gun boomed but the Mavals continued their attack and the gorge remained unassailable.

Baji recovered from the shock and asked, seeing a small cloud of smoke in the air, 'Has the cannon been fired?' He could barely stand now but that was the only question Baji kept asking. As a soldier tried to give him a helping hand to get up, he said, 'So what if I am wounded by a bullet? Raje has not reached the fort yet—how can Baji afford to die?'

Baji rushed to the entrance of the gorge, brandishing a sword. The enemy soldiers were taken aback seeing a wounded Baji standing there and at that moment, the cannons from the fort boomed.

Baji had a smile on his lips and he muttered, 'Raje has reached the fort. We have won!' Saying so, he collapsed. Masood's men stormed the gorge and attacked like wolves. The Mavals had been courting death for nearly twenty hours now. They were blessed that their efforts had not been in vain. They had no more energy left to fight.

There was a massacre at the Godhkhind gorge and the entire Maval troop was killed by Masood's men. But no one had any regrets—they had done their job.

It was evening when Raje reached the gates of Vishalgad and ordered the cannon to be fired immediately. Everyone at the fort was overjoyed to see Raje. The Mavals accompanying Raje were tired and sapped of strength. Raje asked the fort-keeper, 'What is the condition of the fort?'

'Maharaj, the fort is strong and well protected. We have enough soldiers here.'

'Our soldiers are wounded and tired. Treat their wounds with ghee and ignore anyone who tries to refuse. No one has eaten for the past twenty hours. Feed them first and then let them rest.'

The soldiers were not worried about their wounds and the pain they caused but they were not willing to subject themselves to the treatment! The only treatment for wounds was to apply a balm of old and rotten ghee, an effective but painful solution. The ghee would not only cure the wound but also prevent it from rotting. The burning sensation was worse than rubbing salt into the wound. Everyone was scared to volunteer for the treatment but they had no choice—they had to obey Raje's command!

Raje could not sleep. He looked at the Maval region as it shone in the evening light. The gorge at Gajapur seemed quiet and he could not see any movement there. Raje was worried and fuming at the thought of Surve and his troops surrounding the fort. Raje had pardoned Surve thinking he was loyal to Raje but Surve had not hesitated to join forces with Siddi Johar.

Raje came back to the palace. The fort-keeper had organized the treasury and other valuables for inspection but Raje merely sat on his chair looking worried. Everyone knew what had happened in the Gajapur gorge but no one dared to spell it out.

The fort-keeper came in followed by a wounded and limping soldier. Raje got up and helped the soldier to sit. The soldier was in a daze and nearly fainting. Raje splashed some water on his face and someone brought a mashaal closer to his face. He opened his eyes and seeing Raje, he tried getting up.

Raje held him and said, 'Tell me what happened!'

'Raje, Baji fought like a tiger waiting for the signal from the fort confirming your safety. His body was so full of wounds that it could not be wounded further. Masood had a rifleman and Baji took the bullets on his chest.'

The wounded soldier gasped for breath.

Raje asked, his voice choked with emotion, 'Then what happened?'

'Baji fell down and we pulled him back. The fight continued. Baji came to his senses and asked, "Has the cannon been sounded?" Realizing that you have not yet reached the fort, he got up immediately and no one could stop him. He moved towards the gorge saying, "Raje has not yet reached the fort. So what if I am hurt? When Raje has not reached the fort yet, how can this Baji die?"'

Raje could not stop his tears.

The wounded soldier continued, 'At that moment, the cannon was heard. Hearing that Baji shouted, "Raje has reached the fort. We have won! Raje, my salute!" and then he collapsed. Everyone had lost the will to fight and it was a massacre. I somehow managed to reach here but Raje, we did win!'

The wounded soldier's neck twisted to one side as he fell down. He was dead. Raje sobbed uncontrollably as he laid the soldier on the ground. He used his shawl to cover the soldier's body and said, 'Baji, you are no more! You have made Godhkhind a pure place. It is paavan now. We shall call it Paavankhind from today!'

The next day, Raje watched the scene below from the ramparts. Masood and Surve were busy trying to organize another attack. Raje realized that they were planning to surround the fort. He came into the palace with his fort-keeper and gave the orders. That night, his soldiers went down from two sides of the fort. Surve and Masood had never imagined that the Maratha soldiers would come down and fight. The Maratha soldiers took the opportunity of the stormy weather, when the enemy troops lay huddled, to attack. There was confusion everywhere and a bloodbath ensued. The Maratha soldiers retreated after the damage was done and Masood and Surve were scared to death.

The next morning, Masood's and Surve's troops looked at the fort with fear in their eyes. They had been at the base of the fort for many days now and the fort now seemed unduly silent.

Raje asked, 'Fort-keeper, have you sent away the cannons?'

'No, sir. You were stuck at Panhala and we felt that it made no sense to use up our ammunition here.'

'Good thinking. Now let us begin the shelling.'

Raje inspected the cannons and ordered the fuses to be lit. The cannons on all four sides of the fort exploded at the same instant. The troops surrounding the fort ran in all directions and after the surprise attack at night, the shelling in the morning created further chaos. Raje watched from the fort as Masood's and Surve's troops ran for their lives. He smiled.

Masood had had enough of the fort. He decided to return to Siddi Johar's camp leaving Surve behind. Surve had no plans to remain there alone and he too marched away towards Siddi's camp. Raje's way had been cleared now.

Raje diverted his thoughts to Shaista Khan and moved towards Rajgad.

Jijabai got news of Shivaji's arrival at the base of Rajgad. He was returning to Rajgad after a gap of many months, having faced many battles and difficult situations. The fort was awash with joy. Ever since the killing of Afzal Khan, Jijabai had been worn down by anxiety for nearly a year.

As Shivaji entered Jijabai's quarters, he bent down to touch her feet. She hugged him affectionately and murmured, 'Shivba!'

'Maa saheb, I have come back thanks only to your blessings.'

'Raje, we have suffered each night. Come inside—we have a lot to talk about.'

That evening Jijabai and Shivaji sat talking while Mahadev was sitting a little away.

Raje said, 'Maa saheb, had your spy not reached in time, we would have been in trouble.'

'Raje, except for this man no one else was able to penetrate the security ring.'

'Mahadev, I am certain that you will be able to find me wherever I am. I am removing you from the group of royal spies from today.'

Shivaji smiled when he saw Mahadev confused.

'Mahadev, I have bigger responsibilities for you now. I need intelligent and resourceful people like you. One never knows the situation one may have to face. You are no longer a spy but my personal bodyguard from now onwards.'

At that moment, Netaji Palkar and Kanhoji Jedhe arrived.

Netaji was hesitant to face Raje as he had not been able to penetrate the enemy flanks at Panhala. They both saluted and stood in one corner. Netaji was avoiding Raje's gaze.

'Maa saheb,' Shivaji said, 'it seems our Senapati is hesitant to face me alone. I wonder why Netaji Kaka has brought Kanhoji along with him.'

Kanhoji tried to save the situation and said, 'I was on my way here when I met Netaji.'

'Kanhoji, I did not know you could meet people on the way so easily! Netaji, had you obeyed my orders and reached Panhala on time, I would not have suffered there for two months. I would not have had the misfortune of hearing about the way your troops were routed. In war, timing is critical. A moment can determine the difference between victory and defeat and one cannot afford to be so careless. However, I am aware of your victory at Shahapur. You deserve praise for the bold attack.'

Netaji was a little relieved hearing Raje's words and smiled.

Shivaji continued, 'But you have performed one task which will wipe away a hundred sins. You managed to hold Maa saheb back from leading the attack. You managed to protect our honour. Kanhoji, in the presence of Maa saheb, I would like to make one request.'

'As you command, Maharaj!'

'Kanhoji, you remember I presented you a gift symbolic of the first honour of this court after Afzal Khan's death?'

'Yes, I do.'

'While I was stuck at Panhala, we had lost any hope of escape when Mahadev reached the fort one night. We worked out an escape plan. Baji Prabhu Deshpande—the very memory breaks my heart— took charge of the escape. We left on a stormy night, and the troops crossed a distance of more than forty-eight kilometres, travelling for hours without a care for food, water, mud or whatever. We were attacked by the Muslim troops at Godhkhind. It was a difficult time and we had no idea that we would encounter Surve and his men. The enemy was on both sides and Baji volunteered to stay back. He and his men had been running for more than twenty hours but they did not care. He said, "Raje, when you reach the fort, sound the cannon. I will then know you are safe. I will hold these Muslims back until then." I reached the fort with a few men but Baji and his men were sacrificed—no one survived.'

Everyone had tears in their eyes and Shivaji took a deep breath and continued, 'Kanhoji, Baji is no more but his valour ... how does one recognize that? I would like that the first role of honour given to you be passed on to his family, but only if you are in agreement!'

Kanhoji smiled and said, 'Raje, why are you hesitating? Thanks to Baji's valour, we have the fortune of touching your feet today. I would most readily give the honour to his family.'

Shivaji got up and hugged Kanhoji affectionately. He said, 'We Marathas are usually willing to sell our souls for the sake of false honours. Your selflessness has at least washed away this black spot.'

Netaji said, 'Maharaj, Shaista Khan has surrounded Sangram Durg at Chakan. Firangoji has been holding the fort for the past one and a half months and we need to send him help without any further delay.'

'I know and we will make a decision tomorrow. I would like to spend at least this day in Maa saheb's company!'

Soyarabai came in then and said, 'Shall we serve lunch?'

'Yes. Today is a day of celebration and I would like Netaji and Kanhoji to join us.'

The meal was served and Jijabai personally supervised it. Raje recounted the tales of the past few months and everyone listened to him awestruck.

'Aba saheb, please wake up!'

Shivaji was having his siesta the next afternoon when he woke up to find the young Sambhaji Raje standing near the bed. He had dozed off and he lifted the young boy gently and put him on his stomach. He asked, 'Bal Raje, who asked you to wake me up?'

'Aai saheb. She is outside,' Sambhaji said, pointing at the door.

Putlabai came in, adjusting her pallu.

Shivaji said, 'Rani saheb?'

'Please don't call me Rani saheb—that title does not belong to me.' Putlabai said.

She said, looking at the door, 'Firangoji has arrived. Maa saheb said that you were sleeping but I thought I would inform you.'

Since Firangoji was supposed to be in Chakan, Shivaji was surprised by the unannounced visit. He said, 'It's good that you woke me up. I will go see him now.'

Putlabai turned to go back when Shivaji said, 'Putla!'

Putlabai stopped and turned slowly. She was tall and slender. Sai had been of a dark complexion but Putla was fair. Sai's eyes had had a smile while Putla's eyes spoke of love and affection and she smiled at him.

Raje said, 'Will you take Shambhu Raje with you? I will change my clothes and go down.'

Sambhaji ran towards Putlabai and they both left Raje's quarters.

Shivaji came down to see Firangoji in conference with Jijabai. He heard Firangoji say, 'Maa saheb, I don't know how to face Raje—I had no choice but to hand the fort over to Shaista Khan. But I was helpless. He dug a tunnel to the gate and then blew it up with explosives. We managed to hold them back for fifty days but everyone was exhausted. I didn't have the courage to face Raje and wanted to kill myself but then I thought I would rather face punishment than commit suicide. That is why ...'

'You did the right thing!' said Raje, as he entered the hall.

Jijabai sat on her seat while Firangoji and Moropant stood in one corner. Firangoji stepped forward seeing Raje and touched his feet.

Shivaji pulled him up and said, 'Firangoji, tears don't become you. Wipe them away.'

'Raje!'

'I am the one who should be ashamed. I was unable to send you reinforcements while you were fighting there alone. And you managed to hold off Khan's mighty army for such a long time! I don't have the words to praise you. Maa saheb, we need to honour Firangoji!'

'For running away from the fort?' Firangoji asked sarcastically. His lips were shivering as he spoke.

'Firangoji, I am not counting the victories and defeats here. I care for valour and determination.'

Moropant said, 'Maharaj, Khan himself invited Firangoji to join him seeing his valour.'

'What is surprising about that? Khan may call him but Firangoji would not go, would he? He is indebted to us from a previous birth. He has to pay back the debt before he can go anywhere. Pant, we need to honour him.'

Moropant stepped out and returned with a tray covered with a shawl. Jijabai uncovered the tray to reveal a sword.

Jijabai said, 'Firangoji, please come here.'

Firangoji's hand shook while accepting the shawl and the sword. He heard Raje say, 'Firangoji, this is not just an honour. It is the responsibility to manage the Bhupalgad from now.'

'Bhupalgad?' Firangoji asked, surprised.

'Bhupalgad is one of our finest forts. It is on the border of Adil Shah's kingdom, and I have built a strong and resilient fort there. I was searching for the right person to manage the fort. Khan has now found one for me!'

All Firangoji could do was smile while tears flowed down his cheeks.

Tanaji, Yesaji, Kanhoji, Firangoji, Netaji and the other sardars had assembled at Rajgad. The rains were almost over and they had no doubt Shaista Khan would make his move soon. Adil Shah himself was expected to march on Shivaji.

Jijabai said, with a worried look on her face, 'Raje, if the Adil Shahi and Mughal troops join hands ...'

'Maa saheb, that possibility is quite remote. Had Aurangzeb decided to help Adil Shah, Shaista Khan would not have wasted his time looting our territories. He would have rushed to Panhala the moment he found out that Adil Shah's troops have surrounded the fort.'

'But do you think Adil Shah and Shaista Khan are going to sit quietly?'

'But they will not move either!' Shivaji said. 'If we start a reconciliation dialogue with Adil Shah, he may be pacified.'

'How do you plan to do that?'

'Bijapur's affairs are not in good health. Afzal's death, Fazal and Rustam Zaman's defeat, the revenue we collected from their territories—all these incidents have made them quite weak. They were unhappy with Siddi Johar when I escaped and have now nominated Rustam Zaman as the Senapati. Rustam is a friend and I can use that friendship to start a dialogue. We can make Adil Shah happy by returning Panhala to him.'

'You want to give back Panhala?' Jijabai asked.

'We can always take it back, Maa saheb. Adil Shah has reached Miraj and if we return one of the key forts, it would please him. Vishalgad will remain with us.'

Shivaji worked out a plan and then sent a messenger to Rustam Zaman for negotiations. In the meanwhile, Shivaji focused on pending work. He visited Kalyan and was pleased to see his ship anchored in the ocean. Abaji Mahadev was standing next to him. Shivaji said, 'We need to spread our wings wider and need more ports in our control. I want to see a hundred such ships roaming the seven seas just the way the firangis do.'

'To be frank, Maharaj, it was because you never showed any indifference to our work and we never fell short of cash, luckily.'

'It is Bhawani's grace! We have the Kalyan treasury at hand.'

Trayambakrao Bhaskar came in one day, upset over the plans of handing back Panhala. He said, 'Raje, I left the fort only because you ordered. Else, I would have held out Siddi Johar's forces for many more months.'

'I know, Trayambakrao, but it is not possible to fight two formidable enemies at the same time. You are aware that in a battle, retreating is as important as moving forward. I am equally sad about giving up Panhala but we will get it back. We still have time for that. I hope you did not have any problems leaving the fort?'

'No, Siddi Johar was very accommodating. He allowed all of us to leave without creating any trouble for us. This act has made Ali Adil Shah, Rustam Zaman and Siddi Johar very happy.'

'They don't know that their happiness is not going to last long!'

The pact with Adil Shah reduced Raje's burden by half and he could now focus on Shaista Khan, and his spies were constantly updating Shivaji of Khan's movements.

The monsoon had ended and, as predicted, Shaista Khan moved his camp to Pune and settled in the Lal Mahal Palace. Shivaji was angry but in his heart of hearts, he smiled on hearing the news.

The moment Shaista Khan arrived in Pune, Shivaji sent Vishwanath Dabir to him with a letter. He called Kanhoji Jedhe and said, 'Shaista Khan has come to Pune and is actually occupying our Lal Mahal. He is not going to leave now that the rains have stopped. We cannot afford to confront him.'

'I agree, Maharaj.'

'I have sent our messenger to Khan, but I am sure he is not going to be convinced with sweet talk. It is difficult to guess his intentions. I want you and your Deshmukhs to find out what Khan has in mind. Khan would be reassured if he sees the Deshmukhs near Pune joining him and may take them into confidence.'

Jedhe left to put the plan into action. Soon, Jedhe would come to the fort often to meet Raje. In one such meeting, Shivaji sensed that Jedhe was restless but was unable to fathom the reason. He said, 'Kanhoji, if something is troubling you, why don't you tell me what it is?'

Kanhoji hesitated for a moment. He cleared his throat nervously and said, 'Raje, your loyal sardar Haibatrao Shirmalkar's father-in-law Khandoji Khopade has been in hiding for the past year—since Afzal Khan's death. He is scared to death and has taken refuge in Haibatrao's house. He came to me ...'

'And what ...' Shivaji asked.

'Raje, he has suffered enough. Let him find shelter at your feet.'

Khandoji Khopade, for whom Raje had done many favours, and who had gone and joined forces with Khan. He had fought against Raje. The same Khandoji had guided Khan!

Shivaji erupted with anger. 'Kanhoji, you are siding with that traitor? With that haramkhor Khandoji? He did not know where his loyalty lay! He turned against us and joined the enemy. He deserves to be cut into four pieces. How can you plead his case?'

'Raje, I have given my word to Haibatrao. You may punish me instead of Khandoji and pardon him.'

Raje was overcome with emotions and said, 'Kanhoji, don't take responsibility for Khandoji's crimes. How can you compare yourself to that traitor who was willing to barter his motherland? For your sake alone, I will pardon his life. Go and bring him here.'

Kanhoji left the fort delighted. When he returned, Shivaji was not keen to meet him but Khandoji was persistent. Raje had given his word to Kanhoji and suffered Khandoji without saying anything, and Kanhoji misinterpreted Raje's silence as a tacit approval.

One day, seeing Raje alone in his quarters, Khandoji came in.

Shivaji asked, 'Khopade, how have you come here without any warning?'

Khandoji smiled and in an embarrassed voice said, 'Raje, there was something urgent I wanted to discuss with you. I asked Pant where you were and he said I would find you here.'

Khandoji continued, 'I made the mistake of joining Khan. You pardoned me and allowed me to serve you here and I am grateful. After all, ordinary men do make mistakes.'

'Who are you referring to?'

'Who else? I am talking of our own Kanhoji Jedhe!'

Raje got up and fixed his gaze on Khandoji and said, 'Khandoji, what are you saying? Speak openly!'

'Well, I wish you were a little careful about trusting him.'

'Khandoji, please be clear. I don't like these riddles.'

'Raje, have you checked where Kanhoji is these days? Who does he meet and what does he do?'

Shivaji was losing his patience. He stared at Khandoji.

'Let me explain,' Khandoji hurried. 'He hobnobs with Shaista Khan. I may have gone and joined forces with Afzal Khan but not in this fashion. I was open about it. But this Kanhoji! He is your friend in the day and spends his nights at Lal Mahal!'

'Khandoji!' shouted Raje. Shivaji was shaking with anger. He called for the guards and screamed, 'Arrest this haramkhor!'

Khandoji Khopade was taken by surprise. 'Raje!'

'Silence! I pardoned you. And now you are speaking against the person who begged on your behalf?'

Shivaji turned around and ordered the guards, 'Cut off the right hand and left leg of this traitor.'

Within moments, Khandoji's limbs were amputated. There was blood all over and his screams could be heard across the palace. Shivaji watched calmly, his face holding no sympathy for Khandoji. He said, 'Take this fellow away and give him medicines. See that he does not die.'

When Kanhoji heard of the treatment meted out to Khandoji, he could not believe his ears. He came running to the fort, angry and agitated. He presented himself to Raje and asked, 'Raje, is that the way you treat someone who has been pardoned? What is the value of my words? You have betrayed me, Raje! If you cannot fully forgive someone, then you should not have pardoned him.'

'Kanhoji, I had nothing against him.'

'Then why did you order his arms and legs cut off?'

'Kanhoji, there are people like you who are willing to give their lives for me. There are others who are waiting for the opportune moment and are selfish. I have to manage both but people like Khandoji are traitors. I took Khandoji back into our fold hoping he would change but he, on the contrary, was trying to poison my mind. I knew the truth and hence, I was not swayed but others can be influenced with such malicious gossip. I had no choice, Kanhoji.'

Kanhoji realized the gravity of the situation and his anger subsided. He said, 'Raje, it is his destiny. I was wrong.'

Both of them were silent for some time. Shivaji asked, his voice choked with emotions, 'Kanhoji, are you angry with me?'

Kanhoji smiled and said, 'Raje, you were trying to protect my reputation. How can I be angry with you?'

Shivaji smiled. There was no burden on his conscience now.

Everyone was surprised to see Shivaji in the kitchen in the evening. Jijabai was sitting on a low stool while some maids were busy cleaning vegetables. Putlabai and Soyarabai got up, adjusting their pallus over their heads. Shivaji indicated to Jijabai that he wanted to speak to her and waited outside. Every moment was becoming difficult for him as he stood waiting impatiently.

Seeing him beaming with joy, Jijabai asked, 'Shiva, what has overcome you?'

'Maa saheb, I received a letter from Maharaj saheb today!'

'Really? What does he say?'

'Maa saheb, Maharaj saheb is coming to visit us. Can you believe that?'

'Now don't pull my leg!'

'I am not joking, Maa saheb! Thanks to my deal with Adil Shah and the increasing influence of our power, Maharaj saheb has got the permission to go on a pilgrimage and visit us. He has already arrived in Tuljapur for darshan of the devi as we speak.'

'Devi darshan? But I thought Khan ...'

Shivaji smiled. 'Maa saheb, our pandits at Tuljapur are quite bright and have made us proud. Their quick thinking has protected our pride, prestige, honour and our family deity. Hearing that Khan was reaching Tuljapur, they removed the main idol and put another one in its place.'

Jijabai was overjoyed hearing this. 'Raje, we must honour them as soon as we have the chance. When is Maharaj saheb arriving?'

'I assume he will come via Pandharpur and Jejuri.'

'But what about Shaista Khan?'

'Don't worry about him. I will keep him busy with my correspondence. In any case, he will not dare do anything till Maharaj saheb is here. He knows his prestige in the south and the support from Emperor Shah Jahan that Maharaj saheb enjoys.'

Jijabai could not contain her happiness. She was going to have the good fortune of welcoming her husband home after nearly twenty years. The priests suggested that their first meeting should be in the temple and that she should see his face in a reflection in a pot of molten ghee. Shivaji suggested they meet at the temple in Jejuri.

Sakhubai, Mahadji and Bajaji were invited to the fort. Kanhoji Jedhe's joy knew no bounds and he reached the fort the moment he got the news. He went with Tanaji and Yesaji to receive Shahaji Raje at Pandharpur.

Meanwhile, Shaista Khan was kept engaged in various meetings in Pune. Shivaji would send letters in a tone which was servile and humble. Khan would receive expensive jewellery and garments at each meeting. Shaista Khan was thus convinced that Shivaji, despite his huge force, did not have the courage to confront the Mughals. Shivaji had treated the Mughal forces differently from the way he treated the Adil Shahi forces. And as Shivaji's behaviour towards the Mughals was friendly, the emperor too carried the same impression as did Shaista Khan.

Shivaji had posted hundreds of his men along the route to Jejuri for information of Shahaji Raje's progress. Netaji Palkar, accompanied by eight thousand foot soldiers, was asked to reach Jejuri and receive Shahaji Raje.

Shivaji was lost in his memories of the trip to Bengaluru. He remembered his father's face vaguely as he stood in his room. He was lost in these thoughts when Soyarabai entered his room.

He said, 'I was thinking of the events from twenty years ago. Remember? The day I saw my father for the first time? And how I was married to you to fulfil his wish?'

'I consider myself lucky, Raje. I am not burdened by my childhood memories as I moved away from home very early.'

Shivaji did not respond. He was in a nostalgic mood that day and continued to lie down and recall the events of the past.

Jejuri looked beautiful with fresh green grass covering the meadows. The shining black steps leading to the temple shone in the sunlight. Hundreds of tents stood fluttering at the base of the fort. At the centre of the camp was a lovely tent with a golden canopy, and a saffron flag fluttered in the wind proudly.

Shivaji performed an elaborate puja of Khandoba and distributed alms to the poor.

Mankoji Dahatonde and other officials waited for Shahaji Raje to dismount. Mankoji bent down and touched Shahaji's feet, who hugged him affectionately and said, his voice choked with emotions, 'Mankoji, we finally meet! I am so happy!'

Mankoji said, 'Welcome, Maharaj!'

Shahaji Raje hesitated for a moment and said, looking around, 'I don't see Raje!'

'I beg your pardon, Maharaj. This meeting was as per the religious protocol suggested by the pandits to prevent any mishap ...'

'Oh, I understand! Let us go now. I am eager to meet him.'

Shahaji Raje stood in the temple hall after finishing his darshan. A huge tray with a lamp in it was left in the hall. He looked at his image in the pool of molten ghee kept in a bowl in the tray. Four more faces appeared. One was a copy of his with the same sharp nose, broad forehead and lovely talkative eyes! The child must be Yuvraj! And the young woman must be a daughter-in-law, he surmised. Jijabai, as always, stood coyly without saying a word. The faces were smiling, and the temple bells rang loudly, heralding the important event. Kanhoji and Mankoji wiped their tears.

Shahaji Raje got up. He had crossed sixty years of age and one could see a hint of grey in his hair. But he was as handsome as before. Shivaji stood there expectantly and Shahaji Raje was reminded of his own youth. He stood there watching his son, unable to speak.

Shivaji came forward slowly and then bent to touch his forehead to Shahaji's feet. Shahaji Raje blessed him as he patted his back with trembling hands. He pulled Shivba up and hugged him tightly. He could not utter a word and continued to hug him tightly.

After a while, Shahaji Raje managed to find his voice. He had been impressed with Raje's manners, the way he had bent to touch his feet. He said, 'Raje, though you are grown up now and have turned into a man with many accomplishments, I am impressed the way you show your respect to the elders.'

Shahaji Raje sat in his tent and Jijabai, Soyarabai, Putlabai and others were in attendance. Sambhaji was enjoying the attention sitting on his grandfather's lap. Shahaji Raje asked, looking at his daughter-in-law, 'Sunbai, do you remember me?'

Soyarabai blushed and Shahaji Raje said, 'You need not feel so shy! You had started crying during the ceremony and we had to take you around the fire with your feet wrapped around my waist!'

Everyone laughed and Shivaji said, 'I suggest you rest a while, Maharaj saheb. We are available at your command.'

All the others left except Jijabai.

'Rani saheb!'

Shahaji Raje got up and paced the floor, his hands clasped behind his back. He did not know what to say. Farzand Shahaji Raje, the man who was never in doubt in any situation, was speechless! He stopped and turning his head, exclaimed again, 'Rani saheb!'

Jijabai did not respond.

'Rani saheb, I stand here with my head bowed. I am ashamed to face you. I don't even have the courage to look at you!'

Jijabai looked up and saw him tormented with guilt.

Shahaji Raje continued, 'Do you remember? When you had requested to take Sambhaji Raje with you to Pune, I haughtily replied, "Leave Sambhaji here and take care of Shivaji. Let us see who does a better job."?'

Shahaji Raje could not speak further. There was a lump in his throat. He managed to hold back his tears and continued, 'Rani saheb! You were all alone and yet you have made a man out of Shivaji. And despite all my power and privilege, I was unable to save Sambhaji. I am unable to get over the guilt.'

'There is nothing to credit me for. It was with your blessings that Shivaji was able to achieve so much.'

'It is your greatness to give credit to others! What have I done to help Shivaji? In fact, he is the one who helped me. His pact with Adil Shah helped me greatly. He is never bothered about himself. Worried that my acts may invoke the displeasure of Adil Shah, I often failed in performing my duties towards my son. I could not live with the guilt any longer and was eager to come here.'

Jejuri glowed that night in the presence of all the royal guests. The steps leading to the temple were lit up with lamps burning on both sides. The rows of lamps created a beautiful fluttering line of lights in the silence of the night.

After camping in Jejuri for two days, Shivaji requested Shahaji Raje to come to Rajgad. As they reached Rajgad, Shivaji requested Shahaji to enter the fort in a special palanquin that was waiting, its arms decorated with jewels and seat piled with lovely soft dhurries. Shivaji requested that Shahaji Raje step into the palanquin and, removing his shoes, Shahaji got in. Shivaji took his father's footwear in his hands and walked barefoot behind the palanquin. The bugles announced the arrival of the royal procession at the gate.

Shivaji guided Shahaji Raje to a seat in the durbar hall. Seeing the shoes in his hands, Shahaji Raje said, 'Raje, it is I who would be proud to wear your shoes! Put my footwear down!'

Shivaji introduced all his friends to Shahaji Raje and soon, dinner was laid out. As per custom, rangoli were drawn around the plates. Shahaji sat with his grandson in his lap. Shivaji stepped forward and tied a mogra garland to his father's wrist and Shahaji felt a teardrop on his hand. He looked up and exclaimed, 'Raje, I see tears in your eyes!'

Shivaji said, 'It was because of my impertinence that you were captured and these wrists were tied.'

'Raje, don't say that! You did what I could not manage. You have made me proud by fighting the Adil Shahi and Mughal troops. The handcuffs were as light as these mogra garlands. Don't be so hard on yourself!'

The meal began and Jijabai was happy seeing everyone enjoying the meal in a relaxed manner. The royal women were in attendance, ensuring that everyone was properly fed. Different delicacies continued to arrive from the kitchen.'

Shahaji Raje took a tour of the office, the fort and other areas. He was satisfied seeing the operation and Mankoji and Kanhoji regaled him with Shivaji's exploits.

Shivaji had sent his hunters into the forests and each day, fresh meat would arrive at the fort for a feast. A week had passed since Shahaji Raje's arrival. While they were eating one evening, Shahaji Raje asked, 'Raje, do you hunt?'

Shivaji replied, a little embarrassed, 'I would like to but I don't have the time ...'

'I understand,' Shahaji Raje said. 'I would love to go on a hunt. My youth maybe spent but I still have the urge to fight a wild boar. The thrill of a chase on horseback with a spear is great. I am willing to try that at any age.'

Shahaji Raje had brought many jewels and gifts for the entire household. He turned towards Shivaji and said, 'Raje, I have something precious for you.'

A servant stepped forward with a tray with a sword with a jewelled handle. Shivaji sat on his knees to accept the sword with both hands. He touched it to his forehead reverently and stood up.

'I have heard a lot of praise of your Bhawani sword. It has done you proud. Take this as a gift from me—I have named it Tulja.'

'I shall pray to it daily along with the Bhawani sword.'

Shahaji came for darshan to the devi temple at the foot of the fort when he asked Moropant, 'How many forts does Shivaji have?'

'We have sixty strong forts, Raje!'

'And what about the cavalry?'

'More than fifteen thousand,' Netaji replied.

'Raje, I am told that you have a few ships too. Is that so?'

'Yes,' Shivaji replied.

'That is good. But I suggest that you increase the cavalry. Do you remember the shloka I taught you?'

Shivaji recited the shloka in Sanskrit which meant the strength of a king are his horses and the more horses he has, the stronger he is.

Moropant said, 'Maharaj, every time Raje inspects the cavalry, he recites this shloka.'

'Moropant, the one who understands the meaning of this shloka will never stop expanding his kingdom. Raje, I came here and met you. I am very happy. Do you know what I promised Khandoba at Jejuri? I would place a gold idol at the temple when I see Raje's Swaraj. We need to fulfil my promise.'

'Pardon my impertinence, Aba saheb,' Shivaji said, 'but the Swaraj is not yet complete. We need to fortify it further. On one side, Shaista Khan is waiting to teach us a lesson and on the other, Adil Shah is restless.'

'This is a part of raising a kingdom. Don't let it deter you. If you were not a formidable enemy, the Mughal and Adil Shahi troops would not have been so worried. These men have foresight—Aurangzeb was aware of your growing strength even when he was a Subedar in the Deccan and he had warned Adil Shah. Don't be worried about Shaista Khan. I am impressed that you have managed to keep them at bay. I am convinced that you will win.

'Raje, make Raigad your capital—you won't find a better place. I am managing Karnatak. Ekoji Raje will look after that after I am no more. He is like me—a simple fellow at heart,'

Shahaji Raje smiled and continued, 'He may not be as smart as you but he will look after the territory well. You are the eldest now. Take care of him. The day these two territories are joined, your kingdom will extend from Thanjavur to the Narmada. That day is not far away and I hope that my dreams are fulfilled by you. However, I cannot stay here for long. I will, unfortunately, have to leave soon.'

'Why? Are you bored so soon?' Shivaji asked, a little disappointed.

'Of course not! Seeing your fame and prestige has made me feel ten years younger and invigorated. But if I stay longer, Adil Shah will become suspicious. The day you killed Afzal and entered Adil Shah's territory was the day I arrived in Bijapur from Karnatak. There was chaos in the durbar.'

'Why, what happened?' Mankoji asked.

'The rumour was that Shivaji would attack from one side and I from the other. The rumour mill will be working overtime now that I have visited you.'

'But did Adil Shah not give you permission to come here?' Shivaji asked.

'Yes, he did but it was with the understanding that I would pacify you and make you understand the repercussions of taking up cudgels against him. He has agreed to honour you by making you a sardar of a ten-thousand-strong force. Of course, I will never ask you to accept that. I have impressed upon him the importance of having the powers in the Deccan united together in keeping the Mughals at bay. Adil Shah seems to be agreeable to that logic and I am sure that once he agrees, at least one part of your problem will be solved.'

Shivaji was pleased listening to the wisdom and diplomacy which his father demonstrated. He could not have asked for more!

As they all sat down for dinner, Shahaji Raje said, 'Raje, I must admit that your Maa saheb has brought you up very well.'

Jijabai blushed and said, 'He is just like you, Raje!'

Shahaji Raje laughed. 'Not at all! There is a lot of difference between us. I am a rajbhogi but he is a rajyogi. The day I return from an exploit, I look for ways to entertain myself. But Raje? He returns from one campaign and plans another the next day. He has all the makings of a true king.'

Shahaji Raje let out a deep sigh and said, his voice a little worried, 'Raje, you removed a great burden from my mind by killing Afzal. It was he who had handcuffed me and was responsible for the death of Shambhu Raje. But I still have one wish left.'

'Tell me, Aba saheb! What is it?' Shivaji asked eagerly.

'Baji Ghorpade!' Shahaji Raje said. 'That treacherous bastard! He kept me in the dark. I regret that I was deceived by him! I was serving under Adil Shah and so was he. I kept quiet and did not do anything.'

Raje said, his voice taking on a serious tone, 'Maharaj saheb, I promise you, I will have your revenge.'

'I am sure you will,' Shahaji Raje said.

Shahaji Raje left for Bijapur within a few days and while he was leaving, Shivaji could not stop his tears. He placed his head on Shahaji Raje's feet and said, 'Whatever I have is at your feet ...'

A sob escaped Shahaji Raje and he hugged Shivaji tightly. He kissed his forehead and wiping his tears, he took out a pearl necklace. He put it on Shivaji and hugged him again.

As he mounted his horse, Shivaji bent low in an elaborate mujra. Shahaji acknowledged it with a nod and then spurred his horse. The cavalry followed suit. The horses galloped away and all Shivaji could see was the cloud of dust left behind. He stood there watching the cloud dissipate for a long time, his tears blurring his vision.

BOOK FOUR

The fort seemed empty and desolate. Raje's father had visited for just a fortnight but his presence and the conversations with him had doubled Raje's enthusiasm and vigour. He never openly admitted it but he missed his father sorely.

It had been a year since Shaista Khan had made camp in Pune. All the forts, except for Chakan, were now back under Shivaji's control. After the rains, Khan made plans to capture Kalyan and take charge of the ships there. He entrusted the job to his sardar Kahar Talab Khan.

Shivaji explained the situation to his council of ministers and the unanimous advice was to stop Khan from moving to Konkan and confront him at Kalyan–Bhiwandi. Shivaji smiled and said, 'Let us see what guidance Bhawani Mata gives us.'

A month after Diwali, Bahirji reported, 'I am told Khan's forces will attack tomorrow.'

Shivaji asked, as he paced the floor, 'Do we know which route Khan is planning to take?'

'Yes. He plans to reach Konkan via the Umbarkhindi route passing Lohgad.'

'Did you say Umbarkhindi?'

'Yes.'

'Bahirji!' Shivaji said, smiling widely, 'The Lord has blessed us by giving Khan the right ideas!'

That night, Raje slept satisfied knowing that he could tackle the Khan successfully. Shivaji set out the next morning after taking Jijabai's blessings.

He said, 'Maa saheb, Khan will get a slap on his face once victory falls in our lap. He has been looting and vandalizing our territory. A defeat will teach him to think twice before attacking our territory.'

The trumpet announcing the move was sounded and the sound of horse hooves filled each corner of the fort. Shivaji came down the fort where Netaji was ready with the troops.

'Netaji, have you dispatched the cannons?'

'Yes, I have sent forty small ones ahead.'

'That should be enough. Let us move.'

They moved at a rapid pace. Umbarkhindi was a deep gorge with the sides of the mountains kissing the skies. There was a mountain wall on one side while the other side had gaps in it giving a glimpse of the plunging deep valleys. Dense forest covered both sides with the narrow gorge snaking its way through.

Shivaji stood observing the gorge in its natural and pristine beauty. The soldiers had taken vantage positions and were ready for the attack. The snipers were positioned at high places with a clear vision of the approaching enemy. The cannons were placed at strategic points. Shivaji was in his camoflauge dress as he toured the jungles while Netaji inspected the arrangements. They all waited eagerly for Kahar Talab Khan's men to arrive.

The spies brought news of the impending arrival of the enemy. The entire forest was bathed in silence. Khan's advance party came first to inspect the gorge and, finding it safe, signalled for the caravan to move ahead. Khan's huge army moved slowly as the cannons, carts, elephants, foot soldiers and others lumbered along the way. The curves were dangerous and their march was slow.

Khan was sitting astride a black horse, accompanied on one side by Amar Singh and Raibaghan on the other. His guards followed close behind, their swords unsheathed and shining in the sun. The last of the camels entered the gorge. The entire valley seemed peaceful and even the wind had stopped blowing. The sun was now high in the sky, bathing the valley in warm sunlight.

Kahar Talab looked around and said to Raibaghan, 'What a beautiful place!'

Raibaghan said, 'It may be beautiful Khan saheb, but this silence is disquieting.'

At that moment, a trumpet sounded somewhere deep in the forest. It was followed by another one from a different direction. Within moments, the entire forest was filled with the sounds of bugles and trumpets. Kahar Talab, Raibaghan and Amar Singh looked around, a mixture of fear and surprise on their faces.

Kahar Talab shouted, talking to no one in particular, 'What is this? Who is making this noise?'

Unperturbed, Raibaghan said, 'Khan saheb, the mystery of the silence has been solved. Shivaji has surrounded us.'

Raibaghan unsheathed her sword and said to Amar Singh, 'You stay near Khan saheb. I will take a look.'

Raibaghan spurred her horse when the cannons boomed and the entire Mughal army erupted in chaos. The cannon balls were picking their targets. The trumpets continued to blow, creating a noise which was unbearable. Not a single Maratha soldier had been spotted yet. The soldiers who tried to flee into the forest were being picked up by sniper arrows. The gorge was filling up with corpses in no time. Khan watched the massacre as he stood in between two cannons. His guards surrounded him to give him some cover.

Raibaghan came to report and said, 'Khan saheb, the gorge has been blocked from both sides. We are trapped! '

Khan shouted, losing his cool, 'Destroy the enemy!'

'But where is the enemy?' asked Raibaghan. 'It is we who are being destroyed. I cannot see anyone!'

'Chase them into the jungle!'

'Those who did have not come back—snipers are killing them!'

There was chaos everywhere. The cannons were targeting the carriages and one of the carts carrying the royal treasury was attacked. The cart exploded throwing jewellery all over. One could see pearl necklaces strewn over the mud. But no one had the time to go after them! The soldiers were worried that they would each be the next target from the incoming arrows. It was mayhem across the gorge and Khan trembled with a mixture of indignation and fear.

Raibaghan said, 'Khan, this is the result of our audacity at entering such a difficult terrain controlled by Shivaji.'

'Raibaghan, I need a way out,' Khan pleaded.

'There is no escape from a crocodile's jaws. You have brought the army into the clutches of a lion. All our efforts and victories so far have been nullified.'

'Raibaghan, you must have courage!' Khan's voice was now desperate.

'Courage? Khan saheb, at least you should not teach me to be courageous. When the Alamgir Badhshah built Jagjivanpura in Aurangabad, he named it after my son. He bestowed the title of Raibaghan on me when he saw the valour I displayed. Khan saheb, courage is important when it leads to results. Else, it is useless bravado.'

'Raibaghan, what is your advice now?'

'You ask for advice? If Shivaji makes up his mind, not a single soldier will survive. Your experienced marksmen are no use here—they cannot see the enemy and are all at the mercy of an invisible enemy.'

Kahar Talab Khan was aware of this and he could hear the screams of the dying each moment. He was losing hope. He shouted, 'Do whatever you can, but save us! This Shivaji is not a human. He is a Satan!'

Raibaghan smiled. 'Khan saheb, send your emissary to Shivaji to negotiate an immediate ceasefire.'

'Will Shivaji agree?' Khan asked.

It was not a Mughal custom to spare the enemy. In fact, the Mughal army enjoyed killing their trapped enemy and derived a sadistic pleasure from it. Khan was suffering the same fate today.

Raibaghan said, 'Shivaji is a just king. He is large-hearted. He would never attack an enemy who is willing to surrender. It's why he is famous.'

'Then send an emissary immediately. I am willing to negotiate and surrender.'

An emissary was dispatched immediately with a few men wearing white clothes. They entered the forest shouting 'Ceasefire!' as they made their way into the deep jungle. They were surrounded within a few minutes by Shivaji's men. The attack on the gorge, however, continued.

It was afternoon by the time Khan's emissary reached a camp near the mountaintop. In a small clearing in the forest, he saw Shivaji astride a horse, looking radiant in camouflage. The emissary bent low, almost touching the ground, and saluted Shivaji thrice with a traditional mujra. He covered his hands with a green handkerchief as a mark of respect and said, 'I have come here to pay my regards to Raje on behalf of Khan-e-azam Kahar Talab Khan saheb and Raibaghan saheb.'

'Give me the message of the brave Kahar Talab Khan and Raibaghan.'

'Khan saheb repents his mistake, because despite your love and affection, he acted in haste on the advice of Shaista Khan. He regrets having entered your territory.'

'My love and affection?'

'Maharaj, Kahar Talab Khan is an old friend of Farzand Shahaji Raje. We beg you to acknowledge this friendship and ask you to pardon Khan saheb. It is our ardent prayer.'

Shivaji smiled and said, 'It is good of you to remember old friendships so soon! Give my regards to Khan saheb and Raibaghan, and tell them that we never attack an enemy who has surrendered. My men and I have suffered a lot and we expect to be compensated duly. The attack will continue till I hear from him, and I shall wait here for your answer.'

The emissary bent in mujra and stepped back. He hurried back to Khan who immediately agreed to Shivaji's conditions. The emissary returned with royal jewellery boxes loaded on to a horse. A young boy also accompanied the emissary. He was a handsome youth, and wore a bright yellow turban with a jewelled crescent adding to its beauty. He also wore an embroidered waistcoat with narrow cotton trousers. A sword hung on his side, its handle decorated with lovely gems.

The youth recognized Shivaji who sat atop a white steed. The armour on Shivaji's chest added to his aura. The two quivers of arrows on his back gave an appearance of wings. A bow was slung on his right shoulder. The ash mark on the forehead was a soothing antidote to the terrifying armour.

The emissary saluted and then opened the boxes to display their contents. One was full of gold coins, the other filled with silver coins and the third box had precious gems and jewellery. Shivaji raised his hands and Netaji signalled to one of the soldiers to blow the trumpet. Soon, a succession of trumpets blew and within moments, the gorge stood silent as the attacks stopped. The jungle was cloaked in an eerie calm once more.

Shivaji said, 'Ask Khan saheb to leave our territory immediately. Ask him not to make the mistake of attacking us again. Warn him that this part of our kingdom is the shining jewel in our crown and that no one has the strength to take it from us. You must have realized how foolish it is to try doing so.'

The youth standing behind the emissary continued to look at Shivaji without batting an eyelid. He stepped forward, his hand on the hilt of his sword. Netaji's hand moved to his sword but Raje indicated to him to stay back. The young man stepped forward and bent in mujra. He removed his sword and held it in both his hands stretched forward.

Raje asked, 'What is the meaning of this?'

'I am honoured to see your large-heartedness. I request you to accept this as a token of my gratitude.'

Raje smiled and looked at the two hands holding the sword. He said, 'I think it would be unfair to accept the sword of a brave sardar like you. I don't have the right clothes to honour you with and it would have been my pleasure to do so. I congratulate you on your daring. No wonder Aurangzeb has given you the title of Raibaghan.

The youth was none other than the brave lady Raibaghan! Her hands trembled as she said, 'Maharaj, how did you recognize me?'

'That was not difficult,' Shivaji said. 'Your fair hands and the tattoo on your forehead were a giveaway. Notwithstanding that, I recognized you the moment you arrived. Who else would have the courage to come here?'

Raibaghan was dumbfounded.

Raje continued, 'Tell Khan that I am glad I have had the good fortune to meet a brave lady like you. I am reminded of Bhawani Mata when I hear of your exploits. I would like to honour you properly as soon I have the opportunity and I hope you will pardon me today.'

Raibaghan returned with the emissary, impressed and overwhelmed with Shivaji's behaviour.

Khan and his soldiers made a hasty retreat soon thereafter. Shivaji ordered that all the dead men, including the enemy, be given an honourable burial. Aware that Shaista Khan would be enraged on hearing about this defeat and likely to attack Konkan, Shivaji asked Netaji to guard Bhorghat well.

Shivaji assembled his troops on returning to Rajgad. Each day was critical. He issued orders to his spies to move in advance and also divided his troops into two, keeping one with him.

Seeing this Jijabai asked, 'Raje, you have just returned from one campaign. Should you not wait for some time before leaving on another?'

'Maa saheb, Shaista Khan will have lost sleep on hearing of the defeat in Umbarkhindi. Netaji is already holding fort in Konkan and will not allow Khan to reach Raigad–Mahad. We cannot afford to give Khan any respite. He should know what we are capable of.'

'Then are you planning to attack him?'

'Of course! But just not right now. Jaswant Singh of Palvan is trying to trespass us. Remember, when was held up at Panhala, the Surves too sided with our enemy? They need to be taught a lesson. The English, who fought against us, need to be contained. Once we defeat the foreigners, Khan will know the true strength of our forces.'

Just then, Shambhu Raje ran in and asked, 'Can I come with you?'

'On the campaign?'

'Yes, Maa saheb gave me this—see?' Shambhu Raje showed him a small sword.

Jijabai and Shivaji smiled. Picking Shambhu Raje up, Shivaji lovingly said, 'This fellow cannot even pronounce "sword" properly but wants to come for a battle! Raje, you don't have too many days to enjoy your games. Enjoy them while they last! Later, you will have to do what I am doing today.'

Shambhu Raje would not give up his demand and insisted on coming along. Raje was at his wits' end trying to pacify him when Shambhu started crying and said, 'Aba saheb is a bad man!'

Jijabai explained gently, 'You must not speak that way to your father, Bal Raje!'

Shivaji said, 'Maa saheb, he seems to have a wild temper.'

Sambhaji was about to burst into tears again when Jijabai, diffusing the situation, hugged him and said, 'If you want to go on a campaign, where is your shield?'

'Shield?' Sambhaji asked, wondering where he would get that from.

'You cannot fight without one.'

Sambhaji had no answer.

Jijabai hugged him and said, 'Bal Raje, we have asked the blacksmith to make you one. The moment it is ready, you may go on a campaign.'

Sambhaji went off, excited at the prospect of going to battle soon.

Jijabai said, 'He may have his tantrums no doubt, but he will listen if you have the patience to talk to him. I wish Sai was here.'

The memory of Saibai sent a shiver down Raje's body. He walked away, his head bent in thought.

Shivaji and his men marched on towards Konkan the next day. The news of Shivaji's victory at the gorge had spread far and wide and he did not even have to attack to bring the prosperous cities of the Konkan region under his control—they surrendered even before he reached city limits. Shivaji would appoint new ministers to manage the cities and move ahead. His next stop was Palvan.

Jaswantrao of Palvan was mortally afraid of Shivaji's impending attack. He had helped Siddi Johar when Shivaji was surrounded and he ran for his life. Shivaji entered Palvan and captured the Dabhol Port under the control of the Dalvis.

He was camped at Chiplun, which was famous for a temple of Parashurama. Shivaji had darshan and after distributing gifts to the Brahmin priests, moved to Devrukh. The Surves of Shringarpur, the Sawants of Kudal and the Dalvis of Palvan were all well within Raje's territory. Shivaji had no intention of either fighting them or making allies. But he was keen that they join him in his campaign. He knew that the Surves had supported the Muslims when he was surrounded in Panhala but he sent his emissary to them nonetheless. His message was simple:

'I am leaving on a campaign and am leaving a small platoon of my troops at Sangameshwar. I would like that you take care of the platoon till I return and offer them help if need be.'

The Surves were relieved to receive this message as they had feared the worst. They accepted the responsibility with pleasure and sent back the reply:

'I am your servant and would be happy to serve you. Please pardon any mistake from my side.'

Shivaji was satisfied with the reply and decided to convert them into his allies once he returned from his campaign.

Tanaji was holding fort at Sangameshwar and Pilaji Nilkanth joined him soon. After specific instructions about managing the platoon at Sangameshwar, Shivaji moved forward to Rajapur with an army of a thousand cavalry and three thousand foot soldiers. He sent his emissary to Rajapur after surrounding the town to meet him. The rich and powerful of Rajapur came forward to meet Raje but most were unwilling to compromise and pay him anything. Letting them off without a fine, Shivaji waited for the firangi traders.

Shortly, four or five English gentlemen arrived and walked arrogantly into the tent. They removed their hats with a flourish and bent in salute. Raje sat there, observing them. They had long hair while their white waistcoats were up to the knees and they wore long narrow boots.

The translator said, 'Raje, the moment the British traders got wind of your arrival, they came to pay their respects.'

Shivaji acknowledged their presence saying, 'You have come to see me without a formal invitation—I am honoured.'

Revington, one of the British traders, said, 'Your friendship is dear to us and to our company.'

'Oh, I see! In that case, we know each other well!'

The traders were taken aback.

Shivaji explained, 'We had an agreement at Miraj when we had returned whatever we had captured—including your men. Isn't this Gifford the same person we captured?'

Revington smiled and said, 'We cannot forget your blessings, sir.'

Raje's anger erupted and he said, 'What disloyal men you are! Barely had the ink on the agreement dried when you moved your cannons to Panhala to fight against me. If you had had any value for your honour, you would have thought twice before allowing your flag to flutter on the battlefield.'

The accusation was a lighting strike. Revington wiped his face nervously with his handkerchief and said, 'There seems to be some misunderstanding, Raje!'

'Silence! I will tell you why you went to Panhala. You presumed Siddi Johar was strong and you knew that Shaista Khan was ready to attack. You wrongly presumed that Shivaji's end was near and thought it was a godsend to support the Muslims and finish me off!'

Shivaji's anger was directed at Revington and he stared at him and said, 'Revington, I believe you are far-sighted, aren't you? I am told that you have a piece of equipment with which you can see things in the distance. You must have taken that along when you reached Panhala.'

Shivaji was silent for a moment and said, his voice laced with sarcasm, 'Is this what you call your trading philosophy? Is this why you left the shores of your own country? What do you trade in—your wares or your honour? If this is your attitude, it will lead to destruction and sorrow one day.'

Shivaji stood up and said, 'I'm sorry, I cannot pardon you.'

'Raje, we are willing to pay whatever you ask for,' Revington pleaded.

'Are you doing me a favour?' Shivaji snapped back in anger. 'Arrest these bastards! They dared to show their flag and bombard us. Their company and them both need to be taught a lesson!'

Shivaji stepped out of his shamiana and ordered the loot of all merchants who had not paid their dues to him to be confiscated. He said, 'Loot the firangi camp and arrest all the firangis. If anyone tries to use their weapons, don't hesitate to kill them.'

Turning, he said in a low voice to a havaldar standing nearby, 'Find a man by the name of Balaji Aavji.'

The confiscation of goods continued till late in the evening and soon heaps of items were laid down for Raje's inspection. The loot included precious items such as jewellery, spices, brass, gold, sandalwood, deer musk, saffron, and rhino horns. Raje ordered Revington and his colleagues to be jailed at Songad and the rest to be sent to other forts. The English had received a fitting reply to their treachery.

Soon, the havaldar came in and reported, 'We brought Balaji Aavji as per your command.'

Raje was eager to meet him and said, 'Present him immediately.'

The man was brought into the tent and he was shivering with fear. Raje heard a woman crying and asked, 'Who is crying?'

'It is Balaji's mother, Maharaj.'

'Send her in too.'

An old lady ran in. She was accompanied by three other men. She flung herself at Raje's feet and said, 'Raje, we are poor people. We have nothing to give you.'

Raje lifted her up gently and said, 'Mother, don't worry. I have summoned Balaji for work and not to punish him.'

She was relieved on hearing this and said, 'Raje, how shall I recount my horrific tale? My husband was a Diwan under Siddi Johar and one day Siddi lost his mind and ordered my husband and his brother to be put to death. My three sons and I were to be sold as slaves. The servants took pity on us and we were sent to Rajapur. My brother, Visaji Shankar, was a trader here and he bought us without letting anyone know that we were related. That is how I managed to raise my children.'

'You do not have to suffer anymore,' Raje said. He looked at an elderly man standing behind and asked him, 'Are you Visaji Shankar?'

Turning towards Chitnis, Raje said, 'Chitnis, return his payment. They are our men and you should ensure that they are not put to any trouble.'

Raje turned to Balaji and said, 'Balaji, after listening to your mother, I am convinced that it was you who wrote all those letters describing the atrocities being committed in this city. Is that right?'

'Yes.'

'I am thankful for your efforts. We do not campaign to loot cities and we need people like you to administer our territories. We would like you to be a part of my administration if you agree.'

'It would be my good fortune, Maharaj!' Balaji touched Raje's feet.

Raje said, 'Get up! You and your brothers, along with your mother, should come to Rajgad. Chitnis, ensure that their expenses are taken care of. I will tell you about your new responsibilities when we reach Rajgad.'

Raje was planning to decamp and march ahead from Rajapur when he received the news of Vithoji's arrival from Sangameshwar. Raje could not believe Vithoji's words when he said, 'As per your instructions, Tanaji and Pilajirao were guarding Sangameshwar. One night as they were sleeping peacefully, Jaswantrao of Palvan and the Surves of Shringarpur attacked the cantonment. A battle ensued for three hours. Tanaji fought bravely and by dawn, the Surves had to run for their lives.'

This was the same Surve who Raje had pardoned and asked to take care of Sangameshwar. He had taken good care, no doubt! Raje decided to go back to Sangameshwar.

Tanaji got the news of Raje's arrival and went to meet him. Shivaji was pleased by the way Tanaji and his men had repulsed the attack. He asked, 'Tanaji, where is Pilajirao? I can't see him.'

Tanaji smiled. 'Raje, I have tied him to a boulder! He was running away scared and I had no option but to hold him.'

Everyone laughed, but Raje did not join in. He said, 'Bring Pilajirao here.'

Pilajirao came in, his head bent with shame. Pilaji was from the Nilkanthrao family of Purandar, who had been associated with Raje ever since he had taken over Purandar.

Pilajirao bent in mujra and Raje patted his back and said, 'Pilajirao, there is no need to feel ashamed. It is quite normal to feel fear when one faces the enemy for the first time. When I killed Afzal and returned to the camp, I was still shaking with fear. Tanaji, let there be one more opportunity and you will see how Pilaji fights like a tiger. I am sure of this.'

Changing the topic, he asked, 'Where is Surve now?'

'He is at Shringarpur. Raje, we did not have your orders or I would have already taught him a lesson.'

'Tanaji, we can do that any day. But the Surves and Sawants are our people. We need to give them an opportunity to reform themselves.'

'They have been given enough opportunities but look at the way they have shown their loyalty!'

'Have patience, Tanaji.'

Raje sent his messenger to Surves with the message, 'Suryarao, I am deeply hurt that you have attacked the cantonment without provocation. This behaviour is unpardonable, but I am letting it go. You have also given shelter to Jaswantrao who betrayed us. I am planning to capture his territory. I ask you to meet me at Pali the moment you get this message. All will be pardoned then.'

Shivaji had sent the note with the best intentions because he was keen to get Surve on his side. Surve sent a reply saying, 'You go ahead and I will join you.'

Shivaji marched to Pali and his troops captured Pali without any opposition. The fort of Chitradurg was renamed Mandangad. Pali was taken over but there was no news of Suryarao yet.

Shivaji lost his patience and said, 'Surve is getting too big for his boots!'

Tanaji agreed and exclaimed, 'You are absolutely right! There is no point in being nice to them. They need to be treated like cattle. What about Jaswantrao?'

Raje smiled and said, 'Jaswantrao? When the Surves are taken care of, where is the question of Jaswantrao surviving? Tanaji, let me tell you an old fable from the Puranas: Takshaka, the snake king thought he could hide behind Indra when Janamejaya was performing the sarpa yagna. He did not realize that Janamajeya would give orders to burn Takshaka to ashes along with Indra. Jaswantrao and his Indra, Surve, are both going to face the same fate!'

It was summer and the Konkan region was boiling in the humid heat. Raje and his troops marched towards Prabhavali without any resistance on the way. Once Raje moved towards Pali, Surve thought that his troubles were over. He disbanded his troops and was at ease. However, he soon received the news of Shivaji's march towards them and both Jaswantrao and Surve lost their nerve. They took their personal belongings and ran away from Shringarpur.

On hearing of their escape, Shivaji exclaimed, 'Cowards!'

He entered Shringarpur and reached the palace, marching through empty streets. The troops took charge of the palace and Shivaji kicked the throne lying vacant in the durbar hall in disgust and said, 'That coward Surve does not need this anymore.'

Trayambak Bhaskar was put in charge of the town and Shivaji left for Rajgad.

Shivaji was surprised to find Soyarabai in his chamber early in the morning.

'Maa saheb is waiting for you,' she said. Shivaji came to Maa saheb's chamber to find her drowned in anxiety. She said, 'A short while ago I got the news of Mankoji being taken seriously ill.

Shivaji said, 'I met him the day before. Yes, he did seem very tired.'

'He is not getting any younger and this rainy weather adds to his woes,' Jijabai added.

Shivaji went to Shivapur with Moropant and Mankoji was indeed looking weak. He held Shivaji's hand tightly and said, 'Raje, Khan's atrocities have increased greatly. We need to contain him.'

Shivaji was overwhelmed with emotions. Mankoji, despite his bad health, was worried about the Swaraj! He said, 'You get well first, Mankoji. We can care about these things later.'

'I don't think I will get better now. My age is catching up fast.'

'Don't talk like that! If people like you don't bless me, how will I accomplish my tasks? I need you with me!'

'Maharaj, I am quite confident of your capability but not of my own now. I am blessed by your visit. Please give my regards to Maa saheb.'

After giving instructions to the attending physician, Shivaji returned to the palace with a heavy heart.

Kanhoji had died long back. There were doubts about Mankoji's health. Dadoji, Kanhoji, Mankoji: they were Raje's three strong pillars. He wondered how he would manage without any of them.

Raje was lost in these thoughts as he reached the Devi temple, where he found Moropant waiting for him accompanied by a fair-skinned stranger. He was a man in his early thirties, sporting diamond studs in his ears. The man bent in mujra on seeing Shivaji.

'Moropant, do I know this man?'

Moropant replied respectfully, 'This is Kulkarni from the Mosa valley. He desires to have an appointment with you.'

Shivaji asked, 'Why do you want to meet me?'

Kulkarni folded his hands and said, 'Maharaj, I am unable to run my household. We are three brothers but none are married as we do not have any money. We are Brahmins and hence cannot beg. I was hoping that you could give me a job in your office—it would be a great obligation on my family. You will be blessed for having helped a poor Brahmin.'

Raje listened to the youth without interrupting and said, 'You are a Kulkarni, isn't it? What happened to your pay from the royal treasury?'

The Kulkarnis were part of the administration and were given hereditary rights over the part of revenue they collected on behalf of the Swaraj. Their duties were to collect revenue, levies and taxes from the area given to them and credit the same to the royal treasury. To protect their respective areas they would also maintain a small troop of soldiers. The income, mostly extracted from agricultural land or area given to them as a vatan, was offered towards their remuneration.

The youth was scared the moment he heard the question. He said, 'Maharaj, I do not have a complaint against anyone. I have got what I deserved. I just wish to serve under you.'

'What happened to your vatandari?' Shivaji's voice was stern now. 'Answer me without hesitation!'

Kulkarni took a deep breath and said, 'Maharaj, while it is true that we are Kulkarnis, the debts taken by my father are a burden on us. The interest is so high that we had to pledge our Kulkarni and Joshi titles and our pay to the moneylenders. We are homeless today thanks to the debt.'

Raje smiled. He said, staring at the youth, 'It is quite an ironic mix of the moneylender's grip and your family's casual attitude. Who is this shrewd moneylender of yours?'

Kulkarni was afraid of that precise question. He knew that he could not avoid it and said, 'Maharaj, I don't hold a grudge against anyone.'

Raje said, his voice rising, 'Tell me the name of the sahukar.'

Kulkarni had no option but to divulge the name, 'He is your Peshwa, Shamrao Nilkanth. He has the lien over my title.'

Raje was taken aback on hearing the Peshwa's name. He looked at Moropant but saw him looking down, avoiding his gaze. Raje said to Moropant, 'Meet me privately.'

That evening, when Moropant presented himself, Shivaji said, 'Moropant, look into this matter and get to the bottom of it. But do it discreetly.'

Shivaji was upset for the next four or five days. Jijabai was quick to notice and asked, 'Why do you seem so preoccupied?'

'Maa saheb, you know how much I hate this vatandari system. I am trying desperately to abolish it and let the people live in peace. And now I find that my own men are enjoying the old system. What should I do?'

'If the accusations are true, you cannot have such men serve under you,' Jijabai said, without a moment of hesitation.

Raje turned to look at Jijabai. He was smiling.

'Maa saheb, I am always happy when I talk to you about my problems.'

Within a few days, Moropant reported back. Raje called an emergency meeting and in the evening, the Peshwa, Amatya, Dabir and other officials came in. Netaji and Yesaji Kank too were invited. Everyone was wondering why Raje had called for such an urgent meeting and they were waiting for Raje to arrive.

However, Shamrao Nilkanth Peshwa seemed distinctly uncomfortable. He knew something was amiss. He had just returned from a campaign at Janjira where he had been routed badly by Siddi Khairyat.

Shivaji came into the durbar looking grim. He said, 'This meeting is in honour of our Peshwa Shamraopant.'

Everyone turned towards Shamraopant.

He said, adjusting his coat, 'Maharaj, you called for the meeting for me?'

'Yes! You know how to manage money and are an old hand at it. When I have a doubt who else should I reach out for?'

Shamraopant did not know how to respond and kept quiet.

'I hate this vatandari system. I am trying my best to eliminate it and here you are, encouraging it?'

Shamraopant recoiled in fear. He said, desperately trying to defend himself, 'Maharaj, you are mistaken. Someone seems to have complained falsely against me.'

'Shamraopant, don't lie to me. I know that you had your eyes on the Kulkarnis of Mosa valley. Is it not true that you used your position as Peshwa to usurp and take charge of the rights there?'

Shamraopant pleaded, 'Maharaj, have mercy! I beg of you to pardon me and give me another chance. I am returning the vatandari right away.'

'Do you have a choice? Shamraopant, you returned from the Janjira campaign defeated by the enemy. I never said anything. You were trapped by Siddi's words and were captured. You managed to escape on the promise that you would not step into that territory again. That too I am willing to pardon. There are times when one has to deal with such situations. But this crime is unpardonable.'

'Maharaj!' Shamraopant beseeched.

Raje stared at Shamraopant, who looked despondent. He said, 'Shamraopant, you are our Peshwa. I am not Lord Indra and do not have a thousand eyes. I see through your eyes. I trust you to manage the affairs of the kingdom. But if you start behaving in a manner not befitting your post, then you have no option but to step away from such responsibilities. I don't think our people would be safe under your administration. I have decided to take away the responsibility with immediate effect.'

The bold decision was a surprise to everyone. Shamraopant looked up and said, a little agitated, 'Maharaj, I would request you to relieve me of office duties as well.'

Raje was unperturbed and said, 'Shamraopant, don't think you can use such pressure tactics. If you cannot manage the office affairs, that is your choice. Are you trying to embarrass me? I'd recommend you think twice—it will be impossible to get your office duties back once you give up your post.'

Shamraopant came to his senses and said, 'Maharaj, I am sorry. I made a mistake. I take back my words. Please pardon me.'

'I am appointing Narhari Anandrao as the Peshwa in place of Shamraopant. And Anandrao's position will be taken by Annaji Dattto. Shamraopant, you have been our Peshwa since the beginning. Taking that into consideration and in order to avoid a stain on your career as the Peshwa, your seal will be used de facto, but Narhari Anandrao will be the Peshwa de jure.'

Raje appointed Narhari Anandrao and Annaji Datto to their respective roles. The ceremony was carried out with an additional prerequisite of having a personal palanquin.

The news of Mankoji Dahatonde's death was indeed sad. Shivaji had grown up with Mankoji because this affectionate man had been the Senapati from the beginning. Shivaji instructed that Mankoji's last rites be performed in a manner befitting his status.

Shaista Khan had been sitting on his plans because of the rains but Raje knew that he could not relax. Shaista Khan was disgusted with the small and irritating attacks by the Marathas across the state. The defeat of Kahar Talab Khan too rankled in his mind. He sent his sardar Namdar Khan to attack Kalyan–Bhiwandi.

The moment Shivaji heard the news, he marched forward with Krishnaji Babaji and Vaghoji Tupe. He met Khan at the ridge near Pen and the sudden attack made Khan's troops run for their lives. But Krishnaji was killed in battle while Tupe was wounded, forcing the Marathas to retreat. Shivaji knew that though there was no clear victory, the enemy had been greatly demoralized and intimidated which, for the time being, was a moderate success in itself.

The constant presence of the Mughals was a disturbance to the ryots, who were losing their cattle and sheep by the dozen. Within no time, people began migrating to the Konkan region for fear of losing their lives. Shivaji's heart wrenched at the thought of people moving away from their homes and land, and he could not sit by and merely watch. He was desperate to find a way to rout Khan.

The East India Company, on the other hand, continued to make demands for Shivaji to release their men captured in Rajapur. Shivaji had released Revington earlier due to bad health but he did not survive very long, and three Englishmen had died in captivity. Shivaji decided to release the rest as he believed that the English had learned their lesson.

That summer, Raje received news that Netaji Palkar was wounded in a clash with Namdar Khan.

'They met near Supe,' Moropant explained. 'Netaji fought bravely but it was of no use. He had to retreat while Sarfaraj Khan and Namdar Khan chased him and managed to capture three hundred horses.'

'Where is he now?'

'He is arriving here in a palanquin.'

Sounding exasperated, Shivaji exclaimed, 'What do I do with this man! He has a mad streak of bravado in him and does not think twice before attacking.'

The physician came in and gave his diagnosis—though he had lost a lot of blood, Netaji would be fine.

Shivaji went to see Netaji the next day. Seeing Raje, Netaji tried to get up. Shivaji rushed forward and held his arm saying, 'You are not supposed to move!'

Netaji had tears in his eyes. Shivaji gently wiped the tears and said, 'Kaka, you are my Senapati! Tears do not suit you. You lost some horses and had to retreat. Why do you feel so bad? I have said this often: I am not enamoured by victory or defeat. What I admire is the perseverance. You have shown this quality and that's enough!'

Even though Shivaji had managed to reassure Netaji he knew that the defeat was difficult to swallow. There was enormous strain on the army. On top of it, the spies got the news that the people at Kondana were likely to stage a revolt. It had been more than three years since Shivaji had managed to rout the Mughals anywhere effectively. And thus, Shivaji's thirty-third birthday was celebrated amidst such worries.

A few weeks later, it was Gudi Padwa, the Marathi New Year, and Rajgad was decorated all over with traditional gudis. They shone brightly against the sky, bright cloths fluttering in the wind. Jijabai called Raje for the puja. While sprinkling the traditional rice, he wiped his eyes.

Jijabai asked, 'What is the matter, Raje?'

'I was remembering someone.'

'Who were you thinking of?'

'Who else could I be thinking of now? Thanks to my weakness, my subjects are roaming homeless in the forests. I wonder how they would be celebrating Gudi Padwa today.'

He got up and, without speaking another word, returned to his quarters.

'Maa saheb is talking to someone called Gyanu. She asked you to come meet him as well.'

Raje had just finished his puja and entered his chamber when Soyarabai came looking for him. He said, 'Gyanu the gardener? You should have told me sooner!' He left without waiting for answer, leaving Soyarabai astonished.

As Raje entered Jijabai's chamber, Gyanu rushed forward to touch his feet. Shivaji asked, 'Gyanu, what brings you here today?'

'Maharaj, we can leave only when we are thrown out of our jobs. Otherwise, we are prisoners.'

'Prisoners? What are you saying, Gyanu?'

'I am still a gardener in the Pune palace, but I cannot leave the palace without asking for permission.'

'Then how did you manage to come here?'

'I told them that my child was unwell and I had to see him. I had to meet you. My Raje may have forgotten me but how I can I forget him?'

Gyanu was an old man, nearly sixty years old, but he stood ramrod straight.

Shivaji asked, 'Gyanu, how is your garden?'

'Raje, Khan has despoiled the palace completely. Do you remember the puja room? Khan sits there and eats whatever he wants! He has converted your quarters into his harem. The mogra flowers meant for the Lord are being used to decorate the concubines. In place of shlokas, one hears dancing and songs now. Raje, Pune has lost its glory.'

Raje was visibly disturbed. He merely said, 'Each dog has its day, Gyanu.'

'I don't know what you mean, Raje. All of Pune has been turned into a cantonment. We do not see our own men anymore. Beef is being taken into the palace—right in front of the Ganesha temple! What can a man do when he sees such blasphemous acts? I could not watch it anymore and that's why I came here. I hope you don't mind my bluntness.'

'Gyanu, I understand how you feel, and I am sure we will find a way out.'

'My lord, we cannot wait for these things to happen on their own. Rise up and finish off Shaista Khan. He is not an elephant—he is a lazy, fat bull. Catch him by the horns and kill him.'

Shivaji, looking at Gyanu as if he had heard some secret, said, 'Come, Gyanu. Let us go and speak in my quarters.'

They sat alone together for a long time. When Shivaji left his chambers in the afternoon, he had a strange glint in his eyes. Gyanu the gardener returned to Pune that evening.

Two months had passed since then. Netaji Palkar had recovered and was able to walk now. Shivaji's spies sent regular updates from Pune regarding the timings of the change of the guards at Lal Mahal, the number of soldiers deputed on patrol and other such details. While Raje did not discuss his plans, everyone knew that something big was being planned.

A month before Dussehra, Firangoji came in to make his report.

'Firangoji, what is the news?' Shivaji asked.

'The day fixed is for ashtami. The daughter of the havaldar of Pune is getting married.'

'Shivba! What is going on? What marriage are you talking about?' Jijabai asked.

Shivaji smiled but was silent.

Turning to Firangoji, Jijabai said, 'Raje does not answer my questions these days. He is detached and preoccupied, only going around the fort with his men and talking to them for hours. I see the spies coming in every day but Raje does not tell me anything. I am not privy ...'

'You are exaggerating, Maa saheb,' Raje said, smiling. 'I will tell you the moment I finalize something.'

'What plans?'

'I have decided to attack the Lal Mahal Palace.'

'Lal Mahal?' Jijabai asked. 'With the entire city of Pune full of Khan's men?'

'That might be so,' Raje said, 'but we are not going to attack the city. We are going to attack Khan.'

'But how?'

'It is possible, Maa saheb, with your blessings. I have realized that Khan sends his sardars out of town on campaigns but does not himself step out of Pune. Even when I routed Mahabat Khan, Shaista Khan did not step out to take revenge. He has rendered scores of our people homeless, who are now forced to roam around in jungles. And other people like Sambhaji Kavji have fallen prey to the lure of riches and have joined forces with him.'

'And so you have decided to go down this route?'

'There is no other choice! I defeated Kahar Talab Khan and Namdar Khan with no effect on Khan. Each passing day is adding to our losses, and it won't be long before we lose Konkan.'

After a pause, he continued, 'Khan would never dream of entering Lal Mahal. If I kill Khan, his troops will run for their lives, and we will get back what we lost.'

Jijabai was lost in thought.

Shivaji said, pleading for her approval, 'Maa saheb, do you not agree?'

'Raje, I am not against the idea, but the thought of you entering the palace, amidst all the soldiers, is very disturbing.'

'Why do you think I will be alone? I will have Tanaji, Firangoji, Sarjerao and my guards.'

Jijabai smiled. 'Raje, don't try to pacify me. With more than a lakh soldiers in the Pune cantonment, the idea of storming the palace to kill Khan sounds ludicrous.'

Firangoji said, 'Maa saheb, we are willing to take the risk but Raje is not convinced. He wants to lead the attack himself.'

'Maa saheb,' Shivaji said, continuing his argument, 'no one knows Lal Mahal better than me. No one else can do this job. I was blessed by the Devi in my dreams and I have no doubt that I will return victorious.'

Jijabai took a deep breath and said, 'Raje, I am convinced that you will accomplish whatever you have put your mind to, but the mother in me is always afraid. I won't stand in your way but remember—I will be waiting for you.'

Raje said, his voice choked with emotion, 'Maa saheb, I understand how you feel—a mother always grabs a child in fear instinctively. But very rarely does one have the good fortune of having a mother who supports her child, despite the dangers in fulfilling one's duty. I am blessed to have been born to you.'

Taking a pause, Shivaji continued with renewed confidence, 'I will enter Pune on ashtami, after a brief halt at Kondana.'

'But what about Ram Navami?'

'I will celebrate the victory at Kondana that day. Maa saheb, the month of Ramadan is also beginning. The fasting soldiers will be tired and sleepy in the night after their dinner. The guards will be relaxed.'

Firangoji exclaimed, 'Raje, we never thought of this!'

'It is not enough to think of the strength of your troops when attacking an enemy. We need to take into account festivals, traditions and the other nuances of the enemy's culture. If someone makes the mistake of attacking a Maratha during Dussehra, he should not be surprised if he is repulsed strongly!'

There was no time to lose now, and Shivaji got busy finalizing the plans for the attack.

It was Panchami in March, when Raje took Jijabai's blessings and marched from Rajgad towards Kondana. The sun burnt fiercely and not a leaf stirred. The horses frothed at the mouth, with the exhaustion of the long march adding to their thirst. Raje was accompanied by Netaji, Firangoji, Balaji, Chimnaji and Moropant. The men were not aware of the intricate details of the plan except for the fact that they were on an important mission, and Tanaji and Yesaji waited with their men at Kondana.

The moment they reached Kondana, each man was given his specific responsibilities and tasks to carry out. Raje opened the discussion with his plans for attacking Khan. Only Firangoji was aware of the plan in advance, and everyone was excited on hearing the plan.

Tanaji said, 'Maharaj! It is a wonderful plan! This old man has been getting bored just sitting here!'

'Khan would not even dream that we would plan such a thing,' Balaji commented.

'I agree, Balaji, and it is not an easy task. Even if one person fails or hesitates, each one of us will die. Tanaji!'

'Ji, Maharaj?'

'You leave tomorrow. Keep your men ready to be part of a marriage procession at Katraj. You have to enter Pune in the afternoon with the requisite pomp and show, and Mahadev will be with you. Is that understood?'

'Yes.'

'And Yesaji, you have to enter the city with the carts before nightfall. If you are questioned, you should answer saying you are bringing carts with hay. Vithoji?'

'Yes?'

'Keep a hundred bullocks ready in the valley with torches tied to their horns. The moment you hear the trumpets at midnight, light the torches and move towards the fort.'

'Maharaj, what about you?' asked Firangoji.

'Moropant and Netaji will wait with their men at the designated place, and Sarjerao Jedhe, Balaji and Chimnaji will accompany me.'

Balaji and Chimnaji were thrilled on hearing that they would be accompanying Raje.

'Balaji and Chimnaji, you are my childhood friends and we grew up together in Lal Mahal. No one else knows the palace as well as we do. Firangoji, you need to hold fort here, is that understood?'

Firangoji was upset at not being a part of the action at Lal Mahal. He nodded half-heartedly and replied, 'Yes, Maharaj.'

'There is no need to be upset, Firangoji. When I return, I expect Khan's men to be in pursuit. Keep your men ready—along with the cannons, they will be a great help.'

Raje had meticulously planned the entry of all the men and how they were to introduce themselves if questioned. The excitement among the Marathas was palpable.

The next day, the marriage procession reached the checkpoint at Katraj. A groom was sitting astride a horse while a hundred-odd men danced to the beat of drums. They had swords at their waists and were enjoying the festivities. The guards, after a cursory glance at the procession, waved them in.

At the same time, a group of horsemen entered Pune from the other side of the river. The guards challenged them and asked, 'Who goes there?'

'We are Jadhav's men. We are returning after some reconnaissance.'

Jadhav's camp was on the other side of the town and the horsemen were allowed to enter the city without further questioning. At two o'clock in the afternoon, a few bullock carts arrived at the Katraj checkpoint. The carts were loaded with hay, and a few horsemen escorted the carts. On seeing the guards enquiring, the havaldar shouted from his cabin, 'Can't you see they are carrying hay? Let them in and don't waste your time!'

The carts entered the gates without any obstacles and the same scene was played out with the guards at the Kota gate. No one suspected anything.

Shivaji sat in a small hut in the woods close to the Katraj checkpoint. He could see the dense forests spread all over. Shivaji was accompanied by Ibrahim Khan, a Pathan, and his men. They were a part of the plan to raid

Shaista Khan. The Pathans, accompanying Raje, were tall and handsome and were a formidable presence. The forest was quiet in the hot sun—the birds too were quiet that afternoon. From afar, the deep call of a Bharadwaj bird pierced the silence.

Clouds were gathering on the eastern horizon. A light wind started blowing, soon increasing in intensity and the call of the peacocks could be heard. Suddenly, the winds turned cold and flashes of lightning streaked across the sky, illuminating the ground for a few moments. Without warning, there was a shower of hail stones.

Shivaji, watching the dance of nature, said, 'This storm reminds me of the night I was fighting Rustam Zaman at Kolhapur. All you could hear were the rumbling of the cannons, the clanging of the swords, the raining of bullets from the guns and the continuous beat of the horse hooves.'

After a while, the rains stopped. The thunder continued and the lightning flashed occasionally. Mahadev came in and reported, 'Everything is going as per plan. No one has been stopped and they all have reached Pune.'

Within a few minutes of the sunset, the forest was covered in darkness while flashes of lightning continued to illuminate the eastern sky intermittently. Raje put on his chest armour, wearing a long coat over it. He had his head armour on below his head gear. The Bhawani sword looked magnificent hanging on his left side while a small dagger and a knife were tied on to his right side.

The Pathan sardar Ibrahim Khan displayed a charismatic persona, wearing a bright-red turban crowned with a diamond-studded gold leaf. He wore an embroidered long coat and equally elaborately embellished trousers. A sword and dagger were tied to the side of his waist.

Raje said, 'Ibrahim, you are my sardar now, and I am your servant—is that understood?'

'Ji, Huzoor.'

'Come on, let us go.'

Raje said a prayer to Bhawani Mata and the horses moved in the darkness of the night. As soon as they reached the main road, Raje ordered the torches to be lit. The torches were held in long brass holders and burnt brightly in the wind. The two men holding the torches near Ibrahim Khan led the group. Soon, they reached the checkpoint.

Ibrahim raised his hand for the troops to stop as soon as he reached the checkpoint and, with his hand on the waist, shouted at the chowkidar, 'How many of you are here?'

'Nearly fifty men, Huzoor,' the chowkidar replied, unsure who the man on the horse was. He assumed it must be one of Shaista Khan's important sardars returning to Pune.

'Be vigilant. Understand?'

'Ji, Huzoor.'

Ibrahim spurred his horse and the men moved forward. The guards heaved a sigh of relief when the horsemen vanished in the darkness ahead.

It was late in the night when the group reached Pune. The soft light of the ashtami moon spread across the land. The guards at the gate heard the horses and came out adjusting their guns. One of the guards asked, 'Who goes there?'

One of Ibrahim's men stepped forward and slapped the guard hard, shouting, 'Badtameez! Don't you recognize Khan saheb?'

The other guards hastily bent in mujras and salaams. The road was now clear. Ibrahim moved forward in a casual yet dignified manner as if nothing had happened. There was silence everywhere except for the intermittent warnings of the guards parading the area. Most of the Mughal troops were tired after the day-long Ramadan fast and were fast asleep after a heavy meal.

Any guard encountering the group would salute and mutter 'Parwadigaar' before moving away. The Maratha plan seemed to be working well and finally they reached the town near the Lal Mahal that was surrounded by the guards. Raje dismounted near Gyanu's cottage and knocked on the door and it was opened immediately.

There was a total lull in the courtyard of the palace. A few minutes ticked by.

In the garden, one of the guards asked, 'Who goes there?'

'It is me, Gyanu the gardener,' Gyanu replied.

The guard came forward, unaware of the danger lurking around. Mahadev, standing behind Raje, took out his dagger. There was a slight scraping noise of the dagger cutting across skin, and Gyanu quickly rushed forward to cover the guard's mouth. There was not a sound as the guard went limp and fell to the ground.

From the kitchen, the noise of the utensils being washed could be heard. It was the cook, busy preparing the troops' pre-dawn meal so that they may begin their fast. Raje indicated with his finger, pointing at the kitchen, and five men stealthily entered it. The cooks were dead before they realized what had happened to them and the noise of the utensils stopped within moments.

Gyanu came back with a ladder and pointing to a window which seemed shut, he said, 'I have loosened the hinges. Just push it gently.'

Raje looked at Mahadev, who climbed up the ladder and pushed the window, which opened with a loud, grating noise. Everyone stood rigid, fearing the worst. Mahadev came down and Raje indicated to Balaji and Chimnaji to move forward. They went in first, followed by Raje and the others.

Raje knew the palace well. The room they had entered was once his bedroom. There were curtains all over and many small corners had been created for Khan's wives. Khan's begums and their handmaidens were asleep while a lamp burnt brightly. A few women had woken up hearing the noise and were stunned to see strangers brandishing swords in the room. The men were taken by surprise by the half-naked women who were staring at them.

Suddenly, one of the women screamed, her voice piercing the stillness of the night as it reverberated across the palace rooms. The scream was cut short as a sword sliced her neck. One of the maids showed the presence of her mind and rushed to snuff out the lamp and more screams erupted as soon as the lamp was shut. Raje's men struggled to stifle the noise. Raje did not waste time and moved ahead, slicing through the curtains in search of Khan.

Khan woke up to the sounds of the screaming and picked up the gun on a table nearby. One of Raje's soldiers collapsed as Khan opened fire. Khan was about to jump out of the window when his begum snuffed out the lamp. There was noise of screaming and screeching in the darkness. Shivaji's men tried to stop the screams and went on tearing the curtains in search of Shaista Khan. The watchmen and the guards who came their way were slaughtered. Raje saw Khan near the window and attacked him with his sword but was not sure if his blow had been fatal. He heard Khan shriek and then disappear in the darkness.

The entire palace was in chaos. Khan's son, Abdul Fateh, rushed to save his father and was killed instantly. Shivaji signalled his men and the trumpeters at the door began to sound their trumpets. Raje's men reached the town square and announced their victory.

Ibrahim's men were waiting for the signal and Shivaji's men guarding the palace attacked the guards posted there and killed them quickly. Shivaji stepped out of the palace and mounted a waiting horse, to gallop as fast as possible out of the city.

Ibrahim, fooling Khan's men, shouted out orders, 'Khan saheb is dead. The enemy has run away. Chase them. Catch them!'

The men galloped in the direction Ibrahim pointed. Ibrahim, along with his men, galloped shouting, 'Catch them. The enemy has escaped.' The cantonment was in an uproar. Raje's men too followed the troops in the front shouting, 'Catch them. Kill them!'

Raje's men blew the trumpet the moment they came out of the city. The trumpets in the forests reciprocated the signal.

At one of the gates, the guard was asked by Khan's sardar, 'Did the enemy escape from here?'

'No, Huzoor!'

Khan's sardar was confused. At that moment, one of the men pointed in the direction of the forest saying, 'Huzoor, look!'

The sardar looked in the indicated direction to see flaming torches moving in the forest. His anger boiled over and he unsheathed his sword and screamed, 'Traitor!'

The sardar ordered his men to chase the torches and Raje's men followed the sardar for a while, who simply assumed that they must be his own men. At a turn in the forest, Raje's men moved towards Kondana while the sardar and his own men continued to chase the burning torches deeper into forest, eager to capture the enemy. To their surprise, when they finally overtook the burning torches, they realized they had been fooled. They had been chasing the bullocks with torches tied to their horns while they had assumed all the while for them to be Maratha soldiers. He knew he had been outwitted.

Dawn was breaking over the eastern sky on the day of Ram Navami as Shivaji reached Kondana. He folded his hands in obeisance at the rising sun.

The Lal Mahal Palace, once a place of pride for Khan, was in ruins. The begums sat beating their chests around Abdul Fateh's dead body. The bodies of the dead begums, maids and other guards were lined up covered with cloth. Shaista Khan was wounded in the attack and three of the fingers on his right hand had been cut. He looked at the hand as it was being bandaged by the royal hakim. The sudden attack in the dead of the night had shaken him deeply.

The cantonment had not recovered from the attack either. No one could believe that Shivaji had had the temerity to attack Lal Mahal. Khan called for an urgent meeting of his sardars, and blamed their lackadaisical attitude for the attack. Shaista Khan was a worried man; he did not know how he would face the emperor now. He was related to Aurangzeb and he knew that the emperor would find Shivaji's audacity an affront to the Mughal throne itself. Without wasting time, Khan decided to attack Kondana.

Shivaji, anticipating such a move, had ordered the gates of the fort to be left open. No one, and not even the Maratha flag, was seen on the ramparts when Khan's troops reached the fort. Seeing the open doors and an apparently unprotected fort, Khan's men decided to enter without fear. They assumed Shivaji and his men had run away in fear of Khan's retribution. The Mughal troops reached the fort led by an elephant carrying the Mughal flag.

As they began the steep climb, they were suddenly surprised by shouts of 'Har Har Mahadev!' echoing all around. They could not believe their eyes when a saffron flag all at once fluttered from the fort. Soon, the cannons erupted. Scared of the booming cannons, the elephant leading the troops, tried to turn back. Shivaji surveyed the battle below as he stood on the ramparts with a smile on his face.

Shaista Khan heard of the fate his men met at Kondana. Unable to believe that they had been deceived, he now viewed each one of them with suspicion. He screamed at the assembly of his sardars and said, 'I cannot believe Shivaji could come walking into my palace without the involvement of my own men. He's had the guts to come straight into my bedroom and attack me! The next time, he will simply cut my throat! I am done with this city—I am leaving Pune!'

Khan began preparations to move to Aurangabad, and within three days he had left Pune, ordering Jaswant Singh to stay behind.

After taking care of the men wounded in the attack on Lal Mahal, Shivaji left for Rajgad. He was disappointed to hear that the attack on Shaista Khan had not been completely successful and had left Khan merely wounded. Jijabai, however, was very happy to see Shivaji return safely.

Within eight days of attacking Shaista Khan, Raje marched towards Konkan and captured Rajapur, Kudal, Vengurla and other territories, finally reaching the sea. The rains had begun and there was news of the Mughal forces having reached Mahad. Raje decided to turn back. There was not much to gain monetarily in this campaign but Raje had managed to increase his influence in the Konkan region and establish his superiority over the Kudal Sawants. He returned to Rajgad in the rains.

Shaista Khan's three-year reign in Pune had destroyed the Pune province. The villages were deserted as the farmers and peasants had moved to the Konkan region. Jaswant Singh continued to hold on to Pune while Raje was unable to collect the kind of revenue he wanted from the Konkan region. His finances were stretched with the burden of an ever-expanding cavalry and army of foot soldiers. It was necessary to find ways to increase revenues and a campaign was the dire need of the hour. The only question was—where should they attack?

One of the sardars suggested, 'How about Karnatak?'

Raje shook his head and said, 'We don't want to upset Adil Shah. Shaista Khan will attack us again someday for revenge, and we cannot afford to have Adil Shah against us at that time.'

'Then what should we do?' Jijabai asked.

'Jagdamba will show us the way,' Shivaji sighed.

That evening, Bahirji came to see Raje, who told him, 'Bahirji, I have some work for you. I want the Mughals to compensate the monetary loss they have caused us.' The next day, Raje spent a long time with Bahirji who left the fort late in the afternoon.

It had been four months since Bahirji's departure when one afternoon Yesaji, Tanaji and Netaji came to Rajgad. Netaji said, 'Tanaji, Raje seems to be making a big plan.'

Tanaji replied, 'I think so. Raje has summoned the troops and there have been messages going all around. He inspected the cantonment personally last evening.'

'But I am unable to understand what the plan is,' Netaji commented.

Raje was waiting in the office. He had with him Prataprao Sarnobat, Anandrao, Moropant, Nilopant, Annajipant and others.

Raje said, as soon as everyone was seated, 'Netaji, we are leaving tomorrow.'

'Where are we going, Maharaj?' Netaji asked.

'We have an opportunity to make peace with the Mughals. We can help Aurangzeb by supporting Mahabat Khan at Patan. It is a good opportunity to keep Aurangzeb at bay for a while.'

It was disappointing news for those who had assembled. They were unable to understand Raje's urgency in helping the Badshah. Shivaji did not elaborate further and left the room.

That evening, as Raje entered Jijabai's quarters, she asked, 'Raje, I am told that you are going to help Mahabat Khan.'

Asking Mahadev to stand guard outside, Shivaji entered Jijabai's quarters and said, 'Maa saheb, I cannot afford to bear the strain of the expenses anymore. Shaista Khan drove our people out of their homes. I need enormous amounts of money to get them back.'

'But where do you plan to get the money from?'

'I have found a source—it has an unlimited supply of wealth. I am going to slake my thirst from this spring.'

'Don't speak in riddles!'

'Maa saheb, I am going to attack Surat.'

'Surat?'

'You heard me right! Surat is a cash cow for the Mughals. Their revenue is in lakhs just on account of taxes. It is the main port from where the Haj pilgrims leave for Mecca. I have decided to loot Surat and reduce our debts.'

'Raje, isn't that Mughal territory? And also, Surat is so far away!'

'For the past four months, my spies have been sending me information. Surat is safely ensconced in Mughal territory, but with no forts and soldiers guarding it. Surat is like a Mughal queen roaming freely in the royal gardens without any fear. They would never dream of an attack there.'

'Do you expect any trouble on the way?'

'I don't think so. Shahzada Muazzam is preparing to face me in Aurangabad as per the information his spies have given him as I have deliberately created that impression. The Portuguese at Goa fear an attack from us at any moment and are scared to death. The Adil Shahi troops are constantly alert.'

'You have managed this well! Your own Senapati is not aware of your plans. Don't you trust him?'

'Don't mistake me, Maa saheb. This is not a lack of trust—I am just being very cautious. Our spies are aware of my plans. They are, as we speak, spread across Surat, waiting for us. Our ships are moving into position around Surat and we have no time to lose now. I know the burden of managing a campaign all alone, and of a thousand men willing to lay down their lives at my command.'

Jijabai said, as she stood up, 'Raje, take care and come back victorious. We will be waiting for you.'

'Maa saheb, I will win this battle in a manner that will be unsurpassed. I am going to recover all our past losses. The wealth we capture will blind your eyes with its shine and our strength will multiply manifold. I can just imagine the smile on your face when I return.'

They came out of the palace and Mahadev stood guard at the door.

Jijabai asked, 'Is Mahadev accompanying you?'

'Yes, of course! He has become my shadow—how can I go without him?'

The next morning, the fort woke to the sound of trumpets blaring. The bugles and horns followed as Raje left Rajgad. It was a cold winter morning as they descended from the fort, and a contingent of eight thousand foot soldiers began their march towards Surat. Raje reached Trimbakeshwar and moved further after darshan at the temple. They would halt in the jungles during the day and march at night. The Maratha troops made remarkable progress without a word to the outside world.

The lovely fort at Surat sat perched on the banks of the Tapti River. It was a small but strong fort and the town of Surat, fanned out behind the fort, was on flat land. There was no boundary wall encircling the town, which spread over a mile both in length and breadth. There were a few moats around the fort, dug long ago, but they had not been used for ages now. Surat was flanked by the ocean on one side and the mighty Mughal empire on other. There was no need for any other protection.

Aurangzeb received an annual tax revenue of ten lakhs from Surat each year as Surat was the business centre of the country. Englishmen, Turks and many other foreigners had set up their trade in Surat. The Mughal sardar Inayat Khan ruled over Surat without a care in the world. The Englishman James Oxenden had a camp set up on the other side of the river, and he had an office near the mouth of the river. The smaller boats would bring in goods from the larger ships on the river. Similarly, goods from India would leave by the same route. And so, all the rich traders had huge homes along the riverside.

The watchman in the watchtower was basking in the warm morning sun, and there was a nip in the air. The harbour was silent as there was not much traffic that morning. The harbour was closely guarded by the Mughal troops who collected taxes for all goods entering and leaving the port.

A casual labourer, called a Momin colloquially, stood near the octroi post stood when a guard asked, 'Momin, why are you standing here?'

The Momin replied, 'I wonder if there will be much work.'

'There isn't much work expected today. You may as well take a break.'

'I took leave yesterday too—not a ship in sight. I don't think I will make any money today.'

The guards laughed and the worker walked away slowly, smiling to himself.

In the meanwhile, Babul stood outside Oxenden's house, adjusting the saddle on a horse. He had come to Surat five months ago in search of work. The English saheb was happy with him and had given him work near the harbour. While Babul was busy shoeing the horse, a stable hand and two other servants came and stood near him. Hearing a noise, Babul stood up to see Oxenden saheb leaving for office. He saluted smartly.

'Babul, finish your work fast. The poor animal is waiting for the other shoe to be fixed.'

The stable hand suddenly asked, 'Babul, there used to be a beggar here. I don't see him anymore'

Babul was taken aback for a moment and asked, 'Which beggar?'

'The one who used to sit there under that tree,' he said pointing in the same direction.'

Babul said, as if he was trying to remember, 'Oh, that fellow? I shooed him away. I allowed him to sit there out of sympathy, but he was trying to steal from the stables.'

The stable hand laughed. The beggar had become friends with everyone in the last four months, and would be seen in each corner of the city. But he had now vanished.

Babul finished fixing the shoe and got up, admiring the horse, and asked casually, 'Looks like there are no ships in the port today.'

'What have you got to do with it?'

'We have to take care of our families. We need money. If there is no cargo to unload, we do not earn our day's wages. We cannot manage a living by hammering horse shoes alone.'

The stable hand smiled and said, 'You are right, brother. But I went to the wharf this morning and there aren't going to be any ships today or for the next two days. Anyway, I will see you later.'

'And what about my money?'

A few days later, Babul stood at a crossroad in town when a shadow fell on him. He lifted his head to see Ramsharan standing there. He seemed tired.

'What happened, Ramsharan?'

'I am tired of working at the oil extraction plant.'

'Why?'

'My head reels seeing the bullock go round and round. I am going round in circles even in my sleep.' He looked around and continued, 'Virji Hora's goods are expected to arrive in a few days hopefully. Anyway, I will go home now.'

It was late afternoon when two riders were seen galloping towards the Subedar's house.

Subedar Inayat Khan was enjoying a lovely siesta when he was woken up. An irritated Inayat Khan waited for the spies to present themselves. He rested his head against the large cushions and stifling a yawn, asked, 'What is it?'

'Huzoor, Shivaji has reached Gandevi. He has a huge army with him.'

Inayat Khan was wide awake. Shivaji? In Gandevi? That was just a few miles away. Impossible! Inayat smiled, 'You fool! How can you imagine that Shivaji would care to come into Mughal territory? Have you seen with your own eyes?'

'No, Huzoor. But I saw the way people were running about and the kind of confusion created in Gandevi. I came to inform you immediately.'

'Idiots! Shivaji could not have come this far through Mughal territory without being questioned or stopped earlier. Henceforth, don't come to me with such baseless news.'

The spies left but the news of Shivaji's arrival spread among the townsfolk. By evening, there was more news—Shivaji was a mere mile away from Surat. Inayat Khan was worried now and another rider brought still more news, 'Huzoor, one of our sardars has left for Ahmedabad to get help from the Mughal forces.'

Inayat Khan was happy with this piece of news but the city was tense. People gathered at various places and whispered among themselves. The English and other representatives of the traders and merchants came to Inayat Khan's place for a meeting and requested permission to move away from the city.

Inayat Khan said, 'You are here for the benefits of trade and when we are faced with impending danger, you want to run away, is it? If you desert the city, what would be our fate? You cannot leave and I too am going to stay right here.'

'But ....'

'I don't want to hear anything. Shivaji has not arrived and I am told that one sardar has already left for Ahmedabad to get help. There is no need to worry.'

The English and the Dutch officials had a tête-à-tête among themselves and decided to move their women and children to safety. They had heard of the way Shivaji had captured Rajapur. But soon, a messenger arrived to Inayat Khan's house and his man announced, 'Huzoor, Shivaji's messenger has come with a message.'

The messenger was ushered in. One of Inayat Khan's men read the letter:

'Before noon tomorrow Shivaji will reach your city. You are thus requested to hold discussions with the merchants Baharji Bohra, Haji Kasam and Syed Baig and decide the amount of money you will pay us. If you refuse, we will be forced to use our might to destroy your city.'

The foreigners looked at Inayat Khan in disgust and they stormed out of his palace, and the next morning Inayat Khan took shelter inside the fort with his family. He carried all his personal belongings and wealth with him. The moment the merchants heard of Khan's escape, they too ran towards the fort. Inayat Khan allowed them to enter the fort after collecting huge entry fees.

The Subedar had run away! The top merchants had followed suit. There was chaos everywhere. Where would the ordinary people go, the river and ocean on one side and Shivaji's eight-thousand-strong army on the other?

The English were preparing to fight their own battle. They wanted to protect their harbour at any cost. The cannons were readied and Oxenden decided to march with his two hundred men, surprising everyone and giving the locals some confidence. The men in the harbour were scared by seeing the people running around.

Seeing them making arrangements to leave, one of the chowkidars asked Babul, Ramsharan and Momin, 'What, you too are running away?'

'What do you expect? Shivaji ...'

'What is Shivaji going to do you? He has many rich men to plunder.'

'Our lives are precious and you are going to be in trouble.'

'Why do you say that?'

'Your sardar Inayat Khan has locked himself in the fort. You will face the Marathas first.'

'Go away!' the chowkidar said, feeling a little scared.

In a while the guards too vanished, finding their escape routes.

By noon, the sound of horses approaching Surat sounded like a sheet of torrential rain rapidly moving towards the city. Shivaji's eight-thousand cavalry pitched their camp just outside the city and a tent was pitched in the shade of a mango tree for Shivaji.

Raje looked in the direction of Surat. The white dome of the masjid was visible from a distance. Bahirji Naik came followed by Babul, Ramsharan and Momin who were really Vithoji Manke, Appa Ramoshi and Abdul Qadir. They bent in mujra as Raje asked, 'Vithoji, how is Surat treating you?'

'Maharaj, Surat is waiting for you!'

'Do we expect any resistance?'

'Who would resist? The Subedar is hiding in his fort, but the English are ready to attack.'

'How many of them?'

'Around two-hundred-odd.'

'And the Mughal forces?'

'None at all. There are no guards either!'

'We have sent a message for the ransom. If they agree, we need not loot the town. Let us wait.'

It was evening but there was no message from Surat. Shivaji said, 'Netaji, take five hundred men and go into the city. I want to strike fear in the hearts of the men when you loot the town. Let us see if this puts some sense into their heads. Moropant ...'

'Ji, Maharaj.' Moropant stepped forward.

'Send a letter to the Englishmen. Demand a ransom of three lakh rupees. Tell them that we do not have any enmity against them, and we are fighting the Mughals.'

Oxenden replied promptly and said, 'Tell Shivaji Raje that we are traders and do not have liquid cash. But we can pay in form of spices or cloth. You must promise not to destroy our goods. But if you try to harm the harbour or the godowns, we will retaliate. We await your reply.'

Raje smiled reading the message and said, 'Saheb seems to be large-hearted. He knows that we cannot carry loads of cloth or spices home. For the time being, don't touch the Englishmen. Scare the Subedar by sending our troops to the base of the fort, and don't allow him to get out. We will wait till tomorrow morning before we begin to loot the city. Moropant, what is the news from the harbour?'

'It is in our control.'

'Raje, look!' Mahadev pointed with his sword in the direction of the town. Two trails of smoke could be seen billowing from Surat. It was getting dark.

'Netaji seems to have started his work.'

It was night when bullock carts stacked with utensils and other kitchen equipment reached the camp. The number of troops to be fed were not small. There were many carts full of fodder for the horses, and a herd of goats followed soon for meat. It was a winter night and a hundred small fires burnt across the camp. Raje sat in his small tent with a small fire inside for warmth. Netaji returned from Surat with each rider carrying bags full of gold coins and jewellery. The loot was spread out in front of Raje.

'Netaji, did you loot the entire town in one evening?'

'No, Maharaj. This is just from the octroi house and a few other houses. We set fire to just two houses as per your command.'

'We were able to see the smoke. Netaji, we will wait till dawn tomorrow. Any movement from the English camp?'

'No. All seems quiet.'

'Divide the cavalry into two. Each soldier should have another horse along with him to carry back the loot. Our spies will guide them around the town.'

It was dawn as Raje stepped out of his tent. He had draped a white shawl around himself and Mahadev was trying to revive the dying fire. Shivaji was about to give orders for the looting to start when he spotted five men being escorted towards his tent. The man in the middle seemed like a man of cloth, a Reverend Ambrose. An interpreter accompanied him.

Shivaji said, 'You and your fellow Christians need not have any fear. Rest assured that you are safe.'

Father Ambrose had come to recommend the name of a businessman in Surat who had amassed a lot of wealth but was known for his large-hearted and charitable nature. Raje entrusted one of his men to ensure that the businessman's shop and house were not touched. Father Ambrose returned a happy man.

As soon as he left, Shivaji instructed Netaji, 'Ensure that the women children, masjids, all places of worship irrespective of the religion, are not sacked either.'

He then issued the orders the men had been waiting for, as he pointed in the direction of Surat. 'Ravage the city of Surat which stands as a symbol of Mughal arrogance. Collect her wealth for the Swaraj. Go!'

The soldiers eagerly galloped towards Surat. The streets lay deserted, empty of the usual hustle-bustle of the morning. All doors were tightly shut and the spies escorting the soldiers pointed out the rich businessmen's homes and guided them through the streets. One could hear screams of the women as the soldiers looted the houses. A whip usually did the job in case the businessmen refused to hand over their riches. Now they were more worried about their health rather than their wealth! They were arrested and sent along with the loot towards the camp.

The loot continued till noon. The houses were burnt using oil collected from the oil merchants and the sky was filled with smoke rising from Surat. The camp was becoming full of the loot and the prisoners that accompanied it. Raje stood near his tent, standing below a tree. The loot was piled in front of him while the clerks were busy sorting gold, silver, jewels and other such valuables.

More than half the city had been looted by sundown. The houses being set on fire continued to belch out huge clouds of smoke. The rich merchants had taken shelter in the fort while their houses continued to burn. The soldiers found twenty-eight kilograms of pearls apart from other riches in one merchant's house! The Maratha troops enjoyed the loot they continued to amass without any resistance.

Worried that the Marathas may attack the fort, Subedar Inayat Khan ordered the cannons to fire. The cannon balls fired from the fort fell on the city, destroying it further. It was ironical that the Subedar, responsible for protecting Surat, was accelerating its destruction.

By nightfall, the burning city was a fearsome sight. Huge balls of smoke continued to spiral heavenwards and fires burnt everywhere. Havelis and houses were tumbling down as they burnt away. The black smoke had made the day look like evening and now the fires made the night seem brighter than day!

The loot began again at sunrise the next day. The Englishmen got the news that Shivaji's ships had arrived in the harbour. They were scared but were also relieved on hearing that Shivaji had ordered that their jetty and ships not to be touched. The Subedar, on the other hand, was a worried man—worried about the flak he would face from the Mughal emperor. A restless Inayat Khan decided to send an emissary to Shivaji. The emissary left the fort with four soldiers on horseback.

As Shivaji was busy supervising the loot, Tanaji came in with a few men and said, 'Maharaj, we caught two traders trying to cross the river with a few barrels. When we questioned them, they tried to escape saying the barrels contained oil but we opened them to find that they were full of gold coins. We managed to confiscate thirty such barrels!'

'Our ships are arriving any moment now. Load the barrels into them.'

The traders turned out to be the same men whom Raje had pardoned the previous day because they had pleaded that they were very poor. They now begged for mercy. 'Raje, please pardon us this once. We are willing to pay whatever you ask.'

'Tanaji, behead them—they deserve nothing less.'

At that moment, the emissary from the Subedar reached Raje's camp.

'They seemed to have finally woken up. Bring him here.'

The emissary bent low in mujra as he entered Raje's tent.

'Why are you here?' Shivaji said.

'Raje Shivaji! I have been sent here by Inayat Khan, the Subedar of Surat and representative of the Mughal durbar. Subedar's message is: "You are warned that your actions will only increase the wrath of the emperor. You are thus asked to return all the loot at once. If you do so, the Subedar will put in a good word in your favour to the emperor."'

'And ...'

'The Subedar is also willing to give you appropriate compensation. You need to return all the loot first.'

'Is that all?' Raje asked.

'Yes.'

Raje stood up. His face was stern and he had lost his earlier smiling countenance. He growled, 'Shame on you! Your Subedar ran away like a coward when we marched into town and is hiding in the fort. And you have the temerity to ask me to return the loot? We will do whatever we want in Surat. Who will stop us?'

'I will show that I am not a coward!' and so saying, the emissary took out a dagger and leapt at Raje. Mahadev, standing alert, cut off the emissary's hand in one deft stroke of his sword. The emissary lunged at Raje with his bloodied hand and fell on him. The guards pushed the emissary away, but there was a red patch of blood on Raje's shoulder. The news that Raje was wounded spread like wildfire in the cantonment and within minutes, there was a massacre as the soldiers took revenge by killing the captives.

Raje ran towards the camp to stop the massacre. He wanted to let the soldiers know that he was safe and stop the massacre. By the time everyone realized that he was well, many prisoners had died. Raje returned to his tent exhausted. He was annoyed at Inayat Khan's emissary's foolishness. He ordered severing the hands of twenty-two of the captured men. Six of them had lost their lives in the earlier massacre.

Raje said, 'Continue looting Surat and do not spare anyone. Collect only gold, silver and coins.'

While the loot continued, Shivaji's soldiers managed to capture an emissary en route to Delhi to meet Aurangzeb. He had a large amount of jewels, being sent to the Mughal emperor as a token of appreciation, with him. The looting of Surat continued till the end of the third day. The ships were loaded on the fourth day. The value of the gold, silver and gems amounted to crores.

In the meanwhile, the news of Mahabat Khan marching towards Surat with a huge army reached Raje. While releasing the prisoners, Raje said, 'Give this message to your Badshah and your Subedar: Your Surat is "badsurat" now, ugly and barren. This is the land of the Hindus. You are currently ruling in the Deccan and in Delhi. Those lands are not yours either. One day, we will prove that they belong to the Hindus.'

With the blowing of the trumpets, the Maratha cavalry moved out of the sacked town. Surat, a shining jewel in the Mughal crown, and a city resplendent with its wealth just four days ago, had now been reduced to resemble a smouldering, burning log.

En route to Rajgad, the Marathas celebrated Makar Sankranti and they were all eager to reach home. Raje had marched right into the heart of Mughal power and wealth and collected loot worth crores of rupees. He was now eager to hear praise from only one person—Maa saheb!

Raje could imagine Jijabai holding a traditional tray at the gate of the palace, waiting to welcome him. He spurred his horse forward in eager anticipation. Seeing Rajgad looming large in the distance, Shivaji forgot his tiredness as he increased his pace. He barely acknowledged the salutes as he climbed up the fort. Trumpets and horns announced his arrival. He glanced at the saffron flag and was a little disappointed to see it lie limp against a windless sky. As he dismounted, he saw Firangoji and was surprised to see his hair unruly, his head uncovered.

Firangoji's whiskers quivered with emotion as he received Raje with tears in his eyes.

Raje asked, dismounting hurriedly, 'Firangoji, what is the matter?'

'Raje! The elder Maharaj saheb ...' He left his sentence incomplete.

Maharaj saheb had left the world forever! Controlling his emotions, Shivaji asked, 'Firangoji, how did this happen?'

'Maharaj saheb had gone on a campaign with Ranadullah Khan and Sarja Khan to Bidnoor. They had camped at a place near Shimoga. Maharaj saheb went out to the forest when he spotted a tiger. He chased the tiger on horseback when ...'

'What happened then?' Raje asked, his voice trembling.

'He was a very talented rider, but the horse tripped and Maharaj saheb was tossed up like a flower high in the air. He died on the spot.'

Firangoji hugged Raje tightly. The tears would not stop now. After a while, extracting himself from Firangoji's embrace, Shivaji asked, 'Maa saheb?'

Firangoji said, wiping his tears, 'Raje, what can I say? Maa saheb wanted to commit sati. The preparations were made as well but everyone tried to convince her to wait until you return. But she is insistent on jumping into the fire.'

'Did she plan to commit sati before seeing me?' Raje asked, unable to believe what he had heard. He turned and rushed towards the palace.

The palace was cloaked in a strange silence. No one dared look up as Shivaji rushed towards Maa saheb's quarters.

He stopped at the door. Maa saheb sat on the floor wearing a green sari. She had green bangles on her hand, and the other queens sat around her.

Jijabai looked up and seeing her Raje exclaimed, 'Shivba!' as she hugged him tightly.

After a while, Raje asked, 'Maa saheb, were you planning to leave me?'

'Raje, you are not a young boy anymore. He is gone and there is no further need for me to stay alive.

Jijabai spoke with such determination that Shivaji was scared. She was everything to him! He said, 'Maa saheb, birth and death are predestined. One cannot force either of them. It is you who taught me this! Maharaj saheb is not here anymore for me to display my exploits to. If you also go away, whom shall I show my valour to? Maa saheb, I have never done anything without your advice and counsel. I cannot go on any campaign without your blessings. If not for me, Maa saheb, you need to live for the Hind Swaraj. Who else but you can bless the formation of the Swaraj?' Raje could not hold back his tears.

Jijabai said, wiping his tears with her fingers, 'Raje, don't trap me with your words.'

Raje sensed a little hope in her voice and continued, 'Maa saheb, I mean it!' He touched her feet and said, 'Maa saheb, I am bound to fulfil my promise of creating a Swaraj. I shall not have a moment's rest till it is formed. I will fulfil the oath Maharaj saheb made to Khandoba. Give me your blessings!'

Jijabai hugged Raje, much to his relief, and he knew that the danger had passed. A light breeze of happiness touched Raje in the midst of the deep sorrow of his father's death.

The rituals and other formalities to mourn Maharaj saheb were over but Raje was worried about Jijabai's health and would spend as much time with her. The young Sambhaji was helping this cause by playing with her.

Jaswant Singh was still camped outside Kondana but Shivaji was not worried. It was a strong fort and he smiled at Jaswant Singh's dogged yet foolish determination. All the while that Raje had marched on to Surat, looted it and returned, Jaswant Singh had continued to camp outside Kondana.

Jaswant Singh knew that it would be impossible for him to capture Kondana once the rains began. He tried attacking the fort but was repulsed with equal intensity. Around the same time, his ammunition store caught fire and killed a few soldiers. The twin mishaps were enough to send Jaswant Singh back to Pune. He had lost his nerve after five months of unsuccessful attempts.

This was welcome news for Shivaji, who reached Kondana the very next day to honour the soldiers who had fought the Mughals valiantly.

The loot from Surat and the Mughal failure to capture Kondana was a great boost for Raje. His strength had increased manifold. Raje decided to recoup all his losses since Shaista Khan's conquest and ordered Netaji to attack the Mughal territories. He marched himself on Ahmadnagar province. The attack on Ahmadnagar had been held in abeyance since his attack on

Junnar. He managed to ravage the province right up to Aurangabad. By then, the winters were over and summer was in full scorch.

One day, as the summers were ending, Jijabai sent Raje a message:

'I have been informed that Khavas Khan has again decided to march against you from Bijapur, supported by Baji Ghorpade. I am sure Amba's blessings are with you. Don't let Baji get away this time.'

Raje touched the letter to his forehead reverently and said, 'Yesaji, Adil Shah has gone against his word and has asked Khavas Khan to attack us.'

'Shall I send word to Netaji?'

'No,' Raje said. 'It will take time for Khavas Khan to cross Konkan—we are prepared.'

However, Shivaji was shocked to find out that the Adil Shahi sardar accompanying Khavas Khan was none other than his younger brother, Ekoji Raje Bhosale! Baji Ghorpade was in Mudhol and had not yet joined them.

Shivaji said, 'Yesaji, my own brother is marching against me. The Kudal Sawants, Baji Ghorpade and we are of the same caste but we all behave differently. I tried bringing the Sawants into our fold but they rush to betray us at the earliest opportunity. It was Baji Ghorpade who ensured that Maharaj saheb was arrested. Ghorpade is now resting, let us make help rest forever! We need to reach Mudhol at the earliest!'

Raje and his men reached Mudhol before sunset. The village slept peacefully that night, unware of Shivaji's presence. One of Raje's men knocked on the door of Baji's haveli. Before the servant could react, the men had entered. Baji Ghorpade sat up wide-eyed as Shivaji entered his room.

'Who are you?' he asked.

'Don't you recognize me? People call me Shivaji.'

'Shivaji?'

'Yes, son of Shahaji Raje.'

Baji could sense his death approaching and he tried to get up when a sword pushed him back. Baji said, trying to gather some courage, 'It is not honourable to kill a sleeping enemy. Give me time to get up and fight.'

'You ungrateful traitor! Do you dare tell me the rules of a fight? Did you not remember these rules while arresting Farzand Shahaji Raje? You traitor! Did you not arrest Maharaj saheb while he was sleeping? He was hurt and fell unconscious in the scuffle, but you did not hesitate to handcuff him. Are you now teaching me the rules?'

Baji was mortally afraid and crouched on the floor.

Shivaji looked at him with disgust and said, 'Baji, I am waiting for you downstairs. Pick up a sword and come face me. I will be waiting.'

Baji emerged from his room, a sword in his hand. He was an expert swordsman, and Raje knew he was taking a risk. The two men sparred for a while, and Shivaji was only waiting for an opportune moment. Soon Baji was on the ground, Bhawani having pierced his chest. He was dead before his body touched the floor. Shivaji said, 'Destroy the village. I don't want this treacherous man's memories lingering here.'

Night turned into day as the flames from the burning houses reached the skies and three thousand people were massacred in Mudhol. It was sheer good luck for Baji's wife, who had left the previous day for her village Dahir with her sons Maloji and Shankarji. Raje had not only managed to avenge insults to his father but also fulfilled Jijabai's desire.

Raje reached Kudal where Khavas Khan waited, unaware of the attack on Baji. Raje descended on Khavas Khan's troops as soon as they reached Kudal. Encamped in a narrow area, the troops were quickly surrounded. Khavas Khan had not expected to be attacked in the dead of the night. He had heard of Shivaji's cunning ways and believed him to be the devil and was seeing the devil in action now! Soon, Khan was looking for ways to escape rather than fight, and the moment he heard about Baji's death, he ran for his life.

Lakham Sawant lost his nerve on hearing of Khavas Khan's escape. He managed to collect his personal belongings and his family and escaped from Kudal to take shelter with the Portuguese. But the firangis were not willing to give him refuge, which left Sawant no option but to surrender to Raje. He reminded Raje of their common caste while pleading for his life and wrote:

'You are a Sawant too—we share the same Bhosale gotra. We are like your children!'

Raje's temper cooled down a bit. Sawant had surrendered to Raje earlier and had helped him in the early days of his expansion. Raje could not forget that he had been a traitor but still managed to get him back into his fold. The Sawants promised their loyalty once again and the episode was over. The territory of Konkan was free but Raje knew he had to increase his naval capabilities and so, he paid a visit to the Malvan region.

Raje stood at the edge of the ocean, at the harbour city of Malvan, watching the ocean, and Tanaji and Manaji More stood nearby. Raje was overwhelmed at seeing the waves crashing on to the shore, the water spraying like a shower of pearls as it dashed on the rocks. Raje saluted the setting sun and said, 'Manaji, there is no guru like this ocean. My mind expands when I come here, thoughts erupting and crashing on the shore of my mind. We should be like the ocean—it knows that it can't erode away the shore but it hasn't stopped trying. It does not concede defeat and continues relentlessly whether it is day or night, high tide or low tide.'

Sleep eluded Shivaji that night. He could see the ocean and hear the waves crashing. His kingdom had now expanded and the Konkan coast was under his control. He had the ships to guard the coast but the real ruler of the seas was Siddi Johar in Janjira. He had Danda–Rajpuri and Janjira under his command, giving him a huge advantage in naval terms. Shivaji needed to establish control over some strategic ports to give him absolute control over the waters.

At dawn, he said to the guard standing outside, 'Ready my horse and send a message to Tanaji, Gangaji Mangaji and Manaji More to come with me for a ride.'

The morning mist was still in the air and the soil was wet with dew as Shivaji stepped out with his soldiers. Raje rode along the shore, the waves crashing noisily on the beach. Tanaji and others followed behind. No one said a word. The rising sun glinted in the waves. Raje suddenly pulled on the reins—he could see a blot on the horizon. He said, pointing in the same direction, 'What is that?'

Everyone looked to the horizon but no one was able to make out. Tanaji spotted a fisherman and spurred his horse towards him. The fisherman was scared seeing the soldiers riding towards him but Tanaji brought him to Raje.

The fisherman, seeing Raje, bent to touch his forehead to the ground.

'What is your name?' Shivaji asked.

'Savji, sarkar.'

Shivaji pointed in the direction of the spot on the horizon and asked, 'What is that?'

The fisherman said, following the direction in which Shivaji was pointing, 'It is the Kurate Island, sarkar.'

'How big is it?'

'Quite big.'

'Can you row to that island?' He asked Tanaji to inspect the island and report back.

Raje was restless. He could not get the huge black rock jutting out in the ocean out of his mind. It was late afternoon when Tanaji and the others came back. All of them were smiling. Shivaji asked eagerly, 'Tanaji, what did you see?'

'Maharaj, the island is fantastic. There is solid black granite everywhere, and the entire area must be around two square kilometres.'

Raje was thrilled. Manaji added, 'And the beauty of the island is that there is a sweet water spring as well.'

Raje looked at Manaji and asked, 'Really?' He could not believe his ears.

'Yes, Maharaj. We tasted the water. It is a perennial spring and the water is really sweet.'

'It is God's grace,' Raje said. 'You don't know the value of what you have done today. I am going to visit the island. Get the men ready and gather as many boats as possible.'

The afternoon sun glinted off the water and the waves continued to rush towards the shore. Raje's tent at the edge of the shore fluttered in the wind. A dozen fishermen walked proudly behind Raje while Tanaji, Manaji and Gangaji walked along with the soldiers. Raje continued to ask Savji questions. 'How deep is the water? Do the boulders get covered in a storm? How high is the high tide?'

A few dozen boats waited at the shore for the group, and there were a few canoes too. Raje got in first and was followed by the others. He stood at the edge of the boat as it moved forward, swaying with the waves. The fine ocean spray drenched Raje as he waited eagerly to reach the island. The boats touched the rocky, jagged shore and Raje folded his hands in salute before jumping out of the boat.

Raje was thrilled to see the huge expanse of boulders and granite. He could now see an unfulfilled dream taking shape. He inspected the area and was happy about drinking the sweet spring water. He said, 'Tanaji, we had decided to raise a fleet and had control of the coastline from Gokarna to Mahad but we did not have adequate protection. We were afraid of Siddi's ships or the firangis' attacks. We have a place to dock our ships now—this is the place.'

Tanaji said, 'Maharaj, Kurate Island is blessed!'

'No, on the contrary, we have got this island as a blessing.'

Raje looked around and muttered, 'We have found a place which has no equal. Siddi will be worried now. We need not pay taxes to the Portuguese, and our ships will be safe here. Tanaji, the day is not far now when we will rule the seas.'

Shivaji seemed filled with a divine energy. He had the look of someone building a nation, someone who would fulfil the promise of a Maratha state. Raje returned to his tent but could not forget the island—he could think of nothing else. He would gather a few fishermen each morning and reach the island. Raje honoured the men for having discovered the island and decided to extend his stay at Malvan.

The local pandit consulted his almanac for an appropriate date for Raje to perform the bhumi puja. He reached the island with hundreds of fishermen and with his sardars and soldiers. He set a gold-crusted coconut adrift in the water and the waves engulfed it in an instant, as if acknowledging the gift with gratitude. Raje folded his hands in prayer to the ocean. Raje laid the foundation of the fort to the chanting of mantras. The entire island reverberated to the sound of trumpets and drums.

Raje got down to the task of assembling the best craftsmen in Malvan. He managed to collect five hundred workers to build roads, a couple of hundred ironsmiths and another three thousand men to work on the island. A small town soon came up as the workers started building the fort. Money poured in to ensure that work was not disrupted.

Tanaji could not hold himself back and asked, 'Maharaj, are we not spending too much?'

'Tanaji, we looted crores of gold in Surat. What else should we use the treasury for? A strong fort is our real treasure. Once we secure our kingdom on all fronts, there will be no dearth of money.'

The Portuguese had extended a hand of friendship during the Konkan campaign. Raje decided to test them and asked for their best and most skilled men from Goa to help build the fort. They promptly sent a hundred of their best men. Raje appointed Subedar Govind Vishwanath Prabhuji as chief supervisor.

The work progressed with remarkable speed. Molten lead was used to fortify the foundation. Five hundred Malvan soldiers guarded the island day and night. Raje could now store his ships, cannons and gunpowder without any worry. It was Siddi who was losing sleep now. Raje had ensured that he would not create any mischief and personally supervised the construction for a month before moving out of Malvan. He returned to Rajgad satisfied with the progress of the construction.

The temple reverberated to the chanting of the Vedic mantras. The Shiva lingam was consecrated with milk, and Raje performed a puja of the weighing scale. He looked at Soyarabai and she got up, adjusting her pallu. Raje requested Jijabai to move towards the weighing scale. He was barely able to control his excitement. He seated Jijabai on one weighing pan and then went and stood near the empty one. Soyarabai stood near Maa saheb. Putlabai, Sagunabai, Kashibai, Gunwantabai and the others stood close by. The moment had arrived, and all eyes were on Raje now.

Overwhelmed with emotion, Raje looked at Maa saheb as he removed his earrings and dropped them in the pan. He then removed the jewel-encrusted gold leaf and his turban and put them into the tray.

Jijabai could not hold her tears back—she was truly blessed. With a son like Shivaji, she could not have asked for more. Her body trembled with gratitude as she looked at Shivaji. Bereft of all jewellery and with just a bright tilak on his forehead, he looked more handsome than ever before. For a brief moment, Jijabai was happy that he had removed his jewellery. Such a bright star needed no other adornment.

Raje cupped his hands and began pouring coins into the pan. The trays of gold coins were being emptied one after another. Everyone was now eagerly watching the scales and the pan Jijabai sat in kept going up. Raje's eyes were filled with tears of joy. The crowd could not hold back their tears either. Raje added a few more jewels and soon, the scales were balanced. The crowd cheered and the resonating sound of the trumpets filled the air. The horns and other bugles pierced the skies.

Jijabai's lips quivered. Her hand shivered as she patted Shivaji's head as he bent to touch her feet. They hugged each other and could not hold back their tears.

Jijabai said, 'Raje, I am truly blessed today.'

Raje could not speak. He tried to speak, his hand moving in the air. He managed to mumble, 'Maa saheb, I am but a poor soul. Who am I to give anything? I tried to weigh a diamond in gold—what is so praiseworthy about this?'

Jijabai was now fully satisfied about the man Raje had become. Sonopant Dabir sat watching them, his eyes filled with tears.

Raje turned towards him and said, 'Sonopant, please get up.'

Pant was taken aback and asked, 'What for?'

'One should not ask questions at such auspicious occasions.' Taking him gently by the hand, Raje moved towards the weighing scales.

'Please sit here, Pant.'

The old man, already bent with age, started trembling. He said, 'Raje, why are you mocking an old man like me?'

'Sonopant, you have spent your whole life in service to my family, until this body of yours has withered away. If I now want to weigh it in gold coins, can you really object? Please sit down.'

The ceremony was repeated and Raje and Jijabai donated the coins to the poor and needy.

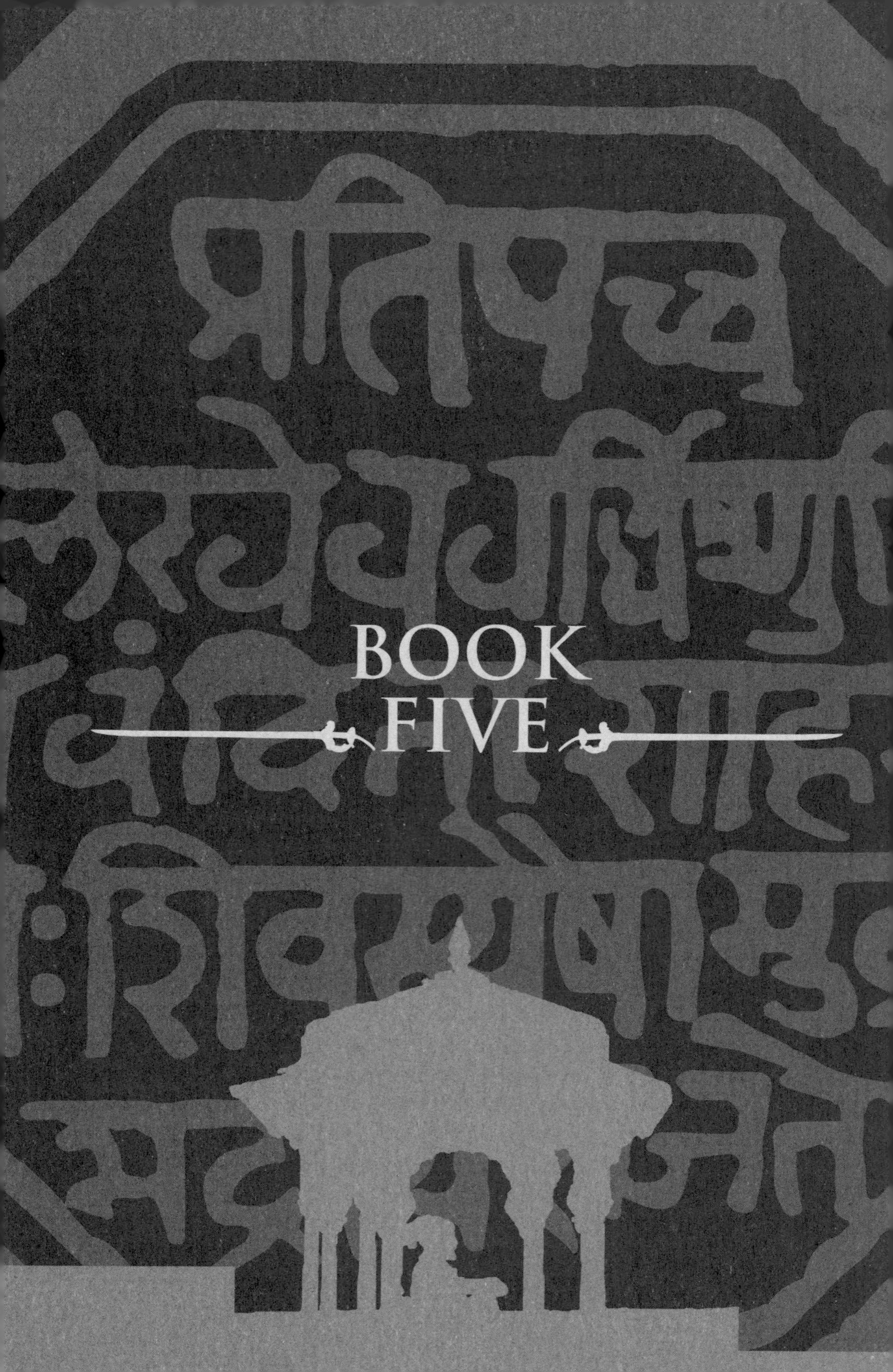

BOOK FIVE

Aurangzeb's anger had many reasons to rise, from the defeat of Shaista Khan and Jaswant Singh to the looting of Surat. While he maintained a cool demeanour, he was furious inside. Shaista Khan had begun the campaign with nearly seventy thousand men. He had spent more than a lakh hons during this time but had returned with nothing. To make matters worse, he had lost a few fingers in the battle. Shivaji's sacking of Surat had been a big blow to the Mughal foreign trade.

After hearing about Surat, Aurangzeb announced in court, 'It is no surprise that a cunning and bold enemy like Shivaji is able to loot our territories when we employ foolish sardars like Inayat Khan. I am aware that a lot of people in the durbar sympathize with Shivaji. I would be happy to have an ambitious man like him join us, and would be willing to forgive his past mistakes if he joins my durbar.'

Shivaji's increasing strength and the threat that he posed to the Mughal territories was a matter of worry for Aurangzeb and he knew that if Shivaji was allowed to flourish unchecked, the entire south of India would soon be out of the control of the Mughal empire. He thus decided to send his senior-most commander Mirza Raja Jai Singh to rout Shivaji.

Aurangzeb assembled a huge army and told Mirza Raja Jai Singh, 'Raja saheb, the situation is such that either you or I must take charge personally. Thus, I am giving you the task of defeating the Marathas. Return only when you rout him completely. Diler Khan will accompany you for additional support.'

Jai Singh accepted the responsibility, even though he knew the real reason for Diler Khan accompanying him. After all, he was a Hindu and could be trusted only to a certain extent! He began his preparations in earnest and did not make the mistake of making premature claims like Afzal Khan and Shaista Khan. Mirza Raja Jai Singh was nearing sixty and had spent his entire life managing political equations. He was aware of Shivaji's strength. He knew that he had able sardars like Qutubuddin Khan, Ugrasen Kachwaha, Gazi Baig and others. The artillery was being supervised by a trained Italian technician named Niccolao Manucci. He knew that he was facing a cunning and shrewd enemy. As a precaution, he called four hundred Brahmins to perform various havans and pujas to appease the gods before leaving Delhi.

Jijabai had returned to Rajgad with Shivaji after the tula ceremony at Mahabaleshwar. The spies brought the news that Jai Singh was marching towards Aurangabad with Diler Khan, eighty thousand soldiers and five thousand Pathans.

Pant said, 'Raje, Afzal and Shaista Khan may have been reckless but this Rajput is a shrewd fellow. I suggest we meet him and negotiate rather than confront him.'

'I am also in no mood for a confrontation. I am told he is marching with an army of eighty thousand which will increase manifold once he enters the Pune–Supe region. His forces, scattered there, would join him and his strength will cross more than a hundred thousand. I know that he is an intelligent and a capable soldier and an honest and determined person. We will depend on the Lord to show us the way.'

Raje sent messages to all the forts asking them to store adequate quantity of grains and ammunition. Hundreds of new spies were inducted into the spy network to ensure that the movement of the Mughals was tracked. Raje ordered his ships to move towards Malvan, prepared for battle.

'Raje, why are you directing your ships towards Malvan?' Jijabai asked.

'Maa saheb, Mirza Raja's attack is imminent. It would be quite expensive for us. I know that the loot we managed from Surat and Ahmadnagar would not suffice but we have a window of opportunity. Ever since Adil Shah and the Raja of Bednur have formed a pact, there has been no fighting in that area. I have heard that the port of Basrur is rich, and I would like a chance at looting it!'

Raje dispatched four thousand men towards Gokarna and rode to Malvan himself. The construction of the Janjira Fort was taking shape and the foundation was in place. The sea was dotted with three huge ships and another eighty-five small ones. Raje stepped on to a ship. It was armed with cannons, and the troops followed Raje and he ordered them to move.

The anchor was lifted and the sails swelled in the wind. It was the maiden voyage for these ships, and Raje was eager for a victory. He said, looking at Moropant, 'Pant, we need to have hundreds of ships in these waters. It will protect us from any invasion from the sea.'

The armada stayed close to the land. The Portuguese ships coming in from Goa were worried about such a large armada and dared not challenge them.

The port of Basrur awoke from their slumber to see a flotilla of saffron flags in the ocean and chaos was created to the cries of 'Shivaji has come!' The Marathas entered Basrur while the people were still coping with the news. They offered no resistance and Shivaji collected the loot and loaded it on to the ships. Then, having loaded the booty into the ships, he moved to Gokarn Mahabaleshwar for a darshan. Keeping only a dozen boats for crossing the rivers on the way, he sent all the ships back and moved towards Karwar along the sea coast.

Holi was approaching and so was Raje's thirty-fifth birthday. He was now stepping from an age of youth and dreams, enthusiasm and courage to a more mature age and wanted to celebrate the same with an appropriate victory. The Karwar harbour had English ships anchored there, and it was Shivaji's plan to loot them.

One of Adil Shah's sardars, Sher Khan, who happened to be at Karwar, heard of Shivaji's impending arrival. He had no troops and was worried about the confrontation. But he was a shrewd politician. He gathered all the rich merchants together and collected a huge amount of money to send Shivaji as a token of welcome. Shivaji acknowledged this cunning strategy and sent a message to Sher Khan: 'You have managed to secure the safety of the town. Now please help me to capture the English ships.'

Sher Khan relayed the message to the English sailors, who were scared for their lives. He managed to collect a huge ransom from them. Shivaji, in turn, decided not to attack the ships and accepted the ransom money.

One day, Kudtoji Gujar and Raghunathpant came to Raigad to see Raje. He asked, 'Did you meet Jai Singh?'

'Yes, Huzoor. He seems to be a gentleman, his grey hair matching his maturity.'

'Did you give him my letter? Was he wild with anger while reading it?'

Raghunathpant shook his head. 'In fact, he smiled and said, "Tell your Raja that the Mughal army has the capacity to destroy the might of any enemy. The earlier you surrender, the better will be for you."'

Shivaji was lost in thought for a moment. He looked up and said, 'Would he be ready for a negotiation?'

'I don't think so,' Raghunathpant said.

Shivaji smiled. 'Pant, he may not be ready now but may be in a few days. Shaista Khan too had come here with the same idea, but by the time he captured Chakan, he had changed his mind. Jai Singh too will undergo the same experience. How large is his cantonment, by the way?'

Kudtoji Gujar said, 'It is massive, spread over a few villages. The cannon and ammunition depot is enormous. I saw one of the cannons being pulled by eighty oxen! A firangi called Manucci is supervising the cannons. His son Kirat Singh is with him along with able sardars like Diler Khan, Daud Khan, Sisodiya, Itimad Khan, Raja Subhan Singh Bundela and many others.'

'He has come fully prepared it seems! Alert all the forts. I will reach Purandar the day after tomorrow as that is the nearest and most likely to be surrounded first. Kudtoji, what is the situation at Kondana?'

'Maharaj, Kondana is strong and fully capable of defending itself. You need not worry.'

Shivaji was in a hurry now. After issuing the necessary instructions, he reached Purandar and the fort erupted with joy on seeing him. Murarbaji Deshpande, the fort-keeper, was one of the few men that Raje trusted implicitly. Murarbaji was a tough soldier with thick whiskers, a deeply tanned face with bright eyes staring angrily at the enemy—he was a sight to behold. He was eager to serve Raje and waited for his instructions.

'Murarbaji, we expect the enemy to attack us and in all likelihood, Purandar will be the first in line. The enemy is strong, and it is your responsibility to defend the fort.'

'Maharaj, till I hold the fort, you may rest assured the enemy will not be able to step in.'

'I know. Keep them engaged for months. They need to know that it is not easy to enter Shivaji's domain. Do you need anything from me?' Raje continued.

'Not at the moment, but we may run short of ammunition if we continue to hold them for a long time.'

'Don't worry on that count. I will send across adequate ammunition the moment I reach Rajgad.'

'Maharaj, we have enough grain, and the fort walls are strong. They will not be able to make a dent here,' Murarbaji said, a little overwhelmed with emotion.

Raje hugged Murarbaji and this was enough to make the man's chest swell with pride and increase his confidence. Raje returned to Rajgad immediately.

The rays of the evening sun shone brightly on Raja Jai Singh's golden tent with the Siddi soldiers standing guard outside. He sat on a well-appointed baithak. His hair shone with the bright red tint of mehendi. He was in his sixties but his face reflected the handsomeness of a man who had aged well. His huge whiskers added to the fullness of his face. His sharp nose accentuated his red cheeks while his bright eyes expressed themselves clearly without a word being spoken. He was a true Rajput in looks. A few maids stood on the side gently waving fans. Kirat Singh stood respectfully on one side, his hands behind his back. Raja Jai Singh was lost in thought, his eyes closed, when the sound of a trumpet disturbed his reverie. He looked at Kirat Singh who said, 'Diler Khan is on his way.'

Jai Singh looked towards a corner of the tent where a set of turbans were kept ready. Kirat Singh quickly handed one to Jai Singh, who put his turban on and stepped out of the tent. They could see Diler Khan and his men marching towards them.

Diler Khan dismounted the moment he saw Raja Jai Singh. He was wearing an embroidered coat with pathani trousers and shoes and a matching embroidered pathani cap. He walked with the confidence of a well-trained Pathan sardar. His curly beard only added to his imposing persona. Raja Jai Singh acknowledged his salute and said, 'Come in, Diler Khan! I have been waiting for you to arrive.'

Diler Khan eased himself on to a diwan inside the tent and accepted a glass of wine from one of the maids. Kirat Singh and some others stood in attendance nearby. After the courtesies were exchanged, Diler Khan said, coming straight to the point, 'Raja saheb, what are your intentions?'

'I have been waiting for you, in fact, to discuss that.'

'My spies have reported that Shivaji's strength lies in his forts. Without them, he is nothing.'

'Is capturing him that easy?'

Diler Khan stared at Jai Singh. He was calm and continued to return his stare.

'The enemy can never be more powerful than our emperor's army.'

'I know that. But we should not repeat the mistakes made earlier.'

'If I may say so, the previous campaign was fought with a timid heart. That is why we lost.'

'That is not true.' Jai Singh said. 'Shaista Khan had a large number of soldiers with him. Capturing the fort at Chakan was a simple affair and yet it cost us a lot. Jaswant Singh had surrounded the Kondana Fort but it drained our resources quite a bit. The Mughal army was in this region for more than three years and it cost us crores of hons. And we got nothing in return.'

'Raja saheb, let us forget the past. I have decided that we will attack Purandar. If we manage to get it, the rest will follow without much trouble.'

Jai Singh nodded and said, 'Diler Khan, I admire your eagerness but that alone is not enough in politics. Let us not go after the forts. If we fail to capture them, we will lose our honour.'

'What great idea do you have in mind then?' Diler Khan asked, a little agitatedly.

Jai Singh continued, ignoring the barb, 'Shivaji has invested all his resources in the forts. We will expend a lot of energy while capturing them. You see, a rat has fifty holes to hide in. If we close one, he would escape from the others. But if we fill the holes with water, he will eventually have to come out. We need to find a suitable rat trap.'

'I don't understand.'

'We need to attack his villages, his people, stop the resources which support the forts. He will be forced to come out in the open.'

'But how long can we fight this way?'

Jai Singh's face turned hard. His smile vanished as he spoke, 'Diler Khan, I have seen many seasons more than you. I am not used to prolonging any battle for years on end. We can gain control of Shivaji's territories in a mere eight days. Spread your men all around and ask them not to show any mercy. Let us start today. Is that understood?'

'I don't agree with you!'

'I hear you but let us go ahead with this plan for the moment.'

Diler Khan returned a little disappointed. Jai Singh had ordered his troops in groups of five and ten thousand to attack Supe, Junnar, Loni, Pune, Shirval and other places. The sardars were instructed that in case they found Shivaji leaving the fort, he should be chased back into the fort and not allowed to come to the rescue of his men.

From the next day, the entire Maval region was in turmoil. The men feared the sound of horse hooves. Villages were turning into bonfires and the screams of the women abducted from the villages were heartrending. The cattle were herded and driven away. Within days, the entire region was in ruins.

Raje's troops attacked the Mughal army whenever they got the opportunity, looting the camp and running away before the entire cantonment could assemble itself. Raje had given his men strict instructions not to engage in a battle.

Diler Khan, however, was becoming increasingly restless by the day and was eager to attack Purandar. He was not in favour of Mirza Raja Jai Singh's plan. Jai Singh recognized his anxiety and allowed him to march towards Purandar. Within fifteen days, Diler Khan reached the base of the fort with his huge army. The cannons at the fort welcomed Diler Khan with a shower of ammunition and Diler Khan had to return fire from a safe distance. His men were moving forward through trenches and inching closer to the fort base. Jai Singh was happy with the progress.

One evening Diler Khan returned to Jai Singh's camp, tired and dusty. It had been eight days since they had surrounded the fort but the progress had been minimal. The only thing being spent was the ammunition and all they had achieved was raising huge columns of dust. Raja Jai Singh asked, 'Diler Khan, how are you progressing?'

'Well equipped as we are, we have tightened the siege.'

'Diler Khan, if you believe that you have surrounded the fort so well, how did one contingent of Shivaji's troops find its way up the fort?'

Diler Khan erupted, 'That was because of Daud Khan's treachery.'

'Diler Khan, capturing a fort, and especially one that belongs to Shivaji, is not an easy task. You lay mines but the enemy finds a way to douse them. They have also found a way to enter your trenches and destroy three of your cannons. We cannot fight such daredevils with the sheer strength of our numbers.'

'I have ensured such loopholes will not exist in the future. I am confident of that.'

'But how long will it be before we capture the fort?'

Diler Khan had no answer. He answered in a complaining tone, 'Raja saheb, you are seeing for yourself—I am trying my best but these Maratha rats are adamant on holding out.'

'Now do you believe me? This is what I have been saying all along, but you were eager to teach them a lesson. The rains are likely to start any day and once it starts pouring, I will be blamed for getting our army stuck in the mud. And, if that is not enough, I will also get a sound scolding from Alijah!'

Diler Khan looked at Mirza Raja Jai Singh and erupted, 'Impossible! I shall burn the fort of Purandar to ashes.'

'By when?' Raja Jai Singh asked coolly.

Diler Khan retorted, 'Raja saheb, do you not trust me?'

'Silence!' Jai Singh said, his fists curling in frustration. 'Shut up! Don't you know you are talking to Mirza Raja?'

He continued, 'Diler Khan, it is not enough to hate the enemy. We need to find the right strategy.'

Diler Khan stood up and said in a beseeching tone, holding his cap in his hand, 'Mirza saheb, give me one last chance. I will now return only after I capture Purandar. I take your leave now.'

Diler Khan stepped out of the shamiana. Mirza Raja Jai Singh smiled—he knew Diler Khan would not lose now!

The atmosphere at Rajgad was tense. Everyone's faces were creased with worry. Many sardars, having managed to escape the Mughals, were returning with the latest updates. Each piece of news added to the fraught atmosphere. Raje conferred with Moropant, Raghunathpant, Annaji Datto, Tanaji, Yesaji, Kudtoji Gujar, Anandarao and Jijabai.

Raje looked at the assembly and said, 'We are in a dire situation now. Mirza Raja is a cunning man. He has started looting our territories while he continues to hold Purandar. Our womenfolk are being carried away, our villages burnt, and innocent farmers murdered. And here I am—sitting in the comfort of a fort!'

'But what will Jai Singh gain from the plunder?' Annaji asked.

Raje turned towards Annaji and said, 'It is a strategy to make our men lose faith in us.'

Raghunathpant said, 'Maharaj, we may have managed to kill Afzal and fool Shaista Khan but this Rajput king is a shrewd man. My advice would be to start negotiations.'

'I am not against it, but he is looking for complete surrender and not a peace treaty. He is bent on capturing Purandar.'

Yesaji said confidently, 'Purandar has the capacity to keep the enemy at bay for a year at the least.'

'If we have a year, we will be able to think of a better plan. It is the Lord's kingdom and His responsibility. He will take care of us but at this moment, I feel helpless.'

Jijabai was listening to this exchange silently. She let out a deep sigh and said, 'There is no reason to be so hard on yourself, Raje. Did you not donate gold to ensure that we get the Lord's blessings? Was that all in vain?'

Raje smiled. 'Maa saheb, Mirza Raja performed the koti chandi homam, the most powerful of the fire rituals dedicated to the goddess Chandika, and donated crores of coins. He seems to be ahead of us.'

Jijabai asked, 'How do we make him change his mind?'

'It is difficult. He is a true Rajput. He will not go against the hand that feeds him. Had he been chasing our forts, I would not have been worried because he would spend a lifetime trying to capture all of them. But he is not one to give up so easily.'

Jijabai retorted, 'Raje, I have never seen you so defeatist.'

Raje replied, his voice steady, 'Maa saheb, I am not saying this out of frustration. I believe that it is better to be realistic than live with false pride. Mirza Raja's confidence is not because of his troops. He did not become arrogant when Aurangzeb took off his knee long robe and offered it to him. Aurangzeb also placed a diamond medal in his turban. '

'What is your plan then?' Jijabai asked.

'I have not planned anything. I am trying to observe the enemy's movements but have not been able to understand their tactics. However, I trust in Jagdamba, Who has always helped me out of the clutches of defeat. I will not lose my faith in Her in these troubled times.'

The conference was over, and everyone left without saying a word. Raje stood alone in his room. He turned at the sound of footsteps to see Kudtoji Gujar standing at the door. Raje asked, 'Kudtoji, what brings you back?'

'Maharaj, Mirza Raja is trying to entice our people. On receiving the news that something has gone wrong in the Javali camp, Netaji Palkar urgently left for it.'

'Without informing me?'

'I am told Mirza Raja has been successful in wining him over to his side. He also managed to get the two Koli brothers, Atmaji and Kahar Koli, to join him with three thousand of their troops from Purandar.'

Raje was stunned hearing the news. He let out a deep sigh. 'One must admire Mirza Raja. He managed to bring Kulab Shah, the Adil Shahi sardar, and the rajas of Ramnagar Peth and Chotiya over to his side even before he even got to Pune. He managed to rouse Shivappa Nayak and the Nayaks of Basavapattan against us. He cajoled the firangis to send their ships against ours. He challenged Afzal Khan's son's pride, asking him to avenge his father's death. And now he is planning to take my own men.'

Kudtoji stepped forward and touched Raje's feet. Raje looked at the tears streaming down his cheeks and said, 'Kudtoji! You are my best commander. It does not suit an army commander to cry like this.'

'Maharaj, I will be blessed to see these feet again but if I don't come back alive, consider this my last mujra. Don't worry about Mirza Raja.'

Raje's body stiffened. He asked, 'Kudtoji, what exactly do you have in mind?'

'Rest assured, Maharaj,' Kudtoji said. 'I beg you, in the name of Bhawani, not to say another word to me.'

'You ask too much of me, Kudtoji!' Raje said, shutting his eyes in anguish. When he opened them, Kudtoji had left.

Raje spent that whole day in great anxiety. When he returned to his quarters late in the evening, he saw a lamp burning near the puja room. The lovely rhinestone Shiva linga shone in the light of the oil lamp. Raje bent down praying, and remained there for a long time. Later, he moved to his bed and lay awake, his mind in turmoil. He drifted into sleep late in the night.

All of a sudden, Raje woke up with a start to find his body drenched in sweat. The window panes shook as the wind blew hard. Streaks of lightning illuminated the room intermittently. The puja room shone in the lightning while the wicks of the lamp swayed in the wind. The idol of Jagdamba played hide-and-seek as the flashes of lightning lit her up. The clouds rumbled with the deep sound of thunder. Raje stepped out into the balcony to see dark clouds covering the sky. The winds were hot but there was no sign of rain. He turned to look at the idol. He stepped forward and bent down in obeisance, his forehead on the ground. The thunder seemed to be echoing in his room.

Raje stepped out of his quarters and moved towards Jijabai's room. He seemed to be in a trance. He shouted, as he reached Jijabai's quarters, 'Maa saheb! Maa saheb!'

Manohari came out running. Seeing Raje, she stepped to one side while Raje moved straight into the quarters. Jijabai stood near her bed while Manohari was busy lighting the lamps. Hearing Raje shouting in the middle of the night was enough to send a shiver down Jijabai's spine. Sweat broke out on her forehead. She asked him, 'Raje, what happened?'

'Water ... please!'

Manohari poured water into a tumbler. Raje touched it to his lips and drained it in few quick gulps.

'Maa saheb!'

'Shivba! Did you dream of something?'

'It was not a dream, Maa saheb!' Raje tried to explain. 'I was lying down when I woke to find the entire palace lit up. I wasn't sure whether I was awake or dreaming. Jagdamba stood there and her voice seemed to be coming from somewhere deep within. I can remember her words clearly.'

'What did you hear, Shivba?' Jijabai asked, eager to hear the Goddess's words.

'Mata was telling me ...' Raje said, his eyes wide and fists clenched. 'My son, these are tough times. You cannot kill Jai Singh, but you need not worry. I will take care of your troubles—it is my responsibility. I have not handed over the kingdom to you for one generation. It is to be taken care of for the next twenty-seven generations. I will find a way to take care of you.'

Raje let out a deep sigh. 'That is what I heard. And there was no one else in the room, except for the sound of lightning and thunder.'

Jijabai looked perplexed, 'Lightning and thunder? What are you talking about?'

Raje looked at her confused.

'It is silent everywhere. Even the curtains are still. There has been no wind or thunderstorm.'

Raje said, 'Maybe it was a dream then. I suppose I just imagined it.'

Jijabai couldn't contain her emotions. She said, her voice quivering, 'Raje, you have been lucky enough to be granted darshan of the Goddess. You have been assured of victory by Jagdamba personally. Now go and get some rest.'

Raje returned to his quarters lost in thought. The night was still, and there was no sign of any wind. He was feeling relieved. He soon dozed off into a deep sleep.

It was late in the evening when Mirza Raja sat playing chess in a tent especially set up for the game. A gust of cool air passed through the tent. Mirza Raja's opponent was lost deep in thought, toying with a pawn in his hand. After a while, he smiled and said, 'Raja saheb, you won. I lost!'

Mirza Raja laughed aloud and Manucci, his opponent, stood up to leave. He bent to take permission and left the tent. Mirza Raja stepped out to see torches burning in the cantonment. He slipped on his shoes and walked towards his shamiana. Two Siddi soldiers walked behind, spears in their hands. As he was about to reach, he spotted someone running in the darkness towards his tent. Mirza Raja shouted, 'Catch him alive!'

Within seconds, the intruder was arrested. Mirza Raja instructed the guards, 'Bring him inside. And don't allow anyone else in. Understood?'

Mirza Raja was taken aback by the sudden attack but he managed to mask his emotions. He entered his shamiana and looked at the daring intruder who had planned to kill him. A guard removed the cloth covering his face. Seeing his face, Mirza Raja exclaimed, 'Didn't you accompany Shivaji's messenger?'

Kudtoji was silent. Mirza Raja indicated to the guards to leave the tent. Kudtoji looked around nervously. Mirza Raja said, 'What would you have achieved by killing me?'

Kudtoji licked his lips before answering. He was feeling a little relaxed now. He said, 'Saheb, I had come here to do my job. But it seems the Lord favours you—you would not have survived otherwise.'

Mirza Raja smiled, 'I am aware of His mercy, or I would not have been able to defeat Shivaji.'

'The victory is still far away.'

'Not at all. In fact, it is within reach. Otherwise people like you, who love your Raje so much, would not have dared to attempt something so foolish.'

Kudtoji wondered how Mirza Raja had guessed that. He did not answer.

Mirza Raja laughed out loud and said, 'Are you surprised? It seems you have not understood your Raje yet. He would not have tried something so foolish. Had he planned it, I would not have been alive. Remember Afzal and Shaista Khan? I am impressed at your boldness and I would like you to join me. Name your price.'

'I would rather sacrifice my life instead.'

'I knew you would say this! You are free to go now. Do you have a horse?'

'No.'

Mirza Raja clapped twice. A servant came in and he was instructed to arrange a horse for Kudtoji. Mirza Raja placed his hand on Kudtoji's shoulder and said, 'Don't be afraid. We will not betray you. My men will accompany you out of the cantonment. The horse is a gift to you. Tell your Shivaji Raje that I am never for a moment relaxed when I am in enemy territory. It would be easier if Raje had come himself. Ask him to meet me before it is too late.'

Kudtoji was impressed with Raja Jai Singh's personality and his behaviour. He bent in mujra and left the cantonment.

Mirza Raja sat in his shamiana enjoying wine when Kirat Singh entered. He asked, 'I heard that you were attacked?'

'Who can dare to attack me?'

'Who was in your tent then?'

'You don't have the liberty to question me; nevertheless, I will tell you. Shivaji's key aide Gujar had come to meet me. I expect reconciliation soon.'

'I too have good news for you. Diler Khan has captured Vajragad. I will take your leave now.' He turned and left.

Mirza Raja leaned back on a pillow, satisfied. Events were panning out well.

Kudtoji Gujar stood facing Shivaji. Raje could not believe the events he had narrated. Kudtoji recounted, 'Mirza Raja behaved with grace and also gifted me a horse. He is a large-hearted man.'

Raje smiled. 'Kudtoji, I am happy that you were able to return unharmed. But I was worried sick. I am certain your rash behaviour is going to cause me agony sometime in the future. You need to manage your emotions better. How are the conditions in Mirza Raja's camp?'

'They are confident of their victory.'

Raje let out a deep sigh. Kudtoji bent down to take Raje's leave when he said, 'Wait, Kudtoji.'

Raje acknowledged Kudtoji's actions by giving him the traditional dress and sword to him as a mark of honour. 'Kudtoji, I am now going to call you Prataprao. It suits your personality!'

Prataprao bent down in mujra. He was now Prataprao Gujar. He turned around to leave when Tanaji entered. 'Maharaj, we have had another blow! We have lost Vajragad!'

Raje was stunned at the news. Vajragad was like a twin to Purandar, which was now within striking distance for the enemy. They were confident that the fort would sustain the enemy attack for a year but the enemy had managed the feat within mere thirteen days.

Raje said, 'Our worst fears have come true.'

At night, Raje sat in his quarters brooding over the matter when Jijabai entered. He got up, and said, 'You could have sent for me. I would have—'

'The lamps were lit long time ago. When I asked Soyara where you were, she said you were alone in your quarters. Is it true that we lost Vajragad?'

'Yes, and I don't think we can manage to hold on to Purandar either. Maa saheb, I have decided that we should negotiate with Jai Singh.'

'But Mirza Raja has asked for unconditional surrender, hasn't he?'

'I will try to not let it reach that state but I cannot be sure. If we manage to reach a treaty before we give up Purandar, we will regain some manner of control. If we lose Purandar, we will be at his mercy.'

'Shivba! What sort of trying times are these?'

'Maa saheb, don't lose hope yet. I have been blessed by Jagdamba Herself. Whenever troubles have reached their peak, we always find a way out. Purandar is still safe, and Murarbaji will not give up so easily!'

'Whom do you plan to send for the negotiations?'

'We have to be cautious. Let me try some other trick. Let us see if that works.'

Raje sent his trusted spy Karmaji with another letter to Mirza Raja. The letter said, '... the emperor stands to gain much from me. I am, after all, a servant of the Badshah. Instead of wasting your time in this rocky and barren Konkan region, I would suggest you focus your energies on targeting Adil Shah. I am willing to help you in your efforts.'

Raje's attempt was to divert the Mughal army to Bijapur. He waited for Jai Singh's answer eagerly. The spy soon returned with the letter. Raje asked Raghunathpant to read it aloud.

'The Badshah's army, huge and innumerable as the stars in the sky, has been deployed specifically to defeat you. Don't be smug and bank on your rocky and hilly terrain. Our foot soldiers and cavalry will smother this terrain into flat land. If you are worried for your life, you will be willing to work as a servant of the emperor. If you accept that your men should be happy too, give up these forts. If you don't, the results will be disastrous and you have only yourself to blame.'

Raje was stunned by the reply. Many letters and replies were exchanged but Mirza Raja was unwilling to negotiate. Raje was not worried about

Purandar. Tanaji was guarding it with three hundred of his key men. He had only one hope left—nature would soon bring the monsoon.

The loot continued in Raje's territories, adding to his woes. Purandar continued to be battered each day. Raje sent a word that he was willing to send his commander and his son for discussions but Mirza Raja was not willing to speak to anyone but Raje himself. He warned Ranghunathpant, 'I have no right to sign a treaty. But if Shivaji is willing to come and stand before me and accept his crimes, I may be able to send a recommendation for his pardon.'

Raje sent word that he would meet Jai Singh in person. Mirza Raja was overjoyed, and he promised Raghunathpant that no harm would come to Raje. The date for the meeting was fixed. Mirza Raja summoned Diler Khan and explained the situation to him. Diler Khan was annoyed that he had not been consulted. He was further surprised when Mirza Raja instructed that they withdraw their troops from Purandar. He erupted with anger, 'Mirza saheb, we have worked hard to surround the fort and you are asking us to withdraw at the last moment? We will capture it another few days.'

'You have been saying this for quite some time now. Even if it were possible, I don't want it.'

'Why so?'

'Shivaji Raje wants to surrender before he loses Purandar. His dream is still intact. If he loses Purandar, he may not be willing to surrender. He will go wild with anger and we will lose a golden opportunity.'

'Raja saheb, you are right but ...'

'Silence! Diler Khan, you have spent many days trying to capture the fort. It is going to start raining soon. We can fight against men but not against nature, and I am not willing to risk it. If we are able to negotiate the surrender, well and good. If not, you are free to pursue your line of action. So let us withdraw from Purandar till we conclude our negotiations with Shivaji.'

Diler Khan left seething inside but he did not have the courage to argue or show his anger. He had no choice but to agree to Mirza Raja's command. In the meanwhile, Mirza Raja eagerly waited for the meeting with Shivaji.

The mrigashira nakshatra had set in but there was no sign of the rains; nor had the cool westerly winds begun to blow. The western sky was filled with dark clouds making the air humid.

Raje had returned to Rajgad and after a month of prolonged negotiations, the meeting was fixed for the ninth day of the Ashad month. Raje became increasingly restless as it approached. He was not sure of the outcome. He decided to move Jijabai and Soyarabai to the safety of Kondana.

Jijabai asked, 'Why are we moving now?'

'Maa saheb, when we get down to negotiating, the possession of Kondana will surely come up. I will have an excuse to deflect if you are there. Shambhu will stay at Rajgad and you move to Kondana. It is not a good idea to have the entire family in one place.'

'Raje, I am not comfortable about your meeting with Mirza Raja.'

'What are you worried about?'

'I hope he will not betray us.'

Raje looked directly into her eyes and said, 'Maa saheb, you need not worry. He is a Rajput and will live up to his word. When Diler Khan captured Vajragad and presented the captured soldiers to Mirza Raja, he could have killed them as per tradition. Instead, he ordered their release, and without punishing them either!'

'He seems to be a large-hearted man.'

'That was a political move though.'

'Political?'

'Yes,' Raje said, 'it was his way of making us aware of his large-heartedness. I am sure Mirza Raja will take care of me but Diler Khan is a rascal and a traitor. I cannot be sure what he will be up to.'

The next day, Raje made arrangements for Jijabai and Soyarabai to move to Kondana. He sent out instructions to each fort and gave detailed instructions to Moropant, Annaji Datto, Prataprao Gujar, Yesaji and Manaji. He selected Anandrao, Nirajipant, Nagoji Farzand, Bahariji Farzand, Krishna Joshi and Vishwasrao to accompany him. Mahadev, his personal bodyguard, was ready as always. Raje left the fort as per plan to meet Mirza Raja.

Mirza Raja sat in the shamiana specially constructed for the meeting with Shivaji. Two lovely embroidered seats were prominently visible in the tent. Handcrafted hookahs were kept alongside the seats. Incense sticks were lit in a golden incense burner. Rugs decorated the floor and the golden shamiana seemed ready to receive its royal guest. Mirza Raja had personally supervised the decoration. A few Rajput soldiers, with traditional turbans and their long beards split in the middle, flowing down to both sides of the chest, had been selected to stand guard. Each held a naked shamsher sword in his hand. Ugrasen Kachwaha was responsible for the entire arrangement. The Siddi soldiers guarded the shamiana on the outside. Any unknown person anywhere near the tent would be thoroughly questioned and searched.

Mirza Raja sat there thinking. He wore a saffron turban and an embroidered blue kurta and a churidar completed the attire. A navaratna necklace hung around his neck. His white hair added to the grace of his sixty years. His long sharp nose, thin lips and bright eyes enhanced his personality. A saffron tilak adorned his face. He came out of his reverie on hearing the sound of the cannons. He turned towards Ugrasen Kachwaha and asked, 'Has Diler Khan commenced his attack?'

'Yes, as per your orders, sir.'

'After all, Shivaji Raje needs to be welcomed in style!'

Ugrasen smiled, and Mirza Raja was satisfied. The cannons boomed loudly as Diler Khan continued his assault on Purandar. The sun had risen high in the sky when a messenger brought the news, 'Huzoor, we have managed to make a breach near one of the gates of the fort.'

'Good! Continue the assault.'

Mirza Raja took a long drag from his hookah, lost in thought once again. Udayraj Munshi and Ugrasen waited in attendance outside the shamiana. Soon, Jani Baig came in and said, 'Shivaji is within sight of the cantonment.'

'Who is accompanying him?'

'I don't see too many men. A few are carrying his palkhi and there are five or six guards at the most.'

Mirza Raja asked Udayraj and Ugrasen to receive Shivaji and instructed them, 'Please allow Shivaji Raje to proceed only if he is willing to surrender unconditionally without any weapons. Else, he may return. If he is agreeable to terms, let him proceed towards the shamiana.'

Mirza Raja prowled restlessly inside the tent. Kuchwaha returned soon and reported, 'Shivaji is coming in.'

'Where is he?'

'He must be just outside the tent now.'

Mirza Raja stepped out to see Shivaji walking towards him with his hands folded and covered by a white shawl. Forgetting protocol, Mirza Raja stepped forward. He was surprised to find Shivaji had a faint smile playing on his lips. He removed the white shawl covering his hands and asked, 'Raje, what is this?'

Shivaji answered, 'Mirza Raja, you set a condition of complete and unconditional surrender. I am just following your instructions. I would have no hesitation in meeting a respected Rajput like you with my hands folded or even down on my knees.'

Mirza Raja did not allow Shivaji Raje to speak further. He engulfed him in an embrace. When Shivaji Raje extricated himself from the bear hug, Mirza Raja said, holding his hands, 'You have managed to keep the Delhi sultanate at bay with a lot of earnestness. You must show the same eagerness to now work for the durbar. Come, let us go in.'

Shivaji Raje stepped into the shamiana. Anandrao stood outside waiting with Raje's shoes. Mirza Raja escorted Shivaji to his seat and then sat down opposite him. Shivaji sat there comfortably, and returned his stare without blinking.

Shivaji looked regal in his white turban enhanced with pearls. The lovely diamonds in his earrings gave off a light blue tint as they shook slightly. His thick beard and the tilak between his eyebrows added to his charming personality. He was about thirty-five years old but the luminescence of youth shone brightly. He wore a white embroidered angarkha and a saffron shawl was tied around his waist. He was not carrying any weapons and he wore tight trousers like narrow pyjamas. Many thoughts raced through Mirza Raja's mind as he observed Shivaji Raje.

This was the same Shivaji who killed Afzal! He had the courage to enter Shaista Khan's room and attack him. He challenged the supremacy of the Mughal emperor who had routed both the Nizam and Adil Shah. He is capable of making the emperor in Delhi lose sleep.

Mirza Raja had met many people who were arrogant in their victory, but he was meeting a person with the courage to look him in the eye even while he surrendered for the first time. He smiled and said, 'Raja saheb, I have been waiting for you. It was nice of you to come, but I don't see Gujar around. Quite a daredevil he is, isn't he?'

'Courage is praiseworthy if it leads to a result,' Shivaji replied.

'That was bad luck, was it?'

Raje continued to smile. 'Everything is fair in politics. Who knows, I may be the next victim yet?'

Mirza Raja said, slapping his thighs, 'It will not happen on my watch. I treat my guests with a lot of care.'

'I am a Maratha! Had I not been confident of your integrity, I would not have come.'

Mirza Raja was happy about his candid reply. He wanted to test him further and said, 'Raje, I don't see your Bhawani today. You are not carrying your sword today?'

For a brief moment, Jai Singh could see anger flit in Shivaji's eyes. But Shivaji replied without hesitation, 'Sometimes it is better for weapons to be given a rest.'

'Well done! That is a good answer.' Mirza Raja continued, 'Remember that you are still quite young. Shahzada Aurangzeb became an emperor thanks to this Mirza's efforts.'

'How can I forget? In fact, that is the tragedy,' Shivaji blurted.

Mirza Raja's eyebrows arched up as he thundered, 'What do you mean?'

Shivaji Raje said, 'It is quite clear. It would have been better had you seated yourself on the throne of Delhi rather than give it to Aurangzeb. He does not want any Hindu to challenge him. He cannot think beyond Islam. Had you been the emperor, you would not have had the need to come south. Instead, I would have happily come to meet you and handed over my kingdom. I would have been happy to be your slave for generations to come.'

Mirza Raja was stunned at Shivaji's blunt and emotional reply. He glanced around and screamed, 'Hold your tongue, Raje! This Mirza Raja is a servant of the emperor and I will not tolerate any words against the Delhi durbar.'

Shivaji Raje let out a deep sigh and said, 'I am sorry. I did not realize that a slave does not have the right to express his views freely. I seek your pardon.'

Mirza Raja clapped once and a servant entered with a tray of fruits. Mirza Raja cut an apple into two pieces saying, 'Raje, pick up any piece.'

Shivaji picked up both the pieces much to Mirza Raja's surprise. 'There is no doubt in my mind. I believe that a person lives or dies as per the Lord's wishes.'

The cannons continued to boom loudly. After a while, Raje could not hold himself back and asked, 'Mirza Raja, what is that noise?'

'It is the sound of the attack on your Purandar Fort.'

'But have I not agreed to a complete surrender?'

'We will continue the shelling till it is implemented.'

Raje was about to get up when Mirza Raja said, 'Wait! There is no need to get up.'

A servant lifted the flaps of the tent and Shivaji was wide-eyed at the view. He could clearly see the Purandar Fort burning, and his heart ached at the sight.

Mirza Raja said in a taunting voice, 'Raje, see how your prized possessions in Deccan burn. We erected this tent especially for you to get an uninterrupted view.'

Shivaji sat watching as the fort was enveloped in flames. He stood up, as if in a trance, and stumbled forward, holding one of the pillars for support. He suddenly turned around. Mirza Raja continued to sit with a smile playing on his lips.

Shivaji said, 'Mirza Raja, I will give you Purandar but stop this attack.'

'You are planning to give me Purandar?' Mirza Raja asked. 'It is already taken, Raje! Within a few minutes, you will see our flag fluttering there. Speak of your other forts if you will.'

Raje said, letting out a deep sigh, 'I will, but please stop this attack.'

Mirza Raja looked at him with penetrating eyes and said, 'I may consider it if you make a proper request.'

Shivaji's eyes burned with anger but he controlled himself and with great effort, he said, 'Mirza Raja, I beg of you to stop this attack and save my people's lives.'

Mirza Raja asked Kirat Singh to stop the firing, and he immediately conveyed the message to Diler Khan.

That evening, Shivaji dined with Mirza Raja but he could barely manage to eat. Each mouthful felt like poison. His mind was occupied with Purandar. The cannons had stopped booming and a little later the messenger brought the news of Korde having come to meet Shivaji. He bent down in mujra as he stepped into the tent.

Shivaji asked, 'Korde, has the fort been vacated?'

'No, Maharaj. Havaldar Naik is not willing to act unless there are specific instructions from you.'

'Ask Naik to vacate immediately. And ask Murarbaji to see me.'

'Maharaj!' Korde exclaimed. 'Murarbaji fell in the battle!'

Raje was stunned by this news. Korde bent in mujra and stepped out of the tent. Mirza Raja looked at Raje, who stood there with tears flowing down his cheeks. His fists were clenched while the tears continued to fall on the carpet below.

Mirza Raja stepped forward and, putting his hand on Raje's shoulder, said, his voice full of sympathy, 'Raje, are you crying because you lost one man? This is the nature of war.'

Shivaji looked at Mirza Raja and shouted, 'Anandrao!'

Anandrao stepped inside the tent. Shivaji said, 'Anandrao, bring Korde back.'

Shivaji wiped his tears. Mirza Raja stood watching Shivaji. Korde came into the tent and Raje said, 'Korde! Mirza Raja wants to know how our Murarbaji fell. Please tell him.'

'Maharaj, I was with Murarbaji and the enemy was attacking with full force when he heard that Bale Killa was in danger. He ordered the doors to be thrown open. He marched out with fifteen hundred Mavals, taking the enemy by surprise. They began to retreat as Murarbaji moved forward. Diler Khan had to beat a hasty retreat and return to his camp. Murarbaji continued to chase the enemy and reached the Pathan camp. Maharaj, I have not seen a daredevil like him. Diler Khan came forward to challenge him. He managed to stop the battle for a moment shouting, "I can see that you are a true soldier. You should not risk your life in such fights. I promise you a sardar's post if you drop your arms now."

'"Who the hell are you to bribe me? I am Shivaji Raje's soldier!"'

Korde continued, 'He charged at Khan and there was massacre everywhere. Seeing him attack Khan, a Mughal sniper let loose an arrow which met its mark as it passed through Murarbaji's neck. We returned with his body back to Bale Killa.'

Korde stopped and Raje indicated that he could leave. He looked up and his eyes reflected the many emotions racing through him. He asked, wiping his tears again, 'Did you hear that? I knew this had transpired when I heard of his death. My men will not succumb to an easy death. They have a common goal and they don't work for money. Each and every of my men is worth his weight in gold and any loss saddens me.'

Mirza Raja did not dare to look at Shivaji and stared at the carpet. A few moments passed in silence when Mirza Raja said, 'Raje, you must be tired. Go, rest, and we will begin talks in the night.'

Shivaji stepped out of the shamiana with a heavy heart.

Ugrasen Kachwaha showed him the way to the tent made for him. Shivaji was exhausted, both in body and mind. Tears welled up in his eyes and he slumped on the bed.

That evening, Shivaji strolled around the cantonment and reached the tent where Mirza Raja was waiting for him. Seeing him, Mirza Raja came out and led him inside by the hand. Udayraj, Ugrasen and a few firangis sat inside waiting for them. Mirza Raja introduced Manucci.

Shivaji acknowledged his salute and said, 'Is he not the one in charge of the artillery?'

Mirza Raja exclaimed, 'Oh! You know all about him?'

Shivaji smiled in reply.

Mirza Raja said, 'He is not only an ammunition expert but also a good chess player.'

Raje smiled and said, 'Then we will get along well. I too love playing chess.'

Mirza Raja suggested a round of chess. Afterwards, the servants announced that dinner had been served. They returned to the tent after dinner. The shamiana was brightly lit with oil lamps. Hiroji and Anandrao stood next to Shivaji. Pant announced the arrival of Udayraj Munshi and Surat Singh Kachwaha.

They entered and bent down in mujra. Raje asked, 'Shall we?'

'Where to?' Udayraj asked.

'Begin the negotiations?'

'We have come for only that purpose. Mirza Raja has sent us to work out the details.'

'And what about him?'

'He will not be present.'

Raje was silent for a while and then he said, 'Let us go ahead.'

Udayraj put forth his demands, taking Shivaji by surprise. Mirza Raja demanded every single fort and the money looted from Surat. Shivaji found himself firmly trapped in their vice-like grip. He had to finally relent and agree to hand over twenty-three of his forts and four lakh coins to the Badshah. All that was left with him was the region of Tal Konkan from where he expected no revenue to be collected. He knew it would be impossible for him to manage his own expenses. Shivaji proposed capturing Adil Shah's territory towards Balaghat in order to expand his borders and he was given permission to do so but at the cost of paying forty lakh rupees. This was to be paid in annual instalments of three lakhs each.

Udayraj asked, as he picked up a goblet of wine, 'Raje, what about your title and position?'

Shivaji had been fearing the question for a long time. He could not accept the fact that he would be working under a Mughal Badshah. It was like an eagle working for a crow!

He said, 'Udayraj, I accept all your conditions but please do not force me to work under the Badshah.'

'But why would you be opposed to working under him?'

'Please don't misunderstand,' Shivaji pleaded. 'I have lived without caring about the Badshah all this time. I am a Maratha and cannot face him. He has agreed to pardon me, thanks to his large-heartedness but I am a criminal in his eyes. I would rather that my son is given an appropriate job with the Badshah. I am sure he will do a great job. I would never dream of betraying the Badshah and I would be happy to just be by myself. I don't need a mansab or any other job.'

Udayraj relented, much to Shivaji's relief. And so, the negotiations ended late in the night.

The next morning, after his daily puja, Shivaji was ready to meet Mirza Raja who received him warmly.

'Raje, you have been very wise. Please accept my congratulations.'

'Rajaji, it was a tough negotiation.'

'But nothing compared to the crimes you have committed.'

'I am aware of that.'

'Raje, our understanding is not only about agreeing to these conditions. You have to implement them as well.'

'I know.'

Mirza Raja was aware that Diler Khan was unhappy about not being consulted throughout these proceedings. However, he did not want him to get take offence and requested Raje to meet Diler Khan.

Shivaji asked, 'Raja saheb, I have negotiated with you. Why do I need to meet Diler Khan now?'

'Now that you have surrendered completely, it is advisable not to be rash. Diler Khan is a close confidante of the Badshah. But you need not be afraid of him.'

Shivaji smiled, 'I am not afraid of Diler Khan. I will go and meet him as per your orders. But I request that I am sent with the protocol due to me.'

'What do you have in mind?'

'I would like to meet him under your protection. Diler Khan would not then dare to do anything foolish.'

'A person who has surrendered cannot be given any special treatment.'

Raje could not control his anger and erupted, 'Then don't blame me if something happens.'

'What are you talking about?'

'Rajaji, you are like a father figure to me. You are a Rajput and I can tolerate anything you say. But if Diler Khan decides to act funny, I will not hold myself back. I don't want to create trouble for you; and hence, I asked for your protection.'

Mirza Raja stepped forward and taking Shivaji by the shoulders said, his voice choked with emotion, 'Raja saheb, it is a tragedy that we met in these trying circumstances! I cannot think of being harsh with you.'

Mirza Raja sent Shivaji to Diler Khan with due protocol. He left with Raja Jai Singh on an elephant decorated with a silver-canopied howdah. Diler Khan was happy to see Shivaji coming to meet him. He presented Shivaji with an expensive sword, and the meeting went off cordially, contrary to Shivaji's apprehensions.

Mirza Raja's shamiana was decorated lavishly. The seating was on soft lush carpets. He welcomed Raje and they both sat down while the other sardars took their seats. Mirza Raja said, 'Raje, we are presenting a Rajput song in celebration of the successful treaty between us.'

'But I have no knowledge of music and songs.'

'Don't worry, Raje! A warrior like you will find these songs enjoyable.'

Mirza Raja clapped once and a tall Rajput wearing a traditional turban stepped forward. He had a kanjira, a local Rajasthani instrument, in his hands. He sat down in the centre of the assembly while another musician accompanied him on the dholak.

Mirza Raja made the introductions, and said 'Raje, this is Hira Singh. He has a rich baritone voice and you will love his songs. Hira Singh, sing a song and make our Raja saheb happy.'

Hira Singh bent his head to acknowledge the request and tuned his instrument. He sang a famous love song, very popular with the Rajputs.

When Hira Singh finished singing, Mirza Raja asked, 'Raja saheb, did you like the song?'

'It was a nice tune,' Raje answered.

'Raje, the meaning is quite subtle. A young soldier wearing a saffron turban had told his beloved the exact day of his return. She waited for him, counting the days on her fingers. One day, she forgets the count and sits there numb, not knowing what to do. Her beloved suddenly arrives and she looks at him with loving eyes.'

'Wah! It is really a lovely tale!'

'This song is a Rajput treasure, Raje.'

'I can understand that,' Shivaji said. 'Rajaji, I too am homesick hearing this song. I should leave tomorrow.'

Mirza Raja smiled and the evening ended.

The draft of the agreement was ready the next day. Mirza Raja asked, 'Raje, the agreement is in place. It is now the time for implementation, isn't it?'

'As you say. I will not go back on my word.'

'I have no doubts about that. Let us begin today itself.'

'As you command,' Raje said.

Raje selected his key men and orders were issued to vacate key forts like Rohida, Lohgad, Isagad, Tok and Tikona. Mirza Raja sent his sardars there to take charge. He said, nodding with satisfaction, 'Raje, while going to Rajgad, please hand over Kondana. I will send Kirat Singh with you. Let him come to Rajgad and return with Sambhaji. He will be staying here.'

Hearing that, Shivaji Raje was uneasy but Mirza Raja assured him, 'Don't be uneasy, Raje. I will take care of him as if he were my own son. But he needs to stay here. I hope you understand.'

Shivaji let out a deep sigh and said, 'I understand. I will send Yuvraj.'

Raje made plans to return to Rajgad. He was bid farewell with all fanfare. Mirza Raja gifted him two finely decorated horses and an elephant. Mirza Raja said, 'Raja saheb, don't worry. It is for your own good that you are now working under the Badshah.'

'I will take your leave,' Shivaji said, as he struggled to check his tears.

Mirza Raja hugged Raje suddenly. They both could not hold back their tears. Mirza Raja said, 'Raje, wipe your tears. Everything will be well. I have sent messages to the Badshah, and he will respond soon. You will be welcomed in Daud Khan's camp. Please accept his hospitality and then move forward.'

The sending-off ceremony took place in Daud Khan's camp. Raje sat in a palanquin while the cavalry was led by Ugrasen Kachwaha and Kirat Singh. The sky was filled with dark clouds and cool winds blew. It had not yet begun to rain.

The palanquin moved rapidly and by afternoon, Kondana was in sight. Raje kept staring at the saffron flag fluttering on the fort. Kondana was the gateway to the Konkan. It was from here that he had managed to secure the release of Maharaj saheb. It was from Kondana that he had taught Jaswant Singh a lesson and established the superiority of the Mavals. This favourite fort of Raje's was now going to be a part of the Mughal empire.

Raje was restless because of such thoughts. The trumpet at the first gate announced their arrival. The palanquin moved forward as each gate received him with an official welcome. Raje stepped out of the palanquin. Morpopant, Anandrao and others were there to receive him. He acknowledged their mujras but went into his quarters without a word. The men accompanying Raje were surrounded by their comrades at Kondana and they spoke in whispered tones.

Soyarabai received Raje and he asked, 'Where is Maa saheb?'

'She is waiting in her quarters for you.'

He washed his feet and Manohari hurriedly tried to wipe them with a towel. Raje asked Soyarabai, 'How is Maa saheb's health?'

'She is fine. And she has been eagerly waiting for you all morning.'

'I will see her now. In the meanwhile, please pack our things. We will be leaving for Rajgad today.'

'Today itself?'

'Yes.'

Raje did not continue the conversation and went to Maa saheb's quarters. He went in and touched her feet. Her lips trembled as she blessed him.

'Were you able to sign the treaty?'

'Yes.'

'What has been decided?'

Raje took a deep breath. His face was rigid when he said, 'What was there to decide? The one who surrenders has no choice. Mirza Raja did not leave anything for us. He will get twenty-three forts and four lakh hons. Including Kondana. All we are left with are Raigad, Rayari, other ten forts and a province which will yield about a lakh of hons as revenue.' He smiled ironically as he continued, 'I suggested we capture Adil Shah's territory but I have now been given the additional responsibility of ensuring that we get forty lakh revenue from those very territories.'

'Was there anything at all in our favour?'

'Of course! I was asked to work for the Badshah but I managed to wriggle out of that. Instead, Yuvraj will be an employee there with a mansab of five thousand. Isn't that enough?'

'Shivba!'

'It's not just that, Maa saheb! He will be in Mirza Raja's custody till we implement the treaty in full.'

'Raje!'

'I had no choice. I have not come across a seasoned politician as Mirza Raja Jai Singh—this is his style. I know that he had used the same tactics when he made the kings of Ranagar Peth and Chotiya surrender.'

'Raje, what are we left with now?' wailed Jijabai.

'Nothing but patience.'

Jijabai was in tears and Shivaji hurriedly continued, 'Maa saheb, please don't cry. I am so tired and unable to bear the tears in your eyes. We need to vacate the fort and move to Rajgad immediately.'

Shivaji turned to return to his quarters. There was activity everywhere with palanquins being readied. Everyone was rushing around but there was not a sound to be heard. The preparations were complete before sundown. Jijabai sat in her palanquin and they began their journey down the hill. Raje walked along her palanquin, followed by Kirat Singh. Raje was about to step into his palanquin when Kirat Singh bent low in mujra.

Raje returned the mujra and said, 'Kirat Singh, we will be meeting often now. There is no need to salute with a mujra. Let Mirza Raja know that we have handed over Kondana.'

Raje's palanquin reached the main exit door when Raje looked up to see the saffron flag fluttering. Kirat Singh said, 'Raje, your flag is still flying on the fort. With your permission, may I remove it?'

'Thank you for reminding me, Kirat Singh. I will order its removal right away.'

Shivaji climbed up the steps. The saffron flag fluttered in the wind. Shivaji bent in mujra for a final salute to the flag as tears flowed down his cheeks. He untied the knot and the flag slithered down to the ground. He folded the flag neatly and carried it back.

Shivaji turned around to find Kirat Singh standing there with his head bent. Shivaji quickly wiped his tears and got down the steps. The palanquin moved as soon as he stepped in. Shivaji sat there holding on to the flag as he looked down at the floor.

It was nightfall by the time they reached Rajgad. Raje stopped in his tracks seeing Putlabai standing there to welcome him traditionally with a tray and lamp.

Putlabai stepped forward when Raje said, 'Putlabai, wait!'

She was surprised to see Raje's expression and her hands shivered as she held the tray.

'Rani saheb, there is no greater insult that welcoming a defeated husband.'

Raje pushed the tray away before she could say anything and walked to his quarters. The sound of the doors being closed followed by the loud noise of the bolt locking the door reverberated in the fort. There was silence everywhere. Moropant, Kachwaha and others in the next courtyard were awake talking among themselves. The rest of the fort was silent.

It was dawn but Jijabai continued lying on her bed. She did not feel like getting up. Her head throbbed. She opened her eyes to see Sambhaji standing there.

He said, 'Maa saheb, are you not feeling well?'

Jijabai could not hold back her tears at seeing Shambhu. She hugged him tightly and starting sobbing. The eight-year-old was terrified and asked, 'Maa saheb, what happened? Why are you crying?'

Jijabai wiped her tears and said, 'It was just that I have not seen you for a few days. I am fine now. Go and play!'

The day progressed and it was noon when Manohari came with Putlabai carrying Maa saheb's lunch. Jijabai said, 'My dear, I am not hungry. I am not feeling well.'

Putlabai covered her face with her pallu when Jijabai asked, a little worried, 'What happened, Putla? Is everything all right?'

'Maa saheb, what should I do? The door to Raje's quarters is still closed. No one is able to eat. No one speaks anything or tells me anything.'

'Maharaj has not opened his door yet?'

Both of them nodded. Soyarabai entered the room and Jijabai asked, 'Soyara, is it true that the doors to his quarters are still closed?'

'Yes.'

'Then why are we sitting here?'

Soyarabai erupted, 'What are we supposed to do? When I call, I don't get any response.' She left fuming with anger.

Jijabai said, getting up with effort, 'Why didn't you send for me if you were unable to do something?'

She went and stood near the door to Raje's quarters but could not get herself to shout. She steeled herself for a moment and then said, 'Shivba! Open the door, it is me. Open the door.'

A few moments passed. She could hear footsteps and then the bolt moved. But the door did not open. Jijabai stepped forward and pushed the door. She stopped dead in her tracks.

Raje stood with his back to the door. His hair was dishevelled and his hands were clasped behind the back, his fists clenched.

Jijabai exclaimed, 'Raje!'

She heard his gruff voice say, 'Maa saheb, please leave me alone. Your Shivba is not here. Nor is your Raje. They both were sacrificed at the altar of Mirza Raja yesterday.'

'Shivba!'

'Maa saheb, please leave me be. I am not sure whether I should live or die. I feel that death would be more acceptable.'

Jijabai's heart broke listening to Raje but she wiped away her tears. She spoke with an edge in her voice, 'Raje, if you are so fond of death, why did you involve me in your pursuits?'

Raje unclasped his hands and slowly turned around. Jijabai was shocked to see the state in which Raje was. His eyes looked dull and the glow on his face was gone. Raje looked at her and said, 'Maa saheb, when have I involved you?'

'You might have forgotten Raje, but I cannot. When your father left us, I was prepared to accompany him but you stopped me. You fell at my feet and said, "Maa saheb, don't leave me. I need someone to be proud of my exploits. I am bound by my oath to establish the Swaraj." Have you forgotten that, Raje? If you don't believe in your oaths, then you should not have taken one. Did you make me stay back to see this day?'

'No, Maa saheb!' Raje's lips were trembling as he spoke. 'I nursed many dreams and I hoped I would be able to establish my Swaraj with your blessings. Was that a crime? I was dreaming of the Hindavi Swaraj and now, I am reduced to being a slave to the Mughals. The forts which I captured without caring for my life, and rebuilt with my own hands, are now in possession of the Mughals. I managed to get people to work on barren lands and made them prosperous. I have now handed over my own son, my flesh and blood, to the Badshah. Maa saheb, my dreams are shattered. My identity is no more! Why should I then live?'

Jijabai's face was hard. She could not bear to see Raje's fragility. She said, looking directly into his eyes, 'Raje, you are telling me stories of tragedy and loss? Your father left me when I was seven months pregnant. You were born in an unknown land in someone else's house. My elder son was with my husband. I was alone with no support. How did I live?'

'You were just six years old. I stayed in the barren fort of Pune holding your hand. I was the landlady of a barren village! But did I get scared? Raje, the Pandavas had to bear fourteen years of exile. Even Lord Ram had to go through this. If the gods had to endure hardship, who are you and me to question our fate? People who are scared of troubles cannot dream of creating the Lord's Swaraj, Raje!'

'Maa saheb!'

'Don't say a word! You don't feel like living, do you? Prefer death to living? If you feel this way, then pick up your sword and march over to

Mirza Raja right now. Listen to me! I am willing to see you being sacrificed on the battlefield but Raje ...' Jijabai faltered for a moment. She continued, her words laced with sarcasm, 'But Raje, I cannot bear the blemish of giving birth to a coward. I am leaving now. Raje, I don't want to see your face. You may do whatever comes to your mind.'

She turned and started walking away with slow, heavy steps.

Raje ran and fell at Jijabai's feet. He said, clutching her feet, 'Maa saheb, please! The world may be against me but you can never leave me. I made a mistake. I should have never said those words. Don't punish me so harshly. Please forget whatever I said. I promise you, I won't forget the oath I took. I ...' Raje stopped, fumbling for words.

Jijabai bent down, her hands shivering. Tears flowed down her cheeks. She lifted Raje up and said, 'Shivba! My dear son!'

And for a time, they were lost in each other's embrace, and their tears continued to flow.

That evening, Raje came into the meeting room and enquired about Ugrasen Kachwaha. Everyone felt relieved seeing him smile once more. He went to Jijabai's quarters and said, 'Maa saheb, I will retire for the night now.'

'Is it true that Shambhu will be leaving tomorrow?'

'Yes, but you need not worry. I have Mirza Raja's word on his safety.'

'Who is accompanying him?'

'I am sending Netaji along with him.'

Raje went to his quarters for the night. The next morning, he sat in his room alone. He had summoned Shambhu, who came in and asked, 'What is it, Aba saheb?'

'Bal Raje, I wanted to speak to you. You are not a child anymore. You need to take charge of some responsibilities for me. Are you ready?'

'Yes,' Shambhu Raje said, nodding his head innocently.

Raje smiled. 'See that you don't go back on your word.'

'Not at all. Tell me what I must do and I will do it.'

Raje hugged and kissed him on his cheeks. He said, 'Bal Raje, I have signed a treaty with Mirza Raja. Till the treaty is executed, you need to stay with him as Yuvraj.'

Sambhaji Raje was a little scared and asked, 'All alone?'

Raje hesitated for a moment and said, avoiding his gaze, 'A raja is alone most of the time. You must make a habit of it. So, will you agree to go?'

'Yes.'

'And one more thing, Bal Raje! When you leave, Maa saheb, your Aai saheb and others will be there to say goodbye. You should not cry then even if you feel like it. Remember, a Yuvraj does not cry!'

Bal Raje stood up in attention, his chest swelling in pride and said, 'Aba saheb, I will not cry.'

'Well done, my son! Live with pride and honour in Mirza Raja's house. You are going to be granted a panch-hazari mansab. Don't demand anything of him, and you can address him as Aajoba. Your Netaji Kaka will be with you. Listen to him and do whatever he says. You may go now.'

Bal Raje left the room. Raje closed his eyes but could not take away the image of Bal Raje. He couldn't stop the thoughts from swirling in his head. He is such a young, innocent child. I am sending him as my guarantee for executing the treaty! What a shame! Is it his fault that he is the eldest and the Yuvraj? He is being used as a pawn in the chessboard of politics. Is that the meaning of being Yuvraj?

I promised Sai that I would take care of him like a flower in one's hand. I promised never to leave him alone and now I am teaching him to be alone and behave like an adult! Is that taking care of him? He is the living memory of my Sai. I hope that stays the same.

Raje closed his eyes but could not hold back his tears.

Mirza Raja has dealt us such a blow. The most difficult part of the treaty was the condition that Shambhu Raje had to be left with him. I wish I were an ordinary man and didn't have to bear all of this. If the treaty is not executed for some reason, I hope he remains safe.

The preparations for Sambhaji's journey were made but Raje remained in his quarters. Sambhaji came to say goodbye and Shivaji felt suffocated seeing him at the door. A mere lad of nine! Will I see him ever again if God forbid the treaty were not executed as per plan?

Sambhaji looked a Yuvraj in the true sense of the word. He wore a turban, an angarkha and trousers. A sword on one side, a shield on his back and a dagger completed his attire. He stood there, waiting for Raje.

Raje stepped forward when Sambhaji bent and put his head on Raje's feet. Shivaji's hands shivered as he caressed his back. He managed to steady himself and said, 'Remember what I told you!'

Bal Raje nodded his head and left the room. Raje closed his eyes as the tears flowed down. The palanquin was ready in the courtyard. Netaji and others were standing around as Sambhaji sat in the palanquin. Everyone bent down in mujra and the procession moved forward. The cavalry followed on both sides while Netaji, Urgasen Kachwaha and a few others led the way. The palanquin disappeared within moments as it turned around the fort.

Raje could not hold himself back as a whimper escaped him. He stood clutching the window grills, his head resting on the walls. He did not try to hold his tears back at all.

The western sky was filled with dense clouds while strong winds blew everywhere. There were clear signs of imminent rains. Mirza Raja had moved his camp to the Purandar Fort. It was late afternoon and he sat in his palace while Diler Khan, Udayraj Munshi and others were in attendance. Mirza Raja seemed pleased at the turn of events. He said, looking at Diler Khan, who seemed in a pensive mood, 'Diler Khan, Shivaji has surrendered thanks to your courage.'

'Yes, it would seem so,' Diler Khan said.

Mirza Raja was aware that Diler Khan was not very pleased with the treaty. Diler Khan was not convinced about Shivaji honouring the treaty.

Mirza Raja said, 'Khan saheb, believe me, if Shivaji joins us, it would improve the prestige of the Delhi durbar. I have left him with no choice. We have managed to get all the strong forts. The territory is under our control and to top it all, his young son Sambhaji is going to be with us till the treaty is executed.'

'If only that happens ...' Diler Khan left his sentence incomplete.

'It will happen that way. It has been agreed upon.'

'There is a difference between agreement and execution, Raja saheb. I don't trust this Shivaji for a moment!'

Mirza Raja was uncomfortable with Diler Khan's argument. At that moment, a messenger came in and announced, 'Kirat Singh and Kachwaha have reached the base of the fort.'

'What about Sambhaji Raje?' Mirza Raja asked.

'I have no information about him.'

Diler Khan was smiling. He asked, 'Rajaji, didn't Kunwar Kirat Singh go to take charge of Kondana?'

Mirza Raja nodded and Diler Khan continued, 'It seems he has managed to take charge within a day itself. Why has he returned after taking charge?'

Mirza Raja was nonplussed and had no answer. Diler Khan stopped smiling, seeing his face turn red with anger. Mirza Raja said, 'I don't have answers to your questions, Diler Khan. Let Kirat come and clear the confusion. And bear in mind that if Shivaji has changed his mind, I have enough power to rout him once more.'

Mirza Raja sat thoughtfully as he sucked on his hookah. Diler Khan fidgeted about in his place waiting for Kirat.

It was evening when Kirat Singh finally entered the palace. Mirza Raja was looking in admiration at the young lad who had accompanied Ugrasen Kachwaha.

Sambhaji was busy observing the palace. He noticed Mirza Raja staring at him and looked questioningly at Ugrasen, who indicated with a slight nod. Sambhaji stepped forward stopping a few yards in front of Mirza Raja. He bent low in mujra.

Mirza Raja smiled and said, 'Welcome Sambhaji Raje! I have been waiting for you. Come sit near me.'

Sambhaji Raje stepped forward and Mirza Raja affectionately made him sit close to him.

Mirza Raja asked Kirat Singh, 'Has Kondana not been vacated so far?'

'It was handed over the moment we reached the fort. Raje made arrangements and they all left for Rajgad. The Mughal flag is flying high on the fort and is being managed by Shahid Khan.'

Mirza Raja looked at Diler Khan who avoided his gaze. Mirza Raja asked Sambhaji Raje, 'Will you stay with me here?'

'I will stay with you here, Aajoba saheb!' Sambhaji Raje answered.

Surprised at being addressed thus, Mirza Raja asked, 'Who told you to call me grandpa?'

'My Aba saheb.'

'Ugrasen,' Mirza Raja said, 'Make arrangements for Sambhaji Raje in my quarters. He will stay with me.'

Netaji Palkar stepped in at that moment and bent low in mujra. Mirza Raja looked at the man who had just entered. His personality was magnetic.

Kirat Singh introduced him and said, 'This is Netaji Palkar. He has come with Yuvraj.'

Mirza Raja smiled, 'Kirat, Shivaji's men are smart, and don't be fooled by their looks. He is not a guard. He is Shivaji's commander. His exploits merit him to be called another Shivaji. After all, Shivaji would not send any ordinary person to accompany Yuvraj. Netaji, don't you agree with me?'

Netaji smiled politely but kept quiet.

The lamps were being lit in the evening and seeing them Sambhaji Raje folded his hands in namaskar. He got up and touching Mirza Raja's feet said, 'Aajoba saheb, please give me your blessings.'

Mirza Raja was charmed by the young boy's manners and upbringing and hugged him affectionately.

The rains continued unabated. Rajgad was covered in clouds and mist every now and then. Streams of water flowed down the ramparts, giving the impression of many small waterfalls.

Shivaji sat with all of his sardars and the assembly consisted of Moropant, Annaji, Anandrao, Tanaji, Yesaji and others. As per the treaty, most of the forts had been handed over in a period of less than two months. The sardars and other soldiers were now returning to Rajgad. The kingdom was gone but the army remained. Raje had managed to raise a huge army of trusted men and wondered how he would take care of them.

Annaji Dattoji said, 'Raje, we are left with twelve forts and a revenue of a lakh of hons. It is not possible to manage the entire territory and the army with such a small sum.'

'So what do you suggest?' Raje asked.

'I suggest we reduce the army. After all, they are our men. They will return when called.'

'How easily you suggest this!' Raje commented, smiling wryly. 'And that too for such an important issue. Ever since Shaista Khan captured our territory, people have lost their lives, their livelihood, their villages, but they haven't lost their faith in us, and nor have they left us. I know they will come back when we call them but if we do this, how do we face them later? Annaji, we will never do this.'

'But Raje, how are we to manage such a huge force?' Anandrao asked.

'Anandrao, we have twelve forts and the territory around them. Use this opportunity to strengthen these forts. Let all the soldiers move to the forts. They will not be a burden on us. After all, the Lord has provided for us till now. Anandrao, Prataprao, Yesaji and Tanaji, I want you to take charge of the arrangements. Leave a few key soldiers at Rajgad and let the men move to the other forts before they suffer too much in the rains.'

Raje got up to move to his quarters when he heard someone say, 'Maa saheb has asked for you.'

Raje turned to see Putlabai standing at the door. He sighed deeply and followed her. Jijabai's mental state was the same as Raje's. Raje's heart broke seeing Jijabai's forlorn face. She was unable to reconcile the fact that Sambhaji Raje was in Mirza Raja's custody till the treaty was fully executed.

Jijabai asked, as Shivaji stepped in to her quarters, 'Any news of Bal Raje?'

He said, letting out a sigh, 'None. But I am sure he is fine.'

'Raje, a child was sent across as a guarantee for the treaty—can you ensure his safety?'

'Maa saheb, I have told you this earlier and will say it again; Bal Raje is safe there. Had I not been sure of it, I would not have steeled my heart and sent him.'

'I leave it to you to decide what is right,' Jijabai said with a sigh.

'Maa saheb, believe me. Mirza Raja is a man of honour. He will not allow any trouble to befall Bal Raje.'

'I don't know how much you should trust an enemy. You are praising the same person who captured you.'

'Please don't misunderstand me, Maa saheb! You need to understand the enemy. Mirza Raja is loyal to Aurangzeb and will not do anything against him. But if you leave that part of it aside, there is no one as compassionate as him. He is large-hearted and true to his word.'

'I am eager to see Bal Raje,' Jijabai insisted.

Raje stared at Jijabai and said, 'Let me see what I can do.'

Raje stepped out of the quarters. He sent a letter to Mirza Raja which the messenger carried immediately. The rains continued to pour incessantly.

After two days, there was still no reply from Raja Jai Singh. Shivaji was resting in his room in the afternoon when he was awakened by a noise. It was Manohari at the door, smiling. She announced, 'Bal Raje is here.'

'What? When did he arrive?' Raje asked, getting up.

'Just a few moments ago. He is in Maa saheb's quarters.'

Raje went into Jijabai's quarters to find Bal Raje sitting on her lap. Soyarabai, Putlabai and Sagunabai hovered around while Netaji Palkar was in attendance, standing in a corner. Sambhaji bent down in mujra seeing Raje and then touched his feet.

Netaji said, 'Mirza Raja agreed to send him the moment he received your letter but the rains were incessant. He is deeply attached to Bal Raje. He was worried that he may get wet and fall ill. Hence, he ordered us to leave only when the rains stop.'

Bal Raje stepped forward pointing to his necklace, 'Aba saheb, when I was leaving, Aajoba gave me his necklace.'

'It is really lovely,' Raje said. Turning towards Netaji, he asked, 'Who else has come with you?'

'No one,' Netaji replied. 'Rajaji said, "Take Bal Raje to Rajgad and stay as long as you wish to. Come back when you are comfortable. I am fine with that."'

Shivaji threw a knowing glance at Jijabai, who avoided his gaze. Raje said, 'You see, Maa saheb? I don't normally falter in my assessment of people.' Raje stepped out of the quarters with a smile on his face.

Mirza Raja decided to visit Kondana the moment the rains stopped. He was keen to see the fort which had been able to successfully withstand Jaswant Singh's attack. He was satisfied seeing the huge, strong fort. After a proper inspection and an overnight stay, he returned with Jaswant Singh to his camp. He received a farman for Sambhaji Raje from the Delhi durbar. He sent a message for Sambhaji Raje to return immediately. The next day, Sambhaji Raje arrived at the cantonment and accepted the farman with grace. As part of the mansab, he was entitled to a revenue of five thousand, upfront payment of rupees two lakh and permission to use the emperor's insignia. Sambhaji Raje was now officially a Mansabdar under the emperor.

Mirza Raja had fulfilled one dream and was now eager to fulfil the other. He had seen the restlessness in Shivaji's eyes and wanted to put him at ease. He started a correspondence in this regard with Aurangzeb. He soon received news of the royal farman which he had been eagerly awaiting. Shivaji was in Tal Konkan at that time. Mirza Raja dispatched a messenger immediately to summon Shivaji.

Raje presented himself at the cantonment the moment he got the message. He was received with great joy by Mirza Raja.

'Raje, you are very lucky. My wishes have been fulfilled.'

'I am happy too. I am honoured that Sambhaji Raje has been made a Mansabdar.'

Mirza Raja stepped closer and said, his voice full of joy, 'Raje, the Badshah has sent out an urgent farman inviting you to the durbar.'

'But I am not in his employment! I know he is large-hearted, but I have no right to accept the farman. It is Sambhaji who is employed by him.'

Mirza Raja was taken aback by Shivaji's diplomatic refusal and said, his voice a little harsh, 'Are you planning to refuse the royal invitation?'

Shivaji realized his folly and quickly changed track. 'I am sorry, that's not what I meant. I have received an honour I don't deserve, and I was nonplussed for a moment. It is easy to accept such honour but difficult to maintain it.'

Mirza Raja smiled. He stepped forward and shook Raje's shoulders and said, 'Believe me, it is best that you are in the employment of the Badshah as it is in everyone's interest. I was keen that you do not incur his wrath and was doing my best to get you invited. You are lucky to have received the farman. Let us give it the respect it deserves.'

'Rajaji ...'

'Don't worry, I will make all the arrangements. Diler Khan is a part of the inner coterie of the Badshah but he has never received such a farman till date. It is quite obvious that people are surprised at the honour that is being bestowed on you. It will add to your prestige.'

Shivaji had no choice but to nod his head in acceptance. But he was restless. He had routed Shaista Khan, had fought with all his might against the Mughals and had weakened Adil Shah. Now he was being summoned by the Mughal court. The farman would carry the respect, the honour and special recognition bestowed by the Badshah. It would carry a mehendi-stained handprint of the emperor himself. Protocol demanded that one was barefoot and sitting on one's knees as a mark of respect while accepting the farman.

Shivaji could not hold back his anger. He curled his fists desperately trying to control it. Mirza Raja's sardars were praising Shivaji's good fortune and congratulating him. All Shivaji could do was force a smile on his lips.

A specially designed farman badi, a place to receive the royal farman, was set up a few miles from the cantonment. On the appointed day, Shivaji walked towards the new farman badi accompanied by Mirza Raja's son Kirant Singh and Jani Baig.

The sun rose high in the sky while the green Mughal flag fluttered on the shamiana. The cavalry stood in attendance on both sides of the shamiana. Assuming that Shivaji was overwhelmed with joy, Baig tried to explain the protocol to be followed while receiving the farman. Shivaji somehow managed to hold back his tears and looked at his trousers which had been stained with mud while walking barefoot for a mile.

Kirat Singh said excitedly, on hearing the trumpets, 'I think the farman has arrived.'

Swallowing his pride Shivaji bent down on his knees. His tears fell on the hot soil and vanished instantly. The trumpets and other instruments now were shrill in their welcome for the farman. The camel carrying the farman was made to sit down while Kirat Singh and Baig stepped forward and received the farman with great care and handed it over to Shivaji's outstretched arms with elaborate dignity and respect. Shivaji touched the farman to his forehead as the guns fired in salute. As Shivaji stood up, Kirat Singh exclaimed, seeing his tear-filled eyes, 'Raja saheb, what's this? Why are you crying?'

Shivaji smiled, wiping his tears with his fingers, 'Kirat Singh, one doesn't cry only in moments of sadness. One can also cry when happy.'

On their return, Mirza Raja gave Shivaji a hero's welcome. Diler Khan and other sardars were in attendance in the shamiana erected specially for his welcome. He was, after all, one of them now! Everyone praised the royal clothes and armour sent for Raje, while there were murmurs of discontent among the sardars who had toiled day and night for the Mughal emperor but never received such honours. But no one dared to speak out against the emperor. Everyone went out of their way to praise Shivaji. He had been given the title of Raja by Aurangzeb. Mirza Raja asked Shivaji Raja to sit down when he noticed that he did not have any weapon at his side.

'Raja saheb, where is your sword? Your clothes do not become you without your favourite sword.'

Shivaji smiled, 'Rajaji, I have surrendered. Your orders were that I should come to you weaponless. I know one looks incomplete without a sword, but it is better than being insulted and asked to remove it in full view of the court.'

'Raje, I swear in the name of the Lord that it never occurred to me that I should ask you not to carry your weapons. I apologize for the misunderstanding.'

Mirza Raja called for Kirat Singh and whispered something in his ears. Kirat Singh left the tent in a hurry. Wine was served and everyone enjoyed the evening. Shivaji sat there sipping from his glass of juice. Soon, Kirat Singh came back followed by a servant carrying a tray covered with a velvet cloth. A jewel-encrusted sword and a matching dagger lay in the tray. Mirza Raja presented both of them to Raje.

At that point, Mirza Raja looked regal—a broad, saffron tilak on his forehead, bright eyes below the white bushy eyebrows, sharp and aquiline nose and the luscious whiskers which shivered as he spoke. All of these reminded Raje of Maharaj saheb. Before Mirza Raja could realize what was happening, he bent down and touched his feet.

Mirza Raja hurriedly lifted him up. 'Raja saheb, what's this?'

Raje said, 'I ask for your blessings.'

'What for?'

'You have given me back the sword which I had lost. Bless me that I never have to lose this again.'

Mirza Raja became emotional on hearing Raje's words. He patted his back and said, 'Raja saheb, so shall it always be. I always remember a couplet during such times:

'A man should make himself so powerful that while writing the decrees of destiny on his forehead, God would ask, "My child, tell me what you want it to be!"'

Mirza Raja sat through the evening chatting with Raje. Many thoughts flitted through Mirza Raja's mind. He asked, 'Raja saheb, the rains have ended now. I intend to march on Adil Shah. Alamgir too has expressed the same desire.'

Shivaji was stunned on hearing Aurangzeb's plans. Both the Adil Shah and Qutb Shah dynasties were Muslim but he never had imagined that the Mughals would decide to attack them.

Mirza Raja commented, 'I am sure you are surprised to hear about my decision. If I am able to rout Adil Shah before I return to Delhi, the emperor's reign would extend all over Hindustan. Alamgir would be mighty pleased with me.'

Shivaji nodded. 'When do you intend to start the campaign?'

'Quite soon. I want you to help me in this campaign.'

'What help can I provide?' Shivaji asked. 'I am a Raja for namesake, with neither a kingdom nor an army!'

'That was till yesterday. Now you are a Raja. Sambhaji is a Mansabdar now. If you come with your army to support us, we would be convinced that you are involved in the mansabdari. I can recommend that the territories captured from Adil Shah be put under your control.'

'I cannot raise an army so quickly. There are resources involved and I will need some time.'

'Raja saheb, don't worry about money. I will give you two lakh rupees tomorrow. Don't hesitate thinking it is gratis. I shall recover it from your jagir later. I suggest that you leave tomorrow and return with your troops at the earliest. We shall leave on the campaign once you arrive.'

Shivaji nodded and left for Rajgad the very next day. He sent out orders for the troops to gather the moment he reached Rajgad. Normally such an order would create a flutter of excitement but none was visible this time!

After issuing the orders Shivaji came to his chambers, lost in thought. He had dictated a letter to Balaji Awaji addressed to Mirza Raja assuring him that he was busy gathering the troops. He turned towards the door and saw Jijabai enter the room accompanied by Sambhaji. Raje got up seeing Jijabai. Balaji stepped out of the quarters discreetly. Raje hugged Sambhaji and said, 'Maa saheb, you could have sent word to me. I would have come down to meet you.'

Jijabai said, 'What is the point in calling you now? You don't share anything with me. I wouldn't find out anything any way.'

'Maa saheb, I shared everything with you when I had lots to share. Now I tell you what is essential. I have no control over anything now.'

'Raje, one must face sorrow with courage.'

'Maa saheb, where do I get this strength from?' Raje paced the room. He stopped suddenly and turned towards Maa saheb and said, ' I received the farman. Look at the strength a mere piece of paper carries—to walk barefoot to receive the farman, to wait patiently at the shamiana for it and then, to receive it on bent knees without daring to look up! After all, it is the Badshah himself represented in the summons!'

'Raje!'

'Let me finish, Maa saheb! After receiving the farman, one has to touch it to one's forehead and then come back to the shamiana. I have never seen such an insulting act. Mirza Raja has gifted me a sum of two lakh rupees to make the trip to Delhi.'

'Did you accept the invitation?'

'That is the only weapon in the hands of a fallen soldier!'

Seeing tears in Jijabai's eyes, Shivaji exclaimed, 'Maa saheb! Are you crying? You did not want a disheartened son about to commit suicide, did you? You wanted one who could face these things squarely. Then why are these tears in your eyes?'

Maa saheb wiped her tears away and a strange glint came into her eyes. She said, 'Shivba, it is all right to celebrate one's defeat. Imagine the mental torture the mighty Arjuna went through when he donned the dress of the dancer Brihannala. And what did the majestic Bheema think when he had to put on the apron of a cook? What went through Yudhishthira's mind when he had to lift Kichaka's slippers with his own hands? Raje, it is those who face calamities with courage that find a brighter future. A man's destiny is determined by his ability to face problems with dignity. They are the ones who are blessed by Bhawani. Have faith in her blessings, Raje!'

'I too live by those hopes, Maa saheb,' Raje said.

Sambhaji stood in the room listening to them with a quizzical expression on his face. Shivaji said, turning to him, 'Maa saheb, our Sambhaji Raje is a Mansabdar now. I am going to lead his troops and march against Adil Shah with Mirza Raja. Bal Raje, will you lend me your troops?'

Bal Raje did not understand Raje's question and asked innocently, 'Shall I come along too?'

Raje hugged Sambhaji and said, 'I hope you never have to go on such campaigns. You would not be able to bear such sorrows.'

Sambhaji wiped Raje's tears with his soft, small palms and asked, 'Aba saheb, are you crying?'

'Yes, Raje. It is my good fortune that I still have Maa saheb's shoulder to cry on. Go and play outside now!' And turning towards Jijabai, he said, 'Maa saheb, I am tired. I will go and rest a while. Don't send anyone to my quarters.' Raje turned towards his quarters on tired feet.

Mirza Raja's cantonment was soon turning into an ocean of soldiers. Men were joining from all over. Raje arrived with six thousand of Sambhaji's soldiers and seven thousand of his own men.

He had a tent specially erected for him. He would play chess with Manucci, who would often come to see him, and would hear a lot of news from him. Raje was impressed with the firangis coming to India across many seas and oceans. Manucci was a fair and good-looking young man. His eyes shone with the brightness of intelligence and Raje liked watching them exhibit a myriad of emotions when he would trap him in the game of chess. Raje looked up, sensing someone in the tent, to find Mirza Raja entering. He got up hurriedly when Mirza Raja said, 'Please continue with your game, Raja saheb.'

Shivaji knew that Mirza Raja would not come in unless he had something urgent to talk about. He said, 'I am tired and was planning to stop the game in any case.'

'Don't leave your game half-finished.'

Shivaji blurted out, 'There is a different pleasure in leaving a game midway.'

'I do not understand.'

Recovering quickly, Shivaji said, 'Please ignore what I said.'

Manucci left the room after gathering the chess pieces.

Mirza Raja said, 'I suggest that we leave tomorrow. It is a good day.'

'As you desire,' Shivaji said, nodding.

'Raje, you know this territory better than anyone else. I suggest you lead the march.'

'As you command.'

'I was expecting exactly this reply. I will go now—there are many other things to wind up.'

The next morning, they woke up to the sound of trumpets announcing their departure. The entire cantonment was filled with the trumpeting of elephants, the neighing of horses and the moaning and groaning of carts as they moved the cannons. Shivaji reached Mirza Raja's tent at the crack of dawn. He was accompanied by Netaji, Prataprao, Anandrao and Yesaji. Mirza Raja stood waiting with Ugrasen, Daud Khan and Diler Khan.

'Come in, Raje. I was waiting for you. I was wondering where we should start our campaign.'

Shivaji was dumbfounded, much to Diler Khan's pleasure who said, 'Let us begin with Phaltan.'

'Phaltan?' Shivaji asked, a little surprised.

'Yes. Isn't it controlled by Adil Shah? Once we capture Tathwad and Phaltan, the road to Bijapur is clear.'

Shivaji agreed without allowing his emotions to show. He knew Diler Khan's ploy. Shivaji's daughter Sakhu was married to Mahadji of Phaltan and Shivaji, as Mahadji's father-in-law, was being given the task of attacking him. Shivaji instructed Netaji to attack Phaltan and the troops moved forward at once.

Mirza Raja's elephant decked with gold and silver jewellery was ready for battle. The huge silver bell hanging from his neck gave out a tinkling sound while the howdah on his back was decorated with soft embroidered cloth. A ladder was placed when Mirza Raja said, 'Raja saheb, let us go.'

'I will follow you in my palanquin.'

'No, I suggest that you accompany me on my elephant.'

Shivaji climbed into the howdah following Mirza Raja. An umbrella protected them from the sun. The guards walked alongside. Diler Khan and his sardars could not tolerate the affection Mirza Raja showed towards Shivaji.

Soon, the troops moved into Adil Shahi territory. They reached the banks of the Nira River. The troops attacked Phaltan and within no time, the town was captured. The fort of Tathwad too was captured. Mirza Raja was impressed with Shivaji's capabilities and he sent a letter of praise to the Delhi durbar.

The troops had now reached Tal Konkan, capturing Adil Shahi territory along the way. Ikhlas Khan's army was routed by Shivaji's men but Adil Shah's men were ready to repulse the attack. They poisoned the waters in the countryside to prevent the Mughals from moving forward. The Mughal forces, heady with their victories, came nearly ten kilometres from Bijapur to find the Adil Shahi forces attacking them with such ferocity that they had to fall back. Many sardars and around fourteen thousand men lost their lives.

Mirza Raja was disturbed at the news. He was unable to understand the reason for such a defeat. Diler Khan entered the tent while Mirza Raja sat pondering over the defeat.

Diler Khan erupted, 'Rajaji, now do you believe me?'

'What?'

'The reason for this defeat? This is Shivaji's ploy. You pardoned him as a Maratha but how he has betrayed you!'

'Diler Khan!'

'You don't believe me? You allowed Shivaji to take charge and he put our troops at risk with the Adil Shahi army. How can you trust a man whose brother is fighting on the other side?'

'Whose brother?' Mirza Raja asked.

'Shivaji's brother! Ekoji Raje is Shivaji's brother and is leading the Adil Shahi troops. Raje, our troops will lose faith if we allow this to continue.'

Mirza Raja was stunned into silence. He did not know how to react.

Diler Khan continued, 'Rajaji, will you listen to my plan?'

'Tell me, Diler Khan,' Mirza Raja replied quietly.

Diler Khan looked around to ensure they were alone. He asked the guards to move out of the tent and said, 'This is the right time to remove this thorn permanently. It is easier when we are in a battle.'

Mirza Raja asked, his anger erupting, 'What nonsense are you talking, Diler Khan?'

'Mirzaji, leave the task to me. I will do it in a manner such that there won't be any suspicion.'

'Shame on a stupid plan! It is impossible!' Mirza Raja said, clenching his fists.

Diler Khan continued, keeping his emotions in check, 'Shivaji is not a fool. He has the confidence of a lion and the daring of a wild buffalo. He will never allow you to rest in peace. This thorn needs to be removed.'

'Silence!' Mirza Raja screamed, his body shaking. He said, pointing at Diler Khan, as he took a few steps back, 'Diler Khan, I am a Rajput. I have given my word to Shivaji Raje. If Shivaji is harmed, I would not be able to do justice to the Sultanate. Keep that in mind.'

Diler Khan tried to interrupt when Mirza Raja continued, 'Don't say another word now! The troops under my command and I have the Shahenshah's support. Don't think on these lines again, Diler Khan. These are my orders. Leave!'

Diler Khan left but a seed of doubt lingered in Mirza Raja's mind. He realized Shivaji was not safe among the Mughal army. He went to Shivaji's tent and taking a seat, Mirza Raja said, 'Raja saheb, I did not see you earlier; and hence, I came to meet you.'

'Rajaji, I don't have any face to show you.'

'Defeat and victory are part of the battle. One defeat does not make you a loser. I know you fought with all your might.'

'I have a request to make.'

'Tell me.'

'I request that you hand the command over to someone else. I am willing to fight under another person's command, and it would be best for the troops too.'

Mirza Raja admired Shivaji. He knew what was going on in his mind. He said, 'We cannot make these changes now. If we lose, you will be blamed.'

Shivaji was silent for some time. He said, 'Shall I suggest something? Give me an independent campaign to take charge of. I am familiar with the Panhala region. I will go and rout the territory and Adil Shah would be forced to send his troops there to control the trouble.'

Mirza Raja was agreeable to this suggestion and nodded. He was happy that Shivaji would be safer on his own campaign. Within a few days, Shivaji's men were ready to move towards Panhalgad.

Shivaji divided his troops into two groups, one managed by Netaji and the other by himself. He said, 'Netaji, I want you to reach exactly five days from now and meet me at the base of Panhalgad. We will attack the moment you arrive.'

Raje reached Panhalgad as per plan but Netaji was nowhere to be seen. The valley was swathed in the fog of a winter night. Raje was worried that their presence may be spotted by morning. He decided to attack with the help of Tanaji and Yesaji. The troops climbed up the hill. The doors of the fort opened suddenly and the attack was repulsed by a large force, and Shivaji's troops had to make a hasty retreat. They managed to find shelter in Vishalgad, but had lost nearly a thousand men in the attack. It was a big blow to Shivaji.

Shivaji sat there, nursing his defeat, unsure of his next steps. He got the news of Netaji's arrival the next afternoon. He was fuming with anger waiting to hear Netaji's excuse. Netaji was his commander, a close aide and a family member. But his trust-worthiness had, of late, become dubious. He had let Shivaji down at the last moment during Afzal's attack. And now it was because of Netaji that Shivaji had lost a thousand men. If only he had come on time ...

He asked, the moment Netaji arrived, 'Netaji, why are you late?'

Netaji was aware of Raje's temper. He knew that Raje normally addressed him as Netaji Kaka. He said, 'Raje, I am only late by a few hours.'

'A few hours? Netaji, you of all people should not be making such a comment. Don't you know that in battle each minute counts? I reached as per our plan but you were nowhere to be seen. We had no choice but to attack and we lost a thousand men. You are responsible for this loss!'

'Am I?' Netaji asked.

'Then who else is?' Raje countered, fuming with anger.

Netaji could not dare to return his gaze. He said, 'I had an entire army with me. I was not alone.'

'Enough of these excuses, Netaji. It does not suit a commander like you.'

'Your Senapati?' Netaji blurted out.

Shivaji could not hold his temper any longer. He screamed, 'What did you say?'

'Raje, we once fought under your command. Now you have joined the Mughals and Mirza Raja is the commander. Sardars don't have a Senapati.'

Raje was shaking with anger. He shouted, 'Netaji, please take your words back.'

Tanaji rushed in to control the situation, but Netaji brushed him aside and said, 'I am not used to taking my words back like you, Raje. I am a Maratha.'

Raje was stunned by the attack. He rushed forward and pulled out the sword hanging by Netaji's side. He said, 'Netaji, don't show me your face anymore. I don't need people like you. Leave before I behead you!' The fort reverberated with Raje's screams. He turned his back to Netaji. He had lost a dear one!

The defeat at Panhalgad hurt Shivaji deeply. He turned his forces towards Phonda and decided that he would return only after he won the fort. Mirza Raja had retreated to Parinda after being defeated at Bijapur. Diler Khan had taken an oath that he would not turn back till he captured Bijapur. Netaji, who had now joined Adil Shah's troops, led the attack from Bijapur.

Mirza Raja was contemplating his next move when he received some bad news—Qutb Shah had realized that he would be the next target and thus, he had joined forces with Adil Shah along with fifty thousand of his men. Mirza Raja summoned Diler Khan and they discussed the next steps.

Diler Khan said, 'Rajaji, it seems you are not aware of a bigger threat.' As Mirza Raja looked at him askance, he said, 'Shivaji Raje's commander Netaji has joined Adil Shah.'

'I heard that they had had a bitter argument,' Mirza Raja commented.

Diler Khan said with a wry smile, 'This is a cunning move from Shivaji. He first lost precious Mughal forces at Bijapur and then moved to Panhala. Now he is on the way to Phonda. I don't understand how long we are to tolerate his nonsense.'

'Diler Khan, what exactly are you saying?'

'I am telling you the truth. The same Shivaji, who was able to capture these forts with a handful of men, is now unable to capture despite such a huge force? Believe me, Netaji has joined Adil Shah and one day we will hear that Shivaji too has joined them.'

'If that happens, he will not be spared,' Mirza Raja thundered.

Diler Khan's laughter echoed in the tent. All the sardars present were surprised and Mirza Raja asked, 'Diler Khan, what is so funny about this?'

Diler Khan managed to hold his laughter back and replied, 'Rajaji, what else can I do? Please pardon my indiscretion, but if Shivaji joins forces with Adil Shah, what can you really do? If Qutb Shah, Adil Shah and Shivaji join hands, not a single Mughal soldier will be spared. How then can we teach him a lesson?'

Mirza Raja shivered. There was some logic in what Diler Khan was saying. He dispatched an urgent message to the Delhi durbar: 'Now that Qutb Shah and Adil Shah are fighting together, it is imperative that we send Shivaji up north. It is urgent that we dispatch Shivaji towards Delhi.' Mirza Raja was waiting for a reply from Delhi when the news of Shah Jahan's death reached them. Aurangzeb was now emperor in the true sense of the word.

Shivaji had planned to capture Phonda but the defences there were strengthened by troops sent by Adil Shah. He returned from Phonda red-faced. He received an urgent summons from Mirza Raja.

'Raje, don't feel bad about the defeat. I am aware that you tried your best.'

'It is your magnanimity that you are tolerating my failures.'

'Not at all,' Mirza Raja consoled him. 'I am in my sixties now. I have lost and won many battles. I know that luck plays a role in success. I called you here with a particular request.'

'Please command me.'

'Would you swear to obey?' Mirza Raja asked.

Raje was silent for a moment and then said, 'Raja, I too am a Rajput. My word is my oath.'

'Rajaji, I have conveyed the message of your exploits to the Delhi durbar. Now that Shah Jahan is dead, Aurangzeb is the true Badshah. He wishes that you and Sambhaji attend his birthday in Agra.'

'Sambhaji and I?'

'Yes, it is better to meet him in person. After all, both of you have received a royal farman. Protocol demands that you should visit him and pay your regards. I am sure Aurangzeb will treat you with dignity and honour that you deserve.'

Shivaji was lost in thought. What if he was cheated in Agra? There could be danger to their lives. He expressed his doubts and said, 'Rajaji, I agree that there is a question of protocol. But what if there is some perfidy?'

Mirza Raja came close to Raje and said, 'Raje, believe me. There is no danger to your life. I am bound by my oath to protect you. I will ensure that there is no danger at all.'

Shivaji agreed, 'I believe you and will visit Agra. Though I must wonder why I am going there in the first place!'

Mirza Raja said, 'I did whatever I had to do. Now it is up to the Badshah. Who knows, he may be mighty pleased with you and give you the subedari for south. I wish it happens because your wishes too would be fulfilled.'

'I am willing to try my luck.'

Mirza Raja was pleased. He said, 'The Badshah's personal representative Jani Baig will accompany you. I have sent word to Ram Singh who will take care of all the arrangements. My trusted aide Tej Singh Kachwaha will accompany you till Agra. And yes, I forgot to tell you, the Badshah has sent a sum of one lakh rupees for your travel expenses. You may make arrangements for the journey now.'

Shivaji got up and said, 'Rajaji, I wish to make a request. I may be overstepping my limit but I request you not to trouble my other territories when I am in Agra.'

Mirza Raja hugged Shivaji and said, 'Don't worry on that count. I will ensure your territory is safe. I will wait for you to return.'

Shivaji took leave of Mirza Raja and returned to Rajgad.

'Raje, I heard you are going to Agra?' Jijabai asked.

Everyone present had been shocked on hearing the news. Raje had casually mentioned it when sitting with Moropant Pingle, Sonopant Dabir and Jijabai.

Shivaji replied with a smile, 'Maa saheb, what's so surprising about that? After all, Aurangzeb is a now a full-fledged Badshah. Sambhaji is a Mansabdar and I have received a royal farman. Should we not go and pay our regards?'

'Don't taunt me!' Jijabai retorted.

Raje was silent for a while. He said, 'Maa saheb, I have not forgotten the dream of Hindavi Swaraj. But just living in status quo would not solve the problem. I have decided to take advantage of the situation and see if we can benefit from it.'

'How can we benefit?' Jijabai asked.

'If Aurangzeb is really pleased with me, he may make me the Subedar of south India. Then we can be relieved of Mirza Raja and raise our own kingdom back again. Isn't it a great benefit?'

Everyone was silenced by Raje's logic. But Jijabai would not be convinced. Her mother's heart refused to listen to Raje's logic. She was not convinced of the need for the visit. She muttered, 'Raje, but the dangers ...'

'Don't worry. I have Mirza Raja's word that we will not be betrayed. Aurangzeb would not dare to go against Mirza Raja's words. Had it not been for Mirza Raja's promise, I would not have acquiesced to make the trip.'

There was no further argument and Raje had very little time to plan. He left the next morning on a visit to his forts, giving instructions to each saying, 'Be alert and take care of the forts as before. We need to be extra careful and not allow a single moment of weakness. Those standing alert will be amply rewarded and those who show any laxity will not be tolerated. Follow Maa saheb's orders without fail.'

Raje toured his territory and returned with Moropant to Rajgad. He called his most trusted men together—Firangoji Narsala, Hiroji Farzand, Niraji Ravji and Trimbakji Sondev. He distributed responsibilities among them. Under Jijabai's command, Moropant Pingle was nominated as Peshwa, Nilo Sondev as Mazumdar and Prataprao was made the Senapati.

The fact that Raje would leave with Yuvraj for Agra was difficult for Jijabai to accept. She said, her voice tinged with concern, 'Raje! You are not going be there, nor Yuvraj. How will I manage everything?'

'Don't worry, we will return safely. But the kingdom needs to be protected in the meanwhile. After all, that is more important than me or Yuvraj. I need you to be the same Maa saheb who used to manage everything when I was young.'

Moropant asked, 'Raje, who will be accompanying you?'

'Oh, I forgot to mention! Raghunath Korde, Trimbakji Sondev Dabir, Madari Mehtar, Baji Jedhe and Niraji Ravji would accompany me. I have also asked the poet Parmanand to come with us.'

The people whose names were mentioned were thrilled. But Yesaji, Tanaji and Firangoji were disappointed. Raje said, 'Yesaji, you need to take care of our kingdom. The rest of you need to stay with Maa saheb and watch everything with a hawk's eye.'

Raje selected a total of three hundred and fifty men including many spies. Even the palanquin bearers and other servants were handpicked.

Jani Baig and Tej Singh, who were to accompany Raje to Agra, presented themselves at Rajgad. Jijabai selected an auspicious day for their departure in consultation with the pandits. Nearly five months had gone by since the farman had been received. Shivaji was to leave on the ninth day of the Phalgun month. There was a lot of activity with trunks being packed and people running around everywhere, much to the excitement of Sambhaji.

Manohari was packing Raje's travel clothes under the supervision of Soyarabai. She said, 'Put this with the other headgear. But I wonder whether Raje would be able to find these later.'

'Why, he has Mahadev with him, who knows everything,' Manohari replied. 'Frankly, Rani saheb, Raje does not have any idea about his clothes. He will wear whatever you keep ready for him!'

Soyarabai let out a deep sigh. 'Forget the clothes. He does not have any idea of the household either!'

'It seems I am the topic of conversation today,' Raje said as he entered the room. Manohari left the room at once, covering her face with her pallu. Soyarabai and Shivaji were alone. He came near her and Raje was attracted to her fair skin, her bold eyes and her daring attitude. He said, 'Are you not sad that I am leaving?'

'No. Why should I be? You have to go. Do you have a choice?'

'Not everyone understands that,' Shivaji said.

Soyarabai said, smiling. 'Where do we ever stay in one place for a long time? We women have to get used to this.'

'Yes, you are right!' Raje agreed.

Soyarabai continued speaking but deep down Raje was a little disturbed but he could not pinpoint why. He said, 'Rani saheb, you are the eldest. I would suggest that you help Maa saheb in her office. She is getting tired.'

'I will, if Maa saheb does not object.'

'I will tell her,' Raje said.

'I will take leave now,' Soyarabai said and was about to leave when Shivaji pulled her back with his hand on her shoulder. He asked, 'Would you like me to get you something when I return?'

'What shall I say? I am told that you get good perfumes in the north. Get me some if you have the time.'

Raje laughed out loud. Soyarabai was taken aback and asked, 'Did I say something wrong?'

'Oh no! That would be the only good thing I would do during my trip. Why would I forget?'

Soyarabai blushed and left the quarters. Raje's artificial smile promptly disappeared.

It was late night when Raje returned to his room and it was lit by a few lamps. He saw someone sitting on his bed. He came closer to find Putla there. He asked, 'Is that you, Putla?'

Putlabai got up and Raje turned her face towards his and asked, 'Putla, what is the matter?'

Putla could not hold back her tears as her body was racked with sobs. Raje hugged her and said, caressing her back, 'Come on now! Wipe your tears.' He continued, 'It was good that you came in, Putla. I wanted to ask you something.'

'What is it?'

'What shall I get for you?'

'Will you get me what I want?'

'Of course, please tell me what it is!'

'Do you promise?'

'Yes! Now tell me.'

She raised her eyes to look at him. Raje was eager to hear her wish and pleaded, 'Tell me! What is it that I should get for you?'

'I want you to come back safe,' Putlabai said, a sob escaping her lips.

Raje was silent. He said, 'It is a tough job. But I will do it on one condition.' She looked up surprised. Raje said, smiling, 'You will not keep any fasts for me. And you will not cry.'

'What sort of condition is this?'

'When I return, I want to see my dear ones happy.'

'Don't worry about me,' she said as she got up. 'I will leave now. It is getting late, and I was only waiting to see you.'

Raje called her name softly as she turned to leave, 'Putla!'

'Yes?'

'Will you do one thing for me?'

Putlabai did not reply but waited for him to continue. Shivaji said, his voice choking with emotions, 'Maa saheb is getting old. Take care of her. She needs someone to be her support and console her. I know you can do it and that I can leave without a worry. Would you?'

'You have shown faith in me. I am blessed,' Putlabai said and left without turning back.

Raje went to bed relieved.

Raje got up in the morning and when he returned after puja, he found Manohari busy packing his things. He asked her, 'Have you packed the sphatika linga from the puja room?' Raje would not leave without the quartz linga for his daily puja.

'Yes, in the morning itself. Shall I go now?'

'Yes.'

She turned to leave but bent down quickly and touched Raje's feet and he touched her head. She got up with tears in her eyes. Raje said, 'Don't worry, Manu. I will return safely. I would not allow your efforts to go in vain. Take care of Maa saheb.'

Raje came down to find Sambhaji Raje decked up and ready to leave. Sambhaji was nearly nine years old now. Raje commented, 'The royal durbar will be pleased to see you.'

Raje and Sambhaji went to the puja room and touched their foreheads on the ground. Maa saheb was there and they touched her feet. She could not hold her tears back and hugged Shivaji tightly.

Raje managed to get himself out of her clasp and said, 'Don't worry, Maa saheb. I am going into the enemy's den fully aware of the dangers. Don't get upset by the rumours which are likely to go around. I will return safely.'

'Take care of the child.' Shivaji was about to turn when Jijabai spoke again, 'Wait a moment.' She brought a shawl out and handed it to Raje.

He asked, 'What is this for?'

'Raje, this is the shawl Bal Raje likes to sleep with.'

'But would it not be too hot for a shawl?'

'Bal Raje likes the warmth which this shawl provides.'

Shivaji picked up the shawl and left the palace with Sambhaji.

While on the way to Agra, Shivaji received another farman from Aurangzeb that read: 'People in Agra are waiting for you and you may arrive to receive our hospitality. You will be sent back with honour ...'

Special clothes were sent along with the farman, and Shivaji was pleased to receive the farman and the clothes. The Mughal officers would visit Shivaji wherever he camped, ensuring that food and other necessities were taken care of. Aurangzeb had instructed them in advance that the guests should be treated as if 'the emperor himself were travelling'. The journey was thus without any trouble.

The whole city of Aurangabad seemed quite eager to meet Shivaji Raje. There were thousands on the road waiting to see Shivaji. Suddenly there was a shout, 'He has arrived ... he has arrived.'

Aurangabad's soldiers marched into the town, clearing the crowds with shouts of 'Clear the paths!' An elephant led the procession with a silver howdah on which the saffron flag fluttered. The embroidered symbol of the sun and moon on the flag shone brightly in the daylight. The elephant was followed by cavalry soldiers decked up in a similar fashion and they were followed by foot soldiers. The royal palanquin was behind the soldiers.

Shivaji sat in the palanquin embellished with silver work. The palanquin legs and top were golden in colour. A similar palanquin followed carrying Sambhaji. All the palanquin bearers wore a similar dress with their Turkish turbans attracting everyone's attention. The guards surrounding the palanquin brandished naked swords and long-nosed rifles. Two men followed the palanquin with long umbrellas to provide shade. Shivaji's key aides followed on elephants behind while the rest of the entourage consisted of carts and camels with their luggage.

The citizens of Aurangabad were pleased to see Shivaji. Sambhaji, with his good looks, captured the imagination of the population. Seeing the handsome young boy, many Hindu women cracked their knuckles on the sides of their heads in a gesture to ward off the evil eye.

Aurangabad's Subedar Shafshik Khan was an arrogant man and though he had received the farman sent to Shivaji, he sent his nephew to receive Shivaji. He believed that a Maratha zamindar did not deserve anymore. His nephew received Shivaji in a tent and said, 'I welcome you on behalf of Subedar Shafshik Khan. He has invited you to his haveli.'

Shivaji asked, 'I hope the Subedar is not unwell.'

'By the grace of Allah, he is fine.'

'Why don't you lead us to our tents where we can get some rest?'

'Would you not visit Subedar's haveli?'

'No. We would like to visit our tents.'

The Subedar's nephew led the way to the area in the royal gardens specially created for their stay. He then ran to the Subedar to give him Shivaji's answer. The Subedar, waiting with his officials, finally understood the meaning of Aurangzeb's farman to 'treat him as if the emperor himself were travelling'. He realized his folly and was worried that Shivaji may narrate this incident at the Delhi durbar. He rushed to the royal gardens and welcomed Shivaji with all grace and humility. Shivaji was pleased with the reception and also agreed to visit the Subedar's haveli.

Shivaji visited the haveli the next day. Everyone present was impressed with his humble nature. He spent a few days at Aurangabad and then proceeded on his journey. The Subedar personally escorted the entourage till the borders of the town.

The journey was uneventful with pleasant weather. Sambhaji hounded Hiroji Farzand with a million questions as he marched along his palanquin.

The fort of Daulatabad was visible now. The majestic fort stood strong in the flat grounds covering it. Shivaji could not take his eyes off the fort. The green Mughal flag fluttering on the top of the fort pierced Shivaji's heart. The Vijayanagara empire had been reduced to dust by the Mughals and so had Daulatabad's riches. The Mughal juggernaut had reduced everything to ashes. Shivaji was worried about whether he too would meet the same fate. The very thought sent a shiver down his spine. He let out a deep sigh. The fort-keeper of Daulatabad stood outside to welcome Shivaji but he declined his invitation and proceeded further.

Within a month of Raje's departure for Agra, a heartbreaking piece of news reached Shivaji. Netaji had now joined Mirza Raja's army and was awarded a panch-hazari mansab by Aurangzeb. Shivaji was deeply hurt by the news and was quiet for a long time.

The next morning, while making plans for their departure, he told Niraji Ravji, 'We will cross Grishneshwar on our way. It is where the Bhosale family deity resides, and I would like to halt there.'

Niraji nodded his head in agreement and a few soldiers were sent in advance to make preparations.

As the temple came into view, Shivaji became increasingly eager. He said, as he got off the palanquin, 'Sambhaji, I would like to cover the rest of the distance on horseback. Will you come along?'

'I will, Aba saheb!'

The horses were made ready. A cool breeze through the dense green forest blew and Tej Singh Kachwaha said, 'Raje, this is the Badshah's favourite place. When he was the Subedar under the Shahenshah, he would camp here very often. I am told that he loves this place.'

Raje looked around and said, 'I agree. But one does not like this place just because it is beautiful. There is something else that attracts one to such a place.'

'I am unable to follow you, Raje.'

'I too am unable to explain properly. I feel that there is something linked to the Badshah here. Anyway, let us move ahead.'

The golden spire of the temple glistened in the sun. It was late afternoon by the time they finished their puja. Raje was pleased and he sat with Sambhaji on the floor of the temple.

Niraji had just arrived when Raje said, 'Pant, isn't this a lovely place?'

'Undoubtedly. Raje, I am told there are some beautiful caves quite close by in the hills.'

'Then let us visit them.'

'There is the fear of wild animals there, though.'

'They are not going to eat us, are they?'

Hiroji Farzand said, 'We will carry a few torches. That should be enough to scare them away.'

'Let us go,' Raje said, getting up.

They moved through dense forests, and the sunlight barely reached the forest floor. The guide expertly guided them through the dense paths and they soon arrived at a clearing. Everyone stopped dead in their tracks. There was a gap in the forest and the caves, carved out of the mountainside, were clearly visible. All eyes were glued to a huge cave, the entrance of which was flanked by carved elephants.

The guide said, 'This is Kailash Mandir. The rest of the caves are not accessible but this is the most important one.'

The majesty of the Kailash Mandir was evident as they approached the cave. There were massive sculptures inside the cave, and Raje stood admiring them. In one, Parvati sat on Shiva's lap. In another, Ravana was trying to move the Kailasha Mountain. Shivaji's hands were folded in namaskar.

'One must admire Ravana who dared to move Kailasha to make way for his mother. I wonder who these sculptors were.'

'I am told that many millennia ago, Vishwakarma, with the help of priests, sadhus, gandharvas and Hindus made these caves and sculptures,' the guide explained.

'Quite obviously, such beauty would not be possible without the blessings of the gurus,' Raje said. 'Wah, Nirajipant! I am blessed to have visited this place.'

They decided to rest at Grishneshwar for the night, camping in the precincts of the temple. They had dinner outdoors and then rested in the open air. Shivaji, though, could not sleep for a long time. The sculpture of the Kailasha Mountain had taken over his mind!

The heat worsened as their journey continued. There was a distinct change in language and the garb of the people as they moved northwards, and a clear Mughal influence was now visible. Raje listened to the dialect attentively. He was familiar with the Hindustani language, but now paid attention to the nuances. Due to the increasing heat, they would travel from dawn till noon and then after a break, travel again from the late afternoon till sunset. The water supply, carried by the camels, was not sufficient to quench their thirst.

They reached Asirgarh to be warmly welcomed by the fort-keeper. It was the same Asirgarh Fort, after capturing which Emperor Akbar had exclaimed, 'I have opened the doors to the south now.'

The fort-keeper was overwhelmed with emotion and remarked when they departed, 'Raje, I am blessed with your visit. Let us together promise to serve under the Badshah for generations to come.'

Shivaji had to bear such insults as he moved towards Agra. He had been given a sum of one lakh rupees for his travel assuming that he may not be able to afford to bear the expenses for offering royal gifts in the Agra Durbar. And now, here was a fort-keeper who was willing to pledge his future generations in the service of the Badshah! He left Asirgarh with a heavy heart.

The fort of Gwalior, under Raja Man Singh, caught Shivaji's imagination. It was a beautiful yet powerfully built fort. He wondered whether he would be able to construct such forts back home. They were approaching Agra now and Shivaji wondered what fate had in store for him. The sun continued to burn fiercely.

They crossed the Narmada and the Chambal rivers and were now close to Agra. Jani Baig had sent word of their arrival ahead. Raje was expecting a senior sardar to receive them, and he looked at the group of soldiers arriving. There was a Rajput soldier followed by four others. The soldier dismounted and bent low in mujra saying, 'Raja saheb, Kunwar Ram Singh has sent me to welcome you.'

'And you are?'

'Raje, this humble servant is called Munshi Girdharilal.'

Shivaji did not know whether to laugh or cry. A mere clerk to welcome him! It was preposterous!

Munshi Girdharilal sensed Shivaji's hurt feelings and said, 'Raja saheb, I would like to tell you that Kunwar Ram Singh, Mirza Raja's son, was to personally come and receive you but has been engaged with some royal duties. I would like you to follow me to your accommodations. Kunwar Ram Singh will join you the moment he is relieved of his duties.'

'Is the royal durbar tomorrow?'

'Yes.'

Shivaji entered the city of Agra fuming. The fact that there was no one to receive him irked him and did not bode well for the events to follow. They were asked to make themselves comfortable in Mulukchand Serai. The serai was neat and clean but Shivaji's mind was restless—the signs were not encouraging. He got up early the next morning and waited for Ram Singh. Many processions entered the city but there was no sign of a welcome for him. He was increasingly getting restless now.

The city of Agra shone with signs of Mughal prestige. The outskirts of the city were dotted with the amps of sardars who had come to pay their respects. Aurangzeb believed in simple living but he ensured that the visitors were well taken care of. Aurangzeb had a political motive behind such hospitality. His father Shah Jahan was dead and he was to be crowned the emperor now, but in the process, he had acquired a bad reputation.

He had put his father in prison, making many senior sardars unhappy. He had come to the throne by ensuring that his brothers were taken out of his way. People supporting his brothers had been eliminated too. Having been too restless to watch his father die, he had finally resorted to poisoning him, and this was known to many.

Aurangzeb wanted to ensure that his fiftieth birthday celebrations and his accession to the throne were excuses to win some friends. The famous Peacock throne had been specially sent from Delhi to Agra. He decided to meet Shivaji in the Diwan-i-Am, the common man's hall of audience, to put Shivaji in his place.

He had nominated Ram Singh and Mukhlis Khan to meet Shivaji on his arrival at Agra. The day Shivaji was to arrive, Ram Singh was deliberately given royal guard duty, which was a duty no one could refuse. Ram Singh was thus forced to send Girdharilal to receive Shivaji. Ram Singh was restless and waited for his duty to get over and pay his respects to Shivaji.

Shivaji was angry at seeing Girdharilal the next morning, who tried explaining the situation. He pleaded, 'Raja saheb, I beg of you not to take offence and request that we leave immediately for the durbar. We are already late.'

Shivaji had travelled all the way from the south for this and did not want to ruin the moment. He also did not want to waste more time arguing and they all left immediately. The sun was high in the sky. Shivaji was carrying the items to be placed before the emperor when he would be welcomed with him. The crowd on the streets looked at the Maratha king as he sat erect on his horse moving towards the durbar hall.

Even the right path turns out to be the wrong one when fate is against you! Such was the state of Girdharilal when he realized that Ram Singh had not told him which route to take to reach the durbar. Ram Singh and Mukhlis Khan were rushing to meet Shivaji through the Firoza Bagh route while Girdharilal and Shivaji Raje were travelling through a different route. Ram Singh realized his mistake and sent his men to intercept Shivaji en route. It was a hot sunny day when they met in the crowded bazaar and embraced each other.

Ram Singh said, seeing Shivaji's entourage, 'Raja saheb, it is quite crowded up ahead. I suggest you leave the elephants near my camp and we move forward. There is no point in any further delay.'

Shivaji agreed and moved along with Kunwar Ram Singh and Mukhlis Khan.

The Agra Fort shone in its glory with the lovely red sandstone minarets. The guards at the entrance were alert and scanned each and every individual entering the fort. The gatekeeper allowed them inside the fort after checking their credentials. Shivaji did not have time to look around. Hearing the trumpets, Ram Singh urged them to move faster. Seeing the crowd of sardars assembled in the gardens outside the Diwan-i-Am, Ram Singh realized that the special durbar at the Diwan-i-Am was over. The durbar for which Mirza Raja had specially sent Raje all the way to Agra was over.

Aurangzeb had moved to the Diwan-i-Khas, or the Hall of Private Audience. Ram Singh sent the message of Raje's arrival through Wazir Jaffar Khan. Aurangzeb sent Asad Khan Bakshi to meet Shivaji.

Shivaji's eyes took some time to adjust to move from the bright sunlight to the dark and cool halls of the Diwan-i-Khas. Aurangzeb sat on an elaborately embroidered chair. Vetiver curtains hung all around, sprinkled with water, provided a cool ambience and prevented the harsh sunlight from entering. Soldiers stood at attention on the sides while two maids waved a fan slowly.

The men present there were a select few, chosen by the Badshah himself. Wazir Jaffar Khan was one of them. Raja Jaswant Singh stood there with his head bent low. Aurangzeb wore a heavily embroidered, pale green angarkha. His white cummerbund was embroidered with fine silk while his headgear shone with the diamonds reflecting the light of the lamps. A huge pearl necklace completed his attire. Raje stood there looking at the Badshah in all his glory. Jaffar Khan stepped forward followed by Shivaji. Aurangzeb sat there observing them.

Aurangzeb stared at the slightly short yet magnetic persona of Shivaji. The servants presented the 'nazar', the traditional way of honouring someone. The tray consisted of a thousand coins, two bundles of two thousand rupees and five thousand rupees. Shivaji stepped back and Sambhaji stepped forward to present a tray with five hundred coins and two bundles of a thousand and two thousand rupees. They both bowed, presenting their mujras.

Shivaji stood at attention while Aurangzeb continued to watch them silently. The emperor seemed tired after his meeting in the Diwan-i-Am. At a signal from Jaffar Khan, Shivaji went and stood behind Jaswant Singh. He was trying to control his anger. Everyone was given the royal paan as symbol of their loyalty but the true symbol, the royal gift from the Badshah was given to the chosen few such as Bade Shahzada, Jaffar Khan and Jaswant Singh.

Shivaji had been silently bearing every insult ever since he had met Mirza Raja. Now, he had travelled all the way to Agra only to be insulted once again. He could not bear the fact that he was not honoured by Aurangzeb. He was being treated as a lesser mortal compared to Jaswant Singh.

He asked, his voice loud, as his eyes burnt in anger, 'Ram Singh, who is this person standing in front of me?'

The court could not believe that someone had spoken in such a loud voice. Protocol demanded that when in front of the Badshah, one would keep one's eyes fixed on the ground and speak only when spoken to and after covering one's mouth with a handkerchief. And here was someone who had the temerity to speak loudly! The court shivered with fear.

Ram Singh whispered, 'Raja Jaswant Singh!'

Shivaji continued, his voice as loud as before, 'Really? The same Raja Jaswant Singh whose army ran away when they confronted me? And this person now stands ahead of me?'

Ram Singh begged Shivaji to stop with folded hands. But Shivaji's anger erupted and he said, 'I simply can't tolerate this!'

Ram Singh was mortally scared and held Shivaji's hands, entreating him to stop.

Shivaji brushed his hands off, shouting, 'Never!'

Turning his back to the Badshah, he marched out of the Diwan-i-Khas, and Sambhaji Raje followed. The durbar was stunned into silence. Ram Singh hurriedly saluted and stepped back without showing the Badshah his back till he was out of the hall. Outside the hall, Shivaji sat on the floor with his head resting on his palms. Ram Singh ran after him shouting, 'Raja saheb!'

Raje raised his left hand to interrupt him and said, 'Don't say a word, Kunwar! Is this the reason you got me here? I am ready to be beheaded but I would not go back to meet the Badshah again.'

Aurangzeb listened to the conversation outside. He instructed Multafi Khan, Akhil Khan and Mukhlis Khan to bring Shivaji back. 'Give him the royal honour and ask him to come back.'

They rushed out of the hall and tried to cajole Shivaji Raje, further angering him.

'I did not come here just to receive the royal honour. I was made to stand behind Jaswant Singh. Why? Merely to insult me? My son is a panch-hazari Mansabdar under the Badshah. He can be made to stand wherever the Badshah wishes him to. But I am not a servant of the Badshah!'

'Raja saheb!' Mukhlis Khan tried to interrupt.

'Your Badshah may kill me if he wishes. But I would never serve under him.'

The three of them returned, unable to convince Shivaji. They explained the situation to the Badshah when Ram Singh said, 'Alijah! It seems the hot Agra weather has not suited Raje. May he please be pardoned.'

'I can understand his feelings,' said Aurangzeb. 'Ram Singh, please sprinkle my special gulab jal on him to cool him down. Please request him to come back. We will then talk.'

Ram Singh returned to Shivaji's camp and asked him to sit down. Shivaji's body continued to tremble. Ram Singh was worried. After all, he was responsible for Shivaji's well-being. He said, 'Raja saheb, you should not have lost your temper.'

Shivaji's angry glare bore into Ram Singh 'Why don't you say this to the Badshah? There is a limit to which a person can bear insults. There are enough men in the durbar to introduce me. There are many who have lost fighting against me ...'

'But Raje, this could lead to ...'

'Since when have Rajputs done anything keeping the results in mind?'

'I think there has been a misunderstanding,' Ram Singh tried to say.

'What do you mean? The durbar seems to have ignored simple protocol. A mere clerk is sent to receive me when I arrive in Agra. I am then asked to stand with mere sardars of no ranking and deliberately ignored when the royal welcome is being showered! And you say that there was a misunderstanding?'

Ram Singh let out a deep sigh and said, 'Please hear me out! This is just your bad luck. I was supposed to receive you but I was called for royal guard duties which I could not refuse. Even the Badshah did not realize it. In the morning, we missed each other and were late. Who knows how things would have turned out if you had presented yourself in the Diwan-i-Am? The emperor was waiting for you, in fact. It is possible that he may be upset that you did not come there on time. But he did not show his irritation. He accepted your presents.'

'And in return insulted me?'

'What insults are you talking about, Raje?' Ram Singh said bitterly. 'Do you know Mirza Raja himself stands in the same place where you stood today?'

'Ram Singh, you seem to be forgetting,' Raje said, 'your father is a servant under the Badshah. I may have surrendered but I am an independent king. Aurangzeb may have felt good about honouring me with the title of Raja but that is what I have always been known as!'

Shivaji stood up and said, putting his hand on Ram Singh's shoulder, 'Ram Singh, I am prepared for any outcome but I don't want to embarrass you. I will listen to what you say.'

Ram Singh returned to his camp, which was nearby. Niraji, Sondev, Hiroji Farzand and the others were worried hearing the chain of events. It was nightfall soon.

The coronation ceremony and the birthday celebrations went off as grandly as planned. But the event in the Diwan-i-Khas was a blot on the festivities.

A Hindu king came into the court and insulted the Badshah and had the temerity to walk away! The news spread all over, and no one could believe it.

Aurangzeb sat in his bedroom wearing a simple white muslin kurta and trousers. A chain of beads moved slowly in his right hand while he twirled his moustache with his left hand. A few queens, Jaffar Khan, and Jaswant Singh were in attendance. A smile played on Aurangzeb's lips as he moved the beads one by one.

Jaffar Khan said, 'Alijah, one is punished for speaking out of turn in the durbar. And this Kaffir has had the temerity to come and shout at you and then walk away, showing his back to you! You cannot allow this to go unpunished. If you do, people will lose respect for the crown. We cannot allow such disrespect. Islam would be in danger, and how will we manage the empire then?'

Jaswant Singh said, in support of Jaffar Khan, 'My lord, Jaffar Khan is right. Of course, Your Highness will make the final decision. But a loyal soldier cannot tolerate such insults to the crown!'

Aurangzeb smiled and asked, 'Jaswant Singh, what do you suggest?'

'My lord, Shivaji must be punished.'

'Yes, yes. I see the point.' Playing with his beard, he turned to one of his queens and asked, 'What do you say, Begum Saheba?'

'What should I say? The person who looted Surat, cut Shaista Khan's fingers and insulted you in your durbar cannot be spared.'

Aurangzeb continued to move the beads in silence for a while. He was the emperor of India but he was not swayed by personal insults. He was thinking of Mirza Raja—Mirza Raja who managed his entire empire from Kabul in west to Assam in the east and from Kashmir in the north to the southern states. Mirza Raja was his loyal commander! Everyone waited with bated breath. He looked up after a while and said, 'This too shall pass. Allah has given us another gift. Are you aware of that?'

Those in attendance looked askance. Aurangzeb continued, 'The sweet gift called sleep. It is now inviting me. If you don't mind, I would like to sleep for a while.'

He stifled a yawn while his lips prayed,

Bismillahir Rahmanir Rahim .... I begin my day in the name of God, the most beneficent and the most merciful. There are no Gods but God and His prophet. O Saviour of Mankind, be merciful, be blissful ...

After a couple of days, Kunwar Ram Singh came to meet Shivaji in the afternoon. Shivaji's anger had subsided in these two days. He had realized that it was not wise to irritate the Badshah in his own territory. As advised by Ram Singh, he had written to the Badshah, though he was not sure how Aurangzeb would respond. Much to Ram Singh's relief, he was welcomed with a warm smile from Shivaji.

'What is the news from your durbar, Ram Singh?'

'It is still a little heated up there! The sardars who are against Mirza Raja are trying to rouse the Badshah against you. Shaista Khan's begum is adding fuel to the fire.'

'And what has been the result?'

'Alampanah is an ocean of love. It is not easy to create ripples in his heart of kindness. I have put in a word and also asked Jaffar Khan to speak in your favour. I suggest you meet him.'

'What?'

'Raje, you created this trouble. I suggest you forget your ego for a while and do as I say. I am responsible for your well-being and I want to fulfil my duty properly.'

Raje smiled, 'Kunwarji, I will do as you say but just don't ask me to present myself at the durbar again.'

'Let us go out for a bit of sightseeing today.'

'With pleasure! Niraji!' Shivaji said, 'We will go out to see the city.'

They all mounted their horses while the guards followed behind. At the Taj Mahal, Shivaji was wide-eyed seeing the beautiful architecture shining in the slanting rays of the evening sun. He had heard a lot of praise of the Taj and he was dumbstruck by its beauty. 'It's so beautiful!'

'I was sure you would love it. That is why I got special permission from Wazir Jaffar Khan.'

'Only a blind man can not appreciate such beauty,' Shivaji said. 'But why do you need permission to see the place?'

'You cannot enter the sanctum where the royal treasure is buried as per instructions from the elder Shahenshah.'

'Oh, I see!'

'There is no parallel for this building anywhere in the world. Shah Jahan built this in memory of his wife, Arjumand Banu. About twenty thousand men worked on it for fifteen years. The marble came from Makrana, and the Shahenshah was buried here after his death.'

'Aba saheb! We too must build something like this,' Sambhaji said.

Shivaji caressed his back saying, 'Bal Raje, you are still very young but try to understand this: Every person who ascends to a throne wants to leave behind something which the coming generations will remember him by. They try and build these things for a place in history. But a true king must lead a life such that he does not have to resort to building things for people to remember him by.'

'Your advice is quite sound,' Ram Singh nodded with a smile.

'It is better, then, not to have such monuments,' Hiroji uttered.

Shivaji turned immediately and said, 'Hiroji, don't jump to such conclusions either. It depends on how you look at things. I was talking about the concept of a monument. I never criticized the beauty of the Taj Mahal.'

Everyone was silent. Shivaji continued to be mesmerized by the beauty and stared at the Taj for a while.

Nirojipant said, 'There is a grandeur here which befits this Mughal monument but it still lacks the pious beauty of a Hindu temple.'

'I told you, it depends on your outlook. How different would the monument look if I had told you that it represented the four evils—lust, anger, pride and jealousy?'

Shivaji asked, turning to Ram Singh, 'Kunwarji, are the foundation stones made of marble too?'

'No, Raja saheb, the foundation stones are but ordinary stones.' He asked, a little hesitantly, 'Pardon my curiosity but I wonder why you ask that?'

'Please don't be so formal with me. Your father, Mirza Raja, considers me his son. You are like my brother then!'

'Raja saheb, I must have shown this monument to scores of people but you are the first one to ask this question; and hence I wondered why you ask.'

Shivaji was silent for a while. He let out a deep sigh and said, 'Kunwarji, thousands of stones lie below to support this beautiful monument. Millions will see and admire the beauty of the marble masterpiece but no one would realize the sacrifice made by the ordinary stones to support the marble blocks. I am reminded of my efforts to build the Swaraj and the thousands who have sacrificed their lives for it. When we get our Swaraj, I will be commemorated and praised but very few will recall the sacrifice made by the thousands of loyal troops. Seeing this I was suddenly reminded of them. Anyway, let us go in.'

They washed their feet and entered the mausoleum. The lovely marble graves were embellished with jewels and stones. A fakir sat with a huge fan made of peacock feathers. The smell of incense sticks and perfume wafted through the thick air. Shivaji folded his hands in veneration and Sambhaji followed suit. Ram Singh could not believe he was seeing Raje with his head bent in prayer. He wondered whether it was the same person who had stormed out of the durbar just a few afternoons ago.

Shivaji said, recognizing Ram Singh's confusion, 'Kunwarji, the soul who built this knew the true value of beauty. He understood the value of love. What is wrong in bending down to such a soul?'

They had just come out of the narrow room when Hiroji asked, 'I wonder how much it cost to build this.'

Raje replied, 'One does not calculate the cost in war and love.'

They returned to their camp to see cannons being placed around. Thousands of horses were all around. Shivaji noticed a rider coming towards him. He was wearing a green jacket and a typical Muslim dress and rode stylishly, his left hand on his waist while the right hand held the reins.

He smiled indulgently at Shivaji's men with their naked swords and said, looking at Raje as he bent his head in salute, 'Shivaji Raje! This humble servant is called Siddi Fulaad Khan. I am sorry to tell you that I have been sent to guard you and your camp with five thousand of my men.'

Shivaji was shocked to hear that. This was the same Fulaad Khan who was known as the 'one with no heart'. He was a broad-chested hunk of a man.

Shivaji said, 'Khan saheb, you may do your job. After all, we are both under the Badshah. You may guard us and we shall remain like prisoners here.'

Fulaad Khan was surprised by Shivaji's nonchalant attitude. He bowed and left. At that moment, Sambhaji came running and asked, 'Aba saheb, why have so many horsemen come here?'

The innocent question was enough to break Shivaji's resolve. He blurted out, 'We have been cheated. We have been trapped!' And his tears flowed—he could not resist them anymore.

Fulaad Khan and his men guarded the camp from the outside while Ram Singh's men were inside. Shivaji was impressed with Aurangzeb's cunning. It was clear that they could not escape easily now. He decided to put his mind to work—he had to find a way out of this.

When Ram Singh came to meet him, he said, 'Ram Singh, do you agree with me now? This is what Aurangzeb has had in mind since the beginning.'

'I am deeply disturbed, Raje,' Ram Singh said with tears in his eyes. 'I have conveyed the message to my father. I can only do so much.'

Shivaji knew that Ram Singh was not at fault. He said, 'I am not blaming you. Now listen to me. I know that your word has no value in the durbar. Don't take anymore responsibility on my behalf.'

'Raja saheb!'

'Listen to me carefully, Ram Singh! Tell Aurangzeb that Fulaad Khan has surrounded Shivaji and that he cannot escape. He does not need you anymore. Relieve yourself of this responsibility.'

Ram Singh got up quickly. He could not shirk his responsibilities so easily. He said, his eyes filled with tears, 'Raje, it is your large-heartedness to say so but I am, after all, a Rajput. I have given you my word and you have accepted me as your brother. How can I leave you like this? Whatever, has to happen, let it.'

Ram Singh continued, before Shivaji could interrupt, 'Raje, don't worry. My trusted men, Tej Singh, Arjun Singh, Sukh Singh Nathawat, are here to guard you. They will keep a constant vigil.'

Raje let out a deep sigh. He went to see Ram Singh off and then assembled his own key men. They were happy to hear his plan, and their hopes were renewed.

The next day Ram Singh came in to find Shivaji in a foul mood. His men were gathered around while he shouted, 'Get out all of you! You are all good-for-nothing. I don't want to see you here.'

They all left with their heads bent low. Ram Singh asked, 'Raja saheb, what happened?'

'I don't need them anymore. What use are they to me? Whatever has to happen will happen—why involve them?'

Ram Singh came out of the tent to find the men removing their tents. They said, 'We are moving out.'

Ram Singh told Niraji, 'Let your men camp in the gardens behind my haveli.'

Niraji was taken aback. He was aware that Raje had a plan and Ram Singh's request would spoil the same if he were to get involved. When Niraji told about Ram Singh's reaction, Shivaji muttered, 'These Rajputs have no brains! That is why they continue to work under the Mughals!'

Shivaji called Fulaad Khan the next morning and welcomed him with great protocol. He was surprised at Shivaji's behaviour. Shivaji smiled and said, 'Fulaad Khan, I have nothing against you. You are, after all, bound by the emperor's orders. You are just doing your duty.'

'Raja saheb, you are wise to understand—'

'I have called you here with a specific request.'

Fulaad Khan was suddenly alert and asked, 'What request?'

'I am trapped here and I cannot afford to feed so many of my men. I want to request the Badshah to allow most of my men to go back, leaving just a few. I want to keep only ten or fifteen of them.'

Siddi Fulaad Khan was overjoyed and conveyed the message to Aurangzeb, who could not believe that Shivaji wanted his men to go back. He ordered the release of hundreds of Shivaji's men. Aurangzeb wondered what Raje had in mind. He was watching each and every move by Shivaji carefully. He had wondered earlier why Shivaji had brought only a few elephants. The request for release of his men was something he could not fathom. He sent out precautionary orders to all districts around Agra, 'If Shivaji escapes, he must be captured immediately and imprisoned.'

When the orders came from the Badshah himself, Ram Singh reluctantly agreed to let Shivaji's men go. Mahadev was one of the men who were supposedly going back, and as were many other spies.

Shivaji had managed his first step well.

Aurangzeb was waiting for a reply from Jai Singh. A letter had arrived with the request that Shivaji be treated with respect. Aurangzeb was formulating an appropriate reply when he received a strange request from Shivaji, expressing his desire to renounce everything, become a sanyasi and visit Kashi. His plea was that he was deeply disturbed and wanted some peace of mind.

Aurangzeb laughed and sent a reply, 'I have no objection to your being a sanyasi. A sanyasi can stay anywhere; I suggest that you make yourself comfortable in my fort at Allahabad. Subedar Bahadur Khan will take care of you. You may spend your days there praying to your lord.'

However, Shivaji's ploy did not materialize and two months had passed by, when the great poet Parmanand came to visit Shivaji from Allahabad with a Brahmin poet, Kalash. Shivaji asked Kalash to stay back and they spoke till late in the night. The poets left after two days and Shivaji gifted them a few elephants. Aurangzeb heard of the incident and was convinced that Raje was really inclined to becoming a sanyasi.

The rains had just begun, increasing the humidity in Agra. Shivaji wistfully remembered his homeland—the dense green forests, hills covered in green and the rains drenching the forts and creating instant waterfalls as the water cascaded down the ramparts. The misty clouds would create a loving cover protecting the forts. A loving cover!

'Maa saheb! How must she be spending her days, the poor soul,' Shivaji mused.

Shivaji's mind was restless. Many thoughts flitted through his mind. A man gets impaled on his own ego! I was hopeful of Alamgir's large-heartedness. I came here with the hopes of being the Subedar of the south and taking back my kingdom the moment Mirza Raja and Diler Khan turned northwards. But my hopes have been shattered. I am now trapped here thanks to the Badshah.

Raje smiled wryly at his thoughts. Who would decide right and wrong? Aurangzeb? Why would he give me the subedari of south? He killed his own kin, and did not hesitate to poison his own father. Why would he show me any pity? I wonder why he has still kept me alive. Aurangzeb is taking time to decide. There has to be some other plan. He knows a delay could cost him his future. And yet, he has decided not to act. I wonder whether it is my sheer luck which is keeping me alive. But if that is the case, then why has Bhawani Mata not shown me the way forward yet?

Shivaji got up from his bed. He saw Sambhaji Raje sleeping soundly and thought, Look at this blessed soul! He sleeps without fear for his life. He has no knowledge of the spectre of death hanging on our heads or the guards outside the camp. He can sleep soundly leaving all responsibilities to his father. Then why should I not trust my Jagdamba Ma?

Maa saheb! She must be spending her days at the feet of the Lord, shedding tears and wishing us well. What if something happens to us here?

Shivaji could not bear to think further as he paced the room. We are stuck here in this foreign land. What must be the condition of the forts back home? Annaji, Moropant, Prataprao, Tanaji and the others must be sick with worry. On top of it, there would be rumours spreading thick and fast! The rumours of my death would shake the core of their hearts. Hopefully, my spies would have reached Agra by now. I hope the news of my arrest does not lead to a revolt at home.

Raje stopped for a moment and then thought, But who would revolt and against whom? Annaji, Tanaji, Moropant—there were many people who were capable of it but these men? Would they ever lead a revolt? Impossible! Instead they would be spending their energies trying to manage the forts. They would be giving Maa saheb false hopes and promises, trying to pacify her restless mind.

Raje continued pacing the room. I brought a thousand men with me. Luckily, they have escaped arrest now. Hopefully they will be waiting for me at different places. Poor Ram Singh is not aware of all this.

Raje's thoughts hardened. I need to escape from here somehow. But how do I do this?

Raje's mind was busy. He remembered Samarth's words, 'If things have to be done, then they should be done!' Raje also recalled Maa saheb's words when he had gone to show her the farman sent by Aurangzeb, 'Raje, learn to celebrate your losses too. The true victor is one who is able to face such defeats and come out victorious. You need to have faith and accept such things. Faith will show you the way forward.'

Raje felt better. His mind took a different turn now. Even the Pandavas managed to escape from captivity. Why should I not be able to find a way? Krishna escaped from Kansa's jail in a meer basket. Vasudeva was able to take him away despite so many guards. They all slept soundly as he was taken away. Even the Yamuna receded to allow him to escape. I am lucky that Alamgir has kept me alive. I need to find a way now.

Shivaji moved a wick in a lamp and joined another one with it. The lamp burnt brightly. His face too was shining brightly in the light of the lamps!

Shivaji and his men sat in conference. There was a hint of optimism in the air. Shivaji welcomed Ram Singh as he presented himself. 'Ram Singh, what is the news from the durbar?'

'Everything is fine.'

'I too am relaxed, thanks to the blessings of Alamgir.'

Ram Singh was surprised to hear that. Shivaji smiled. 'You need not look so surprised. After all, there is no one as relaxed as one in captivity. There are thousands of men guarding me!' Changing the topic, he asked, 'Have you managed to relieve yourself from your duty?'

'Not yet.'

'Ram Singh, you are like a younger brother to me. I suggest you request that you be relieved as soon as possible. I don't want you to have this responsibility. After all, he is a Badshah. One never knows when he would change his mind.'

Ram Singh was lost in thought. Shivaji sensed his hesitation and asked Pant, 'Where is Bal Raje?'

Gopinathpant answered, smiling, 'He is inspecting the guards along with Fulaad Khan.'

Shivaji laughed out loudly, 'Look at the irony. I am captive here and Yuvraj is a free bird, inspecting the guards! How lucky he is!'

Ram Singh joined the laughter, 'It is true, Raje! He is really lucky. Alamgir too likes him a great deal and asks me to bring him to the durbar often. In fact, he has asked me to bring him there today as well. He is a favourite in my house too.'

'I know that Alamgir is large-hearted. Who would treat an enemy's son with such love and affection?'

Ram Singh said, 'Raje, do you recall meeting Manucci?'

'Manucci?'

'Yes. He is in charge of my father's artillery. I believe you met at Purandar.'

Shivaji immediately remembered him and said, 'What a man! In fact, we are friends! His company was a great pleasure in days of turmoil. Where is he these days? Has he come here?'

'No. But he has sent an artist with a letter of recommendation.'

'An artist?'

'Yes, a painter. He has painted portraits of many at the durbar. Alamgir has given permission for him to meet you.'

'It is indeed kind of the Badshah. What is the painter's name?'

'Mir Hassan.'

Mir Hassan presented himself and bent in mujra to Ram Singh and Shivaji. He waited for Raje's instructions. Shivaji looked at Ram Singh and said, 'Ram Singh, what a coincidence! When we were to hand over Purandar, I met a pandit, Shivram, from the north. He looked at my horoscope and predicted I would be free within eighteen months. Instead of being a free man, I am now not sure if I will leave Agra alive. Now Manucci has sent me a painter. Sometimes fate is cruel, isn't it?'

Shivaji was quiet for a moment before he burst out laughing, 'Perhaps there is irony in it. I may not remain here but the painting will remain forever!'

Shivaji laughed but Ram Singh did not join the laughter. Shivaji said, trying to hide his own anxiety, 'What is the need to worry, Ram Singh? One day everyone has to die, isn't it? At least a painting will keep my memory alive.'

Ram Singh felt a little relieved. He said, 'Raja saheb should not speak like this. Maybe Jahanpanah may change ...'

'Ram Singh, anything is possible. Let this painter come anytime he wishes to. It will be a good distraction for me.'

The next day onwards, Mir Hassan would come to Raje's room and paint a portrait of him. Raje seemed to be in a talkative mood and would spend the hours chatting with him. Ram Singh, on the other hand, was worried sick of the dangers that lay ahead.

He was ruing the day when Mirza Raja had given him the responsibility of Raje's well-being. The Badshah had been contemplating a campaign down south and Ram Singh was to keep an eye on Shivaji. But Mirza Raja had advised that Ram Singh should ask to accompany the Badshah. He was in agreement with Raje's advice of relieving himself of the responsibility as soon as possible. Aurangzeb did not agree at first but later acquiesced to his request and relieved him of the job. Ram Singh heaved a sigh of relief. For Shivaji too, it was a load off his mind. He was now free to plan his escape.

One day, Mir Hassan came with a painting of Shivaji sitting astride a horse surrounded by many guards including a few Muslims.

'Mir Hassan, I must admire your art. You have managed to recreate my image with outstanding similarity. But where did these Mughals come from?'

'Huzoor, I saw you accompanying Ram Singh to the Shahi durbar. That image was captured in my mind.'

'Wah! Beautiful! Niraji ...'

Niraji came forward and presented Mir Hassan with a large sum of money and some rich clothes. Mir Hassan stepped forward to present the painting when Shivaji said, 'Mir Hassan, keep this with you. If you wish, you may hand it over to Manucci. It will serve him as a reminder of me.'

Mir Hassan soon left, and within a few days, Raje looked more and more well-disposed.

A few days later, the news that Shivaji had taken ill spread and soon reached Aurangzeb's court. He immediately sent his physician but Shivaji seemed to have lost the will to live and was not in the mood to take any medicines. He had agreed to take medicines suggested by a village doctor. The only people with him were Hiroji Farzand and his manservant Madari. He was now bedridden all the time. Fulaad Khan would enquire about his health whenever possible. In order to get good wishes and blessings, Shivaji started sending crates of sweets to the various ministers in Aurangzeb's court and the crates were being sent daily.

Shivaji had managed to bribe many of Fulaad Khan's men who had called on him while Fulaad Khan was blissfully unaware of these developments.

Aurangzeb, on the other hand, was now quite relaxed as far as Shivaji was concerned. Shaista Khan's begum and others were now creating a false image of Shivaji. 'Shivaji is a shaitan! He can walk through walls! He can jump a few hundred feet. He can vanish at the drop of a hat!' and such were doing the rounds.

'If he can do all this, why is he still languishing in that jail?' Aurangzeb asked, unconvinced of Shivaji's supernatural abilities. He was now waiting for his final act. The haveli of Raja Vitthaldas was being readied. Aurangzeb had planned to move Shivaji there and then kill him.

Ram Singh came to know of this plan and met Shivaji on the pretext of enquiring after his health, only to find that Shivaji did not have any fever but complained of body ache. Ram Singh seemed restless. He said, 'Raja saheb, your health has taken a turn for the worse at the wrong moment.'

'Why do you say that?' Shivaji asked.

'I have heard about a plan to kill you in Vitthaldas's haveli. I feel so helpless! I am unable to help you,' Ram Singh said, as he started crying.

After getting up with a lot of effort, Shivaji hugged Ram Singh and said, 'Please don't cry. If possible, please do one thing for me.'

'Tell me, Raje!' Ram Singh said eagerly.

'Convey my regards to everyone at your home and take care of Sambhaji Raje.'

'You don't worry on that count, Raje!' After a pause, he added, 'There is one thing I can do to help you. The day you are to be moved to the haveli, I will send a message through Fulaad Khan saying, "Don't come to my house. The Badshah does not approve." That will be a signal to you. I don't know what else I can do for you.'

Ram Singh left and Raje was lying on his bed when Madari, Hiroji, Ramkishan and Jiva Joshi came in. They were busy packing the sweet baskets.

The baskets were always thoroughly checked at the gates. One of the baskets was sent to Fulaad Khan's house.

The next day, the poet Kalash came to meet Raje. He had a saffron cloth tied to his head, while the tilak on his forehead and his fair skin gave him a radiant look. Raje was speaking to him at length when he realized someone at the door. It was Fulaad Khan.

Raje called out from his bed, 'Come in, Fulaad Khan.'

Fulaad Khan came in and said, 'Raja saheb, I came to personally thank you for the sweets.'

'Please have a seat. There is no need for thanks. Please meet Kalash, a renowned Brahmin from Kashi. He can read horoscopes, and I was asking him when I would get well.'

Fulaad Khan smiled and said, 'Instead why don't you enquire about when you would be released?'

Raje's eyes penetrated Fulaad Khan for a moment and then he said, smiling, 'Fulaad Khan, isn't that rhetorical? I am trapped here under the Badshah's instructions. I cannot escape while you guard the camp! A bird cannot escape the Badshah's prison and no one can dare escape your guards!'

Siddi Fulaad Khan swelled with pride on being praised. He said, showing his bright white teeth and smiling widely, 'Raja saheb, that is a fact!'

'I know! I was not praising you. I was merely stating facts.'

Sambhaji Raje came in at that moment. He said, looking at Shivaji Raje, 'Aba saheb! I had gone to Ram Singh Kaka's house. We went to meet Alijah and look what he has given me! His dagger! See!'

Bal Raje showed the dagger. The sharp edge glinted in the light. Raje said, 'Be careful, Bal Raje. Royal daggers are sometimes poisonous.'

'Aba saheb, I asked for a dagger for you when Alijah said something like "He is such an innocent boy!"'

Everyone laughed. Shivaji said, 'Bal Raje, the Badshah was praising you.'

Fulaad Khan had been guarding Raje for weeks now and he was impressed with the way Raje treated everyone. He was not able to understand Raje's exemplary behaviour. He said, 'Raja saheb, it is unfortunate that I am guarding you as a prisoner. Had the Badshah been as large-hearted to you as he is to Sambhaji Raje, you and I would have been great friends in the court.'

'I still believe that our relationship is the same. I am wise enough not to blame you just because you are guarding me.'

Fulaad Khan took his leave, and the moment he left, Raje hugged Sambhaji and said, pointing at Kalash, 'Do you recognize this gentleman?'

'I do,' Sambhaji said, nodding.

'Then don't forget him. You should listen to whatever he says.'

'Yes, Aba saheb.'

Kalash patted Sambhaji's back and said as he moved out of earshot, 'Raje, you have given me such a big responsibility!'

'I am sure you can manage it well. You need not come back now. Hiroji will meet you at the right time.'

Kalash left and Shivaji went back to his bed.

Shivaji's health continued to deteriorate. There was no improvement despite the medicines. One afternoon Fulaad Khan came in to enquire. 'How are you feeling, Raja saheb?'

'Just about managing!' Raje said, sighing, as he tried to get up.

'You can't give up like this! Allah is merciful! Raja saheb, you were to meet Ram Singh, weren't you?'

Raje did not show any surprise. He said, 'I am tired of my ill health. I thought I would feel better in his company.'

'Raja saheb, Kunwarji has sent a message asking you not to come as the Badshah is not in favour of it. I too feel it is better that you don't visit him.'

'As the Lord wishes!' Raje said, 'That was the one place I could go and spend some time. Anyway, I will sleep now.'

Fulaad Khan left and Shivaji shot out immediate instructions to Madari, Farzand, Joshi and the others. Sambhaji was sent over to Ram Singh's place with Joshi. Raje told him, 'Sambhaji, go over to Ram Singh Kaka's place. And don't go to the court with him. Listen to whatever Hiroji or Kalash Kaka say. Take care of yourself.'

Sambhaji left and Raje asked Arjun Singh, 'Are the baskets ready?'

'Yes.'

'I hope all the men are trustworthy.'

'Yes.'

'All right then. Arjun Singh, you will accompany us till the borders of the town. We will then find our way from there. Call the men in.'

Arjun Singh called a man inside. He was one of the workers. Arjun Singh said, 'He is deaf and dumb.'

Raje sat on his chair. While his beard was being shaved, Hiroji got into Raje's clothes. No one from a distance would have doubted it was not Shivaji, who quickly changed into a workman's clothes with a red turban on his head.

Shivaji's bearing changed completely. All instructions were clear. He patted Madari's back. Madari started pressing Hiroji's legs as he would do for Raje every day.

Hiroji said, 'Raje, take care!'

Raje pressed Hiroji's hand lightly. He sat in the room where the other workmen would come to fill up the sweet baskets.

The sun had set now. There was a clamour outside as the guard duty was being changed. Arjun Singh indicated to Raje and he joined the third row of workmen carrying out the sweet baskets. The baskets were being sent out one by one. Raje joined the queue and was out in a few minutes. The baskets were checked at the gate. The guards allowed them to go once they were sure that the baskets were okay. The men moved with rapid steps and soon were out of the camp.

Arjun Singh led the way and soon, they reached a narrow road leading to the bazaar where a fakir sat singing. Raje dropped a coin into his bowl. Another worker quietly joined the crowd and squeezed in behind Raje to share his load. Raje gently stepped out of the crowd and watched as the baskets moved out of sight within minutes. He heard a voice say, 'Come on, we need to move fast.' It was the fakir.

Raje joined the fakir as they meandered through the streets. They entered a house after negotiating a few turns. The house belonged to a potter. Raje said, seeing Kalash, 'Bal Raje?'

'He is fine. He will be out of Agra city by now,' Kalash said. 'The moment they hear of your escape there will be enquiries everywhere. They will stop anyone with a small lad. Mahadev is accompanying Bal Raje and they are on their way to Mathura.'

'But what if someone recognizes them?'

'He is bald and dressed like a poor Brahmin boy—no one will give him a second glance.'

***

Hiroji Farzand slept with his face towards the wall. Madari sat near his legs, massaging them. The lamps burnt brightly when Arjun Singh came for guard duty. Joshi too joined the guards while Fulaad Khan's men peeped inside. They saw Raje sleeping as usual. Raje's turban and sword were visible near his bedside. It was late at night now, and Raje had refused food. They could hear Raje's whimpering. Madari continued to massage the legs when he whispered, 'Hiroji, will you ask me to stop now? I am tired!'

'No, continue massaging. I don't want anyone to have any doubts,' Hiroji replied.

Madari continued the massage. It was midnight when the guard duties changed. Madari had dozed off by then. Hiroji woke him up early in the morning and said, 'Get up now.'

Hiroji stepped off the bed and changed back into his clothes. He put up a fat pillow on the bed and arranged the same to look like Raje sleeping there. That morning, when the guard peeped in, Hiroji signalled with his fingers on his lips to request silence because Raje was in a deep sleep.

They got up after a while and stepped out of the tent. While leaving, he told the guard outside, 'Raje did not sleep the whole night. He is sleeping now. I will get some medicines for him. Don't disturb him till then.' They both stepped out of the camp.

It was daylight now but the tent seemed to be silent. Anyone approaching the tent was told that Raje had been not able to sleep the whole night, and that they should let him sleep now.

The sun was high in the sky. There was no noise from inside. The guards were suspicious and worried. The men who had gone to get the medicines had not returned yet. They could not take the silence anymore and called for Fulaad Khan. He came in immediately to find Raje sleeping. His turban and sword were at the bedside. He seemed to be sleeping peacefully and Fulaad Khan was reluctant to disturb him. He called out gently, 'Raja saheb!'

There was no response.

'Raja saheb!'

The silence was complete.

He came near the bed and lifted the bedsheet covering Raje. It was as if the heavens had come falling down. Fulaad Khan could not believe his eyes. He shouted, 'Ya Allah! The devil has escaped!'

Fulaad Khan could not hold back his anger and kicked and insulted the soldiers around. He then went to Ram Singh's house, who could not believe what he was hearing. They knew they were both in trouble. Ram Singh went to the durbar to report without any delay.

Aurangzeb was in the Diwan-i-Khas with the Wazir and maulvi in attendance. He was pleased to see Ram Singh and remembered the plan he had for Shivaji that day. He was going to move Shivaji that evening to the haveli and that would be the end of him. He said warmly, 'Come in, Ram Singh.'

Ram Singh stood there with his head bent low. He was normally in good spirits, and Aurangzeb was surprised to see him like this. He asked, 'Ram Singh, why are you so glum?'

Ram Singh looked up, his eyes moist. He said, 'Jahanpanah, there is bad news. Shivaji has escaped.'

Aurangzeb could not understand the meaning of Ram Singh's words for a moment. He threw the chain of beads from his hands and screamed, 'How did he escape?'

'He was being guarded as always but this morning, we found that he was not in his room.'

Aurangzeb's temper knew no bounds. He called Fulaad Khan, who took the oath in the name of the Holy Quran that Shivaji had just disappeared into thin air—he had vanished! Aurangzeb knew Fulaad Khan's loyalty and immediately blamed Ram Singh, 'Ram Singh, this is all your fault!'

'I ask for mercy, Jahanpanah. I wish to point out that my men were guarding inside while it was Fulaad Khan's men who were guarding the camp outside.'

Aurangzeb dispatched his men in all directions to search for Shivaji and Sambhaji. He was confident that they both would be found soon. They searched in all the houses including the potter's where Raje had camped earlier. But they could not find them.

Ram Singh's men were caught and punished but they could not shed any light on what had happened. Unfortunately, Tryambakpant and Raghunathpant were caught in the search. Fulaad Khan vent his anger on them and tortured them to no avail. They caught Parmanand who was on his way home with the elephants gifted by Raje. He too was captured and taken back to Agra.

Aurangzeb behaved like a man possessed. He was unable to believe what he had just seen and heard. Had Shivaji really vanished as described by Fulaad Khan? He wondered whether Shivaji could walk through walls and materialize elsewhere. He was not willing to take chances with his own life and ordered strict security around himself. A maulvi accompanied him all the time. Ram Singh's mansabdari was removed and Mirza Raja was ordered to capture Netaji.

The news from Aurangzeb's durbar reached Raje regularly while in hiding. It had been nearly three weeks since their escape when Raje decided to step out in the garb of a mendicant. Others followed suit but their hearts melted seeing Raje. Shivaji said, sensing their trauma, 'Niraji, my wish has been fulfilled. I have wished to be a mendicant for a long time. At least I am now wearing his garb. By the time I really become worthy, it might be too late!'

He continued, 'You know the language of these people, don't you?'

'Yes.'

'That is why I selected you to accompany me. Now you are our leader. You are "Kalyan" and I am "Anand". We all are your disciples.'

Raje gave each one a new name. They left in pairs. Raje made them leave in different groups, and go in different directions. They all left Agra within a few days. They knew that there would be strict vigilance towards the south; and hence, they moved northwards.

Raje halted at a dharamshala for the night. They lit a bonfire for warmth and to cook food. A man sat in one corner wearing a silk shirt and trousers. He had a small cloth tied to his head. He seemed to be keenly observing them.

The next morning, they were preparing to leave when the man came towards them, 'Maharaj, pardon me but I need your help.'

Nirajipant looked at him and asked, 'What do you want?'

'I am a perfume seller. I have expensive perfume from Kanauj,' he said, opening a box of perfumes.

Everyone laughed. Nirajipant said, 'We are mendicants. Even ash is a burden for us. What use is perfume to us?'

Raje was listening to the conversation intently. He interrupted, 'I have been looking for kewda perfume for a while now.'

Everyone was stunned into silence.

The perfume seller asked, 'You want kewda?'

'Yes.' Raje looked into his eyes and exclaimed, 'Kalash?'

'Ji, Maharaj!'

'Wait for us near Mathura. We will reach there shortly.'

Kalash got up to leave. Raje dipped into his bag and gave him a few coins. Everyone present was wondering what the exchange was about. Raje explained, 'That was Kalash. "Kewda" was the password!'

They all reached Mathura soon. Moropant Pingle's brother-in-law Krishnajipant and his brothers, Kashirao and Visajipant, took the responsibility of taking care of Sambhaji. They had got the news of Raje's arrival in advance through Kalash. Sambhaji, in his Brahmin attire, was unable to recognize Raje and his men, much to Raje's relief. The plan was to let Sambhaji stay in Mathura and send him to Pune only after the others had reached. The group now moved to Kashi.

Raje's mind was not at ease despite reaching Kashi. Kalash took care of their stay but Raje was restless. He was desperate to reach his Kashi—Rajgad—and the one who had bought him to this world, Maa saheb!

The Padmavati gate at Rajgad was silent. There was no one in the courtyard. Moropant, Balaji and others were busy with their work. Jijabai was in her puja room as usual. She would spend most of her time there, often fasting. She was getting weaker by the day. Her forlorn look was unbearable to others yet they had no words to console her. The men tried their best to prevent rumours from reaching her.

Moropant sat in his office. It was noon when he was told that a rider had come to meet him. Moropant got up to receive the rider and could not believe his eyes. It was Mahadev! He ran to hug him tightly. He asked eagerly, 'How is Raje?'

'He is safe!' Mahadev replied.

'Where is he?'

'I don't know.'

'What do you mean?'

Mahadev recounted the events in Agra and how they had escaped from the camp. He said, 'As instructed by Raje, I crossed Narwar Ghati and waited for orders. As soon as I got the news of his escape, I came here.'

'What are his orders?'

Mahadev said, 'Raje had told me, "Mahadev, the moment you hear of my escape, go to Rajgad. They will search everywhere for me. I will have to find a way to reach there. When you reach Rajgad, tell Moropant that Raje has escaped and that he has reached the fort. They should fire cannons in celebration of my arrival. Give this message and he will understand the rest."'

Moropant had tears of joy in his eyes. He said, 'I am blessed to be able to serve him. You are his spy, Mahadev! Did you not understand his message? It is so simple. The moment we celebrate Raje's arrival, the news will reach Aurangzeb and they will stop searching for him. Raje will then be able to find his way back home without much trouble. You wait here! I will inform Maa saheb and then you can meet her.'

Moropant stepped into Maa saheb's quarters. Jijabai sat in the puja room with Putlabai in attendance. 'Maa saheb, I have some news for you.'

'Don't tell me your troubles now. Whatever it is, tell Soyara.'

Ignoring protocol, Moropant sat next to Jijabai and said, 'Maa saheb, Raje managed to escape and is on his way here now.'

'Who told you all this? Have you been dreaming?'

'Maa saheb, Mahadev is here.'

As soon as Mahadev entered, Jijabai fired a barrage of questions. He tried his best to answer as well as he could. Jijabai paid obeisance in the puja room. Moropant asked, 'Shall I give the signal for the cannons to fire?'

'Wait for the night. Send a palanquin down the fort and let them come back with some riders. Get the guards in place, and the next morning announce his arrival with the cannons.'

That night, Moropant went down with the royal palanquin and returned a few hours later. The curtains were drawn. The news spread—Raje had arrived! The cannons boomed, announcing the good news. Raje was ill but had managed to reach home! Mirza Raja got the news and immediately informed Aurangzeb. The fort was being strictly guarded under the supervision of Moropant. No one could leave the fort and each visitor was to be screened carefully.

Shivaji Raje negotiated his way through various states like Chanda, Indore and other parganas in the garb of a mendicant. The landscape was now getting familiar, giving him hope. It was nearly a month since they had escaped from Agra. The aches and pains of the journey were soon forgotten. A small village was nestled between dense vegetation. Smoke was coming out of some of the houses, possibly from the kitchen. Niraji said, 'Raje, let us rest here.'

The four mendicants moved towards the village. The villagers welcomed them while curiously looking at them. There was no dharamshala in the village but one of the villagers welcomed them into his house. Raje was overwhelmed at their hospitality and said, 'Maharaj, these people are so welcoming.'

'Anand, it is a Hindu tradition to welcome a guest at the door. It is thanks to such hospitable people that mendicants like us are able to survive,' Niraji replied.

The farmer's wife came out and after placing a few dry beans for the visitors, she went inside. The farmer pointed towards the beans and said, 'Please eat them, Maharaj.'

They asked, 'What is your name?'

'I am Ravji Patil.'

'So are you the Patil?' Niraji asked.

He laughed, 'Maharaj, we were Patils but lost everything to the Mughals. Now we just carry the title!'

'This would not be your state for long, don't worry,' Raje said.

'What?'

Niraji said, 'Patil, Anand can predict the future and his predictions are always correct.'

Patil got up and touching Raje's feet and said, 'Anandji, I hope what you say comes true for this poor farmer. May God bless you!'

That night, the Patil's wife served a simple hot meal of bhakri and some vegetables. Seeing the hot food Raje said, 'Aai, may the Lord bless you!'

She looked at Raje and said, her anger rising, 'Eat what you get. If we had been better off, we would have served some sweets too, but Shivaji has taken away everything from us!'

Everyone was taken aback but they kept their cool. Raje asked, 'What has Shivaji done?'

'We are the ones stuck under the Mughals. What is our fault? Shivaji Raje's sardars—Prataprao, Anandrao and Telengrao—they are creating havoc everywhere, looting villages after villages. The Badshah had captured Shivaji, I believe. He should have died there, but I am told he has escaped.'

'Has he?'

'Haven't you heard?'

'How are we to know? We are simple folk,' Niraji said.

'Not only has he escaped, but he has reached the fort too. They sounded the cannons on his arrival.'

'I see,' Raje said. 'But is it true what Aai is saying?'

Patil said, 'Oh, don't listen to the womenfolk. They make a mountain out of a molehill. These Mughals have created chaos all over and so everyone gets blamed for it.'

Raje finished his meal and then spread out a mat to sleep. They left early the next morning. Within a few days, Raje realized that he had reached his territory—the familiar landscape, the mountains, the orchards and the distant forts!

Niraji said, 'Raje, we have reached our territory now. It is okay if we let our identity be known.'

'No, Niraji! Not till we reach the fort.'

Niraji was silent. The sun was high in the sky as the four mendicants walked along their way. Niraji signalled them to stop. They could hear horses galloping towards them. Soon, a group of soldiers on horseback emerged, led by a sardar. The mendicants stood on one side of the road. The soldiers stopped while the sardar dismounted and looked closely at the mendicants. Raje immediately recognized his commander Prataprao, who looked at them and said, 'Sirs, where are you from?'

'We are from Kashi.'

'Then why are you headed south?'

Niraji fiddled with his stick and replied, 'Beta, we are simple souls. We have nothing to own or possess. Wherever the feet takes us we go there.'

'Maharaj, we are facing one problem. Can you tell us whether we will be able to overcome that?'

He pointed at Raje and said, 'Beta, Anand can predict the future very well. Ask him whatever you wish to.'

Raje was stunned but did not say anything.

Prataprao came forward and said, 'Maharaj, please bless me.' Prataprao looked at the mendicant. Raje looked every inch a bairagi with his saffron turban, body covered with ash and a chain of rudraksha beads on his chest.

'Beta, what is your problem?'

Prataprao glanced in the direction of his soldiers and asked, 'Maharaj, is it true that you know of the past and future?'

The mendicant was enraged. He looked angry and said, 'Are you testing me? I know you very well. You are Kudtoji, isn't it? Raje gave you title of "Prataprao" and I can see a thousand men under you. You are the commander. Listen! Raje has not yet reached the fort. It is untrue that he has reached. I believe you want to know when Raje would reach the fort.'

'I am blessed, Maharaj!' Prataprao bent down to touch Raje's feet. 'Maharaj, please pardon me. That is true—Raje has not yet reached the fort and I wanted to know when he will be arriving.'

Anand closed his eyes and then let out a deep sigh. He looked at Prataprao and said, 'Beta, there is nothing to worry. Your Raje is fine.'

'But when will we meet him?'

'Very soon. I can see you touching Raje's feet within this week.'

Prataprao was overjoyed. He folded his hands in namaskar and said, 'Maharaj, if this is true, I will raise my hands heavenwards in praise of the Lord.' He glanced at the gold bracelets given by Raje to him and said, 'I will gift these gold bracelets to you. They were given to me by Raje himself.'

'I would be glad to receive them.'

Prataprao asked, 'But Maharaj, where would I find you?'

Raje raised his hands up and said, 'Don't you worry. I too will be there when you meet Raje.'

Prataprao bent low in namaskar and then marched on with his soldiers. Niraji could not hold his laughter anymore and burst out laughing.

Raje said, his face grim, 'Niraji, I hope Maa saheb will recognize me.'

'Raje, a mother will not fail you. Someone who looks at your feet all the time may not recognize you but the one who looks into your eyes can never fail to recognize you.'

They finally could see the imposing structure of Rajgad. The sun was high in the sky. Niraji said, 'Raje, only our good fate has got us here!'

'Yes, Niraji! It is all due to the blessings of Bhawani Mata. There is one soul there whose blessings we need now. Let us move fast. I cannot rest till I have darshan of those feet.'

Raje reached the first gate and the guards came forward, seeing some mendicants. The havaldar asked, 'Where do you want to go, Maharaj?'

'We are on the way to the fort to collect some alms,' Niraji answered.

'I am sorry. I cannot allow anyone inside.'

'Are you saying there are restrictions for us too?'

'I am sorry, sir. These are strict orders of the Peshwa. I need his permission.'

They were nonplussed. They wondered what to do next when they saw Prataprao, Anandrao and Telangrao coming towards them on their horses. They spotted the mendicants and Prataprao ran forward to touch their feet. He said, 'Maharaj, why are you standing here?'

'I have come here for some alms but we were stopped. We were told that Shivaji Raje's mother is very generous. We are keen to meet her.'

'Maharaj, I will ask someone to escort you in.'

Prataprao gave instructions and the escort took them up the fort. Jijabai was in her puja room. The idol of Jagdamba stood there silently while Jijabai put some bilva leaves on the Shiva linga. She continued to chant 'Shiva Shiva' as she did her puja. Her hands shivered while her body shook involuntarily out of weakness and old age. This puja was her daily ritual.

Moropant came into the room and hesitated, seeing her in the puja room. He coughed to attract her attention.

Jijabai turned and asked, 'Yes, Moropant? Come in.'

'Maa saheb, there are four mendicants at the door. They are requesting to meet you.'

Jijabai picked up the bilva leaves saying, 'Give them whatever they ask for. I am tired of doing everything—donation, giving alms, trying out different pujas. And I am still unable to see my Shivba! I cannot close my eyes for a moment. Send them back with good wishes and a nice donation.'

Moropant went back but the mendicants were adamant to see Jijabai. Moropant came in and informed that they were unwilling to accept anything till they met her.

Jijabai kept the tray on the floor and said, 'I will see them. I don't want their curses upon me.'

She got up with a lot of effort. Moropant ran and put out his hand forward to support her. Jijabai recovered and said, 'See, I seem to be losing balance now.'

'Maa saheb, you must stop fasting now.'

'Then why don't I die?' Jijabai erupted. She continued talking to herself, 'Where will that poor lad be? Shivba can take care of himself but my heart goes out to Bal Raje!'

Moropant wiped her tears. Jijabai did not notice that. He said, 'Maa saheb, after you meet the mendicants, I request you to come to the main hall.'

'Why, do you want to say something?'

'We need to take some decisions.'

'I will come. Wait for me.'

Jijabai walked into the courtyard, supported by Putlabai. Moropant walked on the other side. She came out into the courtyard.

Raje got up seeing Jijabai. He was seeing his mother after so many months! She was wearing a white sari, and her hair had also turned white. Raje had tears in his eyes seeing her so old and tired. He walked swiftly climbing the steps and put his head at her feet. Moropant and Putlabai gasped in surprise while Jijabai tried to walk back a few steps.

'Oh, this is a bad omen. Since when did bairagis start touching someone else's feet?'

She heard him say, 'Maa saheb, don't you recognize me?'

A million shivers passed through her body. She had been waiting to hear this voice! Moropant and Putlabai watched intently. Jijabai stared at the face of the mendicant. The bright eyes, they bent down as soon as they met her gaze. The same broad forehead and the lovely nose!

Maa saheb exclaimed, 'Shivba!'

The next moment she hugged him tightly. Shouts of joy erupted in the courtyard. Moropant and Putlabai ran inside when they saw Manohari at the door.

'What happened, Rani saheb? Why are you running?'

Putlabai hugged Manohari and kissed her before she realized what was happening! She said, blushing, 'He is back!'

Jijabai came into her room with Raje, who said, 'Maa saheb, please sit down now. We will speak at length later.'

Jijabai said, wiping her tears, 'I was praying to Lord Shiva when you arrived in the same avatar!'

The inner quarters were filled with the queens and maids. No one was bothered about protocol. Raje took Jijabai's permission to step out and meet them. Everyone had surrounded Niraji in the office. They bent down in mujra seeing Raje enter. When they lifted their eyes, they saw Raje crying.

Prataprao could not believe his eyes. He asked, 'Maharaj, is that you ...?'

'Yes, it is me. Did I not tell you that I too would be present when you meet your Raje? But tell me Prataprao, you are my Senapati but you still failed to recognize me?'

Raje looked at Prataprao, Anandrao, Telangrao, Annaji, Balaji and Moropant who stood there in attendance. He was overwhelmed with emotions. He said, putting his hand on Prataprao's shoulder, 'I am truly indebted to you. I was away for months but you did not leave anything to chance and have manged to control things well. I will never be able to repay this debt. Annaji, Moropant—this is your strength. I know you can manage without me!'

Raje could not speak further. His voice was choked with tears.

Annaji Datto said, 'Maharaj, where is Bal Raje?'

Raje looked at Niraji. He curled his fists and said, 'You have asked something which I was dreading telling you till now.' Raje closed his eyes and said, 'Bal Raje has left me and gone away!'

Raje opened his eyes to find shock on everyone's face. Raje turned sharply to find Jijabai standing at the door. She had got the answer to the question she had come to ask! Raje exclaimed, 'Maa saheb!'

Jijabai turned back, crying. She moved forward with rapid steps. Raje did not know what to do. He turned and followed her into her quarters. Jijabai sat on the edge of the bed weeping uncontrollably.

'Bal Raje! How could you leave me? Whose permission did you take before doing this?'

The palace, whose joy knew no bounds a few minutes back, was enveloped in a deep sorrow. The shock was unbearable. The queens were uncontrollable with sorrow.

Raje said, 'Maa saheb, listen to me for a moment.'

Jijabai brushed off his hand and said, 'What do you want me to listen for, Raje? And what else is there to listen to now? An innocent life has been lost in the politics played out by his elders! You should have remembered the promise you made to Sai!'

There was no privacy in the palace. Raje looked around and asked Jijabai, 'Maa saheb, please come into the puja room.'

'Puja room? Whom shall I meet there? My balkrishna is no more! What is the point of going into an empty room?'

Raje was unable to hold back his tears. He held her arm firmly and made her stand up. He took her to the puja room and closed the door from inside. He said, 'Maa saheb, will you please hear me out?'

Jijabai was surprised at his tone. The idol of Bhawani shone in the light of the lamps. Raje was saying, 'Maa saheb, I wanted to tell you later but have no choice but to tell you now. Bal Raje is safe!'

Maa saheb gasped with shock, 'Shivba!'

'I swear in the name of Jagdamba that he is safe. It is not safe for him to come back yet and hence, he is hiding in Mathura. The news of his death should be kept alive. Until he negotiates his way back here, we need to continue with the charade.'

'Raje!'

'Listen to me, Maa saheb! I am bound by my oath to protect him. I cannot rest till he is back. The news of his death will reach Delhi and they will stop searching for him. He will be able to return home safely.'

'Shivaji, these politics of yours are too testing for us poor souls!'

'Maa saheb, you too have to participate in this game of politics. We cannot afford to let anyone know the truth. His life depends on it.'

Raje escorted Jijabai out of the puja room. She went and lay down on her bed while Raje moved to his quarters. The wailing sound from the queens' quarters continued for a long time.

It had been a month since Raje's return to Rajgad but he had not recovered fully. The heat, the long journey and the constant anxiety had taken a toll on his health. It had been more than four months since Raje's escape from Agra. He was feverish every few days. The physicians continued their medicines but it was a recovery. Raje was being briefed daily by Moropant, Annaji, Balaji and Prataprao. Raje was overwhelmed by all the love and affection he received from everyone. The men who had accompanied him to Agra too were returning, and he was apprised of the events in Agra.

Ram Singh's mansab had been cancelled the day Raje escaped. His jagir had been taken away and he was banned from appearing in the durbar. Raje felt bad that Ram Singh was being punished needlessly. He wondered how sad Mirza Raja would be right now.

It was late afternoon when Raje woke up. Soyarabai sat in one corner of the room, busy with her embroidery work. She looked beautiful, engrossed in her task. Raje continued looking at her for a while. She looked up to meet his gaze. Raje asked, 'When did you come in, Rani saheb?'

'A while back, but you seemed to have dozed off.' She continued, smiling coyly, 'It seems you are in a good mood today.'

'Rani saheb, happiness is infectious. You seemed happy; and hence I too am happy!'

'I had requested you to bring me some attar, the Mughal perfume. But you forgot, didn't you?'

'I did.'

'You could have, if you had tried,' she added with a sigh and then moved to the door.

'Remember I got the silk cloth from Surat? But this time was different. Though I did get what the younger queen wanted.'

At that moment Putlabai came to the door. She hesitated seeing the elder queen inside when Raje said, 'Come in, Putla. You were the cause for a fight just now.'

'It is each one's fate,' Soyarabai said in a resigned tone.

Putlabai was nonplussed and kept standing at the door. Raje said, 'It was just that Rani saheb had asked me to get her something which I forgot to but I got what you had asked for.'

Putlabai laughed and said, 'It was nothing. I just told him to bring himself back safely, that's all.'

Soyarabai could not hide her anger. Her nostrils were flaring and she turned red. She got up picking up her items saying, 'Anyway, as far as there is someone to do the worrying, why should it bother me?'

Soyarabai left in a huff. Putlabai said, 'As such, she is against me anyway. You have only added fuel to the fire.'

'I was just joking. Just ignore her temper.'

Raje adjusted the wick in the lamps and they started burning brightly. He said, 'Putla, I lost something, and I am troubled because of it.'

'What?'

'I forgot the Shiva linga which I used to pray to every day. In the hurry to leave, I forgot to carry that one thing with me.'

At that moment, they heard someone calling, 'Aba!'

Raje's face lit up. He said, 'Oh, Sakhu has come to see me!'

Raje ran to the door as Sakhu entered. He hugged her affectionately as she touched his feet. She touched Putlabai's feet and burst out crying.

'Sakhu, hold yourself together. Maa saheb has been crying all these months. We need to now steady ourselves.'

Sakhubai wiped her tears. Raje asked, 'Have you come alone?'

She shook her head. 'No, Mama saheb has also come with me.'

'Why don't you bring them here? Bajaji is not an outsider.'

Sakhubai and Putlabai went down to receive Bajaji. Raje was delighted to see Sakhu. She resembled Sai so much!

Mahadji followed Bajaji into Raje's quarters. Both father and son bent in mujra, and Raje said, putting his hand on Bajaji's shoulders, 'Bajaji, please forgive me.'

'Why, what happened?'

'I had to march on Phaltan when I was with Mirza Raja. But my hands were tied.'

'Maharaj, please don't worry about that,' Bajaji said. 'I got my self-esteem back only due to your efforts. I can never forget that.'

'That is your large-heartedness,' Raje said. 'But I have big ambitions. And I cannot afford to have people like you in the enemy camp.'

'Raje, my jagir may belong to Adil Shah but this soul is yours. Call me in the middle of the night and I will make myself available. Raje, I was overjoyed hearing of your return. But one eye weeps while the other one smiles.'

'What can we do? It is our fate,' sighed Raje.

After a few days, Raje's health improved and he started moving around. He soon left for Phaltan with Mahadji. He returned after a few days and heard that Pilajirao Shirke had come to see him. He was Yesubai's father. Raje went down to meet him.

Pilajirao was Raje's age. They had met last at Sambhaji Raje's wedding in Shringarpur. It had been a political alliance and not celebrated with much fanfare as both Sambhaji and Yesubai were very young. Raje got up the moment he saw him entering. Pilajirao was a man of soil, a strong Maratha. The twirl of the moustache at the ends suited his personality. But Raje could not bear to see how very tired Pilaji looked. The moment Raje put his hand on Pilaji's shoulder, he started crying. Raje made him sit down and said, 'Pilajirao, control yourself.'

'How do I do that? Raje, I was so happy to hear of your return. I assumed that we would hear of Sambhaji Raje soon as well. They were only children when they married, but now she understands everything. How can I tell her not to wear sindoor or her mangalsutra?'

'Pilajirao!'

'Raje, I don't have the courage. I have not told anyone but came here to meet you. I have come to take Sambhaji Raje's shoes.'

'Shoes?'

'Yes, I am a Maratha of the Shirke family. We believe in sati. There is no other option for her.'

A shiver ran down Raje's spine, and his throat went dry.

Pilajirao said, 'Raje, when I left she was playing in the garden. She asked me where I was going and she said, "Bring something back for me." Now I am going to take back his shoes!' Pilaji said, between his sobs. 'Raje, what shall I tell her? She is cursed.'

'Please don't speak like that, Pilajirao!' Raje said, putting his hands over his ears. He went and hurriedly closed the door, his face flushed. Pilajirao looked at him questioningly. Raje came near him and asked, 'Have you told anyone at home about Sambhaji Raje?'

'No, I did not dare to.'

Raje told Pilaji the truth under an oath of silence. He was overjoyed by the news. He got up, his body shaking and unsheathed a sword. He said, giving it to Raje, 'Please take this!'

'I don't understand.'

'On my way here, I went for darshan to our family deity, Bhaveshwari. I took an oath that whoever tells me that the news is false would get the sword as a reward.'

Raje hugged Pilajirao tightly and made him sheath his sword.

Raje was surprised seeing Jijabai at the door to his quarters that evening. He asked, 'Maa saheb, what brings you here?'

'Raje, I am told Pilajirao came to see you. I could not bear to meet him.'

'I can understand that, Maa saheb. I have now sent my loyal men to bring Sambhaji Raje back.'

'Is that so? When will we see him?'

'We cannot afford to rush these things, Maa saheb. We need to be cautious.'

'Any news of Netaji?'

'The only thing I know is that as per Aurangzeb's orders, he was to be captured and sent to Delhi.'

'I pity the poor girl—Saguna is really taking this to heart.'

'It is Netaji's fault. Rani saheb has done no wrong.'

'But won't she feel bad? After all, Netaji is her uncle,' Jijabai said. She changed the topic and said, 'See that you bring Bal Raje back soon.'

'I am not worried about Bal Raje. I am worried about Madari, Hiroji, Raghunathpant and Trayambakpant. These are men who risked their lives for us. It sends shivers down my spine thinking of their fate. I hope they return soon.'

Jijabai could not say anything after seeing Raje's worried face. She left the room quietly, leaving Raje to his thoughts.

Raje sat for dinner along with Jijabai. Sakhubai sat nearby while Putlabai, Soyarabai, Sagunabai and Kashibai stood. Raje was recounting his journey back to Rajgad while they listened to his anecdotes with tears in their eyes. Raje said, 'Maa saheb, it is so difficult to be a mendicant. It is not easy to stand in front of a house and shout, "Give me alms!" It really tests your ego.'

'I don't want to hear of your troubles.'

Raje smiled. He looked at the door and found Madari and Hiroji entering.

'Madari! Hiroji!' Raje exclaimed and got up to hug them. The queens started to leave when Raje said, 'No one needs to leave. Had it not been for Madari and Hiroji, I would not have been here. They risked their own lives to save mine.'

Raje sat back down on his chair. He looked at the bag Madari carried and asked, 'Madari, it looks like you are carrying some loot from Agra!'

'Yes, Maharaj. You will be happy to see what I am carrying.'

'Show me,' Raje said eagerly.

Madari opened his bag and Raje's excitement knew no bounds when he saw what was inside. It was Raje's Shiva linga. He held it gingerly and put it on the desk. Everyone folded their hands in namaskar. Jijabai said, 'Raje, isn't this the one you pray to every day?'

'Yes, it is! And I was just ruing the fact that I could not carry it back with me. Madari, how did you ...?'

'Maharaj, this is the only thing I could manage to carry back.'

'This gives me the most happiness! Hiroji, tell me the latest news.'

'It is not good news, Maharaj.'

'Tell me,' Raje said.

'Raghunathpant and Trayambakpant were caught.'

'What?'

'They were caught by the search party the same day you escaped. I am told that Kavi Parmanand and Pandit Kalash too were caught.'

'Oh God! I got my Shiva linga back but the tridev were caught. I wonder how they are being treated.'

'And the other news is that Mirza Raja has left for Agra and that some other commander will take his place.'

'Poor Mirza Raja! Maa saheb, we must find the right opportunity to honour these two brave men. What they have done is invaluable. Madari, Hiroji, please rest now. We shall talk later.'

They both left, bending in mujra, and Raje continued his tales of Madari and Hiroji.

It was nearly a week since Pilajirao's visit when Raje left Rajgad in a hurry. He was accompanied by Tanaji, Suryaji, Yesaji and Prataprao. But no one knew the reason behind his sudden departure. Two days later, the news arrived that he was at the base of the fort. Everyone waited eagerly for Raje to come up to the fort. They were overjoyed to see Sambhaji astride another horse next to Raje! A few palanquins accompanied the group. They all waited eagerly for the procession to reach the fort. No one could believe that they were seeing Sambhaji alive.

Manohari was like a woman possessed hearing the news. Putlabai could not hold back her tears and Soyarabai was stunned to say anything. Only Jijabai remained calm. She prepared the tray to receive Bal Raje with all honour. She told Moropant, 'Moropant! Please honour him by showering him with gold coins. Let his golden feet enter this palace!'

They reached the first gate to the sound of bugles and trumpets. He was welcomed with traditional curd rice balls. The women washed his feet, and all the queens stood in line to perform an aarti for him. Moropant stepped forward and showered him with gold coins. Bal Raje stepped into the palace and acknowledged the mujras of everyone present.

Jijabai stood at the door and the moment he came near her, she hugged him tightly. Her tears drenched his coat. Jijabai led Bal Raje by the hand and made him sit on her lap. Raje said, 'He is no longer a small boy to sit on his grandmother's lap.'

'Everyone present burst out into laughter. Bal Raje moved away shyly when Jijabai said, encircling him with her arms, 'Shut up, Raje! He is still a child to me.'

Raje stepped forward and tried to remove his cap. Bal Raje resisted strongly.

Jijabai asked, 'Why, Sambhaji?'

'Ask him.'

Bal Raje removed his cap to expose his bald head. Everyone present laughed and he hid his face in Jijabai's pallu out of shyness.

Raje said, 'Maa saheb, you cannot visualize how he was dressed. He had a dhoti wrapped around his waist, a small shirt and this bald head of a Brahmin boy!'

'Keep quiet now, Raje! You too shaved your beard for the mendicant's disguise. After all, both are the Lord's guises, aren't they—one of Shiva and the other of Vaman!' Jijabai then kissed Sambhaji's forehead lovingly.

Raje stepped out followed by Moropant, Krishnajipant, Keso Trimod and the others. Krishnajipant's wife Parvatibai and Kashipant's wife Lakshmibai too were present. Raje introduced all of them to Jijabai saying, 'Maa saheb, we can never redeem their favours in our lifetime. This is Moropant's brother-in-law, Krishnajipant. They stay in Mathura. And this is his brother Kashipant. They took care of Sambhaji there. Krishnajipant accompanied us till Varanasi and Keso Trimod got Bal Raje here. But Kavi Kalash, who managed to get Bal Raje to Mathura, is now in Aurangzeb's custody.'

'How was he caught?' Moropant asked.

'As per the plan, he left Bal Raje in Mathura and returned to Agra to avoid any suspicion. Unfortunately, the Badshah arrested him.'

Raje asked Moropant to see the men off after giving them lavish gifts. Raje said, 'Moropant, Raghunathpant and Trayambakpant are still in the custody of the Badshah. Tell their families that we will try to get them back safely. I know they must be worried.'

The arrival of Bal Raje had created an atmosphere of enthusiasm and excitement. Jijabai's weakness disappeared. Sambhaji was being pampered to death with the love and affection of seven mothers and a doting grandmother.

Raje was back to work, engrossed in getting his army back into shape. Yesaji, Tanaji, Prataprao, Moropant, Annaji, Suryaji and Firangoji were working with renewed vigour. Arms, ammunition and horses were being purchased. There was a constant buzz of activity in the fort.

One day, Moropant came in to say, 'Maharaj, Krishnarao Naik wishes to meet you.'

'Who is that?'

'He is Netaji's Naik. He had defected along with Netaji. When Mirza Raja left, Naik was arrested.'

Raje erupted in anger and said, 'Moropant, tell him that we are not interested in adding such people to our army. We will take only loyal men into our fold.'

A week after Sambhaji's return, Raje summoned Moropant and Balaji. Annaji too came along.

'Annaji, it's good that you have come as well. I have decided to write an important letter today.'

'To whom, Maharaj?'

'Moropant, Annaji, what would be Aurangzeb thinking about since the time I escaped?'

'He'd be wondering when you would revolt against him.'

'Exactly!' Raje said, slapping his thigh. 'Our territory has been drastically reduced since the signing of the Treaty of Purandar. There are still a few Mughals left here but Mirza Raja has left for Agra. If we revolt now, it would not take long for Aurangzeb to attack us. We cannot afford to make enemies with the Mughals, Adil Shah and Qutb Shah at the same time. Our kingdom is still new. We have suffered losses in the last few campaigns, and we should find a way to turn our enemy into an ally. We may derive some borrowed strength from such an alliance.'

'But how is that possible?' said Annaji, expressing doubt.

'I am going to send a letter to Aurangzeb, reinforcing my loyalty to him.'

'But do you think Aurangzeb will accept it?'

'Of course! He has spent a lot of money in Mirza Raja's campaign without any results in his favour. He will not be keen to try his hand in the Deccan again so soon. He will agree to our proposal.'

'But does that not mean being under the Mughals again?' Moropant asked.

'Doing nothing does not mean we are not capable of action. We only need to buy time.'

Raje dictated the letter and said, 'Balaji, arrange to dispatch the letter today itself.'

The next morning, Raje came to Maa saheb's room after his daily rituals. He was smiling when he touched her feet.

Jijabai asked, 'Raje, there seems to be a lot of activity in the fort today.'

'I have called everyone for a meeting and I want you to come along.'

The men were waiting for Raje but no one knew the reason why they were there. They all bent low in mujra seeing Raje and Jijabai enter.

The moment they took their seats, Moropant said, 'Raje, Mirza Raja is active again. He has met the sardars at Pune, Supe, Indapur and other areas. He has warned them that those who oppose the Mughals will be strictly punished. We cannot afford to ignore such threats.'

'Moropant, I am sure Mirza Raja cannot stay in the south for long.'

'Maharaj,' Prataprao said, 'this is an opportune moment. We are waiting for your orders—we cannot sit here twiddling our thumbs.'

'Before we make any moves, we need to strengthen ourselves. While I was returning from Agra as mendicants, we were having dinner at a village. The old lady who fed us served us some dal along with rice. Before I could manage to stop it, the dal flowed all over the leaf plate. The old lady laughed and said, "You seem to be just like Shivaji." I asked her why she said that, and she replied, "Shivaji too is like you. He has not bothered to fortify his territories from all sides and he is trying to expand his kingdom. You need to create a protected boundary even for eating rice and dal."'

Raje continued, 'That reminds me, Moropant! We stayed at a Patil's home one night on the way to Rajgad, and the Mughals had looted his property. Nirajipant knows his address. Please ensure that he is taken care of.'

'Yes, Maharaj,' Moropant nodded.

Raje described his vision for the new kingdom. He explained the need for the right combination of cavalry, foot soldiers and armoured cannons. Everyone listened intently.

Maa saheb said, 'We should have thought of this much earlier. We would not have been in this situation if we had done so.'

'I agree. A fort with a strong fortification remains protected against cannonballs. Similarly, a well-protected kingdom is immune to outside attacks. I now understand why Mirza Raja had appointed someone like Manucci to look after the ammunition. He is the best man for artillery.'

The conference was over and everyone dispersed to do their respective jobs so that the plan could be implemented. Shivaji had laid down the rules: 'The troops will move soon after Dussehra. They will spend eight months raiding other territories and return during the monsoon. No soldier is allowed to marry or have a relationship with a woman during this time. Those who disobey this order will be beheaded. Those who hide loot from the campaign will be dealt with severely.'

Raje's dream was now taking shape. His strength increased every day. He was constantly updated on the news from the Delhi durbar. Mirza Raja had been routed in the south while the Afghans in the north were a cause for concern for Aurangzeb. Shivaji was amused at Aurangzeb's plight and was confident that he would agree to his proposal.

He had just finished his evening rounds when a messenger came running in, announcing the arrival of Raghunathpant and Trayambakpant. The slanting rays of the setting sun illuminated his smiling face as he waited for them to arrive eagerly. They seemed to have changed so much! Tears welled up in his eyes. He could see the torture they had suffered so courageously. Shivaji battled to hold back his tears. They both came in and bent in mujra. Raje could not speak as he was overwhelmed with emotions. His tears were now flowing freely.

Addressing Moropant, Raje said, 'Pant! I am fortunate to have regained two of my gems that I had lost some time back. The Lord has now relieved me of my oath. Raghunathpant! You must be tired. We have a lot to talk but that can wait.'

'Maharaj!' Raghunathpant said. 'I have some good news—Aurangzeb has agreed to your proposal.'

'I realized that he had the moment I saw you. I am happy that things are working out the way I hoped. Get some rest now.' Raje said, wiping the corner of his eyes.

That night Raje sat with Jijabai and others. Raghunathpant and Trayambakpant recounted their story, and those listening could not hold back their tears. They were angry listening to the tricks Aurangzeb played to convert them to Islam, but they were willing to sacrifice their lives rather than convert. The pride on the listeners was evident.

Raghunathpant said, 'Maharaj, I handed over the jewellery we had carried along with us to Mulchand, hoping that it would be kept safe and returned later.'

'What happened then?' Maa saheb asked.

'Maa saheb, Raje handed over the jewels to Mulchand who, in turn, gave them to his munim. But when the munim heard of Raje's escape, he gave them back to Mulchand, who was mortally scared and gave them to Aurangzeb. Aurangzeb sold the jewels as he did not want to touch a Kaffir's wealth and distributed the money he received among the poor.'

'Pant,' Raje said, 'Aurangzeb has sent my two most precious jewels back to me. What more do I want? I am not sad that I lost the treasure. And, in any case, we will take them back soon!'

For a long time there was silence. Everyone looked at Raje expectantly.

Moropant said, breaking the silence, 'Raghunathpant, is it true that Netaji has been arrested?'

Everyone turned to look at Moropant, and Raje's eyes held disgust.

Raghunathpant looked at Raje for a brief moment and then, lowering his head, said, 'Netaji has converted to Islam.'

It was a rude shock to everyone present. Raghunathpant continued, 'Netaji could not tolerate the torture. He had to resort to conversion to save his life.'

Bal Raje, sitting next to Maa saheb, said, 'It would have been better to accept death.'

Everyone turned to look at Bal Raje.

Raje said, sighing deeply, 'This is what happens when you are not true to yourself. He left us for a meagre mansab under Adil Shah and then left him when Mirza Raja offered a panch-hazari mansab. Now to save his life, he has deserted his religion. This clearly is his fate!'

However, Raje was deeply hurt by Netaji's actions. The next day, Raje went to Jijabai's quarters but stopped at the doorstep. Sagunabai sat next to Jijabai while Jijabai caressed her back. She was sobbing with her head in between her knees.

Jijabai said, seeing Raje,

'Come in, Raje!'

Sagunabai got up wiping her eyes. Raje touched Jijabai's feet and said, looking at Sagunabai, 'What happened?'

'The poor girl!' Jijabai said, 'She is unable to stop crying since she heard about Netaji's conversion.'

'Netaji has become a Muslim. How is this her fault?' Raje asked.

'That is what I am telling her! But Netaji Kaka's actions have hurt her deeply.'

'There is nothing we can do about it. Let it go, Saguna.'

Sagunabai left, and Raje was about to leave as well when Jijabai called out, 'Raje!'

'Yes?'

'It is not enough to look after the kingdom alone. You need to look into household matters too.'

'I don't understand.'

Jijabai smiled. 'Saguna would have been very happy had you personally told her about Netaji. They are always waiting for word from you. See how happy Soyara is since the time you have asked her to take charge of the office affairs!'

'They are being groomed under your supervision. Why should I interfere?'

'Don't change the topic. Thanks to your encouragement, Soyara has taken charge. Saguna, Putla and Kashi look after the household. But you need to encourage them.'

Shivaji said, in an embarrassed tone, 'It is my fault. I shall look into it.'

Raje did not wait to see Jijabai's broad smile.

The treaty with Aurangzeb was a big relief for Shivaji. He decided to organize affairs in the undisciplined Konkan region. The money received from Shambhu Raje's mansab was enough to manage the daily expenses but there were other expenses due to the frequent raids on Adil Shah's territory. Shivaji demanded an additional lakh of revenue. Aurangzeb agreed and allowed Shivaji to get back his Deshmukhi, and thus allowing him to collect taxes.

When Shivaji was about to make plans for Konkan, he received news of an attack on the Rangana Fort by Adil Shahi troops. Shivaji had captured Rangana just a year ago and had posted Subedar Ravji Pandit as the fort-keeper. Adil Shah took advantage of the fact that Shivaji was still operating under the treaty with Aurangzeb and sent his troops to capture the fort. Shivaji was furious and he ordered his men to return the attack.

The orders were executed immediately and Prataprao, Tanaji, Yesaji, Suryaji, Firangoji and Telangrao reached the fort. They were worried after hearing the news from Rangana. They all waited in the afternoon for Shivaji to arrive.

Prataprao said, 'If we lose Rangana, the Bijapurkars will be emboldened.'

'But who is talking about losing Rangana?' asked Shivaji.

Telangrao said, 'Such a strong enemy is not ...'

'Shut up!' Raje interrupted.

Everyone was surprised at Raje's injection—he had never used such language before.

'Haven't we learnt anything from our treaty at Purandar? We must hold on to our forts. Our earlier strategy of giving up forts and then recapturing them won't work anymore. It is only when we repulse an attack that the enemy knows our strength. We need to make a show of it. Only then the enemy would not dare attack again. We were taught this difficult lesson by Aurangzeb!'

'Are you planning to march to Rangana?' Jijabai asked.

'There is no other option. But there is something which worries me. The troops laying siege to Rangana are led by Adil Shah's Bahlol Khan and my cousin, Ekoji Raje.'

'Since when have you put family before your Swaraj, Raje?' Jijabai asked.

'Maa saheb, I have your permission now, and we will prepare to march.'

Shivaji moved towards Rangana as per plan. His troops joined him en route. Bahlol Khan and Ekoji Raje's troops were in great numbers but Ravji Pandit was holding his own, and he waited for Raje to join.

It was a late summer day, humid and stuffy. The sky was filled with lightning and soon, the rains began. The Adil Shahi forces scattered, trying to protect themselves from the downpour. This was the moment the Marathas were waiting for and soon the shouts of 'Har Har Mahadev!' rent the air as Raje's troops poured out from all over from the mountains. Bahlol Khan and Ekoji Raje tried to repulse the attack in vain, and the Muslim troops ran for their lives.

Bahlol Khan and Ekoji Raje decided to withdraw rather than lose more men. Raje had managed to save his fort, and he soon returned to Rajgad after having strengthened the security arrangements at Rangana.

Raje's triumphant return from Rangana infused a new energy into the troops. They had regained some of their lost pride. Raje was now determined to protect his kingdom with renewed vigour. New recruits were being added, the cavalry increased and weapons were being produced. The rains did not stop their activities.

It had been two weeks since the return from Rangana. One evening, Shivaji returned from a visit to find Moropant, Niraji, Annaji and others waiting for him. He said, 'Moropant, the rains have now receded. I suggest we visit Konkan.'

He continued, 'Konkan is not yet stabilized. I received a letter from Pilajirao yesterday. We will need to break the stranglehold of the Desais of Konkan to proceed. Prataprao, what is your view?'

'You need not bother yourself, Raje. Just give us the orders and we will take care.'

'Don't be so impatient, Prataprao. We need to plan our campaigns keeping other things in mind. Aurangzeb's son Muazzam has taken charge as the Subedar in Aurangabad. Mirza Raja may have gone back but he has been replaced by Raja Jaswant Singh and other sardars. We are yet to finalize our treaty with the Mughals. We must wait till then.'

Jijabai came in unannounced. Everyone got up. She took her seat and said, 'I have bad news.'

'Why? What happened?'

'Mirza Raja is dead. I am told he died while he was camping at Burhanpur.'

Raje was stunned. Mirza Raja dead! All his memories came flooding back and he was in tears.

Moropant said, 'Maharaj, it was not due to natural causes.'

'Then?' Raje asked, surprised.

'Jai Singh was deeply disturbed by the way Aurangzeb had treated Ram Singh. The appointment of Muazzam as Subedar was another blow. He was already ill when he reached Burhanpur, and I am told Aurangzeb's men poisoned him.'

Raje listened without saying a word. No one knew how to respond.

Jijabai said, 'This is more treachery from Aurangzeb.'

'Maa saheb, don't blame Aurangzeb.'

Everyone was surprised at Raje's words.

He wiped his tears and said, 'Aurangzeb is a true politician. He cares for results and not emotions while Mirza Raja was just the opposite. He cared for people, loyalty and the honour of the throne. Jai Singh saved Aurangzeb in the battle against Shuja. While Mirza Raja went about protecting the honour of Delhi, it was still Mirza Raja who captured Dara Shikoh's son, Sulaiman. Had it not been for Mirza Raja, Aurangzeb would not have ascended the throne in Delhi.'

'And this is what he got in return?' Jijabai asked.

'Aurangzeb is a shrewd man. He didn't hesitate to kill his brothers and father. Mirza Raja should have recognized his true nature. He did not judge Aurangzeb well. It was owing to his defeat in the south and my escape from Agra that Aurangzeb had lost his mind. He, in a fit of emotion, ordered putting Mirza Raja to death.'

'Why?' Moropant asked.

'Because Mirza Raja is a loyal soldier; an emotional person. It would not have been long before he revolted against Aurangzeb. He could not afford Mirza Raja's enmity. Hence, he found an opportune moment to eliminate him. Mirza Raja, whose commitment to the emperor was unquestionable, lost his life to politics. It will be difficult to meet such a great soul again!'

It was a great relief to Aurangzeb that Mirza Raja had died. However, in the Deccan, Muazzam and his commander Jaswant Singh were uncomfortable. The fact that they did not have the capability to fight Shivaji made them restless. Muazzam sent a letter of recommendation for Shivaji to Delhi and Aurangzeb promptly sent his blessings as well. Muazzam was relieved and dispatched a messenger to Rajgad immediately.

Raje accepted the request and decided to send Sambhaji Raje to accept the mansab. The preparations for the journey began and Raje selected the sardars who would accompany Sambhaji Raje.

Raje went to meet Jijabai in the evening. Soyarabai, Putlabai and Kashibai stood in attendance there. Raje said, 'Maa saheb, our Sambhaji Raje is going to be a Mansabdar finally!'

'Aba saheb, won't you be coming along?' Bal Raje asked.

Raje said, 'Bal Raje, don't worry. You are not going alone. Our Senapati Prataprao Gujar will be there with his troops. If things don't turn out right, don't hesitate to capture Aurangabad!'

Bal Raje laughed, a little relieved.

Jijabai asked, 'Is Prataprao really going with him?'

'Maa saheb, our Yuvraj cannot be sent alone. It seems that Shahzada Muazzam is keen to extend his friendship. The Mughals should know that our prestige is not restricted to the panch-hazari mansab they are bestowing on him.'

Jijabai felt relieved after listening to Raje.

The festival of Navratri was celebrated with a lot of gaiety. Bhai Dooj was selected as the day for Sambhaji's departure. The moment Sambhaji left for Aurangabad, Raje sent his spies to Konkan and Goa. Adil Shah was worried ever since he had been defeated at Rangana. He extended a hand of friendship and Raje finally agreed to sign the treaty. Apart from other conditions, he agreed to pay Raje three lakhs annually.

After receiving the mansab, Sambhaji returned to Rajgad with great honour. He was now officially a member of the Mughal durbar with the title of a panch-hazari Mansabdar. Shahzada Muazzam had welcomed Sambhaji with honour and respect.

Prataprao recounted, 'The Shahzada gifted us horses, elephants, jewellery and expensive clothes.'

'Well, that is quite nice!' Raje exclaimed, satisfied with the turn of events.

Niraji said, 'We surveyed the mansab in detail. He has a territory in the region of Waradh as his jagir and has a potential of more than fifteen lakh hons of revenue.'

Raje was satisfied and relieved. He said, 'Niraji, you have managed a huge task. We will have some respite with the treaties with the Mughals and Adil Shah. We can now take care of the expenses for the troops, and our plans can be executed.'

Raje laid out his plans in the next few days. The Desais in Konkan were creating a lot of trouble, Lakham Sawant, Keshav Prabhu and Keshav Naik being foremost among them. Shivaji decided to resolve the issue of the Desais once and for all.

Prataprao raised a doubt and said, 'What if they decide to take refuge in Goa?'

'I hope they do! These firangis have been pampered a lot. They have converted more than eight thousand Hindus. We will use the excuse of the Desais taking refuge there to teach the firangis a long-overdue lesson.'

Raje marched to Konkan and, as expected, the Desais took shelter in Goa. Shivaji marched onwards, not sparing anyone. Four priests were hanged, and he captured nearly thirteen hundred soldiers and destroyed Portuguese ships.

It was while Raje was camped in Dicholi that Padre Gomalu Martis and Ramoji Kothari came to negotiate a treaty. Raje could not afford to spend much time in this territory and agreed to the terms and conditions as he had gotten what he wanted. He released the captive soldiers, and the conversions were stopped by the priests.

The defeat of the Portuguese sent a message to the English too. They knew that it was dangerous to cross Shivaji, and they were aware he had a treaty with both the Mughals and Adil Shah. They soon sent their emissaries to Rajgad to win Shivaji over.

Within a month of returning from Konkan, one afternoon, Raje got the message of the arrival of a few Mughal soldiers. He came into the courtyard and they bowed in mujra.

Moropant said, 'Maharaj, the soldiers have come from Aurangabad to inform us that the royal farman will reach in two days.'

'Is there another farman for Bal Raje?' Raje asked.

'It is for you,' Moropant clarified.

Raje was lost in thought for a moment. He said, 'All right, take good care of the messengers. I will write a letter to Shahzada Muazzam.'

Raje sent out orders to receive the farman. A farman badi was erected at the base of the fort.

Shivaji told Bal Raje, 'Shambhu, you should receive the farman on my behalf. You know the routine, don't you? The moment the camel arrives carrying the farman, you have to move forward, rest on your knees and receive it with both your hands while your head remains bent low. Then you have to touch the farman to your forehead and keeping the farman on your head, return to the fort accompanied by trumpets and drums.'

The Rajgad fort was decorated to receive the farman. There were flowers and rangoli everywhere. The doors were strung with mango leaves to announce a welcome in the traditional manner. Raje ensured that each and every thing was in order.

Jijabai was unable to tolerate his indulgence and said, 'Raje, should you welcome the farman with such pomp and gaiety?'

Raje sighed and said, 'Maa saheb, this is part of politics. The news of our wholehearted welcome will reach the Badshah, and he will be convinced that we do not bear any ill will. I have lots of plans, Maa saheb, and I have to tolerate these things for the sake of those plans.'

Sambhaji Raje left to receive the royal farman. He was accompanied by the sardars, the Senapati, and other important officials. Raje waited at the fort.

The farman was kept on a low stool covered with embroidered silk. Raje asked Moropant to read it aloud. The farman praised the high office of the royal durbar and Raje understood its contents, even though they were in Farsi: 'We are pleased with you; and hence, we are bestowing upon you the title of Raja. You are advised to work more than your duty. This will enable us to bestow further largesse upon you in times to come.'

The Mughal sardars accompanying the farman hugged Raje. He then asked that the letter from Shahzada Muazzam be read out. The letter stated, 'Shivaji Raje! I trust you and have communicated the same to our Badshah. He has, thus, been large-hearted and has bestowed upon you the title of Raja. I am pleased with the same and am sure that you will do the title justice.'

Raje expressed his happiness and praised the Shahzada. He then bid the sardars farewell after giving them appropriate gifts.

Raje went to meet Jijabai that evening. The farman, the jewel-encrusted sword and other items were placed in front of Jijabai.

Niraji said, 'Maharaj, please pardon my impertinence, but I fail to understand your happiness at this farman from a man who wanted to kill you.'

'Niraji, a person of your stature should not make such comments. In fact, I admire Aurangzeb's wisdom. Despite my escape, he is going out of his way to please me, forgetting his own ego. We need to learn from him.'

'Well, it is only because you survived ...'

Raje smiled ruefully and said, 'Moropant, we cannot afford to think of ifs and buts in politics. We need to take decisions as the situation demands. Often, one may have to regret a decision not taken or taken for their entire life. Aurangzeb has got this chance to insult me only because I escaped. He will have to pay for it dearly. He will regret it for the rest of his life.'

The farman had taken on a new meaning now. Everyone looked at Raje eager to know what he would do next. There was a mixture of pride and curiosity in their eyes.

Shivaji appointed Prataprao as the administrator for Sambhaji Raje's mansab. He left with five thousand for his men for Aurangabad. Muazzam had agreed to take care of the expenses of managing the troops. The mansab too was generating income. Shivaji was happy that his monetary situation was under control.

Having taken care of the troops, Shivaji turned his attention to the citizens. He expressed his views in a meeting when Annaji said, 'Raje, if you abolish the vatandari system that has existed for generations, the landlords will be displeased.'

'Not the common people though!'

'How do we run the administration without their support?'

'I understand,' Raje said. 'Lazy rulers are happy to impose the vatandari system and collect whatever they get from the ryots. They do not bother to find out how the ryots are being treated. We need to abolish this system which is eating into the very foundation of good administration.'

'Raje, we can do this in steps.'

'Annaji, step by step is not what I want. This way, we will never meet our objectives. These Patils, Khots, Kulkarnis, Desais, Deshmukhs, Deshpandes, Mirasdar, Jagirdars—they are holders of the estates, and the poor ryots are in their grip. There is no one to help them. After all, am I not supposed to be their king? Or am I Raje for only the vatandars? Annaji, this kingdom is the Lord's kingdom.'

'But what crime have the vatandars committed ...' Annaji was interrupted mid-sentence by Raje.

He continued, 'Ask what crime they have not committed. I have been seeing this since my childhood. I will not tolerate the ryots being exploited. The estate holders have become insolent. They have their huge mansions, fortresses and weapons. They are ready to side with the enemy anytime. We need to stop all their bonuses and give them a fixed income. Destroy all their mansions. Issue orders that they cannot build such luxurious havelis anymore.'

'But what about the temples?'

'The rule applies to everyone. The shrines are no exceptions. Henceforth, all the expenses for the shrines—oils, oblations, holy baths, etc.—will be taken from the royal treasury. The same rule applies to the pirs and the mosques. The Brahmins, pandits, Vedic scholars and others will get food, clothing and money for expenses from the government. Their job is to accept this and spend their time in prayers for the welfare of the state.'

Annaji looked incredulous but dared not ask questions. He could not believe that Raje had thought through the whole situation. He asked, out of curiosity, 'And what about the ryots?'

'Annaji, I have grown under the guidance of Dadoji. What does a simple ryot want? A good meal, a place to sleep, implements to till his land, a few animals and some clothes to protect his modesty. He is content if he gets that. He tills the soil and harvests the crops but what does he get in return except debt? They borrow to survive and then live the rest of their lives repaying their debts. I have witnessed these complaints since childhood. We need to do something for them. Henceforth, the harvest will be split into five parts—two for the treasury and three for the ryots. Map all the land and allocate it to the villages appropriately. If new ryots come in, give them the necessary implements and animals to till the soil. Give them good seeds. If required, help them out for a few seasons till they are able to reap a good harvest. After all, I am no Raje without them. Collect revenues only after you inspect the harvest. If you do this, you will get their blessings, and we all will be happy.'

There was no stopping Raje now. The ryots were happy though the landlords resented the relentless supervision by Shivaji. There was dissent in some places like Chinchwad, which was an important religious centre. They resented Raje's interference despite his assurances that they would get the funds required to maintain the temple. On seeing their reluctance, Raje said, 'I assumed you were mendicants and that you had no interest in the estates. In case you are not keen to run the temples, give the task to me.' That shut them up finally. Raje's dream of a Hindavi Swaraj was now finally taking shape.

It had been three months since Sambhaji's acceptance of the royal farman. Pilaji Shirke visited Raje along with Yesubai, bringing excitement and happiness to Shivaji's life. After having settled her there, Pilaji left after getting necessary instructions from Shivaji about keeping an eye on the movements in Konkan region. Within a month of her arrival, Yesu had endeared herself to everyone in the household. She was learning the scriptures well under the same priest who had taught Sambhaji earlier. Raje would take her out for evening rides once a while.

One evening, Sambhaji came in to meet Jijabai and said, touching her feet, 'Maa saheb, I came to say goodbye.'

'Where are you off to?' Yesu asked.

Jijabai said, looking at her indulgently, 'Yesu, one should not ask when someone is leaving. He is going for his riding sessions, by the way.'

'I too would like to go.'

'You think riding is fun? But if you like, ask your father-in-law.'

Before Sambhaji could react, Yesu had left Jijabai's quarters and walked towards Raje's quarters. Jijabai watched her, smiling to herself. 'She does not fear anyone, have you noticed?'

Sambhaji continued to look at the carpet, not knowing how to react.

Raje was talking to Soyarabai when Yesu appeared at the door. Seeing her, he said, 'Come in! What brings you here?'

'I came to ask for your permission to go for a horse ride with Sambhaji Raje.'

'Oh, is that so?' Raje asked, smiling at Soyarabai. 'You may, if you give me a hug.'

Yesu rushed in without hesitation. Soyarabai was taken aback at the boldness of the young girl. She said, after Yesu had left, 'Now, don't you think that's a bit brash?'

'I am happy she is so, Soyara. Don't you see how she has adjusted to the household so well? It is a great relief. I hope she does not lose her innocence very soon,' Raje said, holding her hand.

Soyarabai blushed. She gently extricated her hand from Raje's grip and left the room.

That evening, Raje stood at the ramparts observing the region at the foothills of the fort. Spirals of smoke from the villages indicated the activity below, and it was a pleasant sight. Raje remarked, 'It tells me the land is fertile and our men are busy tilling it.'

That evening, Bahirji came in to report on the activities from Goa. 'The death of the Portuguese viceroy is an important development. He was personally responsible for many converting to Christianity.'

The news of the death of Viceroy Conde de Sao Vicente was a boost to Raje's morale. That very evening he made plans to attack Goa. He did not need more than five hundred men for this task. He sent Bahirji and a few spies ahead while he decided to camp at Narve along the Panchganga River.

The next morning, realizing that he had forgotten to carry his Shiva linga for his daily puja, he enquired after a Shiva temple nearby only to find one in an extremely dilapidated condition. By the time Raje completed his puja, a bael leaf floated down onto his ritual.

It was a sign from heaven—the bael leaf was Lord Shiva's favourite! Raje decided to rebuild the Saptakoteshwar temple. The work had started in earnest when Bahirji came from Goa, looking crestfallen. He said, 'Raje, our plans were exposed and our men got caught. The new viceroy slapped our emissary and then threw all of them out of the city limits.'

Despite the setback, Raje decided to stay in Narve. Scanning the horizon he said, 'It is a pity that a handful of men from across the seas are able to take over a city thanks to the fluid loyalty of our own men. Thousands get converted to Christianity and we see our own temples being despoiled and destroyed. What a pity our own people are the cause of our downfall!'

After ensuring that the temple was being rebuilt with care, Raje turned towards Kudal. He said, as he spurred on his horse, 'We will certainly return one day, Tanaji. We will show these firangis what we are capable of!' In the evening, he reached Kudal and camped there for the night.

The next morning, a beaming Moropant came to Raje and said, 'Maharaj, I have good news. The Sindhudurg Fort is ready.'

'Wah! I have been waiting eagerly for this day. Come on, let us not wait anymore.'

The camp moved immediately and soon, they reached Malvan. The waves, in the light of the morning sun, seemed gentle, as if creating small steps for Raje to reach Sindhudurg. He could not take his eyes off the magnificent fort, built on the Kurate Island, an imposing structure which resembled a giant turtle basking in the sun. Raje was reminded of Vishnu's incarnation as the Kurmavatar.

Raje stepped into a boat and as the boats moved towards the fort, Govind Vishwanath Prabhu, the leader, stepped forward to receive him. Raje, overwhelmed by the sight of the imposing fort, took the gold chain off his neck and gifted it to Prabhu as he bowed to receive him.

Raje said, patting his back, 'Prabhu, you have added a precious pearl to the string of the Swaraj. I feel blessed and am eager to see the fort now!'

As Raje moved through a narrow passage, trumpets and kettle drums announced his arrival. Raje touched the threshold, bending in mujra, before entering. He inspected the small houses and ammunition store before he reached a well. Raje folded his hands in namaskar. It was really a miracle to have a well with sweet water on an island in the sea!

'Moropant, this is truly God's gift to us. Is the water supply enough?'

'Yes, Maharaj. We haven't faced a water crisis in the last three years. The water tastes really sweet.'

It was noon by the time Raje finished his inspection. In the distance, he could see the Malvan coast. He said, looking at Annaji, 'This fort will make the Abyssinians think twice now. The Sawants of Wadi too will not dare indulge in piracy. We must build our naval strength now and take charge of the entire Konkan.'

Spending nearly a crore of gold coins, Raje performed the house-warming ceremony of the fort in a manner befitting the magnificence of the fort. After suitably rewarding the labourers, he appointed Rayaji Bhosale as the fort-keeper.

That evening, Raje stood on the ramparts watching the waves lash at the walls of the fort in the light of the dying sun. A kaleidoscope of colours had filled the sky as the sun rushed eagerly to plunge into the western horizon. Lost in his thoughts, Raje stood looking at the waves for a long time. He said, letting out a deep sigh, 'You know Moropant! Sindhudurg is a perfect example of the indomitable spirit of the Marathas. The waves may try repeatedly to crush the walls and the clouds their best to drown it but the fort stands unperturbed, with a well full of sweet water for its residents, and secure in the knowledge that its walls can challenge the strongest of the cyclonic winds.'

For an evanescent moment Raje was restless before he stepped down the ramparts ... the waves continued their pounding as everyone followed Raje down the steps.

A satisfied Raje returned from Sindhudurg. His mind now turned to Siddi of Janjira. It was an appropriate time to rout Siddi when key enemies like the Mughals, Adil Shah and the English were not much of a concern. Raje decided to launch a dual attack from land as well as the sea. Entering Siddi's territory from the north of Mahad, Raje descended with his forces and looted Danda–Rajpuri and captured many forts on the way.

Siddi, having heard of Raje's attack, had locked himself up in his fort at Janjira. He was about to surrender when three of his comrades drummed up support and managed to ward off the attack till the rains began. Realizing that it would be impossible to capture the fort during the incessant rains, Raje was forced to retreat. Stationing a few ships in the creek a few miles from Janjira to ensure that Siddi remained under threat, he returned to Rajgad.

The last six months had seen two unsuccessful campaigns. The first one was Goa and now, at the last moment, he'd had to retreat from Janjira. But Shivaji was content knowing that he'd been able to restore the temple at Saptakoteshwar and that he had captured Danda–Rajpuri, a strategic point in the creek near Janjira.

The rains had nearly ended and one evening, after having been served dinner by Soyarabai, Raje strolled in the courtyard outside his room. Soyarabai, standing nearby, looked beautiful in a lovely black Chandrakala sari. Raje glanced at her as he said, 'I have got a gift for you.'

'Really?'

'I paid a goldsmith at Danda–Rajpuri to buy this for you,' he said, as he gave her a gold girdle.

Soyarabai said, blushing red, 'I love the gift but you have given it to me at the wrong time. I am not in a position to wear this anymore!'

It took a moment for Raje to grasp the meaning of her words. He said, holding her hand, 'Soyara, what you are giving me is far more precious. I don't mind you not wearing it for some time.'

Soyara, abashed at Raje's words, quickly turned and left before he could stop her.

As the rains abated, Raje took some time to inspect the progress of work at Rajgad. He returned to Rajgad to find everyone a little tense. Veterans like Annaji Datto stood with their heads hung.

Raje asked, 'What's the matter?'

'Raje, Aurangzeb has demolished the Kashi Vishwanath Temple.'

It was a bolt from the blue, stunning Raje into silence. Annaji continued, 'Aurangzeb also razed the Shri Keshav Dev Temple in Mathura to the ground. He has imposed the dreaded jizya tax again. Maa saheb is very upset and has not touched even water for the last two days.'

Raje rushed to Jijabai's quarters. As he entered, he exclaimed, 'Maa saheb!'

Jijabai managed to get up, her hands shivering as she said, 'Raje, Aurangzeb has managed to take his revenge. I feel orphaned now.'

Raje's heart wrenched at Jijabai's anguish. He could not hold back his tears. Others, standing at the door, were in tears too. After a while, Raje managed to get a hold of himself and said, 'Maa saheb, I take an oath today—I will never pardon Aurangzeb. From this day, he is my sworn enemy and I shall not stop till I rebuild the temple he has so mercilessly destroyed.'

'Raje! Don't get carried away and ...'

'No, Maa saheb, I am not saying this in the heat of the moment. I wish Mirza Raja were alive today. Aurangzeb has imposed the jizya tax to crush the very spirit of Hindus. There are twenty conditions in jizya, including not allowing you to rebuild a temple which has been previously destroyed; any Muslim has the right of entry into any Hindu shrine or household; Hindus cannot name their children after Muslims; they cannot keep weapons at home or wear jewellery; a Hindu cannot build a house near a Muslim household; nor can they lament aloud the death of a loved one. If we don't find a way to nip Mughal arrogance in the bud, it will be impossible to do so later.'

'But what can we do?'

'Quite a few things, Maa saheb! A single spark can start a fire. We need to make the people revolt in such a way that the Mughals are forced to turn their attention to the Deccan. Once they are here, we will teach them a lesson.'

A wave of delight passed through those in attendance. Annaji said, 'Just command us, Raje, and we shall ensure that not a single mosque survives.'

Raje said, 'Annaji, let not anger overrule your wisdom. Let us not take an eye for an eye. Balaji ...'

'Ji, Maharaj?'

'We need to send an urgent message to Delhi. Bring your pen and paper.'

When Balaji returned, Raje dictated a letter: ' ... you have destroyed our most sacred temple Kashi Vishwanath and had the audacity to build a mosque in its place. You must be gloating over your actions, but you must realize that while you may be the emperor in the north, it is we who rule the Deccan and it would not take much time for us to destroy all the mosques here and build temples over them. You may call yourself a Muslim but we seem to understand Islam better than you.

'What good is a religion if it does not tolerate and respect others? How can you call yourself a true Muslim when you forcibly convert Hindus and impose taxes like jizya? We are not going to tolerate such deeds anymore. I shall rest in peace only when I have overthrown you and rebuilt the temples you have mercilessly destroyed. I hope your god gives you the strength to face us!'

Raje paused for a moment when Jijabai said, 'Shivba!'

'Maa saheb, we cannot afford to be weak now. It is because of the majority of the population being afraid that such men have the courage to commit atrocities. If only Mirza Raja had shown the courage to turn his back on Aurangzeb! Bullies get emboldened when the meek back out. We cannot allow this anymore.'

Jijabai remained silent and did not say a word.

Raje, restless after his dispatch to Aurangzeb, decided to act immediately and got busy strengthening his forces. He issued orders to collect as much ammunition as possible. That evening when Raje was at the summit of the fort, he was surprised to find Prataprao Gujar and Ravji Somnath there. They were supposed to have gone to Aurangabad to oversee Sambhaji's jagir.

Seeing Raje's reaction, Prataprao Gujar said, 'Raje, there is nothing to worry about. When we reached Aurangabad, we found that Aurangzeb had issued orders for us to be captured. He did not know that Shahzada Muazzam does not support his father; and hence, we were alerted in advance. We left the city immediately and returned here.'

Raje heaved a sigh of relief. Prataprao continued, 'Maharaj, Ravji managed to loot some Mughal territories before reaching here.'

'Is that so?' Raje asked.

'What else could I do, Maharaj? I remember Aurangzeb had taken back the one lakh rupees he had promised for our travelling expenses to Agra. I thought it was right that I collect the same by looting Berar on my way back. However, I managed twenty lakhs!'

'That's fantastic!' Raje exclaimed, slapping Ravji's back.

'You have taken the lead in thumbing our nose at Aurangzeb. Our troops can now be taken care of for the next two years, and we have Muazzam on our side. It is a good beginning indeed.'

The Maval region, which had lain comatose for the last four years, now throbbed with a renewed sense of life and vigour. Young men were eagerly joining Raje's forces. Swords, hanging on walls and rusting, were now being sharpened. The atrocities of the Mughal empire had reached their zenith and every day, Raje would find more and more men eager to join him.

Raje put forth his plan. 'Let's first capture the forts we lost. We had surrendered twenty-seven forts to Mirza Raja and he has rendered them defenceless by destroying their ramparts. It would be an easy task for us. Moropant Peshwa, Nilopant Mazumdar and Annaji—you need to use your political wisdom to recapture them. The hill forts can be taken by our Mavals.'

One fine morning, as per the plan, Raje directed the first batch of his troops to enter Mughal territory. He was helped greatly by Prataprao, the Senapati, who had united all the scattered Marathas and made them into one cohesive force.

Raje, under his own supervision, selected two thousand men including expert marksmen and those who knew how to use the spear well. Dressed in gold-embroidered turbans and specially designed angarkhas, they looked regal.

Jijabai asked, 'Raje, what will these men do?'

'Guard me.'

'So you have finally started taking care of yourself?'

'Maa saheb, till my task is complete, I cannot afford to allow myself to be caught unawares. Till the Lord's task is complete, I cannot be lax.'

That evening, Jijabai met Raje as he returned from his inspection of the fort with Tanaji, Yesaji and Suryaji. Jijabai, despite her age, stood erect as she addressed Raje, 'What is the plan now?'

'We have been deliberating where to begin, Maa saheb.'

'Come with me,' Jijabai gestured as she moved towards the ramparts. Pointing to the magnificent Kondana Fort, she said, 'That is where you should begin!'

Raje was taken aback and exclaimed, 'Kondana?'

'Yes! I see that every morning and my heart aches to know that the enemy occupies it.'

'Maharaj, that's it! We shall recapture it now,' Tanaji said excitedly.

For a moment, Raje was lost in thought. Kondana and Purandar were the two forts which the Mughals guarded zealously. Kondana's fort-keeper Udaybhanu, a tough Rajput, guarded his fort with two thousand selected men. It was not an easy task to retake the fort.

'Are you worried, Raje?' Jijabai asked.

'I wonder if we should ...' Raje hesitated.

'Let us not think of it then. We can always plan later.'

'Maa saheb, this is an opportune moment to snub the Badshah,' Tanaji interrupted. 'It is decided now! Let us take Kondana.'

'It is not a task in which we want to fail,' Raje countered.

Tanaji fell at Raje's feet, much to his surprise, and said, 'Raje, I have never asked you for anything. Please grant me my wish.'

'What do you want, Tanaji? You are my most precious jewel. What can I give you?'

'Let me lead the charge on Kondana. If I lose, you will never see my face again!'

'Tanaji!' Raje muttered as he, choked with emotions, was unable to say anything more.

The next morning, Tanaji formally took leave of Raje. Suryaji was to accompany him.

As he bent to touch Jijabai's feet, she said, 'Tanaji ... take care.'

'Don't worry, Maa saheb!' Turning to Raje, he said, 'Raje, look out for our signal on the night of Navami. You will know that we have won.'

Raje patted his back saying, 'I will be awake and waiting for your signal, Tanaji.'

Tanaji stood up proudly. Raje could not help admire his straight posture, his chest puffing out proudly and his luxuriant whiskers adding to his personality. For a brief moment, their eyes met and then, turning abruptly, Tanaji left. Raje stared at his retreating figure for a long time.

Raje received news over the next four days of Tanaji having summoned the Mavals for the attack. He knew that Tanaji was familiar with the fort.

The dark, imposing and tapering precipices, the strong fortifications which he himself had constructed—Raje was aware that the task was fraught with danger. All Raje could do now was pray for Tanaji's success.

The day of Navami arrived. Raje, unable to contain his anxiety, felt time was crawling by. The night sky, resplendent with stars, could not soothe his tormented mind as he kept looking at the imposing fort.

Raje was surprised to see Jijabai enter his quarters.

'Maa saheb, you haven't gone to sleep?'

'I couldn't.'

Sleep eluded everyone as they sat expectantly, unable to do anything except wait.

As the gong announced the midnight hour, Raje said, 'Maa saheb, I suggest you sleep for a while. I am sure Tanaji will win.'

'How can I sleep when our beloved men are busy fighting?'

Raje went back to the terrace and looked out in the darkness. He was about to turn when a flickering flame at Kondana attracted his attention. He shouted, 'Maa saheb, we have won! The fort is ours!'

Pointing in the direction of the fort, he said, 'Have you seen a better constellation in the sky than this? Look at the flame announcing our victory. I need to go now. I have promised to meet him at the gates.'

'At this hour?'

'Yes! I cannot wait to meet him now, Maa saheb! I must go.'

Raje descended the fort and mounted his horse. The soldiers were waiting for him. Within minutes, they vanished in the darkness. Dawn was just breaking over the horizon as they reached the base of Kondana. The Mavals, seeing their Maharaj, saluted. To Raje's surprise, no one said a word and the silence, as they entered the fort, was unbearable. Seeing a crowd, he turned towards it. The men moved aside. It was a sight Raje had not imagined.

Tanaji lay on the ground as if in deep sleep. His face looked serene despite the wounds on his cheeks and temple. Raje glanced at the blue scarf around his neck. He had gifted Tanaji the scarf when he had left for the attack. A sob escaped Raje's lips as he could not control his tears.

'Oh, Bhawani Mata!' he exclaimed.

With trembling hands, he removed the scarf. Tanaji! He had been a constant companion since the beginning. He had played a crucial role during Afzal's attack. Memories came flooding back and his tears flowed unchecked.

'Tanaji!' Raje exclaimed. 'Why did you lie to me? You promised that you would be at the gates to receive me! Why did you not keep your word?'

He turned to Suryaji and asked, 'What happened?'

He said, his voice barely audible, 'Maharaj, we had managed to climb up the walls of the fort with around three hundred men when the soldiers guarding the fort woke up. By the light of the torches, they started attacking us. Tanajirao managed to confront Udaybhanu. They both duelled and in the process, Udaybhanu managed to break Tanaji's shield. As they both collapsed to the ground, our Mavals, losing heart, started running away.'

Jotyaji said, pointing to Suryaji, 'Seeing the men run, Suryaji took a sword and before the Mavals could realize what was happening, he cut off the ropes with which they had climbed up. "How dare you think of running away when your saviour lies on the ground?" he screamed. The Mavals, realizing their mistake, attacked the Rajputs with renewed vigour and soon, we captured the fort.'

Raje looked at Suryaji who could not stop sobbing.

The moment Raje's hand touched his shoulder, Suryaji said, his voice choking with anguish, 'Maharaj!'

Raje was barely able to control his own tears. He said, 'This is not the time to shed tears, Suryaji. Tanaji has made us proud. He fought like a lion and we shall call this fort Sinhagad henceforth to honour him. But we have one more task to do. That alone will allow Tanaji's soul to rest in peace.'

Raje stood up and walked towards the high point on the fort where the green Mughal flag fluttered. He said, turning to Suryaji, 'What are you waiting for? Remember Tanaji had promised that he would capture the fort?'

Raje took out a saffron flag tied to his cummerbund and said, 'I took this flag down when I had to hand over our fort to Mirza Raja. I have carefully preserved it all this time. Now you need to do Tanaji's job. Hoist our flag!'

Soon, as the sun rose in the sky, the saffron flag fluttered in the wind. Raje's chest puffed up with pride and, turning to Yesaji, said, 'Send a message to Maa saheb. We won the fort but lost our lion!'

Raje returned to Rajgad after making necessary arrangements at Sinhagad. He knew that he had managed to wake a sleeping giant. The act of taking Sinhagad was going to provoke the Mughal might into action. He knew that he had to act fast now. There was no time to rest or lament the loss of dear ones.

Jijabai too had no time to grieve Tanaji's death. Shivaji and Tanaji had been childhood friends but Soyarabai's advancing pregnancy took all of Jijabai's time as she took care of her delicate condition.

Ten days after the capture of Sinhagad, Raje sat in his quarters alone, anxiously waiting for the delivery of the child. Soon, Putlabai came in and said, 'It is a boy!'

'Wah!' 'Pointing to a bag of pearls, he said, 'I was planning to give this to the person who brings me the news but you have already got what you deserve.'

'I don't understand.'

'You already have me, Putla! What else can I give you?'

'Putlabai blushed. At the same time, Manohari entered. Seeing Raje's smiling face she realized that he had already received the news.

'Here, this is for you, Manu,' Raje said, giving her the bag of pearls.

That evening the priest arrived to suggest a suitable name for the boy.

'The child was born in a breech position,' Raje said, turning to Maa saheb. 'We will now breach the Mughal might too,' he quipped, laughing at his own joke.

The drums soon announced the name of the newborn—Rajaram.

The very next day, the capture of Purandar spread cheer among the Marathas. Nilopant, after taking charge of the fort and having captured the Mughal fort-keeper, Sheikh Raziuddin, had sent him to Rajgad. Raziuddin, mentally prepared to be beheaded, was pleasantly surprised when Raje released him with due respect, in light of the happy occasion.

The Maratha troops, under Raje's command, were now creating havoc in the Mughal territories. Raje attacked Mahuli Fort, personally leading the charge but the Rajput fort-keeper turned out to be a capable leader who managed to repulse the attack. Raje had to beat a hasty retreat, losing a thousand men in the process. It was a loss which he found difficult to accept.

He turned his sights towards Kalyan and Bhiwandi and managed to take these under his command. Soon, many other territories were captured. Alarmed by the many victories of the Marathas in the region, the fort-keeper at Mahuli appealed to the Mughal Badshah for help but was ignored. Fearing the worst, he deserted his post and was succeeded by another sardar, Alvardi Beg. It was the opportunity Raje had been waiting for and the Marathas soon entered the fort, killing Alvardi Beg and two hundred of his men. The saffron flag fluttered over Mahuli.

The monsoon season had been a great help to Raje. He had captured Kondana, Purandar, Kalyan, Lohgad, Mahuli, Karnala, Rohida and many other forts in that time. The looting of territories in Waradh and Khandesh had made his treasury richer by a few lakh gold coins.

Raje was aware that the capture of territories was one aspect of expanding an empire but managing them was a totally different matter. He ensured that each fort was managed by the right set of people. Each fort was also sufficiently fortified with arms and ammunition. It was crucial that the regained territories remained with the Marathas now.

Raje decided to put Nilopant in charge of administrative matters of the kingdom. Nilopant was well versed in both warfare as well as administration. He broached the topic with him one evening and said, 'Nilopant, I suggest you oversee the territory from Mahuli to Indapur, Chakan and Kadim.'

Nilopant, a soldier at heart, was a little disappointed hearing Raje's request. He said, 'Would it not be better if someone else managed these territories while I lead the men in the field?'

Raje said, holding his hand, 'Nilopant, I understand what you are saying but believe me, I need people like you who are effective administrators and also understand battle. It is a job I cannot hand over to anyone else.'

Nilopant nodded silently. He knew Raje was speaking from his heart. He said, 'I have one request; please ensure that my share of the revenue is less than that of the Peshwa.'

Raje was overwhelmed by Nilopant's words. He knew his men would never take up a job for the sake of money. This integrity was what made Raje confident of his men, and secure in the knowledge that those managing the administration would count each penny before spending it.

That night, Raje told Jijabai, 'Maa saheb, I want to visit Raigad.'

'Let the rains subside. What is the hurry?'

'Maa saheb, we are sure to have a direct confrontation with the Mughals soon and there is no fort better equipped than Raigad. We are safe at Rajgad right now but it is too close to Pune for comfort. Raigad, with its strong walls and tall ramparts which literally kiss the skies, is a safer place. We have fortified it well. We need to shift our capital there. And I shall ensure that you are comfortable there. We are building a beautiful haveli for you at the base, in the Pachad village.'

Jijabai was overwhelmed and agreed immediately. The next morning, Raje left for Raigad.

Raje was received warmly by Hiroji, who was in charge of the construction at Raigad. Raje declined to use a palanquin and decided to walk up the fort. 'This way, I will be able to take a closer look at your work,' he quipped.

'Maharaj, however minutely you may look, you will not be able to find a flaw. I will live only for a few years but the fort will stand for generations to come,' Hiroji said confidently.

'Spoken like a true soldier! Hiroji, I have nothing to worry when I have men like you with me.'

As he walked up the narrow path leading to the main gate, Raje's forehead glistened with sweat. The climb had been steady and difficult, turning and twisting at various places. 'Hiroji, you have chosen the path well,' Raje said, as he paused to take a breath. 'You can even leave the doors open at night, safe in the knowledge that even if the enemy manages to reach here, they will have no energy left to fight!'

The sun was high up in the sky but the cool air at the top of the fort was pleasing. The clouds seemed to kiss the ramparts as they passed by. Raje stood on the bank of a large tank, the waters of which reflected a few minarets. A five-storied minaret caught his attention. He asked, turning to Hiroji, 'Can you read minds as well, Hiroji? I have always loved the beauty of the Gwalior fort and wanted to build similar minarets one day. You have done precisely that!'

'It is all thanks to Moropant, Raje. He is the one who guided us.'

'I knew it! He has great foresight and perceptiveness. He is responsible for the layout of Pratapgad.'

The fort was well designed, and there were residences for ministers, a place for the market, stables, ammunition storage yards and other facilities. Satisfied with the visit, Raje stayed four more days. As he stood at the ramparts one evening, surveying the valley below, pointing in the direction of a fort, he said, 'You can see the Konkandiwa Fort, which has long protected Raigad. We have Lingana in the north-east, Torna in the east and one each in the north and north-west.'

While returning, he instructed Hiroji to build houses for the Brahmins, guards and other sardars. These men would grace the fort and make it even more prestigious.

Hiroji said, 'Raje, we have already spent a lot of money and I was not sure if Moropant would have approved of such expenses.'

'Don't worry about money, Hiroji,' Raje said, placing his hand on Hiroji's shoulder. 'We have the Badshah's bank of Surat close at hand whenever we are in need of money! I am eager to shift the capital soon so let us not leave any stone unturned.'

Enthused by Raje's words, Hiroji said, 'I have three hundred men working here. I will add another two hundred. You may shift here anytime you wish.'

A satisfied Shivaji left the fort the next morning.

A fortnight after inspecting Raigad and a few days before Diwali, Shivaji camped with more than twenty thousand men near Kalyan in preparation for his attack on Surat.

The city of Surat seemed peaceful when Raje reached the outskirts, a mere ten miles from the city. An English spy, having got the news of the impending attack, had warned his men, who promptly moved their goods to the dockyard at Swali. The Mughal Subedar on the other hand, despite having got the news, dismissed it as a mere rumour. He had just three hundred men guarding the city. The city had not learnt its lesson since the previous attack, except for the addition of a fortified city wall.

The news that 'Shivaji has come!' spread when the Maratha troops were at sighting distance. There was a sense of general chaos and the residents ran amok to save their belongings and lives. It was Diwali, and the city woke up to a deathly silence as the rays of sun tried to penetrate the fog which engulfed the havelis. Except for a few stray dogs, the roads were empty, as the citizens huddled in their houses, fearing the worst.

Ghiasuddin stood at the gates with his men, his eyes searching the rice fields for the Marathas. Despite the cold morning, he was sweating. He glanced at his men, who were nervously looking at each other and as he loosened his jacket buttons, he said 'Shivaji will never come here. It is all rumours and nothing else!'

'Subedar saheb,' one of the soldiers shouted.

'What is it?'

'Look ...' the soldier said, pointing in the direction of the rice fields.

Ghiasuddin strained his eyes but could see nothing. Within moments, a rumbling noise was heard and, as their worst nightmares came true, a long line of horsemen emerged from behind the trees.

'Shivaji has come!' someone screamed from the crowd.

It was a chilling sight. The noise stopped suddenly as a few thousand cavalrymen waited a few hundred yards from where Ghiasuddin stood. Giving instructions to his sardar to stop them, Ghiasuddin ran inside the city to hide in what he believed were the safe confines of his fort.

Shivaji, astride his white steed, instructed Prataprao to take charge of the city. 'Anandrao and Vyankojipant, you create a blockade. I shall camp here and wait for you. Take care not to pick a fight with the English and the Dutch. We are here to loot and not fight.' Pointing his sword in the direction of the city, he said, 'May the Goddess Bhawani be with you!'

The chant of 'Har Har Mahadev!' filled the skies as the Marathas stormed the city. The loot began in earnest and soon, heaps of gold, silver and other precious jewellery were laid before Shivaji. The English, fearing for their lives, had launched a counter-attack and had killed many Marathas.

At Raje's insistence, the Dutch had remained neutral. The king of Kashgar had taken refuge inside the French factory and his treasury was an added bonus which the Maratha troops received without any resistance. The burning havelis and markets gave the city a golden halo as it burned in the night, the light of which could be seen for miles around. The loot continued for three days. It had been an extremely successful raid, the total loot accumulating to more than a crore gold coins. It was time for them to return.

While returning, Shivaji warned the merchants that if they did not pay him twelve lakh rupees annually they would have to face the same fate once again. The city heaved a sigh of relief as the Maratha soldiers retreated, leaving them to gather whatever was left behind.

The caravan moved slowly back towards Pune because the carriages lumbered with the weight of the loot. As they neared Nashik, they received information that the Mughal sardar Daud Khan was marching towards them. Raje pushed the troops to cross the Chandwad hills through the Kanchana–Manchana pass and stopped for the night.

Prataprao, aware of Daud Khan's might, suggested, 'Maharaj, wouldn't it be better if we continue to march ahead?'

'That is not necessary, Prataprao. Let the booty move ahead with two thousand men and reach Rajgad. We shall wait for Daud Khan here. We must let the Mughals know that we do not run away!'

Raje's troops, nearly fifteen thousand strong, were ready in the wee hours of the morning for the Mughals. Raje, clad in brocaded armour and holding the dandpatta, the long, double-edged sword, surveyed the flat plains ahead as he mounted his horse. The Mughals were said to be a mere five thousand or so but they were a force to reckon with as they carried ammunition and elephants.

The Mughal troops led by the able sardar Ikhlas Khan crossed the pass, confident that the Marathas would have run away on hearing of their arrival. The sight which greeted him shook him. Spread across the fields was a huge Maratha army poised to attack them.

As the Mughals descended, the Maratha troops retaliated and within no time, more than three thousand Mughals had been killed. Ikhlas Khan was routed while Daud Khan beat a hasty retreat to save his remaining forces.

That evening, as they camped for the night, Raje asked, 'How many men did we lose?'

'Just three hundred, Maharaj,' Prataprao answered as he nursed a wound on his arm.

At that moment, a messenger came in and said, 'Maharaj, Daud Khan has taken refuge in the hill. His men are busy burying the dead.'

Anandrao sensed an opportunity and said, 'If you permit me, I will take my troops and finish them off.'

'No, Anandrao. We do not behave the way they do. We have already defeated them. Send their two ministers, who are in our captivity, back with due respect and let us move our wounded soldiers to Kunjargad. I too shall go there.'

Raje personally attended to the wounded soldiers and ensured they were resting. He also received the news that Moropant, who had not been able to take Shivneri, had finally managed to capture Triambakgad. At this, there was also confusion within the Mughal camp. Daud Khan's son Ahmad Khan and Jaswant Singh did not see eye to eye while Shahzada Muazzam and Diler Khan were becoming careless. It was a good opportunity to take advantage of. Raje set out on a new campaign, and this time the target was the city of Karanja, the ancient city near Akola, nearly five hundred kilometres away from Kunjargad.

Karanja was primarily a trading centre, and was known for its riches. The campaign was a complete success and Raje's troops, after looting the town for nearly three days, had to load the booty onto four thousand bullock carts and mules. With a booty of more than a few crores of gold coins, Raje returned to Rajgad, capturing the fort of Salher on the way.

Jijabai was eagerly waiting to meet Raje. She said, as he touched her feet, 'You must be tired.'

'On the contrary, Maa saheb, I wish I had wings so I could show you our territory and the flags fluttering on our forts now.'

Jijabai hugged him affectionately. She said, as she ruffled his hair, 'I can see it in your eyes! I don't need your wings.'

At that moment Sambhaji, hiding behind a pillar, came forward and said, 'Aba saheb, I am told you managed to steal an elephant from Daud Khan?'

'Who told you so? We found the poor elephant grazing alone in the forest and bought him here.'

'Shivba, he may be young, but you should not lie to him,' Jijabai reprimanded gently.

'You will understand better when you grow up,' she said, turning to Sambhaji.

'He is grown up enough, isn't he? He is thirteen now, and it is time he took charge of some duties.'

'What do you have in mind?'

'I am going to give him some administrative tasks once we move to Raigad.'

It was time to move to Raigad now. Subhanrao, the fort-keeper at Rajgad, was overwhelmed with emotions and was unable to speak. Raje said, 'Subhanrao, it is not easy to leave you. I have many memories attached to this place. It was from here that I went to meet Afzal Khan, and I defeated Shaista Khan from here. It was from this fort that I had gone to meet Mirza Raja.'

His tears flowed without hesitation, and Raje put his hand on Subhanrao's shoulder, and said, 'There are some memories that will remain buried here forever!' He could not continue and, without turning back, mounted his horse and rode away.

The work at Raigad was completed before the monsoon. Keeping the monsoon and Jijabai's health in mind, Raje made arrangements for her in a haveli at Pachad. Sambhaji had taken charge of some parts of the administration and would make regular visits to Jijabai's quarters.

As the month of Shravan ended, Raje paid regular visits to the forts nearby and inspected them. He was in Mahad to see how fortification work was progressing when he received some shocking news—Pune had been raided by Diler Khan, Bahadur Khan and Mahabat Khan. They had mercilessly killed everyone above the age of eight, whether man or woman. Having burnt the city, they had left Pune reduced to ashes.

Raje was furious and when he reached Pachad, he told Jijabai the news.

'Raje,' she asked, 'were we not warned of their attack?'

'We knew they would attack but we never expected them to resort to such brutalities. We had looted Surat and Karanja and I had expected them to respond one day. This is why I was keen to move to Raigad at the earliest. I am told Aurangzeb has issued orders to march on us. At this moment, the Mughals have surrounded Salher.'

'Raje, what does that mean?'

'There's nothing to worry about, Maa saheb. Our forts are well equipped and we can hold the enemy at bay.'

Raje issued orders to Prataprao to go to Salher and break the siege. Moropant Peshwa was to join from Konkan to support him.

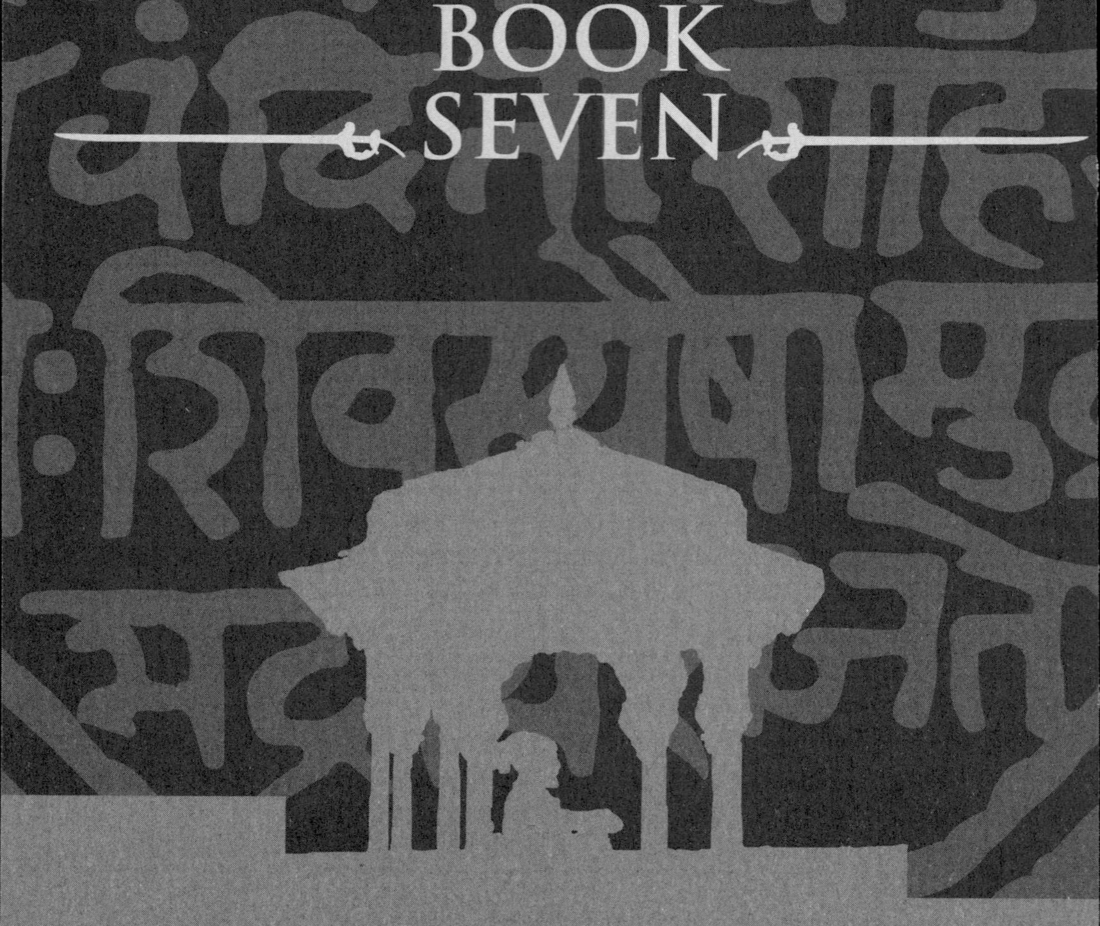

BOOK SEVEN

Calamity seemed to have the effect of increasing Raje's fervour. It was clear that the Mughals were determined to capture Salher. On Raje's orders, all the Maratha troops from across the regions gathered near Salher, keeping a safe distance lest they alert the Mughals. The plan was to attack from two sides—one from above and the other from below the ghat on the Konkan side.

The Maratha spies kept a close watch on the Mughal camp of nearly fifty thousand spread across miles. The cantonment, used to the largesse provided by the emperor, believed in living in style. With such large amounts of money and manpower at hand, the Mughal sardar Ikhlas Khan's complacency was understandable. The Maratha fort-keeper rose at dawn to watch the siege below. It was a daily affair now. The Mughals would shell the fort for a while, followed by a few troops attempting to scale the wall, which was followed by further shelling till nightfall. Despite this happening every day, there was little effect evident on the strong walls of the fort.

The next morning, as the Mughal camp slowly awakened, the neighing of horses alerted the soldiers. But it was too late. With shouts of 'Har Har Mahadev!', the Marathas pounced on the sleeping enemy. While the Mughals scrambled to the saddles of their horses and get their elephants ready to fight, the Maratha troops had reached the camp and begun the slaughter. The air was filled with the piercing screams of wounded soldiers while weapons clattered and the elephants trumpeted in fear. The massacre was over before it could begin. Ikhlas Khan managed to escape but twenty-two of his key sardars have been taken captive. The Marathas captured six thousand horses, a few hundred elephants, a few thousand camels and lakhs of jewellery and precious stones.

Raje stood at the ramparts of the Raigad fort eagerly awaiting news from Salher. On seeing the messenger arrive, he hurried towards him. Accompanying the messenger, Balaji, with happiness writ large on his face, said, 'Raje, we won! We captured thousands of horses, elephants and goods worth lakhs!'

'Well done! That is great news!'

'The enemy lost thousands of men. But so did we, Raje,' Balaji said, unable to face him.

'Oh, is that so?' Raje muttered. 'What else?' he asked, seeing Balaji hesitate.

'We lost Suryarao Kakade.'

Raje was overwhelmed with sorrow on hearing of Suryarao's death. 'The battlefield is not willing to relent till we sacrifice something in return!' Gathering his emotions, he said, 'Balaji, let us go to the office. We need to reward the messenger.'

As soon as they reached the office, Jijabai, eagerly waiting for news, came out.

Raje said, as he looked at Sambhaji, 'Yuvraj, as you are managing the affairs of the administration well, it is appropriate that you give a gold wristlet to this messenger.'

Jijabai, ever alert, could detect a sad note in Raje's voice despite his best attempt to sound normal. She asked, 'Raje, what is the matter?'

It was enough to bring tears to Raje's eyes. But before he could speak, Jijabai said, 'We have lost one more sardar, haven't we?'

Raje did not know how to respond. Gathering himself, he said, 'Maa saheb, I don't know if I can shoulder this responsibility well.'

'What do you mean?'

'Maa saheb, on a single word from me, my men are willing to lay down their lives. I fervently wish that the sacrifice of thousands of these men at the altar of Swaraj does not go to waste. The men who died did their job, but I have to take it forward. Sometimes I fear that I may not be ...'

'Don't worry, Raje!' Jijabai interrupted. 'I believe in Almighty, who will fulfil our wishes.'

Diler Khan had been shaken up by the attack at Salher. The Mughals had retreated from Salher, fearing the worst. Aurangzeb, enraged by the news, wrote a strongly worded note to Bahadur Khan, who had been made the Subedar:

'It would have been better if you had sacrificed your life in battle rather than sending me this message. The Portuguese and Abyssinians are flattering Shivaji, offering him gifts. I am sure, if you worked together, you can rout the Marathas in no time.'

Bahadur Khan replied:

'I am disheartened that you cast aspersions on my loyalties. This is the same Shivaji who managed to escape from Agra with his son, despite the strictest security arrangements under your command. You would appreciate our situation if you knew what conditions we operate under here. Shivaji has sent his Muslim emissary, Kazi Haider, to meet us. I am sure we can find a way to improve relations with him.'

Bahadur Khan's reply infuriated Aurangzeb further, and he ordered him to arrest Shivaji's emissary. While the orders were being sent to Bahadur Khan, Raje received Moropant, Prataprao and others, as they reached the fort victorious.

After offering them gifts, he said, 'Moropant, our men have shown exemplary courage. We lost Suryarao unfortunately, and I must visit his house and pay my respects.'

'Raje, there is one more house you must visit,' Moropant said. 'That of Ramaji Pangera, the fort-keeper at Kanhergad. While Diler Khan was making plans for Salher, he turned to Kanhergad. Ramaji, on hearing that Diler Khan was marching towards him, came down the fort with a mere six hundred Mavals and attacked them. After an intense battle, where all of them suffered heavily and finally lost their lives protecting the fort, Diler Khan and his men turned away unable to face the brave Mavals. The twelve-hundred-odd Pathans had no choice but to retreat.'

Raje was deeply saddened. He wondered how many more lives would be sacrificed for his goal. He said, his voice trembling, 'In a way, it is good that Pangera is no more, because even the gift of our entire kingdom would have been paltry in lieu of what he did for us. He was there with me when we fought Afzal Khan, and now he has laid down his life for Kanhergad. I must visit his house without any further delay!'

'Maharaj,' Moropant continued, 'I am told Bahadur Khan has now been made the Subedar.'

'That does not worry me. He is like a dog who is satisfied with a mere bone thrown at him. We can tackle him any day.'

'What about the sardars we have captured at Salher?'

'We will do what we have always done—release them honourably and give them royal clothes and gifts. We have no enmity with them anymore.'

The meeting was over and while others walked away, Raje stood at the ramparts, looking down at the valley. His mind was filled with thoughts of Pangera.

Despite the summer heat, it was pleasant at the top of the fort in the evening. Raje sat there conferring with Annaji, Balaji and Moropant when Sambhaji came in.

'Aba saheb, I have been asked to call you to inspect the stables. They are ready now.'

Annaji said, 'Yuvraj, we are busy discussing some other plans. Is it that urgent?'

A dejected Sambhaji said, 'I leave that to Aba saheb to decide.'

Raje, realizing that Sambhaji was hurt, said, 'Come on, let us go. After all, he is only doing his job.'

While going to the stables, he entered the quarters to take Rajaram for a ride.

Soyarabai said, 'I suggest you don't take him out. The wind is cold.'

'Rani saheb,' Raje said, trying to keep a smile on his face, 'I know what I am doing. We need not worry about his health so much that we make him weak. He is my son too and a Maratha as well.'

'Yes, you are right. But you have two and I have only one.'

The taunt pierced Raje's heart. For a moment, he struggled to control his emotions and letting go of Rajaram's hand, he said 'Rani saheb, it would have been better if you had not said that.'

Without waiting for Soyarabai's response, he turned abruptly and left the room.

It was late afternoon and the sun burned brightly on the fort. Raje was inspecting the stables being built for the elephants as he was escorted by

Hiroji. He said, 'Hiroji, you have done a good job, no doubt, but we have no use for the elephants here at the fort. We don't have the time to take care of these beasts. I believe our strength is our cavalry and our ability to camp in the open.'

'Maharaj, elephants add glory and prestige to the fort, don't they?'

'Hiroji, they are one of the reasons for the Mughal defeat. A howdah is the perfect target for an archer and once the commander falls, the troops run for their lives.'

At that moment, a shout of 'Jai, Jai Raghuveer Samarth!' attracted everyone's attention.

Raje turned to find a man walking confidently towards him. He was clad in saffron clothes and, folding his hands in namaskar, said, 'My name is Diwakar Gosavi, and I come with a message from Samarth Ramdas Maharaj.'

Raje was overjoyed to hear this. He said, 'Please wait a minute, and let me bring Maa saheb here as well. I am sure she will be keen to hear what Samarth has to say.'

As they assembled in the hall, Raje asked Moropant to read the message out aloud. It read:

'You, the one with the determination as solid as Mount Meru, the one who protects everyone—you are a shriman yogi. Your greatness and your benevolent acts; they are but countless. You are the true king of the people. You live in the hearts of the people; with your conduct, reasoning, generosity and righteousness you surpass everyone in your conscientiousness. Shrines were destroyed and Brahmin houses desecrated; our religion under threat from aggressors. But you, the incarnation of Lord Narayana, is here to protect us. There is no protector like you. You are the one Maharashtra looks up to. You are the one whose glory will spread the world over; you have annihilated the wicked and protected the good. You are truly, the benevolent king. Kindly excuse me, for I write to you unsolicited.'

Raje could not believe his ears while Maa saheb was in tears. She said, 'Raje, how lucky we are to be praised by Samarth Maharaj!'

'No, Maa saheb! It is a huge responsibility Maharaj has vested in me. He has reminded me of my duty. He has forgiven me despite my mistake.'

'Mistake?'

'Yes, I have committed a great blunder. A great saint like him moves about our kingdom and his followers are ever ready to help us at each step. Yet, unfortunately, I have not met him yet! Maa saheb, the sooner I meet him, the better it is! I have to meet him and seek his blessings.'

'I wish I could accompany you, Raje. But my health does not permit me. Please meet him and convey my regards. It is my desire that I receive his blessings before I die.

After honouring Diwakar Gosavi, Raje gave him a letter for Samarth Ramdas Maharaj, expressing his desire to meet him at the earliest.

On getting the news that Samarth Ramdas Maharaj was living near Shinganwadi in the Chaphal province, Shivaji made plans to meet him. Samarth's hermitage was in a mango grove with thickets on all sides. It lay nestled in the lap of the Sahyadris in the beautiful valley of the River Koyna, where nature was in full bloom. Diwakar Gosavi received Shivaji when he arrived at the hermitage.

The ashram had low huts with clean and pristine courtyards. A beautiful cottage made of grass and leaves near a huge peepul tree caught Shivaji's attention. Ramdas Samarth stood outside a beautiful garden, his matted hair, fair complexion and piercing eyes in his smiling face creating a welcoming aura around him. He held a rosary in one hand and a crutch under the other arm. Raje was delighted to see him and when he bent down to touch the guru's feet, he felt his hand on his arm, sending a shiver through his body. He heard him say, 'I have been waiting for you, Raje.'

Shivaji looked up. He could see powerful arms around which a rosary was tied. Samarth lifted Raje gently by his shoulders and hugged him. He said, 'Raje, I feel blessed after meeting you. It is like meeting Lord Ram.'

It was impossible for Raje to stop his tears. He said, gathering his thoughts finally, 'Please pardon me, Samarth.'

'Shivaji! Look at me!'

Raje looked at Samarth to find him smiling. He said, putting his hand on Raje's shoulder, 'Shivba. You may not have met me earlier but I know you well. You are a rajayogi, a shriman yogi! I have no words to describe you but I am sometimes bewildered by your commitment. I wonder how you manage to keep it constant.'

Raje, unable to speak, just looked at Samarth who continued, 'This province is under the control of Adil Shah. Why do you take such risks to meet me? I wrote to you as I appreciate what you have done but you need not have put your life at risk to meet me.'

'My life is not that precious!'

Swami held Raje's wrist tightly saying, 'Be patient, Raje, and never say that again. What you have undertaken is of great importance. I am a devotee of Lord Ram and my job is to spread his word but words alone are not enough, Raje. What you are doing is crucial, and my words are incomplete without your deeds. I was about to send you a message but I was told that you were already on the way.'

Raje then introduced Moropant and Prataprao Gujar. Samarth said, 'I was pleased the way you handled the siege at Salher. I hope you always show such valour. There is a lot of work to do yet.'

'It seems Maharaj has all current information!' Raje said, impressed with the swami's knowledge.

'It is not divine intuition! Your men have engaged many of my ascetics and they seem more involved in politics than spiritual pursuits. I thus get all the current information. I also want to say that you need to be careful. I don't think your friendship with Adil Shah will last long. You irked Khavas Khan in Kudal. He has a lot of influence in the Bijapur durbar.'

Soon, on a cue from Raje, Moropant asked his men to present covered trays to Samarth. They overflowed with gold and silver coins.

Seeing them Samarth said, 'Raje, for an ascetic like me, a loincloth is my only necessity. What I need from you is your love and commitment.'

'Commitment?'

'Yes, Raje. Men like you are born to fulfil a mission.'

'Samarth, please tell what you want me to do.'

Samarth smiled. He said, 'Raje, a king is like a cloud which showers the earth with water. You must do the same to your people.'

Samarth called one of his disciples, Kalyan, and said, 'Raje is our guest. Please ensure his men are taken care of.'

'My men are carrying their supplies including fodder for the animals. Please do not worry.'

Samarth said, 'I know. I also know that your men never harm people wherever they travel and that makes me very proud.'

Their conversation continued for a while and then Raje went to the hermitage for the night. For the next two days, Raje attended discourses by Samarth Ramdas on spirituality, wisdom and detachment. Raje requested Maharaj to bless him, which he gladly did. Raje felt he had been spiritually enlightened.

The next afternoon, sitting outside Samarth's cottage, he asked, 'Maharaj, have you seen God?'

Samarth looked up, surprised. He continued, 'Raje, the aim of life is not to meet or perceive God. To know oneself is the ultimate aim—that is where you will find God. Had I found God, I would not have exhorted you to find him.'

'Does it mean that a preceptor has no place in life?'

'A guru is a guide, to show you the right path. We are both travellers on the journey of life.'

'But then why haven't you recommended any prayers or mantras for me?' Raje asked.

'You have a mission to fulfil—to set up the Lord's rule on this land. Raje, love everyone and protect your dharma. This is your duty and I am sure the Lord will help you reach your goal.'

In the presence of Samarth and the divine atmosphere of the hermitage, hours passed by as Shivaji and his men listened to Samarth's words. All their woes were forgotten.

It had been four days since their arrival, but Raje did not want to leave the hermitage. Sensing this, Samarth said, 'Shivba, tomorrow is an auspicious day and I suggest you leave. If I hold you back any further, the entire kingdom will curse me. Also, your mother waits for you eagerly.'

Raje said, overwhelmed by emotion, 'Maa saheb was very keen to meet you but her health did not permit her to come. She sends her salutations. She said she was keen to get your blessings before she breathes her last.'

Samarth closed his eyes for a long time. When he opened them, they were filled with tears. He said, 'Raje, your Maa saheb is a blessed soul, and I am eager to meet her. Tell her I have received her wishes and that Lord Ram will fulfil her desires.'

The next morning, as dawn broke, Raje was restless. Seeing tears in Raje's eyes as he touched his feet, Samarth said, unable to contain his own tears, 'Shivba, please don't cry!'

'Maharaj, my life is blessed because I had the chance to meet you. I don't feel like leaving and would like to spend the rest of my life at your feet. When will I see you again?'

Samarth looked at Raje and said, caressing his back gently, 'Raje, I am with you at all times—remember that! Focus on the challenges ahead and the mission you need to fulfil.'

'Gurudev!'

'Carry on now, and you can meet me whenever you want to.'

Samarth went inside his hut and returned in a few moments carrying something wrapped in an ochre-coloured paper. He said, 'Raje, I am an ascetic and have nothing to offer you. Sitting in the caves at Shivthar for nine years, I wrote *Dasbodh*. I dictated it to Kalyan who made it into a manuscript. It was possible with the blessings of Lord Ram only. I made a copy of the manuscript and kept it for you. *Dasbodh* is the philosophy of my life—please preserve it carefully. Whenever you find yourself in trouble, read this. I am sure Lord Ram will show you the way. Raje, with the *Dasbodh*, I have given whatever I have to give!'

Raje touched the *Dasbodh* to his forehead reverently. As tears flowed down his cheeks, he took leave of Samarth.

The next morning, Raje and his men left at the crack of dawn. Even after two days of travel, all Raje could think about was the time he had spent with Swami Samarth Ramdas. The summer heat was intense but they continued their journey. On reaching a riverbank, they stopped near a mango grove. Sensing that Raje was looking for a place to rest and eat, Prataprao Gujar said, 'Give me a few minutes, and I will search for some palash leaves to make a plate for our meal.'

Raje smiled. 'Prataprao, you seem to forget that we are Marathas who have often times eaten while riding. Just hand the bhakri over to me.'

Prataprao opened the bundle of food he was carrying. It was a simple meal of raw onions, green chillies and jowar bhakri. As they dismounted to drink from the river, Prataprao said, pointing in the direction of a village at the base of the hills, 'Ramaji Pangera was from that village—Korjai.'

'He lived so far away from the fort?'

'Raje, your orders were clear—the fort-keeper should not be from a village near a fort. We found Ramaji here.'

As they reached the village, a small affair of about twenty-five huts, the villagers, worried at hearing the horse hooves, were tense as the cavalry arrived. They watched Raje with a mixture of awe and curiosity. Prataprao guided Raje to Ramaji's house where his father, Maruti, rushed to receive them. He bent to touch Raje's feet when Raje said, 'Baba! You are supposed to bless us and not touch my feet.'

The old man was rendered speechless. Raje guided him to sit on a parapet on the verandah outside the house. Soon an old woman, apparently Ramaji's mother, his widow and a small boy of about twelve years came out of the hut. They all touched Raje's feet.

Raje could not believe the joy with which they all received him.

Maruti said, 'Raje, we are truly blessed. You have come to this poor man's today!'

'Baba, don't call it a poor man's house. This is the house of Ramaji, who fought tooth and nail to chase Diler Khan away.'

Hearing Ramaji's name, the old man's eyes filled with tears.

Raje said, trying to hold back his own tears, 'Baba, please don't cry.'

'I am not crying, Raje,' Maruti said, wiping his tears. 'It is only because of my son's valour that we have had the good fortune of being visited by you.'

At that moment Ramaji's younger brother Rupaji came in.

Raje smiled dejectedly and said, 'Baba, we survive at the cost of men like Ramaji. What is the use of admiring men like me?'

Maruti said, 'Raje, don't say that. Boys like Ramaji have the courage to fight only because they know you are there to take care of everyone. The poor live because of you, Raje.'

'What have I done for you, Baba?'

'Ask me what you have not done! Earlier the Kulkarnis, Patils, Desais and Jagirdars used to take everything away from us. Now, your administration supports us and we get bullocks to till our land. As a rule, your men take only two parts of the produce. If you ask for three, we would readily part with it.'

'Baba, I have everything I want. When men are willing to lay down their lives for me, what else can I ask for?'

As Raje got up to leave, Prataprao handed to Maruti a bag of coins.

'If this is compensation for the death of my son, I don't need it, Raje. I have my land and house and I have your support. What more do I need?'

'Tell me, what can I do for you then?'

'Let Ramaji's younger brother, Rupaji, join you—that will be our reward.'

Raje's eyes were filled with tears. He said, holding Maruti's hand, 'Let him stay and help you till the land. This too is required to strengthen the Swaraj.'

'This old man still has a lot of strength left! Take him with you, I beseech you.'

Raje nodded and said, 'Rupaji, you are now drafted into the army. Use the money for your household, and then meet me at Raigad soon. I shall inform you about your duties there.'

Rupaji, inducted as a Shiledar, a cavalryman, touched Raje's feet in gratitude. The entire village accompanied Raje and his men till they reached the riverbank.

As they mounted their horses, Raje said contentedly, 'Prataprao, today has been a golden day in my life.'

Shivaji returned to Pachad to find Annaji Datto there. Jijabai normally stayed at the foothills of the fort at Pachad as the humid weather atop the fort during monsoons did not suit her.

'You must be supervising Maa saheb's arrangements here, I suppose,' he asked Annaji.

Annaji's answer surprised him as he said, 'Yes, and I was on my way to Mahad to summon the physician Diwakar Vaidya to the fort.'

'Why, what happened?' Raje asked, suddenly alert.

'Yuvraj was wounded on a hunt.'

Raje's heart skipped a beat. He asked, 'When? How is he now?'

'This was yesterday. Yuvraj was told about a tiger creating havoc in a village nearby. When he confronted the tiger, he charged ahead and killed him with his sword. But in the process, he was wounded but not badly hurt. Our physician called for Diwakar Vaidya.'

'And you left Yuvraj to manage the fort in the meanwhile?' Raje said, stunned.

'Ibrahim, Yesaji, Rupaji Bhosale—they are all there and ...'

'I am not interested in names,' Raje shouted, raising his hand to cut off Annaji mid-sentence.

Raje mounted his horse and raced up the mountain to reach the fort. The trumpets at the main door announced his arrival but he had no time for the salutes and mujras and he galloped towards Sambhaji's quarters. He jumped down the horse and rushed indoors. Sambhaji was lying on a bed while the physician, Jijabai and the others stood nearby.

Raje asked the physician, 'How is Yuvraj?'

'There is nothing to worry about. Except for a deep gash on the shoulder, which will take a week to heal, he has only a few minor scratches.'

Raje wiped the sweat off his forehead and looked at Sambhaji, who smiled, further enraging him. He said, 'Whose permission did you take before going out on a shikar? And what experience do you have to charge at a tiger directly?'

Turning to Yesaji, he asked, 'Yesaji, you were present. And so was Ibrahim Khan. How could you allow him to take such a risk?'

Seeing Sambhaji silent, he shouted, 'Sambhaji Raje, answer me!'

Sambhaji's face was flushed. He looked at Maa saheb who said, 'Raje, please go to your quarters.'

Raje looked at Maa saheb at the unexpected command. He said, 'But Maa saheb ...'

'Please do not say a word. Just go!' Jijabai interrupted.

Raje was taken aback and left the room. He entered his quarters and stood with his hands behind his back, looking out of the window. He could see Soyarabai playing with Rajaram, splashing water near the water tank. But he was in no mood to greet them. At that moment, he heard footsteps and turned to see Maa saheb enter.

She asked, 'Are you still angry?'

'No, Maa saheb.'

'Raje, Shambhu is wounded. Should you berate him at such a time?'

'Do you think it gives me any pleasure to do so? But there are times when I fail to understand you.'

'Why do you say that?'

'You remember when I used the elder Maharaj's gun and shot a tiger sitting on the ground? You scolded me to no end. In my huff, I had refused dinner but you did not care. You were so strict with me but it seems you are allowing Shambhu to get away with anything. It is not good to pamper him so much, Maa saheb. I am worried that he may not be able to handle his responsibilities well.'

Jijabai was agonized to hear Raje's words. She said, 'Shivba, you don't realize—I would have questioned Sai had she been alive. Remember, you are lucky to have a mother. Shambhu isn't.'

Over the next week, Sambhaji recovered well. Raje would peep into his room once a while but he did not say much. Towards the end of the week, Raje was in his quarters chatting with Soyarabai and playing with the young Rajaram. Putlabai too was there when Raje asked, 'Where is Maa saheb?'

'She is in her puja room.'

'I escaped from Agra but it seems Maa saheb has not given up her fasts and puja. Each time I ask, she is either fasting or busy with something else.'

At that moment, Sambhaji stepped in. Raje said, looking at him, 'And Maa saheb now has found this new god to worship!'

Sambhaji, unable to understand, looked at Raje suspiciously. He stepped closer and sat on his knees to touch Raje's feet. Raje patted his back and head lovingly. Feeling his wet hair, he smiled and said, 'Oh, it seems the physician has allowed you to have a bath.'

Sambhaji stood up. He was a young, tall and handsome lad of fifteen with a broad chest. Raje felt proud seeing the young Yuvraj.

He said, 'Sambhaji, I don't derive any pleasure from scolding you. But I want you to know your responsibilities. You need to be careful. I have so many plans lined up and someone like you needs to take them forward. I am not forbidding you to hunt but next time you want to go, ask me. I shall come along!'

'Aba saheb!'

Raje hugged Sambhaji and caressed his back. He said, not realizing that Putlabai and Soyarabai were in the room, 'I am bound by the promise I made to Sai, Shambhu! If I cannot fulfil it, I have no right to live.'

Realizing that his other queens were around, he quickly wiped his tears and said, 'Sambhaji, check if Annaji is in the office. Tell him I will join him soon. We have to make arrangements for Maa saheb to go to Pachad.'

Sambhaji Raje nodded and left with Rajaram holding his hand. Raje, looking at them as they exited, said, 'These two are like Ram and Lakshmana. I am sure they will fulfil my dreams.'

With his increasing power, Shivaji wanted to ensure that his forts were kept secure. This required lakhs of rupees to be spent. He directed that a part of the revenue collected from various districts be credited to the state treasury.

In the meanwhile, Prataprao Gujar sent a letter to Surat on behalf of Raje. The letter read:

'You are hereby asked to pay four lakh rupees to us. Your emperor attacked our lands and we were forced to maintain a huge army. This money would be used to meet such expenses.'

The letter was a veiled threat that if they did not pay up, the Marathas would attack Surat once again. Ever since Mahabat Khan and Shahzada Muazzam had been recalled to Delhi, the Deccan was being managed by Diler Khan and Bahadur Khan. However, since their defeat at Salher, Aurangzeb had been annoyed with them. In order to pacify Shivaji, they sent a Brahmin emissary. Raje welcomed him and, in turn, sent his trusted clerk

Kazi Haider to meet Bahadur Khan. Raje was not in the mood to attack Surat and preferred to negotiate a treaty.

Aurangzeb, already enraged at his commanders, sent them a letter: 'You should work with all of Shivaji's enemies like Adil Shah, Qutb Shah, the Portuguese and the Abyssinians. How long can he hide in his fort? Soon, we will defeat him.'

Bahadur Khan replied, 'This will not work as Shivaji has many forts where he can hide. Secondly, he uses the inaccessible land between the mountainous regions to grow hundreds of maunds of corn, which can feed them for a hundred years. Thus, we have sent our emissary to negotiate with him. He too has sent a Muslim emissary in return. Please allow us to sign a treaty.'

Aurangzeb was further enraged by their letter and replied in a scathing manner. Bahadur Khan and Diler Khan were bewildered, not knowing what to do next. To pacify Aurangzeb, they made a show of nominally arresting Shivaji's emissary.

Raje smiled when he heard about this. He said, 'Poor Alamgir! He cannot expect such sardars to defeat me. They are mere labourers working like bullocks fed on oil cakes.'

Shivaji needed the treaty for some respite from his relentless activities. He was sure that Bahadur Khan or Diler Khan would not create trouble. He was also aware that the Mughals were losing their hold on the Deccan. He directed his soldiers to attack and loot Mughal territories with more vigour.

At that time Shivaji received the news of the death of the Golconda Sultan, Abdullah Qutb Shah. He was succeeded by his son-in-law, Abul Hassan Tana Shah. Shivaji immediately asked Nirajipant to meet the new Sultan at Golconda to ensure that the earlier treaty was honoured. As expected, Tana Shah agreed and Nirajipant returned with sixty-six thousand hons against the annual pact of one lakh.

The news of another death reached Shivaji. Ali Adil Shah was succeeded by his five-year-old son, Sikandar Jahan. The Abyssinian chief, Khavas Khan, was named regent. Shivaji knew that Khavas Khan did not favour Marathas and sooner or later, he would attack. Preparing himself for a surprise attack, he recalled his emissary Punde from the Adil Shahi court and issued orders to Prataprao and Anandrao to return home. The plan to attack Adil Shahi power was finalized. The target was the Panhala Fort.

Shivaji knew he needed a foolproof plan. He had lost a thousand men the last time he had attacked Panhala and he could ill afford to make such a mistake again. Sheer bravado would not work and he got busy thinking about an ingenious plan. It had been more than six months since meeting Samarth Ramdas. One evening, while returning from his evening darshan, walking along with Annaji Datto, Ganaji and Prataprao, Raje said, 'I have been thinking—Khavas Khan is no friend of ours and he will attack sooner or later. We need to pre-empt him.'

'Raje, just command me and I will burn the country down,' Prataprao said, his hand on his sword.

'Patience, Prataprao!' Raje said, smiling. 'We need to do something which will make them think twice before attacking us again.'

'You mean Panhala!' Annaji Datto muttered.

'You read my mind!' Raje exclaimed.

'Please command us,' Prataprao and Ganaji said, stepping forward.

'Prataprao, mere recklessness will not get us the fort. We have lost a thousand men earlier, and we need to plan well this time.'

Raje returned to his quarters a little later and was surprised to find Annaji waiting there. He asked, 'What is it, Annaji?'

'Raje, I am sure we can easily take Panhala with a planned attack. I would like to lead the charge.'

Raje thought about a moment and said, 'Let me think over it.'

The next morning, as the sun rose in the eastern sky and all the sardars had assembled as per Raje's orders, and after receiving the symbolic betel leaf, Annaji took leave of Raje, who said, 'Annaji, I am entrusting the campaign to you; Prataprao will support you. Take your time, but come back successful.'

The others were a little disappointed. Annaji, his joy knowing no bounds, left the fort soon after.

Annaji Datto camped at Rajapur. The news from the spies visiting Panhala was not encouraging. It was guarded by nearly two and half thousand soldiers. The fort was tall and magnificent, with strong doors and an alert fort-keeper. Annaji knew he could ill afford to be reckless. It was nearly a month since he had set up camp but he had not found a way to attack the fort.

Raje too was worried that Annaji had not been able to make any progress. As he stood on the ramparts of Raigad, looking at the silhouette of the mountains in the distance, he noticed the striking Konkan Diva Fort which stood out sharply in the fading light. That night he hardly slept and the next morning he called Kondaji Farzand and said, 'It has been more than a month since Annaji went to Rajapur. We need to find a way to take Panhala.'

'Please tell me how I can be of use,' Kondaji pleaded.

'I want you to go to Rajapur.'

The next morning, Raje received Kondaji formally as he entered the office and bent in mujra. Raje slipped a gold bracelet on to Kondaji's arm, who was overwhelmed and touched Raje's feet.

'Maharaj!'

'Don't say a word, Kondaji. You are now the rightful owner of this bracelet and will ride in a palanquin.'

Seeing Yesaji smile, Raje asked, 'Why are you smiling, Yesaji?'

'Raje, I have seen people being felicitated after they have won something. Today, we have witnessed a felicitation before anything has been achieved.'

Yesaji had spoken what others felt too. Raje, quiet for a while, put his hand on Yesaji's shoulder and said, 'Giving Kondaji a job is tantamount to his achieving it. But I always wonder if I will see these men again, the ones who are willing to lay down their lives for me. If we wish to felicitate Tanaji today, is he here for us to do so?'

Raje's words stunned everyone into silence. Raje continued, looking at Kondaji, 'Capture Panhala, but come back safe. We have lots of other plans for you and we cannot afford to lose you!'

Kondaji marched out, increasing Raje's worries further. Moropant had sent a huge amount of loot from the Nashik region but Raje's mind was elsewhere. He could not think of anything other than Panhala. Fifteen days had now gone by since Kondaji's departure.

A few days later, Raje was pleasantly surprised to receive a messenger from Panhala who handed a bag to him. Reading the letter inside the bag, Raje was overjoyed and tears flowed down his cheeks. He said, 'Give this messenger a hundred gold hons. We have captured Panhala!'

Looking at the messenger, he asked, 'What is your name?'

'Mankoji.'

'Mankoji, were you with Kondaji when he conquered Panhala?'

'Yes, I was.'

'Then narrate the account of his courageous fight. I want to hear how he did it.'

'Maharaj, Kondaji had made a detailed plan. Kondaji and sixty of us stormed the fort in the night.'

'What? Just sixty of you?'

'Yes, Maharaj. We had studied the fort well. Some of them managed to climb the walls and then threw the ropes down for others to climb up. It was late and in the inky darkness, we could not see our own hands. There was just a single man with a torch patrolling. Our arrow pierced him and he died before he fell on the floor. We all then blew the horns we carried with us, making a huge noise. The fort woke up but no one dared come up, fearing us to be ghosts! At the signal of a whistle and our cries of "Har Har Mahadev!", we all charged in and a carnage followed. Kondaji beheaded the fort-keeper with two strokes of his sword, and that was the end of the battle! Pant was waiting at the door which was opened soon and we took charge of the fort.'

'That is unbelievable!' Raje exclaimed. 'I was unable to capture it but you sixty ghosts have performed a miracle,' he added. Raje got up from his seat and said, 'We must leave for Panhala tomorrow. I am sure the Adil Shahi troops will retaliate and we need to be prepared.'

Raje left the room and walked towards his quarters with a smile of satisfaction on his face. After many weeks, Raje slept soundly that night.

The next morning, at the crack of dawn, Raje got up and first visited the temple at the fort. As he returned from his darshan, the sun peeped over the eastern horizon, just behind the mountains. The early morning fog had descended into the valley. Raje could see small rivulets as they flowed down to the valley from Konkan Diva's mountainous side. It was a wonderful sight. Raje said, turning towards Prataprao who walked with him, 'Prataprao, we managed to capture Panhala. It is a huge relief for me. Our previous defeat had irked me no end.'

'But the Adil Shahi troops are going to be restless now.'

'But that is what I want! We have Qutb Shah's men on our side. Once we defeat Adil Shah's army, we will rule over the entire Deccan. We can then think of how to tackle the Mughals.'

Soon, Raje descended from the fort to reach the haveli at Pachad. Touching Jijabai's feet, he said, 'I apologize, Maa saheb. I got tied up with some arrangements and that's why I'm late.'

'Don't make a fuss of it. At this age, I should be spending all my time in prayer but I cannot resist being involved in your campaigns. At times, I wish I was at Raigad instead of sitting here in Pachad.'

'Then why don't you come to Raigad?' Raje said. He looked at his mother, her neck shaking a little with age, the crow's feet around her eyes showing.

'Shivba, I am in my seventies now. My daughters-in-law are there to look after you. Who knows how long I will last?'

'Maa saheb!' Raje exclaimed, unable to say anything further. The next morning, Raje marched towards Panhala.

The news of Raje's arrival spread cheer in Panhala. Annaji dispatched Kondaji along with his troops to receive Raje, and seeing him, Kondaji dismounted and walked towards him. Walking with a straight back and sporting a saffron turban, he stepped forward with a sword in his left hand. His face was flushed with a mixture of pride and modesty as he removed his shoes before taking the final few steps to meet Raje.

Raje asked, as he hugged Kondaji, 'Where is Annaji?'

'He is waiting at the gate of the fort.'

'Come on, let us not keep him waiting.'

Mounting their horses, they galloped towards the fort. The kettledrums and horns announced their arrival long before they reached the fort. Annaji rushed forward and showered gold flowers on Raje's head who, overwhelmed with emotion, was dumbfounded.

Annaji said, 'Maharaj, let us go in.'

Raje glanced at the main gate for a moment and looking at them, he said, 'You two have won the fort. You must lead us in. You deserve the honour, Subedar Kondaji.'

Annaji and Kondaji could not believe their ears.

Raje said, 'Now what are you waiting for?'

As they entered the fort, the drums and trumpets celebrated their arrival while the guns boomed across the fort.

Annaji said, 'Raje, we managed to capture the fort with minimum damage. We would like you to inspect our loot. There is immense wealth we got hold of.'

'I will see that later. Show me my sixty warriors first, for they are our real wealth.'

The warriors were given lavish gifts and honoured individually. Raje assured the safety of the prisoners and pardoned most of them. Panhala was finally in his control and he did not intend to lose it again.

The capture of Panhala had ignited a renewed sense of purpose in Raje. He had issued orders to Prataprao to gather as many troops at possible.

Prataprao was a little surprised and asked, 'Maharaj, why do you want to bring so many of our soldiers here?'

'Prataprao, you are my commander-in-chief. I did not expect you to ask such a question! The moment Khavas Khan finds out that we have captured Panhala, he will be itching to teach us a lesson. We need to put fear in their hearts before they decide to do anything.'

Raje's plans were put into action and, apart from fortifying Panhala with more troops, they managed to capture the forts at Parli and Satara within the next few weeks. The captures also led to a rich haul of gems and jewellery, which were loaded up into many bullock carts and deposited at the treasury at Raigad. Khavas Khan was further enraged when he heard of this and ordered his senior commander Bahlol Khan to attack Shivaji. He was given command of nearly ten thousand soldiers. Khavas Khan ordered his commanders at various cantonments to send reinforcements for Bahlol Khan.

When they heard of Bahlol Khan having left Bijapur and being camped at Umrani a few miles from Bijapur, Prataprao said, 'Maharaj, let us wait for Bahlol Khan to come here. We will teach him a lesson.'

Raje said, a little dejectedly, 'Prataprao, we cannot wait for him to come here. He will bring reinforcements with him. We need to attack him when he expects it the least.'

Prataprao stood up as Raje gave him his jewel-encrusted dagger from his waistband. Receiving the same with a mujra, Prataprao said, 'I will return after defeating him.'

The next afternoon, Prataprao and his men left with the trumpets announcing their departure. The force disappeared in a cloud of dust as they galloped away towards their goal.

Marching through Miraj, Prataprao rapidly covered the distance of nearly a hundred miles to reach Umrani. They surveyed the camp surreptitiously and, then, in the dead of the night, managed to take over a lake which supplied water to the camp. The next morning, Bahlol Khan's men woke up to find that they had been surrounded and that they had not a drop of water to drink. With the heat getting worse as the day progressed, their thirst added to the soldiers' anxiety.

Finally, Bahlol Khan decided to lead the charge. Sitting in a howdah atop an elephant and swinging a naked sword, his troops marched forward to the shouts of 'Deen! Deen!' Suddenly, the march stopped, much to Khan's surprise. A deathly silence prevailed for what seemed like an inordinately long period. Shading his eyes, Khan looked into the distance to see soldiers charging from all directions. The next moment, cries of 'Har Har Mahadev!' pierced the silence.

Like hail falling on tin roofs, the Maratha soldiers fell on Khan's troops and a fierce battle erupted. Khan, seeing the Marathas moving inwards in a circle from all directions, and killing his men as they marched forward, lost all his resolve. But he had no way out.

By sunset, he hurriedly sent his messenger to Prataprao with the message, 'I did not march on you of my own will but on the orders of the Sultan. Please assure Shivaji that I shall never go against you again.'

Prataprao's heart melted at the appeal and allowed Khan to return. Raje was overjoyed to hear of the Maratha victory but was clearly disappointed with Prataprao who had allowed the enemy to escape. He sent him a note demanding an explanation: 'Why did you allow Bahlol Khan to go scot-free when my explicit instructions were to kill him? On whose instructions did you do this?'

More than a month had passed since the defeat of Bahlol Khan. The monsoon had set in, and strong, cool winds blew on Raigad. The news of Raje's arrival had reached the fort and everyone eagerly awaited his return. After ensuring that Maa saheb was comfortable at Pachad, Sambhaji had ascended the fort and was waiting for Raje.

That afternoon, he was resting in his quarters when Yesubai came in with Rajaram. They got along well and Rajaram loved to play with her. She chatted for a while, sitting at the edge of the bed when she suddenly got up seeing Soyarabai at the door. Adjusting her pallu, she was about to leave when Soyarabai berated her. 'How many times have I told you not to feed

Rajaram unless I tell you to?' she said, looking at a plate of sweets kept on a table.

Turning to Sambhaji she said, 'Raje asks me to involve myself in the administrative work but here you are, attached to your chamber. Annaji told me that an English envoy has arrived but you haven't found the time to move out of your chamber yet. Shouldn't you be more involved in administrative matters?'

Soyarabai left the room, dragging Rajaram behind her, before Sambhaji could react. Yesubai was bewildered. She asked, 'Why was Aai saheb taunting you?'

'She is part of the family,' Sambhaji said, trying to make light of the situation. 'Only strangers would not speak their mind. Now, I need to go the office and look into matters as she said!' Sambhaji left quickly leaving a dumbfounded Yesu behind.

On reaching the office, Sambhaji found Annaji reading a letter. He enquired whether everything was in order and Annaji nodded in response. Sambhaji asked, 'Any news of Aba saheb?'

'No. He has left Panhala but is visiting a shrine for a holy dip and will then come here.'

'You are lucky to be his confidante. You know everything,' Sambhaji said, sighing. He continued, 'I am told there is an English envoy waiting to meet me?'

'Not here, but at the foot of the fort.'

'Then please bring him here.'

'Please do not misunderstand, but I thought it is better that Raje meets him.'

'Why?' Sambhaji asked, raising an eyebrow questioningly.

'The envoy is a cunning fellow. He has come here with his own demands. It is better that ...'

'I can handle it. I have met many such merchants and their envoys before.'

'They were mere merchants. This man is an emissary and showing such eagerness ...'

'Annaji!' Sambhaji said, raising his voice a little. 'I am the Yuvraj here and am managing the administration under Aba saheb's orders. If you are worried about my age, let me remind you that that Aba saheb was younger than me when he captured Rohideshwar.'

'That was different,' Moropant muttered.

'Why? Did he appear from the sky suddenly?'

'Raje!' Annaji exclaimed.

Sambhaji realized he had spoken out of turn. He said, 'I should not have said that. Annaji, let the English envoy meet me here. If I slip up, Aba saheb will take care of it.'

'The envoy is here to ask for compensation towards the damages inflicted by us at Rajapur. Prataprao had closed down their factory at Hubli. He is sure to raise these issues.'

'Let him! We will tackle them,' Sambhaji said. He asked, changing the topic, 'Has Kondaji returned?'

'Not yet. He is still at Panhala.'

'He is a real hero. He managed to capture the fort with a mere sixty men. I believe you entered through the main door, didn't you?'

Annaji's forehead creased for a moment before he replied. 'That is true. But finding a way to enter is as difficult as entering the fort, Raje.'

Sambhaji smiled. 'Annaji, it requires some courage to face death.' Sambhaji turned to leave without waiting for Annaji to reply.

The moment Sambhaji had left the room, Moropant said, 'At times I am more scared of Sambhaji Raje than Raje himself. His aim is perfect and he hits where it hurts the most.'

'After all, he is a hunter,' Annaji said, sighing.

The next morning the envoy Tom Nichols along with his interpreter Shamaj came to the fort. Nichols was dressed in typical English fashion with socks, narrow trousers, a full-sleeved coat and a silk scarf around his neck. His grey smiling eyes twinkled as he looked around, and his hand stroked the cap he had placed on his thighs. His fair skin in the heat of the subcontinent had turned ruddy.

They all stood up as Sambhaji entered. He waved with his hand for the envoy to sit, pointing to a chair nearby. Nichols bowed and then stood up to request compensation for the closure of the English factories at Rajapur and Hubli. He asked to be allowed to transport timber and fuel without paying taxes.

Sambhaji listened to him with an expressionless face. He said, after hearing the envoy patiently, 'I shall think about it and also apprise Maharaj when he returns in two or three days. The humid weather here will not suit you and I suggest you stay at the base. I hope your stay at Pachad has been made comfortable.'

The Englishman bowed once again and left.

As expected, Raje returned within the next three days. He was a little unwell with fever and cough. He said, as he rested on his bed, 'Bal Raje, I am told you heard the envoy out patiently without letting him know your thoughts. That is good diplomacy!'

Sambhaji was surprised to find that his father had already been apprised of the meeting. Before he could react, Shivaji said, 'Shambhu, I heard it from Annaji. I have not descended from the heavens with supernatural powers!'

Sambhaji said, a little hastily, 'I apologize.'

'What for? What you said is absolutely correct. I too learnt from my experiences. I also learnt that it is good to take benefit of someone else's experience. Anyway, Annaji, let us meet the envoy tomorrow. Shambhu, what do you think he wants?'

'He is demanding compensation for the closure of their factories at Rajapur and Hubli.'

'I see! By the way, how is the elder Rani saheb? I am told she is not well. Did you visit her?'

'No, I was busy ...'

'Well, you should have.' Raje did not elaborate further and seeing him being quiet, Sambhaji quietly stepped out of the room.

The next morning, Nichols was presented in front of Raje. He stood up as soon as Raje's arrival was announced and bowed on seeing him enter.

Raje said, as they took their seats, 'Tell me what we can do for you.'

'While we were negotiating a treaty, your men attacked our factory at Hubli. Our president is now in two minds about the future of our factory.'

Raje smiled, irking the envoy who continued, 'Were you aware of the men looting our factory?'

'We are keen to keep friendly relations with the English.'

'Then why this attack?'

'How can you be sure that it was our men who attacked?'

'I can prove it!'

'Things happen sometimes inadvertently.'

'You had promised to compensate us for the attack at Rajapur.'

'I have not denied that.'

'Similarly, we request you to look into Hubli too.'

'That is not possible!'

'Why?'

'I had given you my word for Rajapur, but you must recall why we attacked Rajapur in the first place. You allowed the enemy to use your cannons against us. Why are you getting involved in the politics of this country?'

Nichols swallowed nervously. Raje looked into his eye and said, 'When we looted Surat, we were insulted by your men, a mere thirty of them. We could have easily taken over your harbour and destroyed your ships but we wanted to extend a hand of friendship. It seems you are forgetting that.'

'We too are keen on being friends. I am told your ships are due to arrive from Mecca. I am sure you would not wish that we capture them?' The English envoy asked, the threat masked in a question.

Raje was unflustered. He said, 'Sure, go ahead. If such a thing were to happen, I can promise you not a single ship of yours would be able to land on Indian shores ever again. I know you gave refuge to Siddi Sambool at your harbour in Mumbai, lest you forget we have an eye on all your activities.'

Nichols had not expected such a calm but decisive response from Raje. He said, trying to improve the situation, 'Maharaj, there seems to be a misunderstanding. Sambool begged for our help but we refused.'

Raje remained silent. Assuring Nichols that he would consider his requests, Raje bid him farewell. In the meahwhile, Raje's troops had captured Satara, much to his satisfaction. He was now waiting for the rains to end.

Soon it was time for Dussehra. For the Shastra puja, the worship of weapons, all types of arms—from a simple dagger, sword, sabres, spears and lances to tiger claws—were on display. Sambhaji took Rajaram, holding his hand, for a tour of the weapons. He said, pointing towards one, 'Look! This sword was gifted by Mirza Raja to Aba saheb. And the one over there—that was the same tiger claw used by Aba saheb to confront Afzal Khan.'

Rajaram was looking at Sambhaji's sword intently. Seeing his small sword next to it, he made a face. He said, 'Will you give me yours?'

Before Sambhaji could answer, he heard someone say, 'Swords are never requested for—they must be demanded.'

Sambhaji turned to see Soyarabai coming in. He said, greeting her, 'But one needs to wrest them from enemies—not from brothers.'

Putlabai was impressed by Sambhaji but Soyarabai was not silenced easily. She said, 'And what if the brother does not give you one?'

Sambhaji, unperturbed by the barb, replied, 'If that happens, he is not really a brother then.'

He walked out with Rajaram in tow.

Putlabai, unable to contain herself, said, 'Such a fine pair! Their love for each other is amazing.'

Soyarabai muttered under her breath but loud enough for Putlabai to hear, 'Well, I wonder sometimes whether the wise are clever or the ignorant are gullible.'

Raje's arrival at the fort spurred everyone into action. All the queens were waiting for him—Soyarabai, Sagunabai, Kashibai and Putlabai. He said, looking at Soyarabai, 'I will take both Sambhaji and Rajaram to the base of the fort. When Maa saheb comes here tomorrow, they can accompany her.'

He picked up his sword kept along with the puja items and sheathed it at his waist, after touching it reverently to his forehead. As he was tucking his dagger onto the other side, he said to Sambhaji, 'Why don't you ask Bal Raje to tuck your sword at his waist and see how it looks?'

Sambhaji helped Rajaram but the sword was much too long and dragged on the floor when Rajaram walked. Everyone laughed, irritating Rajaram, who said, 'Aai saheb, I don't need this sword.'

Putlabai tried to defuse the situation by saying, 'Don't worry! You can carry it when you are older, Bal Raje.'

Raje smiled saying, 'But then Shambhu Raje too would have grown up, isn't it?'

Soyarabai knew Raje was directing his comment at her and she got up in a huff and left without saying a word. Raje, along with his two sons, descended from the fort to meet Jijabai.

Once the Dussehra festivities were over, Raje focused his attention on Satara. Camping at the village of Kudir, a few miles from Karwar, he directed his troops to loot the territories of Bijapur. After a gap of three months, after having collected vast amounts of loot, he returned to Raigad.

A few days after returning to Raigad, Moropant informed Raje of a letter from Nashik. 'It is from our priest, Anant Bhatt Kavle,' he said.

'What is it regarding?'

'He has informed us about the expected arrival of Pandit Gaga Bhatt, a very well-respected Vedic scholar.'

'His visit would be a blessing for us. Please ensure that our head priest visits Nashik and accompanies him here. He must be honoured suitably.'

Raje received Gaga Bhatt near Mahad, a few miles before Raigad. As soon as the palanquin was put on the ground, Raje stepped forward to receive him. Gaga Bhatt stepped out of the palanquin. He was a fair, slightly plump man. His head was covered by an embroidered yellow scarf while a red shawl was draped around his shoulders. He wore a white dhoti with a red silk border. A big mark on his forehead added to the intensity of his black eyes. A ring of topaz on one finger and a golden ring in another caught the attention of those waiting to receive him. He walked in his wooden sandals and touched Raje's shoulder affectionately and muttered his blessings as Raje bowed reverentially.

Gaga Bhatt was pleased to be received with such respect. This was the same Shivaji who had taken an oath at the temple of Rohideshwar of creating the Hindavi Swaraj. Gaga Bhatt's pleasure knew no bounds because he was being hosted by such a man.

A few days later, Gaga Bhatt said, 'Raje, I have come here with a specific purpose. Tomorrow, after sunrise, at an auspicious time, I will tell you the reason for my coming here.'

Everyone had assembled in the main hall, where a raised seat had been created for Gaga Bhatt. Jijabai and Raje were seated next to him, followed by Sambhaji and Rajaram. The queens and others sat behind. The ministers and other officials were seated at the end. As soon as Gaga Bhatt's arrival was announced, Shivaji got up followed by the others. Folding his hands, Raje requested Gaga Bhatt to take his seat. The priest removed the scarf from his head and then, looking at the audience and sighing deeply, sat down. After a while, he said, 'Raje, the only thing a Brahmin normally demands from a king is a donation. But I have come here with a specific purpose.'

Raje said, folding his hands again, 'We are blessed with your visit. Please command me.'

Gaga Bhatt said, 'Raje, I have come all the way from Kashi. Word of your deeds has reached there too. In our Bharatvarsha, there have been rulers like Chandragupta Maurya, and kingdoms like Vijayanagara and Devagiri which were toppled by foreign invasions at their peak of glory. There is no kingdom worth mentioning which can be called a Hindu kingdom. I see hope in the Deccan because of you. The way you rebuilt your kingdom after the unfortunate treaty at Purandar gives us great hope. I am here to ask for something. Let me see if you can fulfil that!'

Raje did not know how to react and remained silent.

Gaga Bhatt continued, 'My ancestors established the Kashi Vishwanath Temple. Its destruction by the Muslims led to a great famine and my ancestors rebuilt the same. I am here to beg a boon from you and I hope you will not turn me away.'

Jijabai, listening to the priest, was a little worried.

Seeing her reaction, Gaga Bhatt smiled and said, 'Aai saheb, it has been a long-standing Kshatriya tradition to protect priests. Vishwamitra came to Dashrath to appeal to him for protection. Your kingdom is spread from the Tungabhadra to the Narmada, and you need a royal seal proclaiming it. We need to convince the people that there is a Chhatrapati, a protector, who will look after the Hindavi Swaraj. This is possible only with the formal coronation of Raje, declaring him the Chhatrapati. This is the special request I wanted to make of you.'

Jijabai's eyes filled with tears. Those in attendance were awed at the prospect of a formal coronation. Raje shuffled his feet nervously and looked at his mother who nodded her acceptance.

Annaji said, 'The revered pandit has spoken all our minds.'

Gaga Bhatt was relieved to see that his suggestion has been accepted. He said, 'Raje, I am eagerly waiting for your consent. Please speak your mind.'

Raje stood up and said, 'I have never gone against the advice of my priests. Your wish is my command. But I have a request.'

'Please tell me, Raje.'

'I want this ceremony to be carried out under your supervision. Your blessings will make a big difference.'

Gaga Bhatt raised his hand in benediction and said, 'It is our duty, Raje, and I shall be honoured to do so.'

Raje turned to Moropant and said, 'Please inform Samarth. Let us get his blessings as well. Please invite Anant Bhatt here. His presence would be a great benefit to all of us.'

After further discussions and having given his blessings, Gaga Bhatt retired to his residence. The fort now throbbed with a renewed energy.

The idea of the coronation had invigorated each and every person in Raigad. A king was being crowned after a few centuries and was the talk of almost each household. Anant Bhatt had opined that since Shivaji's tonsure ceremony had not been performed, he was deemed a Shudra. The necessary purification ceremonies needed to be carried out before his coronation. Gaga Bhatt, determined to see Shivaji formally sit on a throne, ensured that all doubts had been suitably answered. His knowledge of the scriptures and deep understanding of the rites allowed him to carry out all the rituals without any objection.

The preparations for the ceremony had begun in earnest and large amounts of gold had been ordered to create a special throne for the occasion. Shivaji Raje may have inadvertently killed many Brahmins in his battles and raids and a special ceremony was performed to absolve him of such sins.

While all these preparations were on, Shivaji's mind had turned to Panhala. He was aware that Bahlol Khan was preparing to attack the fort and would disregard the treaty at Umrani. Raje decided to reach Panhala as soon as possible.

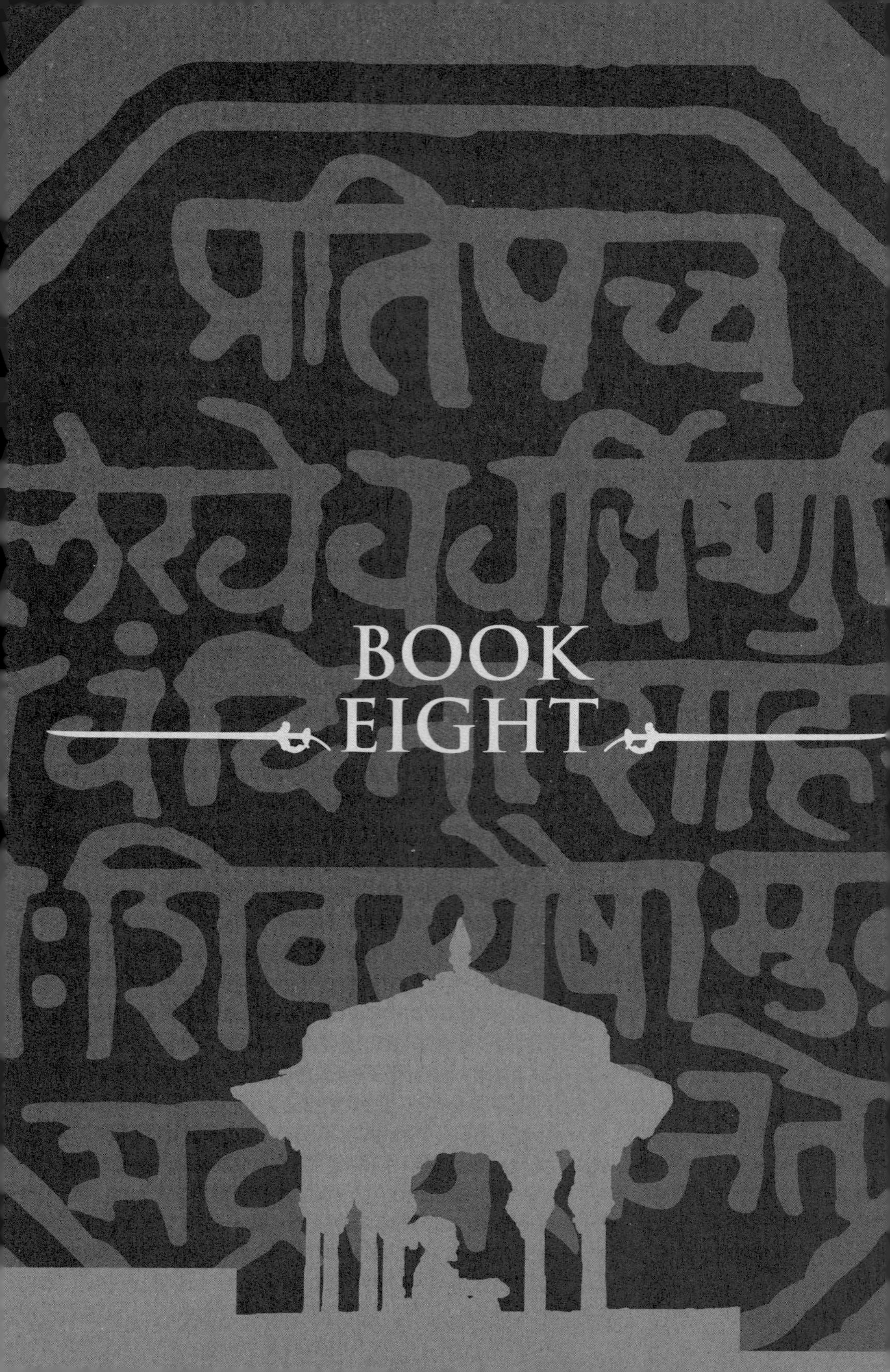

BOOK EIGHT

Nearly a month had passed since Anant Bhatt's arrival. In the early hours of one morning, Raje was walking around the fort. He asked, looking at Moropant, 'We have selected this fort for the coronation ceremony but I wonder if there is enough place to organize the event.'

'Don't worry about that, Maharaj,' Moropant said. 'We cannot find a more suitable fort. This place is as pure as Kailash itself. Not a drop of blood has despoiled this place. And as far as arrangements are concerned, with the existing accommodation and the tents and temporary accommodation being constructed, we can accommodate at least a lakh people. We are well prepared.'

At that moment, a messenger arrived with a letter from Prataprao.

'Please read what my commander has to say,' Shivaji said, after going through the letter.

'When Prataprao had the chance to capture Bahlol Khan at Umrani, he allowed him to retreat and now, the same Khan is planning to attack him. Prataprao is asking for our advice. What shall I tell him? That we are willing to lay out a red carpet for Bahlol Khan? We are holding the coronation ceremony—we may as well gift the kingdom to Khan on that occasion.'

Shivaji Raje's temper was well-known and no one dared speak. He said, looking at Annaji, 'Send a strongly worded letter to Prataprao and tell him that I cannot afford to have an enemy disturbing us when we are busy with the ceremonies here. Order him to arrest Bahlol Khan, put him in chains and drag him here to Raigad.'

In a few days, Raje received another message from Prataprao. The letter stated that while Bahlol Khan was hiding in a valley near Nesari, he was worried about the Maratha attack. Prataprao requested that he be sent more men to ensure that the attack was successful. He was certain that he could defeat Bahlol Khan if he received more support.

Raje, already irritated with Prataprao, screamed, 'Stop it, Annaji!' Turning to his scribe, he said, 'Write this down verbatim: You have disappointed me with your behaviour. I am unable to understand why you allowed Khan to escape when you had the chance to capture him in the first place, and all these problems could have been avoided. Asking for more help does not become you. Please don't show your face to me unless you defeat the Bijapurkar troops!'

The messenger left but Raje was not able to sleep peacefully that night. The next morning, he asked Annaji to send a letter to the troops camped at Chiplun to help Prataprao at the earliest. He said, 'I am restless since I read Prataprao's letter. If Bahlol Khan attacks, I shall personally go to Panhala as soon as Shivaratri is over.'

Shivaratri arrived, and despite it being winter, the sky was cloudy, creating a gloomy atmosphere. After returning from the temple, Jijabai said, 'I don't know why but the garland that I tried putting on the idol fell down twice. It is not a good omen!'

Raje was restless and would look out of the office window to check if the messenger from Prataprao's camp had arrived. He got up when he saw Anandrao come in hurriedly and asked, 'Has he defeated Bahlol Khan?'

'No.'

'Tell me what happened, Anandrao?' Raje almost screamed, seeing Anandrao's dull face.

'Raje, we attacked Bahlol Khan but could not defeat him. Your commander kept his word though.'

'And why has he not come himself to tell me this?'

Anandrao could not hold his emotions in check as tears streamed down his cheeks. He managed to mutter, 'Our commander and his six sardars died in the battle, Maharaj!'

Raje asked, his voice almost a whisper, 'Tell me exactly what happened!'

'We had surrounded Khan. Our commander was waiting for reinforcements but then he received your letter. He said, after reading it, "Such a small force will be no match for Khan's but you can tell Maharaj that I fought as per his command."'

Raje's lips shivered. He clenched his fists, trying to hold back his tears.

Anandrao continued, 'We tried to dissuade Prataprao but he paid no heed and galloped away with six of his sardars. They attacked the ten-thousand-strong army. As we feared, they all lost their lives. We had no option but to retreat.'

Anandrao sat down on the ground, sobbing. Raje sat down next to him, numb after listening to Anandrao. This was the same Prataprao who had not hesitated once while attacking Mirza Raja.

Seeing Jijabai enter, Raje lost his composure and said, 'Maa saheb, I am responsible for Prataprao's death. A man of dauntless courage, he has sacrificed his life to follow my orders!'

Jijabai tried her best to console Raje but she could not stop his tears. The next morning Raje came into the office red-eyed but with a resolute expression on his face. He said, 'Anandrao, I am going to avenge Prataprao's death.'

'Maharaj, the coronation ceremony is approaching and I suggest ...'

'On my order, Prataprao laid down his precious life. While Bahlol Khan is still roaming free, do you think I care about the coronation ceremony?'

Everyone present was worried that Raje may personally lead the campaign against Khan. Anandrao stepped forward and said, touching Raje's feet, 'Give me a chance, Maharaj! Hansaji Mohite and I—we want to teach Khan a lesson and we shall not show you our faces if we fail.'

Raje hugged Anandrao and said, 'I don't want to hear anyone say that again! Take whatever help you need and finish off Khan but return safe. I will be waiting for you.'

Hearing the drums in the distance, Raje said, looking at Annaji, 'Ask the drum beaters to stop that noise. Our Prataprao is no more and I wish to mourn his death.' He turned and left with a heavy heart.

The preparations for the coronation ceremony were going on in full swing. The golden throne was being fabricated by the best artisans and jewellers. Shivaji Raje was a little worried about the lakhs of hons being spent on the coronation ceremony and felt uncomfortable about so much money being wasted. On expressing his doubts, Moropant replied, his chest puffing in pride, 'Raje, leave managing the expenses to me. Our treasury has enough to spend on ten such coronations.'

Raje asked, turning to Annaji, 'I haven't seen Shambhu Raje since the morning.'

'I am told he went down the fort last night,' Annaji said.

'Why?' Raje asked, a little surprised at Shambhu not informing anyone about his whereabouts.

At that moment, Sambhaji stepped in and saluted.

'Where were you, Shambhu?'

'I was at the base of the fort. I had received news from my spies of our victory over Bahlol Khan.'

'What?'

'Yes, Aba saheb! Anandrao and Hansaji didn't attack Bahlol Khan directly, as he had taken help from the Mughal sardar, Diler Khan. Instead, they attacked his jagir, looted his bazaars and picked up cartloads of wealth. They ravaged Bahlol Khan's territory and, as we speak, Anandrao is returning here with a pair of elephants and five hundred horses captured in the battle as booty—not to mention the tons of other wealth we have got along with them.'

'Oh, that is fantastic news!' Raje exclaimed.

'Aba saheb, I got the news last night and I went down to ensure that that I personally received the heroes.'

'Well, that was very good of you!' Raje said, happy at Sambhaji's conduct.

'Now welcome the triumphant warriors here,' he added.

As soon as Anandrao entered, Raje stepped forward and tucked a crest into his turban. 'Your success has helped me to relieve a little bit of the pain caused by Prataprao's death. Welcome back,' he said, hugging him affectionately.

To add to the celebrations, another piece of good news came in the same day; Raje's naval troops had defeated Siddi at Janjira. It was indeed a happy day!

The preparations at the fort were progressing at a rapid pace. Artists were busy decorating the walls of the palace with new paintings and all the havelis, houses, mansions and other buildings were being renovated. Fifty thousand people were estimated to attend the ceremony. Kashibai, having taken ill, was shifted to the haveli at Pachad on instructions from the physician. She was being looked after by Putlabai and Sagunabai while Soyarabai and Maa saheb supervised the work at the fort.

Raje had one more worry—he had not been able to select a suitable successor to Prataprao as the Senapati. He needed to fill the post soon. He was worried that the Adil Shahi and Mughal troops may take advantage of the temporary lull in activity and attack during the coronation ceremony.

That night, Raje sat in his quarters with Annaji, Moropant, Yesaji and Sambhaji. Raje said, 'I have lost Prataprao. We need someone in his place now.'

Annaji said, 'Maharaj, may I suggest something? I nominate Anandrao who defeated Bahlol Khan and proved his worth.'

Raje said, smiling, 'If victory in wars was the only criterion, we have many such heroes. Kondaji and you won at Panhala while Moropant showed his bravery at Salher besides Yesaji and Hansaji. A Senapati needs to have foresight, be thoroughly familiar with the kingdom, have the trust of his men and show loyalty to the kingdom. Netaji was a daredevil and had the men's trust but his shaky loyalty to the throne made him unworthy of the position. Prataprao was loyal to the core but his eagerness to prove the same cost him his life.'

'Aba saheb, if I may ...'

'Yes, please.'

'I feel Hansaji Kaka would be a worthy choice. He has a calm temperament and is very loyal.'

'How do you know that he is loyal?'

'He is related to us but has never demanded a position. In fact, he shared the credit for having the battle against Bahlol Khan along with Anandrao but instead of coming here, he preferred to look after his duties in Chiplun.'

Raje said, his face turning a little grave, 'I will think over it. I will visit Chiplun as soon as possible.'

As everyone took leave for the night, Raje said, 'Sambhaji, please come with Anandrao to meet me in the morning. And don't mention it to anyone.'

After Sambhaji left, Raje lay down on his bed for a long while as sleep eluded him.

The next morning, as Raje returned from darshan, he found Firangoji waiting for him. He said, accepting his salute, 'Why were you waiting for me? You should have sent a message. What brings you here?'

'I heard about the coronation ceremony and could not wait to see you.'

After chatting for a while, Raje was about to get up but found Firangoji hesitating. He seemed to be wanting to say something more. Raje said, 'Please speak your mind, Firangoji. I can see you want to say something.'

'Raje, this old man has spent his entire life in your service. You are going to have a coronation ceremony, but I will not be there to witness it.'

'Why do you say that?'

'You are asking me why? You were the one who issued the orders—"Protect the forts with utmost care and don't allow the smallest of negligence in your duties. Else you will not be spared ..."'

Raje laughed loudly and said, 'I know I have issued the orders but it does not mean you won't be present here. How can the ceremony take place without you? Now, please ensure that you depute someone to Chakan in your absence and make yourself available here at the earliest.'

Firangoji got up and saluted. At that moment, Sambhaji came in and seeing Firangoji, rushed to touch his feet. Firangoji said, 'Shambhu, my child, what are you doing?'

Raje looked at both of them admiringly. 'Firangoji, Yuvraj did what was appropriate. Else, you would not have addressed him as "my child". You have seen him as an infant and seen him grow. Why shouldn't he touch your feet?'

Raje told Sambhaji, 'Take Firangoji around the fort. And ask him to return here soon for the ceremony. Firangoji, I will take your leave now.'

Later, Raje and Sambhaji met in their private room with Anandrao. Raje said, 'Anandrao, I have called you here for a reason. I wanted to know why Hansaji went straight to Chiplun and did not come here.'

'Raje, realizing that the sardars at Chiplun were disturbed after hearing about Prataprao's death, Hansaji did not want to take any chances and left immediately.'

'You should have informed me.'

'You were busy and Hansaji was taking care of Chiplun. I thought there was no need to bother you.'

'Anandrao, we must remember that our troops consist of a diversity of castes. It is a bundle of thousands of minds tied together by the rope of trust. A single thread breaking loose can create havoc.'

A servant entered hurriedly then and said, 'Maharaj, Putla Rani saheb has called for you urgently.'

Raje was red with anger. He shouted, 'Can't you see I am busy? Tell her I will come when I am free.'

The servant bowed and left the room. Raje continued his work and went to the palace much later. He said, the moment he entered, 'Putlabai, I have other things to do than select garments for you. What was the hurry?'

'Some things are sometimes more important than anything else,' Putlabai retorted.

Raje was taken aback to hear her answer. Her face was red with indignation as she tried to hold back her tears. He asked, his voice soft, 'What is the matter?'

'She did not ask for anything in her life. All she wanted was to see you once!'

'What? Are you talking about Kashi?'

'That's good! At least you remember her!'

'Don't talk in riddles. What happened?'

'She could not wait any longer!'

Raje did not speak any further and walked out of the room. A palanquin bearer rushed to help but he brushed him aside and continued walking down towards the gate. Moropant, seeing Raje walk all alone, ran to be by his side.

At the gates Raje jumped on to a horse and galloped all the way down to Pachad. By the time he dismounted at the haveli, the horse was foaming at the mouth. Leaping off the horse, he rushed inside to find Jijabai waiting for him. He entered the room without saying a word to the wailing ladies. Tears in his eyes, Raje stood in the hall a little away from Kashibai's bed, his gaze vacant. He lamented, 'Kashi! She came in a new young bride and was soon lost in the crowd. Following Mughal customs, Maa saheb had me marry many others but she did not say anything. She hardly spoke to me and now she never will again ...' Raje's voice faltered.

At a solemn ceremony, Kashibai's body was consigned to a sandalwood pyre. Cold winds blew as Raje stood looking at the burning pyre, his eyes unblinking. Firangoji said, 'Maharaj, please step back a little. The flames may singe you.'

Raje looked at Firangoji for a long time. He said, his voice choked with grief, 'The flames have already touched my life. Moving back will not make any difference now.'

A fortnight had passed since Kashibai's death but Raje was unable to overcome his guilt. He sat in his quarters alone when Putlabai walked in.

Raje turned to see her but did not say a word. A sob escaped her lips as she came near Raje's bed. He asked, 'Putla, what is the matter?'

'I don't know how to tell you—I made a mistake.'

'What are you talking about?'

'I was near Kashi's bed. I should have called for you much earlier.'

Raje touched her chin gently and said, 'Putla, I am not angry at you. Don't torture yourself.' He continued after a moment, 'You know she taught me a lot. I may be known for my conquests but I have failed as a husband, Putla. I could not spend a few minutes with her when she needed me most. I wonder what went through her mind at the end. Did she say anything, Putla?'

'She said she was lucky to have you as her husband and was happy that you would have a coronation. She wished she could have been there for the ceremony but she was content. She said, "I wish to see him before I go." When I said I would personally go and call you, she held my hand and said, "No, don't disturb him—he is busy with his meetings."'

Raje's tears continued unabated. He said, wiping them, 'Putla, my people consider me their god but here I am, unable to spend such precious moments with my wife. I could not fulfil such a simple wish! I conquer forts and win battles but I am a failure in my own house!'

As he got up to look out of the window, Raje said, 'It seems my men have arrived. I must leave for Chiplun now. I will be back soon.'

Despite the scorching summer, the cantonment at Chiplun bustled with activity. Each solider was busy polishing his weapons, grooming the horses and cleaning the tents. Hansaji Mohite and his sardars ensured that everything was spic and span for Raje's inspection. The journey of a hundred miles from Raigad to Chiplun would not take more than a day and they waited patiently for Raje. Soon, a messenger came galloping in and announced his arrival. Hansaji and his men rode out a few miles to receive him.

The soldiers, lined up along the entrance, bowed in mujra as they welcomed Raje. It was a glorious evening as the sun set in the western horizon, leaving a golden sky behind. Raje inspected the lines the next day and was satisfied seeing the arrangements. As he was about to leave, a young man looking at him attracted his attention. He asked, 'What is your name? You look familiar.'

The young man hesitated and before Hansaji could answer, Raje said, 'Oh, are you not Ramaji Pangera's brother?'

Hansaji smiled. 'Maharaj, you recognized him!'

Raje said, his voice filled with pride, 'Who can forget Ramaji's valour and the way he fought Diler Khan! How can I afford to forget him?'

'His brother too is equally brave, Raje. He was one of the main heroes in our battle against Bahlol Khan.'

'And yet he is a mere trooper? Pangera, I am promoting you!'

Pangera, delighted at the sudden promotion stepped forward and saluted smartly.

After the inspection, as Raje rested in his tent, he said, 'Hansaji, the camp is running quite smoothly. What made you rush here?'

'The spies had reported a disturbance and I did not want to take any chances.'

'Well, now that things have settled down, I am keen to appoint a Senapati. Whom do you suggest?'

'I think Anandrao is a good choice. He knows our territory, has proven his loyalty and knows the tactics of war well.'

'What about you?'

'Maharaj, mere loyalty or love for the country is not enough. It is a huge responsibility. I will not disobey your command but I am happy with what I am doing.'

'Let us see,' Raje said, without further comment.

A further two days' inspection provided Raje a much-needed break before he returned to Raigad. As he was preparing to leave, the sardars at Chiplun requested a meeting.

'They have all come with the request to attend your coronation ceremony, Raje,' Hansaji said.

'I am overwhelmed by the love you shower on me. But if all you come to Raigad, who will manage the camp? What if the Adil Shahi troops or the Mughals take advantage of the situation?' Raje asked.

For a few moments, no one spoke. One of the sardars, Niyakar, stepped forward and said, 'Maharaj, you may rest assured. We have made all the arrangements.'

'I am pleased with your confidence.'

'Maharaj, I have another request. We want to add another feather to your cap before the coronation.'

'What is it?'

'We want you to be with us when we capture the Kelanja Fort. Our spies tell us that our victory is certain.'

'Hansaji, there is no question of defeat when you are around. It would be the best gift I could receive on my coronation.'

The troops were filled with a renewed enthusiasm because Raje would be with them. Hansaji directed his men and after a fierce battle, they captured the fort. The saffron flag soon flew over the ramparts of the fort. After ensuring that the fort had been taken charge of, Raje decided to return. While inspecting the troops, especially those wounded in the battle, he was impressed seeing a young dashing soldier who stood straight, his spine erect, despite a huge gash on his forehead. The blood had dried flowing down to his chin. Yet, the man stood smiling as he saluted Shivaji. Seeing him, Raje asked, 'What is his name?'

'He is called Mahlari Tandel, and he fought bravely. He is a Dahija, leader of ten men.'

'But why is he here? Should he not be taking care of his wounds?'

'We told him to but he insisted on taking your blessings.'

'I am impressed,' Raje said, patting his back. 'Now onwards you are not a Dahija but a Hazari, the leader of a thousand men. And you will be entitled to a palanquin too.'

Malhari was elated and touched Raje's feet as his tears fell on the ground.

While returning, Raje enquired about the facilities at the cantonment at Chiplun and ensured that the troops were not short of food, clothing or any other requirements. The troops wanted to felicitate Raje personally and each one paid their regards. It took the entire afternoon for the ceremony to be completed.

While leaving, Raje said, 'Hansaji, I am really impressed the way you have managed the camp. The takeover of the Kelanja Fort was another example of your bravery. I am appointing you the commander-in-chief. You shall have the title of Hambirrao.'

Hansaji was felicitated and received the royal commander's clothes, sword and a jewelled aigrette for his turban. Hansaji was now Hambirrao Mohite. That night, having found someone to fill in Prataprao' shoes, a satisfied Raje left for Raigad.

On his return, Raje called a conference and discussed the issues at Chiplun with Annaji, Moropant and Nirajipant. He said, 'The camp needs far more provisions than what they have right now. We need to ensure that they are given adequate rations before the rains begin. At the same time, I want to warn them to be careful about their expenditure. They will have to manage within tight budgets. I will write to Hansaji personally.'

He sent him a letter: 'You are hereby instructed that you need to manage the coming monsoon season with utmost care and ensure that the food stocks are used frugally. Each man will have to sacrifice. No one should harass the ryots for fodder for the animals or for food. The ryots work for our benefit and we cannot loot our own people. Please be careful about the fireplaces lest rats run away with burning wicks while cooking and set fire to the haystacks. Let there be no cases of harassment from the Mavals. No soldier will be spared if he is found violating the laws.'

Moropant was quite impressed after reading the note. He remarked, 'Maharaj, you seem to be very familiar with rural life.'

Raje laughed. 'Moropant, I have spent time with Dadoji who worked with the Mavals and sorted out their problems. We were supposed to be the landlords, but Dadoji taught me how to deal with the ryots. I would not have got companions like Tanaji, Baji, Jiva and Shiva otherwise. I know what poverty is. When I escaped from Agra, I had to survive on begging for alms as I roamed the countryside dressed up as a mendicant.'

Those present were seeing a new facet of Raje's personality.

It was a month since Raje's inspection of the Chiplun camp. Raje had returned to Raigad when Gaga Bhatt called upon him to discuss the preparations for the ceremony. With Jijabai, they went to the Lakshmigriha where the throne was being readied. A lovely pair of scales for the tula ceremony was also being readied. Next to the scales stood silver and golden pitchers, gold vessels and silver square stools and many other such things. A curtain was moved to reveal the throne. It was a fabulous piece of work, octagonal in shape, and studded with precious gems. Lions, with eyes of rubies, adorned the eight corners while a canopy was supported by eight pillars. Chiselled images of fruits, trees, birds and other animals were seen on the pillars.

Moropant explained, 'Maharaj, the throne has been made as per instructions in the scriptures. Thirty-two maunds of gold has been used to make it, not to mention an enormous quantity of pearls and precious stones.'

An intense agony overshadowed Raje's face. He said, 'Could we not have used fewer gems? Each gem I see here reminds me of my gems in war, my companions in each battle—be it Tanaji, Suryaji, Murarbaji, Prataprao or Pangera! They far outshine the gems here.'

Jijabai looked at a sword with a gem-studded hilt and asked, 'Shivba, whose sword is this?'

Raje said, his voice emotional, 'Maa saheb, this is the sword Mirza Raja Jai Singh tucked in my cummerbund while blessing me.'

Moropant led Raje to a raised platform where ornaments were on display.

'What are these for?'

'They are for Tulja Bhawani and the Kasba Ganapati on Maa saheb's behest.'

Raje looked at Jijabai, who said, 'I had made a promise to the Lord when you were imprisoned in Agra that if you came back alive, I would overlay the sanctum sanctorum in Bhawani's temple with silver.'

'Then we must do it! After all, we are going to mint coins for the coronation. We will spend a few more on this cause.' He said, turning to Moropant, 'Please see to it that a lakh silver coins bearing my name are nailed to the floor of the sanctum sanctorum. It is my duty to fulfil my mother's promises.'

Seeing Jijabai overwhelmed with emotions, Raje quickly changed the topic and said, 'These ornaments are really well crafted. Who are the artists?'

'We have heard of the expertise of craftsmen from Jaipur and Udaipur but these are exceptional,' Gaga Bhatt said.

Pride was evident in Raje's face when he said, 'Well, you will find talent if you search for it. What is lacking is our vision.'

At that moment, a man with a tilak on his forehead stepped in. He was wearing a simple dhoti and kurta and had a sharp, pointed nose.

Moropant said, introducing him, 'Maharaj, this is Ramoji Dattoo, the man who built the throne and other things you see here.'

Raje said, taking a ring off his finger, 'I cannot believe the work you have done. Congratulations!'

The day of the coronation was approaching fast. All the sardars and their men were busy with their respective duties. A huge number of guests were expected and special tents, havelis and cottages at the fort as well as at Pachad were being constructed.

Raje, along with Sambhaji, walked along the road leading to the foot of Pratapgad. The palanquin bearers walked along with them. It was the beginning of spring and the palash flowers added to the charm of the dense green foliage around them. The tamarind trees, wrapped in a shawl of green looked lovely. As he reached an open space, Raje stopped, looking at the summit.

Sambhaji asked, 'Aba saheb, shall we rest for a while?'

'Shambhu, I did not stop because I was tired. I was reminded of the day I fought and killed Afzal Khan.'

Sambhaji looked at the spot where Raje's eyes seemed transfixed. A thicket covered it from three sides and it looked intimidating. He exclaimed, 'I cannot imagine it! It must have been extraordinary!'

'Each moment was precious. As I descended from the fort, I cannot tell the thoughts which swirled through my mind!'

'Was it difficult—killing Khan?'

'It was not about killing him, Shambhu! I was worried about his strength, his army and his camp which backed him. We were infants in front of his huge army. We had managed to take over his camps at Supe, Indapur, Wai and the Koyna valley. That night, our strength multiplied manifold—we suddenly had hundreds of guns, thousands of horses and camels, elephants and wealth worth crores of hons. It was all due to the blessings of Jagdamba.'

At Pratapgad, Raje prayed at the temple. He offered a golden umbrella as a decoration for the Goddess. Seeing the lovely parasol bedecking the idol, Raje cried tears of joy. He prayed at the temple for a long time. While leaving he said, 'Shambhu, it is only thanks to Her blessings that we are able to fulfil all our desires. She knew I could not visit Her at Tuljapur and She made a divine appearance one night. I installed an idol of Her here so that I may pray to Her whenever I wished. Wherever I go, Her image stays with me.'

That night, Raje and Sambhaji participated in the performance presented by a group of wandering dancers. The celebrations continued well past midnight and everyone, oblivious to the presence of Raje and Sambhaji, were engrossed in singing. The dancers, with their burning torches, added to the allure of the dark night. The next morning, as the eastern horizon was lit by the rising sun, the festivities ended. Despite having spent the entire night awake, Shivaji was not fatigued as he walked towards his quarters, a smile of satisfaction on his face.

A distance of nearly fifty miles was covered quickly as Raje was eager to meet Samarth Ramdas. As he crossed the gorge, the dense forest gave way to a cool shade. It was here, sitting in a cave, that Samarth had written *Dasbodh*.

Raje crossed the river to see Samarth and his disciples walking towards him. Alighting from his horse, Raje bowed humbly. The sonorous sound of the flowing stream added to the beauty and divinity of the place. It was a wonderful setting while Raje took Samarth's blessings in his cave. A quiver of arrows hung on the wall attracted Sambhaji's attention.

Samarth said, 'Shambhu, don't be surprised. This place has all kinds of dangers—whether from Mughals or wild animals.' He opened one end of his crutch to reveal a shining blade. He said, 'One must know that the compassion of the weak and the non-violence of the meek have no meaning. Only strength gives them meaning. I don't think I need to use these weapons now that our Shivba is going to be made Chhatrapati. Our land will no longer be orphaned. Shivba, I feel blessed that you are going to be crowned soon.'

Raje discussed his plans and apprised Ramdas about the forthcoming ceremony. 'I hope you will be present for the occasion to bless us.'

'You have come to invite me? My blessings are always with you,' Samarth said, his eyes twinkling.

'Samarth, does that mean you are not going to visit us?'

'Do I need to? Gaga Bhatt is well versed in the scriptures and he is a master of the Vedas. What use does he have for someone like me, uneducated and with no knowledge of the sacred books? Additionally, his ego will be hurt. It is best that I do not come.'

'Then what's the use of the coronation if you are not present?' Raje asked dejectedly.

Samarth was overwhelmed with emotions and said, placing his hand on Raje's shoulder, 'Raje, we both have no value for formal affairs but you have no choice. Take this as my order—you must have the coronation ceremony. You know that whenever you need me, I will be by your side. Surrender to Lord Ram and be crowned king. Your dream will then materialize.'

Raje touched Samarth's feet reverently who hugged him lovingly. They were both in tears. There was no need for any words to be spoken.

Raje returned to Raigad, inspecting the camps on the way. The new market coming up at Raigad was full of merchants from Konkan, Karnatak, Marwar and Gujarat. As he climbed up the steps to the fort, he found that the fort had transformed into a new city with all the arrangements to take care of the people expected at the coronation ceremony. Raje was visibly impressed to see an elephant with a golden howdah.

Moropant answered, seeing his quizzical expression, 'Raje, the elephant is Lakshmi's mascot. She is the goddess of wealth. He has to be there when she is!'

Raje laughed. Surveying the fort, he said, 'Moropant, this city is probably more beautiful than Alaka, the heavenly city. I thought I was a dreamer but your imagination takes the flight of an eagle. But we are all dreamers—whether Baji, Tanaji or Shiva the barber who laid their lives down for our dreams!'

Raje was pleased to hear that his daughter Sakhu had come. He said, looking at Jijabai, 'I am happy that Mahadji permitted her to come. He serves under the Adil Shahi court and it is gracious of him to allow her to attend.'

On a tour of the market, set up on the fort for the visitors, Raje noticed singers, musicians, florists and traders of all kinds. He was about to enter the Jagadishwar Temple when a dancer, practising her routine, stopped on seeing Raje enter. He said, 'Don't stop your performance. Carry on.'

Stepping outside, Raje said, 'Moropant, we have attracted a large number of artists here. I have only seen the like in Mathura at the Krishna temple. I want us to patronize such artists. The people will greatly benefit from their art.'

The next morning, a visibly excited Firangoji reported to Raje: 'I cannot believe the way the fort has been transformed. I am waiting for the day of the coronation now!'

Raje was happy to see Firangoji. Yet, he expressed the thought which had been niggling at him. He said, 'Firangoji, I hope the Mughal or the Adil Shahi troops do not take advantage and attack us.'

'Rest assured, Raje, we have taken adequate precautions. And our men are always alert. The Mughals will not have forgotten the way they were routed the last time. They would not dare attack.'

Seeing all his sardars assembled there, Raje was pleased. Yet, he felt the absence of Mahadji and Ekoji Raje. The day of the coronation was almost upon them. Gaga Bhatt and Balam Bhatt performed the thread ceremony for Raje. This was followed by a ceremonial marriage to Soyarabai, giving her the official status of the senior most queen. Ceremonial marriages to all other queens followed.

The atmosphere at the fort was charged with the constant sound of clarions, kettledrums and many other instruments. Musicians and magicians enthralled the crowds each evening while the guests enjoyed sumptuous buffets. The happiness at the fort rose with the growing crescent of the moon.

In the evening, as Raje retired to his room, he stood in the balcony for a while. The innumerable torches burnt brightly, creating a mesmerizing effect in the night. The sound of music from the dance performance at the temple was heard in the distance. In another quarter, a tambourine played. It was a night of festivities. Tired by the events of the past few days, Raje stepped into his chamber to sleep.

It was the day for the tula ceremony, the day Raje would be weighed against gold, silver and other precious stones. It was an important event, a precursor to the main coronation ceremony.

Raje entered Jijabai's quarters and touched her feet. Jijabai held his face in her hands and looked into his eyes. Raje was upset at seeing her in tears. Before he could say anything, Jijabai took a little black lamp and touched it to his cheeks to ward off the evil eye.

Raje laughed, 'Maa saheb, my beard is enough to ward off the evil eye.'

'Now don't turn everything into a joke,' Jijabai chided lovingly, as she wiped her finger on her hair.

Along with the queens, Raje entered the chamber created especially for the tula ceremony. At Gaga Bhatt's signal, Raje stepped into the pan and sat down as the Brahmins, while chanting mantras, poured gold coins into the other pan. Soon, the pan rose, balancing the two. The total number of coins in the other pan exceeded sixteen thousand. To the sound of drums and horns, Raje stepped off the weighing scale and indicated that the coins be distributed among the Brahmins.

The tula ceremony was carried out every day till the day of the coronation. He was weighed in brass, copper, silver, articles of daily use and even vegetables! It was a way to ward off the evil. Thousands of Brahmins at the fort and at Pachad were the beneficiaries. For seven days, the ceremonies went on, finally leading to a day of break. The day of coronation was now eagerly awaited.

The sun rose on the twelfth day of the month of Jyeshtha. As Raje woke to pray to the sun god, he could see the forts of Torna and Rajgad. The coronation was being held at Raigad but the seeds of the dream of Swaraj had been sown at Rajgad. Raje folded his hands in obeisance to the fort where his journey had begun. It was going to be a hectic evening, beginning with the inauguration of the throne, meeting the sardars, and various other events which would go on till the wee hours of the morning.

Along with Soyarabai, Raje stepped into the pandal where a silver-coated oblong chair, made from the wood of the fig tree, called oudumbar, had been installed. Raje, wearing a spotless white dress, was to be bathed in panchamrita, a mixture of water, milk, curd, honey and ghee. As he sat in the chair, Soyarabai and Sambhaji stood next to him. The eight ministers, the ashta pradhans, occupied their respective seats. Moropant stood on the eastern side, holding a pitcher of ghee, while Hambirrao Mohite stood on the southern side, holding a pitcher of milk. On cue from Gaga Bhatt, the bathing ceremony began with Balam Bhatt pouring the waters of the major rivers over Raje. The Brahmins chanted the mantras as the audience watched in awe. Jijabai, unable to see clearly due to her age, was soaking in each moment as she tried to wipe the tears from her eyes.

By midnight, the bathing ceremony was over. Raje was shown his face in a vessel filled with ghee. After putting on auspicious clothes and having worshipped the weapons, he accepted a shield, sword and a bow and arrow offered to him before he stepped into the hall again.

The moment to occupy the throne was approaching rapidly and everyone present waited with bated breath. Raje entered the pandal with Soyarabai and Sambhaji and bowed to touch Jijabai's feet. Overjoyed and at a loss for words, she gently touched Raje's face and then cracked her knuckles to ward off the evil eye.

As Raje moved slowly towards the golden throne, the sardars, dignitaries, guests and everyone present rose to receive him. In the middle of the room was a raised quadrangular pedestal covered with carpets embroidered with gold and silver threads. The golden throne stood in the middle and was visible to everyone.

Just before dawn, as the eastern horizon turned golden, Raje's ashta pradhans led him to the royal assembly. Men holding spears led the group. Raje stood on the first step to the throne and he had hardly glanced at Jijabai sitting to the left of the throne when Gaga Bhatt started chanting the hymns. The other Brahmins in attendance joined in.

Raje moved slowly, taking one measured step at a time, towards the throne. At the final step Gaga Bhatt offered Raje a golden sceptre carved with the head of a lion. Raje accepted it, touching it reverently to his forehead and then, taking care not to touch the throne with his feet, sat down gently. Sitting in veerasana, the warrior pose, with his sword to his right, Raje looked the very image of a king. The tilak on his forehead, his long aquiline nose, his sharp piercing eyes as they scanned the crowd and his majestically tapering beard—all added to the allure of his persona, which those in the assembly could not take their eyes off. The sun, as if in recognition of the new king, rose in the eastern sky showering its light as blessings.

Gaga Bhatt, while continuing to chant mantras, took a gem-studded parasol and held it over Raje's head. As the chanting of the mantras was over, a silence descended over the hall for a brief while as people recovered their breath. The next moment, they heard Gaga Bhatt's voice as it reverberated across the hall:

The great leader of the Kshatriyas,
The saviour of cows and Brahmins,
Hail thee, the one who occupies the throne
Shrimant Shri Chhatrapati Shivaji Maharaj!

The entire audience repeated the words in a loud cheer. Immediately, the dancers took stage.

The news the Chhatrapati, the sovereign king of the Marathas had been crowned, would soon reach people everywhere in no time.

Jijabai got up, unmindful of the tears flowing down her cheeks. Her body shivered as she reached Raje who asked, 'What can I do for you, Maa saheb?'

Jijabai looked at Putlabai for a brief moment and said, 'My dear, take me away from here. I fear my son may get affected by my own evil eye!' Jijabai's sobs were now uncontrollable. A dream, which she had harboured for years together, had come true. It was beyond belief.

As Raje sat on the throne with the priests sprinkling the holy water on him, the sun rose majestically in the sky. It was time for the darkness to be dispelled from the earth.

Moropant stepped forward to make the first offering and showered Raje with eight thousand hons. Gaga Bhatt, Sambhaji and Moropant sat on the pedestal of the throne as the other sardars came one by one to offer their presents in accordance with their rank, prestige and capacity to donate. A raised hand attracted Raje's attention. It was the English envoy Oxenden, accompanied by his interpreter Narayan Shenavi. With a nod, Raje indicated for him to step forward.

Oxenden had come with many gifts—an English chair, a diamond-studded aigrette, a few diamond rings and large pearls. In return, Raje gave a robe of honour to Oxenden.

It was time to visit the temples now. Led by the Senapati, Hambrirrao Mohite, who had taken the place of the mahout, Raje sat in the golden howdah on an elephant and made his way through towards the temple. The trumpets and conch shells announced the beginning of the procession.

The crowd, seeing the newly crowned Chhatrapati, could not contain themselves as they cheered, throwing gulal and coloured powder on each other. Holding their palms together, they looked at Shivaji's new avatar. The elephant was made to sit just outside Jijabai's quarters for Raje to get down. An impatient Jijabai rushed forward to receive him. As Raje put his head reverently on Jijabai's feet, she exclaimed, 'Shivba! Raje!'

Raje said, as he held a tray covered with a silk cloth, 'Maa saheb, I grew up under your protection. It is your blessings and love that made me what I am today. I cannot give you anything to match what you have done for me. But please accept these as a token of my reverence. Please touch them to show your acceptance.'

Jijabai's lips quivered as she touched the tray with shivering hands. She said, tears flowing down her cheeks, 'Shivba, I was never sure if I would see this day. At your birth, the astrologer had predicted that you would fulfil all my dreams. He had assured me that my days of calamities were over. Now that my dream has been fulfilled, I am blessed. I am free to die now!'

'Maa saheb, for god's sake, don't speak thus!'

'Don't worry, Shivba. I have died a thousand times before now. You have put yourself in danger so many times so far! Each time you left on a campaign, I would pray at the Lord's feet. Fear would literally kill me. There were times I wondered whether I would be able to endure the fear.'

Embracing Jijabai, Raje said, 'Maa saheb, you don't have to endure fear anymore. If anything happens to you, this coronation would be useless'

Overwhelmed with emotions, mother and son hugged each other.

Shivaji Raje sat in his quarters, lost in thought. The coronation had come with added responsibility. A hundred thoughts raced through his mind as he contemplated his next steps to consolidate his empire. Outside, those who had come to attend the ceremony were being entertained by magicians from

Bengal, and musicians and dancers who had come from different parts of the country.

Hearing someone clearing their throat to attract his attention, Raje turned. It was Soyarabai. Raje smiled and said, 'Come in! Why are you standing at the door?'

'You seem to be lost in your thoughts. Did you realize I have been here for a few minutes?'

'Soyara, here is a casket of perfumes which I ordered from Karnatak. You had asked me to get some perfume when I had gone to Agra. I could not get it then and these are now for you.'

'Oh, you remembered!'

'A Chhatrapati cannot afford to break his promise, can he?' Raje asked, smiling.

Soyarabai noticed a diamond ring on Raje's finger and asked, 'Where did you get this ring?'

'Oh, this? It was presented to me by the English envoy.'

'How come our diamonds don't shine so much?'

'Soyara, diamonds shine when they are cut and polished. Else, a diamond is a like an ordinary stone. For that matter, the human mind too is like a diamond. It shines only when it is sharpened by wisdom and practical knowledge.'

'Do you mean to say that my mind is not sharp like a diamond?' Soyarabai taunted, her anger plain.

Raje was pained at her reaction. He said, 'Soyara, you need to control your anger. You are now the chief queen and you must shoulder your responsibilities well.'

At that moment Rajaram and Sambhaji entered the room.

Raje said, addressing Rajaram, 'I did not see you during the coronation ceremony. Where were you?'

'He was asleep,' Soyarabai added hurriedly. 'He could not have stayed awake the whole night.'

Rajaram said, looking at his mother, 'No, I did not sleep at all!'

Raje was surprised and asked, 'Bal Raje, where were you then?'

Soyarabai did not know how to deflect the conversation. Before she could speak, Rajaram said, 'Aai saheb did not allow me to attend and was in the Sai Mahal.'

Raje looked at Soyarabai, astonished by Rajaram's answer.

Soyarabai replied angrily, 'What else did you expect me to do? Sambhaji would have been there, next to you, as the prince. What was Rajaram supposed to do? Stand like an ordinary soldier? It is better that he did not attend the ceremony than get humiliated.'

Raje was stunned. He shouted, 'Enough, Rani saheb! Mind your tongue!'

Soyarabai, throwing the casket of perfume on the floor in rage, stormed out of the room.

Shivaji now got busy organizing his council of ministers. Firangoji took leave to return to Bhupalgad. All the eight ministers, Moropant, Annaji, Hambirrao, Trayambakrao, Ramchandrapant, Dattajipant, Raghunathpant and Nirajipant were in attendance. Raje was keen to induct Balaji into his council but he refused and instead requested that he be given the post of his secretary.

Raje agreed and said, looking at Moropant, 'You know, Balaji is very shrewd. He knows that the pen is perhaps mightier than the sword. He has chosen to be my secretary!'

Remembering something, Raje paused and said, 'Please bring Madari here.'

Those in the assembly were surprised to hear Raje call for his Muslim servant. Raje said, sensing their confusion, 'You know, when I was planning my escape from Agra, it was Hiroji who impersonated me and Madari, who knew how to take care of me. They both knew they might be killed but they chose to help me to escape. I need to honour him today.'

At that moment Madari entered the court. Raje stepped forward and took him to the throne saying, 'Madari, it is your sacrifice and love that has allowed me to be crowned king. This throne, weighing thirty-two maunds, is your responsibility now!'

Madari could not believe that he had been given this task! He was overwhelmed with emotions and left with tears in his eyes.

Gaga Bhatt said, getting up from his seat, 'Raje, there is one more thing I would like you to do—our almanacs should start a new year today, that of Shivaji, called Shivashaka.'

Raje approved of the same and addressed Krishnaji, the astrologer, 'Please ensure that the almanac is accurate and that you prepare a treatise on the astronomical periods.'

Krishnanji looked confused and Raje said, 'A lot of Persian words and terms are being used in the almanacs. We must start using our own language in our official correspondence and in court.'

Gaga Bhatt was pleased. He added jocularly, 'So you are now going to spend time creating a dictionary.'

'I did not mean it in jest, Gaga Bhatt. Now that we have a council of ministers, I need to ensure that they take the decisions rather than depend on me. The kingdom cannot be managed by me alone. We have to expand our kingdom now and we need all the support we can get.'

Raje's mind was preoccupied with Jijabai's illness who had been feeling very weak and tired ever since the coronation ceremony and was bedridden. As he moved towards her quarters, he met Nischalpuri Gosavi, the tantric. Raje knew that he had not been happy with Gaga Bhatt's nomination as leader of the coronation ceremony and they did not see eye to eye. One was a scholar of the Vedas and the other a hermit who practised penance. But Raje had to find ways to manage both as he respected their views. Nischalpuri stood facing Raje—he was a symbol of penance with his dried, matted hair, his body covered in ash and with barely any muscles, his body having been withered away in penance. He wore a tiger skin and Raje said, 'I am told you are leaving now.'

'I have to. The time chosen by Gaga Bhatt for the coronation was not an apt one. It is a similar day to those on which your commander-in-chief Prataprao died and so did your queen. Also, the sighting of a meteor was not a good omen. I foresee some difficult times on the thirteenth, fifty-second and sixty-fifth days from now.'

Raje was a worried man. He said, 'You know everything. Tell me, how can we ward off this evil?'

'I will help you, don't worry. If you see any portentous signs, let me know. I will take care of it.'

Raje was momentarily relieved with his assurance but the predictions rankled in his mind and he was restless.

Jijabai was weak with fever. She thought that the weather at the fort was not suiting her and that she would be better off at Pachad. Raje reluctantly agreed, asking Putlabai and Sambhaji to accompany her.

Turning to matters of court, he addressed his council of ministers the next day, 'From now onwards, all decisions will be taken by the council. We must implement what the council says. It is not my sole decision anymore.'

'We are always here to advise ...' Annaji began.

'It is not advice I am asking for, Annaji. I want decisions to be taken by the council. The task is huge and we cannot depend on one person.'

The ministers were a little restless. They knew they had a huge responsibility ahead.

'How much did we spend on the coronation, Niraji?'

'About a crore hons, Raje.'

'Levy an additional tax to recover the amount.'

'I am sure the people will pay that willingly.'

'I don't want the people at large to be taxed. We must recover this from the hereditary landlords like the Patils, Kulkarnis and Deshmukhs. Also, let us not tax the people of Pune who have already suffered a lot since the Mughals raided the city.'

Raje was having his afternoon siesta when he was woken up by Sambhaji. Seeing his teary-eyed face, Raje asked, 'What is the matter?'

'It is Maa saheb. Her health is deteriorating.'

Raje immediately got off his bed.

Moropant, hearing the news, rushed towards him. 'Shall I arrange for a palanquin?'

'No, it is all right,' Raje said, 'I will walk down.'

The servants ran ahead as Raje walked down briskly towards Pachad. As soon as he reached Jijabai's quarters, Raje asked, 'Maa saheb, have you taken any medicine?'

'Sambhaji has sent a message to Ganga Shastri at Mahad. But Shivba, what is the point in torturing this body anymore. A leaf, once withered, has to fall down someday, isn't it?'

Raje did not respond. He was waiting for the physician to arrive. By evening, everyone including Soyarabai, Rajaram, Sagunabai and others had assembled at the haveli at Pachad.

Ganga Shastri arrived the next day. After checking her pulse, he was silent for a while, his face sombre.

'Vaidyaraj?' Raje asked.

Ganga Shastri took some time to respond, adjusting his turban, clearing his throat and fiddling with his medicine basket. He said, finally finding his voice, 'Maharaj, I am just a physician. I can treat an illness if there is one. But I cannot treat someone with no ailment.'

'I don't understand, Vaidyaraj.'

'I can give her some medicines to satisfy you but she needs to decide whether she wants them. If she does not want to live, we can do nothing.'

Raje left the room and walked into an adjacent room, worried that he may burst into tears in front of everyone. Recovering after a while, he asked Sambhaji to take Rajaram away. As he sat near Jijabai's bed, his tears flowed freely. He felt Jijabai's weak hand holding his palm.

She said, 'Shivba, you are not a child anymore. These tears do not become you. Remember, you held me back when I wanted to fling myself on your father's funeral pyre? You said you wanted me to witness your victories. Now you have been crowned Chhatrapati. I have seen everything now.'

'Maa saheb!'

'Shivba, can I live through your lifetime? It is a blessed soul who leaves the world after witnessing her son's valour and achievements. And even if I die, it is only my body which is mortal. My thoughts, wishes, blessings—they are all with you. Please don't shed tears when you think of me. My soul would be tortured seeing you so. Just turn back and you will know that I am there with you, like your shadow.'

Jijabai took a pause and then continued, patting his back, 'Rajaram and Sambhaji—they are still immature. You will need to manage Sambhaji. I did what I could. But now you need to take care.'

The effort to speak had tired Jijabai. She was still for a while, her eyes closed. Seeing her drifting into sleep, Raje stepped out of the room silently.

A strange fear of death had enveloped the haveli. Nirajipant had called a few Brahmins who chanted their mantras softly, adding to the sombre mood. The feeling of being orphaned overwhelmed Raje and he could not stop tears from flowing.

After a while, Jijabai opened her eyes. Seeing Raje sitting next to her she said, 'Raje, you need to rest now.'

'Maa saheb, how are you feeling?'

'What can I say? I asked you not to shed tears, didn't I? Now wipe them away. I have been lucky to have witnessed all your valour. It is better to be detached now.'

'Maa saheb!'

'Shivba!'

Seeing Sambhaji near her feet, Jijabai tried getting up a little. He was sobbing uncontrollably. She said, 'Shambhu dear, don't cry now.' Turning to Raje, she said, 'Shivba, I am worried about this child. You need to take care of him. Please don't berate him even if he errs. You need to be compassionate. He does not have his mother to look after him.'

At that moment, Annaji rushed into the room saying, 'Maharaj, Samarth is here!'

'Who?'

'Samarth Ramdas Swami.'

Raje got up hurriedly.

Jijabai said, 'This is my good fortune. I will finally be able to see him.'

Raje rushed out of the room. Nirajipant was waiting outside. Raje asked, 'Where is Samarth?'

Niraji pointed in the direction of Samarth Ramdas as he walked up the steps to the verandah.

Rushing to meet him, Raje fell at his feet. Samarth lifted him up as he muttered his blessings. He asked, 'How is Aai saheb's health?'

Raje could barely answer and the words choked in his throat. Samarth too was overwhelmed with emotions and said, putting his hand on Raje's shoulder, 'Whatever happens, it is Lord Ram's wish.'

'The vaidyaraj too has given up, Maharaj. I don't know what to do. I ...' Raje's voice was barely audible.

Hugging him Samarth said, 'Raje, hold yourself together. Let us go in.'

As they walked towards Jijabai's chambers, Raje asked, 'Have you come alone?'

'My disciples will soon follow. I was impatient and rushed when I heard of her condition.'

As soon as they entered the room, Jijabai made an effort to get up and said, 'Samarth, you have come! I am blessed.'

'Don't exert yourself, Aai saheb! I had made a commitment to Shivaji Raje; and hence, I had to come. I am a mere ascetic, Mother! I pray to Lord Ram and he shows me the way.'

Jijabai was abashed. She folded her hands and said, 'Maharaj, now that I have met you, there is nothing else I want. But Maharaj ...'

'Please command, Mother!'

'Don't embarrass me ...'

'I don't lie, Mother. Your greatness makes me say so!'

Jijabai smiled. She said, 'I am worried about Shivba. He needs a guardian and somebody's affection. I entreat you to be his guardian.'

Samarth's face turned serious. His eyes were agonized for a brief moment and then he said, his voice a little hoarse, 'Mother, I don't think I am capable of doing that. You have proven that you were a true mother to an illustrious son. To me, he is not a king—he is God incarnate! He is the result of the tapas of many like me. He has descended here like Lord Ram to create heaven on earth. But you need not worry. He is capable of managing himself. Our land, religion and God—they are all quite safe in his hands. This is Lord Ram's will too.'

Tears flowed down Jijabai's cheeks as she heard Samarth's words.

'Mother, just focus your attention on Lord Ram now. He will take care of everything. I will take your leave.'

Jijabai folded her hands as Samarth left the room.

As night fell on the haveli, the torches flickered in the winds. Jijabai was gasping for breath and there was a flurry of activity everywhere. Samarth sat on his tiger skin, lost in deep meditation. A holy fire burnt before him. At midnight, a loud wail erupted from the chambers. Tears trickled down Samarth's cheeks as he continued to sit in his meditation.

The next morning, after the funeral rites, everyone returned to the haveli. Not a single person could stop their tears. Jijabai had touched everyone's lives and they now felt an immense void. A huge presence had suddenly vanished, leaving everyone at a loss.

Raje's sorrow knew no bounds. He had not stepped out of his quarters ever since returning from the funeral. Sambhaji too was in a state of deep sorrow. His mother had died when he was very young and Jijabai had been his surrogate mother. He was now orphaned once again.

Moropant was worried. He sought Samarth's advice.

Samarth said, 'What can I do, Pant? I understand his loss and while I may be a sanyasi I am human. I am not able to bring myself to go to him. Death is inevitable but such a relationship is extremely rare. She was not just his mother but his best advisor, his moral support and the one who shaped his personality. What can words do to soothe his soul? He has to find his own way out of this.'

Moropant was in tears. He said, 'Everyone looks to Raje for support. He cannot sit alone in his mahal while the rest are looking for him. We need to do something. I beg you!'

Samarth said, 'I agree with you. Let me try speaking to him.'

Raje was lying down on his bed when Samarth entered the room. Hurriedly getting up, Raje touched Samarth's feet. As Samarth pulled him up by his shoulders, a sob escaped Raje's lips. He was uncontrollable now, as if he had been waiting for Samarth's touch. They stood embracing till Raje's sobs subsided.

Samarth said, 'Raje, you need to control yourself now.'

Raje shook his head. 'It is not possible, Maharaj. Maa saheb is dead—I have lost everything.'

'Raje, I understand. Death is inevitable from the moment you are born. See how lucky she was—she was able to see your coronation. How many mothers can say they left the world with such satisfaction? And how many sons can give this contentment to their mothers? This is when you should feel blessed rather than cry for the departed soul. Do you think her soul will be happy to see you morose?'

'The mind agrees but the heart is unwilling.'

Samarth's voice turned harsh. He said, 'Then you are the one who is responsible for her death.'

'Me? What did I do?'

'Had you not got your coronation, she may have survived, however frail and bent with age, waiting for the day her Shivba would ascend the throne. But you fulfilled her last desire. She had no further reason to live. She left, all her wishes fulfilled.'

Raje wiped his tears, realizing his folly.

Samarth said, 'I am leaving now, Raje. Shed your ignorance. You have the huge responsibility of your people on your shoulders and you have neither the right nor the time to be selfish about your own personal sorrows.'

Samarth left with a heavy heart, knowing that he had assigned a huge task to Shivaji. In the haveli at Pachad, a lonely Shivaji sat on his bed. He felt alone, terribly alone now.

Raje busied himself with making donations to Brahmins and feeding the poor, but there was no respite from his sorrow. The gap was impossible to fill. Each day, the sardars would stream in to express their condolences and it would trigger Raje's tears over and again.

One night, Raje woke up to find himself shivering and damp with sweat. Putlabai stood nearby. He asked, 'What happened?'

'You were shouting "Maa saheb, Maa saheb!" in your sleep. I rushed when I heard that.'

Raje could recall the dream vaguely. Maa saheb, dressed in a white sari had woken him up and indicated him to follow her as she turned to leave the room. Raje had shouted her name to stop her. At that moment he had woken up. Raje was upset. He said, 'I search for her everywhere but I am not able to find her. Now that I've seen her in my dreams, you come and wake me up? Can you not leave me alone and let me be with her even for a moment?'

Putlabai was shocked by Raje's words. All she could manage to do was stifle her sobs by pushing her fist into her mouth as she rushed out of the room.

It was a rainy morning. The monsoon was now gathering strength and it poured the whole day. Annaji came to meet Raje. He said, 'Raje, we need to move to the fort now.'

'Why? Who says so?'

'The order was given by the younger queen.'

Raje's anger erupted. He asked, as soon as Putlabai entered the room, 'Who did you ask before giving these orders?'

Putlabai looked straight in his eyes and said, 'Since the coronation, you have not visited the fort. People are waiting for you to take charge but no one dares to say anything.'

Raje said, his voice in a mocking tone, 'So you decided to instruct me, did you? Perhaps you have taken Maa saheb's place?'

Putlabai's face creased with pain. She said, now angry at the needless assault, 'No one can take her place. She is no more and she will not be here anymore, in case you don't know.'

'Rani saheb!'

'I am trying to tell you the truth but you won't listen. You can stay here forever but you will not find her. Had you been the head of one family, I would not have said anything. But you head a million families. Just because your mother is no more, can you ...' Her voice trailed away.

'Enough, Rani saheb!' Raje's voice was tired. He had no energy to fight anyone. He said, in a resigned tone, 'Annaji, get the palanquin ready. I will move to the fort now.'

'Let the rains subside a little.'

Raje laughed. Putting his hand on Annaji's shoulder, he said, 'Since when have we stopped because of the rain? We have to get drenched a lot in the future. There is work to do. Come on now!'

The palanquin bearers moved at a rapid pace. Through the pouring rain, Raje could see the hazy outlines of Raigad.

The celebrations at Raigad had ended abruptly due to Jijabai's demise. Soon, the temporary residences and the bazaars erected for the coronation were wound up. It added to the desolate atmosphere at the fort, which were made worse by the rains.

It had been more than a fortnight since Jijabai's death when one afternoon, after his siesta, Raje woke up to find it raining outside. Manohari informed that Rajaram had a fever. While going to Soyarabai's quarters, Raje stepped into the verandah. It was a pleasant afternoon, and the valley looked serene and beautiful. A little distance away, Raje could see Putlabai standing near the window of her quarters, lost in thought. For a moment, he thought of calling out to her but decided against it.

Stepping into Soyarabai's quarters, he found Rajaram on the bed.

'What happened, Bal Raje?' Raje asked, fondling his hair gently.

'Just a little fever, Aba saheb. I got drenched the other day when we came up the fort. Where is Dada Maharaj,' Rajaram asked.

'I too was wondering where he is. I haven't seen him since the morning.'

'How will you?' Soyarabai said. 'He is in Pachad.'

'He misses Maa saheb. Maybe he went ...'

'He went to enjoy some dance and songs,' Soyarabai interrupted.

Raje raised an eyebrow questioningly. Soyarabai continued, 'After he invited some dancers for the coronation ceremony, he has asked them to stay back. He goes down to the haveli to enjoy their music.'

'So what is wrong with that?' Raje asked. 'He is young. Let him enjoy the music if he wants to.'

'That is why I haven't mentioned this to you earlier because I knew you would take it lightly. You only listen to the younger queen in any case.'

'What about it, Rani saheb? Please speak your mind.'

'Would you have come here in the pouring rain had she not insisted? And poor Rajaram, he fell ill after having got drenched.'

Raje realized that it was better to stay silent. He got up and left. He remembered Putlabai standing at the window. He turned towards her quarters, and at that moment, Putlabai came out smiling.

'What were you doing at the window? You seemed lost in thought.'

The gusts of wind were making it difficult for Putlabai to manage her sari and her hair. She tried desperately to control them much to Raje's amusement.

Raje said, 'You seemed preoccupied. Tell me what is on your mind, Putla.'

'You know how women think ... I was worried ...'

'Worried about what?'

'Your coronation is over and it is the highest honour you have received. The sun always dips once it reaches the zenith. The full moon too has to wane. And so, I was worried about our future.'

'Does the moon worry about waning? Does the sun stop rising each day knowing that it has to set by evening? If nature does not worry, why should we bother?'

'Well, we can be worried about the incoming rain,' Putla said, as she saw a sheet of rain approaching them.

They ran towards the shaded part of the verandah but were drenched before they could reach it. At that moment, a soldier ran with two umbrellas. Raje said, smiling at Putlabai, 'Look! Now that I am a Chhatrapati, I don't even have the liberty of getting drenched in rain at will.'

While retiring for the night, Raje noticed a lamp burning in one of the quarters. He asked Putlabai, 'Isn't that Sambhaji's mahal?'

'Yes, it is. But he is not here. Yesu is awake.'

'It is quite late. What keeps her awake so late?'

'She reads the Eknathi Bhagwad each night.'

Raje looked at the lit window for a long time and then dozed off. The next morning, on his way to the temple for darshan, he asked the guards to send for Yesu. When she arrived he asked, 'Yesu, Yuvraj is never around but should you not, as my daughter-in-law, accompany me to the temple?'

Yesu smiled in reply. They both mounted their horses and went to the temple. The guards followed at a respectable distance. On their return, Raje said, 'Yesu, you are grown up now. Maa saheb is no more and you must take on the responsibility of looking after my successor. I am entrusting you with a responsibility. In my absence, my seals will be under your care. I am sure you will handle the responsibility well.'

A surprised Yesu said, 'But Aba saheb, this responsibility is ...'

'I know! Don't worry. I will let Shambhu know. He may act irresponsibly at times but I am confident you never would.'

Yesu blushed. Raje patted her forehead lovingly and said, 'You came in here as a young bride but grew up like a daughter. I know you have the capability to take care of Shambhu. My blessings are with you!'

In response, Yesubai bent to touch Raje's feet and left without saying a word.

That afternoon, Raje was told that Sambhaji had returned to the fort but did not present himself. He asked Annaji that evening while going to the temple, 'I am told Yuvraj has gone to Pachad. Is that so?'

'Yes, Maharaj.'

'Does he go there to listen to the singers?'

'Yes.'

'Why did you not tell me about it?'

'Maharaj, he is short-tempered and I did not want him to feel that I was complaining about him. Later, I thought it was proper to tell Soyarabai Rani saheb about it.'

'It would have been better had you told me. He is my successor and we have to ensure he does not fall into bad habits.'

The next day, Sambhaji sent in a request to meet Raje. On being granted permission, he presented himself.

Raje asked, 'Since when have you been seeking permission to meet me?'

Sambhaji stood with his head bent, unable to face his father.

'I am told you were in Pachad, enjoying the music and dance?'

'I am sorry, Aba saheb. Please pardon me,' Sambhaji said, rushing to fall at Raje's feet.

Raje let out a deep sigh and said, 'Shambhu, I know you enjoy music. But your behaviour upsets me. It has been less than a month since Maa saheb left us and here you are, engrossed with the dancers!'

A sob escaped Sambhaji's lips. He said, 'Aba saheb, I don't know what to do! Maa saheb's absence is difficult to bear. My mind was in such turmoil ...'

Hugging Sambhaji, Raje said, 'Shambhu, is this the way to forget Maa saheb? When you went down the fort at night, her soul would have followed you, knowing you might be in danger. Don't you know how much she cared for you?'

Sambhaji was in tears. He said, 'I apologize, Aba saheb.'

'I can forgive any mistake but you cannot repeat mistakes. You are, after all, my successor. You need to be careful. We cannot live our lives the way we wish, Shambhu! Wipe those tears now.'

Shambhu was relieved and managed a smile.

At that moment Yesu came in. Raje said, pointing at her, 'Yuvraj, I have given her the responsibility of taking care of my seals in our absence. You and I will be on campaigns, and someone needs to take care of them. I hope you don't mind.'

Sambhaji smiled in reply and then stepped out of the room. Yesu too followed coyly. Raje laughed seeing them blush. It was the first time since Jijabai's death that Raje's laughter was heard in the fort.

It was nearing a month since Jijabai's death. Mahadev, Raje's trusted spy, came to visit and the fort was agog with news of a campaign which would be announced soon. The monsoon was at its peak, and Raje issued orders to Hambirrao, Moropant and Anandrao to organize their troops and be prepared. The meeting, with Anandrao, Hambirrao, Annaji, Moropant and other ministers, was in progress and Sambhaji too was present. Raje asked, 'What is the position of the Mughals?'

'Aurangzeb has recalled Diler Khan and has sent his trusted commander Bahadur Khan to the Deccan now.'

'And he has renamed the fort at Pedgaon Bahadurgad, hasn't he? They think we have been lax since the coronation. We need to teach them a lesson.'

'Maharaj, the rains are at its peak. Would it be sensible?'

'Yes, it is the right moment. How much did we spend on the coronation?'

'Nearly a crore hons.'

'I am told Bahadur Khan has collected nearly a crore of rupees in taxes. He has nearly two hundred thoroughbred horses. We need to capture them before they are dispatched to Delhi. Apart from that, I want Moropant to go to Kalyan and Bhiwandi and bring a quarter of the tax collections from the Vasaikars. Annaji will go to capture Phonda at the same time. I will be leading the campaign against Bahadur Khan.'

'What about me, Aba saheb?'

'Shabbash! I am happy that you have asked me about this. A restless mind sometimes needs a campaign to divert its attention. Anandrao will accompany Yuvraj, and your task is to create terror in the Mughal territory of Bhaganagar. We must teach them that we are always alert and have not gone to sleep since the coronation.'

He continued, looking at those present, 'This is my plan—what does the council think?'

Everyone nodded and when the others departed, Moropant stayed back and said, 'Raje, Yuvraj has asked the singers to leave after paying them a handsome amount.'

'I am aware.'

'Oh?'

'I am also aware that you adjusted the amount paid to them against the coronation ceremony, didn't you? Moropant, you may see him as Yuvraj but I look at him as a father would!'

In a few days, Moropant was ready to leave. Sambhaji came to meet Raje before leaving. Raje said, 'Shambhu, take care of yourself and don't show bravado where it is not required. You are now a responsible sardar and have to ensure you return safe. I shall be waiting for you.'

Raje met Hambirrao and said, 'You must draw Bahadur Khan out. Take two thousand men and see that Bahadur Khan comes out of the fort to attack you. I will, in the meanwhile, attack his fort with eight thousand men and take over the treasury.'

'And shall we challenge Bahadur Khan to battle?'

'No. We don't want to lose a single man now. The treasury is our target. The English came with their presents during the coronation. The Mughals did not. We shall collect one crore hons and two hundred horses as our gift from them! It would be a fitting gift from the Mughal emperor, don't you think?'

Hambirrao replied, 'Maharaj, do you expect the Mughal Badshah to retaliate?'

'I don't think so. I doubt whether he would even notice such a small amount being looted!'

Raje was lost in thought as Hambirrao took his leave. He was thinking of Alamgir.

The monsoon had not yet reached Delhi. The clouds, however, had gathered, making the weather oppressively hot. In the Diwan-i-Khas, the fountains gurgled, creating a cool environment around the hall. The vetiver screens were constantly being watered with rose essence. In the centre of the hall sat Aurangzeb, looking into a few papers.

Two servants with hand fans made of peacock feathers stood on the side, waving them gently. Jaffar Khan and a few other sardars stood at a respectable distance. Aurangzeb smiled, reading one of the letters. The news from Iran was good. He said, 'It seems things in Iran are under control.'

Jaffar Khan replied, 'Alampanah, we are taking care of that territory.'

'Who are we to take any care? Allah is great and merciful,' Aurangzeb replied while the sardars nodded vigorously.

'And what about the Deccan,' Aurangzeb asked, turning to Jaffar Khan.

'The Adil Shahi dynasty has been taught a lesson and will not dare to oppose us. If you say, we can annex it to our empire.'

'No, I don't intend to annex the territory. It is good they know their limits. But when I said Deccan, I was asking about Shivaji. What about him? You seem to be taking him lightly.'

'I beg your pardon, Jahanpanah. Bahadur Khan is there now.'

'And what is he doing about Shivaji?'

Jaffar Khan smiled. 'What can he do? I was laughing when I heard about what he's been doing.'

'What about it?'

'Well, I am told that he had a pandit from Kashi and held a coronation. Now, isn't that ridiculous? He makes a laughing stock of himself.'

Jaffar Khan did not notice the change of expression on Aurangzeb's face. He was busy recounting the tale of the coronation when he stopped mid-sentence. Aurangzeb's face had turned pale, and before others could see his tears, he abruptly got up and left before the sardars, who had bent to perform an elaborate mujra, could straighten up. With two sardars in tow, Jaffar Khan ran behind Aurangzeb.

Entering his room, he was surprised to find Aurangzeb lying on the carpet and crying, praying to Allah. 'Parwardigar, for what crime are you punishing me? Did I not perform my namaaz properly? Please give me the strength to bear this insult. Please help me!'

'Jahanpanah!' Jaffar Khan exclaimed, when he saw the emperor in such a helpless state.

Refusing Jaffar Khan's hand to help him get up, Aurangzeb stood up.

Jaffar Khan said, 'Jahanpanah, what will Shivaji gain by holding a coronation? There are many fools who have tried the same thing and have been shown their place by the Mughal sultanate.

Aurangzeb said, 'Enough, Jaffar! Don't talk nonsense. Shuja and Salim held coronations, but they had a right to the Mughal throne in some form or other. Don't take Shivaji's coronation lightly. Don't you realize that it is a direct affront to Islam?'

'Alijah, where does Shivaji stand in comparison to the Mughal throne? If we cannot find a way to sign a treaty with him, we will defeat him and ...'

Jaffar Khan stopped mid-sentence as Aurangzeb laughed hysterically and said, 'That traitor!'

Jaffar Khan nodded saying, 'That is true, Alampanah. He is a traitor! That idol worshipper!'

Aurangzeb stared at Jaffar Khan. Realizing that he had made a mistake, Jaffar Khan looked down at the carpet.

Aurangzeb said, 'I was not calling Shivaji a traitor. I was talking about you! You want to sign a treaty with him? Don't you realize that he may die but his throne will live on?'

Aurangzeb raised his hands in the air praying and said, his voice pleading with Allah, 'Parwardigar, don't doubt my faith in you. Please trust your most faithful servant—I beseech you!'

Turning to Jaffar Khan and the sardars he said, 'You have already shown your impotence by allowing Shivaji to escape from Agra. Now, before I lose my temper and order you beheaded, get out of this room!'

The sardars hurriedly saluted and left. They did not dare to turn back and see Aurangzeb standing alone in the hall, lost in his thoughts.

The monsoon had ebbed a little but the sun was still playing hide-and-seek behind the clouds. Raje left for Pedgaon as the rains, albeit reduced to a steady downpour, continued to fall. The entire region seemed covered under water.

At the banks of Bhima River, Raje and his troops halted for a while. The river was in spate with the brown water gushing forth at great speeds. Bahadur Khan's cantonment looked peaceful, the soldiers resting with nothing to do in the wet weather.

Standing guard at the entrance of the fort at Bahadurgad, the gatekeeper noticed two turbaned horsemen galloping towards him. Soon they reached the gate and while dismounting, they said, 'Quick! Close the gates. The Marathas are on their way!'

Bahadur Khan was sent a message and soon enough, his spies reported seeing a contingent of Maratha soldiers marching towards Pedgaon. 'How many of them are there?' Bahadur Khan asked.

'Two thousand, Huzoor.'

'Is that all?' Bahadur Khan was surprised to hear that.

'Huzoor, they are known to travel light with a small contingent.'

Bahadur Khan laughed as he caressed his beard. He said, 'Sound the bugles.' He had finally got a chance to teach the Maratha rats a lesson, he mused.

Soon, at the sound of trumpets and horns, a ten-thousand-strong cavalry left the fort, leaving only a few men to guard the fort behind. On the outskirts of Pedgaon, he spotted the Maratha contingent which, to his surprise, turned and started to gallop away when they saw the Mughal troops. Bahadur Khan was surprised. He had heard of the Marathas and their treacherous ways but this was the first time he had seen an enemy run away without bothering to challenge him. He commanded his men to chase them. For hours, they raced to catch up with them, but soon the Marathas had stretched their lead to an extent that was impossible to bridge.

Bahadur Khan ordered the men to stop and said, 'Cowards! They have run away, those Marathas!'

Dreaming of the way he would have tortured the rats if he had caught them, Bahadur Khan cantered back towards his fort. As they came within sight of the fort, he was surprised to see black smoke billowing from the fort and the cantonment around. Spurring his horse on, he galloped all the way. The fort seemed desolate. The door was wide open and the half-burnt tents in the cantonment flapped miserably in the wet wind. Bahadur Khan, aghast to see the carnage asked, as he spotted a solider coming his way, 'What happened?'

'Those Marathas,' the soldier said, sobbing, 'they came and looted everything while you were away.'

A furious Bahadur Khan realized that he had been tricked by Shivaji's men as he chased them needlessly across the muddy plains. A few miles away, Hambirrao, astride a horse, galloped as Raje and the troops moved at rapid pace towards Raigad. Two hundred of the thoroughbred steeds and a crore of gold coins of loot was the reward they carried with them. Soon, Raigad was in sighting distance!

The campaign at Bahadurgad was a major success. As planned, Moropant had created havoc at Kalyan–Bhiwandi, spreading terror among the English and Portuguese. After Bahadurgad, Raje's men moved to Junnar while Annaji was at Phonda. The entire region was being shaken up. While good news poured in, Raje was eagerly waiting for Sambhaji's return.

It had been a month since the campaign at Bahadurgad, when one day, in the wee hours of the morning, Raje woke up to the trumpets announcing Sambhaji's arrival. Raje eagerly reached the office but was told that Sambhaji had gone to his quarters, having entered through a side gate.

'Anandrao, what happened to Yuvraj?'

Anandrao smiled. 'We had reached Bhaganagar as instructed by you. We were confronted by the Qutb Shahi troops and I asked Yuvraj to turn back. Much against his wishes, he turned back. But in his anger, he refused to talk to me for the rest of the way. He feels that he has returned without fighting and is ashamed to show his face to you.'

'Oh, so that's what is going on! Well, in that case, let me go see him,' Raje said, as he walked towards Sambhaji's quarters.

Sambhaji was sitting on his bed while Yesubai stood nearby. Seeing Raje enter, Sambhaji got up and saluted, and stood with his head bowed.

Looking at Yesu, Raje asked, 'Have you not welcomed your husband in the traditional manner with an oil lamp and tray?'

Sambhaji erupted with anger and said, 'What for, Aba saheb? A hero is welcomed home—not a coward.'

Raje smiled. 'Who says that running away is the mark of a coward? It is often a wise thing to do. It is not easy to do and needs courage.'

'Huh! If only Anandrao had not forced me to turn back.'

'Yuvraj, I had asked you to loot the territory and not to fight the Qutb Shahi?'

'What impression would they have of us, seeing us run away like that?'

'That is irrelevant. We got what we wanted. Don't mourn your so-called defeat—I have faced many of them. I cannot forget the way I had to run from Panhala and it taught me many lessons.'

Sambhaji smiled, much to Raje's relief. Turning to Yesu, Raje said, 'Now, please welcome your husband properly. He is a hero and needs to be welcomed appropriately.'

As Raje stepped out of Sambhaji's quarters, a visibly relieved Sambhaji hugged Yesubai, much to her embarrassment.

The rains had ended, turning the land green. Raje supervised the construction of a new stable at Pachad where he housed five hundred select horses. As he sat in his office one evening, he remembered Nischalpuri's prediction. While Raje did not believe in bad omens, many felt that the day of the coronation, chosen by Gaga Bhatt, had not been a very auspicious one.

Raje said, looking at his sardars, 'Lord Rama was crowned at a very auspicious time, yet he had to go into exile for fourteen years. We lament the death of our commander Prataprao but we forget that he fought a ten-thousand-strong enemy force. Maa saheb left us but hers was a life well lived. What more could she have asked for?'

Knowing that the sardars did not want to leave anything to chance, Raje relented in sending the word for Nischalpuri. He was a master of tantric rites. Amidst the loud chanting of mantras, Raje was asked to ascend the throne once again. A satisfied Nischalpuri blessed Raje, and said, 'It is because of your qualities that the land will flourish for another three hundred years, Chhatrapati! The power of the invading foreigners will be routed in the interim.'

Raje descended from the throne and instinctively turned to the right. Having walked a couple of steps, he realized that Maa saheb, who would usually be sitting next to him, would not be there to bless him. There was no one at whose feet he would now place his head for blessings! Holding back his tears, he left for his quarters.

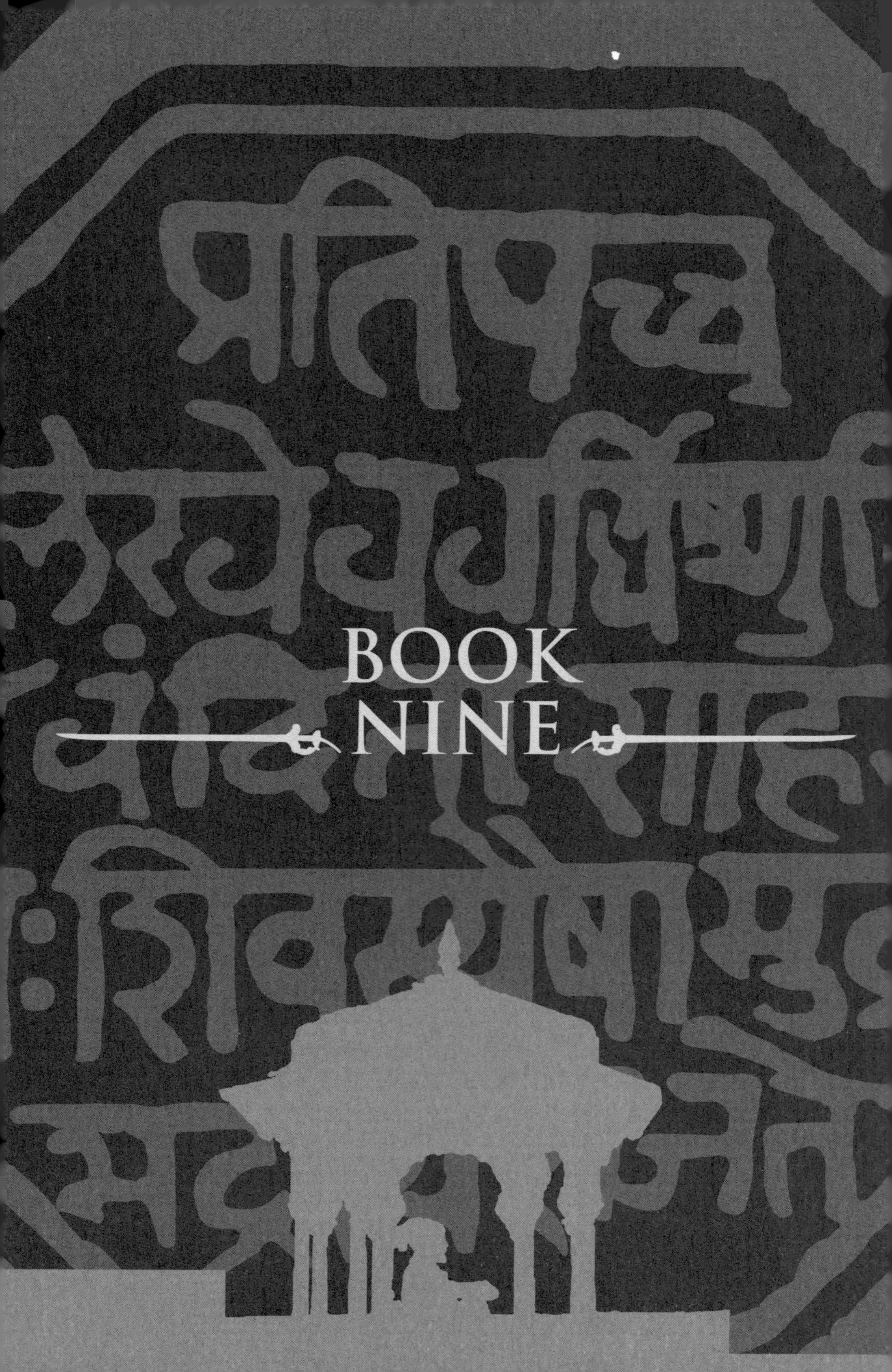

BOOK NINE

Winter was approaching fast, and fog covered the hilltops in the morning. The next campaign was now being planned. It was decided that Raje would personally lead a campaign to Khandesh while Anandrao would lead a contingent towards Surat to create havoc there.

For nearly three months, Raje campaigned in Khandesh. Anandrao's forces, in the meanwhile, were confronted by nearly four thousand Bhils in Ramnagar region near Daman and, despite negotiating to pay them a lakh of rupees, Anandrao and his men had to return. He joined Raje in Aurangabad, and the attack on Surat was thus temporarily abandoned.

Halting at Erandol, Raje ordered the troops to march on the English factory. The Mughal officer Keshagi tried his best to face the Marathas but had to finally run away. Raje was thus able to enter Burhanpur without any resistance and returned to Raigad with a large loot.

The winters had ended now. The English tried their best to demand compensation from Shivaji but to no avail. Apart from the Mughals and the Adil Shahi court, Shivaji was worried about another enemy—the Siddi of Janjira. He held sway over the Arabian Sea, leaving Shivaji's ships under constant threat. With a view to counter Siddi, Raje decided to build a fort, Padmadurg, at Kasa near Rajpuri. He instructed his admiral Daulat Khan to send a naval force to protect the men as they built the fort. Soon, the fort was ready and Raje named Subhanji Mohite as the fort-keeper. Sambhaji's thread ceremony was performed around this time as well. It was to be done during the coronation ceremony but had been delayed due to Maa saheb's demise.

Within a fortnight of Sambhaji's thread ceremony, a surprise attack by the Mughals at the Kalyan–Bhiwandi area also worried Raje. It was something he had not expected them to do. That evening, he called a meeting of the council. He said, as the men assembled, 'I am told that Bahadur Khan has been furious ever since we looted his camp, which was expected. I know he is lazy and does not have Diler Khan's grit, but his attack on Kalyan proves that he is getting ready to act.'

'What do you propose we do, Aba saheb?' Sambhaji asked.

'We must reconcile with Bahadur Khan. Begin peace talks with him, and say that we are ready to pledge allegiance to the emperor and surrender seventeen forts. Also, say that I am willing to send my son to serve under him if he promises a mansab of six thousand. But all of this on the condition that the territory south of the Bhima River will remain ours.'

'I will never serve under the emperor!' Sambhaji exclaimed.

Raje smiled and said, 'You will have to go, my dear! It is for the good of the kingdom.'

'I would rather fight and die than give in so easily.'

Raje smiled, seeing Sambhaji's reaction. He said, 'Shambhu, I was only pulling your leg. These are negotiation tactics, and we need to buy time. Even if Bahadur Khan agrees, he has to wait for the final orders to come from Delhi. Till then at least, we will have peace and can complete our operations in Karwar.'

Sambhaji was visibly relieved to hear Raje's plan.

Raje's estimate was right. Bahadur Khan, weakened by the constant attacks from Shivaji's men, had no strength to counter the attacks. To add to things, he was worried about the emperor's wrath. The proposal for a treaty from Shivaji Raje was an opportune one and he did not waste any time in writing to Aurangzeb, who was then camping in Punjab, to send a farman in Sambhaji's name.

Raje, seeing that his ploy had worked, decided to start a new campaign and, after asking Sambhaji to be stationed at Raigad, planned an attack on Phonda.

On arriving at Rajapur, he dispatched forty ships to Vengurla. Raje had suffered a defeat here at the time of his negotiations with Jai Singh. Annaji too had failed to capture it. Determined not to lose this chance, they marched with a huge army of fifteen thousand cavalry and nearly an equal number of foot soldiers. On reaching Rajapur and then going via Kudal on to the outskirts of Phonda, Raje dispatched two thousand cavalry and five thousand foot soldiers to lay siege to the fort.

The summer was at its peak and the coastal humidity made matters worse. The fort-keeper, Muhammad Ikhlas Khan, despite having food supplies to hold out for nearly four months, decided to counter the Maratha attack.

The Portuguese in neighbouring Goa were becoming concerned about the situation. They had promised to remain neutral but were worried that Raje may turn his attention to them once he captured Phonda. They managed to instigate the Desais on the border areas to attack the Marathas. The Desais were routed quickly and the Maratha soldiers chased them right into the Portuguese territory. The Portuguese, having captured Raje's emissary, sent ten vessels loaded with food as relief to those trapped in Phonda but these were intercepted by Raje's men. When the viceroy was demanded an explanation by Raje, he pleaded innocence. Raje knew that the Portuguese would now not interfere anymore and he focused his attention on capturing the fort.

Despite repeated attacks, the strong walls of the fort did not fall. There had been many casualties and Raje was worried that he may lose more men if he kept trying the same tactics. He called for five hundred ladders and asked Ibrahim Khan to lay mines near the walls.

On the day of the attack, the soldiers at the fort were taken aback by a sudden lull in the activities and many looked out from the ramparts, wondering whether the Marathas had decided to retreat. Suddenly, three deafening blasts penetrated the sky and in no time, the wall had been breached. Ibrahim Khan was the first one to attack with the Maratha flag in hand. Soon, the Maratha soldiers, shouting 'Har Har Mahadev!' charged in and captured the fort.

Ibrahim Khan presented himself to Raje after the capture. He could barely salute as his right shoulder was wounded and Raje was overjoyed to see him. He said, 'You have shown great valour. You are now the fort-keeper of Phonda.'

After making necessary arrangements at Phonda, Raje moved on. He had set his sights on Karwar now.

In the forests of Marai, near Pachad, Sambhaji had been enjoying a hunting expedition for two days. The summer was in full swing and the Savitri River, now reduced to a stream, looked miserable. As Sambhaji galloped towards Raigad, the horses frothed at the mouths, the dry and sweltering heat taking a toll on everyone. Sambhaji got emotional when the haveli at Pachad came into view.

'Shidoji!' He called out to his aide.

Sambhaji said, when Shidoji came near, 'You carry on. I will take darshan of Maa saheb and join you.'

Spurring his horse, he entered the precincts of the haveli. A soldier saluted standing there but Sambhaji was lost in his thoughts as he entered the gardens, now looking deserted. The gloomy atmosphere was in stark contrast to the hustle and bustle in the place when Jijabai had resided here. He moved his horse towards Jijabai's samadhi, and dismounted. He gently moved his fingers over the pedestal. The tulsi plant swayed in a light wind. With a heavy heart, Sambhaji abruptly turned and mounting his horse, galloped towards Raigad. He did not want to linger there any longer, memories flooding his mind and making him restless. As he raced towards Raigad, he spotted a well and a beautiful lady standing near it, holding a pitcher. He pulled the reins sharply, making the horse rear. Sambhaji had not seen a more beautiful face.

Unable to take his eyes off her, he asked, as he wiped the sweat off his face, 'Can I have some water for my horse?'

The young woman, without saying a word, poured the pitcher into a small pit. As the horse drank, Sambhaji, stroking the horse gently, looked at the woman's sensual and curvaceous figure. Quite to his surprise, she did not look away.

He said, as he moved towards her, 'You have quenched my horse's thirst. What about me?'

For a moment she looked angry and then suddenly, she smiled sweetly, and said, 'Please go before someone sees us here.'

Sambhaji was not one to listen to orders. Giving in to his request, she poured the water from the pitcher into Sambhaji's cupped hands. Hurriedly looking around to see if they had been spotted, she seemed in a great hurry to move.

Sambhaji said, wiping his mouth, 'I have never tasted such sweet water. Thank you.'

'Masters should not say that!'

'So you do recognize me! What is your name?'

'Godavari.'

'Do you come here every day?'

Godavari did not reply but her silence conveyed the answer Sambhaji wanted.

'I will be here tomorrow. I will meet you.'

Sambhaji mounted his horse. As he spurred, he turned to look at Godavari who continued to stare at him. Galloping towards Raigad, he wondered whether he had been dreaming. Her face continued to wreak havoc in his mind.

The next day, Godavari came to the well as usual and was restless at not seeing Sambhaji around. Waiting desperately for him, she looked around as she continued to wash her clothes. Soon, she heard footsteps and Sambhaji emerged from behind a tree.

She asked, not knowing what to say, 'Where is your horse?'

'I tied him a little away. His thirst is quenched. It is I who is thirsty!'

As she moved to give him some water, Sambhaji said, raising his hand, 'No, that won't quench my thirst.' He held the edge of her pallu. 'Godavari, I could not sleep all night!'

Extricating herself from his grip, she said, 'The receiver should not harass the one that gives.'

Sambhaji took out a necklace he was wearing and gave it to her.

She shook her head saying, 'I am visiting my parents—I cannot take that.'

'What shall I give you, Godavari? Something that you would remember all your life. Tell me!'

'If you insist,' Godavari said, a little hesitant, 'then I'd like to experience you as closely as possible!'

Sambhaji was quiet for a moment and then said, 'I shall fulfil your wish. I will return soon.'

He returned to the fort. The blazing sun hardly mattered to him. On reaching the fort, he received news of Raje's capture of Phonda. An excited Sambhaji said, 'Please let the cannons announce Raje's victory.' He turned to go to his quarters.

As he stepped into his room, Yesu asked, 'Are you planning to go out tonight again?'

'Yes. I am told a tiger is prowling nearby. If you keep my secret, I will go.'

A braid of champak flowers attracted his attention. Picking up the braid, he said, as he inhaled the scent deeply, 'This is so lovely. And it is intoxicating too, isn't it?'

At that moment, the cannons boomed announcing the victory.

The news of further victories was reaching the fort daily. Within fifty days of capturing Phonda, Raje had captured Akola, Kadra and Karwar and merged them into the Maratha kingdom. Karwar was known for its slave trade. As soon as the territory was merged into the kingdom, Raje said to Prataprao, 'The practice of slavery is a shameful one. We must stop it immediately.'

Prataprao said, 'You may be right, Raje, but we must be patient. The trade occurs in Bijapur and Hubli too. The English, the Bijapurkurs and the Mughals are all involved in it.'

Raje was perplexed. He asked, 'I can understand the inclination of the Mughals and the Bijapurkars. Why do the English need slaves?'

'They have a fascination for Indian dwarfs, Maharaj.'

'I see! I am not going to allow this to persist in the kingdom of the Lord. We must impose heavy taxes on the trade so that it stops automatically. Please issue orders immediately to this effect.'

After staying in Karwar for a few days, Raje decided to return to the fort. A large portion of coastal Konkan was under his control now. As the monsoon advanced towards the Western Ghats, Raje started his return march to Raigad.

At Raigad, Sambhaji's midnight excursions had become a regular affair, much to the anxiety of the elders, but no one dared question him.

The rains were in full swing now. As Sambhaji was getting ready to leave one night, Yesu asked, 'When are you likely to come back?'

'Tomorrow—or the day after for sure.'

'Have you informed my mother-in-law?'

Sambhaji replied casually, 'Tell her I have gone out for some recreation.'

As he was about to leave, he saw Soyarabai standing at the door.

She asked, 'Where are you off to?'

Seeing Sambhaji raise an eyebrow questioningly, she said, 'Oh, I am sorry. You must be going on an important mission and I should not have asked.'

'Well, I am going to receive Aba saheb, who is expected any day.'

'Why did you not say that?'

'The custom here at the fort is that till he comes to the fort, no such news must be made public.'

'I see!' Soyarabai left, fretting and fuming.

Yesu asked, as soon as she was out of earshot, 'Why did you snub her? People get hurt for the smallest of reasons.'

'Well, Aai saheb is the one who hurts others. It is my misfortune that I was born first. She will never forgive me for that!'

Yesu, overwhelmed with emotions, could barely say anything. Sambhaji did not wait for her to respond and left.

The western sky was filled with dark clouds, threatening to burst open at any moment, as Sambhaji waited with his horsemen for Raje to arrive. The air was warm and humid. Sambhaji dismounted after seeing Raje at a distance. Raje too dismounted and hugged Sambhaji affectionately. He said, putting his hand on his shoulders, 'Is everything all right?'

'Ji, Aba saheb.'

Raje turned to Hambirrao and said, 'You know, it would have been fine had Sambhaji met me at the fort but to be honest with you, I did wish that he would receive me here!'

Hambirrao smiled and said, 'You are fortunate to have your wishes fulfilled!'

'Our soldiers wait impatiently for the rains and are eager to reach home before that. Yurvraj, let us go to the fort now.'

As they rode towards Pachad, Raje ordered the troops to take the horses to the stables.

Sambhaji said, 'Aba saheb, would you like to rest for a while? It is terribly hot now.'

'What? Wait now? No, we'd better make our way to the fort.'

As they crossed the well where Sambhaji had met Godavari, Sambhaji said, 'Aba saheb, you must drink the water of this well. It is very cool and tasty.'

Godavari was standing nearby and filled the pitcher to serve Raje. She said, 'I do not have any other vessel with which to serve you'

'Don't worry,' Raje said, as he cupped his palms for her to pour water in.

Wiping his mouth, Raje said, 'It is indeed very tasty. What is your name, dear girl?'

'Godavari.'

'It suits you. The one who served us water! Where are you from?'

Hambirrao stepped forward and said, 'Maharaj, she is the daughter of Dinkarpant and is related to Annaji.'

'Oh, is that so? Please see that when she leaves for her father-in-law's home, she is given a blouse piece and a coconut. Let us go now.'

Godavari watched as the horses galloped away. Her heart was overflowing with love and affection.

Torrential rains lashed Raigad. The rivers were in full spate, and mist covered the mountains throughout the day. In the meanwhile, Raje was busy with his spies, gathering information for his forthcoming attack on Janjira. He was only waiting for the rains to recede.

Raje had been at Raigad for more than a month when one morning, the news that Bahadur Khan's envoy was on his way to meet Raje reached the fort. The envoy was provided with a separate residence and a date was fixed for an audience with Raje. As he waited in court for Raje to arrive, he glanced at the dazzling throne with its precious gems and stones. Wearing a Mughal turban and a silk kurta on loose trousers, he admired the beauty of the throne and asked, a little bewildered, 'Does Shivaji Raje have so much wealth? Where did you get this throne?'

The question was asked to Nirajipant, who said, 'We did not get it. We got it made with thirty-two maunds of gold, not to mention the hundreds of gems and precious stones.'

The envoy was perplexed. He wondered why such an affluent king would want to willingly hand over his forts and serve under the Mughals. Just then, a sentry announced Shivaji's arrival. The court rose. Shivaji Raje walked in, flanked by ushers who held golden spears. As Raje turned to sit on the throne, the envoy bent thrice in an elaborate mujra. Ramchandrapant introduced him and said, 'The envoy of Mughal Subedar of the Deccan, Khanjahan Bahadur Kokaltash Jafarjung is here in our durbar.'

'I am glad to welcome the envoy of Bahadur Khan.'

The envoy stepped forward and clapped his hand once. The servant standing behind him holding trays covered in silk came forward. He removed the covers and the trays were full of gold coins and precious items. Shivaji stretched his hand forward in acceptance. The envoy, licking his lips nervously, chose his words carefully before saying, 'Huzoor, my master Bahadur Khan had made a plea on your behalf to Emperor Aurangzeb and he has been kind enough to forgive all your offences. He has asked you to surrender the forts and send Sambhaji Raje to accept his mansabdari.'

Raje smiled. 'I don't think he sent me a message. "Order" would be a more appropriate word.'

The envoy was taken aback and said, swallowing nervously, 'Ji, Huzoor.'

Raje's smile vanished and he said, his voice now threatening, 'Order? Bahadur Khan has the temerity to send me this order? It seems he has forgotten how we looted the fort. What makes him think we are going to surrender and accept their servitude?'

'But Huzoor ...' The envoy began.

'Shut up and listen! Leave before I lose my temper.'

As Raje stood on the dais, the envoy hurriedly saluted and vanished from the durbar.

As he left the fort, he wondered how he was going to convey the message to Bahadur Khan. He had come with hopes of serving the Mughal farman and had been dreaming of the rewards on his return. Aurangzeb, in anticipation of the treaty, had promoted Bahadur Khan and had sent him an elephant as a gift. He now prayed fervently that Bahadur Khan had the courage to bear the way Shivaji had insulted him. Unmindful of the lashing rains, the envoy hurriedly left the fort.

Raje had been planning a campaign against Janjira for the moment the rains stopped. It had been nearly a month since Bahadur Khan's envoy had left. The spies had provided some crucial information which Raje shared with a select few sardars including Moropant, who was asked to lead the campaign. Moropant reached the fort.

The English envoy Austin reached the fort demanding compensation for the damage they had suffered at the hands of the Marathas. But he had to return without any promise of the same. Raje was in no mood to compensate the English. Annaji had reached Pachad but had not reported to the fort yet. Assuming that he must have been tired after a long campaign, Raje did not summon him. But after a few days, when there was no information regarding his visit, Raje sent a message to Pachad asking him to meet at the fort.

It had been a week since the summons to Annaji. One afternoon, as Raje sat in his quarters, planning the forthcoming campaign, Soyarabai, who was sitting next to him, stood up to leave.

'Where are you going?'

'What is the point of sitting here? You are far away, lost in thought and planning something or the other. Do you even recognize that someone is sitting next to you? I often feel you belong to no one!'

Raje said, a little hurt at the accusation, 'Soyara, I am destined to carry out the Lord's wishes. All I can think of is the Swaraj. When on a campaign, there is a constant watch at my door and patrolling with the light of the torches. Yet, I feel like a prisoner—lonely and trapped. Now that Sambhaji is a grown man, I was hoping to relax a little.'

Hearing Sambhaji's name, Soyarabai extricated her hand from Raje's.

He asked, 'What is the matter, Soyara?'

Just then, Manohari came in to announce the arrival of Moropant, who soon came in and saluted.

'Pant, where is Annaji? I have not seen him yet. Is he not well?'

'No, he is fine,' Moropant said, hesitating to say anything further.

'He is ashamed to face you,' Soyarabai added, much to Raje's confusion.

'What has he done to feel ashamed? Why don't you speak up?'

'It is not Annaji who has committed the offence,' Soyarabai interjected.

'Rani saheb!' Moropant exclaimed.

Ignoring him, she continued, 'Yuvraj did something which Annaji is trying to hush up.'

A puzzled Raje asked, 'Can you please elaborate?'

'He kidnapped a Brahmin girl, who happens to be related to Annaji. He has forcibly kept her in the Lingana Fort.'

'Rani saheb!' Raje screamed.

Soyarabai was unperturbed. 'Well, those are the facts and the whispers are soon going to spread.'

Raje said, turning to Moropant, 'Please bring Annaji here. I want to nip this episode in the bud.'

The next morning, Annaji presented himself. Soyarabai was present when he came into Raje's chambers. He was barely able to make eye contact with Raje and kept his head low. Raje asked, his voice filled with anguish, 'Annaji, it seems you don't consider me someone you can confide in.'

Seeing Annaji silent, Raje asked, 'What I hear—is that true?'

Annaji nodded saying, 'Maharaj, after all I am a mere servant and Yuvraj is going to be my next master. You may punish him now but sooner or later, you will reconcile, leaving me in the lurch. The loss my relatives suffered may not be made good. It is best my people assume the girl to be dead and remain silent.'

'It is a grave error, Annaji! Sambhaji may be my son and the heir to the throne, but you shoulder the responsibility of the kingdom. In this matter too, you need to take ownership.' His face resolute and his fists clenched, Raje continued, as his voice took on a harsh tone, 'We shall decide the matter tomorrow in court.'

Soyarabai said, 'I don't think you should solve it that way.'

'Why not?'

'Because I believe nothing is going to come out of it. All it will attract is unwanted attention.'

'Rani saheb, if Yuvraj is proven guilty, he will not be spared.'

'Really?' Soyarabai laughed, her tone derisive. 'You will at best reprimand him.'

Raje closed his eyes for a moment. 'If he is found guilty, he receives the same punishment meant for any other person who commits the same crime. He will be blasted with a cannon.'

'Maharaj!' Annaji exclaimed, unable to even imagine the scene.

'You may go now,' Raje said, waving his hand. 'I don't want to hear anything else.'

Turning his back to the door, Raje stood, lost in anguish and turmoil. Putlabai, standing at the door and listening to the conversation, did not have the courage to talk to him and left, covering her mouth with the edge of her sari. Outside, the rains lashed with all their intensity, wreaking havoc on the fort.

Soyarabai was busy in her apartment when Rajaram came in and said, 'Aai saheb, may I go out to play with Dada Maharaj?'

'No. Please play in the courtyard here.'

A dejected Rajaram left the room.

'It is better to be childless than have such a son,' Soyarabai commented to no one in particular.

The maid in the room said, 'The calumny has spread all over the fort. No one feels like eating.'

'I have been wondering about it for a long while—ever since I saw him leaving the fort at odd hours.'

Noticing Putlabai enter, she became silent.

Putlabai wiped her tears and said, 'Elder Rani saheb, I need your help. We need to find a way to extinguish the flame before it engulfs all of us.'

'What do you want me to do?'

'Yuvraj will listen to you. I fall at your feet and take an oath in the name of your son!'

'Withdraw that oath! Aren't you ashamed to swear on the life of my son for the sake of that vagrant?'

Putlabai's anger erupted. 'I am not asking you for Yuvraj's sake but for the sake of our husband. He will not be able to bear this.'

'Such sympathy for your husband! It is good that you are childless or ...'

'Rani saheb!'

'Now, just shut your mouth and don't interfere in this matter.'

'I will leave then,' a dejected Putlabai said.

'I never called you here in the first place.'

Putlabai, affronted by Soyarabai's taunt, left the room. The maids, watching from the sides, giggled as Soyarabai said, 'What compassion she has for her husband and the wayward son!'

The taunt was not lost on Putlabai. She could not believe the words she had just heard. As night descended and lamps had been lit outside, Putlabai was able to breathe a little easy, having gotten a hold over her emotions. She said, as she saw Manohari enter to light the lamps, 'Manu, is Yuvraj in his chambers?'

'Yes.'

Gathering her courage, Putlabai reached Sambhaji's room. He sat on the floor, his head between his knees. Yesu stood nearby, sobbing.

Putlabai said, as she saw Sambhaji getting up on her arrival, 'Yuvraj, will you do what I ask you to?'

'Yes, Maa saheb.'

'Go to Raje's chamber right now and fall at his feet, begging for mercy.'

'Will he ...'

'Don't argue. Just do as I say.'

'I have no one to go to! I don't have a mother or a father and that Annaji, the cheat, has complained ...'

'Yuvraj! You have made a mistake and you want to accuse others of being cheats?'

Sambhaji could not hold back his tears as Putlabai ruffled his hair affectionately. She asked, 'So are you going to see him or not?'

'I will—if you come along.'

'Come on then.'

As they both reached Raje's chamber, they found the door closed. Mahadev, standing outside said, his head bowed, 'Maharaj has asked me not to allow anyone to enter his chambers.'

Putlabai, ignoring Mahadev, knocked twice. There was no response. As she turned, she found that Sambhaji had already left. Letting out a deep sigh, she turned to return to her chamber.

It was a dreary morning, with the sun hidden behind the clouds with a constant drizzle. There was an eerie silence in the fort. Moropant, Annaji, Niraji and others sat in the office.

Moropant said, 'Annaji, we cannot change what has happened. We must find a way to save Maharaj now.'

Annaji sat, letting out a deep sigh, 'Tell me, what I should do? Should I go and tell Raje that I willingly entrusted the girl to Yuvraj?'

'I am not saying that,' Moropant said, fighting emotions. 'We understand your dilemma but we know how much Maharaj loves Yuvraj. Raje holds women in high regard and will not hesitate to punish anyone who commits a crime against them. Now, Yuvraj is in the dock, and Raje will order the cannons to blast him away. We have to save Yuvraj to save Raje.'

'Let me see what I can do,' Annaji said, 'I will try my best, but I doubt he will listen to me.'

In his quarters, Raje was getting ready. Putting on his headgear, he adjusted his cummerbund as he tucked in his sword and dagger. Bowing to the idol in the room, he wiped his eyes and was about to leave when Mahadev came in and said, 'They are all assembled in the meeting room.'

'Tell them I am on my way.'

At that moment, Yesu walked in and, falling at Raje's feet, started crying. Raje stood with his eyes closed, as his face twisted in agony. He said, his voice almost a whisper, 'Yesu, get up! My misfortune is worse than yours. Yuvraj has committed a grave mistake and I cannot save him. I can only pray to Jagdamba to give me strength. You too should do that. I don't know what else to tell you.'

As he turned to leave, Yesu hugged his feet and said, 'Please bless me.'

Raje curled his fists as he tried to hold back his tears and said, 'I pray that Jagdamba gives you the strength to endure this pain. Now, please let me go!'

Without looking back, he left the room.

The meeting room was silent as he entered and sat down. No one dared speak. Putlabai and Soyarabai sat behind a split bamboo curtain. Raje said, 'Bring Yuvraj in.'

Sambhaji came in accompanied by Hambirrao Mohite. He stood there, his face pale.

'Annaji, please read out Yuvraj's crime.'

Annaji stepped forward. He said, 'If you will excuse me, Maharaj ... is it not too soon to ...'

'Annaji, you heard me! Read out the crime at once.'

Annaji was in a dilemma. He looked at Yuvraj.

'Speak, Annaji! You need not be worried about anyone's status here.'

'Maharaj,' Annaji began, licking his lips nervously, 'Yuvraj kidnapped a Brahmin girl and kept her in his custody at the Lingana Fort.'

Sambhaji cast a burning glance at Annaji but the next moment, he lowered his eyes.

'Sambhaji Raje, do you admit your offence?' Sambhaji looked at Raje but did not speak.

'Tell me if you kidnapped a married Brahmin girl?'

'I did.'

'And that you kept her in your custody at Lingana.'

'Yes.'

A wave of shock went over those in attendance. Raje said, struggling for words, 'Do you know the punishment such an offence carries?'

'Yes, I am aware.'

'Please tell me what it is.'

'The accused is thrown down from a precipice or is gunned down.'

'And despite knowing this you transgressed?'

Sambhaji looked at Raje. He said, 'Maharaj, if I am treated as a mere offender in your court, I have nothing else to say.'

'Shut up!' Raje shouted. 'I am not interested in listening to justifications for your sin.'

Hambirrao stepped forward with his hands folded and said, 'If I may, Maharaj, may I request you to allow Yuvraj to defend himself?'

The assembly was surprised at Hambirrao's courage.

Raje said, with a dejected smile, 'Yes, he may.'

Sambhaji said, 'I did keep the girl at Lingana but I did not kidnap or dishonour her. She came of her own volition. I deny these accusations.'

'What proof do you have?' Hambirrao asked.

'You can ask the girl herself.'

'Hambirrao, I don't know whether to cry or laugh at Yuvraj's recklessness.'

'Maharaj, we want to ensure that no one is denied justice. We will conduct a full enquiry and come back with a report.'

'All right. Annaji, please go to Lingana tomorrow and bring the girl to me. I will take a final decision after talking to her.'

The assembly heaved a sigh of relief seeing that the matter had been delayed.

Raje continued, as his gaze pierced Sambhaji, 'Whatever the case may be, Yuvraj has admitted that he kept a married woman in his custody—that is a crime. As punishment, I am ordering that his necklace of cowries representing Jagdamba be removed immediately. His sword, which is meant to protect the weaker sex, must be confiscated as well.'

Annaji stepped forward. For a brief moment, Sambhaji's fist curled tightly around the hilt of his sword. But the next moment, he accepted his punishment. The cowries scattered on the floor and his sword was flung to one side.

Raje said, 'Till the matter is decided, the doors of the fort will be closed to Yuvraj.'

Raje, in his state of turmoil, reached his quarters, followed by Putlabai.

She asked, as soon as they were inside the room, 'Are you satisfied now? That poor boy—he has neither a mother nor Maa saheb to help him. Where will he go now?'

'Rani saheb!' Raje exclaimed. 'You seem to be ignoring his crime.'

'Who has not committed a crime?'

'This one is unpardonable.'

'You too are guilty then.'

'Me?'

'Did he make any mistake when Maa saheb was around? There was no one to look after him after her death. Did anyone bother to ask where he was going or with whom? Of course he would slip!'

'Rani saheb!'

'What can a child do when his own father abandons him? I don't deny he made a mistake but rather than carry out an investigation in private, you berated him in public! He is the heir to the throne. How insulting this is for him!' She continued after a pause, 'But who am I to speak? I am not his real mother. Had the elder Rani saheb or Maa saheb been alive, they would have never allowed such a thing to happen. But you are a king with no value for relationships.'

'Enough, Rani saheb!' Raje erupted. 'Had someone else committed this crime, you would have nodded your head when I pronounced the sentence. But that was Shambhu. I have been selfish, looking at my blood ties, when I did not do justice to my duty today. But all I can do is nurse my wounds now. Don't blame me!'

Raje was drained and sat down. The whole episode had been intensely traumatic for him. When he looked up, his anger was gone. He said, his voice hollow, 'Putla, I know you came with Shambhu Raje to see me yesterday. It was the second time in my life that I have not opened the door and that previous time too I was fed up with my life. Yesterday was one such day.'

Putlabai started weeping silently. Putting his hand on her shoulder, Raje said, 'Have courage, Putla. Love cannot be demanded and has to be reciprocated. Our Yuvraj does not know this. I shudder to think of Yesu, poor girl. She must be devastated!'

It was late that afternoon, and Raje was resting in his room. The rain continued to pour relentlessly. Soyarabai and Rajaram walked into Raje's room.

Seeing Raje awake, Rajaram asked, 'I am told you are going to blast Dada Maharaj away with the cannons. Is that true?'

'Yes,' Raje said, trying to hold Rajaram's hand.

Rajaram brushed away Raje's hand and said, 'I don't want to talk to you. You are all evil.'

Raje said, looking at Soyarabai, 'That is true, my dear.'

At that moment Hambirrao walked in. Raje asked, 'Has the girl come?'

'No, Maharaj. There has been a tragedy. When she found out that we are coming to meet her at Lingana, she panicked and jumped to her death from the precipice.'

'Oh, no!' Raje exclaimed. He sat down and said, tears flowing down his cheeks, 'What a tragedy, Hambirrao! The only evidence that Shambhu had has been destroyed. See that Shambhu Raje cannot leave the fort and that he cannot meet me.'

By late evening, the rains lashing the fort seemed to have increased in intensity.

The rainy season was over but the suffocating atmosphere at the fort had not reduced. Sambhaji was seen walking alone to the temple and back but Raje sat alone in his room, feeling tired. He now focused his energies on his campaigns and directed his troops towards Satara.

Moropant and Hambirrao sat talking to Raje when Moropant expressed his desire to visit Kalyan and the surrounding areas.

'Of course. Whom do you intend to take with you? Hambirrao?'

'No, I had someone else in mind—Yuvraj.' Moropant watched Raje's expression closely.

Raje's anguish was evident. He said, 'Pant, you do realize I too am a father and am deeply troubled. The other day, I was visiting the temple and the moment Sambhaji, who happened to be there, saw me, he turned his face and walked away. Can you imagine how I felt? These days, even Yesu comes to my room, takes my blessings and walks away. She barely speaks to me.'

'That is why I want you to pardon him, Maharaj.'

'How can I do that? I have the kingdom to look after. Sambhaji may be my son but he is the future heir to the throne. My heart shudders knowing that.'

Moropant did not say anything.

Raje got up and said, putting his hand on Moropant's shoulder, 'I know how you feel. It is you and the council who have the right to rule the kingdom. From today, Sambhaji is free to go wherever he wishes. There are no restrictions on him. I am planning to leave for Satara soon.'

At that moment, Annaji came in.

Seeing his worried expression, Raje asked, 'Annaji, is there some bad news.'

'Yes, Maharaj. The temple at Pratapgad was hit by lightning.'

'The idol? I hope it ...'

'Don't worry, Maharaj, the idol is safe. A stable nearby, however, got burnt, killing a few horses and the elephant which used to carry the idol.'

'Oh, no!'

Raje sat down dejectedly. He said, 'Well, we are lucky the idol is unharmed. We will have the temple rebuilt soon.' There was a new energy in Raje's voice, taking Moropant and others by surprise.

'Annaji, we are surely getting old now. You remember, we fought our first battle when it was a new moon day. We did not care for the good or bad omens. A simple thing like a lightning falling on the temple scares us today. We must celebrate our victories and not get worried by such acts of nature.'

Everyone smiled, seeing Raje back to his old self.

'Come on, Annaji. Let us go the office. We need to discuss quite a few things before I leave for Satara.'

'What is the need for you to go to Satara?' Annaji asked.

'We must all be out on campaigns. We must secure Kolhapur, Panhala, Satara and Parli before we go. Also, the Janjira campaign is an important one. I feel Satara would be a good place to monitor the same from.'

The task at hand energized each of those present and they all faced their tasks with new enthusiasm.

Raje was getting ready for the Satara campaign when Soyarabai asked him 'When will you return?'

'By mid-summer.'

Rajaram came in and said, 'Dada Maharaj has sent his regards.'

'Really?'

'Yes. He said, "Give my regards to Aba saheb." I asked him to come but he was scared. He said, "Aba saheb may get angry." That is why I came alone to see you off.'

Raje's happiness was evident on his face. He said, 'Bal Raje, only elders who are immature need others to prostrate before them.'

Poor Rajaram did not understand anything and nodded his head.

Taking leave of the queens, Raje stepped out of his quarters. As the bugles announced the departure of the army, Raje rapidly descended from the fort.

After he left, Sambhaji stepped into Raje's room to find Manohari working there. She was busy cleaning the room. Seeing a spittoon below the bed, he asked, 'Why is this here?'

'He is not well these days. He had been coughing regularly.'

'He does not take care of his health, you know.'

Manohari was surprised at Sambhaji's criticism.

Sensing her reaction, he said, 'I don't mean to criticize him. It is just that he is not bothered about his own health while he is busy looking after the kingdom.'

Seeing Putlabai enter, Sambhaji bent low in mujra.

She said, 'Everyone is waiting in the office.'

Sambhaji said, 'I thought I could speak to someone but they are all busy—no one wants me.'

Tears welled up in Putlabai's eyes. She said, 'Don't speak like that ever again!'

Sambhaji was about to say something when she said, 'Now you carry on. They are waiting for you.'

In the office, Moropant, Anandrao, Balaji, Raghunathpant and some others had gathered. Sambhaji was surprised to see Soyarabai present. The sardars saluted Sambhaji when he entered.

Soyarabai said, smiling, 'Come in, Yuvraj. We all are waiting for you. You must be surprised to see me here.'

'Not exactly, Aai saheb.'

'I am not here because I like it. But I was told you don't step out of your quarters and there are things pending to be discussed.'

'Please tell me what they are.'

'I don't know whether to tell you or not.'

'I don't understand.'

'If something happens to you on your campaign, I will be held responsible.'

'That is why I am staying here.'

'Staying here does not change one's character. Can you tell me why the maids who had been appointed to look after the Jagdishwar temple have left?'

Sambhaji was stunned by the insults. The others stood mutely, their heads bowed. No one had liked the way Soyarabai had spoken but they did not dare to oppose her. On the other hand, Soyarabai seemed to be enjoying taunting Sambhaji.

However, she was stunned the next moment when Sambhaji said, 'Aai saheb, there seems to be a misunderstanding. The maids you are referring to did not leave because of me but because of Annaji.'

'What do you mean?'

'They were not given their dues; and hence, they left. You may ask Moropant or Annaji if you wish.' And then Sambhaji continued, his voice steady, 'And allow me to remind you, this is the state office. I am the prince and Aba saheb himself has entrusted me with the administrative matters of the state. I will not tolerate being insulted here.'

'Yuvraj!' Moropant shouted.

'Hold your tongue,' Sambhaji said, pointing a finger at him. 'As far as the maids are concerned, ask them to come back. I did not appoint them—it was Aba saheb who did.'

'Yuvraj!' Soyarabai tried, infuriated at the way Sambhaji had taken charge.

'Aai saheb, it is better that you leave without further ado. If Aba saheb comes to know of what happened here in his absence, I am sure he would not be happy.'

Soyarabai had no choice but to leave mutely.

Moropant left for a campaign to Akola while Sambhaji stayed back at the fort. One afternoon, he was leaving for darshan when Yesu said, 'Come back soon. The elder Rani saheb is leaving now.'

'Where is she going?'

'Satara. Don't you know? Aba saheb is not well.'

'I wish I had been told about it—not because I am the Yuvraj but his son,' Sambhaji said, feeling dejected.

He went to Soyarabai's chambers, and as he entered, she taunted, 'Oh, it seems the Yuvraj from the administration has had the time to come to my room.'

Ignoring her comment, Sambhaji asked, 'Is Aba saheb's health really bad?'

'Yes.'

'Shall I come along with you?'

'Only I have been asked to come.'

'I see!' Sambhaji said, and not knowing what else to say, he left the room.

That afternoon, he met the poet Kalash, who said, 'Don't worry. I know Raje's condition is difficult but he will survive. These are tough times and you need to be strong. The horoscope shows that he will be well soon.'

Sambhaji was hurt despite hearing good news. That evening he met Putlabai and said, 'I have to read horoscopes to know my father's condition now. No one seems worried about what I feel. I am being treated worse than the ordinary servant here.'

Putlabai wiped her tears saying, 'I too am staying back here at the fort. Do you realize how I feel?'

Sambhaji felt guilty for thinking of only himself. He said, sitting close to Putlabai, 'I apologize, Aai saheb. Please don't cry! I am sure Aba saheb will get well soon.'

Putla had found someone to talk to after a long time. She was able to express her emotions, and the tears flowed freely.

The fort at Satara was waking up to a wintry morning, and was enveloped in fog. As the sun rose, the fog slowly dissipated. Despite the morning activities, the fort was silent as no one dared to disturb Raje. Annaji and Yesaji were at the fort. Seeing Hambirrao climb up the steps to the office, they got up. He asked, 'How is Raje? Could he sleep last night?'

'Shivram Vaidya has given him some medicine. He is a little better now.'

'It has been eight days since he has eaten anything. We have tried everything,' Yesaji said. At that moment they saw Shivram Vaidya arriving. They enquired about Raje's health as he reached the office.

The old man, wiped the back of his palm across his luxuriant white whiskers and said, 'He has been better this morning but I need to observe for a few days more. I cannot say anything right now.'

That afternoon, Annaji went to meet Raje. Hearing his footsteps, Raje opened his eyes and raised his hand briefly to call him near. Annaji stepped forward, sitting next to him near the floor. Raje said, his voice barely audible, 'Bring Yuvraj here.'

'What is the hurry?' Annaji said, looking at Soyarabai. 'We will call him when you are better.'

Raje smiled dejectedly and said, waving his hand a little, 'Bring him. I want to see him. I know he is lonely, having been discarded by everyone. I cannot do that to him.'

'Ji, Maharaj,' Annaji nodded and left.

A messenger was dispatched to Raigad with an urgent message for Sambhaji.

That night, the cold was perceptible. Torches burnt at various places. Raje was sleeping soundly in his room when he woke up suddenly and said, 'Is someone there?'

One of the sardars stepped forward.

'Samarth is at the door. He has come to see me.'

The sardar was confused. He said, 'I will call the Vaidya right away.'

'No, not the Vaidya. I am fine now. Go to the door. Samarth is waiting there. Bring him here.'

The message was immediately conveyed to Annaji and Yesaji who were in the office. Annaji said, 'Is he delirious? There has been no message from the guards.'

Just then, a guard came running and announced, 'Swamiji is here!'

Annaji could not believe his ears. He looked up to see Kalyan Swami with a few of Samarth's disciples walking towards the office. Everyone got up to receive Kalyan Swami.

The guard said, 'I heard swamiji's voice and opened the gates to find him standing there.'

'I cannot believe it!' Yesaji exclaimed.

'Why are you surprised?' Kalyan said. 'If Samarth can know of Raje's illness without being informed, won't his disciple know of our arrival at the gate? Come on now! Let us not delay anymore. Please take us to Raje's chamber.'

As they entered Raje's room, Raje folded his hands on seeing Kalyan Swami, who raised his hands in blessing.

'Samarth has sent his blessings to you. When you have your guru's support, what harm can anyone else do?'

Raje's tears flowed down to the pillow. Kalyan Swami rubbed holy ash on Raje's forehead and gently caressed his hair.

Raje said, 'Swami, it is the devotee who should visit the guru but here, the guru is sending his blessings! I am truly blessed. Annaji, there is nothing to worry about now. I am already feeling much better.' Raje's words made everyone breathe easy.

'Bring me a little konji,' Kalyan Swami said.

'He vomits as soon as he eats anything.'

'It won't happen now. Please bring me what I have asked for,' Kalyan Swami repeated.

Kalyan Swami gently served Raje the konji and to everybody's surprise, he managed to drink the whole bowl. After a while, he was in a deep sleep. Everyone was convinced that Raje was truly on his way to recovery now.

The very next day Raje's appetite had improved, and as the days passed, he started to feel better. The tension at the fort reduced considerably. One day, Sambhaji reached the fort. He seemed tired after his journey. As he reached Raje's room, he hesitated to come in for a moment, realizing that Soyarabai and Annaji were inside. As he entered, he was shocked to see Raje, his cheeks sunk in, making his nose look sharper. He was propped up against a pillow and a shawl covered him till the neck.

As he saluted, Raje said, 'It's good to see you, Shambhu. You must be tired. Freshen up and we can then speak at leisure.'

As he left saluting once more, Raje said, 'Annaji, he may be reckless but he loves me. He does seem to realize his mistake.'

'What is the point in the arrow realizing its mistake after it has left the bowstring?' commented Soyarabai.

'Rani saheb, everyone errs but that does not mean we disown them.'

'But what I mean is ...'

'Leave that be for the moment, Rani saheb. I am tired and would like to rest for a while.'

Without waiting for her response, Raje closed his eyes, indicating that the others should leave.

Soon, Raje's strength recovered. One afternoon, as he was taking a nap with the shades drawn, he noticed someone standing near his feet. Barely recognizing the silhouette, he exclaimed, 'Shambhu, is that you?'

Sambhaji did not respond but, holding Raje's feet, he began to cry. Soon, his tears drenched Raje's feet.

'Get up, Shambhu! What happened?' When Sambhaji did not respond, Raje, caressing his head, said, 'You seem to be really worried about me. I am well now and am not someone who gives up easily. Don't worry.'

Sambhaji found his voice and said, 'Am I such a sinner?'

'Sinner? What are you blabbering about?'

'Everyone believes that ... that I have been trying to poison you!'

Raje was alert. He sensed that gossip has been making the rounds. He asked, 'Who says so?'

'There are murmurs all over the palace. I was asked not to meet you alone.'

Raje raised an eyebrow questioningly but he knew who might have said that. He said, 'Raje, you are the future king and have a huge responsibility on your shoulders. You must be careful. When people start playing a game of chess in the house, one needs to be constantly alert.'

'Aba saheb, I beg of you, please tell me that you don't doubt me. If you have even an iota of doubt, I will fling myself from the precipice right away.'

Raje hugged Sambhaji tightly and said, his voice choking, 'Shambhu, when will you understand that if you were dead, I would not want to live even for a day longer? What will I do if you are not here? Wipe those tears now. It does not become a Yuvraj to cry like this. Don't worry; I will make enquiries.'

As Sambhaji stood up to leave, Raje said, 'You know, Sambhaji, this illness has its own merits.'

Sambhaji stood without saying anything. Raje continued, 'It brought you to me. I have had the pleasure of hugging you after a long time.'

'Aba saheb!'

'Will you bring me the small silver box on the table near the mirror?'

Sambhaji brought Raje the box and opening it, Raje took out a necklace of cowries and said, 'Bend down.'

Sambhaji bent his neck. Raje put the necklace on him and said, 'Let bygones be bygones. It is too torturous to relive the past. Now take care of this ornament, the representation of the Goddess Jagdamba, with all your heart. If you wish me to live long, you must take care of yourself.'

Sambhaji prostrated himself, putting his head on Raje's feet.

The next afternoon, Sambhaji and Raje were chatting for a long time. As Sambhaji got up to leave, he found Soyarabai at the door. Saluting briefly to her, he stepped aside to let her in and left.

Soyarabai said, as she stepped in, 'What was Yuvraj doing here at this hour of the day?'

'Why? Is there a fixed time for him to meet me?'

'No, that's not what I meant. But was he not here yesterday too?'

'You seem to know everything!'

Soyarabai was taken aback. She had not expected Raje to question her. She said, 'How are you feeling now?'

'I'm fine. Actually, it's good that you are here—I wanted to share something with you.'

'What is it?'

'It might just be a rumour but I am told that someone is trying to poison me,' Raje said, observing Soyarabai carefully. 'And I am told that ... it could be ...'

'Who? Tell me,' Soyarabai said, eager to hear what Raje had heard.

'Sambhaji might have had a hand in it.'

'I was about to say that as well!' Soyarabai said.

Raje's tone changed suddenly. He said, 'Rani saheb, what makes you believe that he might have? I know how you feel about him—he is only your stepson. You seem to forget that Sai died and gave you the chance to become the senior queen but don't forget that he is the Yuvraj and you need to give him due respect. My spies bring me news from inside an enemy camp. How much time does it take, do you think, to find out what is being discussed in the four walls of this palace?'

'I don't know why you suspect me!' Soyarabai said, trying to defend herself, knowing well that she had been exposed.

'Listen to me!'

'If you don't trust me, then I might as well not stay here,' Soyarabai said, wiping her tears.

'Stop your crocodile tears now. And yes, you may leave for Raigad tomorrow. I don't need you here. Please leave!'

Soyarabai left the quarters but her body continued to shake for a long time.

More than a month had passed since his illness. Raje had recovered fully now and had started taking long walks at the fort. He had asked his sardars to assemble at the office to discuss campaigns which had been in abeyance for a while. Realizing that the people had been worried about his health, Raje dispatched letters to all the fort-keepers, informing them of his good health. Raje's mind was now focused on the long-pending Janjira campaign. The spies were now regularly bringing him news.

One winter morning, a messenger arrived. Reading the letter, Raje smiled and immediately called for a meeting in the office. Sambhaji came in and was relieved to see Raje smiling.

Raje said, 'Sambhaji, I have an important task for you.'

'Please command me.'

'You need to receive an important visitor. His name is Raghunathpant Hanumante.'

Sambhaji had never heard of this person and wondered who this man was and why he was important enough to warrant a personal reception.

Seeing his confusion, Raje said, 'Raghunathpant's father was an important officer in the elder Maharaj's office. After Maharaj saheb passed away, Raghunathpant spent some time with Ekoji, my stepbrother, in Thanjavur.'

'Has Kaka Maharaj sent a message?' Sambhaji asked.

'Your uncle is not that intimate with me, Yuvraj! Raghunathpant was not able to serve under Ekoji for long. When I found out that he was looking for a job, I immediately asked him to come here. After all, such men with experience will be an asset to us.'

Sambhaji descended from the fort the same day with a few horsemen to receive Raghunathpant. At the fort, Raje was waiting for the guest to arrive, much to the curiosity of others. On receiving the message that Sambhaji and Raghunathpant were expected to reach by evening, Raje asked for the durbar to be readied. Wearing his formal clothes, and at the sound of the ushers' announcement, Raje stepped into the durbar, walking slowly to the throne. Everyone bent in mujra.

Taking his seat, Raje asked Raghunathpant to sit down, indicating his place. Raghunath, despite his age, looked dashing in his pink turban decorated with pearls, his south Indian–style dhoti and angavastram casually thrown over his shoulders. His grey eyes sparkled, enhancing his fair skin. His broad forehead and sharp nose indicated a sharp brain to match. His penetrating gaze turned to Raje but he soon looked down, unable to meet Raje's eyes for too long.

Raje smiled and said, 'Welcome, Raghunathpant. I have eagerly been waiting for you.'

'This is my good fortune, Raje. All I ask for is you to bless me.'

After some informal discussions, Raje asked, 'Raghunath, I want you to stay here and work for me.'

'Nothing would please me more, Maharaj. Our family has traditionally been Mazumdars. I too would like to continue doing the same job here.'

Raje nodded saying, 'So be it! Our Mazumdar Niloji Sondev passed away recently, leaving his post vacant. I nominate you to the post with immediate effect.'

Raghunathpant bowed in mujra and left the durbar, happy to be in Shivaji Raje's service now.

Raghunath's arrival gave Raje access to news from the south, including information on Ekoji, who had, since the death of Shahaji, been depending on the locals. Raghunathpant had realized that Ekoji was not interested in the advice of elders like Raje and nor did he like being told about how Shivaji had managed to consolidate his kingdom. Ekoji believed that he needed to be loyal to the Badshah. Raghunathpant had thus found it wise to leave and seek an appointment in the durbar of Shivaji Raje.

Raje was troubled when he heard about the problems with Ekoji. He said, 'It is wrong of Ekoji to insult long-standing employees like you.'

'I tried my best and then decided to leave.'

'Was he willing to let you go?'

'As expected, he snubbed me but I decided to ignore it.'

'I have tried corresponding with Ekoji many times but he does not respond. He does not treat me as his family. I feel I should meet him once. I am, after all, his elder brother and I don't want to forget my responsibility.'

'What stops you then?'

'Nothing. I am just waiting for the right opportunity.'

'It will present itself. Qutb Shah has two capable sardars, Madanna and Akkanna. They are well inclined towards us. I am sure we can try and win Qutb Shah's favour. The elder Maharaj would have been proud to see the way you have expanded your kingdom but the threat of the Mughals in the north remains a big one. It is critical for those in the south to come together. Adil Shah has already realized this and Qutb Shah too would be happy to collaborate. I am sure you can convince Ekoji as well. Your dream of removing the Mughal threat forever and freeing the Kashi Vishwanath Temple from the Muslims will be realized as well.'

'How did you know about that?'

'Maharaj, anyone who knows you would be aware!'

'I have left my dream to the blessings and wishes of Jagdamba.'

That night Raje could not sleep—the prospect of fulfilling his dream was too exciting.

Raje was keeping a close watch on Bijapur where the new Wazir, Bahlol Khan, with the support of the Pathans, was at loggerheads with the previous Wazir, Khavas Khan. Raje decided to move base to Panhala to be in a position to act quickly in case the situation so demanded.

Seeing a couple of sanyasis one day, he wondered if Samarth has sent a message. He asked the office manager, 'Has there been any news from Samarth of late?'

'Yes. Quite surprisingly, he has asked us not to send any material or grains.'

'Why would he say that? I hope we have not offended him in any way,' Raje mused as he walked towards his quarters. The next day, a messenger rode to Chaphal, where Samarth was residing at the moment. A week later, Raje received the message that Diwakar Gosavi was at the gates. Soon, he was ushered in.

Raje asked, eager to know about Samarth, 'How is he?'

Gosavi had read Raje's mind and said, 'Samarth loves you like no one else. There is not a single day that he does not remember or speak about you. You are his most favoured devotee.'

Raje was overwhelmed hearing this. He said, 'I have a request. Could Samarth move from Shivthar cave to either Mahipatgad or Parli? I have a reason to make this request—we may have conquered those places but not the hearts of its people. I want them to know our dream of creating a Swaraj. If Samarth resides there, people would believe him. Also, it would be much easier for me to call upon him anytime.'

'I am sure Samarth will agree to your request.'

A visibly relieved Raje said, 'I shall issue orders to have the place of his choice ready.'

After Gosavi left, Raje gave instructions for the strengthening of the fort at Panhala. In the meanwhile, he received the good news that his men had captured lakhs of hons from the merchants and the English at Athani. The English, who had assumed that Raje had died at Satara, were dismayed by their loss and the knowledge that Raje was back in business.

Raje stayed at Panhala till late summer and his health had improved considerably. Sambhaji was busy in a campaign in a Bijapur territory with Dattajipant.

The Mughals, like Raje, were keeping a watchful eye on the fights in the Bijapur court and were waiting for an opportune moment. The Mughal sardar Bahadur Khan decided to take on the Adil Shahi troops in order to please Aurangzeb. On knowing that Bahadur Khan was advancing towards Bijapur, Bahlol Khan, already demoralized by the defeat suffered at the hands of Khavas Khan earlier, made an urgent plea to Raje for help. Raje's troops managed to ward off Bahadur Khan's attack and Bijapur was saved from the clutches of the Mughals. A satisfied Raje decided to return to Raigad.

As he was preparing to leave, Hambirrao came to meet him, looking crestfallen.

Raje asked, 'What is the matter?'

'Our troops, while returning from Athani, attacked the fort at Belgaum, which was being guarded by the Adil Shahi fort-keeper Anu Khan. Under the pretext of handing over the fort to our troops against a payment of forty thousand hons, he opened the doors of the fort and as our troops entered, his men attacked us. We lost nearly five hundred of our men.'

Raje was silent for a while, dumbfounded by the news, and then he laughed out loud. The laughter sounded eerie in the silence of the court as the others stood silently, unable to understand Raje's reaction. He said, 'It seems we found our match. It is a lesson learnt at great cost. We cannot afford to trust anyone implicitly again.'

The agony crossed Raje's face again as he said, his voice low and filled with anguish, 'Five hundred men! What a way to learn a lesson. Oh Jagdamba!'

Raje returned to Raigad, and the entire fort was there to welcome him. But Sambhaji and Rajaram were conspicuous by their absence. Raje was surprised not to see them and asked Annaji, 'Has Yuvraj returned? Where is he?'

'He must be in his quarters.'

After darshan at the temple, Raje came to Putlabai's quarters and asked, as he handed over his headgear and sword to her, 'How are you?'

'I must ask about your health instead—I had no idea. I found out when Shambhu told me about it.'

'How didn't you hear about it?'

Putlabai shook her head. Raje asked, 'Where is the elder queen?'

'She must be in her quarters?'

'And Rajaram?'

'Him too, I suppose.'

'What about Yuvraj?'

'I suppose he too must be in his quarters.'

'I don't understand, Putla. You don't actually know or are you testing me?'

'No one talks to me. I have no idea.'

Raje said, 'Wah! What a reception! Yuvraj does not come to receive me and no one knows anything! I am going to the elder queen's residence. Are you coming?'

Putlabai looked at the floor. Raje did not wait for her answer and left.

Reaching Soyarabai's quarters, he was received by Rajaram. Raje asked, 'Why didn't you come to receive me?'

'I did not know you had arrived.'

Raje said, patting Rajaram's head, 'My son, lies do not become you. Everyone knows when I reach the fort—the trumpets and horns make enough noise.'

Soyarabai came in and Raje asked, 'I wish you had sent Rajaram to receive me.'

'It would not have made any difference.'

'Why are you so upset? What has happened?' Before she could answer, Raje said, looking at Rajaram, 'Bal Raje, will you bring me some water?'

The maid came in with a tumbler and as Raje was about to drink, Soyarabai said, 'Please don't!'

'Why?' Raje asked, his hand stopped in mid-air.

'Who knows what it may contain?'

Raje desperately tried to control his anger. He said, 'Rani saheb, I swear on Jagdamba that I will never step into your quarters again!'

Dropping the tumbler to the floor, he stormed away. Soyarabai did not imagine that her words would have such an effect. She was dumbfounded as she hugged Rajaram.

Sambhaji was waiting for Raje as he entered Sambhaji's chambers. As he stepped forward to touch his feet, Raje asked, 'Where were you, Yuvraj? I did not see you when I entered the fort.'

'I was in my chamber.'

'Were you not aware of my arrival?'

'Yes, I was.'

'Then why didn't you come to receive me?'

'I thought I would meet you later.'

'I see. How was your campaign?'

'It went well. I have deposited the loot in the royal treasury.'

'I did not ask about that. Don't you visit the office these days?'

'No, no one is bothered about me, and I don't feel like going there.'

'Yuvraj, you don't go to the office because of your likes and dislikes. I have struggled hard to raise this kingdom. Also, I am told you have barred Rajaram from visiting you—why is that?'

'To tell you the truth, Aba saheb ...'

'I am waiting to hear the truth.'

'He is punished if he visits me, and so I thought it is best to forbid him instead.'

Sambhaji had tears in his eyes. Raje said, putting his hand on his shoulders, 'Shambhu, one cannot run a kingdom emotionally. Let us go to the office. Everyone is waiting for us.'

In the office, the sardars were waiting. Raje said, after receiving updates from everyone, 'I intend to try for an accord with the Mughals.'

'With the Mughals? Why?' Annaji asked.

'We need some stability. Nirajipant, meet Bahadur Khan, who, I am sure, must be a little upset over our support to the Adil Shahi kingdom. But he is a greedy fellow. Bribe him and make him believe that you are keen to work under the Mughals. Aurangzeb is busy in the Kabul and Kandahar region right now, trying to quell the rebellion there. By the time he returns, we will buy a lot of time. Moropant, our other enemy is Siddi, who is not likely to be quiet. We need to quash him once and for all.'

'Ji,' Moropant nodded.

After further discussions, Raje stepped out of the office, accompanied by Raghunathpant. As he moved towards the temple for darshan, the clouds had gathered and it was getting dark. Soon a sheet of rain covered the fort, drenching everything. After a downpour, the sun peeped through the cloud cover, and the fort shone in the brightness of the evening sun. The sweet smell of the rain mixed with dust spread all over.

Raje said, looking at the clouds, 'Look at the clouds. They carry all the water they can and then pour it over the thirsty earth. They give away whatever they have. All they can do is get scattered by the wind once they have done their job.'

Raje moved towards his quarters and was surprised to see Soyarabai there, waiting for him. She said, as she wiped her tears away hurriedly, 'I am sorry. I spoke in haste ...'

'You don't need to ask for pardon. I understand.'

'You said you would not come to ...'

'That is right. But you can always visit me here, isn't it?'

'I feel ...'

'Rani saheb, I am tired and would like to sleep now.'

Raje entered his room, leaving Soyarabai standing outside. She hesitated for a moment and then turned to leave. When Mahadev came in to extinguish the lamps, Raje was asleep.

The monsoons were in full swing now. Normally, the troops would be permitted to go home at this time but Raje did not permit the leave. Many were busy with Moropant in Janjira while Nirajipant had gone to Aurangabad to meet Bahadur Khan. News would come in regularly as Raje was apprised of the situation all around.

Raje had just finished his morning chores when he saw Manohari step in.

'Manu, I have not seen you for the last two days. Where have you been?'

'I was in Pachad.'

'Pachad? What for?'

'She was sent to get the work done for Maa saheb's shradh puja,' Soyarabai answered, stepping into the room.

'Oh! It has been two years since Maa saheb left us. How time flies! There is not a single day that I don't think of her. Her absence makes such a big difference here!'

Raje brushed away his memories and asked, 'So, is everything in order?'

'I have asked Annaji to supervise and ensure that everything is taken care of.'

Raje smiled dejectedly and said, 'Rani saheb, what we do after a person is gone is of no relevance.'

'Are you saying the rituals have no meaning?'

'I don't mean that. It is not about remembering her for just one day in a year and following the rituals. It is about remembering her every day. Rani saheb, I wish you would do that—for the good of all of us.'

Mahadev came in to announce the arrival of Balaji.

'So soon? Anyway, send him in.'

Soyarabai left and Balaji stepped in.

'What is the news, Balaji?'

'One of the Mughal sardars, Mohammad Quli Khan wants to meet you.'

'Quli Khan?' Raje asked. He was lost in thought for a while, trying to recall where he had heard his name. Suddenly he smiled and said, 'Oh! Call him to the office and ask the others to assemble.'

'And Balaji,' Raje continued, 'ensure that he does not carry any arms when he meets me.'

'Ji.'

'Who are with him?'

'Four or five cavalrymen and a couple of servants.'

'You may go now.'

A chess board was laid out near the bed. Raje looked at the board and said to himself, 'Sometimes the foot soldier, who makes the first move, does not know that he sacrificed himself to save the king.' He smiled at the prospect of meeting Quli Khan that evening.

As Raje took his place on the throne, he indicated that Quli Khan be sent in. All the sardars including Sambhaji were present in the court, eagerly waiting for the meeting. As soon as the Mughal sardar entered, he bent in a perfunctory mujra. Ignoring the same Raje said, 'Mohammad Quli Khan?'

'Ji, Maharaj.'

'It seems you have forgotten how to salute.'

The Mughal sardar was in tears. He forgot that he was dressed in a Mughal sardar's uniform, complete with the kimosh, the Mughal-style cap, long kurta, churidar and mojadis.

Before he could speak, Raje said, 'You seem to have forgotten that I am a panch-hazari Mansabdar in the court of Badshah Aurangzeb.'

'I beg your pardon, Maharaj.'

'My pardon? Do you realize the kind of anguish I feel when I see you like this? Netaji, you were once my commander-in-chief! Your valour was an example to be emulated by others. You were considered another Shivaji. And now you stand here as Mohammad Quli Khan ...'

'I made a mistake, Maharaj!' Netaji's voice quivered.

Those in the assembly were taken aback. No one had realized that it was Netaji Palkar!

'The moment you saw that we were in trouble, you joined Adil Shah for a mansab of a mere three thousand! And the day Mirza Raja offered you a mansab of five thousand, you shifted your loyalties to the Mughals? And what did they offer to make you change your religion?'

Each word pierced Netaji like a sharp arrow. He finally managed to look up and said, 'Maharaj, I did not do this out of choice. I was forced into it. I tried escaping thrice but was caught. The moment I got the chance, I came to meet you!'

'Who are you trying to deceive, Netaji? I know how to judge men. Are you telling me that in the last nine years, you did not have a chance to escape? Not only did you convert to Islam, you forced your wife and children to adopt the religion, didn't you?'

Netaji's head was bowed. Raje grew angrier with each passing moment. He said, 'Aurangzeb has done you a favour—you are a blot on the Hindu religion.'

Netaji rushed and fell at Raje's feet. 'Please help me, Raje! Please, as a Chhatrapati, allow me to be at your feet. Please take me back, Raje!'

'Get up, Netaji. What is the use of these tears now? I have been given this position by the Lord to create the Swaraj in his name. How can I help someone who has no loyalties, who does not live up to his word and has no faith in his own religion? It would have been better had we met in the battlefield. I am sorry, Netaji, but we don't have place for a traitor here.'

Raje walked out of the room without looking back. Sambhaji rushed to console Netaji, who could not stop his tears and was sobbing like a child.

Putlabai wiped her tears and told Sambhaji, 'Bring Netaji Kaka to your room.'

'Ji,' Sambhaji nodded.

Sambhaji and Netaji conferred for a long time. They stepped out only when the lights were being lit.

That night, Putlabai came to Raje's room. Looking at her grim face, Raje asked, 'What is the matter?'

'Will you give me something?'

'No, I won't. I know you have come here on Netaji's behalf.'

'Whatever said and done, he is my uncle. If you could take him back and ...'

'No, Rani saheb. His crime is too severe to be excused. Please don't plead with me.'

Putlabai was silent for a while. As she turned to go, Raje asked, 'Are you leaving now?'

'Yes. It is getting late.'

'Are you angry with me?'

'Me?' Putlabai said, forcing a smile. 'What right do I have to be angry?'

'What are you talking about?'

'Well, the elder Rani saheb's brother, Bajaji, converted to Islam but he was given refuge at your feet. Netaji has committed the same crime but I should have known my status before pleading with you.'

'Putla,' Raje muttered, 'Wait! Don't go. I wish you would understand. Bajaji was an Adil Shahi sardar and thus was loyal to them. But Netaji? He was one of us! My commander-in-chief! I loved him with all my heart. Yet, he chose to break all bonds. I felt bad when he left us but when I came to know that he had converted to Islam I was really shattered. I have suffered a lot on his account, Rani saheb!'

'I have nothing left to say. I will go now.'

'Wait! Don't go like this. I will take him back.'

'Really?'

'I promise you. For a moment, I forgot that whatever said and done, he is still one of us. It is right to pardon a family member, after all!'

'Are you saying this to please me?'

'There is nothing wrong in doing that, is there? It is your right to expect it from me, Putla.'

'Shall I tell Saguna?'

'Please do so. Tell her Netaji would be welcomed back soon.'

Putlabai's heart brimmed with joy as she rushed to share the good news.

After completing the rituals for Jijabai's ceremony, Raje returned to the fort and brought Netaji back into the Hindu fold following all the necessary rites for atonement. A feast was organized in his honour after a few days. Raje sat next to Netaji, who felt as if he had been reborn. Before the food was served, Netaji stood up and put his head on Raje's feet. His tears drenched Raje's feet.

Raje said, 'Netaji, please get up. Don't think of the past now. Let us look ahead.'

'Raje, I have one last wish. You have taken me back, and I wish to resume my duties.'

Raje looked at Netaji for a long moment. He said, 'That is not possible and I want you not to insist. Feel blessed and devote yourself to the cause of the Swaraj. I am sure you will get what you want soon. I recognize deeds more than blood and your loyalty would not go unrewarded.'

Netaji did not dare to utter another word.

The monsoon was still raging as politics picked up speed. With the help of Madanna from Golconda, Raje was able to sign a treaty with the Adil Shahi regime. The River Krishna was set as a boundary between the two kingdoms. As per the treaty, Raje was to pay a sum of three lakhs and another tribute worth a lakh.

Annaji raised his doubts and said, 'Do you think the treaty will last?'

'You don't need to be an astrologer to predict that it won't. I just need it to last till I return from the campaign in Karnatak.'

With a view to sign a similar treaty with the Mughals, Raje sent Nirajipant to Aurangabad. Raje had given him a free hand to decide the terms with Bahadur Khan at his camp near Pedgaon. While the negotiations were on, Raje received news that Samarth Ramdas Swami had agreed to move to Parli. Annaji came in and said, 'We just got the news from the fort-keeper at Parli. As per your instructions, the fort has been made ready. Parli is lucky. Now it is the abode of saints.'

'I agree. Rename Parli Sajjangad—the abode sanctified by the presence of Samarth.'

As the rains ended, Raje's plans for further campaigns gained momentum and he would spend a lot of his time in discussion with his council of ministers. Raje decided to leave for his next campaign on the day of Dussehra.

It was likely that Raje would be out for months and everyone was anxious to know who would manage the administrative affairs in his absence. Soyarabai had been spending a lot of time taking interest in the administrative matters in Raje's absence. One morning, Raje reached the court. The ministers had already taken their place. Sambhaji too was present. While discussing various plans, one of the ministers asked, 'Who will be here at the fort?'

'Why, Moropant is here. And Yuvraj himself. He is grown up enough now to manage the affairs.'

Sambhaji said, 'I will do my best to manage till you return, Aba saheb.'

Annaji, Moropant and a few others exchanged discreet glances at each other. Sambhaji, aware of this, was smiling.

Raje asked, noticing the uncomfortable silence, 'Please speak your mind, Annaji.'

'I will be blunt but ...'

'I want my council to be honest with me.'

'If Yuvraj is going to manage the affairs of the state in your absence, then I would like to stay home till you return.'

Raje was upset. Sambhaji was red with anger. Except for Hambirrao, all the others did not dare to look up. Hambirrao said, 'Annaji, you cannot insult Yuvraj like this.'

Raje was unperturbed. He said, 'Annaji, Yuvraj is an adult now. He needs to gain experience to be able to manage the kingdom independently in the future.'

'That is fine, provided he does not interfere in the decisions of the council.'

Sambhaji stood up and glared at Annaji, unmindful of Raje's presence, and said, 'Annaji, if you need more clerks and yes-men in your office, I am willing to provide them.'

'Yuvraj!' Raje exclaimed.

'Aba saheb!' Sambhaji continued resolutely, 'I will not tolerate such impudence. And if he stays here, then I may as well leave the fort and take refuge elsewhere.'

'Sambhaji, please control yourself,' Raje urged. 'You are the Yuvraj. How can you talk of taking refuge elsewhere? The Yuvraj and the council of ministers need to work in harmony.'

'Aba saheb, make Annaji understand this.'

'Yuvraj,' Annaji said humbly, 'I want you to understand why I am saying this. I want ...'

'Enough, Annaji! I don't want to hear another word.'

Saluting Raje hurriedly, he stormed out of the office. Those in the court were dumbfounded. Raje took a deep breath and said, 'Annaji, ever since my coronation, I have been taking decisions in consultation with the council. I want to know whether this decision too is your own or a joint one.'

'It is a joint decision, Maharaj.'

Raje glanced at the ministers. They continued to look down, avoiding his gaze.

Hambirrao said, 'I am the commander-in-chief. I too am part of the council but I am not in favour.'

Annaji said, 'Hambirrao, your loyalty is understandable. But surely you realize that managing the affairs of the state is quite different from running a campaign with troops?'

Raje asked, 'Annaji, what is the reason for the rift between Yuvraj and yourself?'

'There is no rift, Raje. It is a question of responsibility. We are being threatened by Siddi on one side and we have enemies like the Adil Shahi troops and Mughals on the other. In case of an emergency, we would need to take quick decisions.'

'Yuvraj can! He is not a child now.'

'There is a difference in not being a child and being a mature adult. We cannot afford to have decisions being taken emotionally. Let me ask you, Raje—if a calamity befalls us, who is going to be held responsible for the failure?'

'I understand, Annaji. Let me think this over.'

Raje left the office but he was disturbed throughout the day, and kept thinking about the matter.

That evening, as Sambhaji sat talking with Kalash, he said, 'I wonder what harm I have done to the council for them to be so against me?'

'A spark can burn a haystack into ashes and can ignite coal to flames. Instead of healing the minds of those whose feelings you have hurt, you taunted them.'

'I don't care. Tell me what I should do now.'

'Maharaj has already accepted the decision made by the council. It is best for you to be away for the next two years, which are full of sorrow for you.'

'My life has been a sorrow since I was born.'

As he turned to go, Kalash said, 'Be careful and don't say something in haste. Maharaj has chosen an auspicious day to leave for his campaign. Don't disappoint him.'

Sambhaji's speculation was right. As soon as he reached his quarters, he received the message that Raje had summoned him. He reached Raje's quarters.

'Come in, Shambhu. I was waiting for you,' Raje said as Sambhaji stepped in.

'Will you hear me out if I say something, Shambhu?' Raje continued, seeing Sambhaji silent.

'You know I will never disobey you.'

'I wish to leave with peace of mind.'

'Do you want me to kowtow to that insolent lot of ministers?'

'Yuvraj!' Raje raised his voice. The next moment he said, his voice low, 'Don't be so angry!'

'I did not flare up, Aba saheb.'

Raje smiled. 'I was not born a prince like you. When I came to Pune, holding Jijabai's hand, it was a barren piece of land. I was taunted as being a Raje only in name. I learnt patience at the feet of Dadoji and Maa saheb, befriending people from all castes. By the grace of Jagdamba, I became a king and organized people together. Can you imagine people like Annaji and Moropant leaving no stone unturned to help me set up the Swaraj? You may have been born a prince and, hence, demand your rights. But the men who fought for me and helped fulfil my dream—don't they deserve to be treated with respect?'

'Does that mean I have no role to play?'

'Did I say that? But you must understand that a king is not a master. He is nothing without his subjects—men, commander and officials. Loyalty is earned and not demanded.'

'I can prove my capability if you give me the chance.'

'I know. I have a plan for you. Select your own men, and don't bother about the expenses. Run the province of Prabhavali independently.'

'I shall!' Sambhaji said, excitedly. 'Please ensure that the ministers do not dabble in the affairs there.'

'You have my word on that.'

A satisfied Sambhaji left Raje's chamber and Raje felt a little better.

On the day of Dussehra Raje decided to march from Raigad. After praying at the temple, accompanied by Soyarabai, Putlabai, Sakwarbai, Lakshmibai, Sagunabai and Gunwantabai, Raje and Sambhaji stepped out.

Raje said, looking at Soyarabai, 'Yuvraj too is going out on an important task. Wish him good luck.'

Annaji and others came to see Raje off. The territory north of Raigad was being managed by Moropant while Annaji had been given the task of looking at the southern territory. The region between Panhala and Karnatak was to be under Dattaji Trayambak. Raje had left Raigad under the command of Ravji Somnath.

Descending from the fort, Raje paid his respects at Jijabai's memorial at Pachad. Hambirraro was waiting outside with Raje's favourite white steed, Vijay. Raje put his hand on the saddle and for a brief moment closed his eyes. Mounting the horse, to the sound of trumpets and horns, Raje raised his hands and said, 'Jai Bhawani!'

He spurred the horse on, and Sambhaji followed close behind. Putlabai and Manohari, standing at the ramparts, watched as the horses galloped away and disappeared from view in no time. Only a curved line of dust, indicating the direction in which they had gone, was visible.

BOOK TEN

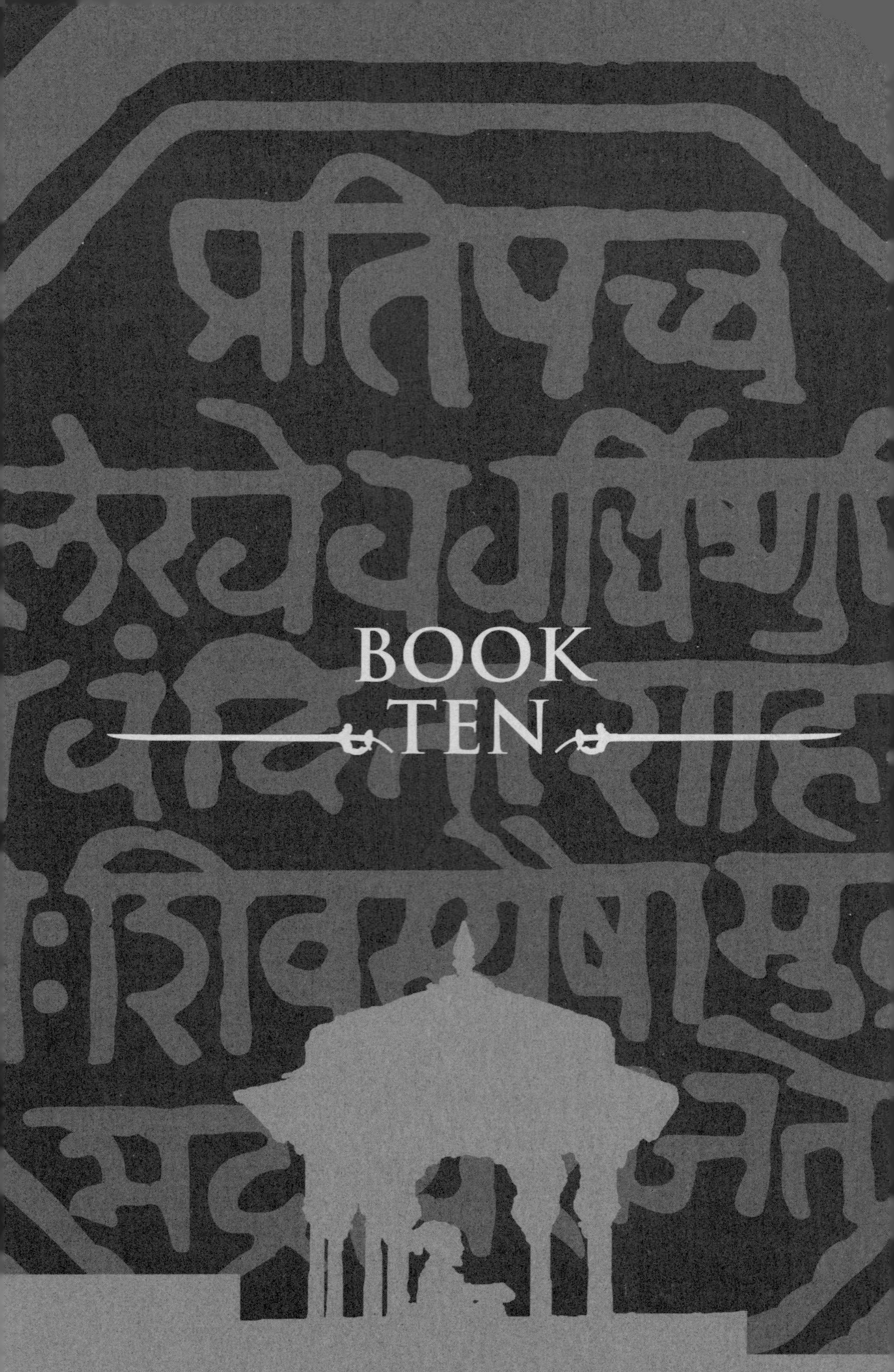

Raje reached Chiplun with Sambhaji. After darshan at the Bhargava Temple there, they reached Shringarpur as planned. The haveli had been readied, whitewashed and decorated for Sambhaji's stay. It was in the middle of dense woods. Looking at the sylvan beauty all around, Raje said, 'Yuvraj, I am sure you will love this place. You can fulfil your desire to hunt here.'

After a moment, he continued, 'But I urge you to be careful. One needs to follow decorum even on a hunting expedition. Remember—even Sita crossed the line and fell prey to Ravana.'

In a few days, Raje had ensured that Sambhaji had organized himself well and that the office was equipped to handle the administration. The day for Raje to leave arrived. He said, as he blessed Yesu, 'I am leaving now. The Subha of Prabhavali will be under Sambhaji's care but I am leaving him under your supervision! I am confident you can manage him.'

'I am a mere woman. What can I do?'

'Yesu, don't underestimate the role of a wife in managing her husband.' As he turned to leave, he remembered something and said, 'Shringarpur is your father's home. I was hoping to meet Pilajirao before leaving ...'

At that moment, a servant brought the news of Pilaji's arrival.

'Wah, it seems Shirke sardar has come.'

As Pilaji entered, he bent low in salute to Raje. Holding his hand, Raje said, 'Pilajirao, you are my son's father-in-law. Don't embarrass me!'

'That is not the only relation we have,' Pilaji said, as he brushed his whiskers with the back of his fist. 'You are, after all, Chhatrapati! Any Maratha would be proud and happy to salute you.'

'That is fine in the court, Pilaji. But you are in Yesu's home right now.' Changing the topic, Raje continued, 'Now your son-in-law is the Subedar of Prabhavali. You must take care of him.'

'You may rest assured, Maharaj. My son-in-law is the Subedar now but what about me?'

Raje raised an eyebrow questioningly. Pilaji elaborated, 'You had promised me something during Yesubai's marriage, remember?'

Raje smiled. 'I had promised you your own subedari when I have a grandchild. I am waiting to fulfil my promise.'

Yesu blushed and ran out of the room while Sambhaji stood there awkwardly, not knowing how to react. The room was filled with Pilaji's and Raje's laughter.

Raje left soon after, and unbeknownst to Sambhaji, he had left men and spies there to ensure that Sambhaji was well protected. He soon reached Panhala, where he was joined by more troops. He divided the army into two parts. One group, under the charge of Hambirrao, was sent to Bijapur while the rest remained with Raje and marched towards Bhaganagar via Satara. Hambirrao kept the Adil Shahi troops busy, looting and creating havoc, while Raje marched onto Bhaganagar unchallenged.

On this march, Raje had taken also elephants, shamianas, tents and camels apart from his regular cavalry—it was a royal procession. As they camped for the night, Raje was restless. North of the River Tungabhadra was the fort of Koppal, popularly called the doorway to the south. Two Pathan brothers, Hussain Khan Miyana and Abdul Rahim Miyana, were in charge of the fort. Raje had asked Hambirrao to capture the fort but he had not received any news yet, which was making him restless.

A few days later, a messenger arrived. He was escorted to Raje's tent immediately.

'What is the news?' Raje asked, eagerly.

'Hambirrao managed to defeat the Pathans. Hearing that Hambirrao was marching on them, Hussain Khan attacked our troops at Yelburga in Gagad province. We managed to capture two thousand horses, a dozen elephants, many camels and a lot of jewellery and precious items. Hambirrao is on his way here.'

Raje was delighted to hear the outcome of Hambirrao's campaign. However, seeing that Balaji was looking crestfallen, Raje asked, 'Balaji, you don't seem to be happy. What is the matter?'

'We lost Nagoji Jedhe in the battle.'

Raje was shocked. Dhanaji and Nagoji were two young soldiers who had been in the battle with Sarjerao Jedhe, their father. Balaji continued, 'When Hussain Khan was surrounded, he managed to escape on his elephant. Nagoji's spear found its mark, piercing the elephant's temple, but Hussain Khan's arrow hit Nagoji right on the forehead. Sarjerao was close by and he pulled the arrow out but by then, it was too late!'

'What a tragedy!' Raje exclaimed.

'Seeing Nagoji dead, Dhanaji attacked Hussain Khan's elephant again and pulled Hussain down, killing him the next instant.'

That evening, Hambirrao came to Raje and said, 'Sarjerao Jedhe and Dhanaji are here to pay their respects.'

Raje stood up and asked, 'What? Has Sarjerao not gone to his village?'

'No. Nagoji was cremated on the battlefield itself. Nagoji's wife, Godubai, committed sati at her village. I requested Sarjerao to go to his village but he did not agree. He said, "No Jedhe has ever returned from a battlefield till the job is done."'

'Call him in,' Raje said.

Raje was waiting as Jedhe entered, walking with his spine straight. He was in his battle uniform, with a sword at his waist and a shield on his back. He came in brushing his whiskers with the back of his wrist. But the moment he saw Raje, he could not control himself and looked at the ground.

Raje rushed to meet Sarjerao and hugged him tightly. When they separated, both had tears in their eyes. Raje held his hand and made him sit on the bed. Seeing him hesitate, Raje said, 'Sarjerao, please don't hesitate. Your son sacrificed his life and your daughter-in-law has committed sati. And yet, you are fulfilling your duty. My head is bowed with respect at your loyalty and devotion.'

'Raje, don't say that! My son has earned his name, sacrificing his life for our cause. He got an opportunity ahead of his father!'

'Sarjerao, how do I repay such loyalties? Balaji, these men are more precious than their weight in gold! As soon as we return to Raigad, issue an order to send a seer of gold every year to the Jedhe family. I shall personally go to your village to console Nagoji's mother.'

Raje then felicitated Dhanaji for his valour and expressed his gratitude.

With Hambirrao's troops joining in, the cantonment swelled to nearly thirty thousand cavalry and twenty thousand foot soldiers. As they entered Bhaganagar, Raje issued strict instructions to all the troops that they were to buy anything they needed with their own money and not indulge in looting. Any soldier found violating the order was to be beheaded, ensuring that no one else would dare disobey.

Qutb Shah was a worried man despite Raje's emissary, Prahlad Niraji, having taken an oath about Raje's intention not to do any harm. When he got the news that Raje had not indulged in any looting, he breathed a little easier. He decided to set up a meeting with Raje. When Raje received the message, he replied with another message: 'Please don't take the trouble. You are elder to me. I shall make myself available at your palace.'

Qutb Shah was happy to read this message, and he asked his Wazirs, Madanna and Akkanna, to meet Raje in his place.

Raje said, 'Hambirrao, you go and meet them first.'

Soon, Raje could see the Qutb Shahi troops approaching the cantonment, and they were nearly thousand-odd in strength. Madanna, wearing a south Indian–style turban and a silk kurta over a dhoti, dismounted from his horse. His forehead was smeared with ash in a horizontal fashion. His eyes, shining in a radiant face, spoke of intelligence. He said, putting his right hand on his chest, 'Victory to Chhatrapati Shivaji! Our Alampanah is delighted that you have come into our territory. This land, known to defeat its enemies, prides itself on its hospitality towards its friends. We welcome you!'

Raje stepped forward and, holding Madanna's hand, said, 'We have corresponded earlier—it is a pleasure to meet you.'

Raje then removed his gold wristlet and slipped it on to Madanna's wrist. 'Let this be the token of our friendship.'

Madanna was overwhelmed. He introduced the sardars who had accompanied him and then they all moved towards Bhaganagar. Traversing the mountainous region and through narrow gullies between rocky cliffs, they soon reached the outskirts of the town where a huge camp had been made ready for Raje's troops. In the centre of the camp was a specially erected tent with a saffron flag fluttering in the wind, indicating Raje's personal accommodation.

As they reached the camp, it was evident to everyone that special care had been taken to lay the roads and create a clean, beautiful atmosphere. Raje entered his tent. Incense sticks, emitting scented smoke had been lit. Madanna and his sardars then bid the Marathas farewell for the night.

In the distance, from his palace at Golconda, the Badshah watched the camp lit up with small fires, reminding him of fireflies in the night. Raje, with his fifty thousand troops were resting for the night. However, the Badshah was restless. He was not going to sleep well that night.

The camp stirred into action as the morning sun rose in the sky. The tents were fluttering in the wind and small fires could be seen everywhere as people went about their morning chores. Raje was received by Madanna and other sardars.

Raje said, 'I would like to meet Qutb Shah in his palace. It would not be right to ask him to meet elsewhere.'

Madanna knew that the Badshah would be pleased as he was worried about stepping out of the safe confines of his palace. A suitable day, a week after Raje's arrival, was selected and Madanna asked, 'Would there be anything you would like to convey to the Badshah?'

Raje said, 'Yes. Like the Badshah, I have also been crowned a Chhatrapati. He should not expect a salute or any such thing from me. We must meet as equals.'

Madanna nodded his head. It was decided that the meeting would take place in the palace at noon the next day.

The city of Bhaganagar now waited with bated breath for the meeting.

On the day of the meeting, Raje and his sardars were dressed in regal finery. They sported a feather on their caps, and the royal elephant was decorated from head to toe in embroidered cloth and gold and silver jewellery. The gold-plated howdah glinted in the sunlight. Raje entered Bhaganagar as the citizens lined up the streets to see who they believed to be the protector of the Qutb Shahi kingdom.

Banners and flags welcomed him as the procession moved through the streets. The area outside the houses had been decorated with rangoli. The citizens watched in awe as the huge procession snaked into the city. These were the famed Marathas who had challenged the Mughals and had defeated Adil Shahi troops. The cavalry cantered slowly while the foot soldiers marched in tandem. The naked swords held by the soldiers struck terror and respect in the hearts of the citizens.

As soon as Raje's elephant came into sight, the men erupted in loud cheers. Raje was astride his white steed, while the men walking alongside held a huge umbrella, signifying his status as a Chhatrapati. At his waist, tied with a saffron cloth was his Bhawani sword and dagger. The mark on his forehead signified his devotion to Lord Shiva.

Holding the hilt of the sword in his left hand and the reins in his right, he moved through the streets at a slow and steady pace, smiling at citizens while they drenched the procession in flowers. The women competed with each other to perform the traditional aarti, holding trays of lit oil lamps. The procession of nearly twenty-five thousand men reached the gates of the fort. The fort had eight doors and eighty-seven bastions. It was a combination of a rock and hill fort. At the gates Madanna stood to welcome Raje.

The inner precincts of the fort were huge, spreading over many acres. It was a mini city with lakes, gardens and even rice fields, which ensured that in the event of a siege or attack, the men inside could hold out for a long time.

On a huge rock stood the royal palace, guarded at each step by armed soldiers A beautiful masjid with its aesthetically carved minarets caught Raje's attention. As he dismounted, he told Hambirrao, 'See that the troops are taken care of. And don't worry about me.'

On Madanna's signal, the bridge over the moat was laid. The soldiers quickly covered the wooden bridge with carpets. Raje walked over the bridge accompanied by Prahladpant, Janardhan Narayan and his personal bodyguards, Somaji Naik and Balaji Dhamdhere.

Madanna, surprised at Raje's decision to take just a few men along, asked, 'Maharaj, are you sure you want the others to ...'

'Madannapant, you cannot mix friendship with suspicion. I have brought the men along as a formality or I would have come alone. Come on now!'

'The Badshah is planning to receive you.'

'No, Madanna. Send him a message that he need not come down. We will meet him in his mahal.'

Qutb Shah, watching the procession from the window of the Angoor Mahal, received the message. He was surprised that Raje was entering with just four men in tow. He was at a loss to find that Shivaji was willing to trust him explicitly. Just then, a servant announced the arrival of Shivaji. Abul Hassan Tana Shah hurriedly moved to the door to receive his royal visitor.

As soon as the men saw each other, Prahlad Niraji announced, 'Ali Ala Hazrat Alampanah Abul Hassan Qutb Shah!'

'The protector of cows and Brahmins, Hindu Badshah Chhatrapati Shivaji Maharaj!'

The two men hugged each other and then Qutb Shah, holding Raje's hand, guided him to his seat. They sat next to each other, with large bolsters for support. Qutb Shah was a handsome man and his light blue eyes sparkled. He was impressed by Shivaji Raje's forceful personality. He tried to ascertain the thoughts behind Shivaji's penetrating eyes as they absorbed everything around. Raje's smile, benign and yet beguiling, confused him a little.

The main hall where they sat was a large, spacious one with the ceiling decorated with frescos and delicate windows covered with satin curtains. Raje was aware that he was being watched by the Badshah's begums from behind the latticed windows. Raje and Qutb Shah kept talking, oblivious of the hours gone by.

Finally Raje said, 'I think I must go now.'

Qutb Shah held Raje's hand asking, 'Are you already bored of my company? I would like you to stay here for a couple of days at least. We will have a chance to talk and enjoy each other's company.'

Raje smiled. 'How can I refuse you? You are like an elder brother to me. It will be my pleasure to stay back and enjoy your hospitality.'

Qutb Shah was pleasantly surprised. He had not expected Raje to accept his request. He truly admired Raje now.

That evening, when they sat for dinner, it was in a relaxed and friendly atmosphere. Qutb Shah had no reservations now. He urged Raje to regale those in attendance with accounts of his Agra escapade, the way he had looted Surat and the dramatic killing of Afzal Khan. After dinner, as they relaxed on a large terrace, the starlit sky above them, Raje's ears picked up the strains of soft, melodious music.

Qutb Shah smiled. 'You must be wondering about the music, I suppose?'

'It is distant, yet so soothing ...'

'Come, let me show you,' Qutb Shah said, getting up.

They walked to the edge of the terrace. Pointing at a building in the distance, nestled between two hillocks beyond a lake, he said, 'Listen!'

The music was emanating from the building which Qutb Shah had pointed to. Raje could not believe his ears and eyes. The building was easily more than a kilometre away. The westerly winds carried the notes to the mahal.

'My father would enjoy the music sitting here on the terrace while the musician would perform there. The original musicians are dead but the tradition continues, especially when we have special guests!'

'I would like to meet and reward them personally. What lovely music they make!'

Madanna nodded in response.

In his quarters, Raje dozed off into a restful sleep, listening to the music, and secure in the knowledge that Somaji Naik, standing guard outside the room, was wide awake, his hand ready at the hilt.

Raje was charmed by the beauty of the palace. Fountains gurgled at various places while water flowed through small channels in the centre of some rooms to keep them cool. The tombs of the royal ancestors were beautifully decorated with velvet and flower garlands. To the north of the fort was a flower garden while next to it were four large wells, deep and full of water.

Three days passed by quickly. They had been busy enjoying music, walking in the beautiful grounds and indulging in the lavish buffets at each meal. Raje's men were enjoying their stay in the camp erected for them. But as three days had passed, they became restless. They had been waiting for a message from Raje and the silence from the fort had begun to make them nervous now.

A worried Qutb Shah met Raje the next morning.

Raje asked, 'Are you not feeling well?'

'I am absolutely fine. But my mind is not at ease.'

'I do not understand,' Raje said.

Madanna replied, gulping nervously as he tried to form the words, 'I am not sure how to put it, Raje. There seems to be some nervousness among your troops and the word is that they might loot Bhaganagar. His Highness is thus worried.'

Raje was lost in his thoughts for a moment and then burst out laughing as he asked, 'And you believed those rumours?'

'I am quite certain of what I heard,' Qutb Shah said.

'You are responsible for these, you know?' Raje asked, taking Qutb Shah by surprise.

'Me?'

'Of course! We have been inside the fort for three days without any information to the troops. They are naturally restless and worried and must have decided to do something. Madanna, ask Hambirrao to meet me immediately.'

Raje said, turning to Qutb Shah, 'If we had to loot the town, we would not have wasted our time showing you our friendship.' Holding his hand gently, Raje smiled at Qutb Shah.

A sound of clap echoed in the room. Raje looked around to find the source when Qutb Shah said, 'It is a signal from the main door of the fort, which I can hear here. Isn't that an architectural marvel?'

'I am impressed,' Raje said.

'What is really impressive is the fact that your troops are restless to get a glimpse of you!'

Soon, Hambirrao was ushered in. He knew the reason for being summoned and came straight to the point after saluting Raje. 'Raje, the troops were a little agitated. They will be happy if they can see that you are safe and sound.'

'The Badshah and I would like to have an inspection. Please ask the troops to be prepared and march next to the fort in a couple of hours.'

'As you command, Maharaj.'

That afternoon, Raje and Qutb Shah stood on the terrace of the Angoor Mahal while the troops marched below. Seeing Raje, there were shouts of joy as they saluted. After the inspection, as they were returning to the inner quarters, Qutb Shah asked, 'What is the strength of the troops here?'

'About forty thousand including the foot soldiers. And another ten thousand support staff.'

'You seem to have come with your entire army.'

'No, not at all. The same number of troops are taking care of the kingdom.'

'I had heard a lot about your men. I'm glad I had the chance to see them today.'

'You must see them in action to know their true worth.'

'I would love to,' Qutb Shah said.

The next morning, a special shamiana was erected in the large field in front of the Golconda fort. At the sound of bugles, the two kings entered the tent and took their seats.

The Maratha soldiers were ready. Displaying various feats with their double-edged swords, they thrilled the spectators. The displays of talent continued for some more time, and by the time they finished, Qutb Shah was mesmerized. But Raje quickly surmised that he was looking for some other talents to be displayed as well.

Qutb Shah asked, 'What about your elephants?'

'We don't keep a large herd of them.'

'The real strength of a soldier, whether a foot soldier or a cavalryman, can be assessed when he sees an elephant charging at him.'

'Each one of my man is equal to an elephant.'

'I am not talking of fanciful description, Raja saheb. I mean real valour.'

'I mean in reality,' Raje said.

'Are you saying your men can fight an elephant?' Qutb Shah asked, a little surprised.

'Without doubt!'

Raje signalled his sardars standing nearby and eight of them stepped forward.

'You may choose any of them,' he said, pointing to the group.

Qutb Shah selected Yesaji from the group, who was the shortest and probably the leanest among them. On cue, an elephant entered the ground. His trumpeting sent shivers down the spine of the audience. He seemed to be in musth as he charged towards Yesaji. Delicately stepping aside, Yesaji moved away from the line of path and the elephant charged ahead, unable to stop itself. This happened a few times. The elephant stumbled and turned to charge again. The crowd cheered each time the elephant missed picking Yesaji up with its trunk. The next time the elephant charged, Yesaji was ready with his sword, gleaming in the sunlight, and he brought it down with force on the elephant's trunk. The sword had sliced it clean and the elephant, unable to bear the pain, trumpeted loudly and staggered towards the end of the field, where he collapsed unconscious.

Raje, holding his breath for the last many minutes, was relieved and hugged Yesaji as he saluted.

Qutb Shah, overwhelmed and impressed with his bravery, immediately offered him a mansab of five thousand and a permanent position in his court were he to join him.

'I am Raje's man. I cannot accept your offer.'

This impressed Qutb Shah further and he pleaded, turning towards Raje, 'Please allow this man to join my court.'

Raje said, touching a necklace with nine gems on his neck, 'How will this necklace look if one of the gems drops off?'

Qutb Shah realized what Raje meant. He knew Raje's navratna, the nine sardars, was his real strength. He asked, 'I saw you perspiring when your man was fighting. Were you nervous?'

'Yes. These men are willing to lay down their lives for me. And anything is possible. I was nervous because I don't want to waste my men on mere entertainment.'

Qutb Shah was now seeing a different facet of Raje's personality. That evening, as they went back to their chambers, Raje made a request to return to his camp.

Qutb Shah asked, 'When do I see you again?'

'I will come whenever you send word to me.'

Qutb Shah bid farewell to Raje with a gift of royal garments, elephants and horses.

The Marathas had stayed in Bhaganagar for nearly a month. Qutb Shah had promised to support Raje's campaign in Karnatak. Raje would be able to use Qutb Shah's artillery and ammunition, which was being managed by foreign gunners. He would also get monetary support of a thousand hons daily.

Qutb Shah was, by nature, a peace-loving man who enjoyed the finer things in life like music, dance and his wines. The drudgery and the hazards of battle were not his cup of tea. The threat from the Adil Shahi kingdom had been a constant thorn and he had been relieved to find a suitable ally in Shivaji. He had readily accepted Shivaji's proposal to bring the three powers in the Deccan together against the Mughal threat.

As Raje took his leave, Qutb Shah said, holding his hand, 'Please give me the same cooperation that your father exhibited in saving the Adil Shahi kingdom.'

'I promise you, it is my aim to crush the Mughal-dominated kingdom. I will not rest till the Adil Shahi, Qutb Shahi and the Maratha forces come together to defeat the Mughals.'

Qutb Shah offered a gift of five lakh hons to Raje. To show his faith in their peace pact, he accepted Prahladpant as the envoy to his durbar. The crowds in the streets gathered to have a last glimpse of the Maratha king. They could not cheer loudly enough as the troops moved slowly through the streets.

That night, as the camp prepared to leave, Raje summoned Raghunathpant and said, 'Send for Balaji. I need to send out an urgent letter.'

As Balaji came in, Raje said, 'We have secured our relations with Qutb Shah now. The Pathans, however, continue to dominate the Adil Shahi court. We cannot expect them to behave rationally. However, if the Marathas in the durbar join hands with us, it can benefit us. Our traditional enemy Baji Ghorpade's son, Maloji Ghorpade, is in Adil Shah's service. I want to reconcile with him, and extend a hand of friendship. I also intend to write to the other sardars as well.'

As he paced in his tent, Raje dictated a letter to Balaji: '... my dear departed father, Shahaji Raje Maharaj, came to Bijapur during the reign of Mohammad Adil Shah and absorbed many Marathas into the administration. One of them was your father, Baji Ghorpade, who later became a minister. Unfortunately, he turned hostile and managed to arrest my father and hand him over to Mustafa Khan. It was also alleged that my father's men killed your father. This is the situation of politics in the Deccan. The first to decline was the Adil Shah's dynasty, which is currently under Bahlol Khan, making the current Shah a mere titular head. Once the Pathans decide to take charge, they will not hesitate to annihilate all native lineages one after another.

'We have a peace treaty with Qutb Shah now. And we are keen that the Maratha people should come together to remove the Pathans at Bijapur. I know it is difficult for you to sever relations and come to Bhaganagar, but I promise you that my only intention is to see the Marathas prosper. I have resolved to unite the Marathas for the sake of their welfare. What more can I say?'

The messenger left the next morning. At the crack of dawn, as the Maratha troops moved out of the camp, they were accompanied by Qutb Shah's sardar Mirza Muhammad Amin with his four thousand foot soldiers, a thousand cavalrymen and his artillery.

Raje and his troops moved towards Karnatak and reached Kurnool, a few miles from the confluence of the rivers Bhima and Krishna, called Nivritti

Sangam. After a dip in the holy waters, Raje donated money to the Brahmins and then camped at Atmakur after crossing the Krishna. Raje was also keen to visit Srisailam.

Within a few days he left with a few horsemen for company. It was the end of winter and the fertile black soil with mango, tamarind and other trees was a pleasant sight. They would spot a herd of deer, which would vanish the very next moment, leaping over the grass. After a few hours of riding, they could see the distant thin bluish line of the mountains of the Nallamala ranges.

Soon, as the forest cover thickened, the topography changed. Tired of seeing the flat plains in Karnatak, the hilly forests were a soothing sight. Raje was reminded of Raigad, nestled in the Sahyadris. By evening, they had climbed the range. The teak, silk-cotton and sandal trees provided a dense cover. The spring, almost upon them, could be seen in the various flowers all around.

As the night fell, the men and horses rested, and multiple fires were lit. Cries of wild animals and birds were heard through the night. They woke up to a glorious sunrise as they started their march again. Soon, the River Krishna was in sight as it meandered through the forests, and dilapidated bastions and remnants of forts dotted the landscape. As they crossed the river, they could see the shrine of Srisailam on top of the mountain.

Raghunathpant said, pointing to the shrine, 'Raje, this place is called Neelganga. From here to Patalaganga, the Krishna flows north.'

The men were surprised as Raje dived into the river and enjoyed a brisk swim against the currents. Spotting a fort in the distance, he asked, 'What is that? Looks like the ruins of a fort?'

'It is, Maharaj. This and a few others were built during Chandragupta's time.'

'What a pity! The Gupta empire was a glorious one.' Raje was in a philosophical mood as he said, much to himself, 'Everything we build is perishable. That is the very rule of nature, isn't it? Yet, we do not change and continue to build forts, hoping they will last forever. We strive hard to protect each man and woman in our kingdom. But what a sacrifice we make for it! I wish our future generations can preserve what we build.'

He paused and, without waiting for a response, said, 'I wish man did not have the faculty to dream! He would not be tortured unnecessarily.'

Pant said, breaking his chain of thoughts, 'Maharaj, the temple, a Jyotirlinga, is a couple of kilometres away on a steep slope. Shall I get a palanquin ready?'

'Why? I will walk the distance.'

They walked from Neelganga to Patalaganga. Raje gasped for breath after walking half the distance. He was out of breath when Pant asked anxiously, 'Raje, are you all right? Shall I order a palanquin?'

Waving his hand to decline the offer, Raje said, as he wiped the sweat off his face, 'I have spent all my life ascending and descending forts. But today, I feel spent.'

'Maharaj, you are not even fifty years old. Why do you say that?'

'Stamina has nothing to do with age. My childhood passed by so quickly that I don't even remember it. I was busy pursuing the Hindavi Swaraj, and I never had the time to enjoy childhood.'

The slope had almost ended and Pant said, trying to encourage Raje to carry on walking, 'We are almost there!'

In the light of the evening sun, the magnificent temple looked imposing as it stood on the flat top of the hill. The arch was an imposing affair. A tent had been pitched near the temple by the advance party. Mahadev came in and saluted, and Raje was happy to see the arrangements. He said, 'We can rest later; I am eager to have darshan now.'

As he entered the courtyard, Raje was surprised to see the size of the temple which included apartments for pilgrims on the side. A life-sized statue of the Nandi bull stood in the middle. There were beautiful sculptures carved in stone everywhere. As he reached the sanctum sanctorum, he could see the imposing Shiva linga with a five-hooded serpent spread out over the idol. Holy water dripped from a jar hanging above. The horizontal marks of ash across the linga overwhelmed Raje as he fell prostrate, tears falling down his cheeks.

It was nightfall by the time they finished their darshan, and the moon shone in the sky. Raje was so taken by the place that he decided to stay in the pilgrims' apartments. Pant said, 'Maharaj, the tents have been readied for you. In a few days, since it is the month of Chaitra, the place will be full on the full moon day.'

'It does not matter, Pant. I don't want to leave this place.'

Yesaji, Balaji, Pant and the others looked at each other helplessly. They knew Raje had made up his mind. As they brought out refreshments, Raje said, his eyes half-closed, 'I don't want anything. I am fine.'

The men were perplexed. Raje's behaviour had changed dramatically. He was silent, hardly speaking. He said, looking at Balaji, 'Will you fulfil a request for me?'

'Please command me, Maharaj.'

'Ever since I have come here, I feel truly satisfied. I have been giving it serious thought. My work for the Swaraj has yielded results, thanks to Jagdamba. But the credit really goes to all of you. The kingdom is safe in your hands. I want you to go back and crown Sambhaji and Rajaram as your kings.'

Yesaji, shocked to hear Raje, could not say anything except exclaim, 'Maharaj!'

Pointing towards the temple, Raje said, 'He is the real Maharaj, not me! I am no longer your king. I want to spend the rest of my life here, at the feet of God. You have to fulfil my request now.'

The men could not hold their tears. Yesaji touched Raje's feet and said, 'If you leave us, where do we go? We too will follow you. We are happy to stay here with you.'

Raje said, as he pulled Yesaji up, 'Do you realize how easy and tempting it is to speak like this? It is late now. Let us sleep.'

The men heaved sighs of relief as Raje fell asleep shortly thereafter. It was sometime around midnight when Raje woke up to find Mahadev, standing guard nearby, a naked sword in hand.

'Mahadev, you too should sleep. We are in the temple of Srisailam Mallikarjuna, our protector. Don't insult him by standing guard here. Go to sleep!'

As Mahadev left, the campus was silent now. After a while, Raje got up and, taking the sword lying next to him, walked towards the temple. Raghunathpant, Balaji, Yesaji and others slept soundly.

Mahadev had left but was not asleep. He was watching wide-eyed. He hurried to wake up Raghunathpant, placing his finger on his lips to indicate silence. Soon, others had woken up and they watched Raje enter the main gate. The silver door to the sanctum sanctorum was closed. Raje knelt and, bending his head, raised his right hand. Scarcely had he placed the edge of the sword on his neck when a firm grip held his hand.

'Maharaj, what is this?'

Raje looked up to see Raghunathpant holding his wrist. Others stood by mutely. Raje said, his voice sounding unnaturally loud, 'Let me be free! If I cannot stay here, I want to at least offer my head at his feet.'

Raghunathpant trembled. He said, 'Maharaj, committing suicide is a sin!'

An infuriated Raje shouted, 'Who is committing suicide here? I am surrendering myself to the Lord.'

'It is only for the mind to surrender!' Raghunathpant said, his voice calm and steady.

Raje's grip on the sword loosened as it fell with a loud clang on the floor. Yesaji quickly stepped forward to pick it up. They all sat silently. Raje was shivering as he looked at the closed door.

When will these doors open? If one door opens, I see another closing. When will all the doors open? Maybe when the last door is opened, I can go in.

Unaware of those around him, his soliloquy continued. Why is this mind despondent? Why, despite all the pleasures at Qutb Shah's palace, was I feeling uneasy? I established the kingdom as per the Lord's wishes. Is it the future that worries me? Am I worried that it will not last long? Gyaneshwar did not bother whether his Gyaneshwari would be read by others. He surrendered to God and left the world. But these men are gods themselves! They are not mere mortals like me.'

Maa saheb's only desire was to see me build my own kingdom. Her desire was fulfilled when she saw me crowned as a sovereign king. But I seem to be infatuated with my success. My father was as strong as a rock but I could never take shelter under him. My mother gave me all the affection she could but I never asked her for anything. Sai left me before I could even start enjoying my life with her.'

Men are willing to lay down their lives for me but I could not shape my son into someone I could admire! Perhaps I am not capable of winning his confidence. People who were supposed to give me nectar have tried to poison me. I wonder what the meaning of life is—is it conquering lands, invading regions and living a life of constant struggle? We live for perhaps between sixty and a hundred years. I have hardly enjoyed my childhood or my adulthood or even the days of position and authority.

What would it be like if I were to live my life over again? Is this attachment—pining for what is lost and being unable to enjoy the moment? I could have been just a Jagirdar like my father and enjoyed life. But I did not do that. Is ending one's life a selfish act? Do I have a right to end what has been given by the Lord? Would that not be an insult to Him? I must endure whatever comes my way, in whichever form ...

After a while, he was out of his trance. It was morning and the front door was open. Seeing the lovely and unobstructed view of the Shiva linga, Raje's tears flowed unabashedly. He stood up and rang the bell with joy, which spread to all those present. They knew they had their Raje back!

After spending a few days in Srisailam, he ordered a flight of stairs to be built and had the arch at the temple renovated. Raje asked Raghunathpant, as they performed the puja on the full moon day, 'Pant, why were you worried when I said I wanted to stay back here?'

'Maharaj, you would not have lost anything but we would have been orphaned! We would have had no choice but to kill ourselves. The philosopher's stone has no worries, Raje. It is the ordinary metal which worries if it does not turn to gold.'

'If only I could turn everything I touch into gold!'

'You already have, Maharaj! Look at our army of nearly fifty thousand men, and there are lakhs of people waiting for your orders. This is only your magic!'

'No, these are Jagdamba's blessings. Let us light one lakh earthen lamps today. Can you procure them?'

'Yes, we can!'

That night, there was a cloudless sky with a full moon, blazing in its glory. The lamps had been lit everywhere—on walls, on the temple tower and the lamp tower in the temple courtyard. The pilgrims did not know whether to look at the idol or gaze at Shivaji.

After staying a few more days, Raje decided to move on. He stopped for a while at River Krishna to take a final look at the temple. Letting out a sigh, he said, 'Well, we must move now. Such moments are but fleeting. I have seen the Krishna originating in Mahabaleshwar as a thin stream. After cascading over hills, valleys, rocks and being joined by other streams, it becomes what we see here. Thousands wash themselves in it, and yet, I wonder how it remains so pure!'

He continued, before waiting for Pant to respond, 'You know, it remains pure because it is constantly moving towards the sea. The current of human emotions often gets dirtied by desire and lust but the essence of life is pure. Krishna represents the core of human essence. I salute her!'

Folding his hands in a namaskar, he mounted his horse. As Raje crossed the river, the horse hooves splashed through the waters and it appeared that, for a brief moment, the flowing stream had been interrupted.

At Atmakur, Raje's other troops joined him and they moved southwards. Crossing Nandiyal and Kadappa, they reached Tirupati. After a darshan of Lord Venkateswara, they reached Kanchipuram. After a darshan of the temple, they camped a few miles from the Madras harbour.

The Karnatak campaign was to begin from here. What was once Vijayanagara empire was now under the control of the Adil Shahis. Raje's plan was to bring the region under his control. He was particularly interested in the fort of Jinji, one of the strongest forts under Adil Shahi control but Raje was confident of capturing it.

Nasir Muhammad, the fort-keeper at Jinji, was Khavas Khan's brother, the Wazir of Bijapur who was murdered when the Pathans took over. Sher Khan, the Pathan chief in the Deccan, had his eye on the fort but he backed off when he heard that Raje was marching towards it. Raje sent a thousand of his men to Jinji with a message to Nasir Muhammad that he was arriving soon. Nasir thought it was better to hand over the fort to Raje than let the Pathan get hold of it. He agreed to a treaty. Raje, on hearing the news, marched towards Jinji. Nasir Muhammad was given a jagir of fifty thousand in return, and the Maratha flag fluttered atop the Jinji Fort.

The fort was an imposing structure, and the moat around the fort was nearly thirty feet wide and deep. Two perennial streams provided drinking water. The fort, once the pride of Vijayanagara kingdom, was now under Raje's command. After giving orders for the repair and renovation of the fort and appointing Ravaji Nalage as the fort-keeper, Raje decided to move on. He had been at the fort for nearly a week.

In the meanwhile, he received news from Vellore that Qutb Shah's artillery chief, Mirza Muhammad Amin, had left for Golconda. Qutb Shah had assumed that Raje would take over the fort and then, after hoisting the Qutb Shahi flag, merge it into former's jurisdiction. But Raje had no such plans. Muhammad Amin had stopped paying the daily tribute of three thousand hons to take care of his daily expenses.

Marching urgently towards Vellore, Raje reorganized his forces to ensure a siege on the fort there. It was a well-protected fort, with multiple moats, some of which had crocodiles in them. It was crucial for Raje to annex the fort to his kingdom but he knew it was not an easy task.

Nasir, acting on behalf of Raje, tried convincing Abdul Khan, the fort-keeper, to surrender but not wanting to be seen as a coward, he decided to fight. Leaving his troops to continue the siege, Raje returned to Gingee, a distance of nearly eighty miles. Raje's capture of Gingee had shaken up the Dutch, the English and the Portuguese and they started negotiations for reconciliation.

Raje asked the English for antidotes for poison and asked how much they wanted for these. However, the English sent the antidotes without asking for any money. While at Gingee, Raje made plans to target Sher Khan, the Adil Shahi Subedar in the Deccan.

Sher Khan Lodhi's headquarters were at Waligandapuram, near Tiruchirapalli, north of the River Kaveri. He could keep a watch on the Nayaks of Thanjavur and Madurai. He decided to set up an ambush for Shivaji and his forces in Tiruwadi, a few miles from the Kadalur harbour.

The monsoon was about to begin and Raje was keen that he subdue Sher Khan before the rains arrived in full force. Camping within sight of Sher Khan's camp, Raje decided to play a waiting game. He knew that Sher Khan's spies were entering his camp in the guise of fakirs but he did not act, confusing Sher Khan. As expected, Sher Khan's soldiers, seeing the enemy stationed at the door, started losing their morale. Stricken by fear, Sher Khan ordered his forces to retreat.

The moment the news reached Raje, he ordered his men to attack. The Pathans, seeing the Marathas chasing them, fled in fear. Soon, they were surrounded. The air was split with the sounds of horns and Raje's cavalry, who with glinting swords and spears in their hands chased the Pathans. The battlefield resounded with shouts of 'Har Har Mahadev!' Five hundred Pathans were massacred. Sher Khan and his son took shelter in the nearby fort of Bhuvanagiri. But Raje was determined to prevail and soon, a worried Sher Khan sent feelers to negotiate a treaty. He was forced to pay a ransom of twenty thousand hons, while leaving his son Ibrahim Khan as hostage with Raje as he vacated the territory.

The hostilities of Adil Shahi troops in the Deccan stopped with the defeat of Sher Khan. Raje was now free to move around without any hindrance. He was now eager to meet his stepbrother Ekoji Raje and moved southwards.

They camped at Tiruvannamalai. The scenic beauty impressed Raje, and he said, 'What a beautiful village!' looking at Hambirrao.

'Earlier, there were some beautiful temples of Shiva and Samotti Perumal. But after the destruction of the Vijaynagara kingdom, the Muslims built mosques over them,' Hambirrao said.

As they reached the outskirts of the village, the white domes of the mosques, freshly painted with lime, came into view. The destruction was evident even after so many years. A broken idol of Nandi the bull lay in a pit of dust, and a broken Shiva linga lay in the mud. It was a heart-rending sight, and brought tears to Raje's eyes. He said, 'What is the use of building a mosque after destroying a temple? How dare they?'

'Maharaj,' Raghunathpant said sadly, 'the Muslims are proud of their religion. The Europeans too cross the seven seas and propagate their religion but we Hindus seem indifferent to our own faith.'

Raje's face was resolute as he surveyed the ruins. He said, after a pause, 'Demolish the mosques and reinstall our deities. I want a beautiful arch and a thousand-pillared hall in the temple built with the bricks of the fallen Samotti Perumal temple. I shall not be at peace till the deities are reinstalled.'

Hambirrao and Janardanpant could not believe their ears. Janardanpant asked, 'Won't this hurt the Muslims?'

'Did they think of this when they demolished the temples? Tolerance to other religions does not mean being indifferent to our own. We have gotten used to ignoring the demolition of our temples or empires such as Vijayanagara. We don't even feel ashamed when our women are dishonoured. We use our servile cowardliness to justify our honourable life. It has become second nature to us to be passive. We don't hate the Muslims—we have many of them in our armies. The Muslims could have built a mosque anywhere. They had no reason to destroy our temples and build mosques on top of them. I cannot tolerate that. I want you to execute my order without further delay.'

The mosques were demolished and the construction of the temples began at a frantic pace. In the meanwhile, Raje shifted his base to the banks of Godavari near Tiruwadi and sent an invitation to meet Ekoji Raje, who ruled nearby Thanjavur.

Ekoji was reluctant to meet Raje, worried that he may have plans to dominate his kingdom. He first sent his emissaries to get a better understanding of Raje's intentions. Satisfied that the proposed visit was merely to meet each other, he agreed to it.

Within two days of the agreement, Ekoji Raje decided to pay a visit. The nearby temple of Shiva in Tirupatota, a couple of kilometres from Raje's camp, was fixed for the venue. Ekoji arrived, accompanied by Shahaji Raje's stepsons, Bhivaji Raje and Pratap Raje. Ekoji was of medium height and slightly overweight. His demeanour spoke of prosperity—he wore diamond-studded rings and he had tucked a fig leaf in his turban. The brothers hugged each other. After a darshan at the temple, Raje invited Ekoji to the camp.

After a few days of rest and entertainment, Raje found a suitable time to broach the topic. He said, 'Raje, you are younger than me but we are sons of the same father. I came to your territory, but you chose not to help me when I was fighting Sher Khan. Do you not trust me?'

Ekoji did not reply. Raje continued, 'As an elder brother, I could have demanded half of Maharaj saheb's jagir but you did not volunteer my share on your own. I did not want to embarrass you by asking for it. See the way I have developed the Pune jagir, once burnt down by Murar Jagdev. It is now a kingdom. Should you not do the same?'

'You built the kingdom with the help of your men. Isn't it admirable that I continue to hold on to my jagir in a foreign region?'

'Ekoji, my spies have informed me well. It is Sher Khan's gratitude that allows you to run the jagir. I want you to quit your job in Adil Shah's durbar and join me.'

Ekoji was upset. He had not expected Raje to be so blunt. Raje continued, 'Join me as my brother and not in a feudal allegiance. I want you to be the Jagirdar of a Maratha kingdom. It would be a happy situation if we can co-exist together, wouldn't it?'

'What if I refuse?'

Raje was taken aback by Ekoji's comment. He said, his voice taking on an edge, 'I am only advising you as an elder brother, but I would like you to be polite. In the Mahabharata, a family feud flared up and destroyed everyone. If you remain a servant of Adil Shah, I will treat you in a manner that will lead to your destruction. Think it over, and don't be rash.'

Ekoji, though thoroughly frightened, maintained a straight face. After a few days, Raje met him again and said, 'Ekoji, my kingdom is spread from the banks of Narmada to that of the Tungabhadra. But one thing is missing—you!'

'Me?'

'Your presence will be a symbol of remembrance of the elder Maharaj. I am told that the elder Maharaj has left behind twelve tokens. I would love to have my father's tokens or rather, I demand them.'

Ekoji felt relieved that he could probably avoid joining Raje by giving him the tokens. But he was surprised when Kakajipant, his Peshwa, rejected the idea. Ekoji asked, 'Why do you say that?'

'This is a new strategy of Shivaji's. He managed to capture Purandar by coming in as a guest. The way he killed Afzal Khan was also deceitful. He took charge of Gingee but is yet to give Nasir Muhammad the promised fifty-thousand jagir.'

'But I am promising him the tokens and not the jagir,' Ekoji countered.

'Why is Shivaji so attached to Shahaji Raje's ensigns? Don't be fooled by this—he asks for the tokens today. He will ask for the jagir tomorrow.'

'What do you suggest then?'

'He may have subdued the Adil Shahi and Qutb Shahi kingdoms but the Mughals are still a power to reckon with. Shivaji's kingdom is a bubble on water, and it will burst someday. Those who join hands with him will suffer his fate. We are better off being alone and faraway from the Mughals. It is better that we avoid getting trapped in politics.'

Ekoji was worried. He did not know what course of action to take. He said, a little perplexed, 'I will return to Thanjavur and then decide.'

'You will not be able to do that.'

'Why?'

'Do you think Shivaji is going to let you return so easily?'

'Am I a prisoner here?' Ekoji demanded, his face turning red with anger.

'It seems that way to me,' Kakajipant answered.

Ekoji did not wait a single moment longer and with a single horseman for company, he rode to the safety of Thanjavur that night.

Raje could not believe that Ekoji had run away. He summoned Kakajipant, Jaganathpant and the two stepbrothers, Pratap Raje and Bhivaji Raje. 'Is it true that Ekoji Raje has run away?' he asked Kakajipant.

'Yes,' Pant said, a little boldly.

'Why would he do that? Was he worried about being arrested? I don't want the tokens. I asked for them only as a remembrance of my father. What a pity he has run away.'

Dejected that his brother did not believe him, he let out a deep sigh and said, looking at Kakajipant, 'You are his senior advisor. What did you tell Ekoji?'

'I ...' Kakaji hesitated.

'I am sure it was not his idea to run away. You know I can take over Thanjavur just sitting here, don't you? But you probably did not think of it. You can go now,' Raje said, dismissing him with a wave of his hand.

Ekoji's men were sent off to Thanjavur after due gifts of ornaments and royal clothes.

Ekoji's disappearance was a disappointment to Raje and he issued orders to annex Shahaji Raje's jagir to his kingdom. Raje was also able to annex many other territories to his kingdom as he moved towards Thanjavur. The news from Raigad was disturbing. Internal bickering among the Adil Shahi sardars was making the Pathans stronger. Aurangzeb, realizing that Bahadur Khan had not been successful, had asked Diler Khan to take charge.

'Since he has not arrived in the Deccan yet, we need to wind up our campaign and go back as soon as possible,' Raje mused.

It had been a month since Ekoji Raje had run away when Santaji Raje, Shahaji Raje's stepson, came visiting, and Shivaji was pleased to receive him. They sat chatting when Santaji broached the topic of Ekoji. 'I am told he did not obey you.'

'He was not happy with what I said.'

'I had asked Ekoji to meet you the moment I heard of your arrival in Karnatak. But knowing Ekoji's attitude, I did not come along and Bhivaji and Pratapji accompanied Ekoji.'

'Santaji, you must know that being allied with me means facing a new challenge each day. Are you prepared for that?'

Santaji eyed Raje as he brushed his whiskers with the back of his wrist. He said, 'I cannot waste my time here anymore.'

'You must know that I don't hand out jagirs.'

'Who wants a jagir? Just make me a cavalryman and that is enough!'

Raje hugged Santaji and said, overwhelmed with emotions, 'I am happy to have you on my side, Santaji. Why do you want to be an ordinary soldier when you should command a thousand men?'

Raje offered him a mansab of a thousand and inducted him into his team.

The Marathas brought the territories of Kolar, Hoskote, Balapur and Shire from Shahaji Raje's jagir into the Maratha kingdom. After going back to Tiruvannamalai to install a Shiva linga there, Raje celebrated deepotsava, the festival of lamps, on a full moon day.

The troops annexed Ekoji's territory north of the River Kaveri. This yielded an annual revenue of twenty lakhs. A few officials were appointed to manage the territory. Leaving seasoned generals like Hambirrao, Santaji Bhosale and Vithal Atre to look after these new territories, Raje decided to return to Raigad.

'Ensure that the territory is established properly. And don't pardon Ekoji if he tries to misbehave. Let everyone know that we will not tolerate any hostility.'

Within a week of Raje's departure, an infuriated Ekoji launched an attack. Santaji, with six thousand cavalry and foot soldiers, confronted his troops, and they clashed at Amboria. After a pitched battle, Santaji had to retreat, and Ekoji's troops celebrated their victory.

Feeling insulted and worried that he had let Raje down, Santaji launched a counter-attack on the Thanjavur camp. The enemy, caught unawares, ran helter-skelter. Santaji managed to wrest a thousand horses among other loot, and this brought Ekoji to his senses. Raghunathpant started negotiations with Ekoji to keep him occupied. In the meanwhile, Raje wrote a strongly-worded letter to Ekoji:

'... I am on my way to Raigad and I am told that you are being wrongly advised by the Muslims and attacking your own people. However, I am willing to forget the past. You have enjoyed the jagir for thirteen years, and it is time that you entrusted the administration to us and gave us half the money, jewellery, elephants and horses in the jagir. If you agree, you will be given the Panhala district till the banks of Tungabhadra and a revenue of three lakhs annually. I am appealing to you as your elder brother. I want you to accept these terms and be happy. Else, the consequences will be disastrous ...'

Raje kept moving towards Raigad, and at that time, they heard that Bahlol Khan had died and Siddi Masood had been made the prime minister of the Adil Shahi kingdom. There were also rumours of Diler Khan's plan to march on the Bijapur kingdom. Raje decided to reach Panhala soon.

The developments in Bijapur were interesting for Raje. Moropant came to meet Raje at Panhala while Hambirrao reached from the south.

'We have had great success in south right up to Vellore. We now have boundaries touching the Tungabhadra River,' said Hambirrao.

'We are prepared to take on larger responsibilities now,' Moropant added.

'I like your confidence but we cannot be complacent. Siddi is a deceitful fellow and Diler Khan has now come to the Deccan. In my life, I have had two very powerful enemies; one was Mirza Raja Jai Singh and the other, Diler Khan. I cannot forget the treaty of Purandar. Mirza Raja is no more but Diler Khan is very cunning. I came back in a hurry when I heard that he had been sent here or our kingdom would have extended right up to Kanyakumari.'

'We can rout Diler Khan, no doubt,' Hambirrao said.

'I know that. But the matter will not end there. Aurangzeb, one day or the other, is sure to come down to the Deccan himself. We will have to fight the real might of Mughals then. Whoever wins that battle will be the emperor of India. We have to finish off the Mughals and install the idol at the Kashi Vishwanath Temple, and we still have a long way to go. We cannot rest till then.'

'We have some bad news, Raje,' Moropant said. 'Trayambak Dabir passed away.'

'When did that happen?' Dabir was one of Raje's eight ministers and Raje's great counsellor.

'A year ago, in Shivapur.'

'It is unfortunate he is no more when we need him the most. But things have been managed well in my absence over the past one and a half years. Our administration is very strong, thanks to people like you.' Changing the topic, Raje asked, 'How is Sambhaji?'

Moropant was quiet and realizing that something was amiss, Raje asked, 'Go on, Moropant. Don't hesitate.'

'He is quite popular in Shringarpur. In fact, he has given concessions in taxes and the people are happy. But this has led to a deficit in the treasury. Annaji's decisions are not approved by Yuvraj.'

'And ...?'

'I am told he has been initiated to a throne as an independent ruler by the poet Kalash.'

'I don't understand.'

'I heard this from reliable people, Raje.'

'It is an empty mind working overtime.'

'Raje, we are told he is being influenced by some people of the Shakta sect.'

'I see!'

'But there is good news; you are going to be a grandfather soon!'

'That is really good news,' Raje said, smiling. 'Let us go to Shringarpur and see the progress there. We will first have a look at the work at the Padmadurg Fort at Rajpuri and then return to Raigad via Shringarpur.'

At Rajpuri, the English envoy came to pay his respects. The chief of Raje's navy, Daulat Khan, was also present. Raje said, addressing Daulat Khan, 'I am getting reports of the trouble Siddi is creating in our kingdom, kidnapping Brahmins and enslaving them. We cannot wait any longer—I want you to gather all the forces you want and defeat Siddi at any cost. I cannot allow his atrocities any longer.'

Daulat Khan assured Raje that he would take action immediately. Raje said, putting his hand on his shoulder, 'Your confidence reassures me. Let me know whatever you need, and I shall arrange for it.'

After a week at Rajpuri, having inspected the fort, Raje moved towards Shringarpur. It was the hot summer months, and travel through the humid Konkan region was taking a toll on everyone.

Sambhaji, having heard from the advance party of Raje's arrival, came a few miles ahead of the town to give Raje a rousing welcome.

As they entered the haveli, Raje asked Sambhaji in a low voice, 'Is it true? Am I going to be a grandfather?'

All Sambhaji could manage was an embarrassed look. Raje laughed loudly as he patted Sambhaji on the back. Sambhaji was seeing Raje in a good mood after a long time. As they entered the inner chambers, Yesubai came in and managed to bow slightly, her advanced pregnancy making it difficult for her to bend. Yesu looked charming, her pregnancy having added a glow to her face. Seeing Raje staring at her, she fiddled awkwardly with her pallu.

Raje said, affectionately hugging her, 'My dear, I hope you are keeping good health.'

'Yes, Aba saheb.'

'I have missed you ever since I left Panhala. I am going to see my grandson now. I cannot wait!'

'A granddaughter, not a grandson,' Pilaji said, standing a little behind Yesubai. Pilaji was a little embarrassed, having blurted out. He corrected himself saying, 'This is what Kalash tells us!'

Raje smiled. 'Such predictions may come true. Girl or boy, we will be equally happy. If it is a girl, I will believe that Bhawani has been born here.' During meals, Raje said, 'Yuvraj, I was in Karnatak but my mind was here all the time. I was getting constant information about the activities here.'

Sambhaji, Kalash and Umaji Pandit paused to see what Raje would say next. Their faces were tense. Raje continued, 'I am told you have composed poetry in Sanskrit, thanks to Umaji and Kalash. I am pleased to hear it!'

The tension in the room was diffused and the meal continued with laughter and small talk. The next morning, as Raje sat in the makeshift office, he asked poet Kalash, 'How do you see my astrological position at this moment?'

'Your future is bright, Maharaj. I had predicted your win in Karnatak. It has come true!'

Seeing Hambirrao laugh loudly, Kalash asked, a little miffed at the insult, 'Maharaj, I hope you do believe in horoscopes?'

'Yes, I do believe in the position of stars and planets and I enjoy religious ceremonies and make it a point to visit shrines during my campaigns.'

Kalash was relieved to hear that. Sambhaji came and touched Raje's feet. And much to his surprise, Raje made him sit next to him, and said, 'Now I must treat you with all the respect due to a king. You have crowned yourself; and hence you are neither a son nor a Yuvraj anymore.'

'Aba saheb!' Sambhaji said, staring at Moropant angrily.

Raje's expression changed. He said, as he looked at Kalash and Umaji Pandit, 'It is not Moropant's fault. It is you who got yourself crowned as a king without informing anyone. And Kalash, you are supposed to be his advisor. How could you suggest something like this?'

Licking his lips nervously, Kalash said, 'Maharaj, he was insistent. I had no choice.'

'What does that mean? Is he the new Chhatrapati? Will he now take over my kingdom?'

'He was worried and wanted to use this as an insurance against a possible death sentence in the future.'

'Wah!' Raje erupted, his voice dripping with contempt. 'You forget that he is my son and a future king. If decisions had been taken only in a legal framework, he would not have been alive today.'

Raje'e eyes were filled with tears. He said, keeping his hand on Sambhaji's back, who was getting restless by the minute, 'Shambhu, why do you fear that you may be sentenced to death someday?'

Sambhaji touched Raje's feet in reply. Raje continued, 'You are my son, Shambhu. I want you to succeed before I die. You may have been guided by people for whom rites and rituals alone are important, but merely adhering to those does not bring a king to victory.'

'I apologize, Aba saheb! I made a mistake.'

'It does not matter if you made a mistake. To err is not a crime. I am here to rectify it. Promise me—you will err only to the extent that I can correct. The ryots are happy that you waived off their taxes but you must know that a kingdom runs on revenues. You are going to be a father now and you need a greater sense of your responsibilities. But I don't want to dabble in your affairs—you must manage those yourself.'

Raje's attitude towards the situation was a great relief to everyone around. Changing the topic, he started recounting tales from his campaign in Karnatak.

Pilajirao wanted Yesubai's first delivery to take place in her parents' place as per tradition. Raje readily agreed and made arrangements to send the midwives and physicians to look after Yesu.

Everyone at Raigad was eagerly waiting for Raje to arrive. As his palanquin reached the main gate, Rajaram came forward and saluted. He had grown tall and looked dashing in his kurta, a turban and sword tucked at his waist. He was nearly eight years old now. Raje said, as he hugged him affectionately, 'Bal Raje, how tall have you grown!'

'Aba saheb, you came in a palanquin. Are you not well?'

'No, it is just my age, Raje. I cannot walk all the way now. I ride, walk and take a palanquin depending on the terrain.'

The kettledrums and trumpets announced Raje's arrival. The women stood in a line to perform the aarti and ward off the evil eye. Raje was talking about his campaign as he walked towards his quarters.

'It was one and a half years of constant travel and activities, and I got to see various parts of India. How many languages we speak! I believe travel is the best teacher.'

As he reached his chambers, Manohari came in, dressed in a white sari. Raje asked, 'Manu, where is Rani saheb?'

Manohari glanced at the door. Soyarabai was standing there, wearing a green sari, a golden belt adding to her beauty. She was wearing a nose ring, anklets and other jewellery. Raje watched her admiringly, making her blush.

'Is there a festival today?' Raje asked.

'No, why do you ask?'

'I wonder why you are so dressed up!'

'You have come home after a long time. Isn't that reason enough for a celebration?'

'Well, that is true,' Raje said, as he relaxed on the bed. 'I have brought you many things from Karnatak. I will show you in the night, and you will be amazed.'

That evening, as Raje dressed up to reach the court, Soyarabai came in. She was surprised to see Raje wearing a few gold necklaces with ruby and emeralds intertwined. Seeing her expression, Raje said, 'It is a festive day for both of us. You must see the grandeur in the court today.'

The court was full. No one knew the reason for the meeting Raje called.

As he took his seat, Raje said, addressing Hambirrao, 'Do you know why we are here?'

'Maharaj,' he began but did not know what else to say.

Raje got up and took off his necklaces, putting one each on Moropant, Annaji and a few other sardars. They were all surprised, seeing a single wreath of cowries around Raje's neck.

Moropant mumbled, 'Raje, I don't understand ...'

'You deserve far more, Moropant. You managed the kingdom for the last eighteen months in my absence. You have done a wonderful job.'

Rajaram, watching the proceedings, asked, 'Aba saheb, you did not give me anything.'

'I have nothing left to give. But I can give you one thing,' Raje said, as he picked up Rajaram and made him sit on his lap.

Soyarabai was quick with her response, 'Beware, Bal Raje! Else you may suffer the same fate as Dhruva!' She was referring to the mythological tale of Dhruva, who sat on his father's lap. He was the son King Uttānapāda and his wife Suniti, and the king also had another son Uttama, born to his second queen Suruchi. Once, when Dhruva was five years old, he was sitting on his father's lap in the king's throne. Suruchi, who was jealous of Dhruva being heir to the throne, forcefully removed Dhruva from his father's lap. When Dhruva protested and asked why he could not be allowed to sit on his father's lap, Suruchi berated him and said, 'Only God can allow you that privilege. Go ask him.'

The assembly was embarrassed at Soyarabai's words. Soyarabai realized that she should have checked her tongue. Raje said, 'That too needs good fortune. While he may not have gotten a place on his father's lap, Dhruva has a permanent position in the galaxy of stars, I am sure our Yuvraj Rajaram too would get a position similar to Dhruva's.'

That evening, as Mahadev unpacked the large number of boxes, Raje pointed out the lovely saris, brocaded dhotis and many such items. Pointing to a small box, he asked Mahadev to keep it carefully in the chamber.

Soyarabai asked, 'What is that?'

'It is a poison lamp. One that helps to detect poison.'

'Why bring such an inauspicious thing here?'

'A king needs to have these things for protection.' Looking around, Raje asked, 'I don't see Putlabai. Where is she?'

'She went to stay at Raigadwadi. Apparently, the weather here does not suit her.'

'What about her arrangements there?'

'Annaji made them personally. She has everything she needs.'

'The weather did not suit Maa saheb too. I wonder why I am not affected by it.'

The taunt was not lost on Soyarabai. Her face was crestfallen but by the time she looked up, Raje had left the room.

The monsoons were about to set it in. Raje performed the rites of Jijabai's annual shrad at the fort. After the rites, he decided to visit her samadhi in Pachad.

'Moropant,' Raje said, as he left the samadhi, 'build a beautiful garden here. She gave us the shadow of affection. Let her rest under the shadow of trees now.'

As they climbed the pass of Khubaladha, Raje stopped for a while to look at the view. The River Kal flowed below with hills on all sides. The evening sun created a surreal beauty as it penetrated through the dense foliage.

Changing direction, Raje moved towards Raigadwadi. Hambirrao smiled and looked at Moropant. They both followed Raje.

At the haveli at Raigadwadi, there was frantic activity once the advance party had informed them of Raje's arrival. A maid hurried forward with a tray for aarti. After washing his feet in the courtyard, Raje stepped into the main hall. He asked, 'Where is Rani saheb?'

Soon, Putlabai arrived, wearing a simple yet elegant sari. She said, 'Had you given me enough time, I would have made proper arrangements for you.'

'Putla, I was here to pay my respects to Maa saheb. I know you did not leave Raigad under normal circumstances. I am not asking you to explain but I am sorry for whatever happened.'

'I don't need your apologies. I am just happy that you are here.'

'I am glad that after Sai, there is someone else who understands me. I have to leave for Raigad now.'

'It is already late. Why not stay back the night?'

Accepting her invitation, Raje said, 'I will inform the men accordingly.'

Putlabai brought him a glass of kokum sherbet.

'Wah! I am drinking this after many years. Maa saheb used to make it,' Raje said, as he enjoyed the cool sherbet.

'How is Yuvraj?'

'I forgot to tell you—you are going to be a grandmother soon. Yesu is fine and I wanted to bring her to Raigad but Pilajirao requested for her to be taken to his house.'

'And what about Shambhu Raje?'

'He is fine. He was crowned king by that poet Kalash.'

'What?'

'Rani saheb, he did it out of fear, but I am worried about our future,' Raje said, as he got up. 'But you don't worry. I will meet the men in the office now. They are waiting for me.'

The merchants from Raigad had come to pay their respects. Raje met them in the office and enquired about their well-being. That night, a big feast was organized in Raje's honour.

While leaving Raje said, 'Putla, just send word to me if you need anything. If I am not there, ask for Moropant.'

Putlabai nodded. She asked, 'When do we meet again?'

'You know me, Putla. Whenever I feel that the loneliness is unbearable, I will be here.'

Tears flowed down her cheeks.

Raje said, caressing her back, 'These tears don't wash away our sorrows, unfortunately. Don't make this difficult for me. I would take you back to the fort but I don't want you to suffer. Shall I go now?'

'Just give me a minute,' Putlabai said and rushed inside. She came out carrying a pair of shoes. They were marked with spots of kumkum.

Raje asked, 'Where did you get these?'

'You wore these during your coronation ceremony. I had asked Maa saheb to give them to me. She said, "These will give you company for the rest of your life."'

Raje was overwhelmed. Putla said, 'May I make a request? I want you to wear these shoes and walk up to the door. I don't know when I will see you next.'

Raje said dejectedly, 'I don't know why life does not allow me to go in a straight line. I always have to find my way through the twists and turns.'

Wearing the shoes, Raje walked up to the door. He then removed them and put on his other shoes. Putlabai took the shoes in her hand, gently wiping them with her pallu. As soon as Raje left the hall, she lost all her resolve and tears flowed down her cheeks.

Despite the monsoon, Raje's men could not rest. Daulat Khan's army was fighting the Siddis. There were news of Sarja Khan making moves too. Raje was about to leave for the court when Soyarabai came in.

'I was about to call for you,' Raje said.

Soyarabai smiled. 'It is my good fortune that you remembered me.'

'I came in the morning from Raigadwadi, but you were not to be seen. Manohari served me lunch.'

'Why did you not send for me?'

'Some things are done automatically, Soyara. They are not explained. I thought you would know your duties.'

'So it seems the younger queen has complained.'

'Not at all! Why? Did you do anything for her to complain about?'

Soyarabai's cheeks were flushed but she did not reply. As Raje stepped out of the room, he asked casually, 'Have you tried kokum sherbet?'

'Yes. I don't like it one bit.'

'I thought so,' Raje said.

Soyarabai was unable to understand the import of Raje's words as she stood there dumbfounded.

As Raje came into the office, Moropant gave Raje the latest news. 'Sarja Khan has decamped Athani and Raibag,' he said.

'We need to act fast. Hambirrao, go to Bijapur and loot the markets of Gadag. Diler Khan has come here with the intention of destroying Bijapur but the Adil Shahi court still does not understand the gravity of the situation. Let us ensure Panhala is protected properly as I expect Diler Khan to attack it. Moropant, you go into Mughal territory. We must let Diler Khan know that we mean business.'

Raje decided to go to Panhala once the rains had stopped. The Marathas looted the Bijapur kingdom. As the monsoons ended, Raje heard that the combined forces of Jamshir Khan of the Adil Shahi court, Sarja Khan and Siddi Masood were planning an attack on Raje. Smiling, he said, 'It is only a perverted mind which can think like this. Diler Khan is bent on destroying the Adil Shahi kingdom but they, in turn, are attacking us.'

Raje'e health had improved by the time the rains ended. The fort throbbed with energy and vigour.

It was a sultry afternoon with hardly any activity. White clouds floated in a blue sky. The ministers were relaxing in their quarters when a messenger came in.

Moropant asked for Annaji and Hambirrao to meet at the office. Seeing Moropant's anxious face, Annaji asked, 'What is the matter?'

'The news is that Yuvraj is having talks with Diler Khan.'

'This will worry Maharaj greatly. He has just recovered from his illness and this news will be like a thunderbolt. I wonder what we should do.'

They called Mahadev. 'What is Maharaj doing?'

'He had a little fever and is now resting.'

'Call for Rani saheb.'

Soyarabai was told about the situation. She was lost in thought, though she could not hide her satisfaction at the turn of events. She said, 'I will wake him up. You may come in after a while.'

After a while, they went into Raje's chambers. Moropant broached the topic and said, 'Maharaj, the news is not good. We were told that Yuvraj's emissary, Janardanpant, is in Diler Khan's camp.'

'We must arrest Yuvraj immediately,' Soyarabai said.

Everyone turned to look at her. Raje said, 'Rani saheb, you may go. This is a subject of discussion with the ministers. It is not a household matter.'

As Soyarabai left, fuming at the insult, a worried Raje consulted his men. 'Are you sure of the news?'

'It is true, no doubt. But we don't know what they are discussing.'

Raje's face turned optimistic. 'Annaji, Yuvraj may have some vices and play mischief once in a while but he will never be a traitor to our Swaraj. Prince Muazzam and Yuvraj are friends and I know that Muazzam and Diler Khan don't see eye to eye. I would not be surprised if Yuvraj gets Muazzam to our side.'

No one reacted. Seeing them remain silent, Raje was not sure of his own understanding of the situation and said, 'What is your advice, Annaji?'

'I suggest we put Yuvraj under house arrest and arrest Janardanpant.'

'Annaji!'

'I don't see any other way.'

'I know. Had I been feeling well, I would have gone to Shringarpur myself.' Raje was lost in thought. His mind was working furiously now. He said, 'Let our spies go to Shringarpur. Ask Yesaji to stay there. I am ordering Yuvraj to go to Parli. If he goes there, I will see him on my way to Panhala. I need to meet Samarth to clear up the cobwebs in my mind. I will take Yuvraj to Panhala with me. We need to handle this very delicately.' Raje's mind was clouded with anxiety. The fever added to his misery as he shivered involuntarily.

The fort was a hub of activity now, with spies bringing in new reports every day. Yesaji had already set off for Shringarpur, and Raje, despite his ill health, was busy meeting the spies. The gods were being propitiated every day. Annaji came in with good news one afternoon. 'Raje, in deference to your orders, Yuvraj has gone to Parli.'

Raje exclaimed, 'That is the best news I have heard in my whole life. I have been worried sick for the past four days. A suspicious mind entertains all kinds of thoughts. But I knew Yuvraj would not do anything to betray my trust. These are Jagdamba's blessings. Let us illuminate the temple on the coming full moon day with lamps.'

The next morning, Raje decided to leave for Parli. He had a cough but was feeling much better.

'Send an advance party and let Shambhu Raje know I am arriving,' he told Annaji.

Hambirrao came in to the office when Raje said, 'Hambirrao, I was about to call you. We will go to Parli together and from there to Panhala.'

There was activity everywhere. Horses were being readied while the kitchens were busy making supplies. Within an hour, the advance party had left for Parli to inform the watchposts on the way of Raje's impending arrival.

In his chamber, Manohari was busy packing Raje's clothes.

Seeing Mahadev, Raje said, 'Have you packed my gods?'

Soyarabai laughed mockingly at his question.

'Rani saheb, it is the gods who make me what I am. I always take them with me as they give me solace.'

'You have your gods and your campaigns! We don't know how to spend time here.'

'Now good days lie ahead, Rani saheb. Yesu and Sambhaji will be here with my grandson. I am really looking forward to my old age!'

At that moment, Hambirrao, Annaji and Moropant came into Raje's chambers. Annaji was shaking as he said, 'We are undone, Maharaj!'

'What happened?' Raje asked, as Annaji started sobbing.

Moropant said, wiping his tears, 'Yuvraj has just escaped from Parli and defected to the Mughals.'

The news shattered Raje. He held the bedpost to steady himself. His dear prince, Shambhu Raje, had defected to the Mughals, had sought refuge with the enemy! Seeing him slump to the floor, Hambirrao rushed forward and held his hand. The sight was unbearable for the commander. His king, the mighty Chhatrapati was in tears, shattered to the core.

Raje cried, 'Sambhaji Raje, what have you done?' Raje started crying and the men, his sardars could not stop their tears seeing Raje in this condition.

'Where was Samarth? Did Yuvraj not meet him?'

'Samarth was not in Parli when Yuvraj reached.'

All Raje could do was sob like a child. It was a situation he did not know how to handle.

The atmosphere was gloomier than during a funeral. No one spoke, while they went about their jobs silently. Raje had confined himself to his chamber. His face had changed in three days—his eyes looked lacklustre, and he did not seem to have energy for anything. Yesaji and Vishwanath came back and reported to the fort. They had been given the responsibility of taking Yuvraj to Parli. They met Raje in his chambers. Raje said, 'Tell me everything, Vishwanath.'

'We reached Parli only to be told that Samarth had gone out. Sambhaji seemed restless all the while. He took advantage of the situation and left for Mahuli. When we reached Mahuli, Sambhaji Raje declared his intention to join the Mughals. We tried our best to make him understand but to no avail. He disappeared in the night.'

'It is not your fault, Vishwanath. A man, in a fit of emotions, can do anything. Sambhaji Raje has shown us this.'

Yesaji added, 'Maharaj, we chased Yuvraj but the Mughal contingent which had come to receive him was five-thousand strong. We were a mere hundred and had to retreat.'

'That was sensible, Yesaji. It is my fault for having believed that Sambhaji could not do wrong. He must have made the plan well in advance.' Raje smiled, recalling an incident. He said, 'Sambhaji told me once that he would do such wonderful work that it will leave me astonished. I am now stunned!'

Hambirrao suggested, 'Maharaj, we can easily capture Diler Khan's camp.'

'We can; but how do we get the one who has gone missing? The fact that five thousand men came to receive Sambhaji shows he is being protected.'

'What if we write to him?' Annaji said.

'If he had had that much sense, he would not have behaved like this in the first place.'

'But Yuvraj ...'

'What Yuvraj are you talking of? Sambhaji will be a Mughal Mansabdar now and may even march on us. He is not our Yuvraj anymore. Please don't refer to him as that.' Raje stood with his back turned, his fists clenched. He said, his voice sounding hoarse, 'You may go now.'

They all saluted, leaving Raje alone in the chamber.

Bad news always comes together. Soon, the news arrived that Sambhaji had been made a Mughal Mansabdar of seven thousand. Diler Khan was thrilled. Ikhlas Khan accompanied Sambhaji to Karkhamb where he was received warmly by Diler Khan and given the mansab.

Sambhaji left a message for Shivaji: 'I have joined the Mughals and am going to pay my regards to the Mughal emperor in Delhi. I shall come back only to conquer the Sahyadris now.'

Sambhaji's message only added salt to Raje's wounds and each successive piece of news added to his turmoil. His mind was on fire.

It was a lazy afternoon as the fort relaxed. Nearly two weeks had passed since Sambhaji's defection. The servants in the stables had finished their chores and were catching up on some sleep. The elephants swayed gently, enjoying their grass. In the stables nearby, the horses were silently chewing their fodder, snorting and warding off flies with their tails.

The horses first sensed the change as their shiny bodies twitched. They started neighing loudly, waking up the syces. Unable to understand their agitation, they looked around when they heard the elephants trumpeting. The mahout was trying to pacify them, and soon the dogs started barking.

No one could understand what was happening when suddenly, they felt the ground below them shaking. The earth shook to its core. Within moments, everything was quiet as before. The animals had quietened. The destruction, within seconds, was evident everywhere. It had been an earthquake of short but massive intensity.

Raje said, as he looked out of his window, 'An earthquake! That was the only thing missing right now.'

Within a fortnight of Sambhaji's defection, Raje was back to his old self and had started looking into the official matters. He called for a meeting and said,

'I will proceed to Panhala. I know how Diler Khan will react now. I will keep an eye on the movements of the Mughals from there.'

The next morning, Annaji came in with good news, 'Maharaj, we have news from Shringarpur that Yesubai has delivered a baby girl.'

'Is that so?' Raje said, getting up. 'Distribute garments and gold coins to the men who brought the news. I wish Maa saheb was here to see this!'

However, the next moment, reality came crashing down and he said, 'It is better that she is not here. She would not have been able to bear the news about Sambhaji's defection.'

Raje decided to go to Panhala after visiting Shringarpur.

Soyarabai asked, when she heard about the visit, 'Are you still planning to see Yesu's child after what has happened?'

'What is her fault? Why blame her and the child for what Shambhu has done?'

'Don't you think she is involved? He is certainly under her thumb, though he may not listen to anyone else.'

'I am surprised you can say such a thing. I don't think you have understood a man's mind yet.'

Soyarabai fumed for a while and then, realizing that Raje was in no mood to listen to her, left the room.

Shringarpur was asleep, covered in the early morning mist. The haveli was silent when the messenger arrived. Hearing of Raje's arrival, there was a frantic activity everywhere.

Hambirrao received Raje and held the reins as he dismounted. Umaji Pandit and Kalash, along with Pilajirao Shirke, welcomed Raje.

Pilaji said, as he walked with Raje towards the inner chambers, 'After hearing what had happened, Yesu decided to stay back here.'

'I can quite understand that. We have to bear our sorrows with fortitude.'

As Raje entered Yesu's chamber, she fell at his feet sobbing. 'Aba saheb!'

Raje hugged her saying, 'My dear, don't weep. You have a big responsibility on your shoulders now. But I am with you. Things will be fine.'

Yesubai wiped her tears. Raje saw the baby girl and showered gold coins on her crib. He said, as he sat in the chair, 'Yesu, did you have any idea of Sambhaji Raje's plans?'

He had presumed she would not have any idea, but much to his surprise, she nodded and said, 'I did. But he had bound me by an oath.'

'What kind of oath, Yesu? Such promises are not meant to be kept. You should have at least prevented him from going.'

'I tried.'

'Why didn't you appeal to him emotionally?'

'That is beyond me.'

'I know,' Raje said. 'Maa saheb too did not have that capacity. There was only one person but she too is no more. We have to work delicately to untie these knots, Yesu.'

Yesu looked at Raje as he spoke. He had aged greatly in a span of a few months. His eyes, which usually sparkled with intensity, looked cheerless. His cheeks, having sunk in, highlighted the aquiline nose, making it look grotesque. His broad forehead, only carrying the horizontal ash mark of Shiva, now looked wrinkled. He looked weary, old and tired. She said, touching his feet, 'Aba saheb, I hope you don't blame me.'

Raje placed his hand on her back affectionately and said, 'I know you are not at fault, dear. It was I who did not judge him well. The fault lies in our fate.'

Back at the office, he asked Pilaji, 'How could he do this when you were with him all the time?'

'I am ashamed, Maharaj. I am a simple man and know how to deal with an enemy who attacks me. But I cannot comprehend the tricks of cunning and intelligent men. I simply believed him when he said he was on his way to Parli.'

Raje looked at Kalash and said, 'Did you know he was having talks with Diler Khan?'

Kalash's silence was an acknowledgement of his guilt. He said, 'I tried to dissuade him but he did not listen.'

'I have learnt about life the hard way, and I suggest you don't try to fool me. You were the one who crowned him. Now he is not a king but a saat-hazari Mansabdar in the Mughal army.'

Umaji Pandit tried to intervene, 'Maharaj, it is not Kalash's fault but ...'

Raje's eyes burned through Umaji. He shouted, 'Hambirrao, before he utters another word trying to display his knowledge, tie their hands and send both of them to Raigad. They are Brahmins, else I would have ordered that they be dragged all the way tied to a horse.'

The attendants rushed in and arrested Umaji and Kalash before they could react.

The naming ceremony for Yesu's child was performed without much enthusiasm. She was named Bhawani. As Raje sat in his chambers the next morning, he saw Yesu enter with a glass of milk. 'What is this, dear? You should not be walking around. You need to rest and take care of your health.'

Yesu's eyes were filled with tears as she said, 'What harm can come to me if I walk out of my room?'

'My dear, don't cry. Do you understand my situation? Lakhs of families put their trust in me. How do I show my face to them? It is only you who can save the kingdom from dishonour. You cannot afford to cry.'

'What can I do?'

'Sambhaji is fickle and I don't think I can manage to dissuade him from his reckless behaviour. Aurangzeb, seasoned politician that he is, is not easy to predict. We need gentle hands if we have to pick a cactus flower. You are the one who can do it.'

Yesu gave him a confused look. Raje continued, 'You don't know the power you have. You are his wife, a friend and an advisor. Sambhaji will not go against your wishes.' Taking out a tiny golden box from his pocket, Raje said, 'I have brought you a special gift.'

Raje's smile vanished as he opened the box. It was a lovely nose ring. He said, taking it out and handing it to her, 'Here, take this! This was given by Maa saheb to Sai, the eldest Rani saheb. Now it is yours. It is a symbol of pride for the Bhosale family. I know you can keep its glory. And one more thing—at the bottom of the box, there is a small packet which has her mangalsutra. It was preserved despite the heat of the pyre. This is yours now.'

Yesu touched Raje's feet.

'My dear, don't entertain any doubts now. Shambhu is my son and I am not going to abandon him on account of his behaviour.' Raje's voice trembled as he continued, 'How do I tell you, Yesu? He was merely two years old when his mother passed away. I had to meet Afzal Khan and did not even get time to mourn her death. After my coronation, Maa saheb left us. I somehow managed to overcome the sorrow but now—I am once again shattered, Yesu. I don't have the energy even to stand.'

Yesu's tears flowed as Raje continued, 'When I was in Srisailam, I was prepared to offer my head at the feet of the Lord. I wish I had done that!'

'Aba saheb!' Yesu exclaimed, her body shivering with fear.

'You want me to live, don't you? So please do as I tell you—I am leaving my trusted spies here. They will take your message to Shambhu at Diler Khan's camp. Will you do this for me?'

Yesu nodded her head vigorously and said, 'Yes, Aba saheb!'

Raje smiled and patted her back gently as he took the glass of milk and drowned it in one gulp.

The next morning, Raje prepared to leave. He said, 'Do you know there was an earthquake at Raigad? It was due to the little one's birth. The Puranas say that whenever gods and goddesses take birth on earth, the earth quakes.'

Raje soon reached Panhala. He had ordered new guns from the Europeans to fortify Panhala. The Maratha forces were, in the meanwhile, busy creating havoc in the Mughal and Adil Shahi territories. Moropant had managed to take over the fort at Koppal while Anandrao had captured Balapur and Shahapur, which were considered gateways to Bijapur. By then the news arrived that Muazzam, Aurangzeb's son, had been sent as Subedar of the Deccan. Raje extended a hand of friendship to him. He said, 'Now that he and Diler Khan are at loggerheads, this would be to our benefit. Let us see how this turns out.'

Having fortified Panhala, Raje returned to Raigad. One day, Annaji reported, 'There is news of Diler Khan marching towards Bhupalgad.'

'I am not worried. The fort is strong and Firangoji is stronger!' Raje said. He smiled and continued, 'We know they cannot take away even a pebble from our Sahyadris. Sambhaji Raje will soon realize this.'

BOOK
ELEVEN

It had been a month since Bhawani's birth. On a Monday morning, Raje was in his court when Annaji and Jedhe came in. He said, 'Annaji, I think we must wait till the rains end. Diler Khan has besieged Bhupalgad but he has set his sights on Bijapur. I doubt if the Adil Shahi troops would be able to hold out in front of Diler.'

'I hope that the arrogance of Adil Shahi kingdom is crushed.'

'No. That should not happen,' Raje said, much to the surprise of Balaji Jedhe and Annaji.

'Why do you say that?'

'We have gathered our forces at Panhala to help the Adil Shahi kingdom. It is important that the three southern powers stand together when Aurangzeb comes down to the Deccan. Qutb Shah understands this and, soon, the Adil Shahi will also realize this.'

Balaji came in to announce the arrival of Firangoji Narsala.

'Why is he here? That too when Bhupalgad is besieged?'

Firangoji came in, his grey whiskers throbbing on his cheeks. He seemed distraught and the moment he saw Raje, he fell at his feet.

'Why did you leave the fort, Firangoji?'

'I was forced to.'

'Why? Did you surrender to the Mughals?'

Firangoji did not answer immediately, looking down at the floor.

Raje asked, 'By whose orders did you leave, Firangoji?'

'Yuvraj ordered me to.'

'What? Tell me what happened.'

Firangoji said, wiping his tears, 'When Diler Khan stormed the town, the residents took shelter inside the fort. We were prepared for a long siege and give him a fitting reply. But then ...'

'Then what?'

'Sambhaji Raje came forward and, on seeing him, we lost our courage. He ordered us to open the door, threatening to kill our people if we did not.'

Raje's anger was evident as his face turned red. He asked, 'Did you surrender the fort?'

'Yes, Maharaj.'

'I want to know what exactly happened.'

'Sambhaji Raje was to take charge of the fort but Diler Khan went back on his word and chopped off the hands of seven hundred of our men. He snatched jewellery from the women and destroyed the fort.'

'Wah! What a fine thing you have done! You are a veteran general in this army since the times of the elder Maharaj and here you are—surrendering our forts to the enemy!'

'What else could I do, Maharaj?' A helpless Firangoji pleaded. 'Holding the enemy at Bhupalgad was no problem at all. But we had no choice when we saw Sambhaji Raje. I just handed over the fort and came here.'

'It would have been better not to have come at all.'

Firangoji was shocked to hear Raje speak thus. 'Maharaj ...'

'Is anyone there?' Raje shouted, looking out of the room. Two guards rushed in. Raje said, 'Arrest him and shoot him tomorrow before sunrise.'

Firangoji rushed forward and fell at Raje's feet. Raje stepped back when Firangoji pleaded, 'Maharaj, forgive me. I am not at fault.' His face looked pitiable.

Raje could not bear to see him like this. Teary-eyed, he turned away and said, 'I know you are not at fault. Punishment is not given only when you make a mistake. But if many men make mistakes like you did, we would lose our kingdom in no time. Your loyalty is to the kingdom and not to an individual.' Turning to the guards he said, 'Take him away.'

Raje turned his back as he could not bear the sight of Firangoji being dragged away.

Annaji and Balaji stood trembling. They witnessed the entire episode. Mustering some courage, Balaji began to speak, 'Maharaj!'

Before he could continue, Raje said, 'Balaji, I want you to ensure that the order is carried out without any hesitation. Even if Shambhu Bhosale comes to the fort as a Mughal Mansabdar, they must not stop. Else, the guards will not be spared.'

The fort was agog with the news of the punishment pronounced for Firangoji. Everyone knew that Raje had highly regarded the veteran soldier. They could not imagine him being shot to death on Raje's orders. No one dared to enter Raje's chamber. Even Soyarabai had not taken his meals to him. It was evening when Raje heard someone at the door. He asked, 'Who is it?'

Mahadev came in and said, 'Annajipant is here.'

'Send him in.'

Annaji came in and said, 'The younger Rani saheb is here.'

'What? Putla is here?'

Putlabai entered the chamber after a few moments. She was wearing a simple sari without any jewellery and yet she looked arresting. Soyarabai was much fairer than her but there was a fascinating simplicity in Putlabai's beauty which made Raje stare at her for a long time.

She said, bringing Raje out of his trance, 'I am told you have ordered Firangoji to be gunned down. Is the order going to be carried out?'

'That is right. I don't issue orders for them not to be executed.'

'What crime did he commit?'

'Ask what he did not! He surrendered the fort without any justification. If a veteran like Firangoji behaves like this, what else can I do but punish him? There is no offence bigger than being a traitor. The death sentence is the only punishment for such a crime.'

'Is this punishment for all such traitors?' Putlabai asked calmly.

'Of course!' Raje said, a little irritated.

'Even if Shambhu Raje were to return tomorrow?'

Raje was taken by surprise at Putla's question. He was dumbfounded. 'Putla!'

'I ask you; if the punishment cannot be meted out to Shambhu Raje, should you not think it over? You may otherwise repent this decision forever. I only came to tell you this.'

Putlabai left without waiting for Raje's answer. Raje paced restlessly in his room, lost alone in his thoughts. He called for Mahadev.

'Is there anyone outside?'

'Yes, Annaji is here.'

'Send him in.'

Annaji came in. He asked, mustering courage, 'What about Firangoji's punishment tomorrow?'

'It will be meted out as ordered. Anyway, you may go now.' With a heavy heart, Raje sat alone on his bed.

Sleep eluded Raje for a long time. It was long past midnight when he finally managed to sleep. Early the next morning, he woke up sweating. Mahadev, standing guard outside, came in when he heard a noise inside.

'Bring me some water, Mahadev.'

As Mahadev poured water into a cup, Raje asked, 'Is it dawn yet?'

'No, Maharaj.'

'You may go now.'

Raje's mind was cluttered with his racing thoughts. He could not bear the silence in the room. Images of Firangoji haunted him. He remembered the day Firangoji had annexed the Chakan Fort and hoisted the saffron flag atop it. Raje had said, 'I don't want a mere fort, Firangoji. I want men like you.' Firangoji had joined the efforts for the Swaraj that day.

Raje tossed restlessly in his bed. He remembered how Firangoji had fought for two months holding Shaista Khan at bay when he had attacked Chakan. Later, when Shaista Khan had managed to win the fort, he had made Firangoji a tempting offer. But Firangoji had declined, saying he couldn't be a traitor.

Raje could not sleep anymore. He paced his room and went to the window. There was no wind. It was as if time and wind had stood still. Firangoji had been a steady support to Raje throughout his life.

What did you do, Firangoji? Why did you surrender to Yuvraj? Was it attachment? Is that what corrupts a man's mind? But you have committed an offence, and a crime must be punished.

The early morning chirping of the birds attracted Raje's attention. Dawn was about to break.

But man lives by emotions, doesn't he? What must Firangoji have thought when he saw Sambhaji Raje at the door? He could not have shot him! He had played with Shambhu when he was a child. What would I have done had I been in Firangoji's place?

The eastern sky was becoming light now. A brass gun at the Takmak point, the place for executions, was visible to Raje from his window.

Is it not possible for the sun not to rise today? What am I afraid of? Duties cannot be carried out on the basis of emotions. But I cannot stop thinking about what Putla had asked—would I carry out the same punishment for Sambhaji if he returns?

Running barefoot towards Takmak point, much to the surprise of the guards, Raje screamed, 'Stop! Stop!'

All eyes turned towards Raje. Firangoji, tied to the muzzle of a brass cannon stood quietly. The torch bearer was in his position. Raje took a dagger from the waistband of a soldier standing nearby and in one swoop, he cut off the ropes around Firangoji's wrists. He looked at Raje, gasping for breath, his hair dishevelled, beads of sweat on his forehead. Did God look like this?

Firangoji said, trying to hold back his tears, 'Maharaj, why did you rush? This dry leaf had to fall down one day. What difference does it make how I go? It would have been a blessing to have had a death ordered by you.'

Raje could not hold himself back anymore. As tears trickled down his cheeks, he hugged Firangoji tightly and said, 'I don't know what to do, Firangoji. I don't know what to do!'

Raje's anxiety was unending. While he was happy about Anandrao annexing Balapur, he was worried about Diler Khan's march onto Bijapur. A dispatch from Shringarpur came in.

'Yesubai wants to move with Bhawani to Panhala as the weather at Shringarpur is not suiting the child.'

'That is very good news,' a delighted Raje said. 'The humid climate does not suit the baby,' he added. He asked Annaji to immediately make the necessary arrangements. Annaji nodded but was not convinced that Raje's explanation was as innocent as it appeared to be.

Raje had been trying to quash Siddi in Janjira for a long time but the Englishmen's support was helping Siddi. He ordered Mainak Bhandari, stationed at Khanderi, and Daulat Khan, the admiral at Rajpuri, to keep an eye on the English. At that time, the news of Diler Khan knocking on the doors of Bijapur reached Raje. Siddi Masood, worried that he would lose to the Mughals, sent word to Raje to save the Adil Shahi kingdom at any cost.

Agreeing to help, Raje sent a ten-thousand-strong contingent to Bijapur as well as financial help. He sent a message that he would personally be there.

When Raje reached Panhala, Yesubai was already there. Raje asked, 'Any news, Yesu?'

'He has said if he gets assurance ...'

'Shambhu needs assurance? I am the one feeling insecure.'

Seeing Raje in his military attire, Yesu asked, 'Are you going on a campaign? Your health ...'

Raje smiled. 'When it was time for me to enjoy my old age, Shambhu left me and joined the Mughals. Had he been here, I would have sent him on the campaign. But such is destiny! Look at the irony here. I am trying to save the Adil Shahi kingdom when my son is destroying it. Isn't it then better to die?'

'Aba saheb!'

'Don't worry, my dear. My health will improve only if I am out on a campaign.'

While leaving Panhala, Raje instructed everyone that they should receive Sambhaji Raje warmly if he were to arrive. With a contingent of twenty-five thousand men, Raje rushed towards Bijapur.

Raje was approaching Bijapur while the troops, sent in advance, were already engaging Diler Khan. Siddi Masood was happy to see that Raje was reaching out to help and had informed Sikander Adil Shah about the same. But he sent a message that Raje should not come to Bijapur with more than five hundred men.

Moropant said, 'Raje, I feel we must tread carefully. Masood is our traditional enemy and may not hesitate to play foul. Let us be sure of his intentions before we move.'

Raje agreed and cancelled the meeting with Adil Shah and focused on the campaign. Raje was worried that Diler Khan may use his trump card, Sambhaji, and put him in the front, creating a problem for Raje and his men. He decided to move out of Bijapur to wreak havoc in Diler Khan's territories while he was busy in Bijapur.

Crossing the Bhima River, Raje moved to Jalna, near Aurangabad and pillaged the same. Muazzam was stationed at Aurangabad and soon he sent an urgent plea to Diler Khan to return and help. Diler Khan was forced to lift the siege of Bijapur and march back towards Aurangabad.

Raje was returning with a lot of booty from Jalna but was informed that three Mughal sardars were planning to intercept him, with an army of nearly eight thousand men. But one of the spies, Bahirji, found a way to avoid, with a detour of more than three days, the enemy. They reached Pattagad near Nashik, safely covering a distance of nearly three hundred kilometres. Raje renamed Pattagad as Vishramgad after staying a fortnight there.

In the meanwhile, Moropant continued his attacks and managed to loot Dharangaon and even went up to Surat. And there was good news awaiting Raje when he reached Raigad. Sambhaji Raje had abandoned the Mughals and was coming back to Panhala!

The news spread cheer all over. But Raje was worried, lost in thoughts for two days. On the third day, he called for a special meeting with Annaji, Moropant, Balaji, Yesaji, Firangoji and Hambirrao. He asked the guards to not allow anyone else in. He said, as soon as the men came in, 'I have been thinking how to handle Sambhaji Raje's return. I have called you to take a decision about it.'

The ministers looked at each other, not knowing how to react. Raje said, 'My worry is Yuvraj cannot be trusted. He may take a thoughtless decision anytime again.'

Hambirrao said, moving forward, 'Raje, he is your son.'

'I wish you would be clearer about your loyalties.'

Hambirrao was taken aback. He said, 'Raje, have I said anything wrong?'

'Certainly! You are seeing Yuvraj as my son, and that makes you forget the kingdom. Firangoji made the same mistake and as a result, hundreds of our men lost their lives for no fault of theirs.'

'We must give him a chance to improve. I believe he might,' Hambirrao persisted.

'There is no guarantee when you say "might". How can I risk the future of my kingdom?'

'Isn't the kingdom his birthright as well? How can we challenge it?'

'You are making the same mistake again,' Raje said, his voice full of anguish. 'You are the commander and not me. The state belongs to the Lord.

I was crowned Chhatrapati to take care of the Swaraj. But it must go on even when I am no more.'

'Why should we think about that now?' Annaji asked.

'We have to, Annaji. Thousands have sacrificed their lives and many saints have blessed us so that we can achieve what we have. Life is transitory. How can we be sure of tomorrow? We need to decide, before I leave for Panhala, who will be in charge if I were to die.'

'You must decide that, Maharaj. We cannot,' Moropant insisted.

'Why do you say that? You are the prime minister, the Peshwa. Have I not taken every decision collectively ever since I was crowned?'

'We will still leave the decision to you, Maharaj,' Moropant said. 'I agree that Yuvraj may not look after the kingdom with the same sense of responsibility as you did.'

'I am happy to hear that you think the same way. I think Sambhaji Raje should be given the Gingee region and Rajaram the Maharashtra region under your supervision.' Everyone seemed happy with the decision. Raje said, his voice tinged with regret, 'I created such a large kingdom out of nothing. And we are going to divide it now! It is like putting a dagger through my own heart. But anyway, I have to do it. I think Sambhaji Raje would agree. I will convince him and then decide the next steps.'

Raje looked tired and worn out as he stood up. Everyone saluted but Raje was lost in his thoughts as he slowly walked back to his room.

Winter had set in. It had been a month since the looting of Jalna when Raje marched along with his troops towards Panhala. The advance party, led by Hambirrao, had already reached. On reaching the fort, Shivaji asked Hambirrao, who had come to receive him, 'Where is Yuvraj? Has he said anything?'

'He is in his quarters, Maharaj. He has a lot of regret about his mistake. He is young, after all.'

As Raje reached Sambhaji's quarters, he saw him standing outside. Sambhaji stepped forward and saluted thrice, much to Raje's surprise and dismay as he expected Sambhaji to fall at his feet. He only said, 'Come,' and he moved towards the office.

The sun had set and the cold winter fog was rapidly coming in. Raje said, as they entered the office, 'Sambhaji Raje, I am delighted to see you here. You turned your back to me and went to Mahuli on the day of Sankranti. Tomorrow is Diwali and I'm glad you're here.'

'Aba saheb!'

'Why did you do this, Sambhaji?'

'I am really ashamed.'

'Don't say that! I don't want to listen to your excuses. I founded the Hindavi Swaraj to drive out the foreigners who have occupied our land. And you, my own son, defected to the Mughals? You thought you can conquer the Sahyadris? If you had only asked me for what you wanted, I would have readily given it to you.'

'Imprisonment?' Sambhaji asked, his tone taunting.

Raje glared at Sambhaji but he did not lower his gaze.

'Yes, imprisonment! You know the reason why as well. Do you think I like it?'

'I didn't like defecting to the Mughals, either,' Sambhaji said.

'Why do you speak in this convoluted manner, Shambhu? I built this kingdom in the last forty years, while many calamities befell me. But I never wavered. I had to deal with people like Afzal Khan and Shaista Khan. I escaped with you from Agra. But everything was brought to nought when you joined the Mughals. I am so devastated. But by Bhawani's grace, you have come back. I feel good now.'

'I came back for your sake, Aba saheb, and not for the sake of the kingdom. I have lost my status as prince and my subedari now. I have not become a sanyasi, thankfully.'

Raje had tears in his eyes. He said, embracing Sambhaji tightly, 'My boy! Don't speak like this. I have suffered enough already. I wish you would understand what I am trying to say.'

The sudden neighing of a horse startled Raje and he loosened his embrace. A white horse was standing outside in the cold night. Raje said, wiping his tears, as he pointed at the horse, 'You know Moti, my horse? He may be mute but knows the loving touch of my hand on his back. When he sensed that I am here, he broke his tethering rope and came here. But why is it that I fail to deal with you? I thought I fulfilled all your needs. Yet, I suppose I failed somewhere.'

Sambhaji looked at Raje and said, his voice calm, 'Aba saheb, men are not satisfied as easily as animals.'

Raje was startled at Sambhaji's words. He said, in an agonized voice, 'It would have been better had they been.'

The next moment, his agony turned to anger and he erupted with anger and said, 'How dare you speak like this? It seems the Mughal mansabdari has intoxicated you. You lost your mother just two years after your birth but you have Maa saheb's ample love. You have a lovely wife. I initiated you into politics and was happy when you handled that European emissary well. Did you feel that I would not honour the decisions taken by you?'

Raje's words were hot molten lead being poured into Sambhaji's ears. Raje continued, 'After Maa saheb's death, your youth took over your discretion. I too was a young man when the daughter-in-law of the Subedar of Kalyan stood before me. I was to decide the future of that stunningly beautiful woman. I could have easily sent her to a harem or given her to any of my soldiers. But my mind did not allow my heart to rule. Maa saheb was proud of the way I had treated a woman prisoner. But you lusted after a Brahmin girl who had come visiting her parents' home!'

'Aba saheb, I was ...'

'Don't say another word! Self-pity is more dangerous than addiction. You need to look into yourself. The offences you have committed can never be forgiven. And yet, I let you go as I loved you and believed you would improve yourself. But your reckless behaviour continued.'

Raje paused for a breath and continued, 'You did not befriend Annaji and Moropant. Moropant conquered Salher–Mulher and built and renovated Pratapgad. Annaji has dedicated his entire life for the cause of Swaraj. Yet, you called them cunning and insulted them accusing them of deceit. But little did you realize that you are insulting me in the process as these men are equal to me in prestige and position. But they tried to protect you all the time, ignoring your immaturity.

'Look at the men you surrounded yourself with! Men who instigated you to crown yourself. I was intoxicated with bravery while you were getting drunk on a potion of hemp and your harem. Even God cannot satisfy you! You may be my son but I have had to entrust the administration to the council of ministers. You know what agonies I have had to suffer?'

Sambhaji was stunned. He looked blankly at Raje as he continued, 'I wanted to see if you can manage on your own, having been given a Subha. I was away for a year and half and what did I find when I returned? I had returned victorious but was a miserable failure as far as you were concerned.'

'I made a mistake,' Sambhaji said, gathering his voice.

Raising his hands in the air, Raje said, 'It was a huge mistake. The moment I left, you started discussions with our arch-enemy Diler Khan and, to my shock, you joined the Mughals and became a Mansabdar! But if that gives you happiness, I don't know what else to do other than curse my luck.'

Tears flowed down Sambhaji's face. Raje's outburst continued, 'You weep now? What for? You marched onto Bhupalgad and made Firangoji surrender to you. I had ordered his execution.'

'Aba saheb!'

'The order was not carried out. I just could not do it! The mistake was yours and not Firangoji's. He opened the gates and Diler Khan's men cut off the hands of seven hundred of our men, while you were a mute and possibly a willing spectator. They looted everything and destroyed the fort. You are the one to blame—not Firangoji!'

Raje seemed to be speaking to himself rather than address Sambhaji. He said, 'Thousands of women have become widows in our quest to build the Swaraj. Yet, none have cursed us. In fact, I got their blessings wherever I went. But you? At the age of thirty, you have made young mothers and sisters jump into a well, along with their children, to save their honour from Diler Khan. I am told you were also willing to sell the residents of the town as slaves!'

Sambhaji's tears were now unstoppable. He said, 'That is the reason I came back.'

'What a pity that you are still lying. You came back when you heard that Aurangzeb had issued orders to arrest you. Join whoever you want but not Aurangzeb. He will torture you in a manner you cannot even imagine.'

Raje said, putting his hand on Sambhaji's shoulder, 'Shambhu, do you realize that the very idea of your death tears my heart to pieces?'

Raje was exhausted and his hand slipped off Sambhaji's back. Sambhaji fell at Raje's feet and said, as he tried to wipe his tears, 'I don't want you to forgive me, Aba saheb. Please punish me by throwing me off the precipice or shoot me or have me trampled under the legs of an elephant. I am ready for any death.'

'All these punishments are common, Shambhu. For you, there is only one punishment.'

'Tell me, Aba saheb. Tell me what I must undergo.'

Raje looked at Sambhaji for a moment and said, 'You will have to bear my death.'

That evening, as Raje stood on the terrace watching the valley, Hambirrao came in to announce Sambhaji.

As Sambhaji stepped in and touched Raje's feet, Raje said, 'Sambhaji, wipe your tears now. It does not become you to shed tears all the time. I have given the matter a lot of consideration.'

Raje was silent for a moment, trying to construct his thoughts. Sambhaji waited patiently. 'Today, our kingdom is spread from the Tungabhadra to the Narmada and it is not possible to rule over such a vast kingdom easily. Aurangzeb has imposed the jizya tax now and Hindus are being oppressed under his rule. He is likely to descend on the Deccan soon. I had hoped to capture Delhi and re-install the idol of Lord Vishwanath. Now, you need to complete the task.'

'Me?'

'Yes, Sambhaji Raje, you have to do it. I don't know how long I will last now.'

'Aba saheb!'

'A horse can gallop as long it has strong legs, and a wounded horse is a liability. I am the founder of the Hindavi Swaraj and I feel that the best way forward is to bifurcate the kingdom.'

'Bifurcate?'

'Yes. I united thousands of Mavals and ryots to work for the cause but I was not able to unite my family members. The ministers too are divided. The elder Rani saheb is a different matter altogether. This is what I have decided: The region between the Tungabhadra and the Kaveri is the kingdom of Gingee which has rich forts like Gingee and Vellore. It is safe from the Mughals as well. And in case they do invade, the Qutb Shahi kingdom comes first. I want you to manage that.'

Sambhaji was astounded. Raje continued, before Sambhaji could speak, 'And the second half, between the Tungabhadra and the Godavari will be run by a council of ministers till Rajaram becomes a major.'

Sambhaji pleaded, 'Aba saheb, I beg of you not to divide the kingdom. You may entrust it to whoever you want. I will not give you any trouble and shall be satisfied with simple food at home. I want to be in service at your feet. No one else trusts me.'

'I know you mean it. But you should have said this a long time ago. I want to lead a life away from all this now. It is best for all of us.'

'Aba saheb, will you never forgive me?' Sambhaji asked.

'Who am I to forgive you? I don't have the authority. Think of what I have told you. I will go to Raigad and perform Rajaram's thread ceremony and marriage. Once I return, we will discuss and take the right decision. I want you to think about what I said in the meanwhile.'

While leaving for Raigad, he met Yesu and said, 'Don't forget what I told you. You have to assert yourself. That is the only way to keep Sambhaji in check.'

As Raje rode out of the fort, he turned back to look. At the bastion, the saffron flag fluttered and at the gate stood Sambhaji.

A contingent of around two thousand soldiers moved towards Satara. Despite the sun overhead, there was a pleasant warmth. Raje sat in his palanquin, his hand holding the tassel for support. Soon, Parli was in sight and Raje closed his eyes and folded his hands in namaskar.

At that moment the palanquin stopped. Raje peeped out to see Hambirrao running towards the palanquin and he said, 'Raje, Kalyan Swami is waiting for you.'

Kalyan Swami said, as Raje got off and rushed to meet him, 'Raje, we have been waiting for you. Samarth wanted to meet you while you are en route to Panhala.'

Raje was nervous when he heard that. He asked, 'Is he waiting for me? Let us go right away.'

As they walked the way up the hill, Raje saw Samarth standing at the gates of the Parli Fort. Overwhelmed with emotions and with tears trickling down his cheeks, Raje hid his face in his palms as sobs racked his body.

Samarth stepped forward and said, 'Shivba, have courage. Things will be fine by the grace of Lord Ramchandra.'

They reached the hermitage. After a while, Raje and Samarth were alone in the hut. Sitting on a tiger skin, Samarth looked and Raje and asked, 'May I know why you were crying then?'

Raje raised his head. Samarth's right hand was resting on a crutch with a rosary was moving between his fingers. Raje said, 'I had no other choice. I was avoiding you as I had no face to show you. While I was busy working for the Swaraj, our Yuvraj defected to the Mughals.'

Samarth smiled. 'So you thought you could avoid seeing me, did you? Can anything be hidden from your guru?'

'Forgive me, Gurudev! I was confused.'

'Shivba, I understand. That is why I sent Kalyan Swami to wait for you. I am the one responsible for all this agony.'

'You?'

'Yes. When Sambhaji came to Parli, I was not there. If I had been, things would have been different.'

'It is my bad luck!' Raje said, dejectedly.

'Then why pine for it?'

'I am wondering whom to hand over the kingdom to, from the Narmada to the Tungabhadra?'

'Yuvraj has come back now, has he not?'

'Yes, he has. But the ministers don't trust him and Rajaram is still young. When I took the oath at Rohideshwar, I had nothing, but now I have this vast kingdom and the seeds of Swaraj, sowed so carefully, has grown a plant so big that I need an axe now!'

'Why an axe, Raje?'

Raje said, wiping his tears, 'Because of Yuvraj's behaviour, I have decided to split the kingdom into two and entrust the Gingee region to Sambhaji and the rest to Rajaram.'

'So you too are becoming egoistic!'

'Egoistic?' Raje exclaimed.

'To say that you expanded the kingdom and lakhs of people depend on you is a form of ego. You are suffering because of it. Leave it to the Lord to decide how the kingdom will be managed. Why are you worrying about it? You must only do your duty. Therein lies happiness and real satisfaction.'

'How can I be satisfied when I am lonely and have no one to share my sorrows with? I am totally exhausted. The sky remains as high as ever—I miss my mother but I cannot reach her.'

'Shivba!'

'Gurudev, I lived a life of loyalty and responsibility. What sin did I commit to suffer like this?'

Ramdas Swami's face was agonized. He said, 'Raje, you are attached to this world. Each man is born and dies alone. Sorrows are inevitable. Lord Krishna died a horrible death. What sin had he committed? Lord Rama too had to suffer his last moments in a watery grave. Bhishma died on a bed of arrows.'

Samarth's soothing voice made Raje comfortable. He looked up. Samarth said, 'Raje, we are born to suffer pains and agonies. But we must realize that the body is false and as are pains and sorrows. Once you know yourself, you can get out of the bond of life and attain bliss.'

'I don't have that capability. Or, I would not have suffered so much.'

'One has to act, Raje! I gave you the *Dasbodh* so that it can show you the way when you are confused. The gyani does not run after moments of joy. Ignorance is sitting on one's wealth and not being able to see it. We forget to see the presence of the Lord everywhere, whether in the cool breeze, the luminescence of the moon or in the palash blooms in the summer. Till we realize His existence, we do not realize the soul.'

Raje felt better after listening to Samarth's words.

'Raje, don't get entangled in false attachment. Once you know yourself, there is only bliss. The fearlessness with which you met Afzal Khan was a testimony of your belief in the Lord. The moment when you saw the saffron flag flutter for the first time, was it not pure ecstasy? Have you cared to count such moments?'

Samarth saw that Raje was now rapt with attention listening to him. His eyes were closed and his breathing was soft. Watching him sit in this meditative pose, Samarth was overjoyed and called out, 'Shivba!'

Raje was motionless. After a while, when he came out of his trance, he looked at Samarth with contented eyes. Samarth had tears in his eyes. Raje stood up and placed his head at Samarth's feet.

Hugging him affectionately, Samarth said, without bothering to wipe his tears, which flowed freely, 'Raje, you are fortunate that you have attained this position. You have very little time and you should try to realize yourself at the earliest. Don't think about the future. You are already a rajayogi. Now try to become a siddhayogi, the one who is enlightened. That is your true self.'

Raje felt a deep sense of satisfaction after having realized his new identity. With a serene face, he took leave of Samarth.

All of Raigad was agog with the news of Raje's arrival. As his palanquin reached the main square, accompanied by Hambirrao, Moropant and Annaji, the soldiers saluted. Rajaram came running and touched Raje's feet as he wearily got down from the palanquin.

Looking at Rajaram, Raje said, 'You seem to have caught a cold and have fever. Why did you leave the palace?'

'To see you.'

'But what about your health?'

'That is a common thing,' Rajaram said, a little tired.

'Don't neglect your health.'

Rajaram nodded. Raje walked with him towards his chamber. Mahadev stood waiting. Raje handed his sword to Mahadev and then took off his shawl as he sat on the bed.

'Why is Dada Maharaj not here?' Rajaram asked.

'He does not trust me, unfortunately. Anyway, why don't you go out and ask Moropant and Annaji to come here?'

Soyarabai came in at that moment with a maid who was carrying a tray with a tumbler of milk in it.

Raje said, 'I don't want it. Take it away.'

'How is your health?' Soyarabai asked, as she waved a hand to ask the maid to take the tray away.

'Nothing wrong with my health.'

Soyarabai then asked what Raje feared she would. 'How is Sambhaji? Has he come to his senses?'

'He is repenting his deeds. His mind is weak.'

'Despite what he has done, you still say he is weak?' There was malice in Soyarabai's voice as she spoke.

'Such things happen not due to rashness alone. It is also due to weakness.'

Soyarabai said, 'No one except you would have tolerated this.'

'Just leave it, Rani saheb.' Raje did not wait for an answer and left the room. In the office Annaji, Moropant and Balaji were waiting for him. Raje asked, as he took his seat, 'Is the fortification at Khanderi Island finished?'

'Yes, Maharaj.'

'Then why did you not tell me about it?'

'Well, we lost a few men and some ships,' Moropant said, swallowing nervously. 'But Mainak Bhandari and Daulat Khan are fine,' he added quickly.

'Please tell me everything,' Raje said, sighing.

'We had collected the material at Naigaon; Mainak had a hundred and fifty men and four guns but the wall was hardly built to a height of one and half arms when the English ships marched on to Khanderi and tried to obstruct the construction. Our men continued their work. A battle ensued when the English sent their ships. Our navy retaliated and they lost a ship and five men, but we took many of the English prisoners.'

'That is fantastic. Daulat Khan has shown great courage.'

'Maharaj, when we sank their ships, the English launched a fresh attack and sank three of our ships with three hundred men losing their lives and another twelve hundred wounded.'

Raje was pained at hearing this. Moropant continued, 'Daulat Khan continued the construction of the wall around the island and we also changed our strategy and besieged the Rajapur factory. We managed to arrest all the men there.'

Raje admired the courage of Daulat Khan. He smiled and said, 'Carry on. What happened next?'

'That brought the English to ask for a negotiation and they agreed not to help Siddi in the future. Their ships have gone back and we were able to build the wall at Khanderi.'

'You have done a great job. We have created an obstruction between Janjira and Mumbai. We can defeat Siddi and the English later.'

Raje saw Mahadev collecting something from the floor. He asked, 'What is it, Mahadev?'

'The poison lamp broke. I am collecting the pieces.'

'It slipped out of my hand,' Soyarabai said, coming into the room.

'Rani saheb, why are you so upset? We may not need it anymore,' Raje said, laughing.

Soyarabai, surprised at Raje's unexpected answer, was relieved.

Raje had gotten busy after he returned to the fort. His meetings went on till late in the night. Raje received Firangoji when he came into the office and hugged him warmly.

'I was thinking about you, Firangoji. It's good that you came.'

Holding his hand, Raje walked towards his chamber. Rajaram came in and Firangoji stood up to salute. Raje asked, 'Bal Raje, did you bow to Uncle Firangoji?'

Rajaram stepped forward and bent in a low salute. Firangoji hugged him affectionately.

At that moment Soyarabai stepped in and said, 'You have seen the consequences of pampering one prince. Don't do that to another one now.'

Firangoji was startled to hear that and saluted Soyarabai in response.

Raje said, with the intention of dismissing her, 'Please bring some milk and refreshments for Firangoji.'

Soyarabai realized that Raje wanted her to leave and she turned to go without saying a word.

'How is Yuvraj,' Firangoji asked.

'He repents his actions but I feel he is still young.'

'Whatever you may say, he is the heir apparent.'

Raje was surprised to hear him speak like this. He said, 'What are you saying? This throne is not ours. It belongs to men like you who are willing to sacrifice their lives for it. The kingdom should rest in the hands of a person who is responsible and mature.'

Firangoji laughed in response. He said, 'Why discuss this right now?'

'No one can predict death. It can come anytime. It is Yuvraj's behaviour which has got me thinking.'

That night Raje met his ministers in his chamber. He said as they took their seats, 'I met Sambhaji Raje at Panhala. You must be wondering why I haven't yet mentioned it or given you the details.'

Hambirrao said, 'It is not necessary for the king to apprise the commander of everything.'

Raje said, waving his hand for Hambirrao to stop, 'You are my commander and I have taken all decisions ever since my coronation only after discussing them with you. Why? Because the king is not an independent person. He has to listen to the collective voice of himself, his ministers and his commanders. As I was saying, I am hoping that Sambhaji Raje will have become wiser by his experience and he must be given an opportunity.'

The ministers looked at each other. No one spoke.

Finally, Hambirrao said, 'Maharaj, if I may be frank ...'

'Please!'

'Yuvraj must have the trust of everyone here.'

'Hambirrao, you say you want to be frank and yet you beat around the bush. You want to say that Annaji and Moropant do not trust him, don't you? At the time of taking my oath at Rohideshwar, all I had was confidence. I earned trust later.'

Raje heaved a sigh and continued, 'However, I have seen Yuvraj repenting his mistakes many times. He has his hobbies, his fancies and enjoys his luxuries. How can I expect you to trust him when, despite being his father, I don't trust him?'

Annaji said, 'Maharaj, I feel it is the other way round. Sambhaji Raje does not trust us, particularly me. I must part company for the sake of the problem to be solved.'

'Annaji,' Raje shouted, his face stern. 'I know Yuvraj does not like you but the question of you parting company does not arise. Imagine if I were to part my company from you!'

'Maharaj!' Moropant exclaimed.

'Who knows how long I will live? I must be assured that our work would not stop even if I am not around. I was happy to see Yuvraj repenting and had tears in my eyes. But I cannot forget the barber Shiva who came to Panhala and saved my life. Can I forget the six hundred brave men who toiled in rain and mud to take my palanquin through that dark night? And Baji Prabhu who sacrificed his life at Godhkhind to ensure that I reach safely? He waited till I reached Vishalgad before laying down his weapons. Can you understand why I want people whom I can entrust this kingdom to around?'

'Why should you worry about our kingdom?' Annaji said, pride in his voice. 'It has spread from the Tungabhadra to the Narmada. We have an army of more than a lakh. Chhatrapati Shivaji's name brings fear into the hearts of those in the Adil Shahi and Qutb Shahi kingdoms.'

Raje laughed out loudly and said, 'Annaji, you should know better than this. You are my minister! You must know that I am not looking at the Adil Shahi or the Qutb Shahi kingdoms but northwards to Delhi. They are gathering at Aurangabad. Diler Khan has been insulted and I am sure we will have to fight our last battle with Alamgir and it will be a decisive battle. We must be prepared!'

Raje paused for a moment and continued, 'I have proposed that we divide the kingdom between Shambhu and Rajaram.'

'Maharaj,' Firangoji began.

'Don't think I like it, Firangoji. I don't think Yuvraj is going to accept it easily. In the meanwhile, I want to perform Rajaram's thread ceremony and get him married. What do you say, Moropant?'

'I think we can wait. Bal Raje is young.'

'He is a minor,' Raje said, 'but I am getting old. I have very little time at my disposal. Bal Raje will rule with your advice. I have only you all now as my confidantes and counsellors. Our responsibility is very large and we are very few in number! I feel insecure. You must all recognize your strength as early as possible. We don't have much time now.'

Raje got up to leave. 'I will go to bed now.'

They saluted as Raje left. Lying in his bed, Raje was lost in thought as Mahadev came in to put out the lamps while another servant massaged Raje's feet. Soon, he was in deep sleep.

The next morning, Rajaram came in and placed his head at Raje's feet. Hugging him affectionately, Raje asked, 'You seem to be better now.'

'Aai saheb gave me permission to go out.'

'You must now become independent. You can be fit by doing some exercise and eating moderately.'

'But Aai saheb loves me and ...'

'I know she does but blind love is not good. My Maa saheb too loved me but was watchful. If you cannot adjust to the changing climate here, how will you weather the storms and rains when you go out on campaigns?' Patting his head, Raje continued, 'Don't get involved in your Aai saheb's attachments.'

'What a fine lesson!' Soyarabai said, as she entered.

Raje and Rajaram turned to see Soyarabai coming in, and Rajaram was nervous.

Raje said, 'I was only telling the truth. He will soon shoulder a large responsibility and he can't be unhealthy.'

'What responsibility?' Soyarabai asked, suddenly alert.

'The kingdom, what else? Shambhu Raje is at Panhala, and someone must manage things here.'

Hearing that, Soyarabai's spirits soared. She was all smiles.

'I want to perform his thread ceremony and get him married.'

'I was thinking of looking for a suitable girl.'

'There's no need—I have found one. She is Prataprao's daughter. You remember when he had laid down his life in Nesari, I went to his house to console his family? An innocent girl, playing in the courtyard, attracted my attention. Her name, if I remember correctly, is Janaki. Someone remarked that the girl has been orphaned. But a child on my lap can never be an orphan!'

'What about her family?'

'You mean their status? Our kingdom is founded on the sacrifices of people like Prataprao Gujar. And the Malsures, Kanks and Gujars, they all ate at par with us. Anyone who has a relationship with a crowned king becomes a family member.'

Rajaram realized that they were talking of his marriage and ran out of the chamber, a little embarrassed. Soyarabai left a little later, her joy knowing no bounds.

The preparations for the marriage began in earnest. Senior commanders like Hambirrao were sent to Prataprao's village to settle the marriage negotiations and to give invitations to the bride's family. The tenth day of the month of Phalgun was selected for the marriage.

'Do we have enough time to plan it?' Soyarabai said, expressing her doubts.

Raje smiled. 'Don't forget that I am the sovereign king, Rani saheb. If I want it, anything can happen. It is a marriage in the family of Chhatrapati, after all!'

As Raje had said, the entire machinery got into action. And soon, everything was in place. The news of the bride's family having reached Pachad was conveyed to Raje, who went down the fort to receive them personally. Putlabai received Raje warmly at Pachad and offered to serve him his meals and Raje agreed immediately.

She said, 'The preparations for Bal Raje's marriage are in full swing, I am told?' she asked.

'Yes.'

'Is Yuvraj going to attend?'

'What do you think?'

'Maharaj, how can he not attend? He is the elder brother.'

'It seems you trust him a lot.'

Raje asked, changing the topic, 'I hope you got the invitation to the marriage? You are coming, aren't you?'

Putla said, wiping her tears, 'What is the need for an invitation? It is, after all, the wedding of one's own child.'

Raje turned to go. Putla said, her voice agonized, 'Wait a minute! I will come only to see you. If you feel I am not needed, I will stay here.'

Raje raised Putla's chin with his hand and said, looking into her eyes, 'Putla, it is my misfortune that you stay here. But here, at least, you don't get insulted every day.'

'I am willing to suffer anything for your sake,' Putla said.

'Fine then. I will send the palanquin to pick you up.'

Raje was busy writing letters in his chamber when Soyarabai arrived, followed by four servants carrying trays with jewellery. Raje was impressed at the work done by the jewellers. There were dazzling pieces of gem-studded wristlets, bracelets, toe rings, nose rings and such.

'We have many gems in our store, and the craftsmen can make some fancy ornaments if these are not enough,' Raje said, much to Soyarabai's happiness.

'I am told a palanquin arrived at the fort this morning?'

'Yes, I had it sent to bring Putlabai here. She can lend a helping hand.'

Soyarabai was in a good mood and nodded, and said, 'I agree. We must come together on such occasions.' Looking at the letters, she asked, 'Who are you writing to so early in the morning?'

'We have not invited Yesu, Bhawani and Yuvraj yet.'

Soyarabai's expression changed instantly. The tip of her nose turned red with anger as she asked, 'Yuvraj?'

'Rani saheb!' Raje shouted.

'I cannot believe that you are still pampering him,' Soyarabai said, her voice trembling with anger.

Raje said, 'Soyarabai, please calm down.'

'Why should I? Despite whatever he does, I have to call him Yuvraj. He misbehaves with a Brahmin girl and is forgiven. The poor girl commits suicide but nothing happens to Yuvraj.'

'Soyara!' Raje shouted.

'I cannot take it anymore,' Soyarabai continued. 'He joined the Mughals and became their Mansabdar. Yet, you regard him as Yuvraj. What does it mean to our Swaraj?'

'Hold your tongue, Rani saheb! I don't need to be taught politics by my queens. Yuvraj is lucky that he is my eldest son.'

Soyarabai had a twisted smile. She said, 'Do you realize that while he may be the son of the eldest mother, I am the crowned queen?'

'That is just the play of fate.'

'But as per law, Bal Raje, being my son, is the Yuvraj.'

Raje was unable to believe his ears. His face turned pale. Soyarabai, on the other hand, having scored a point, looked triumphant, knowing she had hit where it hurt the most.

Raje said, controlling himself, 'Remember yourself. Don't overstep the position I have given you.'

'Fine then. I will not hold the ceremony if Sambhaji is going to attend.'

The words hurt Raje deeply. He was now more disgusted than angry. 'Rani saheb, in the argument about princely status and succession to the throne, let us not jeopardize the wedding. I was hoping that I would get Sambhaji Raje here on the pretext of the occasion and explain a few things to him.'

'Like what?'

'Sambhaji is a reckless person but he is basically guileless and emotional in nature. If you treat him with love, he may hand over the entire kingdom to Rajaram and go into exile.'

'I presume Sambhaji Raje is not coming for the wedding then,' Soyarabai said, her smile triumphant, as she moved out of the chamber.

Rajaram's marriage ceremony was performed with all the pomp and show befitting the son of the Chhatrapati. The guests were overwhelmed at the hospitality shown to them. As Raje received the gifts given by the Brahmins, they blessed the couple and said, 'Because of this bride, twelve generations of the past and twelve in the future will be uplifted. The girl is now yours.'

Raje was overwhelmed as he hugged the bride's uncle. They were both in tears. Raje said, as he extricated himself from the embrace, 'I miss Prataprao dearly today.'

As the bride and bridegroom moved forward towards the temple, Putlabai, resplendent in a green sari, stepped in to perform the aarti. Seeing her, Soyarabai shouted, 'Bai, don't!'

Everyone around was stunned. Putlabai, looking bewildered, stopped in her tracks when Soyarabai said, 'You are a childless woman. You can't bless the couple on this occasion.'

Snatching the tray from her, Soyarabai moved forward to welcome the newly wedded couple, leaving Putla standing there haplessly. The ceremonies went off as planned but Putla was nowhere to be seen thereafter.

Night had descended on the fort. The marriage celebrations had tired everyone out and the courtyard wore a desolate look. The chiefs sat chatting and enjoying betel leaves, knowing that Raje was relaxing in his chambers.

Manohari, having completed her chores, was passing by Putlabai's room to find only a few lamps burning. She stepped in to light the tall lamp, and as the room turned bright, she was surprised to see Putlabai sitting in the corner, looking out of the window. She had not even changed the sari she had been wearing at the marriage pandal. Her eyes looked tired. Evidently she had been crying for a long time.

She said, before Manohari could speak, 'I feel bad, Manu, that this should have happened in Raje's presence. Bai should have shown some sense.'

'Have you eaten, Rani saheb?'

'No,' Putlabai, said, wiping her tears. 'I will leave the fort and eat. I don't feel like eating anything here now.'

Manohari was about to leave the room when she heard footsteps. Soon, Raje was standing at the door. Putlabai said, adjusting her sari over her head, 'I thought you must have retired to bed.'

'I will stay here tonight, Manu,' he said. 'Send a message to my chamber.'

'I would have come to your room, had you sent for me,' Putlabai said.

'No, Putla. I wanted to see you. I was feeling restless. I see that you have not eaten. Please, will you eat?'

'I don't feel like it,' Putlabai said.

'I feel very restless, Putla. I'm totally fed up, you know!'

Putlabai was surprised to hear his voice sound so tired. Raje held her hand and said, looking into her eyes, 'I am used to my loneliness now, Putla!'

'Maharaj!'

'I am Maharaj to the people, not for you,' Raje smiled dejectedly. 'You know, from the window there, I can see Maa saheb's mansion at Pachad? I can see the sun as it disappears into the valley, though I cannot see it touching the horizon. Just as it rises suddenly, it sets too!' He added, after a pause, 'The way Sai did!'

'I can understand,' Putlabai said.

'I don't know who can, Putla. People believe I have achieved everything by being a Chhatrapati but very few people know the facets of failure in my life. Sai passed away suddenly. Unfortunately, the elder Rani saheb is only interested in being queen and nothing else. Shambhu has never responded to my love, despite all my efforts. That is my biggest failure. He defected to the Mughals and now the elder queen wants to be called the mother of Yuvraj. I am not at all at ease, Putla!'

Putla got up to get a glass of milk for Raje. But by the time she returned, she found that he had dozed off. Extinguishing the wicks of the lamp, Putlabai looked at the reclining figure of Raje. It was already dark outside.

The next morning, as the sun rose, Raje was disappointed to see Putlabai ready to leave.

He said, picking up a shawl from the bed, 'I got this for you,' and stretched his hand to hand it over to her. Their fingers touched each other as Raje's hand lingered for a while.

'I shall come and see you at Raigadwadi whenever I get the time.'

Putlabai responded with tears in her eyes. Pressing the shawl to her breast, she hurriedly left the room. As Raje moved to his chamber, Rajaram met him on the way. He fell at Raje's feet to seek his blessings. Raje moved his hand over Rajaram's back but left without saying a word. On his way to the temple, Soyarabai stopped Raje to say, 'I am told that the priest suggests the marriage party should leave after the new moon day. What do you say?'

'Do as the priest says. I have no interest in it,' Raje said as he walked away.

That morning, as Raje said in the state office, he asked Annaji, 'Where are our troops stationed now?'

Moropant answered, 'Maharaj, my forces are in Nashik–Trayambak region while Hambirrao's are in Karhad–Panhala region.'

Raje asked, 'When is the solar eclipse?'

'After three days,' Annaji replied.

'If the powerful sun god too can be eclipsed, is it a wonder that common men like us have to suffer?' Raje asked rhetorically and, without waiting for an answer, he left the room. He seemed lost in thought.

Moropant came to see Raje in the afternoon, while Firangoji and Raje sat playing chess. 'What is the matter, Moropant?'

'We have news from Aurangabad—Alamgir is descending on the Deccan.'

'We need to strategize right away. Bring Annaji, Hambirrao and Prahladpant to the office at once.'

Firangoji said, moving his fist over his whiskers, 'This old man was getting tired of sitting in one place in any case. It would be good to get some action going!'

Raje conferred with his ministers later that afternoon. Moropant handed over the letter they had received. Glancing at the letter, Raje said, as he stroked his beard, 'What do you make of it?'

'I don't think Alamgir is personally going to move to Aurangabad. His forces may be gathering though.'

'Is this wishful thinking or do you really believe it?' Raje asked Annaji.

Annaji asked, 'Do you believe Alamgir will come?'

'Certainly! I have been expecting it since my childhood and have worked hard in anticipation of this danger. Hambirrao, what is the strength of our army?'

'We have one lakh and five thousand cavalry,' Hambirrao said proudly.

'What about our treasury, Annaji?'

'We have twenty-one lakh gold coins, nearly ten thousand kilos of gold, a large number of gems besides a crore of Chandrama coins, twenty-five lakh specially minted hons and an equal number of other hons.'

'And what about our forts, Moropant?'

'We have the original fifty, and have built another hundred and eleven and captured seventy-nine from Karnatak, totalling two hundred and forty forts.'

Raje could not conceal his joy. He said, 'Moropant, I have been amassing all these for a decisive battle. The ones we have fought so far were not of a decisive nature, but the one with Alamgir will be. Whatever survives will be God's kingdom.'

'If we succeed, our joy will know no bounds,' Hambirrao said.

'There cannot be any ifs and buts, Hambirrao. Ours is the Lord's kingdom. I took the responsibility to create it. I did not allow my desires and passions come in the way of achieving our Swaraj. It is not that I did not make mistakes. But I never coaxed or encouraged these mistakes. Maybe that is why Samarth calls me rajayogi.'

He continued, 'Today, the Rajputs are serving under the Mughals faithfully while in the past they fought with him while their women performed sati whenever they lost. Aurangzeb will want to destroy us off totally. The Rajputs will wait for the right day to take their revenge. I am sure the way things are going on in the north, nobody is resting easy. The Jats are uneasy in Punjab, with the beheading of their guru Tegh Bahadur; the Sikhs are itching for action. I feel I know Alamgir and he knows me better than anyone else. It is my dream to wrest Asirgarh from the Mughals and open the door to the north once closed by Akbar. We will also close the door to the south forever.'

The reference to Asirgarh got the assembly excited. They looked at Raje with a renewed sense of confidence. Raje said, looking at Moropant, 'Ensure you give news from the north regularly, and not just from Aurangabad. We need spies in the north, and Hambirrao, you must be able to predict which route Aurangzeb will take to reach here.'

Hambirrao said, 'I believe he will first come to Aurangabad and then march towards Pune. Even Shaista Khan and Mirza Raja did the same.'

'But I think otherwise. Look at the way he destroyed the temples in Kashi and imposed the jizya tax on non-Muslims. He will come via Tuljapur, Pandharpur, Kolhapur and then to Rajapur. That way he can break up our kingdom and Karnatak into two pieces. The shrines at Tuljapur, Pandharpur, Shikhar Shingnapur and Kolhapur will be destroyed. On reaching Rajapur, the Portuguese and the English would be more than happy to support him. If we cannot protect our shrines, we cannot get the trust of our men.'

The bleak picture painted by Raje made everyone worried. Raje continued, 'The attack on Somnath by the foreigners was not just to loot but also to destroy the faith of the people who will lay down their lives for the sake of their god. If Alamgir wants to destroy our faith, it is easiest for him to destroy our deities before he attacks us.'

'Why should we allow him to do that?' Firangoji asked.

'We should not. I propose to catch up with him before he does so, let us send our forces via the harbour at Dabhol into Gujarat to wipe out the rear of his army. Before Aurangzeb reaches the south we must crush him at Asirgarh in Gujarat. What do you say, Hambirrao?'

'Just command us and we will go, Maharaj!'

'Don't be so impatient! I am expecting Qutb Shah and Adil Shah to help us out for their own selfish reasons. Annaji, you move to Konkan while Moropant goes to Nashik and Hambirrao goes to the Karhad–Panhala region and organize the troops.'

The trio saluted. Raje said, 'Moropant, train the elephants and camels to carry guns. They must get used to the sound of the drums, horns and trumpets. I can imagine our troops shouting "Har Har Mahadev!" as they quash the Mughal forces. But we cannot afford to be careless. Our aim is not to merely defeat Aurangzeb but to destroy the throne in Delhi and install the Lord at Kashi Vishwanath. The hands of my men and the will of the Lord will make it happen.'

Firangoji came forward, tears in his eyes. Raje exclaimed, 'Firangoji!'

'Maharaj, had Maa saheb been alive, she would have performed an aarti for you.'

'I miss her very much today. Not just for her to ward off the evil eye but her mere presence would have been so encouraging.' The meeting ended as the sardars saluted and left.

The next morning, the ministers conferred again, finalizing their plans. Hambirrao asked, 'Maharaj, what about Yuvraj?'

Raje was silent for a while and then said, 'This is the time for all of us to work together. I think that excluding Yuvraj will not be good for us. In fact, he will lead our army. I don't doubt his capabilities.'

The men saluted and left. While seeing them off, Raje said, 'Annaji, Moropant, Hambirrao—be careful. And come back once you have made all the arrangements. I will be waiting for you.'

Raje called for Firangoji. As the old man presented himself, Raje said, 'Firangoji, I have a big responsibility for you. I believe you can make Sambhaji understand his job. He is the Yuvraj. He has grown up in your presence—to an extent, you have reared him, and he respects you greatly. I want you to go to Panhala and talk to him. Ask him to forget the past and use this opportunity presented to him.'

Firangoji's whiskers quivered as he said, 'Maharaj, I will leave for Panhala right away. I am sure I will be able to make him understand.'

An enraged Soyarabai was waiting for Annaji in her apartment. She said, when he walked in and saluted, 'Is that true—what I have heard?'

'Yes, Rani saheb. Raje was quite displeased with Sambhaji and wanted to entrust the governance of the kingdom to Rajaram but he loves Yuvraj a lot. And once Sambhaji Raje meets him, it will not be long before they reconcile. When the Mughals are invading us, Yuvraj will take that opportunity to unite with Raje and all will be forgiven.'

'So what is your advice?' Soyarabai asked.

'I am your servant, Rani saheb. I cannot advise you. These are matters for you to settle among yourself, in private. My advice, if at all I can call it that, is to set aside such misgivings and be happy with your current position.'

'So you too have turned you back on me?'

'You misunderstand, Rani saheb. I am always there to support you but I cannot be disloyal to Raje. As long as Raje lives, I am at his feet.' Annaji saluted Soyarabai, walked back three steps, and left. His last words rang in Soyarabai's ears.

The solar eclipse and the puja thereafter went off as planned. Raje enjoyed the post-wedding feast and other ceremonies. However, within a few days he had fallen ill. His throat was dry and he ran a high fever. The physician was called in and Rajaram and Soyarabai looked restless.

Soyarabai asked, 'Are you not well?'

'Who says so?'

Soyarabai was startled by the question. She said, 'Your face looks drained, and you would not be confined to your bed otherwise.'

'Faces can be deceptive, Rani saheb. Don't worry.'

Soyarabai was enraged and said, trying to control her anger, 'You don't have to be sarcastic all the time.'

'Well, I have been asked to take rest. You may leave me alone now.'

Soyarabai left in a huff. Raje called for Balaji and dictated important letters for the key fort-keepers. By evening, his temperature had come down. Raje believed the fever was due to the exhaustion of the last few days but by night the fever had resurfaced. After a few days, the situation had not yet changed. He was getting weaker by the day. Seeing his deteriorating health, the whole fort was quiet and pensive.

On the fourth day, his temperature had come down a little. He was feeling extremely weak. He said, when Soyarabai came in, 'Please send a horseman to Panhala and inform Sambhaji that I am not well. Call him here urgently, please.'

'Yes, I will.'

The two physicians, Ganga Shastri and Ganga Vaidya, had examined Raje. They conferred and came to a conclusion that it looked like typhoid fever. Ganga Shastri said, 'There is nothing to worry. He will feel better by tomorrow night.'

All those present felt relieved.

Though Ganga Shastri had assured everyone that Raje would return to normal health, his temperature continued to play truant. Soyarabai came in the evening and asked, 'Did you send the palanquin for the younger queen?'

'Yes, I did. Has she arrived?'

'No, I am told she is not keeping well.'

'We both have identical dispositions,' Raje said, as he closed his eyes. Soyarabai left without saying a word.

As Raje slept, Balaji standing nearby could not resist asking Ganga Shastri, who was busy cutting a betelnut for his paan, 'Tell me, Vaidyaraj, the medicine you gave Raje is supposed to be very effective for typhoid. Yet, it has not worked.'

'That is right. I think it may be navajwar, the nine-day fever.'

'Do the symptoms support what you think?'

Ganga Shastri did not respond, focusing on his paan instead. Those around looked grave. It was not a situation they were prepared to confront.

A few days had gone by with the fever rising and falling intermittently.

Raje said, as Ganga Shastri examined him, 'Shastribua, I am not bothered about my lack of appetite but the ups and downs of the fever are becoming unbearable. What is happening to me?'

The physician was holding Raje's hand to inspect his pulse. He said, quickly glancing at Manohari, who went out of the room, 'Maharaj, based on my age and experience, I can tell you that till now, my doses have never gone wrong. But I am at a loss to understand why they have failed this time.'

'You clearly want to say something, Shastribua. Please do—without hesitation.'

'Maharaj,' the physician began, as he licked his lips nervously, 'did you eat something which you should not have?'

Raje's lips quivered. He became restless and asked, 'Is anyone in the room?'

'No.'

Raje smiled and said, 'Don't raise such doubts. I have had similar experiences earlier. I want you to treat me the way you deem most fit. Don't worry about the outcome. I shall recover if the Lord wills.'

The two physicians conferred outside Raje's room. Ganga Shastri was nervous as he wiped the sweat from his face. He was restless, nervous and confused. He said, looking at the other physician, 'Shall we try the gold and pearl vials? We have not given him a dose for vomiting yet.'

'That is right. Let us administer this dose and see.'

The two men prepared the new dose, praying as they did.

The chamber was enveloped in total silence. The dim light of the lamp spread on the floor. It was nearly midnight but Raje was not asleep despite the high fever. His eyes felt heavy. He was desperate to sleep but it eluded him. He mused, My dream was to create the Lord's kingdom. Fifty years! In the process, I lost many great warriors. What was more dear—Kondana or Tanaji?

The dream of Swaraj was incepted when I was a mere fifteen years old. I had seen how the kingdoms of Daulatabad and Vijayanagara had fallen to foreign invasions. I had seen how the jagir at Pune was ruined due to the displeasure of Adil Shah. My strength was limited but I won with unlimited devotion and dedication. So many sacrifices! Men like Baji Prabhu, Prataprao, Murarbaji and Tanaji—they gave up their lives for the cause.

Only those who truly love their land are willing to sacrifice themselves. Shiva the barber was willing to die to save me. Murarbaji, Tanaji and Pangera accepted the challenge. But who assured them that my mission would succeed?

Raje laughed at himself. His thoughts continued. Faith: Its strength is infinite. Like an ocean! But each victory came at a cost. To put an end to my plans, they arrested the elder Maharaj saheb but we did not waver. I went to Agra knowing full well that I was entering the jaws of death. My men like Annaji, Moropant and others stood like rocks and protected the kingdom that remained after the treaty of Purandar. They never believed we would lose.

After escaping from Agra, I wore the disguise of a mendicant, losing my ego. And then the auspicious occasion of my coronation—an event unprecedented in a thousand years. It was an open challenge to the Mughals. But why did we become complacent even before defeating Alamgir?

My own Yuvraj desired power and Rani saheb was only interested in being queen. I reconverted our people who had been forced to adopt Islam. Aurangzeb did the same thing. Is that our concept of loyalty to our religions?

Raje was restless in his thoughts. He was also fatigued. But it is not the same thing! The Mughals came to our land from faraway places while I am a son of the soil, loyal to the land. Otherwise we would not have made Daulat Khan our admiral.

I took care of Shambhu when Sai passed away but I was not able to give him his mother's love. I had promised Sai I would treat Sambhaji with care. I was not able to deal with him with the strict discipline with which I was treated by Maa saheb. I chopped off the hands of a Patil for his misconduct but for a similar offence, I could not punish Sambhaji. Not even when he defected to the enemy camp. It is my failure for not being able to punish my son. It is unpardonable!

Sai passed away but my wounds remain fresh. Kashi's eyes remained unsatisfied while Putla is leading her life in the company of my shoes. Shambhu, dear to me as our family deity, does not know my mind! I have foresight but I am not able to see things close to me! The ministers do not trust Sambhaji's capabilities. And Shambhu does not trust the ministers. What a dilemma!

I gave Sambhaji the independent charge of the Subha at Prabhavali but he did not manage it well. Will he have warriors like Baji and Tanaji and advisors like Moropant and Annaji to fight against Aurangzeb? Does he have the maturity to make his mind tenacious? And the elder Rani saheb believes the junior Yuvraj can lead the men with the support of the ministers. A young lad of ten!

Raje moved his hand across his forehead and his fingers touched the ash marks. He mused, Who knows what is in fate for me? I was planning to give the Mughals a tough fight a week ago and now here I am, lying in bed with a fever! Would the dream of a Hindavi Swaraj remain unrealized if I were to die?

I wonder how Samarth keeps the equanimity of his mind. He calls me shriman yogi but why do I not have the same equanimity? I am not scared of death. My only worry is that the kingdom should survive after me. The kingdom belongs to the Lord. It will survive the Mughal invasion. Even if it does not, the confidence I have given people as Shivaji will remain eternal. That will surely grow.

Raje could sense his sheets being moved. The physician had come to check Raje and was surprised to see him awake. He asked, 'Maharaj, did you not sleep?'

Raje smiled. 'I was staying awake for a peaceful sleep.'

'What do you mean?'

'Nothing. Is it dawn now?'

'Yes.'

'Then the sun should rise soon.'

Raje seemed to be in his own world. The Vaidyaraj, after checking Raje's pulse, walked out of the room. His face could not hide his anxiety.

Raje's deteriorating condition and the seriousness with which Ganga Shastri was attending to it made it clear to everyone that it was not a simple case of fever. Raje was losing more weight each day and was looking visibly emaciated.

Soyarabai sat near Raje's bed while outside, in the verandah, Hiroji, Mahadji and Balaji stood guard. Manohari and Mahadev would take care of Raje, pressing his feet.

That evening, Nischalpuri came with his disciples to ward off evil and touched him with holy ashes. At around midnight, the verandah was silent. Ganga Shastri was dozing while Mahadev stood guard. Manohari slept with her head on the bed, sitting on the floor. Soyarabai was sleeping beside the bed reclining against a bolster. Hiroji was napping with his head between his knees. Suddenly they heard someone cry, 'Moropant, Moropant!'

There was a lot of confusion as it took them a few moments to realize that it was Raje who has calling, and they rushed into the room.

Raje was muttering, 'Moropant, you have done an excellent job but the work at Raigad is incomplete.'

Hiroji called out to Raje but he was in muttering under his breath. His eyes were closed. The physician checked the pulse. As they came out of the chamber, all eyes were on Ganga Shastri.

Yesaji asked, 'Shastribua, please be honest ... how is he?'

'Don't ask me anything,' Ganga Shastri said, blowing his nose. 'I feel defeated. My medicines are not working. Raje is falling into a coma, I fear.'

The soft sobs of those around penetrated the silence of the night.

The next morning, as the fort came to life, all eyes were on Raje's chamber. Soyarabai was in the verandah. She said, heaving a sigh, 'Maharaj has entrusted the whole responsibility to Bal Raje. He is still young and you all must support him; I wish Annaji, Moropant and Hambirrao were here.'

'Rani saheb need not worry. Please command us.'

'Then close the gates to the forts.'

'Yes, Rani saheb,' Balaji said.

'I don't want the rumours to spread. If the news of his failing health goes out, it will create problems. And no one should leave the fort without my permission,' she added.

People were bewildered but did not voice their opinion. They were anxiously waiting for Raje to recover. Raje would be conscious intermittently. He muttered, as he opened his eyes to look at Soyarabai, 'Water ...'

Taking a golden vessel of water, Ganga Shastri helped Raje to sip a little. Raje waved a limp hand towards Soyarabai who stepped forward. He said, 'Why has Shambhu Raje not come yet?'

'I am not sure. He should have.'

Raje looked at Soyarabai fixedly, who struggled not to lower her eyes. He smiled, 'I understand now. The palanquin was sent to bring the younger queen, and she did not come. Nor has Shambhu Raje arrived.'

'Do you think I am lying? Ask Balaji if you wish.'

Raje's expression turned grave. 'Rani saheb, stop it! Shambhu may not like you but he loves me very much—he would have come flying had he been told of my illness.'

Soyarabai angrily glanced at Raje and turned her back. Raje said, 'Shun your anger for this moment at least. Do you think I collected crores of hons for luxury? All my efforts were only for that decisive battle between Alamgir and I. And neither Sambhaji nor Rajaram can fight it. One is thoughtless and the other one immature. If I had been in good health for another year, my wish would have been fulfilled.'

Tears streamed down Raje's cheeks. He continued, 'The kingdom would have been safe after the installation of the Lord at Kashi. But I could not make that happen. Something has gone fundamentally wrong.' Raje closed his eyes but the tears continued to flow.

Yesaji stepped forward and wiped them as he started sobbing. Raje opened his eyes and said, stroking Yesaji's hand, 'Yesaji, you are the one who fought an elephant. Why you are weeping now?'

Yesaji got up hurriedly and pushing the edge of his shawl in his mouth, he rushed out of the room.

Suddenly Raje was restless and shouted, 'Fire the guns ... Baji is fighting tooth and nail and he is waiting to hear the guns. Where is Tanaji? Why is he not around? Tie his hands and bring him before me? How can he leave without my permission?'

It was clear to everyone that Raje was sinking. Soon, he was unconscious and slept fitfully. No one was in the mood to eat or drink. Raje continued to be in and out of consciousness. The Brahmins had begun to recite the Mrityunjaya mantra. That evening, Raje was awake and called the men around. He said, 'Don't lament. You must do whatever that has to be done with full responsibility. If your intent is good, the result will be fine.'

Janardanpant said, 'Maharaj, have courage!'

'I am not afraid of death, Janardanpant. But at this juncture, men like Sambhaji, Moropant, Annaji and Firangoji should have been here. Death rules over time. That Baji Prabhu fought till he heard the guns was only because of time. My escape from Agra was due to the Lord's grace. Today, when I am breathing my last, none of these men are with me. When I escaped from Agra, I wandered as a mendicant and went to Kashi. I felt blessed after the darshan and offered my gems to the Lord. That endangered my life as the priests wondered how a mendicant like me could have such gems. As a result I had to leave Kashi immediately.

'I lost precious men while toiling for the kingdom, accepting success and failure on the way. I surrendered barefoot with my hands tied to the back and my son held as a hostage by the enemy. I faced imprisonment.'

Raje looked at Prahladpant. He said, 'Raje, if Samarth comes to know of it ...'

Raje folded his hands and said, 'Are you a fool to inform Samarth?'

Raje soon dozed off.

That night, the men were alert. The room was lit with a diffused light of the lamps. Seeing Raje clench his fists, Hiroji got up. They knew the symptoms. Raje said, opening his eyes, 'I brought the Ganga from Kashi but it could not reach Rameshwar. All my efforts were wasted. Sai? Where is Sai? Where is my elder Rani saheb? Where do these people go when I need them? Call them!'

The bhajans were being sung outside in the verandah. The rhythmic sound of the tal and the percussion was at a fast tempo. Raje remembered Samarth's words, 'Raje, be introspective. Concentrate on yourself.' Raje remembered the way Samarth had fondly caressed his back when they had embraced each other. Calmed at the thought, he dozed off again.

At dawn, Raje woke up to the sounds of the bhajan. The chamber was silent but he could sense someone pressing his feet. It was Manohari.

'Manu!'

'Yes, Maharaj!'

'Bring me some water, please.'

'Ganga Shastri, standing at the door, brought the water.

'What day is it?' Raje asked.

'Saturday.'

'It is a full moon day, isn't it?'

'Yes, the eleventh day since you fell ill.'

'The Rudras too are eleven, aren't they?'

'Yes, Maharaj.'

'Shastribua, it seems to be a good day. I feel better. You must take some rest. You have done your job. Please go now.'

That morning Shastri administered a dose to Raje and felt his pulse.

Raje smiled, 'What are you worrying about, Shastribua? A collapsing bastion cannot be supported by a peg. Today seems to be a good day. Don't worry.'

Shastri could not utter a word as he watched Raje carefully.

Soyarabai came in and asked, 'Can I do something?'

'I am not seeing who I want to, and am instead seeing those I don't want!'

Soyarabai turned away fretfully. As Shastri stepped out of the room, Hiroji asked, a little optimistically. 'Is he better today?'

Shastri smiled dejectedly and said, 'What you see is different from what it really is!'

The men were speechless. Manohari appeared at the door and said, 'Maharaj is calling all of you.'

They gathered around the bed. Hiroji called softly, 'Maharaj!'

Raje opened his eyes. He looked at Rajaram and said, 'Bal Raje, you have to shoulder a large responsibility now. May Jagdamba be with you! And remember that it is tolerance that makes people great. Don't get tired of it.'

He looked at the men around and said, 'Don't be afraid. Everyone has to die someday. Sit outside and let me remember my Lord.'

They all left silently. Manohari continued pressing Raje's feet. Hiroji was standing nearby, just outside the door. Ganga Shastri was at Raje's feet, looking at him.

Raje said, 'Manu, can you wipe the sweat off my face?'

Manohari wiped Raje's face and as she was wiping his neck, she burst out crying.

'What happened?'

'The wreath of cowries ...'

'It is broken, isn't it?' Raje smiled. 'It seems Jagdamba has withdrawn her support.'

Manohari, tears flowing down, bent to collect the cowries.

'How many cowries have broken?'

'Four.'

'That means I am with you all for four hours more at the most,' Raje said, raising his hands.

A strange fear gripped Manohari. She started weeping.

Raje raised his hand with great difficulty and said, moving his hand over her head, 'Are you weeping for me?' As he held her hand, he saw Saibai's coral ring on her finger. Raje moved a trembling hand over the ring. 'Don't weep, Manu. I could not involve myself in anyone but unknowingly, I got involved in you. Being that as it is, I am going now. Shastribua ...'

Ganga Shastri reached Raje's bed.

'Shastribua, give me the gangajal and the tulsi leaf now. Please put the holy ashes on my forehead.'

Shastri, Hiroji and Manu sobbed silently. Raje sipped the water and Shastri touched his head with the ashes. Taking the tulsi leaf on his tongue, Raje folded his hands. Seeing Mahadev enter, Raje said, 'Mahadev, your watch is almost over now.'

Mahadev could not look at Raje and rushed out of the room, sobbing.

The hymns were now in full progress. Raje was losing his grip over himself. His eyes had a blue tinge in them. 'Alamgir was looking at me peacefully, you know. His eyes had the confidence and power of a cobra, with the ability to penetrate deep into you. There were only two people who could look at me like that—Alamgir and death!'

Raje heaved a deep sigh. Everyone had gathered around the bed. He seemed calm and then he shouted, 'Shambhu Raje never defected to the Mughals. The Yuvraj of the Swaraj, the successor of Chhatrapati and the son of Sai—Shambhu could never do such a thing!'

Raje was coherent after a long time. He looked at everyone but they looked hazy and faraway. He asked Manohari who stood at his feet, 'What are you doing?'

'Pressing your feet!'

'Pressing my feet?' Raje asked. 'I cannot feel anything!'

Manohari had a frightened look in her eyes as she turned towards Ganga Shastri. She put her fingers on her lips lest a sob escape them. Ganga Shastri touched the soles of Raje's feet.

Raje tried to move his hands and mustering all his strength he muttered his last words, 'I am left all alone, very much alone! Sai!'

A Large-hearted Storyteller:
The Works of Ranjit Desai
Vikrant Pande

P.S.

Insights
Interview
& More...

A Large-hearted Storyteller: The Works of Ranjit Desai

Vikrant Pande

Ranjit Desai (8 April 1928–6 March 1992) was born in Kolhapur district of Maharashtra. He was a large-hearted litterateur who engaged his readers at the highest level of emotional dialogue. He started writing soon after his graduation and received an award for his very first short story, 'Bhairav', published in *Prasad* magazine in 1946. He published his short-story collection *Roop Mahal* in 1958. At the same time, he stepped into the world of novels with *Bari*.

In the novel *Bari*, Desai wrote about the tribe of the same name, who traditionally lived in dense jungles and sometimes resorted to dacoity and theft in nearby settlements for their living. They could hardly ever dream of a stable life. The socio-political scenario and exploitation of forest resources significantly changed their way of living and introduced them to new ways and values. In his novel, Desai captured the picturesque environs, the rugged lifestyle, the petty feuds and pleasures, the changing horizon of the tribals in moving and powerful prose, representing them realistically.

Desai wrote several stories about the natural world; some stories are even devoid of human characters. *Morpankhi Saawlya,* a collection of short stories, gives voice to the mute and the inanimate. We are transported to a world we are used to seeing, but we are made to experience it anew, such being the poignancy and intimacy of the narrative voice. There is an element of magical realism in these stories, and even as they end on tragic notes – highlighting survival of the fittest in the natural world – readers are left gasping for more. And yet, Desai executes these surreal stories with constraint so that reality is never too far behind.

In the same vein, the novella *Shekara* tells a story of a jungle squirrel. The novel begins in the pristine jungle and we are given the picture of an idyllic and a simple foraging life of the squirrel, but it takes a drastic turn when a preying fox enters the scene. Ultimately the law of the jungle prevails and the jungle falls back into its own pace, as if nothing terrible happened. Although it is a story of animal survival, the novella is also a parable of our modern existence where there seems to be no sanctuary for the weak, innocent and simple-minded. A gem in Desai's oeuvre, *Shekara* became popular after his death.

Although Desai was adept at describing rural India, and giving voice to its flora and fauna, he is most known for his flair for writing historical and biographical fiction. His book *Swami* is based on the life of Madhavrao Peshwa, the third Peshwa. In the book, Desai explores the subtle relationship between the Peshwa and his wife Ramabai. The novel is as much a retelling of history as it is a story of a young man building his own legacy, fighting against various odds, all taking place against ignominious defeat at Panipat. The novel was made into a popular Marathi TV serial by the same name, earning the author the title 'Swamikar'.

Another masterpiece from the author's repertoire of biographical fiction is of India's greatest painter, Raja Ravi Varma. In writing *Raja Ravi Varma*, Desai wanted to reveal the celebrated artist as a lover, a husband, a businessman and a visionary. He also spent

Novels:

Swami
Shriman Yogi
Abhogi
Radheya
Pawankhind
Mazha Gaon
Samidha
Bari
Raja Ravi Varma
Pratigya
Shekara
Lakshyavedh

much time in researching the novel and took five years to complete it. The sensitivity with which Raja Ravi Varma is portrayed shows how involved Desai was with his subjects. His large-heartedness as a storyteller is also evident in the novel *Radheya*, where he retells the story of Karna, one of the tragic characters from the Mahabharata, to reveal how Karna resides in all of us, thereby asking readers to reconsider the concepts of victory and loss.

Shirman Yogi is perhaps the most-loved book of Ranjit Desai's. He explained how he came about to write his magnum opus on Shivaji thus:

There was a gap of more than seven years between the publication of Swami *and* Shriman Yogi. *I had already started working on* Radheya, *the novel based on Karna, when I was inspired to research on Shivaji by Balasaheb Desai. I realized that I had undertaken a project which would require intense research. I soon found out that Shivaji did not have an official biographer, unlike Aurangzeb who had been portrayed in detail by Jadunath Sarcar. The Europeans had meticulously written about their emperors but there was no dependable material on Shivaji. Most of the writings were not factual and were disposed to melodramatic versions of Shivaji's exploits. While some authors were not assiduous, others like Babasaheb Purandare were steeped in worship, almost like a devotee. Through my research, I discovered the character of the great Maratha warrior. I was so taken by the exploits of the man and soon an image developed in my mind. Here was a king; a multifaceted, multitalented and a complete man. He was not only an ideal ruler and a great leader in war, but also a good administrator. While he was deeply religious, he was secular and allowed other religions to flourish.*

Short story collections:

Roop Mahal
Madhumati
Kamodini
Alekh
Gandhali
Morpankhi Saawlya
Katal
Megh
Ashadh
Vaishakh
Prapat
Sanket
Babulmora
Mekh Mogari

Plays:

Swami
Varsa
Hey Bandh Reshmache
Ramshastri
Dhan Apure
Garudzhep
Shriman Yogi
Loknayak
Sangeet Tanset
Kanchanmruga
Pankh Zhale Vairi
Pangulgada
Tuzhi Vat Pahili
Saawli Unhachi

Ranjit Desai travelled to all the places historically important to Shivaji's narrative to get a first-hand impression of the surroundings. He even met people who showed him the usage of the weapons prevalent during Shivaji's time. Weapons like jambiya or the hooked dagger; axe; spear; bohtati or fighting with spears on horseback; dandpatta, or the gauntlet integrated as a handguard, were studied by the author. Desai also visited the museums in Delhi, Bijapur, Mumbai and Baroda. He got a lot of help from the Kelkar museum in Pune.

One of the problems Ranjit Desai faced was the debate around Shivaji's life and certain events like the death of Shaista Khan. Each event in his life – from his birth to his death – has been interpreted and then reinterpreted from multiple points of view. Though Desai knows that a storyteller's work is not that of a historian's he was aware of the myths that had crept into the life of the great warrior. Ranjit Desai spent four years researching the book. The result was a true masterpiece.

As the translator, I feel truly blessed to have got the chance to get one of Marathi's best-loved novels to more and more people. I hope the readers enjoy the book as much as I have translating it. *Shriman Yogi* was my first translation which I began four years ago purely for the joy of it. I had no idea then that I would be asked by HarperCollins to publish Ranjit Desai's magnum opus. I had translated N.S. Inamdar's *Shahenshah: The Life of Aurangzeb*, and it was interesting to see how Ranjit Desai tackled Shivaji's arch-enemy in *Shriman Yogi*.